INSTRUCTOR'S MANUAL • TEST BANK • TRANSPARENCY MASTERS

Entrepreneurship
A Contemporary Approach
Fourth Edition

Donald F. Kuratko
Ball State University

Richard M. Hodgetts
Florida International University

THE DRYDEN PRESS
Harcourt Brace College Publishers

Fort Worth Philadelphia San Diego New York Orlando Austin San Antonio
Toronto Montreal London Sydney Tokyo

Copyright © 1998, 1995, 1992, 1989 by the Dryden Press

All rights reserved. No part of this publication may be reproduced or transmitted in any form or by any means, electronic or mechanical, including photocopy, recording, or any information storage and retrieval system, without permission in writing from the publisher, except that, until further notice, the contents or parts thereof may be reproduced for instructional purposes by users of *Entrepreneurship,* Fourth Edition, by Donald F. Kuratko and Richard M. Hodgetts.

Web site address:
http://www.hbcollege.com

THE DRYDEN PRESS, DRYDEN, and the DP Logo are registered trademarks of Harcourt Brace & Company.

Printed in the United States of America

ISBN: 0-03-024941-4

7 8 9 0 1 2 3 4 5 6   129   9 8 7 6 5 4 3 2 1

The Dryden Press
Harcourt Brace College Publishers

PREFACE

This *Instructor's Resource Manual* is designed specifically to accompany *Entrepreneurship: A Contemporary Approach* (4th Edition) by Donald F. Kuratko and Richard M. Hodgetts. There are particular features in this manual that we believe make it a comprehensive planning and organizing package for the instructor. These include:

Chapter Outline: Each chapter is outlined highlighting the key items for summary purposes.

Chapter Objectives: The chapter objectives are restated just as they appear at the beginning of each chapter in the text.

Chapter Summary: Each chapter is summarized to give the instructor a brief overview of the chapter's focus.

Lecture Notes: Each chapter has a detailed outline that can be used for lecture purposes. While it is in outline format, the lecture note contains detailed explanations for the instructor to utilize.

Suggested Answers for Discussion Questions (End of the Chapter): Each chapter in the text concludes with a list of discussion questions for the students. This section of the *Instructor's Manual* provides suggested answers that may guide the instructor on critical items to look for in the answers.

Teaching Notes for End-of-Chapter Cases: Every chapter in the text contains two short cases that illustrate some of the chapter material. This section of the *Instructor's Manual* provides suggested answers to each case question that may be helpful in organizing a class discussion.

Additional Experiential Exercise: In addition to the experiential exercises available in the text, this section of the manual provides one or two additional experiential exercises that the instructor may wish to assign. Instructors should feel free to redesign these exercises in any manner to fit their particular class.

In addition to these course assistance segments of our manual, there is a section containing *Instructor's Teaching Notes for Comprehensive Case Studies*. This section begins on page 287 of the manual and presents the suggested teaching note from the actual author of the case. In this manner, the case author's intention can be conveyed to the instructor. We sincerely appreciate those contributions by the authors.

The *Test Bank* begins on page 329 of the manual and contains 25 true/false questions, 50 multiple-choice questions, and 5 essay questions for each chapter. The answers are provided with each question, and the questions have been grouped by topics in the chapter. By doing this, the instructor has not only the answers but also the particular section that the question relates to.

The final part of the manual has the *Transparency Masters* for classroom instruction. These are professionally prepared enlargements of 40 key tables and figures from chapter material.

We are indeed very proud of *Entrepreneurship: A Contemporary Approach,* and the *Instructor's Resource Manual* was designed to enhance the use of our book. Every segment was structured with the professor in mind. We hope you will find the text and manual the most comprehensive and challenging resource in the field today. Your feedback and suggestions are always welcome as you prepare tomorrow's potential entrepreneurs.

ACKNOWLEDGEMENTS

An *Instructor's Resource Manual* of this magnitude takes a great deal of time and effort. A number of people deserve special recognition for their hard work. As always, thanks go to my wife Deborah and daughters Christina and Kellie for their constant support and understanding. In addition, acknowledgement is due to my colleagues at the College of Business, Ball State University, in particular, Neil A. Palomba, Dean, College of Business; Ray V. Montagno, Chairman, Management Department; and Kelli M. Hurley, Executive Director, Midwest Entrepreneurial Education Center, for their encouragement and confidence in my projects.

I would also like to thank Maggie Ailes at Ball State University for her constant help with typing, editing, and word processing.

Finally, a special thanks to my coauthor, mentor, and friend, Richard M. Hodgetts, a dynamic professor whose pace I will always seek to emulate.

Donald F. Kuratko
The Entrepreneurship Program
Ball State University

CONTENTS

Chapter 1	The Entrepreneurial Revolution	3
Chapter 2	Entrepreneurship: An Evolving Concept	13
Chapter 3	Intrapreneurship: Developing Entrepreneurship in the Corporation	25
Chapter 4	Understanding the Entrepreneurial Perspective in Individuals	37
Chapter 5	Developing Creativity and Understanding Innovation	51
Chapter 6	Ethical and Social Responsibility Challenges for Entrepreneurs	65
Chapter 7	Environmental Assessment: Preparation for a New Venture	81
Chapter 8	Marketing Research for New Ventures	93
Chapter 9	Financial Preparation for Entrepreneurial Ventures	109
Chapter 10	Developing an Effective Business Plan	123
Chapter 11	Assessment and Evaluation of Entrepreneurial Opportunities	145
Chapter 12	Structuring the New Business Venture	165
Chapter 13	Legal Issues Related to Emerging Ventures	179
Chapter 14	Sources of Capital for Entrepreneurs	195
Chapter 15	Strategic Planning for Emerging Ventures	211
Chapter 16	Managing Entrepreneurial Growth	225
Chapter 17	Global Opportunities for Entrepreneurs	237
Chapter 18	Valuation of Business Ventures	251
Chapter 19	Management Succession and Continuity: A Family Business Perspective	263
Chapter 20	Total Quality and the Human Factor: Continuous Challenges for Entrepreneurs	277
	Instructor's Teaching Notes for Comprehensive Case Studies	287
	Instructor's Test Bank	329
	Transparency Masters	575

PART I

The Contemporary World of Entrepreneurship

Chapter 1 - The Entrepreneurial Revolution

Chapter 2 - Entrepreneurship: An Evolving Concept

Chapter 3 - Intrapreneurship: Developing Entrepreneurship in the Corporation

CHAPTER 1

THE ENTREPRENEURIAL REVOLUTION

CHAPTER OUTLINE

I. Entrepreneurs - Challenging the Unknown

II. Entrepreneurship: A Perspective

III. Our Entrepreneurial Economy--the Environment of Entrepreneurship
   A. Predominance of new ventures in the economy
   B. Research and education

IV. The Age of the Gazelles
   A. Innovation
   B. Growth

V. The Emerging Trends in Entrepreneurship
   A. Women-owned businesses
   B. Future challenges for women entrepreneurs
      1. Work/home role conflict
      2. Closing the funding gap
      3. Changing preparation
      4. Future research

VI. Minority-Owned Businesses
   A. Future challenges for minority entrepreneurs

VII. Entrepreneurial Opportunities

VIII. Summary

CHAPTER OBJECTIVES

1. To explain the importance of entrepreneurs for economic growth.
2. To introduce the concept of an entrepreneurial perspective within individuals.
3. To examine the entrepreneurial revolution taking place today.
4. To illustrate the entrepreneurial environment.
5. To examine some of the most influential trends in entrepreneurship—women and minorities.
6. To highlight some of the latest trends in entrepreneurial research.

The Dryden Press

CHAPTER SUMMARY

This opening chapter attempts to provide a broad perspective of the entrepreneurial revolution occurring throughout the U.S. and the World. Beginning with a discussion of entrepreneurs challenging the unknown like olympic athletes, symphony conductors, or top gun pilots, the chapter presents the perspective of entrepreneurship as a force that has revolutionized business.

The environment of entrepreneurship reflects a predominance of small firms and new ventures. Over the last few years, there has been a tremendous increase in new-venture activity. There are many statistics that illustrate this fact. For example, during the decade of the eighties (through 1990), new business incorporations averaged 600,000 **per year**. While many of these incorporations may have been sole proprietorships or partnerships previously, it still demonstrates venture activity, whether it was through start-ups, expansion, or development. More specifically, let's examine some of the latest tabulated numbers.

Small firms constitute more than 90 percent of the entire business population. Granted, this figure depends on the definition of the term "small"; however, the IRS reports that 21 million businesses exist based upon business tax returns. Approximately 12 million businesses are those whose **principal** occupation is owning and operating these businesses. Approximately seven million (out of the 12 million) work for themselves without employing anyone else. Of the 5 million remaining firms, only 15,000 employ 500 or more people.

This employment number is important, since the small entrepreneurial firms have created the most **net** new jobs in the economy from 1977 to 1990. In addition, the smallest of our enterprises have created a steady supply of **net** new jobs over the business cycle from 1977 to 1990. It is important to recognize that historically, employment growth in the United States is correlated directly with new business growth. This fact has been traced back to 1960, demonstrating that the new business formations are the critical foundation for any net increase in U.S. employment.

The SBA defines three types of establishments: "small" establishments owned by small enterprises, "apparent small" establishments owned by large enterprises, and "large" establishments owned by large enterprises. An enterprise having 100 employees or fewer is considered small and one having more than 100 employees is considered large. The percentages of small, apparent small, and large establishments are 84.5, 12.7, 2.8 respectively.

It is important to realize the developments in research and education of entrepreneurship. The chapter discusses ten specific developments that have occurred in the last few years. Many institutions have created programs for entrepreneurship research. The research focuses mainly on three areas: entrepreneurship education, outreach activities with entrepreneurs, and entrepreneurship research.

There has been a tremendous growth in women entrepreneurs in the United States. There are many more women starting their own businesses. There are now 4.6 million women-owned businesses generating $278 billion.

There has been a steady trend of women business owners. Women labor force participation from 1972 to 1985 rose from 43.7 percent to 54.7 percent for women 20 years of age and over. Today there are 53 million U.S. women in the labor force. In 1990, women were 45 percent of the labor force and will become 47 percent of the civilian labor force in 2005. In 1970 and 1980, women's share of the labor force was only 38 percent and 42 percent respectively. Projections for the period 1990-2005 indicate that men will leave the labor force in greater numbers than women, by more than 4 million.

Female labor-force participation in all racial groups will rise during the period between 1990 and 2005. Hispanic and Asian women will have the fastest growth, both at 80 percent. Net labor force growth for all women between 1990 and 2005 is projected to be 26 percent. Black women's labor-force growth of 34 percent will also exceed the average for all women. White women will remain the dominant female participants, but their labor-force growth of 23 percent will be lowest among all female groups. Women are expanding into nontraditional industries at a faster rate than the retail trades. The largest percentage of businesses owned by women is still in the service sector (58 percent) with retail next at 24 percent.

More women are preparing for their new ventures. They have more formal training and greater economic opportunities. Changing social mores are influencing the entrepreneurial environment. There will be greater attention to research on women entrepreneurs. Areas that will be investigated in the future will include: individual dimension, organization, process and environment.

In recent years the number of minority-owned firms increased dramatically. Asian-American-owned firms increased 394 percent; Native American-owned firms 40 percent, Hispanic-owned firms 93 percent and Black-owned firms increased 87 percent. Cumulatively, these generated over $78 billion in gross receipts. These statistics correspond to over 1,213,570 minority-owned businesses that in addition to providing salaries for over 300,000 proprietorships, provided paid employment for 836,000 people.

In addition to the weakness in financial areas, the biggest problems encountered by minority entrepreneurs at start-up are obtaining lines of credit, lack of business training, and lack of management experience. While many of these problems continue as the venture grows, they are less frequently mentioned by the same entrepreneurs. Another study reported on the perceived lack of expertise in particular areas for minority entrepreneurs. Obtaining working capital, technical knowledge, recruitment of specialists, and marketing knowledge were ranked as the highest concerns. Again, these areas seemed to improve as the firms grew and matured over time.

LECTURE NOTES

THE ENTREPRENEURIAL REVOLUTION

I. Entrepreneurs—Challenging the Unknown
   A. Individuals who recognize opportunities where others see chaos or confusion
   B. They are compared to olympic athletes, symphony conductors, or top gun pilots

II. Entrepreneurship: A Perspective
   A. More than mere creation of business
   B. Special perspective that permeates individuals

    C. Dynamic forces that have revolutionized business
III. Our Entrepreneurial Economy—The Environment for Entrepreneurship
    A. Predominance of small firms and new ventures
        1. During the last ten years, there were over 600,000 new business incorporations per year.
        2. Small business employment statistics have been steadily rising
        3. Small firms constitute more than 90 percent of the entire business population
        4. Approximately seven million entrepreneurs (out of 12 million) work for themselves without employing anyone else. Of the 5 million remaining firms, only 15,000 employ 500 or more people.
        5. The smallest of our enterprises have created a steady supply of <u>net</u> new jobs over the business cycle from 1977-1990.
        6. Three types of establishments identified by the SBA:
            a. "Small" establishment owned by small enterprise
            b. "Apparent small" establishment owned by large enterprise
            c. "Large" establishment owned by large enterprise

    B. Research and education
        1. The major themes that characterize recent research about entrepreneurs and new-venture creations:
            a. The entrepreneurial and managerial domains are not mutually exclusive but overlap to a certain extent
            b. Venture financing has emerged in the 1980s
            c. Entrepreneurship within large organizations has gained much attention
            d. Entry strategies and career patterns have been identified that show some important common denominators
            e. Entrepreneurs use a great variety of methods in order to achieve success
            f. The risks and trade-offs of an entrepreneurial career have been a subject of keen interest
            g. Women and minority entrepreneurs have emerged in unprecedented numbers
            h. There has been enormous growth of interest in entrepreneurship around the world in the past few years
            i. The economic and social contributions of entrepreneurs have been slow to make immensely disproportionate contributions to job creation and innovation
            j. Entrepreneurship education has become one of the hottest topics at American business and engineering schools
        2. Since 1981 the "Frontiers of Entrepreneurship Research" conference has provided an outlet for the latest developments in entrepreneurship

3. Most university centers for entrepreneurship have focused on three major areas:
   a. Entrepreneurship education
   b. Outreach activities with entrepreneurs
   c. Entrepreneurship research
4. Many universities are expanding programs for entrepreneurship and small business management

IV. The Age of the Gazelles
   A. Fastest growing firms with at least 20 percent sales growth every year from 1990-1994 starting with a base of at least $100,000
   B. Innovation—gazelles are leaders in innovation with responsibility for 55 percent of innovations in 362 different industries
   C. Growth—During the last 10 years business incorporations have averaged more than 600,000 with 1995 experiencing an all-time high of 807,000

V. The Emerging Trends in Entrepreneurship
   A. Women-Owned Businesses
      1. Women-owned businesses generate gross receipts of $278 billion, which is one-tenth of all business earnings
      2. Women entrepreneurs now represent 30 percent of all business ownership in the United States
      3. Women's Business Ownership Act of 1988 established programs to assist development of women-owned businesses
      4. Fifty-three million U.S. women are in the workforce
      5. Receipts from women-owned businesses increased 183 percent between 1982-1987
      6. Women are expanding into nontraditional industries
      7. In 1990 women were 45 percent of the labor force
      8. Between 1990 and 2005 Hispanic and Asian women will have the fastest growth at 80 percent
      9. Between 1990 and 2005 women will account for 62 percent of the net growth in the labor force
   B. Future Challenges for Women Entrepreneurs
      1. Closing the funding gap
         a. One barrier faced by many women entrepreneurs is that of securing initial financing
         b. More venture capitalists are starting to provide financing to women entrepreneurs
         c. This gap will continue to close as financiers begin to realize that they have been neglecting a major source of profitable investments.

The Dryden Press

        d.   Women are beginning to gain more experience in the financial arena and become more proficient at making financial forecasts, structuring financial packages, and negotiating financial terms
- C. Future research
  1. Attention to research will be focused on personal and family-related variables by way of identifying the traits and characteristics of successful women entrepreneurs
  2. Other areas of investigation will include:
     a. Individual dimension
     b. Organization
     c. Process
     d. Environment
- D. Minority-owned Business
  1. Dramatic increases
     a. Asian-American owned firms increased 394 percent
     b. Hispanic-owned firms increased 93 percent
     c. Black-owned firms increased 87 percent
  2. Statistics reveal increases in all minorities
- E. Future Challenges for Minority Entrepreneurs
  1. Education
  2. Capital

SUGGESTED ANSWERS FOR DISCUSSION QUESTIONS
(END OF CHAPTER)

1. Briefly describe the evolution of the term "entrepreneurship."

Entrepreneurship is more than the mere creation of a business. Seeking opportunity, taking risks, and having the tenacity to push ideas into reality are special characteristics that permeate individuals. Entrepreneurship is an integrated concept that has revolutionized the way business is conducted.

2. Describe the predominance of new ventures in the economy.

During the last ten years there were over 600,000 new business incorporations per year. Ninety-nine percent of U.S. businesses can be considered small. The smallest of our enterprises have created a steady supply of **net** new jobs over the business cycle from 1977-1990. It is important to recognize that historically, employment growth in the United States is correlated directly with new business growth. This fact has been traced back to 1960, demonstrating that new business formations are the critical foundation for any net increase in U.S. employment.

3. *What is the record number of new small firms being established?*
   In 1995, there were 807,000 new incorporations, an all-time record

4. *Describe the three types of small business establishments identified by the Small Business Administration.*
   Three types of establishments have been identified by the Small BusinessAdministration: (1) "small" establishments owned by small enterprises, (2) "apparent small" establishments owned by large enterprises, and (3) "large" establishments owned by large enterprises. Small enterprises are defined as having 100 or fewer employees; large enterprises have more than 100 employees.

5. *How have most net new jobs been created in the economy?*
   Small entrepreneurial firms have created the most *net* new jobs in the U.S. economy from 1977 to 1990. In addition, the smallest of our enterprises have created a *steady supply* of net new jobs over the business cycle from 1977 to 1990. It is important to recognize that historically, employment growth in the United States is correlated directly with new-business growth. This fact has been traced back to 1960, demonstrating that new-business formations are the critical foundations for any net increased in U.S. employment. Thus, our employment growth and industry expansions are closely tied to new-venture development.

6. *Identify some of the projected growth industries through the year 2005.*
   Fastest Growing in Output (percentage basis):
   Manufacturers of computer equipment
   Manufacturers of semiconductors, related devices
   Residential care
   Health services, necessary
   Manufacturers of medical instruments and supplies
   Computer/data processing services
   Business services
   Manufacturers of miscellaneous plastic products

   Fastest Growing in Employment (percentage basis):
   Residential care
   Computer/data processing services
   Health services
   Offices of health practitioners
   Individual and miscellaneous social services
   Legal services
   Nursing and personal care facilities
   Elementary and secondary schools

7. *Define a "gazelle" and discuss its importance.*
   A gazelle is a fast growing firm with at least 20 percent sales growth every year from 1990-1994 starting with a base of at least $100,000. Despite the continual downsizing in

major corporations, the gazelles provided 5 million jobs and brought the net employment growth to 42 million jobs.

8. ***Describe the increase in business ownership among women and use actual statistics.***
    Women-owned businesses are the fastest growing segment of small business with an increase from 2.6 million businesses in 1982 to 4.6 million in 1987. Women-owned businesses grew 57.5 percent from 1982 to 1987, and receipts grew during that same period 183 percent. Today women own over 30 percent of all businesses. Between 1990 and 2005, women will account for 15 million, or 62 percent, of net growth in the labor force. In 1990 women were 45 percent of the labor force and will become 47 percent of the civilian labor in 2005. Hispanic and Asian women will have the fastest growth, both 80 percent. Net labor force growth for all women between 1990 and 2005 is projected to be 26 percent. Black women's labor force growth of 34 percent will also exceed the average of all women. White women will remain the dominant female participants, but their labor-force growth of 23 percent will be the lowest among all female groups.

9. ***What are three reasons for the rapid growth of business ownership among women?***
    The rapid growth of self-employment among women is due to: (1) a greater flexibility and adaptability in combining work and family, (2) dissatisfaction with wage and salary jobs, and (3) the availability of business opportunities.

10. ***Why is the "funding gap" likely to diminish during the 1990s?***
    The funding gap will continue to close as financiers begin to realize that they've been missing investments with women. The gap will also diminish when women learn more about financing.

11. ***Describe the emerging trend in minority entrepreneurship. Present some statistical data.***
    In recent years the number of minority-owned firms increased dramatically. Asian-American-owned firms increased 394 percent; Native American-owned firms 40 percent; Hispanic-owned firms 93 percent and Black-owned firms increased 87 percent. Cumulatively, these firms generated over $78 billion in gross receipts. These statistics correspond to over 1,231,570 minority-owned businesses that, in addition to providing salaries for over 300,000 proprietorships, provided paid employment for 836,000 people.
    The number of minority-owned businesses increased in every category between 1982 and 1987. The number of businesses owned by American Indians and Alaska Natives rose from 13,573 to 21,380, an increase of 57.5 percent. The total receipts of these businesses rose 84 percent from $495 million to $911 million. The receipts of businesses owned by American Indians and Alaska Natives accounted for 0.2 percent of all U.S. businesses and about 0.05 percent of total U.S. business receipts.

12. ***Describe the future challenges for minority entrepreneurship.***
    Minority-owned enterprises are not only emerging at a record pace but, more importantly, they are succeeding. One study of the largest black-owned firms found impressive ten-year growth rates, including some reaching 300-400 percent. In a more

recent study, researchers studied the long-term patterns of black and white female-owned businesses and found the "staying" power (longevity) of black-owned firms were equal to that of the white-owned firms. This study pointed out the smaller number of blacks entering into entrepreneurship reinforces that need for increasing entrepreneurial opportunities and education for potential minority entrepreneurs.

TEACHING NOTES FOR END-OF-CHAPTER CASES

VIDEO CASE: TWO WOMEN BOXING: THE ART OF ENTREPRENEURSHIP
(Answers to Questions)

1. *Describe how Linda Finnell and Julie Cohn fit the emerging trend of women entrepreneurs.*

    Linda and Julie are among the 6.4 million women-owned businesses in the U.S. Their retail business is part of the 50 percent control that women exhibit in the retail industry. Linda and Julie employ twelve people, which adds to the statistic that women-owned businesses employ one out of every five U.S. workers.

2. *What potential problems do you think they will face?*

    As their business continues to grow, Linda and Julie will be confronted by growth problems such as access to capital (since the funding gap is a major problem for women) and the need for personnel. Hiring and firing employees as well as expansion decisions are difficult business problems that will confront artists Linda and Julie in the future.

3. *What typical challenges to women entrepreneurs have Finnell and Cohn already overcome?*

    As successful women entrepreneurs, they have already overcome a number of the early challenges such as developing their idea, establishing a retail business, setting up accounts (major industry names), securing funds, and building a solid business reputation.

CASE: BREAKING AWAY

1. *What traits or characteristics would Joan need in order to succeed in this business?*

    Obviously, to be an interior decorator, Joan needs to be creative. She also needs to know the technical skills involved in interior decorating. Technical skills include knowing what supplies to buy, how to coordinate different color schemes, etc. If Joan is going to run her own business, she will have to be highly motivated and possess competent leadership abilities. Joan should also have the sensitivity it takes to work with customers and understand what they want.

2. *How could Joan go about financing her proposed venture? Which avenue would be most available to her?*

    Joan could attempt to get a business loan from a bank. This would depend on things like collateral and her ability to convince bankers that she is a good investment. Joan could

The Dryden Press

resort to equity capital and sell stock in her company. If Joan could not obtain a loan from a bank, she could turn to a finance company, which would mean higher rates of interest. There are also small-business investment companies that are a source of financial assistance. Chances are, if Joan fits into the norm of female entrepreneurs, she will have to rely heavily on personal assets and earnings. Joan may have to take out a personal loan or look to her husband for financial help.

3. *What does Joan need to learn in order to run her new venture most effectively?*

The first thing she needs to realize is that she does not know all there is to know about business, as she told her husband. Joan needs to learn how to develop a business plan and to view the operations in a broader sense. She needs to understand how each part works alone and fits in with the other parts. It would probably be a good idea if Joan obtained some kind of training in handling a small business. She will have to analyze the situation thoroughly and determine how much capital she will need to start the business. Joan also needs to figure out what kind of ongoing costs her business will entail. In addition, Joan should know how to identify and contact potential clients. Finally, and probably most importantly, it will be necessary for Joan to learn about financial planning and seek some kind of assistance.

CASE: A RESEARCH ORIENTATION

1. *What are three research questions Henry could pursue?*
   1. How many hours do women entrepreneurs spend on their businesses?
   2. How has starting a business affected their marriages or relationships?
   3. What kind of influence are the parents as role models?

2. *Discuss any important findings that have emerged in research conducted on minority entrepreneurs.*

   One discovery was that the rate of women entrepreneurs who were college graduates is higher than men and women in general and men managers and administrators. This could explain why a woman would get frustrated trapped in a job that does not make use of her potential. It was discovered that frustration, dissatisfaction, and need for more control were some of the motivators for starting an independent business. These are the same factors that induce men to go out on their own.

3. *Discuss an area of research you think would be most fruitful for Henry.*

   Since the financial aspect of women entrepreneurship seems to be the weakest, it would be most beneficial if Henry pursued this area. He could possibly discover and identify financial avenues that are open to women. The sources could be out there but just not known. Also, it would be interesting to review and analyze why some women-owned businesses succeeded and others did not. This kind of information would help future women entrepreneurs.

CHAPTER 2

ENTREPRENEURSHIP: AN EVOLVING CONCEPT

CHAPTER OUTLINE

I. The Evolution of Entrepreneurship

II. The Myths of Entrepreneurship
   A. Entrepreneurs are doers, not thinkers
   B. Entrepreneurs are born, not made
   C. Entrepreneurs are always inventors
   D. Entrepreneurs are academic and social misfits
   E. Entrepreneurs must fit the "profile"
   F. All you need is money to be an entrepreneur
   G. All you need is luck to be an entrepreneur
   H. Ignorance is bliss for an entrepreneur
   I. Entrepreneurs seek success but experience high failure rates
   J. Entrepreneurs are extreme risk takers (gamblers)

III. Approaches to Entrepreneurship
   A. The schools of entrepreneurial thought
      1. The macro view
         a. The environmental school of thought
         b. The financial/capital school of thought
         c. The displacement school of thought
      2. The micro view
         a. The entrepreneurial trait school of thought
         b. The venture opportunity school of thought
         c. The strategic formulation school of thought

IV. Process Approaches
   A. Entrepreneurial events approach
   B. Entrepreneurial assessment approach
   C. Multidimensional approach

V. Intrapreneurship

VI. Key Concepts
   A. Entrepreneurship
   B. Entrepreneur
   C. Entrepreneurial management

VII. Summary

The Dryden Press

CHAPTER OBJECTIVES

1. To examine the historical development of entrepreneurship.
2. To explore and debunk the myths of entrepreneurship.
3. To define and explore the major schools of entrepreneurial thought.
4. To explain the process approaches to the study of entrepreneurship.
5. To set forth a comprehensive definition of *entrepreneurship*.

CHAPTER SUMMARY

This particular chapter begins with the definition and the proper introduction to entrepreneurship. The chapter stresses the importance historically of entrepreneurship. It provides a basic understanding of the beginning and the modern economic definitions.

To be a successful entrepreneur, an individual must be an independent thinker who is willing to take risks and dare to be different. Personal initiative, ability to consolidate resources, management skills, and risk taking are just a few of the important qualities needed to be a successful entrepreneur.

The chapter continues to define and discuss ten specific myths associated with entrepreneurship. The myths are present because of the lack of research within this particular field. Also, the technology within this field is becoming more advanced and more widely known.

An individual's understanding may be increased by many approaches. Two specific approaches are "macro" and "micro" views. Within each view, there are three "schools of thought." According to this chapter, the "schools of thought" are considered to be a foundation for entrepreneurial theory. Also, there are the process approaches: "entrepreneurial events," "entrepreneurial assessment," and "multidimensional." Entrepreneurial events involve four main factors: initiative, organization, relative autonomy, and risk taking. Through these factors, individuals plan, implement, and control their activities within the entrepreneurship. The entrepreneurial assessment approach involves qualitative, quantitative, strategic, and ethical assessments in regard to the entrepreneur, the venture, and the environment. The multidimensional approach provides fewer distinct categories, giving it a more specific or detailed process approach to entrepreneurship. The approach is divided into the individual, the environment, the organization, and the process.

Before the chapter concludes with the summary, the key factors of entrepreneurship, entrepreneur, and entrepreneurial management are briefly discussed.

LECTURE NOTES

ENTREPRENEURSHIP: AN EVOLVING CONCEPT

I. The Evolution of Entrepreneurship
   A. Taken from the French "entre prendre," meaning "to undertake"

B. An entrepreneur is an innovator or developer who recognizes and seizes opportunities; converts those opportunities into workable/marketable ideas; adds value through time, effort, money, or skills; assumes the risks of the competitive marketplace to implement these ideas; and realizes the rewards from these efforts.
C. Characteristics
   1. Personal initiative
   2. The ability to consolidate resources
   3. Management skills
   4. A tendency toward autonomy and risk taking
   5. Competitive
   6. Goal-oriented behavior
   7. Aggressiveness
   8. Ability to employ human relations skills
D. Historical developments
   1. No single definition of entrepreneur exists
   2. Recognition of entrepreneurs dates back to eighteenth-century France
   3. Until 1950 the majority of definitions and references came from economists
   4. Robert C. Ronstadt said, "Entrepreneurship is the dynamic process of creating incremental wealth"
   5. In present day the word *entrepreneur* has become closely linked with free enterprise and capitalism
   6. Entrepreneurs serve as agents for change, provide creative, innovative ideas for business enterprise, and help businesses grow and become profitable
   7. Considered heroes of free enterprise
   8. Many people regard entrepreneurship as "pioneership" on the frontier of business

II. The Myths of Entrepreneurship
   A. Entrepreneurs are doers, not thinkers
      1. Entrepreneurs have a tendency toward action, but they are also thinkers
      2. Emphasis today is on the creation of a clear and complete business plan
   B. Entrepreneurs are born, not made
      1. Traits include aggressiveness, initiative, drive, a willingness to take risks, analytical ability, and skill in human relations
      2. Entrepreneurship has models, processes, and case studies that allow the traits to be acquired
   C. Entrepreneurs are always inventors
      1. This is a result of misunderstanding and tunnel vision
      2. Many inventors or innovators are also entrepreneurs
      3. Numerous entrepreneurs encompass all sorts of innovative activities
   D. Entrepreneurs are academic and social misfits
      1. This myth results from people who have started successful enterprises after dropping out of school or quitting a job
      2. Historically, education and social organizations did not recognize the entrepreneur
      3. The entrepreneur is now viewed as a professional

E. Entrepreneurs must fit the "profile"
   1. Many books and articles have presented checklists of characteristics of the successful entrepreneur
   2. The environment, the venture itself, and the entrepreneur have interactive effects, which result in many different profiles
F. All you need is money to be an entrepreneur
   1. Venture needs capital to survive
   2. Large number of business failures occur because of a lack of adequate financing
   3. Failure due to lack of financing indicates other problems
      a. Managerial incompetence
      b. Lack of financial understanding
      c. Poor investments
      d. Poor planning
G. All you need is luck to be an entrepreneur
   1. Being in the right place at the right time is always an advantage
   2. "Luck" happens when preparation meets opportunity
   3. What appears to be luck could really be several factors
      a. Preparation
      b. Determination
      c. Desire
      d. Knowledge
      e. Innovativeness
H. Ignorance is bliss for an entrepreneur
   1. Key factors in successful entrepreneurship
      a. Identifying the strengths and weaknesses of a venture
      b. Setting up clear timetables with contingencies for handling problems
      c. Minimizing problems through careful strategy formulation
   2. Careful planning is the mark of an accomplished entrepreneur
I. Entrepreneurs seek success but experience high failure rates
   1. Many entrepreneurs suffer a number of failures before they are successful
   2. Failure can teach many lessons to those willing to learn and often leads to future success
J. Entrepreneurs are extreme risk takers (gamblers)
   1. The concept of risk is a major element in the entrepreneurship process
   2. While it may appear that an entrepreneur is "gambling" on a wild chance, the fact is that the entrepreneur is usually working on a moderate or "calculated" risk

III. Approaches to Entrepreneurship
   A. The schools of entrepreneurial thought
      1. The macro view
         a. Presents a broad array of factors that relate to success or failure in contemporary entrepreneurial ventures
         b. Three schools of entrepreneurial thought
            1. The environmental school of thought

        a. Deals with the external factors that affect a potential entrepreneur's lifestyle
        b. Focuses on institutions, values, and morals
    2. The financial/capital school of thought
        a. Deals with the search for seed capital and growth capital
        b. Views the entire entrepreneurial venture from a financial management standpoint
    3. The displacement school of thought
        a. Holds that the group affects or eliminates certain factors that project the individual into an entrepreneurial venture
        b. Three major types of displacement
            1. Political displacement: Deals with government's policies and regulations
            2. Cultural displacement: Deals with social groups precluded from professional fields
            3. Economic displacement: Deals with economic variations of recession and depression
2. The micro view
    a. Examines the factors that are specific to entrepreneurship
    b. Holds that the potential entrepreneur has the ability or control to direct or adjust the outcome of each major influence
    c. Three schools of thought
        1. The entrepreneurial trait school of thought
            a. The study of successful people who tend to exhibit similar characteristics that would increase successful opportunities
            b. Four factors usually exhibited by successful entrepreneurs
                1. Achievement
                2. Creativity
                3. Determination
                4. Technological knowledge
            c. Deals with the family development idea
                1. Focuses on the nurturing and support that exists within the home atmosphere
        2. The venture opportunity school of thought
            a. The search for sources of ideas, the development of concepts, and the implementation of venture opportunities
            b. Views creating and market awareness as essentials
            c. Deals with the ability to recognize new ideas and opportunities and to implement the necessary steps of action
        3. The strategic formulation school of thought
            a. Emphasizes the planning process in successful venture development
            b. Four major factors in considering the strategic formulation
                1. Unique markets
                2. Unique people

            3. Unique products
            4. Unique resources
      4. Summary of schools of entrepreneurial thought
         a. Knowledge and research available is in its embryonic stage
         b. The field of entrepreneurship uses a number of theories in its growth and development

   B. Process Approaches
      1. Entrepreneurial events approach
         a. Focuses on and includes four factors
            1. Initiative
            2. Organization
            3. Relative autonomy
            4. Risk taking
      2. Entrepreneurial assessment approach
         a. Focuses on the entrepreneur, the venture, and environment
         b. Assessments are made qualitatively, quantitatively, strategically, and ethically
         c. Career stage--early, middle, or late--is also considered
      3. Multidimensional approach
         a. Emphasizes the individual, the environment, the organization, and the venture process
         b. Dimensions that relate
            1. The individual
            2. The environment
            3. The organization
            4. The process
         c. Moves entrepreneurship from a segmented school of thought to a dynamic, interactive process approach

IV. Intrapreneurship
   A. Very few executives understand the concept
   B. Pinchot's definition: those who take hands-on responsibility for creating innovation of any kind within an organization
   C. Major thrust in intrapreneurship is to create or develop the entrepreneurial spirit within corporate boundaries

V. Key Concepts
   A. Entrepreneurship
      1. A process of innovation and new-venture creation through four major dimensions
         a. Individual
         b. Organization
         c. Environment
         d. Process

B. Entrepreneur
      1. A catalyst for economic change who uses purposeful searching, careful planning, and sound judgment in carrying out the entrepreneurial process
   C. Entrepreneurial management
      1. All the rules, things that work, and the kinds of innovations are the same
      2. The techniques and principles of this emerging discipline will drive the entrepreneurial economy of our time

SUGGESTED ANSWERS FOR DISCUSSION QUESTIONS (END OF CHAPTER)

1. Briefly describe the evolution of the term "entrepreneurship."

The word "entrepreneur" is derived from the French "entre prendre," which means "to undertake." Thus, it began as a concept to identify one who undertakes to organize, manage, and assume the risks of business. The risk-bearing part dates back to the eighteenth century when French economist Richard Cantillon matched it with the term "entrepreneur." Economics and entrepreneurship remained closely tied through the years as noted economists such as Jean-Baptiste Say (1803) and Joseph Schumpeter (1934) continued to write about entrepreneurship and its impact on economic development. Over the years various definitions have been used in an attempt to describe entrepreneurship. The twentieth century has linked the term with free enterprise and capitalism, while three specific activities have been recognized that entrepreneurs perform: serving as an agent for change; providing creative, innovative ideas for the enterprise; and helping business grow and become profitable.

2. What are the ten myths associated with entrepreneurship? Debunk each.

   (1) **Entrepreneurs are doers, not thinkers.**
   They are often very methodical people who plan their moves carefully. Today the emphasis is on the creation of clear, complete business plans.

   (2) **Entrepreneurs are born, not made.**
   The recognition of entrepreneurship as a discipline has helped to dispel this myth. Like all disciplines, entrepreneurship has models, processes, and case studies that allow the topic to be studied and the traits acquired.

   (3) **Entrepreneurs are either inventors or innovators.**
   There are numerous entrepreneurs who encompass all sorts of profit-seeking activity. For example, Ray Kroc did not invent the fast-food franchise, but his innovative ideas made McDonald's the largest fast-food enterprise in the world.

   (4) **Entrepreneurs are academic and social misfits.**
   Today the entrepreneur is considered a hero--socially, economically, and academically. No longer a misfit, the entrepreneur is now viewed as a professional.

   (5) **Entrepreneurs must fit the "profile."**
   Many books and articles have presented checklists of characteristics of the successful entrepreneur. These lists were neither validated nor complete. Today we realize that a

standard entrepreneurial profile is hard to compile. The environment, the venture itself, and the entrepreneur have interactive effects, which result in many different types of profiles.

(6) **All you need is money to be an entrepreneur**.
Having money is not the only bulwark against failure. Failure due to a lack of proper financing often is an indicator of other problems.

(7) **All you need is luck to be an entrepreneur**.
"Luck happens when preparation meets opportunity" is an equally appropriate adage. Prepared entrepreneurs who seize the opportunity when it arises often appear to be "lucky."

(8) **Ignorance is bliss for an entrepreneur**.
Identifying the strengths and weaknesses of a venture, setting up clear timetables with contingencies for handling problems and minimizing these problems through careful strategy formulation are all key factors in successful entrepreneurship.

(9) **Entrepreneurs seek success but experience high failure rates.**
Many entrepreneurs suffer a number of failures before they are successful. They follow the adage "If at first you don't succeed, try, try, again." In fact, failure can teach many lessons to those willing to learn and often leads to future successes.

(10) **Entrepreneurs are extreme risk takers (gamblers).**
The concept of risk is a major element in the entrepreneurship process. However, the public's perception of the risk assumed by most entrepreneurs is distorted. While it may appear that an entrepreneur is "gambling" on a wild chance, the fact is that the entrepreneur is usually working on a moderate or "calculated" risk.

3. *What is the macro view of entrepreneurship?*
The macro view of entrepreneurship presents a broad array of factors that relate to success or failure in contemporary entrepreneurial ventures. This array includes external processes that are sometimes beyond the individual's control.

4. *What are the schools of thought that use the macro view of entrepreneurship?*
The environmental school of thought, the financial capital school of thought, and the displacement school of thought

5. *What is the micro view of entrepreneurship?*
The micro view of entrepreneurship examines the factors that are specific to entrepreneurship and are part of the "internal" focus of control.

6. *What are the schools of thought that use the micro view of entrepreneurship?*
The entrepreneurial trait school of thought, the venture opportunity school of thought, and the strategic formulation school of thought

7. *What are the three specific types of displacement?*
Political displacement, cultural displacement, and economic displacement

8. ***In the strategy formulation school of thought, what are the four types of strategies involved with unique elements? Give an illustration of each.***
   (1) Unique markets--College campus businesses would tend to market products college people want and need.
   (2) Unique people--If you were going to open up a car repair shop, you need to know how to repair cars.
   (3) Unique products--Coke differs from Pepsi.
   (4) Unique resources--Middle-easterners have the ability to produce more oil products.

9. ***What is the process approach to entrepreneurship? In your answer, describe the entrepreneurial assessment approach.***
   The process approach to entrepreneurship is a way to examine the activities involved in entrepreneurship by using either an "entrepreneurial assessment" approach or a "multidimensional approach." Both of these methods attempt to describe the entrepreneurial process as a consolidation of diverse factors.
   The entrepreneurial assessment focuses on the process of entrepreneurial activity and includes the following factors: (1) the entrepreneur; (2) the venture; and (3) the environment. All of these factors are assessed quantitatively, qualitively, strategically, and ethically.

10. ***What are the major elements in the framework for entrepreneurship presented in Figure 2.4? Give an example of each.***
    The major elements in Gartner's framework with examples for each are as follows:
    (1) The Individual: Need for achievement, locus of control, risk-taking propensity, and previous work experience
    (2) The Environment: Venture capital availability, presence of experienced entrepreneurs, accessibility of customers or new markets, and proximity of universities
    (3) The Organization: Type of firm, entrepreneurial environment, partners, and strategic variables: cost, differentiation, and focus
    (4) The Process: The entrepreneur locates a business opportunity; the entrepreneur markets products and services

TEACHING NOTES FOR END-OF-CHAPTER CASES

VIDEO CASE: DREW PEARSON COMPANIES: SUPER BOWL CHAMP PUTS A CAP ON SUCCESS (Answers to Questions)

1. *What myth in entrepreneurship does DPC and Drew Pearson seem to debunk?*
   While a number of myths can be applied to this case, the myths of being "born not made," "always inventors," and "all you need is luck" would be three of the most applicable. Certainly Drew Pearson illustrates a person who made his success as a football player and as an entrepreneur rather than someone "born" into it. Obviously DPC does not represent a special invention, therefore dispelling the myth of entrepreneurs always being inventors.

The Dryden Press

Finally, Drew Pearson worked to make his success, as opposed to someone who is "lucky." Luck is when preparation meets opportunity, and Drew Pearson exhibits that statement.

2. *Describe the schools of entrepreneurial thought that may apply to Drew Pearson and his venture.*

From the macro view, Drew Pearson exhibits the environmental school of thought because of his successful experiences in pro football (Super Bowl) that projected him into other professional successes. From the micro view, he exhibits the strategic formulation school of thought because of the unique market that DPC was able to capture.

3. *Using Fig. 2.3, explain how Pearson's venture fits into the entrepreneurial assessment approach.*

DPC is a combination of the entrepreneur (Drew Pearson), the venture (Sports caps), and the environment (pro sports) that all came together at the right stage of Pearson's career to make it a success. Each of these dimensions can be discussed by the class to help illustrate how to assess a new venture.

CASE: PAUL'S FOUR SHORTCOMINGS

1. *Does Paul need to be an inventor in order to be an effective entrepreneur? Explain.*

No, Paul does not need to be an inventor. That idea is one of the ten most commonly known myths of entrepreneurship. Entrepreneurship covers all varieties of profit-making activities and, thus, is not limited to inventions.

2. *How important is it that Paul have a lot of money if he hopes to be an entrepreneur? Explain.*

While having start-up capital is always important in new ventures, it is not the only factor. In fact, many entrepreneurs are able to obtain enough capital through loans because the funding source believes in the managerial ability of the entrepreneur. Thus, having lots of money is not the only key to success.

3. *What is wrong with Paul's overall thinking? Be sure to include a discussion of the myths of entrepreneurship in your answer.*

Paul's overall thinking is caught up in the typical mythical beliefs about entrepreneurship. The myths have arisen due to lack of knowledge and research about entrepreneurs. Therefore, people have simply believed that entrepreneurs are born, not made, and need luck, money, and ignorance to succeed. Paul is reflecting the traditionally accepted "folklore" that still exists due to the infancy of the current research. However, each year the research expands, knowledge increases, and contemporary entrepreneurs realize these weaknesses in the myths.

ADDITIONAL EXPERIENTIAL EXERCISE

"An Actual Start-up"

The students will start up an actual business. Divide them into groups of four. Check with the manager of a mall to see if one Saturday or Sunday he will permit the groups to set up a little contest among themselves. The team that sells the most products and has the most profit after expenses will be the winner and will get some bonus points or a free pizza from you. The product should be perishable so that if the students produce too many items, not only will it hurt their profits, but they will also have to carefully estimate the quantity needed to supply demand. A mall will be a good place to have the contest because students will have to spend a day or two there to get a feel for where the most traffic will be. Their final profits will be affected if they do not know where to set up. It will take some effort on their part if they want to win, and they will have to research their product to get a feel for supply and demand. They will have to find the cheapest way to produce and advertise their product. This will take some research, but it can be a lot of fun. It can be something as simple as the proverbial lemonade stand; however, it will give them a small taste of what it is really like to make decisions about their own business, which in the long run can either make them money or bankrupt the company.

CHAPTER 3

INTRAPRENEURSHIP: DEVELOPING ENTREPRENEURSHIP IN THE CORPORATION

CHAPTER OUTLINE

I. Introduction

II. The Nature of Intrapreneurship
- A. The Need for Entrepreneuring
- B. Corporate Venturing Obstacles
    1. Traditional management practices
    2. Adverse effects
    3. Recommended actions
- C. Factors Apparent in Successful Innovators
    1. Atmosphere and vision
    2. Orientation to the market
    3. Small, flat organizations
    4. Multiple approaches
    5. Interactive learning
    6. Skunkworks
- D. Reengineering Corporate Thinking

III. Specific Elements of a Corporate Intrapreneurial Strategy
- A. Developing the Vision
- B. Encouraging Innovation
    1. Radical innovation
    2. Incremental innovation
    3. Champion
    4. Top management support
- C. Structuring for an Intrapreneurial Climate
    1. Melding individual attitudes, values, and behavioral orientations with the organizational factors of structure and reward
    2. Intrapreneurship training program
    3. Intrapreneurship assessment investment
    4. Organizational factors to consider
- D. Development of Venture Teams
    1. Collective entrepreneurship
    2. Venture team

IV. The Interactive Process of Intrapreneurship
- A. Who Are the Intrapreneurs?

The Dryden Press

            1. Characteristics and traits
            2. Intrapreneurial myths dispelled
        B. The Interactive Process of Individual and Organizational Characteristics

V. Summary

CHAPTER OBJECTIVES

1. To define the term *intrapreneurship*.
2. To illustrate the need for corporate entrepreneuring.
3. To describe the corporate obstacles preventing innovation from existing in corporations.
4. To discuss the intrapreneurship considerations involved in reengineering corporate thinking.
5. To describe the specific elements of an intrapreneurial strategy.
6. To profile intrapreneurial characteristics and myths.
7. To illustrate the interactive process of intrapreneurship.

CHAPTER SUMMARY

Many corporations have gone through changes during the eighties and nineties. These changes have been called a revolution. Due to the infusion of entrepreneurial thinking into large corporations, they learned to tap the innovative talents of their own employees. This new type of business practice is called intrapreneurship. This chapter shows the need for corporate entrepreneuring and describes the elements needed for innovation to exist in corporations, considerations involved in reengineering corporate thinking, strategies for introducing intrapreneurial activity, and the interactive process of intrapreneurial characteristics and traits with organizational characteristics.

In today's rapidly changing market, there is a need for corporate intrapreneuring. There is no room for the "old ways" management. There are many more new competitors that are using new, innovative methods. A modern company must always be ready and willing to accept innovations. Those companies that are unwilling to change will quickly become obsolete. There is also a sense of distrust among the younger employees in older management styles. Entrepreneuring is quickly becoming a more respected career. If a company cannot work with and develop its best people, they may leave. Venture capital is becoming easier to acquire. If young innovative persons feel they are getting stuck in corporate politics, they may leave and try it on their own by starting their own businesses.

Companies need to provide the freedom and encouragement that intrapreneurs need to develop their ideas. A culture with new values has to be developed in order to remain competitive.

It is important to recognize that traditional management practices applied to this new type of culture may cause obstacles to new venture development. Thus, a reinvention of the corporation may be necessary.

Specific strategies for corporate intrapreneuring include the development of a vision, the nurturing of either radical or incremental innovation, structuring for an intrapreneurial climate, and the development of venture teams to enhance "collective entrepreneurship" in the corporation.

The modern corporation is now being forced to seek ways of encouraging in-house entrepreneuring. Management must develop a climate that encourages this way of thinking. Company goals must be clear. There should be a system of feedback and positive reinforcement. Managers need to emphasize individual responsibility and reward on the basis of results. Understanding the interactive process of individual and organizational characteristics is important. The first step is to examine intrapreneurs.

Who are intrapreneurs? They are people with average to above-average intelligence. They are not inventors but rather people who can turn ideas into reality. They are self-determined goal setters who go beyond the call of duty in achieving their goals. They don't see failure as a setback. They learn from it.

Many of the myths of entrepreneurs have come to be myths of intrapreneurs. These same myths have been dispelled. Intrapreneurs are not negative, and they can help a company grow and prosper if allowed to develop.

In today's quickly changing environment, it is necessary to be ready for change—not radical changes, but innovation and keeping up with the times. Those companies that are unwilling to move into the next generation of business by developing an intrapreneuring environment and encouraging innovation will no longer be in business.

LECTURE NOTES

INTRAPRENEURSHIP: DEVELOPING ENTREPRENEURSHIP IN THE CORPORATION

I. Introduction
Today there is a corporate revolution taking place. This revolution is due to the infusion of entrepreneurial thinking into large corporations. This is referred to as intrapreneurship. This allows corporations to tap the talents of innovative thinking from its own employees.

II. The Nature of Intrapreneurship
Intrapreneurship is allowing an atmosphere of innovation to prosper.
    A. The need for entrepreneuring
        1. There is a rapidly growing number of new, sophisticated competitors. Improvements are very common in today's high-tech market. A company must always be ready and willing to accept innovations, or it will quickly become obsolete.
        2. There is a sense of distrust in the traditional methods of corporate management. Since being an entrepreneur is becoming more of a status symbol and more accepted, many companies are losing their best people. They are going out on their own. Venture capital is becoming more widely available for those who wish to go out on their own, thus making entrepreneurship more attractive.

B. Corporate venturing obstacles
   The obstacles to corporate entrepreneuring are usually due to ineffective traditional management techniques. Thus, the adverse effects of management principles applied to new venture development must be considered and corrected. Table 4.1 provides a complete list of the sources and solutions to these obstacles.
C. Factors apparent in successful innovators
   Researcher James Brian Quinn has identified the following factors that exist in large corporations when they have been successful at innovation:
   1. Atmosphere and vision
   2. Orientation to the market
   3. Small, flat organizations
   4. Multiple approaches
   5. Interactive learning
   6. Skunkworks
D. Reengineering corporate thinking
   Companies need to provide the freedom and encouragement that intrapreneurs need to develop their ideas. Managers must learn that entrepreneurship ideas can be developed within their company. Many companies (managers) are using outdated managerial techniques. Doing old tasks more efficiently is not the answer to new challenges; a culture with new values has to be developed. Companies need to start encouraging an intrapreneurial environment from within, in order to remain competitive.

III. Specific Elements of a Corporate Intrapreneurial Strategy
   To create an intrapreneurial environment, it is necessary to reinvent the corporation.
   A. Developing the vision
      The first step in planning a strategy of intrapreneurship for the enterprise is sharing a vision of innovation that executives wish to achieve.
   B. Encouraging innovation
      Two distinct types of innovation exist:
      1. Radical innovation--This type of innovation takes experimentation and determined vision which are not necessarily managed.
      2. Incremental innovation--This type of innovation refers to the systematic evolution of a product or service into newer markets. Both types of innovation require vision and support. There needs to be a *champion* who has the ability to develop and share a vision as well as the effort of *top management* to support the innovative activities. *Intra capital* is a term that refers to special funding set aside for intrapreneurial projects.
   C. Structuring for an intrapreneurial climate
      1. Melding individual attitudes, values, and behavioral orientations with the organizational factors of structure and reward.
      2. ITP= Intrapreneurship Training Program
         Introduction. This consisted of a review of management and organizational

behavior concepts, definitions of intrapreneurship and related concepts, and a review of several intrapreneurship cases.

Personal creativity. This module attempted to define and stimulate personal creativity. It involved a number of creativity exercises and had participants develop a personal creative enrichment program.

Intrapreneuring. A review of the current literature on the topic was presented here, as well as in-depth analyses of several intrapreneuring organizations.

Assessment of current culture. A climate survey (not the research instrument) was administered to the training group for the purpose of generating discussion about the current facilitators and barriers to change in the organization.

Business planning. The intrapreneurial business planning process was outlined and explained. The specific elements of a business plan were identified and illustrated, and an example of an entire business plan was presented.

Action planning. In this module participants worked in teams and created action plans designed to bring about change to foster intrapreneurship in their own workplaces.
   3. IAI= Intrapreneurship Assessment Instrument
   4. Organizational Factors to Consider
      a. Top management support
      b. Autonomy/work discretion
      c. Rewards/reinforcement
      d. Time availability
      e. Organizational boundaries
   D. Development of venture teams
      1. Collective entrepreneurship--When entrepreneurship is diffused throughout the company and individual skills are integrated into a group.
      2. Venture team--Small groups operating semiautonomously to create and develop new ideas.

IV. The Interactive Process of Intrapreneurship
   A. Who are the intrapreneurs?
   They are not necessarily inventors but those who can turn ideas into reality.
      1. Characteristics and traits--Intrapreneurs tend to be action oriented. They move quickly and get things done. They are goal oriented. They are a combination of a thinker and a doer. They combine vision and action. They are self-determined goal setters who go beyond the call of duty in achieving their goals. They do not see failure as a setback; they learn from it and move on.
      2. Intrapreneurial myths dispelled--Many myths of entrepreneurs have carried over to become myths of intrapreneurs.
   B. The interactive process of individual and organizational characteristics.

SUGGESTED ANSWERS FOR DISCUSSION QUESTIONS
(END OF CHAPTER)

1. **In your own words, what is an intrapreneur?**

    An intrapreneur is a person with average to above-average intelligence who has the ability to perceive the big picture. They are not stagnated by structure and have learned how to manipulate it. They are people who like to see things happen, and they like to make them happen. They are self-confident and optimistic. They are willing to work hard with an idea, not needing an authoritative figure over them. They are self-motivated.

2. **What are two reasons there has been such a strong desire in recent years to develop intrapreneurship?**

    A highly competitive market has risen. In order for a company to survive, it must be innovative. Also, many firms that are unwilling to change are losing their best people to entrepreneurship.

3. **What are some of the corporate obstacles that must be overcome in order to establish an intrapreneurial environment?**

    The firm needs to emphasize individual responsibility among its employees. It must have a system of rewards based on results. It must overcome traditional management practices that are too rigid.

4. **What are some of the innovative principles identified by James Brian Quinn that companies need to establish?**

    According to James Brian Quinn, a noted expert on innovation, the following principles are apparent in companies that have been successful innovators: atmosphere and vision; orientation to the market; small, flat organizations, multiple approaches, interactive learning; and skunkworks.

5. **A number of corporations today are working to reengineeer corporate thinking and encourage an intrapreneurial environment. What types of steps would you recommend? Offer at least three and explain each.**
    1. Early identification of potential intrapreneurs. If you have them, use them. Don't let them go to waste, or they will leave.
    2. Top management sponsorship of intrapreneurial projects. If there is no support from the top, what encouragement will that person have?
    3. Promotion of intrapreneurship through experimentation. The full development of an intrapreneurial environment takes time. You must tolerate failure.

6. **What are five useful rules for innovation?**

    Encourage action. Use informal meetings whenever possible. Tolerate failure. Be persistent in getting an idea into the market. Reward innovation for innovation's sake.

7. **What are three advantages of developing an intrapreneurial philosophy?**
   Companies that promote personal growth attract the best people. An intrapreneurial environment allows employees to get the satisfaction of developing their ideas without risk of leaving the company. The company itself will become more competitive. There is higher employee satisfaction.

8. **Identify the four key elements managers should concentrate on to develop an intrapreneurial strategy.**
   The four key elements are: developing a vision; encouraging innovation; structuring for an intrapreneurial environment; and developing venture teams.

9. **Explain the differences between radical and incremental innovation.**
   Radical innovation represents inaugural breakthroughs that have been launched. These innovations take experimentation and vision but are not managed. Incremental innovation refers to the systematic evolution of a product or service into a new market. This innovation can be managed.

10. **Identify the five specific entrepreneurial climate factors organizations need to address in structuring their environment.**
    Top management support; autonomy/work discretion; rewards/reinforcement; time availability; and organizational boundaries.

11. **Why are venture teams emerging as part of a new strategy for many corporations?**
    Because venture teams hold the potential for producing innovative results. The venture team is a small group of people who operate semiautonomously to create and develop a new idea. Working together to integrate individual skills into the group, venture teams are diffusing entrepreneurship throughout the company--this has been termed "collective entrepreneurship."

12. **Of the key intrapreneurship considerations set forth in Table 3.4, which three are of most value to practicing managers? Why?**
    (1) Time orientation is important because a manager has to know that completing a job within the time frame set is important to the intrapreneur.
    (2) The next important characteristic is the tendency to action because a manager needs to know if the intrapreneur is going to be an outstanding employee.
    (3) Finally, an intrapreneur's primary motive is important to the practicing manager because the manager needs to know how important the organization is to the intrapreneur.

13. **How does an entrepreneur differ from an intrapreneur? Compare and contrast the two.**
    An entrepreneur has more risk involved in his/her own business. The entrepreneur is working for his/her livelihood and is much more affected by the fluctuations in the market

than an intrapreneur who faces little risk other than losing his/her job. Both entrepreneurs and intrapreneurs have the same typical myths surrounding them. For example, a common myth both share is that their primary motive is to become rich quick, but the process of innovation and doing things right takes time.

14. **Why is it useful to understand some of the myths that have sprung up about intrapreneurs? Explain, using two of these myths as examples.**

    Intrapreneurs have the same myths about them as do entrepreneurs and as a result have to overcome some preconceived notions that people have. One myth in particular says that intrapreneurs have no morals or ethics, thus placing them in the category with a used car salesman, whereas in truth, they need to have high standards so that community members will trust them. Another myth facing intrapreneurs is that they lack analytical skills. If someone perceives the intrapreneur as being lucky, they may not trust his decisions as easily.

15. **What exactly is the "interactive process" of intrapreneurship? Be specific.**

    After reading and reviewing the specific organizational strategies for intrapreneurship as well as the individual traits and characteristics of intrapreneurs, it becomes apparent that successful intrapreneurial efforts are the result of an interactive process. The decision to act intrapreneurially occurs as a result of an interaction between organizational characteristics, individual characteristics, and some kind of precipitating event. The precipitating event provides the impetus to behave intrapreneurially when other conditions are conducive to such behavior. These influencing factors seem to include some type of environment or organizational change that precipitates or ignites the interaction of organizational characteristics and individual characteristics to cause intrapreneurial events.

TEACHING NOTES FOR END-OF-CHAPTER CASES

VIDEO CASE: SOUTHWEST AIRLINES: POSITIVELY OUTRAGEOUS LEADERSHIP (Answers to Questions)

1. **Describe some of the factors needed to reengineer corporate thinking that Southwest Airlines already exhibits.**

    Southwest Airlines provides the freedom and encouragement for people to develop new ideas. Herb Kelleher has successfully transitioned away from outdated managerial techniques and applies his "management by fooling around" concept that infuses <u>fun</u> into the workplace. Finally, Kelleher instills an innovative environment that encourages people to excel. The "heroes of the heart" award is an excellent example of showcasing that environment.

2. **What specific elements of a corporate entrepreneurial strategy are apparent within Southwest Airlines?**

   Three elements (out of four) seem to be quite apparent at Southwest Airlines: (1) Developing the vision—Kelleher has definitely created a unique vision for this airline; (2) Encouraging innovation—Kelleher believes in the accomplishments of his people and rewards them for it; (3) Structuring an intrapreneurial climate—while Southwest Airlines may not be completely intrapreneurial, the climate is ideal due to top management support, autonomy, and rewards or reinforcement.

3. **How has Herb Kelleher structured a climate conducive to entrepreneurial activity?**

   Kelleher established Southwest Airlines' University for people, where all employees learn trust, cooperation, mutual respect, and good communication. Because of this, Southwest Airlines' climate is conducive for people to interact and develop new ideas. The company's tribute illustrates the intense spirit of the people—"The people of Southwest Airlines are the creators of what we have become, and what we will be."

ADDITIONAL EXPERIENTIAL EXERCISES

"Implementing Intrapreneurship"

Use one hour of class time to ask students to develop and present a plan for introducing intrapreneurship into the corporate setting. Groups of four or five can form to develop the program. Areas that need to be addressed include: developing the plan, implementation, motivating employees to participate, the reward and compensation system, evaluating the plan's effectiveness, making adjustments, goals of the plan, and funding the proposals generated by the plan. The presentations should be judged on thoroughness, creativity, and feasibility.

(OR)

"Intrapreneur - Entrepreneur: The Difference"

Write a report explaining the difference between intrapreneurship and entrepreneurship. Include in the paper definitions of both and profiles of at least two people that you have researched (one should be an intrapreneur and the other an entrepreneur).

The paper should be approximately 3-5 pages in length.

PART II

The Entrepreneurial Perspective

Chapter 4 - Understanding the Entrepreneurial Perspective in Individuals

Chapter 5 - Developing Creativity and Understanding Innovation

Chapter 6 - Ethical and Social Responsibility Challenges for Entrepreneurs

CHAPTER 4

UNDERSTANDING THE ENTREPRENEURIAL PERSPECTIVE IN INDIVIDUALS

CHAPTER OUTLINE

I. The Entrepreneurial Perspective
   A. Who are entrepreneurs?
   B. Research sources on entrepreneurs
      1. Technical and professional journals
      2. Textbooks
      3. Biographies and autobiographies of owners
      4. Books
      5. Compendiums about entrepreneurs
      6. News periodicals
      7. Venture periodicals
      8. Newsletters
      9. Proceedings of conferences
      10. Government publications
   C. Common characteristics associated with entrepreneurs
      1. Commitment, determination, and perseverance
      2. Drive to achieve
      3. Opportunity orientation
      4. Initiative and responsibility
      5. Persistent problem solving
      6. Seeking feedback
      7. Internal locus of control
      8. Tolerance for ambiguity
      9. Calculated risk taker
      10. Integrity and reliability
      11. Tolerance for failure
      12. High energy level
      13. Creativity and innovativeness
      14. Vision
      15. Self-confidence and optimism
      16. Independence
      17. Team building

II. The Dark Side of Entrepreneurship
   A. The Entrepreneur's confrontation with risk
      1. Financial risk
      2. Career risk

3. Family and social risk
  4. Psychic risk
III. Stress and the Entrepreneur
  A. What is entrepreneurial stress?
  B. Sources of stress
    1. Loneliness
    2. Immersion in business
    3. People problems
    4. Need to achieve
  C. Dealing with stress
    1. Networking
    2. Getting away from it all
    3. Communication with subordinates
    4. Finding satisfaction outside the company
    5. Delegating duties

IV. The Entrepreneurial Ego
  A. Overbearing need for control
    1. Business
    2. Destiny
  B. Sense of distrust
  C. Overriding desire for success
  D. Unrealistic optimism

V. Entrepreneurial Motivation
  A. A model of entrepreneurial motivation
  B. Outcomes and expectations

VI. Summary

CHAPTER OBJECTIVES

1. To describe the three major sources of information useful in profiling the entrepreneur.
2. To identify and discuss the most commonly cited characteristics found in successful entrepreneurs.
3. To discuss the "dark" side of entrepreneurship.
4. To identify and describe the four different types of risk faced by entrepreneurs as well as the major causes of stress faced by these individuals and the ways in which this stress can be handled.
5. To examine entrepreneurial motivation.

CHAPTER SUMMARY

This chapter describes the entrepreneurial perspective in individuals. It discusses topics that can be useful in becoming a small-business owner. Most of the topics have to do with personal and psychological traits that are hard to measure but can be identified.

The first part of the chapter talks about where information can be obtained for the potential entrepreneur. Some of these sources are journals, textbooks, books, periodicals, and government publications. These sources can be used to identify characteristics and other things that can offer help in becoming an entrepreneur.

The next part discusses the possible characteristics of successful entrepreneurs. This list is long and ever expanding, and the characteristics are not exclusively the ones necessary to become a successful entrepreneur. Some characteristics are commitment, determination, and perseverance, which are all goal oriented. Also, the drive to achieve can be goal oriented. Other traits are correcting problems and seeking associates for feedback. These are only a few of the many there are.

Some of the traits involved in the risk area indicate that the entrepreneur must be a calculated risk taker instead of a high risk taker. Also, the entrepreneur must have a tolerance for failure; otherwise, there would be no risk. There are other traits that are personal, such as vision, self-confidence, and optimism. These traits can help with self-motivation and attitudes.

The next section describes the dark side of entrepreneurship. This encompasses the risks confronted by entrepreneurs including financial, career, psychic, family, and social. These can lead to many types of stress.

There is a section on stress that discusses four types of stress. These types are loneliness, immersion in business, people problems, and the need to achieve. It also brings up possible solutions to ease the stress, and these are: networking, getting away from it all, communicating with subordinates, finding satisfaction outside the company, and delegating some duties. These, of course, are not sure bets for curing stress, but they can help.

The chapter then discusses the entrepreneurial ego and its negative effects. This is brought about by a false sense of security and invincibility because the business is going well. The traits used to help diagnose this problem are a need for control, a sense of distrust, the desire for success, and external optimism.

The chapter concludes with a model of entrepreneurial motivation that depicts the important factors of expectation and outcome. It is the entrepreneur's expectations and how well the outcomes of the venture satisfy those expectations that keeps the entrepreneurial drive sustained.

LECTURE NOTES

UNDERSTANDING THE ENTREPRENEURIAL PERSPECTIVE IN INDIVIDUALS

I. The Entrepreneurial Perspective
    A. Who are entrepreneurs?

B. Sources of research on entrepreneurs
   1. Technical and professional journals are journals that contain in-depth research on current business concepts. Additionally, these journals are well designed and structured. Examples include the *Journal of Small Business* and *Entrepreneurship Theory and Practice.*
   2. Textbooks on entrepreneurship are books that typically address the operation of small firms and nonprofit organizations. Examples include *New Venture Creation, Effective Small Business Management,* and *Entrepreneurial Strategy.*
   3. Books about entrepreneurship--Most of these books are written as practitioners' "how to" guides. Some deal with the problems facing the individual who starts a business, and others deal with a specific aspect of the subject. Examples are: *Have You Got What It Takes?* and *In the Owner's Chair.*
   4. Biographies or autobiographies of entrepreneurs, such as *Going for It* and *Boone.*
   5. Compendiums about entrepreneurs--These are collections that deal with several selected individuals and present statistical information and/or overviews of perceived general trends. Examples include *The Entrepreneurs* and *The Enterprising Americans.*
   6. News and periodicals--Many newspapers and news periodicals run stories on entrepreneurs either regularly or periodically. Examples include *Business Week, Forbes,* and *The Wall Street Journal.*
   7. Venture periodicals--A growing number of new magazines are concerned specifically with new business ventures. Examples include *Entrepreneur,* and *Inc.*
   8. Newsletters--There are a number of newsletters devoted exclusively to entrepreneurship. The "Entrepreneurial Manager's Newsletter" is an example.
   9. Proceedings of conferences--These are publications relating to annual or periodic conferences that deal in part with entrepreneurship. Examples include *Proceedings of the Academy of Management* and *Frontiers in Entrepreneurship Research.*
   10. Government publications--The United States government publishes a wealth of information on small-business operations. Examples: pamphlets from the Small Business Administration.
C. Additional sources of information about entrepreneurial characteristics
   1. Second source: using direct observation of practicing entrepreneurs can provide insights into their traits and characteristics and provide a profile. Some common methods include interviews, surveys, and case studies.
   2. Third source: the final source on entrepreneurial information is speeches and presentations by practicing entrepreneurs.
D. Characteristics of entrepreneurs
   1. Commitment, determination, and perseverance--More than any other factor, total dedication to success as an entrepreneur can overcome obstacles and setbacks. It can also compensate for personal shortcomings.
   2. Drive to achieve--Entrepreneurs are self-starters who appear to others to be internally driven by a strong desire to compete, to excel against self-imposed standards, and to pursue and attain challenging goals.

3. Opportunity orientation--One clear pattern among successful growth-minded entrepreneurs is their focus on opportunity rather than on resources, structure, or strategy. Their goal orientation helps them with measures of how well they are performing.
4. Initiative and responsibility--Entrepreneurs are willing to put themselves in situations where they are personally responsible for the success or failure of the operations.
5. Persistent problem solving--Entrepreneurs are not intimidated by difficult situations. Simple problems bore them, and unsolvable ones do not warrant their time.
6. Seeking feedback--Effective entrepreneurs are often described as quick learners. Entrepreneurs actively seek feedback. This strong desire might improve their performance.
7. Internal locus of control--Successful entrepreneurs believe in themselves. They believe that their accomplishments and setbacks are within their own control and influence and that they can affect the outcome of their actions.
8. Tolerance for ambiguity--Successful entrepreneurs thrive on the fluidity and excitement of such an ambiguous existence.
9. Calculated risk taking--Successful entrepreneurs are not gamblers. When they decide to participate in a venture, they do so in a very calculated, carefully thought-out manner.
10. Integrity and reliability--Integrity and reliability help build and sustain trust and confidence. Since word of mouth is a valuable tool, a successful small-business owner must be respected in the community.
11. Tolerance for failure--Entrepreneurs use failure as a learning experience. The most effective entrepreneurs are realistic enough to expect such difficulties.
12. High energy level--Many entrepreneurs fine-tune their energy levels by carefully monitoring what they eat and drink, establishing exercise routines, and knowing when to get away for relaxation.
13. Creativity and innovativeness--An expanding school of thought believes that creativity can be learned.
14. Vision--Not all entrepreneurs have a predetermined vision for their firm. In many cases this vision develops over time as the individual begins to realize what the firm is and what it can become.
15. Self-confidence and optimism--Although entrepreneurs often face major obstacles, their belief in their ability seldom waivers.
16. Independence--The desire for independence is a driving force behind contemporary entrepreneurs.
17. Team building--The desire for independence and autonomy does not preclude the entrepreneur's desire to build a strong entrepreneurial team. Most successful entrepreneurs have highly qualified, well-motivated teams that help handle the growth and development of the venture.

II. The Dark Side of Entrepreneurship
   A. The entrepreneur's confrontation with risk.
      1. Financial risk--In most new ventures the individual puts a significant portion of his/her savings or other resources at stake.
      2. Career risk--A question frequently raised by would-be entrepreneurs is whether they will be able to find a job or go back to their old jobs if their venture should fail.
      3. Family and social risk--Entrepreneurs expose their families to the risk of an incomplete family experience and the possibility of permanent emotional scars.
      4. Psychic risk--The greatest risk may be to the well-being of the entrepreneur.

III. Stress and the Entrepreneur
   A. What is entrepreneurial stress?
   B. Sources of stress
      1. Loneliness--Entrepreneurs are isolated from persons in whom they can confide. They tend not to participate in social activities unless there is some business benefit.
      2. Immersion in the business--Most entrepreneurs are married to their businesses. They work long hours, leaving them with little or no time for civic recreation.
      3. People problems--Most entrepreneurs experience frustration, disappointment, and aggravation in their experience with people.
      4. Need to achieve--Achievement brings satisfaction. However, many entrepreneurs are never satisfied with their work no matter how well it was done.
   C. Dealing with stress
      1. Networking--One way to relieve the loneliness of running a business is to share experiences by networking with other business owners.
      2. Getting away from it all--The best antidote could be a well-planned vacation.
      3. Communicating with subordinates--Entrepreneurs are in close contact with subordinates and can readily assess the concerns of their staff.
      4. Finding satisfaction outside--Entrepreneurs need to get away from the business occasionally and become more passionate about life itself; they need to gain some new perspectives.
      5. Delegating--Entrepreneurs find delegation difficult because they think they have to be at the business all the time and be involved in all aspects of the operation.

IV. The Entrepreneurial Ego
   A. The need for control--The entrepreneurs are driven by a strong desire to control both their venture and their destiny.
   B. Sense of distrust--Because entrepreneurs are continually scanning the environment, they may lose sight of reality, distort reasoning and logic, and take destructive action.
   C. Overriding desire for success--This can be dangerous because there exists the chance that the individual will become more important than the venture itself.

D. Unrealistic optimism--When external optimism is taken to its extreme, it could lead to a fantasy approach to the business.

V. Entrepreneurial Motivation
   A. A model illustrating the comparison of entrepreneurs' perceptions
   B. Expectations and outcomes

SUGGESTED ANSWERS FOR DISCUSSION QUESTIONS
(END OF CHAPTER)

1. *Identify and describe the three major sources of information that supply data related to the entrepreneurial profile.*
   The first source of information is publications: technical and professional journals, textbooks on entrepreneurship, books about entrepreneurship, biographies of entrepreneurs, compendiums about entrepreneurs, news periodicals, venture periodicals, newsletters, proceedings of conferences, and government publications. The second source of information about entrepreneurial characteristics is direct observation of practicing entrepreneurs. Through observation, a potential entrepreneur can gain insights into the traits and characteristics of practicing entrepreneurs which will lead to the discovery of commonalities that help provide a profile. The final source of information is speeches and presentations by practicing entrepreneurs.

2. *How do the following traits relate to the entrepreneur: desire to achieve, opportunity orientation, and initiative and responsibility?*
   In most entrepreneurs, these interrelated goals are the backbone that drives them toward the unreachable goal of perfection. In spite of the importance of the remaining ten entrepreneurial characteristics, these entrepreneurial traits--desire to achieve, opportunity orientation, and initiative and responsibility--form the cornerstone for success in entrepreneurial actions. As a result of the incorporation of these traits, high-risk decisions for the average businessperson often are moderate risk for the well-prepared high achiever.

3. *Some of the characteristics attributed to entrepreneurs include persistent problem solving, continuous seeking of feedback, and internal locus of control. What does this statement mean? Be complete in your answer.*
   The underlying variable in these three characteristics is the self-confidence that many entrepreneurs possess. Entrepreneurs feel that impossible tasks just take a little longer. Entrepreneurs learn from their mistakes and setbacks, and entrepreneurs feel that they learn more from their early mistakes than from early successes. Additionally, they believe that their accomplishments and setbacks are within their own control and influence and that they can affect the outcome of their actions.

The Dryden Press

4. *Entrepreneurs have a tolerance for ambiguity, are calculated risk takers, and have a high regard for integrity and reliability. What does this statement mean? Be complete in your answer.*

   Although entrepreneurs get a lot of their needed fuel from the energy that is generated from an ambiguous and risky undertaking, the successful entrepreneur finds ways to channel ambiguity and risk in a credible fashion. Entrepreneurs feel integrity and reliability are the glue and fiber that binds successful personal and business relationships. Moreover, when the community has a positive view of the entrepreneur's integrity, the entrepreneur is gaining the best type of exposure: free promotion.

5. *Is it true most successful entrepreneurs have failed at some point in their business careers? Explain.*

   Yes, the truly successful entrepreneurs have failed an average of two or three times. Failing is an educational process. When a successful entrepreneur fails, he or she does not look at the setbacks in a negative way but as a learning process.

6. *In what way is "vision" important to an entrepreneur? Self-confidence? Independence?*

   Although entrepreneurs are constantly facing day-to-day barriers, successful entrepreneurs never lose sight of their vision. This vision increases the entrepreneur's independence and self-confidence. The desire for independence is a driving force behind contemporary entrepreneurs. Moreover, their belief in their ability seldom wavers. Research has proven that entrepreneurial characteristics are learned, which is the underlying reason small business accounts for 48 percent of the nation's GNP.

7. *There is a "dark" side of entrepreneurship. What is meant by this statement? Be complete in your answer.*

   The dark side of entrepreneurship is a destructive course that exists within the energetic drive of a successful entrepreneur. There are three major traits associated with the dark side of small business: risk, stress, and the entrepreneurial ego. All potential entrepreneurs need to be aware that the dark side of entrepreneurship exists.

8. *What are four specific areas of risk faced by entrepreneurs? Describe each.*

   The four specific areas of risk are as follows:
   (1) Financial risk--Most new ventures take a significant portion of an entrepreneur's savings or other resources. The entrepreneur is exposed to personal bankruptcy.
   (2) Career risk--A question often raised by would-be entrepreneurs is whether they will be able to find a job or go back to their old job if their venture should fail.
   (3) Family and social risk--Entrepreneurs who are married run the risk of an incomplete family experience and the possibility of permanent emotional scars.
   (4) Psychic risk--The greatest risk may be to the well-being of the entrepreneur.

9. *What are four causes of stress among entrepreneurs? How can an entrepreneur deal with each of them?*

   There are four causes of stress: loneliness, immersion in business, people problems, and a need to achieve. To reduce stress, entrepreneurs must define the cause of the stress. After clarifying the cause of stress, the entrepreneur can combat excessive stress by acknowledging its existence, developing coping mechanisms, and probing personal unacknowledged needs.

10. *Describe the factors associated with the entrepreneurial ego.*

    The factors associated with the entrepreneurial ego include an overbearing need for control, a sense of distrust, an overriding desire for success, and unrealistic optimism.

11. *What is the concept of entrepreneurial motivation?*

    Examining why people start businesses and how they differ from those who do not (or those who start unsuccessful businesses) may be useful in understanding the "motivation" that entrepreneurs exhibit during start-up as a link to the sustaining behavior exhibited later. Because motivation plays an important part in the creation of new organizations, theories of organization creation that fail to address this notion are incomplete.

    Thus, while research on the psychological characteristics of entrepreneurs has not provided an agreed-upon "profile" of an entrepreneur, it is still important to recognize the contribution of psychological factors to the entrepreneurial process. In fact, the quest for new venture creation as well as the willingness to *sustain* that venture is directly related to an entrepreneur's motivation. Therefore, one research approach is the motivational process that an entrepreneur experiences.

12. *How does the model depicted in the chapter illustrate an entrepreneur's motivation? Be specific.*

    According to the model, the entrepreneur's expectations are then compared with the actual or perceived outcomes of the firm. Future entrepreneurial behavior is based on the results of these comparisons. When outcomes meet or exceed expectations, the entrepreneurial behavior is positively reinforced, and the individual is motivated to continue to behave entrepreneurially, either within the current venture or possibly through the initiation of additional ventures, depending on the existing entrepreneurial goal. When outcomes fail to meet expectations, the motivation of the entrepreneur will be lower and will have corresponding impact on the decision to continue to act entrepreneurially. These perceptions also affect succeeding strategies, strategy implementation, and management of the firm.

TEACHING NOTES FOR END-OF-CHAPTER CASES

CASE: JANE'S EVALUATION

1. *Which of the three applicants do you think comes closest to having the profile of an ideal entrepreneur? Why?*

    Each entrepreneur is as individual as the characteristics that make up the entrepreneur. An ideal entrepreneurial profile would consist of desire to achieve, ability to solve

The Dryden Press

problems so achievement can continue, ability to remain open to changes and indecisions that occur, tolerance for failure, integrity and reliability, and self-confidence. The applicant that best displays these characteristics is Phil Hartack. Phil is the only applicant that shows a high persistence in problem solving. This will be very benificial to Phil because as an entrepreneur he will continually be working out his business complications. However, his tolerance for ambiguity will help him continue to see the overall picture. The combination of these two characteristics will help him keep a realistic view. His high integrity and reliability displays that he is a responsible person who supports his standards. His high self-confidence shows that he is sure of himself and his values. These characteristics make Phil Hartack the closest to an ideal profile.

2. *To which applicant would you recommend the bank lend money? Defend your answer.*
The recommendation would be for Richard Trumpe. Richard has the highest drive to achieve with a high initiative to accomplish his goals. He possesses a high tolerance for failure, so if he is not successful the first time, he will not give up. His creativity and innovativeness will help him develop new ideas. The new ideas can be continually implemented for the improvement and success of his venture.

3. *Is there anything these three entrepreneurs can do to improve their entrepreneurial profiles and their chances for success?*
The three entrepreneurs in the case study need to improve different areas in their profiles. Robin Wood needs the most improvement in her tolerance for ambiguity. If she does not learn to face the uncertainty of her business, she may find the venture too stressful and be unable to cope. Another improvement area is her persistence in problem solving. Finding options to solve the venture's problems will help Robin reduce the uncertainty. Once Robin learns how to tolerate the inevitable, she will be a stronger entrepreneur. Next is Richard Trumpe. Richard could improve his integrity and reliability. As an entrepreneur, Richard has to stay faithful to his vision for his success. By improving his integrity he will be more likely to be able to stand by his standards. Improvement is also needed in his persistence in problem solving. Solving problems as they occur will help keep the problems from growing. Phil Hartack is the last entrepreneur to be discussed. Phil's weaknesses are in his creativity and innovativeness. He needs to be able to come up with new ideas. These ideas need to then be applied by Phil in his venture. Phil also needs improvement in his drive to achieve because his success will depend on his need for achievement. These are some of the improvements that the three entrepreneurs need to make to improve their profiles and chances for success.

CASE: TO STAY OR TO GO

1. *Identify three major characteristics Mary should have if she hopes to succeed in this new venture. Defend your answer.*
The three characteristics that Mary should have are the desire to achieve, commitment, and

tolerance for ambiguity. First, Mary needs to have a desire to achieve. She needs to determine how to increase the number of clients during the first six months. After that has been determined, she needs to set goals and impose her own standards to help her obtain those goals. Mary has to have a commitment to her new venture. Once she starts the business, she has to be willing to devote her time and energy to it. Her commitment and hard work for her venture will help her succeed. The last characteristic that Mary needs is a tolerance for ambiguity. Since she is just starting the venture, she will be facing uncertainty continually. She needs to learn that surprises and setbacks are going to happen. She cannot let the indecisions of her business overpower her.

2. *How can Figure 4.1 be of value to Mary in deciding if she is sufficiently entrepreneurial to be successful in this venture?*
Mary can use Figure 4.1 to see how she rates on the typology of entrepreneur styles. The matrix will help Mary evaluate and assess her own entrepreneurial profile. She will be able to examine her entrepreneurial level of risk. The conclusions she obtains will help her decide if she has the ability to start her own venture.

3. *Where would she have to be to be successful in the new venture?*
Ideally, Mary would have to be higher in her risk accepting capacity. She would have to learn to increase these skills for her venture. Mary would also have to work on her entrepreneurial characteristics. A few of the characteristics that she needs to work on are tolerance of failure, determination, and commitment, as well as others.

ADDITIONAL EXPERIENTIAL EXERCISE

"Entrepreneurial Characteristics"

This creative exercise is designed to compare and contrast the misconception the public has about small-business owners, and what small-business owners actually encounter in their day-to-day struggle to be their own bosses. The guidelines are simple: the student must conduct a survey of small-business owners and people from the community. Since the surveys will be the same, the student can assess to what degree the community has misinterpreted the small-business owner.

1. Please rate the following entrepreneurial characteristics on a scale of 1 to 5, with 1 being very dominant and 5 being least dominant. Each number can be used only once.

    _____ integrity and reliability

    _____ tolerance for failure

    _____ high energy level

_____ creativity and innovativeness

_____ calculated risk taking

2. Please follow the above directions for the rest of the survey.

_____ vision

_____ self-confidence

_____ independence

_____ team building

_____ managerial skill

3. Rate these four basic risks faced by entrepreneurs.

_____ financial

_____ career risk

_____ family and social risk

_____ psychic risk

4. Rate the sources of risk for entrepreneurs.

_____ loneliness

_____ immersion in business

_____ people problems

_____ need to achieve

5. Rate the best way for small-business owners to deal with stress.

_____ networking

_____ getting away from the business

_____ communicating with subordinates

_____ delegating

6. Rate the following destructive sources on a scale of 1 to 4 with 1 being the most destructive and 4 being least destructive.

_____ the need for control

_____ sense of distrust

_____ desire for success

_____ external optimism

CHAPTER 5

DEVELOPING CREATIVITY AND UNDERSTANDING INNOVATION

CHAPTER OUTLINE

I. Innovation and the Entrepreneur
   A. Innovation is a key function in entrepreneurship
   B. More than just a good

II. The Role of Creativity
   A. The nature of the creative process
      1. Background or knowledge accumulation provides the individual with a variety of perspectives on the situation. This helps the entrepreneur develop a basic understanding of the product or venture to be undertaken.
      2. The incubation process allows the individual to subconsciously mull over the information gathered during the preparation stage. The individual "sleeps on it."
      3. The idea experience is the time when the idea or solution the individual is seeking is discovered.
      4. Evaluation and implementation. Successful entrepreneurs must be able to identify workable ideas that they have the skills to implement.
   B. Developing your creativity:
      1. Recognizing relationships: Many inventions and innovations are the result of the inventor's seeing new and different relationships.
         Example: Adding fruit juice to soft drinks to create "Slice."
      2. Developing a functional perspective: The entrepreneur must begin to look at people and things in the environment in terms of how they complement your attempts to satisfy needs and complete projects.
      3. Eliminating muddling mind-sets: Mental habits that block or impede creative thinking. They include:
         a. Either/or thinking
         b. Security hunting
         c. Stereotyping
         d. Probability thinking
   C. The creative climate: The proper climate must exist for creative owners and managers. Some characteristics include:
      1. A trustful management that does not overcontrol personnel
      2. A large variety of personality types
      3. Enjoyment in experimenting with new ideas
      4. The selection and promotion of employees on basis of merit

III. The Innovation Process
   A. Types of innovation

   1. Invention
   2. Extension
   3. Duplication
   4. Synthesis
  B. Sources of innovation
   1. Unexpected occurrences
    a. Unexpected successes or failures that prove to be a major surprise
   2. Incongruities
    a. Exist when there is a gap or difference between expectations and reality
   3. Process needs
    a. Exist whenever there is demand for the entrepreneur to innovate and answer a particular need
   4. Industry and market changes
    a. There are continual shifts in the marketplace caused by advances in technology, industry growth, etc. The entrepreneur needs to be able to take advantage of any resulting opportunity.
   5. Demographic changes
    a. Arise from changes in population, age, education, occupation, geographic locations, etc.
   6. Changes in perception
    a. Occur in people's interpretation of facts and concepts
   7. Knowledge-based concepts
    a. The creation or development of something new
  C. The major myths of innovation
   1. Innovation is planned and predictable
   2. Technical specifications should be thoroughly prepared
   3. Creativity relies on dreams and blue-sky ideas
   4. Big projects will develop better innovations than small ones
   5. Technology is the driving force of innovation and success
  D. Principles of innovation
   1. Be action oriented
   2. Make the product, process, or service simple and understandable
   3. Start small
   4. Aim high
   5. Learn from failures
IV. Financial Support for Innovation
  A. Venture capital environment
   1. The venture capital funds have increased dramatically during the last ten years.
    a. In 1987 there were 587 U.S. venture capital firms, a 148 percent increase over the previous 10 years
    b. After the stock market crash of 1987, there was a slowdown in the venture capital market

           c. The 1990s have demonstrated a resurgence in the IPO market
           d. Funding levels of venture capital have increased 125 percent since 1991
        B. Government support of innovation
           1. The Small Business Development Act of 1982 provided millions of dollars for smaller companies and entrepreneurs involved in research and development. Forty-five million dollars was awarded in 1983 and by 1995 there were 11 federal agencies that provided over $4 billion.

V.   Summary

CHAPTER OBJECTIVES

1. To examine the role of creativity and to review the major components involved in the creative process: knowledge accumulation, incubation process, idea experience, and implementation
2. To present ways of developing personal creativity: recognize relationships, develop a functional perspective, use your "brains," and eliminate muddling mind-sets
3. To introduce the four major types of innovation: invention, extension, duplication, and synthesis
4. To define and illustrate the sources of innovation for entrepreneurs
5. To review some of the major myths associated with innovation and to define the ten principles of innovation
6. To illustrate the financial support for innovation

CHAPTER SUMMARY

This chapter examines how important creativity is to the entrepreneur. Creativity and how it affects the entrepreneur, the role of creativity, and innovations are the major sections of the chapter.

The first section, innovation and the entrepreneur, is a brief introduction to the creative process the entrepreneur must have to be successful. Innovation is described as not just creating a totally new product but also blending ideas and improving others. The entrepreneur must always be thinking. He/she must ask the questions "what if...?" or "why not...?"

The next section looks at the creative process. This process consists of four phases: (1) background or knowledge accumulation, (2) the incubation process, (3) the idea experience, and (4) evaluation and implementation.

Phase 1 stresses the importance of learning as much about an area of interest as possible by gathering information through reading, conversation, meetings, etc. Phase 2, simply put, is getting away from the problem. Don't get so close that you cannot see the whole picture and consequently miss the solution. Phase 3 is the most exciting because it is when the innovative idea comes together. Finally, Phase 4 looks at the entrepreneur's abilities to identify ideas that are workable and his skills to implement them.

Developing creativity is a process of changing the way you look at things. To do this, you must look for different or unorthodox relationships between people and things. Another way to be more creative is to view people and things in terms of how they can be used to satisfy needs. Finally, just use your brain. Exercise the thought process; the more you use it the more efficient it becomes.

The next major section is about the innovation process. Types, sources, myths, and principles of innovation are all scanned. In addition, financial support for innovation is examined.

Innovation can be broken down into four distinct types. They are invention, extension, duplication, and synthesis. Invention is the creation of a new product, service, or process. Extension is the expansion of a product, service, or process. Duplication is replication of an already existing product, service, or process. Finally, synthesis is the combination of existing concepts and factors into a new formulation.

Sources of innovation, the next topic discussed, deals with the main areas that new ideas come from. Unexpected occurrences, process needs, and gaps between expectations and reality are among the sources. The market is one of the main forces of innovation. In a constantly changing market, new ideas are always presenting themselves. Other sources include demographic changes and changes in perception.

The major myths associated with innovation is the next topic. Five myths are presented and dispelled. They are innovation is planned and predictable, technical specification should be thoroughly prepared, creativity relies on dreams and blue-sky ideas, big projects will develop better innovations than smaller ones, and technology is the driving force of innovation and success.

The chapter describes a number of principles of innovation. The innovator must realize that these principles exist and that they can be learned. One of the principles is to be action oriented. The innovator must always be looking for new ideas. Making the product, process, or service simple and understandable is another example of a principle of innovation. A few more include: make the product, process, or service customer-based; start small; aim high; follow a milestone schedule; and the like. The last but most important principle listed is work, work, and more work.

The final topic of the chapter is financial support for innovation. Two sources of capital are listed, venture capital and government support. The activity in venture capital investment, as well as government support, has been on the rise in the last few years. The chapter goes on to list some supporting statistics. In addition to statistics, the chapter closes by suggesting some government programs where the entrepreneur might get help. Some of those programs are the Small Business Innovation Development Act and the Small Business Innovation Research (SBIR) programs.

LECTURE NOTES

DEVELOPING CREATIVITY AND UNDERSTANDING INNOVATION

I. Innovation and the Entrepreneur
   A. Innovation is a key function in the entrepreneurial process
   B. Innovation is more than just a good idea
      1. Origin of an idea is important
         a. Difference between speculation and extended thinking
         b. Innovation is a combination of vision and perseverance
      2. Entrepreneurs are able to blend creative thinking and logical ability

II. The Role of Creativity
   A. Creativity is the generation of ideas that result in the improved efficiency or effectiveness of a system
      1. Two important aspects
         a. People: Resources that determine the solution
         b. Process: Goal oriented; designed to attain a solution
   B. The nature of the creative process
      1. Creativity can be developed
         a. Some people have greater aptitude
         b. Some have grown in the proper environment
      2. Four phases in creative process
         a. Phase 1: Background or knowledge accumulation
            1. Successful creations preceded by investigation and information gathering
               a. Reading, conversation, attending meetings
            2. Additional investigation in both related and unrelated fields
            3. Ways to develop a creative mind
               a. Read in a variety of fields
               b. Join professional groups and associations
               c. Attend professional meetings and seminars
               d. Travel to new places
               e. Talk to anyone and everyone about your subject
               f. Scan magazines, newspapers, and journals for articles related to your subject
               g. Develop a subject library for future reference
               h. Carry a small notebook and record useful information
               i. Become curious about everything
         b. Phase 2: The incubation process
            1. Mulling over gathered information
               a. Done by doing something totally unrelated
               b. Helpful steps include:
                  1. Engage in routine, "mindless" activities

            2. Exercise regularly
            3. Play (sports, board games, puzzles)
            4. Think about the subject or problem before falling asleep
            5. Meditate and/or practice self-hypnosis
            6. Sit back and relax on a regular basis
        c. Phase 3: The idea experience
            1. Time that idea is discovered
                a. Average person perceives it as the only component of creativity
            2. Ways of speeding idea experience
                a. Daydream
                b. Practice your hobbies
                c. Work in a leisurely environment
                d. Put the problem on the back burner
                e. Carry a notebook to record ideas
                f. Take breaks while working
        d. Phase 4: Evaluation and implementation
            1. Successful entrepreneurs identify ideas that are workable and that entrepreneurs have the skill to implement
            2. Not afraid to fail
            3. Some useful suggestions:
                a. Increase energy level (diet, exercise, rest)
                b. Get an education in business planning and business
                c. Share ideas
                d. Take notice of hunches and feelings
                e. Get an education in selling process
                f. Learn about organizational policies and practices
                g. Seek advice
                h. View problems as challenges
C. Developing your creativity
    1. Improve your creativeness through awareness
        a. Recognizing relationships
            1. Look for different or unorthodox relationships
                a. Perceiving in a rational mode
                b. All things and people relate to other things and other people
        b. Developing a functional perspective
            1. View things and people in terms of how they can be used to satisfy needs
            2. Visualize yourself in complementary relationships to the things and people of the world
        c. Using your brains
            1. Two hemispheres
                a. Right brain understands analogies, imagines things, and synthesizes information

        b. Left brain helps the person analyze, verbalize, and use rational approaches to problem solving
        c. Connected by nerves called corpus callosum
            1. Each hemisphere should be viewed as complementary
            2. Necessary to practice both right and left hemisphere skills
      d. Eliminating muddling mind-sets
            1. "Either/or" thinking
                a. Looking for an unreasonable amount of uncertainty in life
            2. Security hunting
                a. Always trying to take the right path (avoiding risks)
            3. Stereotyping
                a. Looking for or acting on the "average" is using a distorted picture of reality
            4. Probability thinking
                a. Struggling for security causes overuse of probability to reduce risks. Distortion occurs.
   D. The creative climate
      1. Important characteristics
         a. Trustful management, does not overcontrol
         b. Open communication among members of business
         c. Contact and communication with outsiders
         d. Variety of personality types

III. The Innovation Process
   A. Types of innovation
      1. Invention: Creation of a new product, service, or process
      2. Extension: Expansion of a product, service, or process
      3. Duplication: Replication of an already existing product, service, or process. Adding own creative touch
      4. Synthesis: The combination of existing concepts and factors into a new formulation
   B. Sources of innovation
      1. Unexpected occurrences: Unanticipated successes or failures
      2. Incongruities: Whenever a gap between expectations and reality exists
      3. Process needs: Whenever a demand for the entrepreneur to answer a particular need exists
      4. Industry and market changes
         a. Continual shifts in the marketplace caused by consumer attitudes, advancements, and growth
      5. Demographic changes
         a. Trends change in population, age, education, occupations, geographic locations, etc.
      6. Changes in perception
         a. Changes in people's interpretation of facts and concepts

    7. Knowledge-based concepts
        a. Creation or development of something brand new
C. The major myths of innovation
    1. Myth 1: Innovation is planned and predictable
        a. Truth: Innovation is unpredictable and may be introduced by anyone
    2. Myth 2: Technical specification should be thoroughly prepared
        a. Truth: Quite often it is more important to use a try-test-revise approach
    3. Myth 3: Creativity relies on dreams and blue-sky ideas
        a. Truth: Innovators create from opportunities not daydreams
    4. Myth 4: Big projects will develop better innovations than smaller ones
        a. Truth: Smaller groups foster creative ideas better
    5. Myth 5: Technology is the driving force of innovation and success
        a. Truth: Not only source
        b. Truth: Market-driven innovations have the highest probability of success
D. Principles of innovation
    1. Be action oriented; search for new ideas
    2. Make the product, process, or service simple and understandable
    3. Make the product, process, or service customer based
    4. Start small; begin small, plan for proper expansion
    5. Aim high; seek a niche in the marketplace
    6. Try-test-revise; help work out flaws
    7. Learn from failures
    8. Follow a milestone schedule; have a schedule in order to plan and evaluate the project
    9. Reward heroic activity; give proper respect to aid process
    10. Work, work, work!
E. Financial support for innovation
    1. Venture capital environment
        a. During the last ten years the volume of venture capital investment surged
        b. In 1987, there was a 148 percent increase in the amount of venture capital firms over previous ten years
        c. After the stock market crash of October 1987, there was a slowdown in venture capital during 1988 and 1989. However, the 1990s demonstrated a resurgence in the IPO market
        d. By 1995, the funding levels of venture capital had increased 125 percent over 1991
    2. Government support of innovation
        a. Small Business Innovation Development Act of 1982
            1. Means small high-technology firms will receive more federal R&D awards
        b. Small high-tech firms submit proposals through a standard solicitation procedure
            1. Each agency then makes awards to the firms on a competitive basis
            2. Three phases of an R&D award in SBIR program

a. Phase I awards are made for research projects intended to evaluate the scientific and technical merit and feasibility of an idea. Awards generally are $100,000 or less
   b. Phase II awards of $750,000 or less are made for further development of innovation
   c. Phase III is private-sector investment and support that will bring the innovation to market

SUGGESTED ANSWERS FOR DISCUSSION QUESTIONS (END OF CHAPTER)

1. **In your own words, state what is meant by the term "innovation."**
   Innovation means something new or something that has not been done before. It could be thought of as a new idea for a certain type of product or service. Innovation could also be described as an improvement of an existing idea that makes the idea profitable.

2. **What is the difference between an adaptor and an innovator?**
   An adaptor is one who takes the ideas of another and tries to make them profitable. There is no creativity involved because the person is not trying to profit from his own idea but from that of another. An innovator is one who looks for an opportunity on which to capitalize. The innovator researches the need for the idea by finding out the thoughts of the potential customers. An innovator also thinks very carefully about what exactly the innovation has to be in order to appeal to the public.

3. **What are four major components in the creative process?**
   (1) Background or knowledge accumulation: The individual explores the different aspects of a given situation. The individual needs to develop different perspectives to better deal with situations that may arise. By reading, scanning magazines and newspapers, traveling, etc., the individual can accumulate some background knowledge.
   (2) The incubation process: The individual subconsciously "mulls over" the information that has been gathered. The individual can do this by engaging in "mindless" activities such as cutting the grass, exercising on a regular basis, and sitting back and relaxing on a regular basis.
   (3) The idea experience: Often the most exciting part of the process, this is when the idea or the solution the individual is seeking is found.
   (4) Evaluation and implementation: Successful entrepreneurs identify the ideas that are workable and that they have the skills to implement. Further, they do not give up when they run into obstacles.

4. **What are the four steps involved in developing personal creativity?**
   (1) Recognizing relationships--Many inventions and innovations are the result of the

innovator's seeing new and different relationships among objects, processes, materials, technologies, and people. It helps to look for unorthodox relationships among the things and people around you.

(2) Developing a functional perspective--Viewing things and people in terms of how they can be used to satisfy needs and to help complete a project.

(3) Using your brains--The right brain helps the person understand analogies, imagine things, and synthesize information. The left brain helps the person analyze, verbalize, and use rational approaches to problem solving. The functions of both brain hemispheres are important to the entrepreneur.

(4) Eliminating muddling mind-sets--There are a number of mental habits that block or impede creative thinking. Some common mental blocks include "either/or" thinking, security hunting, stereotyping, and probability thinking.

5. *What are the four major types of innovation?*
   (1) Invention--The creation of a new product, service, or process that is often new and untried. Such concepts are "revolutionary."
   (2) Extension--The expansion of a product, service, or process that is already in existence. This involves a different application of a current idea.
   (3) Duplication--The replication of an already existing idea. The entrepreneur adds his/her own creative touches to enhance the idea and better the competition.
   (4) Synthesis--The combination of existing concepts and factors into a new formulation. This involves taking already existing ideas and putting them together to form a new application.

6. *What are the major sources of innovation? Explain and give an example of each.*
   (1) Unexpected occurrences--Unexpected successes or failures that prove to be a major surprise to the firm.
   (2) Incongruities--These exist whenever there is a gap or difference between expectations and reality.
   (3) Process needs--These exist whenever there is a demand for the entrepreneur to innovate and answer a particular need.
   (4) Industry and market changes--Continual shifts in the market caused by technology, industry growth, etc.
   (5) Demographic changes--Trend changes in population, age, education, occupations, geographic locations, etc.
   (6) Changes in perception--These changes occur in people's interpretations of facts and concepts.
   (7) Knowledge-based concepts--Inventions are knowledge based; they are the product of new thinking, new methods, and/or new knowledge.

7. *Briefly describe each of the five major myths commonly associated with innovation.*
   (1) Innovation is planned and predictable. Innovation should not be left to the research and

development department only. Innovation is, in fact, unpredictable and may be introduced by anyone.
   (2) Technical specifications should be thoroughly prepared. Thorough preparation often takes too long. Quite often it is more important to use a try-test-revise approach.
   (3) Creativity relies on dreams and blue-sky ideas. Accomplished innovators are very practical people and create from the opportunities left by reality, not daydreams.
   (4) Big projects will develop better innovations than smaller ones. Larger firms are now encouraging their people to work in smaller groups, where it often is easier to generate creative ideas.
   (5) Technology is the driving force of innovation and success. Technology is certainly one source for innovation, but it is not the only one. Market-driven or customer-based innovations have the highest probability of success.

8. *Identify and describe five of the principles of innovation.*
   (1) Be action oriented. Innovators must be active and searching for new ideas, opportunities, or sources of innovation.
   (2) Make the product, process, or service simple and understandable. People must readily understand how the innovation works.
   (3) Start small. Innovators should start small and then build and develop, allowing for planned growth and proper expansion in the right manner and at the right time.
   (4) Aim high. Innovators should aim high for success by seeking a niche in the marketplace.
   (5) Work, work, work. It takes work, not genius or mystery, to innovate successfully.

9. *Briefly describe two specific sources of financial support for innovation today.*
   The venture capital environment has been taking on a more significant role over the last few years. Venture capitalists are private individuals who are in the business of investing their money in firms that engage in innovative activities. In 1987, there were 587 U.S. venture capital firms, a 148 percent increase over the previous ten years. While 1988 and 1989 slowed down venture capital, the 1990s witnessed a resurgence of the IPO market. Government programs to support innovation have also been on the rise over the last few years. For example, the Small Business Innovation Development Act of 1982 provided millions of dollars for smaller companies and entrepreneurs involved in research and development. The government awarded $45 million for R&D contracts in 1983, and that figure climbed to $4 billion by 1995.

10. *Briefly describe an SBIR program.*
    SBIR programs are designed to help small firms obtain more federal research and development money. The program consists of three phases. In Phase I awards are made to determine the technical feasibility of an idea. Generally, awards of $100,000 or less are made in this phase. In Phase II awards of $750,000 or less are made for further development of the innovation. Phase III is characterized by private-sector investment and support that will bring the innovation to market.

TEACHING NOTES FOR END-OF-CHAPTER CASES

VIDEO CASE: Paradigm Simulation: Reality Bytes in the Virtual World (Answers to Questions)

1. ***Explain how the phases of the creative process apply to the Founding of Paradigm Simulation.***

    Paradigm founders were able to use their knowledge accumulation as software engineers to begin an incubation about computer graphics. They realized (idea) that 3-D simulation wasn't accessible because of the cost. Therefore, they created "Vega," a software tool that enables people to build interactive 3-D visuals.

2. ***What type of innovation would Paradigm be considered? Why?***

    Extension. Since computer graphics software had been so expensive but was already developed, Paradigm's founders expanded the potential market for 3-D simulation by making the software more affordable.

3. ***Identify the source of innovation that best describes the start of Paradigm Simulation.***

    "Process need" would be an applicable source because Paradigm Simulation answered an arising need for 3-D simulation. "Industry shift" could also be considered due to the increased use of 3-D computer graphics.

4. ***How would the principles of innovation be applied to Paradigm's new growth?***

    The Founders of Paradigm Simulation started small, aimed high, made the product simple and affordable, and most importantly worked, worked, and worked to make their company a success.

CASE: POST-IT NOTES

1. ***In developing this product, how did the creative thinking process work? Describe what took place in each of the four steps.***

    The four steps or phases that occur in most creative developments are illustrated in the Post-It Notes case. Each step can be described as follows:
    (1) Background or knowledge accumulation--This phase was exemplified by the 3M manager who had gathered a background of information on adhesives since working for 3M.
    (2) The incubation process--The 3M manager (Art Fry) illustrated this in the choir of his church. He needed a bookmark in his hymnal that would adhere to the page but not tear it. Returning to work he pursued the possibility with members of the research and development department.
    (3) The idea experience--As Art Fry used his new bookmark concept, he realized it might have uses in other areas. For example, secretaries might find it useful in attaching

messages or sending notes on files. Thus, he came up with the idea of "attachable notes."

(4) Evaluation and implementation--The idea was introduced in the 3M Company and when everyone began requesting more of these "Post-it" notes, the birth of a new product was witnessed. Thus, it was through in-house evaluation that the idea developed into production.

2. *Why did the manager have Post-its sent to secretaries throughout the company? What was his objective in doing this?*

The manager (developer of Post-its) had the secretaries try out the product first. If they found it useful and requested more than 3M had, at least an internal market test had demonstrated the usefulness and desirability of the notes.

3. *What type of innovation was this: invention, extension, duplication, or synthesis? Defend your answer. Which of the eight sources of innovation discussed in the chapter help explain the success of this product? Be complete in your answer.*

The Post-it note concept may be viewed as an invention by source since it appeared to be revolutionary. However, it is more appropriately a *synthesis* because Art Fry merely combined the concepts of notes and light adhesive. Both of these concepts already existed, yet it was Fry's innovative combination that produced Post-its.

Of the eight sources of innovation, two actually stand out in explaining the sources of Post-it notes. The "unexpected occurrence" would depict the failure of any bookmark to solve Art Fry's problem when singing in the choir. It was this unexpected and unplanned event which led him to seek out an adhesive that could work. Secondly, the "process need" describes the internal use of Post-it notes and the need it created once the secretaries realized how useful the notes were.

ADDITIONAL EXPERIENTIAL EXERCISES

"Stereotyping"

Think of the following people and see if you can come up with any stereotypical ideas about them:

A 60-year-old factory worker
An oriental college student
A man with a shaved head wearing a robe and carrying flowers
A white middle-aged businessman
A black middle-aged businessman
A house husband
A male hair stylist

Such stereotypes can get in the way of creative thinking.

(OR)

"The Imaginary Animal"

Develop a metaphor that describes the university or college (or even an organization) where students work.

Purpose - This exercise evokes a description of an organization from a dynamic living system perspective.

Directions - With one other person, reach agreement in your answers for the following questions or statements. Write your answers on flip chart paper and draw the animal.

What real or imaginary animal best describes your organization?

Describe what it looks like in detail.
Is it male, female, neither, both?
Describe its temperament: gentle, domestic, wild, unpredictable, etc.
What are its feeding habits, living habits, and routines?
Describe its environment, how it succeeds in competition for food, etc.
What are its strengths, weaknesses, vulnerabilities?
How does it relate to the internal systems that compose it?
Does it use its organs or functions to its advantage or cause harm to them?
How would you adapt or change this animal if you had the power to do so and why?

CHAPTER 6

ETHICAL AND SOCIAL RESPONSIBILITY CHALLENGES FOR ENTREPRENEURS

CHAPTER OUTLINE

I. Introduction
   A. Ethics is a timely topic
   B. The other side of a successful venture
   C. Ethics dates back to 560 B.C.

II. Defining Ethics
   A. Basic rules or parameters for conducting activities in an "acceptable" manner
   B. Problem with implementing definitions, static versus process
   C. Creation of conflict
      1. Inside and outside of organizations
      2. Changes in society

III. Ethics and Laws: The Dilemma
   A. Management rationalizations
      1. The activity is not "really" illegal or immoral
      2. It's in the individual's or corporation's best interest
      3. It will never be found out
      4. Because it helps the company, the company will condone it
      5. Morally questionable acts can be classified as non-role, role failure, role distortion, and role assertion
   B. The matter of morality
      1. Requirements of law may overlap at times but do not duplicate the moral standards of society
         a. Some laws have no moral content whatsoever
         b. Some laws are morally unjust
         c. Some moral standards have no legal basis
      2. Legal requirements tend to be negative; morality tends to be positive
      3. Legal requirements usually lag behind the acceptable moral standards of society
   C. Economic trade-offs
      1. Economic profits versus social welfare

IV. Establishing Strategy for Ethical Responsibility
   A. Ethical practices and codes of conduct
      1. Code of conduct - Statement of ethical practices or guidelines to which an enterprise adheres
      2. Codes are becoming more prevalent

  B. Approaches to management ethics
    1. Holistic approach
      a. Hire the right people
      b. Set standards more than rules
      c. Don't let yourself get isolated
      d. Let your ethical example at all times be absolutely impeccable (most important)
  B. Strategies for ethical responsibility
    1. Ethical consciousness
    2. Ethical process and structure
    3. Institutionalization

V. Ethics and Business Decisions
  A. Complexity of decisions
    1. Decisions have extended consequences
    2. Multiple alternatives exist
    3. Mixed outcomes exist
    4. Uncertain ethical consequences exist
    5. Personal implications exist
  B. Questions used to examine the ethics of a decision
    1. Have you defined the problem accurately?
    2. How would you define the problem if you stood on the other side of the fence?
    3. How did the situation occur in the first place?
    4. To whom and to what do you give your loyalty as a person and as a member of the corporation?

VII. The Social Responsibility Challenge
  A. Social obligation
  B. Social responsibility
  C. Social responsiveness
  D. Environmental awareness

VIII. The Opportunity for Ethical Leadership for Entrepreneurs
  A. Owner's influence
  B. Role model
  C. Ethical concern over specific issues

IX. Summary

CHAPTER OBJECTIVES

1. To discuss the importance of ethics for entrepreneurs
2. To define the term *ethics*

3. To study ethics in a conceptual framework for a dynamic environment
4. To review the constant dilemma of law versus ethics
5. To examine the role of ethics in the free-enterprise system
6. To present strategies for establishing ethical responsibility
7. To introduce the challenge of social responsibility
8. To emphasize the importance of entrepreneurs taking a position of ethical leadership

CHAPTER SUMMARY

Ethics is a delicate and timely topic in the business world of today. It dates back to about 560 B.C., when the Greek thinker Chilon believed that a merchant does better to take a loss than to make a dishonest profit. In today's society, Chilon's way of thinking is still very prevalent. Today's entrepreneurs are faced with many ethical decisions, especially during the early stages of their new ventures. The following summary will examine and highlight the powerful impact integrity and ethical conduct have in creating a successful venture.

What is ethics? Simply, ethics provides the basic rules and parameters for conducting any activity in an "acceptable" manner. In actuality, ethics represents a set of principles prescribing a behavioral code that explains what is good and right or bad and wrong; in addition, it outlines moral duty and obligations. The real problem of this issue of ethics is in the implementation in a dynamic and ever-changing environment because the definition is a static description.

For the entrepreneur the dilemma of legal versus ethical is a vital one. One researcher believes that legal behavior represents one of four rationalizations that managers use in justifying questionable conduct. The four rationalizations are believing that the activity is not "really" illegal or immoral; that it is in the individual's or the corporation's best interest; that it will never be found out; or that because it helps the company, the company will condone it. The reason for the dilemma is due to the fact that these rationalizations are left up to the individual, and ethical conduct may reach beyond the limits of the law. Three relationships between the legal requirements and moral judgment exist. First, the requirements of law may overlap at times but do not duplicate the moral standards of society. Second, legal requirements tend to be negative, whereas morality tends to be positive. Third, legal requirements usually lag behind the acceptable moral standards of society. Due to innovation, risk taking, venture creation, and the creation of new jobs within our free-enterprise system, complex tradeoffs between economic profits and social welfare have been produced. The public's perception may be based on a misunderstanding of the free-enterprise system, for one cannot blame single individuals for the ethical problems in free enterprise.

Because of the conflicts in the free-enterprise system, there needs to be an established strategy for ethical responsibility to which entrepreneurs are committed. Codes of conduct have become more prevalent in businesses today. One study examined motives, goals, orientation toward law, ethical norms, and strategy for three distinct types of management: immoral management, amoral management, and moral management. Another suggested approach, the holistic management approach, encompasses ethics in its perspective. It is a dual-focused approach that includes "knowing how" and "knowing that" and outlines four principles for ethical management: (1) hire the right people, (2) set standards more than rules, (3) don't let yourself get isolated, (4) let your ethical examples at all times be absolutely impeccable. This strategy should encompass three major elements: ethical consciousness, ethical process and structure, and institutionalization.

The entrepreneur is challenged by business decisions each day, and many are complex and raise ethical considerations. There are five reasons why the business decisions of entrepreneurs are so complex: (l) ethical decisions have extended consequences, (2) business decisions involving ethical questions have multiple alternatives, (3) ethical business decisions often have mixed outcomes, (4) most business decisions have uncertain ethical consequences, and (5) there are personal implications in most ethical business decisions. These statements show the need for entrepreneurs to grasp as much information as possible about each major decision.

Over the last three decades, social responsibility has emerged as a major issue. Social responsibility consists of those obligations that a business has to society. The levels of social behavior by companies include social obligation, social responsibility, and social responsiveness.

Environmental awareness has been reawakened during the 1990s. The preservation of our natural resources has become increasingly important, and business is taking the lead with certain initiatives. "ECOVISION" is a term used for a leadership style that is flexible and open to evolving social demands.

Ethics is extremely difficult to define, codify, and implement because of its surfacing of personal values and morality. Entrepreneurs should be very concerned about ethics during the early stages of their venture because decisions may be legal without being ethical and vice versa, whereas sometimes they have to make decisions involving economic tradeoffs. Despite the ever-present lack of clarity and direction, entrepreneurs have a unique opportunity to exhibit ethical leadership during the 1990s and beyond.

LECTURE NOTES

ETHICS AND SOCIAL RESPONSIBILITY CHALLENGES FOR ENTREPRENEURS

I. Introduction
   A. Importance of ethical issues
      1. Scandals
      2. Fraud
      3. Misconduct in corporations
   B. "Ethos": A Greek derivative
      1. Custom or mode of conduct
      2. Challenged by philosophers
         a. Loucks
         b. Sir Adrian Cadbury

II. Defining Ethics
   A. Broadest sense--Ethics provides the basic rules or parameters for conducting any activity in an "acceptable" manner.
   B. Specifically--Ethics represents a set of principles prescribing a behavioral code that explains what is good and right or bad and wrong; ethics may, in addition, outline moral duty and obligations.
   C. Conflict over ethical nature of decisions
      1. Interests inside and outside of the organization
         a. Stockholders
         b. Customers
         c. Managers
         d. Community
         e. Government
         f. Employees
      2. Society undergoing dramatic change
         a. Values
         b. Morals
         c. Societal norms
   D. Ethics: A process rather than a static code--decisions are situational

III. Ethics and Laws
   A. Managerial rationalizations
      1. The activity is not "really" illegal or immoral.
      2. It is in the individual's or corporation's best interest.
      3. It will never be found out.
      4. It helps the company; therefore, the company will condone it.
      5. Types of morally questionable acts: non-role, role failure, role distortion, role assertion.
   B. The matter of morality
      1. Morals and law are viewed as two circles superimposed upon each other.
         a. First area represents the body of ideas that are both moral and legal.
         b. Largest area overlapping the first indicates the vast difference that may exist between morality and law.
      2. Conclusions of legality and morality: Larue Hosmer
         a. Requirements of law may overlap at times but do not duplicate moral standards of society.
            1. No moral content (driving on right side of road)
            2. No legal basis (telling a lie)
            3. Morally unjust (racial segregation laws before 1960)
         b. Legal requirements tend to be negative.
         c. Morality tends to be positive.
         d. Legal requirements usually lag behind acceptable moral standards of society.

The Dryden Press

    C. Economic tradeoffs--economic profits versus social welfare
        1. Generation of profits, jobs, and efficiency
        2. Quest for personal and social respect
    D. Profile: Roger Staubach
    E. Contemporary entrepreneurship
        1. Subway sandwiches
        2. Jogging shoes

IV. Establishing Strategy for Ethical Responsibility
    A. Ethical practices and codes of conduct
        1. Code of conduct--a statement of ethical practices or guidelines to which an enterprise adheres
        2. Codes of conduct are more prevalent today
        3. Improves moral climate of company
    B. Approaches to management ethics
        1. Organizational characteristics
            a. Motives
            b. Goals
            c. Orientation toward law
            d. Ethical norms
            e. Strategy
        2. Management involving organizational characteristics
            a. Immoral management
            b. Amoral management
            c. Moral management
    C. Holistic approach--principles for ethical management
        1. Hire the right people
        2. Set standards more than rules
        3. Don't let yourself get isolated
        4. Ethical example should be absolutely impeccable
    D. Ethical consciousness--key figure is entrepreneur
        1. Open exchange of issues and processes
        2. Established codes of ethics
        3. Setting examples
    E. Ethical process and structure
        1. Procedures
        2. Codes
        3. Goals
    F. Institutionalization--Incorporate ethical and economic objectives

V. Ethics and Business Decisions
    A. Complexity of decisions
        1. Extended consequences
        2. Multiple alternatives

        3. Mixed outcomes
        4. Uncertain ethical consequences
        5. Personal implications
    B. Some pertinent questions of ethical business decisions
        1. Have you defined the problem accurately?
        2. How would you define the problem if you stood on the other side of the fence?
        3. How did this situation occur in the first place?
        4. Whom could your decision or action injure?
        5. What is the symbolic potential of your action if understood? If misunderstood?

VI. The Social Responsibility Challenge--Levels of Social Behavior of Companies
    A. Social obligation
    B. Social responsibility
    C. Social responsiveness
    D. Environmental awareness--"ECOVISION"

VII. The Opportunity for Ethical Leadership by Entrepreneurs
    A. Owners have more influence and leadership
    B. Role model
    C. Ethical concerns vary over specific issues

SUGGESTED ANSWERS FOR DISCUSSION QUESTIONS
(END OF CHAPTER)

1. *In your own words, what is meant by the term ethics?*
    Ethics is the basis of conduct, which is perceived through individual morality and society's norm of what is good or bad and right or wrong.

2. *Ethics must be based more on a process than a static code. What does this statement mean? Do you agree? Why or why not?*
    The statement means ethics must be based on society's differing norms, a process of change. Yes, I agree, because we live in an ever-changing environment where each day is different and each decision has differing alternatives and circumstances.

3. *A small pharmaceutical firm has just received permission from the Food and Drug Administration (FDA) to market its new anticholesterol drug. Although the product has been tested for five years, management believes there may still be serious side effects from its use, and a warning to this effect is being printed on the label. If the company markets this FDA-approved drug, how would you describe its actions from an ethical standpoint?*
    There is nothing illegal about marketing the product because all necessary actions were taken to get the drug approved by the FDA and the benefits must have outweighed the side effects. On the other side, however, marketing the product is not unethical,

because the company is providing information concerning the side effects on the product for the consumer, and therefore, the consumer must make the choice. Management may continue to put more money into the research and development of the product.

4. *Marcia White, the leading salesperson for a small manufacturer, has been giving purchasing managers a kickback from her commissions in return for their buying more of her company's goods. The manufacturer has a strict rule against this practice. How would you describe Marcia's behavior? What would you suggest the company do about it?*

Marcia's behavior is not unethical since she may be trying to gain product loyalty among the managers. Marcia may have misunderstood the rule. The company should not be too harsh on Marcia but should direct its attention toward the managers and suggest they be loyal to the company's goods.

5. *Explain the four distinct roles that managers may take in rationalizing morally questionable acts "against the firm" or "on behalf of the firm." Be complete in your answer.*

The four distinct roles are non-role, role failure, role distortion, and role assertion. There are two roles that apply to questionable acts "against the firm." Non-role examples would include embezzlement and stealing supplies. Role failure includes superficial performance appraisals and not confronting expense account cheating by employees. There are two distinct roles that apply "on behalf of the firm." Role distortion includes bribery or price fixing. Role assertion refers to socially questionable acts such as not withdrawing a product in the face of product safety allegations.

6. *What is a code of conduct, and how useful is it for promoting ethical behavior? Give your reasoning.*

A code of conduct is useful because it sets up ethical standards to conduct company business, outlines ethical behavior among employees, and outlines one's own personal ethics. This allows a business to be successful and individuals to be successful within the company.

7. *Describe carefully the differences between immoral, amoral, and moral management. Explain in detail.*

Under ethical norms, management characterized by decisions, actions, and behavior that imply a positive and active opposition to what is moral (ethical) and that are discordant with accepted ethical principles is known as immoral management. Management that is neither moral nor immoral but whose decisions lie outside the sphere in which moral judgments apply and whose activity is outside or beyond the moral order of a particular code is known as amoral management. Immoral management is selfish and cares only about its or the company's gains, while amoral management is well intentioned but selfish in the sense that impact on others is not considered. Immoral and amoral management also differ in their goals or orientation toward law and strategy.

The goal of amoral management is profitability, and other goals are not considered, while profitability within the confines of legal obedience and ethical standards is the goal of moral management. In amoral management's orientation toward law, law is the ethical guide, preferably the letter of the law, because the central question is what we can do legally, while moral management seeks obedience to the letter and spirit of the law, where law is a minimal ethical behavior, and prefers to operate well above what law mandates. Amoral management gives managers free rein, while moral management lives by sound ethical standards. The difference between amoral management and moral management can also be explained through ethical norms and motives.

8. *Why do complex decisions often raise ethical considerations for the entrepreneur? Give an example.*

    The reasons business decisions of entrepreneurs are so complex are as follows: (1) ethical decisions have extended consequences; (2) business decisions involving ethical questions have multiple alternatives; (3) ethical business decisions often have mixed outcomes; (4) most business decisions have uncertain ethical consequences; and (5) there are personal implications in most ethical business decisions.

9. *Social responsibility can be classified into three distinct categories. Describe each category, and discuss the efforts of entrepreneurs to become more socially responsible.*
    1. Social obligation--Firms simply react to social issues through obedience of the laws.
    2. Social responsibility--Firms are more active in accepting responsibility for social programs.
    3. Social responsiveness--Firms are proactive in social programs and are willing to be evaluated by the public.

    Research is showing that entrepreneurs recognize social responsibility as part of their role in business and are much more critical of their own performance than is the general public. Thus, the stronger influence on the company by the entrepreneur/owner makes a great deal of difference in socially responsive behavior.

10. *Describe the critical threat to our environment as a major challenge within social responsibility.*

    The environment stands out as one of the major challenges within social responsibility. In June, 140 world leaders, along with 30,000 additional participants, gathered in Rio de Janeiro for the Earth Summit to discuss the worldwide environmental problems. Our recent "throw-away" culture has endangered our natural resources from soil to water to air.

    A growing number of businesses are attempting to redefine their social responsibilities because they no longer accept the notion that the business of business is business. Because of our ability to communicate information widely and quickly, many entrepreneurs are beginning to recognize their responsibility to the world around them. Entrepreneurial organizations, the dominant inspiration throughout the world, are beginning the arduous task of addressing social-environmental problems.

The Dryden Press

11. What is "Ecovision"? Outline the specific recommendations for entrepreneurs to consider with environmental awareness.

The term "Ecovision" as a leadership style for innovative organizations encourages open and flexible structures that encompass the employees, the organization, and the environment, with attention to evolving social demands.

Specific recommendations include:
1. Eliminate the concept of waste. Search for newer methods of production and recycling.
2. Restore accountability. Encourage consumer involvement in making companies accountable.
3. Make prices reflect costs. Reconstruct the tax system to a "green-fee" where taxes are added to energy, raw materials, and services in order to encourage conservation.
4. Promote diversity. Continue researching the needed compatibility of our ever-evolving products and inventions.
5. Make conservation profitable. Rather than always demanding "low prices," which encourage shortcuts, there should be new costs allowed for environmental stewardship.
6. Insist on accountability of nations. Develop a plan of sustainable development for every trading nation enforced by tariffs.

12. How can entrepreneurs establish a position of ethical leadership in business today?

An entrepreneur can establish a strategy for ethical responsibility by: (1) hiring the right people because employees who are inclined to be ethical are the best insurance you can have; (2) setting standards more than rules--one can't write a code of conduct that is airtight, so be clear about standards and let people know the level of performance you expect; (3) don't let yourself get isolated--one cannot lose track of markets and competition, especially in his/her own corporation; and (4) let your ethical example be absolutely impeccable at all times. Show people that you care about how the results are achieved. This is known as the holistic approach.

13. Cal Whiting believes that entrepreneurs need to address the importance of ethics in their organizations. However, in his own company he is unsure of where to begin because the area is unclear to him. What would you suggest? Where can he begin? What should he do? Be as practical as you can in your suggestions.

Cal Whiting needs to carefully examine his organization in order to determine actions that might be considered morally questionable. From there he can develop a code of conduct that would represent the ethical positions expected of all employees. Finally, he can follow the four principles for ethical management involved in the holistic approach:
(1) Hire the right people.
(2) Set standards more than rules.
(3) Don't let yourself get isolated.
(4) Let your ethical example be absolutely impeccable at all times.

TEACHING NOTES FOR END-OF-CHAPTER CASES

CASE: LETTING THE FAMILY IN (Answers to Questions)

1. *Has Carmine been unethical in his conduct? What is your reasoning?*

    Carmine has been unethical in releasing "inside information" to certain members of his family for the purpose of gaining extra profits from the sale of additional shares of stock. Thus, the profits are being made with additional knowledge that the outside investors do not have. He is using his position and inside knowledge to gain an unfair advantage on the public investors.

2. *Is it ethical for Carmine to tell his other relatives the good news? Why or why not?*

    The Securities & Exchange Commission (SEC) attempts to investigate and punish what is known as "insider trading," where stock is being purchased and sold with certain information not disclosed to the public. This violation in the SEC is under Rule 106.5; however, as in the case of Carmine, it is difficult to prove. Also, the regulations apply to publicly traded stock as opposed to an initial public offering. Thus, Carmine is absolutely unethical in telling his relatives information that is being used to gain extra profits.

3. *If you were advising Carmine, what would you tell him? Why?*

    In advising Carmine, the SEC regulations (mentioned in question 2) should be explained to him. Also, the situation may not be in violation of any regulations since his company is just preparing for an initial public offering. However, Carmine should realize the violation of ethics in the eyes of outside investors who do not have the information.

CASE: A FRIEND FOR LIFE

1. *Is the recommendation of the marketing vice president legal? Is it ethical? Why or why not?*

    The marketing vice president has recommended that production continue using the substitute fur. While this is not illegal, since there are no laws specifically governing what type of simulated fur is used, it is unethical to delude the public into thinking the product is of high quality when the material is actually of low quality. Especially since the company knows exactly what it is doing in trading away good faith and trust for the sake of profits. Figure 6.2 is useful in understanding this dilemma.

2. *Would it be ethical if the firm used less expensive simulated fur but did not change its slogan of "A Friend for Life" and did not tell the buyer about the change in the production process? Why or why not?*

    No, it would not be ethical since the firm had already produced 26,000 bears with the higher quality simulated fur that lasts seven years. The continued production of bears under the same slogan "A Friend for Life" but with lower-quality simulated fur expected to last only eight months is consumer fraud. Thus, while the legal question may be

The Dryden Press

debated as to the actual fraud, the ethics question is not debatable. This is a prime example of disregard for ethics.

3. *If you were advising Paula, what would you recommend?*

As an adviser to Paula, you should utilize Table 6.2, which illustrates the various approaches to management ethics. The column dealing with "moral management" explains the different aspects of ethics concerned with motives, goals, orientation to the law, and strategy. The strategy segment especially applies to Paula in that she must assume a leadership role when ethical dilemmas arise. In dealing with consumers, enlightened self-interest means that by having concern for others (consumers), you are also taking care of yourself (business) in the future. Thus, Paula will find that either full disclosure to the public of the lesser-quality fur (with a slogan change) or absorption of the extra costs associated with the quality fur are the best options for her to choose.

ADDITIONAL EXPERIENTIAL EXERCISES

"The Ethics Debate"

Assign an ethical business scenario or case study to the students. The students should research and prepare to debate a previously assigned position. An overused example of an actual case is the Nestle's infant formula situation. The advantage of using an actual situation is that the students can see the end result and repercussions.

(OR)

"The Ethical Style of Management"

Each student should conduct two surveys to find the approach of management ethics that two small businesses are utilizing, keeping in mind organizational characteristics such as motives, goals, orientation toward law, ethical norms, and strategy. This will aid in determining the type of management being utilized. The student should come up with one of the three types: immoral management, amoral management, or moral management.

After the surveys are completed (personal interviews are effective), a 2- to 4-page double-spaced paper should be typed showing the significant differences.

PART III

Developing the Entrepreneurial Plan

Chapter 7 -   Environmental Assessment: Preparation for a New Venture

Chapter 8 -   Marketing Research and New Venture Development

Chapter 9 -   Financial Preparation for Entrepreneurial Ventures

Chapter 10 -   Developing an Effective Business Plan

CHAPTER 7

ENVIRONMENTAL ASSESSMENT: PREPARATION FOR A NEW VENTURE

CHAPTER OUTLINE

I. The Environment for New Ventures
    A. Environmental scanning
II. A Macro View: The Economic and Industry Environments
    A. Assessing the economic environment: Key economic environment questions and key entrepreneurial attitudes
        1. Understanding the regulatory environment
            a. Government as a partner to small business
            b. Shift in attitudes and actions of legislators
        2. Trends in policy formation: Milestone laws
            a. The regulatory flexibility act (reg. flex.)
            b. The equal access to justice act (equal access)
            c. The prompt payment act
        3. Other significant public policy developments
    B. Examining the industry environment
        1. Common industry characteristics
            a. Technological uncertainty
            b. Strategic uncertainty
            c. First-time buyers
            d. Short-time horizons
        2. Barriers to entry
        3. Competitive analysis: Taking the right steps
            a. Define the industry
            b. Analyze the competition
            c. Strength and characteristics of suppliers
            d. "Value-added" measure
            e. Market size for the particular industry

III. A Micro View: The Community Perspective
    A. Researching the location
        1. Community demographics
            a. Size of the new venture
            b. Entrepreneurial activity
        2. Economic base
        3. Population trends
        4. Overall business climate

The Dryden Press

      B.   Determining reliance and deservedness
      C.   Examining the use of business incubators
            1.   Four major types
                 a.   Publicly sponsored
                 b.   Nonprofit sponsored
                 c.   University sponsored
                 d.   Privately sponsored
            2.   Business incubator services
                 a.   Management
                 b.   Technical
                 c.   Financial
                 d.   Administrative

IV.   Summary

CHAPTER OBJECTIVES

1. To examine some of the major ways of assessing the economic environment.
2. To review the regulatory environment within which a new venture must exist.
3. To examine the industry environment from a competitive market analysis and strategic point of view.
4. To present the community environment perspective for a local impact understanding.
5. To examine community support in terms of reliance and deservedness.
6. To review the nature of business incubators and their importance to emerging ventures.

CHAPTER SUMMARY

In summary, an entrepreneur should examine both the macro view and micro view of an environment when preparing to start a new venture. There are two major macro areas that should be considered: the overall economic environment and the specific industry environment.

An assessment of the economic environment can help determine if the environment is hostile and if a new venture can compete. It will also aid the entrepreneur to understand the regulatory environment and the new rules and regulations that occur. By understanding these regulations, the entrepreneur may be able to avoid being bogged down in red tape and understand how the government regulations affect small-business ventures more than big business.

In examining the industry environment, the entrepreneur needs to examine the characteristics common to the industry. This may alleviate uncertainties that the entrepreneur has concerning technology, pricing, advertising, and the like. The entrepreneur also needs to examine the barriers to entry that emerge in the industry. A competitive analysis should be performed so that the entrepreneur does not go into a new venture without knowing the competitors' strength, what drives them, and what they can do.

The micro view of the environment should also be examined. First, a research of the location should be conducted. A community demographics study helps to determine the composition of consumers who live within the community. A study of the economic base shows the entrepreneur the opportunities that may be available. Also, a study of the population trends show the growth potential within the community.

Second, the entrepreneur should know how much support the community is willing to give to the new venture and how much it relies on the new venture coming to the community.

Third, the entrepreneur should examine the existence of business incubators within the community. These incubators can provide many support services that could be of use to a new venture trying to succeed.

By examining both the macro and the micro view of the environment, an entrepreneur will be better prepared to enter into a new venture.

LECTURE NOTES

ENVIRONMENTAL ASSESSMENT: PREPARATION FOR A NEW VENTURE

I. The Environment for New Ventures
    A. Environmental scanning
II. A Macro View: The Economic and Industry Environments
    A. Assessing the economic environments
        1. Questions to answer to avoid pitfalls
            a. How many firms are in the industry?
            b. Are they similar or do they differ in size and general characteristics?
            c. Do they serve domestic, foreign, or both markets?
            d. What regulations affect this type of business?
            e. What is the competitive nature of this business?
        2. Attitudes and skills needed for proper assessment
            a. Awareness of external environmental influences on decisions
            b. Ability to integrate traditional business concerns with external environmental influences into comprehensive framework
            c. Skills to solve conflicts
            d. Communication skills
            e. Intellectual skills to analyze and understand issues
        3. Understanding the regulatory environment
            a. Shift in attitudes and actions of legislators
                1. Why?
                    a. Awareness of the valuable impact made by small business
                    b. A move toward deregulation by government

                    c. Efforts by Washington to increase national employment
                    d. Growth in foreign multinationals in the U.S.
            b. Government regulations' effect on small business
                1. Price raises must occur to cover costs
                2. Small business feels the brunt of financial burdens
                3. Competitive restriction
                4. Managers' time is taken up with paperwork
                5. Mental burden and frustration
        4. Trends in policy formation
            a. The regulatory flexibility act
                1. Increase agency awareness of its impact on small businesses
                2. Requires agencies to communicate and explain findings to the public
                3. Encourages provisions of relief for small businesses
            b. The equal access to justice act
                1. Small business and/or government can initiate litigation
                2. Bad faith does not have to be proven
                3. Business does not have to prevail on an issue to receive award
                4. No dollar limit to awards
            c. The prompt payments act
                1. Bills are to be paid in 30 days with a 15-day grace period to all government-contracted jobs with small business
                2. Government cannot withhold entire contracted amount
                3. Only disputed monies can be withheld
        5. Other significant developments
            a. Breakfast series in November 1982 to analyze the unique problems faced by small business
            b. 1986 conference called to reassess policies and the effectiveness of new policies
    B. Examining the industry environment
        1. Common industry characteristics
            a. Technological uncertainty
            b. Strategic uncertainty
            c. First-time buyers
            d. Short-time horizons
        2. Barriers to entry
            a. Proprietary technology is expensive to have
            b. Limited access to distribution channels
            c. Access to raw materials and other inputs may be limited
            d. Lack of experience causes cost disadvantages
            e. Risk

3. Competitive analysis
   a. Consider the number of competitors
   b. Consider the strength of each competitor
   c. Understand what drives the competition
   d. Understand what the competition can do
4. Taking the right steps
   a. Clearly define the industry for the new venture
   b. Analyze the competition thoroughly
   c. Determine the strength and characteristics of suppliers
   d. Establish the value-added measure of the new venture
   e. Project the market size for the particular industry

III. A Micro View: The Community Perspective
   A. Researching the location
      1. Community demographics: Entrepreneur should know
         a. Community size
         b. Residents' purchasing power and disposable income
         c. Average educational background of residents
         d. Types of occupations: percentage of professionals versus nonprofessionals
         e. The amount of entrepreneurial activity in the community
      2. Economic base: Opportunity may be determined by this
         a. Nature of employment
         b. Purchasing trends of consumers
         c. Community dependence on one firm/industry
      3. Population trends: Growth signals include
         a. Chain/department stores in the area
         b. Branch plants of large industrial firms
         c. A progressive chamber of commerce
         d. A good school system
         e. Transportation facilities
         f. Construction activity
         g. An absence of vacant buildings
      4. Overall business climate
         a. Consideration of transportation, banking, professional services, economic base, growth trend, and solid consumer base
   B. Determining reliance and deservedness by community
      1. Questions to answer before entering into business
         a. Are you familiar with the community?
         b. Will there be a positive or negative impact within the community during the start-up period of business?
         c. Do you have the skills in human relations in order to nurture key local contacts?

The Dryden Press

                d.   What steps can be taken to strengthen local support?
                e.   What steps can be taken to reduce local opposition?
         2. How to gain support from community
                a.   Know and further community's reliance or need for venture
                b.   Have an existence of "deservedness" from the community
   C. Examining the use of business incubators
         1. Major types
                a.   Publicly sponsored: Organized through local or regional departments where job creation is the main objective
                b.   Nonprofit sponsored: Organized by private industry, chambers of commerce, or community organizations where area development is the major objective
                c.   University sponsored: Spinoffs of academic research projects where the major goal is to translate basic research findings into new products or technologies
                d.   Privately sponsored: Organized by private corporations where profit is the major goal
         2. Services provided
                a.   Increases the chances of survival for new start-up businesses
                b.   Provides below-market-rate rental space on flexible terms
                c.   Eliminates building maintenance responsibilities
                d.   Allows for sharing of equipment and services that would normally be unavailable or unaffordable
                e.   Increases entrepreneurial awareness of and access to types of financial and technical assistance
                f.   Increases tenant's visibility
                g.   Provides an environment where the entrepreneur is not alone
         3. Community benefits
                a.   Transforms underutilized property
                b.   Creates opportunities for public and private partnerships
                c.   Diversifies the local economic base
                d.   Enhances the local image to become a center of innovation
                e.   Increases employment opportunities

SUGGESTED ANSWERS FOR DISCUSSION QUESTIONS
(END OF CHAPTER)

1. *To assess the economic environment, an entrepreneur would like a number of questions answered. Identify and discuss five of these questions.*
    (1) How many firms are in this industry? This question allows the entrepreneur to establish the potential risk of competition. The more firms there are in the industry, the more likely competition is increased.

(2) Do the firms vary in size and general characteristics, or are they all similar? The size of the firms could dictate the possibility for growth in the industry. The more variations in size, the more potential there is for growth. Firms similar in size could mean that growth is not a wise strategy in this industry.

A wide variety of general characteristics among the firms could mean that rivalry tends to dictate the industry. Similar general characteristics among the firms could allow a new venture to be differentiated.

(3) What is the geographic concentration of firms in the industry—i.e., are they in one area or are they widely dispersed? The closer firms are to each other in an industry, the more intense will be the competitive environment. The further away the firms, the more likely it is that competition will be low.

(4) What federal, state, and local government regulations affect this type of business? Answering this question will make the entrepreneur aware of the different restrictions, laws, guidelines, acts, etc., affecting the industry. Also what kind of problems could develop in the future?

(5) What is the competitive nature of this business? Establishing the way competition reacts to changes in the business could prove fatal to a new venture if the competitive environment is a hostile one. On the other hand, a friendly environment could mean a sharing of knowledge to better position the industry as a whole.

2. ***Briefly discuss each of the following effects of government regulations on small ventures: prices, cost inequities, competitive restrictions, managerial restrictions, mental burdens.***

(1) Prices: Small businesses are often forced to raise their prices to absorb the costs of regulatory compliance.

(2) Cost inequities: Financially, small companies feel the brunt of regulatory burdens more than large corporations.

(3) Competitive restrictions: Putting a greater burden on small business tends to favor big business, thereby subtly encouraging big while discouraging small.

(4) Managerial restrictions: Due to the time devoted to paperwork-imposed duties, the small-business person must sacrifice valuable managerial time to complying with government regulations.

(5) Mental burdens: Postponed projects, wasted time, and managerial failure due to lack of time and energy all begin to take their toll on the small-business person. Frustration leading to depression may spell failure for the business.

3. *How does each of the following legislative acts affect small ventures: (a) the Regulatory Flexibility Act, (b) the Equal Access to Justice Act, (c) the Prompt Payments Act?*

    (1) The Regulatory Flexibility Act: This act recognizes that the size of a business has a bearing on its ability to comply with federal regulations. The law puts the burden of review on the government to ensure that legislation does not unfairly impact on small businesses.

    (2) The Equal Access to Justice Act: This act provides greater equity between small businesses and regulatory bodies. According to this new act, if a small business challenges a regulatory agency and wins, the regulatory agency must pay the legal costs of the small business.

    (3) The Prompt Payments Act: This act is to help small businesses doing work for the federal government collect their money. The act requires that bills be paid in 30 days with an additional 15-day grace period.

4. *Of what value is Figure 7.4 in helping an entrepreneur make a new-venture assessment?*

    It will help the small-business entrepreneur identify some of the major elements of the industry structure that the entrepreneur needs to be aware of.

5. *What are the barriers to entry? How do they affect new-venture assessment?*

    Barriers to entry are things that might prevent the small business from succeeding. Some barriers may disappear as the industry develops, but the entrepreneur needs to be aware of them, just as if he/she were dealing with them on a daily basis for the life of the business. Barriers include: proprietary technology is expensive to access, limited or closed access to distribution channels, access to raw materials and other inputs may be limited, cost disadvantages due to lack of experience and uncertainty, and risk involved in starting up a business instead of investing. If the entrepreneur does not deal with these barriers, he/she may experience problems such as shortages because suppliers cannot meet the industry's need, or the image and credibility of the business may drop because deliveries are not made on time or bills cannot be paid because cash is tied up paying for nonexistent supplies of raw materials. A business cannot continue successfully if these problems are not solved. By addressing and knowing the barriers to entry beforehand, the manager can make sure these problems will not occur.

6. *How could an entrepreneur use Figure 7.5 to conduct a competitive profile analysis? What would the results provide? What types of decisions could the individual make as a result of the analysis?*

    A competitive profile analysis should provide the entrepreneur with information about the competition in regard to the number of competitors and their strengths.

    The results of such an analysis should provide the entrepreneur with helpful information. It can aid the entrepreneur with decisions such as where should he locate, will his business be comparable in size to the competitors, and does his business emphasize the same strengths as the competition or does it offer the community new and different products/services that it desires and can afford.

7. *Identify and describe four of the steps to take when making an industry assessment.*
   (1) Clearly define the industry for the new venture. The need to develop a relevant definition that describes the focus of the new venture is essential. The more clearly the entrepreneur can define the industry for the new venture, the better the chance that the venture will get off to a sound start.
   (2) Analyze the competition. An analysis of the number, relative size, traditions, and cost structures of direct competitors in the industry can help establish the nature of the competition.
   (3) Determine the strength and characteristics of suppliers. The important factor here is to establish the stance of the venture in relation to the suppliers.
   (4) Project the market size for the particular industry. It is important to examine the historical progression of the market, establish its present size, and extrapolate the data to project the likely potential of market growth.

8. *How can the entrepreneur go about researching the location for a venture? What information can community demographics and population trends provide?*

   The entrepreneur can study the community demographics, economic base, population trends, and overall business climate to assess a location suitable for the new venture.

   The community demographics help to determine the composition or makeup of consumers who live within the community. These include such information as size of the community, residents' purchasing power, educational background, types of occupations, who are professionals and nonprofessionals, and the entrepreneurial activity in the community. The population trends identify expanding communities as opposed to long-term declining or static populations.

9. *Discuss this statement: One method of evaluating a community is in terms of reliance and deservedness.*

   The statement refers to the support likely to exist in a given community for an entrepreneur's new venture. The following questions are particularly important in achieving the reliance and deservedness needed for a new venture to be accepted in a community:
   (1) How familiar is the entrepreneur with the community where the venture will be located?

(2) Will the proposed venture make any special positive or negative impact within the community during the prestart-up period or during the start-up period?

(3) Does the entrepreneur have special skills in human relations with which to nurture key local contacts?

(4) What active steps can be taken to strengthen local support and/or minimize local problems during the start-up period?

Answering these questions can help determine the level of support in the community.

10. *What is a business incubator? What are the four major types of incubators?*

A business incubator is a facility with adaptable space that small businesses can lease on flexible terms and at reduced rents. The four major types are as follows: publicly sponsored, nonprofit sponsored, university related, and privately sponsored.

11. *Of what value is a business incubator to a new venture? Explain in detail.*
The value of a business incubator lies in the various services provided to new ventures. Such services are as follows:

(1) Below-market-rate rental space on flexible terms
(2) Elimination of building maintenance responsibilities
(3) Sharing of equipment and services that would otherwise be unavailable or unaffordable: typing, photocopying, phone answering, business planning and financial planning, reception area, conference rooms, and computers
(4) Increase in entrepreneurial awareness of and access to various types of financial and technical assistance
(5) Reduced anxiety of starting a new venture
(6) Increase in business tenant's visibility to the community

TEACHING NOTES FOR END-OF-CHAPTER CASES

CASE: AN INCUBATOR INVESTIGATION

1. *Give a detailed description of a business incubator.*

A business incubator is a facility with adaptable space that new small businesses can rent at below-market rents. Support is available as needed in the form of financial, managerial, and technical advice to the small-business owner. The time is limited to about two years for a new small business to remain in an incubator.

The main benefit to a small business is that there is an increased chance of success in an incubator.

There are different types of incubators. The incubators listed in the chapter are publicly sponsored, nonprofit sponsored, university related, and privately sponsored.

The major services offered in an incubator are low rent, no building maintenance, sharing of equipment and services, and reduced anxiety for starting a new venture.

2. *Identify and describe three benefits a business incubator would offer to Darlene.*

A business incubator could benefit Darlene in many areas. Darlene needs to set up an office with the lowest rent possible; with the reduced rent rates of a business incubator, this will lower her overhead. She will need help in setting up an office and a bookkeeping system. With an incubator she will have the help and experience available to her. With the help and encouragement of a business incubator, Darlene will have more time to spend selling and making money.

3. *Would an incubator be of value to Darlene? Why or why not?*

An incubator could be of some value to Darlene. The value she could receive is reduced rent and help in setting up an office. She may also receive benefit from the encouragement she may get from other businesses in the incubator.

Darlene doesn't seem to need much assistance in selling office supplies. But she will need assistance in setting up an office to handle orders, deliveries, inquiries, bookkeeping, and hiring new employees. I don't believe Darlene will benefit as much as many other small businesses. Many small businesses need more technical and managerial help than she will require.

ADDITIONAL EXPERIENTIAL EXERCISES

"Competitive Analysis"

Have students pretend that they are opening one of the following small businesses in your community. Within that community, conduct a competitive analysis. Make sure to cover the number of competitors, their strengths, what drives them, and what each can do.

Next, address the barriers to entry relevant for you and your business. State what the barrier is and what your plan is to overcome each barrier.

Business choices:
Retail furniture outlet
Small pub or bar with a limited menu
Local travel bureau/booking agency
Small hair-styling salon with independent booth rentals
Family health and fitness gym

(OR)
"Environmental Data"

Have students pick a business in a particular community. The students must then examine the population trends in that community and how those trends influence the business they picked. The students must show references of information taken from the selected sources of environmental data (Table 7.2).

The outcome of this exercise is twofold. First, the students should recognize the impact of population trends on small businesses. Second, they will be exposed to the sources of information available at the library.

CHAPTER 8

MARKETING RESEARCH FOR NEW VENTURES

CHAPTER OUTLINE

I. Marketing Research
   A. Defining the purpose and objectives of the research
      1. Identify where potential customers purchase the goods or service.
      2. Why do they choose to go there?
      3. What is the size of the market? How much of the market can it capture?
      4. How does the business compare with competitors?
      5. What impact does the business promotion have on customers?
      6. What types of products or services are desired by potential customers?
   B. Gathering secondary data
      1. Internal
      2. External
   C. Gathering primary data
      1. Surveys
      2. Experimentation
   D. Developing an information-gathering instrument
   E. Interpreting and reporting the information
   F. Marketing research questions
      1. Sales
      2. Distribution
      3. Markets
      4. Advertising
      5. Products

II. Inhibitors to Marketing Research
   A. Cost
      1. Expensive
      2. Affordable
   B. Complexity (quantitative aspects)
   C. Strategic decisions
      1. Cost
      2. Complexity
   D. Irrelevancy

III. Developing the Market Concept
   A. Marketing philosophy
      1. Production-driven philosophy
      2. Sales-driven philosophy

3. Consumer-driven philosophy
      a. Competitive pressure
      b. Entrepreneur's background
      c. Short-term focus
   B. Market segmentation
      1. Demographic
      2. Benefit
   C. Consumer behavior
      1. Personal characteristics
      2. Psychological characteristics
      3. Five consumer classifications of goods
         a. Convenience goods
         b. Shopping goods
         c. Specialty goods
         d. Unsought goods
         e. New products

IV. Marketing Stages for Growing Ventures
   A. Entrepreneurial marketing
   B. Opportunistic marketing
   C. Responsive marketing
   D. Diversified marketing

V. Marketing Planning
   A. Marketing research
      1. The company's major strengths and weaknesses
      2. Market profile
      3. Current and best customers
      4. Potential customers
      5. Competition
      6. Outside factors
      7. Legal changes
   B. Sales research (questions)
      1. Do salespeople call on their most qualified prospects on a proper priority and time-allocation basis?
      2. Does the sales force contact decision makers?
      3. Are territories aligned according to sales potential and salespeople's abilities?
      4. Are sales calls coordinated with other selling efforts?
      5. Do salespeople ask the right questions on sales calls?
      6. How does the growth or decline of a customer or a prospect's business affect the company's own sales?
   C. Marketing information system
      1. Reliability of the data
      2. Usefulness or understandability of the data

        3. Timeliness of the reporting system
        4. Relevancy of the data
        5. Cost of the system
    D. Sales forecasting
    E. Marketing plans
        1. Appraise marketing strengths and weaknesses
        2. Develop marketing objectives
        3. Develop product/service strategies
        4. Develop marketing strategies
        5. Determine pricing structure
    F. Evaluation

VI. Telemarketing
    A. Advantages
        1. Receptiveness
        2. Impressions
        3. More presentations
        4. Unlimited geographic coverage
        5. Better time management
        6. Immediate feedback
        7. Better control
        8. Less piracy
        9. Lower salary and commissions
       10. Other lower expenses
    B. Disadvantages
        1. Bad habits
        2. Dissension among employees
        3. Turnover in staff

VII. Pricing Strategies
    A. The quality of a product in some situations is interpreted by customers by the level of the item's price
    B. Some customer groups shy away from purchasing a product where no printed price schedule is available
    C. Most buyers expect to pay even-numbered prices for prestigious items and odd-numbered prices for commonly available goods
    D. The greater the number of meaningful customer benefits that the seller can convey about a given product, generally the less will be the price resistance

VIII. Summary

CHAPTER OBJECTIVES

1. To review the importance of marketing research for new ventures
2. To present factors that inhibit the use of marketing
3. To examine the marketing concept: philosophy, segmentation, and consumer orientation.
4. To establish the areas vital to marketing planning
5. To highlight the questions concerning hazards in marketing
6. To characterize the marketing stages of growing ventures
7. To introduce telemarketing as an emerging tool for marketing
8. To discuss the key features of a pricing strategy

CHAPTER SUMMARY

A market consists of a group of people who have purchasing power and unsatisfied needs. The most effective way to gather information about a market is through marketing research. The first step of this process is to define the purpose and objectives of the research. This step identifies potential customers, where they buy products, how large the market is, and what products customers need. The next step is to gather secondary data, which has already been compiled. If this is not thorough enough, then primary data are gathered by observational and questioning methods. Interpreting and reporting the information is the next task. The final step is to come up with questions dealing with markets, consumers, and products.

Four major inhibitors to marketing research exist. First of all, marketing research can be very expensive to the entrepreneur. Secondly, the quantitative aspects scare off many entrepreneurs. Third, some entrepreneurs feel that marketing research is good only for making strategic decisions. Finally, some entrepreneurs feel that marketing research is irrelevant.

In developing the marketing concept, there are three types of philosophies. Production-driven philosophy has production as its main concern and sales as a secondary concern. Sales-driven philosophy concentrates on personal selling and advertising to persuade customers to buy products or services. Consumer-driven philosophy depends on research to find out about consumer wants and needs before production begins. Three major factors affect the choice of marketing philosophy. These include competitive pressure, entrepreneur's experience, and short-term focus of sales-driven philosophy. The second factor in developing the marketing concept is market segmentation. This is the process of identifying a specific set of characteristics that differentiate one group of consumers from the rest. Two major variables in market segmentation are demographic and benefit variables. There are two types of consumer behavior that affect the marketing concept. These are personal characteristics and psychological characteristics. The five major consumer classifications are convenience goods, shopping goods, specialty goods, unsought goods, and new products.

There are four distinct marketing stages in a growing venture. Entrepreneurial marketing has a strategy of developing a market niche and a goal of attaining credibility in the marketplace. Opportunistic marketing strives for market penetration in order to attain sales volume. Responsive marketing tries to develop the product market and create customer satisfaction.

Diversified marketing concentrates on new business development while trying to manage the product life cycle.

Marketing planning attempts to determine a comprehensive approach to creating new customers. The first step in marketing planning is to determine who customers are and their wants and needs through marketing research. The second step is concluding whether the sales force is doing an effective job or not. The third step is the compiling and organizing of data relating to cost, revenue, and profit through the use of a marketing information system. The fourth step is sales forecasting. The next step is the five-step marketing plan, and the final step is evaluation.

Telemarketing is the use of the telephone in the selling of merchandise directly to the consumers. This technique is quickly becoming a major marketing tool due to its low cost. It allows companies to increase potential customer sales due to more presentations. Other advantages are receptiveness, unlimited geographic coverage, and immediate feedback. The major disadvantages include poor telephone techniques, dissension between the field sales staff, and rapid turnover of telephone staff.

After the marketing research is done, the entrepreneur is faced with the problem of pricing the product or service. Some factors affecting pricing strategies are competitive pressure, availability of supply, changes in demand, costs of distribution, and economic conditions. Pricing procedures differ according to the nature of the venture.

LECTURE NOTES

MARKETING RESEARCH FOR NEW VENTURES

I. Introduction--A Market Is a Group of Consumers Who Have Purchasing Power and Unsatisfied Needs

II. Marketing Research--Involves the Gathering of Information about a Particular Market Followed by Analysis of that Information
   A. Defining the purpose and objectives of the research--Specific objectives should be established
      1. Identify where potential customers go to purchase the good or service in question.
      2. Why do they choose to go there?
      3. What is the size of the market, and how much of it can the business capture?
      4. How does the business compare with competitors?
      5. What impact does the business's promotion have on customers?
      6. What types of products or services are desired by potential customers?
   B. Gathering secondary data
      1. Secondary data consist of information that has already been compiled
      2. Less expensive to gather than primary data
      3. Secondary data may be internal or external
         a. Internal secondary data consist of information that exists within the venture such as business records

The Dryden Press

  b. External secondary data are available in periodicals, trade association literature, and government publications
 4. Several problems occur due to the use of secondary data
  a. Data may be dated and less useful
  b. Units of measure in secondary data may not fit current problems
C. Gathering primary data
 1. Primary data consist of new information accumulated through observational methods and questioning methods
 2. Observational methods avoid contact with respondents and can be used economically
 3. Questioning methods involve respondents
 4. Surveys include contact by mail, telephone, and personal interviews
  a. Mail surveys are often used when respondents are widely dispersed and have low response rates
  b. Telephone and personal interviews involve verbal communication with respondents and provide higher response rates
  c. Personal interviews are the most expensive, and people are reluctant to grant them
D. Interpreting and reporting the information
 1. After data are accumulated, they must be organized into meaningful information
 2. Methods of summarizing and simplifying data include tables, charts, and graphs
 3. Descriptive statistics such as mean, mode, and median are also helpful
E. Marketing research questioning
 1. There are several areas in which research questions will be asked
  a. Sales questions deal with competitors and product profitability
  b. Distribution questions deal with distributors and dealers
  c. Market questions deal with buying habits, tastes, and market shares of sales by products
  d. Advertising questions deal with effectiveness and budget allocation
  e. Product questions involve testing market acceptability and packaging effects on sales

III. Inhibitors to Marketing Research
 A. Cost
  1. Marketing research can be expensive
  2. Affordable marketing techniques exist for smaller companies
 B. Complexity
  1. Quantitative aspects frighten many entrepreneurs
  2. Key area is interpretation of the data
  3. Entrepreneurs can obtain help from specialists
 C. Strategic decisions
  1. Some entrepreneurs feel that only major strategic decisions need marketing research support
  2. Sales efforts could be enhanced through research results

D. Irrelevancy
   1. Some entrepreneurs believe that marketing research data either tell them what they already know or are irrelevant
   2. Data that confirm what is already known can be acted upon with more confidence

IV. Developing the Marketing Concept
   A. Marketing philosophy--three types
      1. The production-driven philosophy places production as the main concern and sales as a secondary concern. This philosophy is sometimes used by new ventures that produce high-tech products.
      2. The sales-driven philosophy concentrates on personal selling and advertising to persuade customers to buy the company's product. This approach is taken when there is an overabundance of supply.
      3. The consumer-driven philosophy relies on research to find out about consumer wants and needs before the production process begins.
         a. This philosophy encourages the need for marketing research in order to identify a market and target it.
         b. Although the consumer-driven philosophy is usually the most effective, most ventures don't use it.
      4. There are three major factors that influence the choice of marketing philosophy:
         a. Competitive pressure, the intensity of competition, is a deciding factor in a new venture's philosophy.
         b. The entrepreneur's experience and abilities have an influence on philosophy choice.
         c. The short-term focus of the sales-driven philosophy makes it an attractive approach because of its increase in sales.
   B. Market segmentation--"The process of identifying a specific set of characteristics that differentiate one group of customers from the rest."
      1. The process of segmenting the market can be critical for new ventures with very limited resources.
      2. A number of variables need to be analyzed in order to identify specific market segments.
      3. Two major variables include "demographic" and "benefit" variables
         a. Demographic variables include age, marital status, sex, occupation, income, location, etc., and are used to determine a geographic and demographic profile of the consumers and their purchasing potential.
         b. Benefit variables identify unsatisfied needs that exist in the market and include convenience, cost, style, and trends.
   C. Consumer behavior
      1. Two types of consumer behavior that entrepreneurs must consider are personal characteristics and psychological characteristics.
      2. The five types of consumers are innovators, early adopters, early majority, late majority, and laggards.

3. The next step is to link the characteristic makeup of potential consumers with trends in the marketplace.
4. There are five major consumer classifications of which entrepreneurs should be aware
   a. Convenience goods include staple, impulse, and emergency goods that consumers want to buy but aren't willing to spend time shopping for.
   b. Shopping goods are products that consumers take time out to compare for quality and price.
   c. Specialty goods are those that consumers make a special effort to find and buy.
   d. Unsought goods are those that the consumer doesn't need or look for, such as cemetery plots.
   e. New products are products that are unknown due to lack of advertising or that take time to be understood.

V. Marketing Stages for Growing Ventures--There Are Four Marketing Stages in a Growing Venture:
   A. Entrepreneurial marketing has a strategy of developing a market niche and a goal of attaining credibility in the marketplace.
   B. Opportunistic marketing has a strategy of market penetration in order to attain sales volume.
   C. Responsive marketing tries to develop the product market and create customer satisfaction.
   D. Diversified marketing concentrates on new business development and tries to manage the product life cycle.

VI. Marketing Planning--"The Process of Determining a Clear, Comprehensive Approach to the Creation of Customers."
   A. Marketing research is the process of determining who the customers are, what they want, and how they buy
      1. In marketing research, the following areas are of great importance
         a. The company's strengths and weaknesses offer insights into profitable opportunities and possible problems and help in making decisions
         b. A market profile enables a company to identify its current market and service needs
         c. The identification of a company's current clients helps management find out where to allocate resources. Defining the best customers allows management to achieve a more direct segmentation of this market niche
         d. Through a geographical- or industry-wide analysis of potential customers, a company increases its ability to target this group and turn potential customers into current customers
         e. Identification of competition allows a company to determine the firms that are most willing to pursue the same market niche

- f. Analyzing changing trends in demographics, economics, technology, cultural attitudes, and government policies that may affect customers' needs
- g. Keeping management aware of significant changes in government rates, standards, and tax laws
2. The following are some useful tips regarding low-cost research
   a. Devise a contest that requires customers to rate the quality of your products, and have a drawing for a prize
   b. Attach a questionnaire to the company catalog regarding the quality of your products or service
   c. Give any customer grievances high priority, and follow up with an in-depth interview
   d. Develop a set of questions that can be administered over the phone, asking customers to give their opinions on products and services
   e. Include a questionnaire in product packages
B. Sales Research--The following is a list of questions that need to be answered in sales research
   1. Do salespeople call on their qualified prospects?
   2. Does the sales force contact decision makers?
   3. Are territories assigned according to sales potential and salespeople's abilities?
   4. Are sales calls coordinated with other selling efforts, trade shows, and direct mail?
C. Marketing information system
   1. A marketing information system compiles and organizes data relating to cost, revenue, and profit from the customer base
   2. This information can be useful in monitoring the strategies, decisions, and programs concerned with marketing
   3. Key factors affecting the value of such a system are
      a. Reliability of data
      b. Usefulness or understanding of data
      c. Timeliness of the reporting system
      d. Relevancy of the data
      e. Cost of the system
D. Sales forecasting--"The process of projecting future sales through historical sales figures and the application of statistical techniques"
   1. The process is limited in value because it relies on historical data
   2. As a comprehensive planning process, it can be very valuable
E. Marketing plans--In order to be effective, the marketing plans should follow a five-step program
   1. Appraise marketing strengths and weaknesses
   2. Develop marketing objectives along with short- and intermediate-range sales goals necessary to meet these objectives
   3. Develop product/service strategies
   4. Develop marketing strategies
   5. Determine pricing structure

F. Evaluation
  1. The final factor in the marketing planning process is evaluation
  2. Evaluation allows for flexibility and adjustment of marketing planning

VII. Telemarketing--The Use of Telephone Communications to Sell Merchandise Directly to Consumers
  A. Advantages
    1. Firms may be able to increase potential customer sales, upgrade sales, reactivate old accounts, and support the current sales staff.
    2. Some specific advantages are
      a. Receptiveness
      b. First impressions
      c. More presentations
      d. Unlimited geographic coverage
      e. Better time management
      f. Immediate feedback
  B. Pitfalls
    1. Although there are many advantages to telemarketing, there are also some disadvantages
    2. Poor telephone techniques can undermine the telemarketing strategy
    3. Dissension between the field sales staff and the telephone sales staff can arise
    4. There is a problem of rapid turnover of telephone staff

VIII. Pricing Strategies--Factors Affecting Pricing Strategies
  A. The following factors affect entrepreneurs in the pricing of their products or services
    1. The degree of competitive pressure
    2. Availability of sufficient supply
    3. Seasonal or cyclical changes in demand
    4. The costs of distribution
    5. Economic conditions
  B. Pricing procedures differ depending on the nature of the venture

SUGGESTED ANSWERS FOR DISCUSSION QUESTIONS (END OF CHAPTER)

1. In your own words, what is a market? How can marketing research help an entrepreneur identify a market?

A market is potential customers who have purchasing power. An entrepreneur would not know what type of venture or area to engage in without market research. The market analysis helps tell the entrepreneur what to do.

2. *What are the five steps in the marketing research process?*
   (1) Defining the purpose and objectives of the research--in other words, you need to define precisely the informational requirements of the decision to be made
   (2) Gathering secondary data--these data involve using already compiled data. The two types are internal and external
   (3) Gathering primary data--these data involve gathering new information. The two forms are surveys and experimentation
   (4) Interpreting and reporting information--this segment deals with analyzing and reporting useful information where it is needed
   (5) Marketing research questions--the questions deal in the areas of sales, distribution, advertising, and products

3. *Which are of greater value to the entrepreneur, primary or secondary data? Why?*
   Secondary data are of greater value because they usually contain the information desired and are inexpensive.

4. *Identify and describe three of the primary inhibitors to marketing research.*
   (1) Cost--market research can be expensive
   (2) Complexity--the interpretation of the quantitative aspects of marketing research
   (3) Strategic decisions--cost and complexity are usually tied into major decisions
   (4) Irrelevancy--only a certain amount of research is useful

5. *How would an entrepreneur's new-venture strategy differ under each of the following marketing philosophies: production-driven, sales-driven, consumer-driven?*
   (1) Production-driven--this is based on the belief "produce efficiently and worry about sales later"
   (2) Sales-driven--this focuses on personal selling and advertising to persuade customers to buy the company's output
   (3) Consumer-driven--this relies on research to discover consumer preferences, desires, and needs before production actually begins

6. *In your own words, what is market segmentation? What role do demographic and benefit variables play in the segmentation process?*
   Market segmentation is identifying the factors that classify consumer groups. Demographic factors are used to determine a geographic or demographic profile of consumers and purchasing power. Benefit variables identify the unsatisfied needs that exist in a market.

7. *Identify and discuss three of the most important personal characteristics that help an entrepreneur identify and describe customers. Also, explain how the product life cycle will affect the purchasing behavior of these customers.*
   Consumers are considered to fall into five categories: innovators, early adopters, early majority, late majority, and laggards. Income, education, and time orientation are important characteristics in each of these categories. For example, innovators usually have high

The Dryden Press

incomes, while laggards have below-average incomes. This may be why laggards don't get things as quickly. Early adopter's education consists of college, while the late majority have some high school. Early adopters may understand the theory of supply and demand; the late majority might not. Early majority are present-oriented, whereas laggards are tradition-oriented. Laggards don't accept new methods because they live in the past.

8. *Identify and discuss three of the psychological characteristics that help an entrepreneur identify and describe customers. Also, explain how the product life cycle will affect the purchasing behavior of these customers.*

    Some psychological characteristics are nature or needs, perceptions, and self-concept. Early adopters purchase goods that make others notice them. The laggard purchases only the basic needs for survival. The perceptions of the early majority influence the purchase of goods that make them acceptable, whereas the late majority purchases products for the home. The innovator's self-concept is for the elite things in life, whereas the late majority is concerned with security purchases.

9. *How does an understanding of the way consumers view a venture's product or service affect their behavior? For example, why would it make a difference to the entrepreneur's strategy if the consumers viewed the company as selling a convenience good as opposed to a shopping good?*

    If consumers view a venture's product or service as quality, the consumers would likely desire the venture's product or service. On the other hand, a product of low quality would not be desired.

10. *Identify and describe four of the major forces shaping buying decisions in the 1990s.*
    (1) The continuing increase in educational attainment levels means more knowledgeable, discriminatory purchasing. People are less likely to obtain something that is of a low quality.
    (2) Great discretionary time resulting from reduced work hours means even greater demand for leisure products, travel, and recreational services. People are living more for the joy of the present than waiting to fulfill their pleasures in the future.
    (3) An older, more mature population means purchase decisions will reflect greater conservatism in the search for value and lifestyle satisfaction. Being more mature, people will not buy goods that are not beneficial.
    (4) Higher income attained by traditionally lower-paid blue-collar workers will lead to far greater experimentation in long-standing white-collar purchases such as wines, ethnic foods, and the theater. People in the lower middle class desire the finer things in life.

11. *Most emerging ventures will evolve through a series of marketing stages. What are these stages? Identify and describe each.*
    (1) Entrepreneurial marketing: strategy of developing a market
    (2) Opportunistic marketing: seek a way to penetrate the market
    (3) Responsive marketing: seek to develop the product market
    (4) Diversified marketing: focus on new business development

12. *What does the entrepreneur of an emerging venture need to know about sales research and a marketing information system?*

    An entrepreneur must understand that he/she needs to continually review methods employed for sales and distribution in relation to market research. He/she must understand that information systems can be helpful in monitoring strategies, decisions, and programs concerning marketing.

13. *In developing a marketing plan, what are the five steps that are particularly helpful? Identify and describe each.*
    (1) Appraise marketing strengths and weaknesses, emphasizing factors that contribute to the firm's "competitive edge." By knowing your strengths and weaknesses, you know what to avoid and what not to avoid.
    (2) Develop marketing objectives along with the short- and intermediate-range sales goals necessary to meet those objectives. Setting goals will give you a measure of success.
    (3) Develop product/service strategies. This will determine needs and specifications.
    (4) Develop marketing strategies. These are needed to achieve different goals.
    (5) Determine pricing structure. Determine which customers will be attracted.

14. *How can the entrepreneur evaluate the marketing planning process? Be complete in your answer.*

    Generate reports on customer analysis. The reports should be evaluated based upon performance. The analysis can be compared to sales value, gross sales dollars, or market shares. Only through this evaluation can flexibility and adjustment be incorporated into marketing planning.

15. *How does telemarketing work? What are its advantages? What are its pitfalls? Why is it likely to be a major marketing tool of the 1990s?*

    Telemarketing is the use of telephone communications to sell merchandise directly to customers. Some of the advantages of telemarketing are receptiveness, impressions, more presentations, unlimited geographic coverage, better time management, immediate feedback, better control, less "piracy," lower salaries and commissions, and other lower expenses.

    Some of the pitfalls are: poor telephone techniques can defeat the telemarketing strategy; dissension can exist between the field sales staff and telephone sales personnel; there can be rapid turnover of the telephone sales staff. The major reason for the growth of telemarketing is that it is cost effective.

16. *What are some of the major environmental factors that affect pricing strategies? What are some of the major psychological factors that affect pricing? Identify and discuss three of each.*
    Environmental factors:
    (1) Degree of competitive pressure--in a monopoly where there is no competition, prices are set as desired. In perfect competition, prices are set.
    (2) Seasonal or cyclical changes in demand--some goods are more available in certain

seasons, so the price is lower. During the off-season, prices are higher because goods aren't as available.
(3) Cost of distribution--if the cost to distribute is higher, then the price of the product or service will be a little higher to compensate for the higher distribution cost.

Psychological conditions:
(1) In some situations, the quality of a product is interpreted by customers by the item's price level. Customers believe the higher the price, the higher the quality.
(2) An emphasis on the monthly cost of purchasing an expensive item often results in greater sales than an emphasis on total selling price. Items like cars or stereos, which are expensive, are easier to pay for monthly because few people have the funds to pay the total sales price.
(3) The greater the number of meaningful customer's benefits the seller can convey about a given product, the less will be the price resistance. The customer is more inclined to look at the benefits and ignore the costs.

TEACHING NOTES FOR END-OF-CHAPTER CASES

VIDEO CASE: ROGAINE: MARKETING AN ACCIDENTAL MIRACLE (Answers to Questions)

1. What key marketing research questions were answered by Upjohn in the development of Rogaine?

Certainly the markets, advertising, and products areas were covered. The following questions were addressed.

Markets
1. Do you know all that would be useful about the differences in buying habits and tastes by territory and kind of product?
2. Do you have as much information as you need on brand or manufacturer loyalty and repeat purchasing in your product category?
3. Can you now plot, from period to period, your market share of sales by products?

Advertising
1. Is your advertising reaching the right people?
2. Do you know how effective your advertising is in comparison to that of your competitors'?
3. Is your budget allocated appropriately for greater profit—according to products, territories, and market potentials?

Products
1. Do you have a reliable quantitative method for testing the market acceptability of new products and product changes?

2. Do you have a reliable method for testing the effect on sales of new or changed packaging?
   3. Do you know whether adding higher- or lower- quality levels would make new profitable markets for your products?

2. ***Is there a marketing philosophy that best describes Upjohn's approach to the market with Rogaine?***

   Yes, the consumer-driven philosophy because they relied on the consumer's preferences, desires, and needs <u>before</u> launching Rogaine into the market.

3. ***Using Table 8.3, what consumer characteristics could be used to define Rogaine's market segment?***

   The psychological characteristics: nature of needs, perceptions, self concept, aspiration groups, and reference groups.

CASE: DEALING WITH THE COMPETITION

1. ***Will the information that Roberta is seeking be of value to her in competing in this market? Why or why not?***

   Yes, the information will be of great use because her strategy must develop a niche that will differentiate her from the competition.

2. ***How would you recommend Roberta put together her marketing plan? What should be involved?***

   Recommend a five-step plan that identifies the specific needs of her business. She should first define the purpose and objectives of her research and then gather secondary and primary data. After this she needs to develop an information-gathering instrument to collect the data, and finally, she should interpret and record the information and review it to determine the market she has found. The results should answer questions about sales, distribution, markets, advertising, and products.

3. ***How expensive will it be for Roberta to follow your recommendations for her marketing research plan? Describe any other marketing research she could undertake in the near future that would be of minimal cost.***

   The cost of the plan I described could fit into her budget if she used sources such as her local business bureau, college or university, chamber of commerce, small-business development center, and state agencies that can provide low-cost research ideas and information about her area of business.

The Dryden Press

CASE: FOR COOKS ONLY

1. *From the customer's viewpoint, what type of good is a cookbook?*
    The customer would classify the cookbook as a specialty and unsought good. It is specialty because some people cook for fun or "sport" and enjoy new recipes. However, this item would not commonly be sought after except on special occasions because friends and relatives seem to be the major source of cooking ideas.

2. *Why is Phil's store doing so well?*
    Phil's venture is doing well at the moment because he has a consumer-driven philosophy. This strategy gives the business a long-term advantage in generating sales. In addition, his familiarity with the books gives Phil the technical expertise needed for understanding the particular consumer he wishes to attract.

3. *In his marketing research efforts, what type of information would you suggest Phil collect? How can he go about doing this?*
    Phil should focus on the areas of sales, the market(s), advertising, and products because these factors determine the new ideas or trends that will make the business expand and grow. Secondary research is the way in which this information can be obtained, however, Phil may seek to do some primary research on his own.

ADDITIONAL EXPERIENTIAL EXERCISE

"Surveying Marketing Practices"

Have students go to a small business (retail, wholesale, service, manufacturing) that has 1 to 250 employees and survey the owner on the concepts used in the marketing practices. For example, ask the owner how he/she identifies the target market from secondary data or primary data. Then once you have the major topic, ask related questions from the chapter in the section you have decided on and continue the survey. Once you have the information from your survey, write a 2-3 page, double-spaced, typed paper on what you have learned through the survey related to the chapter. Have students compare their results.

CHAPTER 9

FINANCIAL PREPARATION FOR ENTREPRENEURIAL VENTURES

CHAPTER OUTLINE

I. Introduction
   A. Three resources available to the entrepreneur
      1. Human
      2. Material
      3. Financial

II. The Importance of Financial Information for Entrepreneurs
   A. Key questions are answered
   B. The accounting equation
   C. Three critical statements: balance sheet, income statement, and cash-flow statement

III. Preparing Financial Statements
   A. Operating budgets
      1. Estimating sales forecast
         a. By linear regression
         b. By certain percentage over prior period's sales
      2. Estimating expenses
         a. Cost of goods sold
         b. Fixed variable and mixed costs
   B. Cash-flow statement
      1. Provides overview of cash inflows and outflows
      2. Cash inflows
         a. Cash sales
         b. Cash payments on account
         c. Loan proceeds

IV. Pro Forma Statements
   A. Two kinds
      1. Income statements
      2. Balance sheet

V. Capital Budgeting
   A. Steps
      1. Identify cash flows and timing
      2. Obtain reliable estimates of savings and expenses
   B. Methods
      1. Payback method

        a. Easiest
        b. Ignores cash flows beyond payback period
    2. Net present value
        a. Minimizes shortcomings of payback method
        b. Dollar today worth more than future dollar
    3. Internal rate of return
        a. Cash flows discounted
        b. Must begin with NPV of zero and work backward through tables

VI. Break-Even Analysis
    A. Break-even point computation
        1. Assesses expected product profitability
        2. Determines how many units must be sold at a particular selling price
        3. Approaches used
            a. Contribution margin
                1. Difference between selling price and variable cost per unit
                2. FC = (SP - VC) S
            b. Graphic approach
                1. Deals with total revenue and total costs
                2. Enables visualization of cost structure
            c. Handling questionable costs
                1. Used with difficult-to-assign costs

VII. Ratio Analysis
    A. Key relationships
    B. Measuring and interpreting

VIII. Decision Support Systems
    A. Facilitates financial planning process
    B. Can perform a sensitivity analysis for sales and expenses

IX. Summary

CHAPTER OBJECTIVES

1. To explain the principal financial statements needed for any entrepreneurial venture: balance sheet, income statement, and cash-flow statement
2. To outline the process of preparing an operating budget
3. To discuss the nature of cash flow and to explain how to draw up such a document
4. To describe how pro forma statements are prepared
5. To explain how capital budgeting can be used in the decision-making process
6. To illustrate how to use break-even analysis

7. To describe ratio analysis and illustrate some of the important measures and meanings
8. To describe the value of decision support systems in the management of financial resources

CHAPTER SUMMARY

"Financial Preparation for Entrepreneurial Ventures" explains the importance of budgets, pro forma statements, and break-even analysis. It explains the resources and steps needed in constructing budgets. Formulas that are necessary for budget construction and financial understanding are also given. This chapter communicates the importance of break-even analysis and three approaches to take when conducting break-even analysis. Finally, the chapter touches on the use of a decision support system.

The first part of this chapter explains the importance of financial information for entrepreneurs. Then, the process of preparing an operation budget is covered. The first step in constructing an operating budget is to estimate the sales forecast. This can be done using a statistical forecasting technique such as linear regression. Next, the expenses must be estimated. The first expense that should be estimated is cost of goods sold. This estimation is done in different ways by retail and manufacturing firms. Fixed, variable, and mixed costs are key factors when estimating expenses.

The next budget presented is the cash-flow statement. This financial statement gives the entrepreneur an overview of the cash inflows and outflows during the budget period. The first step in creating the cash-flow statement is to identify and time cash inflows. Cash inflows come from cash sales, cash payments received on account, and loan proceeds.

The preparation of pro forma statements is a key step for entrepreneurs. These statements are projections of the company's future financial position for either a future date or a future period of time. The pro forma income statement is prepared before the pro forma balance sheet. The last balance sheet prepared before the budget period, the cash-flow budget, and the operating budget are all needed to construct a pro forma balance sheet. The accuracy of this balance sheet can be checked by applying the traditional accounting equation: Assets = Liabilities + Owner's Equity.

An entrepreneur can use capital budgeting to help plan for investments that are expected to go beyond one year. These investments are known as capital investments or capital expenditures. Identifying cash flows and their timing is the first step in capital budgeting. Maximizing the value of the firm is the main objective of capital budgeting. It is designed to answer these questions: (1) Which of several mutually exclusive projects should be selected? (2) How many projects, in total, should be selected?

There are three methods used in capital budgeting. The first and simplest is the payback method. In this method, the entrepreneur formulates a maximum time frame for a payback period. All projects with a longer payback period than the time frame allows are rejected. Those projects that fall within the time frame are accepted. The drawback of this method is that it does not consider the cash flows beyond the payback period.

The second method of capital budgeting is net present value. Unlike the payback method, net present value recognizes cash flows beyond the payback period. This method works on the concept that "a dollar today is more than a dollar in the future." The rate used to determine the present value of future cash flows is the cost of capital. The net present value is determined by finding the present value of expected net cash flows and subtracting it from the initial cost of the project. The project with the highest net present value should be selected.

The third method is internal rate of return. In this method, the future cash flows are also discounted. However, they are discounted at a rate that makes the net present value equal to zero. This rate is the internal rate of return. Just as with the net present value, the project with the highest internal rate of return should be selected. This method can be difficult when working with uneven cash flows.

Break-even analysis is used to help the entrepreneur price competitively and earn a fair profit. This technique is used to determine product profitability. It helps the entrepreneur know how many units should be sold at what price to break even. There are three approaches to break-even analysis.

Contribution margin approach is the first approach to break-even analysis. Contribution margin is the amount per unit that is used to help cover all other costs. It is determined by subtracting the variable cost per unit from the selling price.

The second method is the graphic approach. The entrepreneur must at least plot total revenue and total costs. The break-even point is the intersection of these two lines. By plotting two additional points, variable and fixed costs, the entrepreneur can visualize various cost structure relationships.

The last approach, handling questionable costs, was designed specifically for entrepreneurial firms. This lets the entrepreneur see if the product's profitability is sensitive to cost behavior by calculating break-even points for different fixed or variable costs. The entrepreneur can then see if the product will be profitable or unprofitable or if the costs should be investigated further.

Financial statements report both on a firm's position at a point in time and on its operations over some past period. However, the real value of financial statements lies in the fact that they can be used to help predict the firm's earnings and dividends. From an investor's standpoint, predicting the future is how financial statement analysis is useful, both as a way to anticipate conditions and, more importantly, as a starting point for planning actions that will influence the course of events.

An analysis of the firm's ratios is generally the key step in a financial analysis. The ratios are designed to show relationships between financial statement accounts.

Ratio analysis can be applied from two directions. Vertical analysis is the application of ratio analysis to one set of financial statements. Here, an analysis "up and down" the statements is done to find signs of strengths and weaknesses. Horizontal analysis looks at financial statements and ratios over time. In horizontal analysis, the trends are critical. All the numbers increasing or decreasing are particular components of the company's financial position.

Finally, this chapter presents the idea of decision support systems in small business. This technique can help a firm manage its financial resources. Decision support systems help calculate a desired minimum cash balance and the amount of sales needed to meet this minimum balance. It can also calculate different net incomes to see how they compare to targeted profits. Sensitivity analysis can also be done for other levels of sales and expenses. This is an important technique that can give the entrepreneur a more complete view of the financial characteristics on which to base a plan of action.

LECTURE NOTES

FINANCIAL PREPARATION FOR ENTREPRENEURIAL VENTURES

I. Introduction
   A. Characteristics of competitive environment for the entrepreneur
      1. Government regulation
      2. Competition
      3. Resources
   B. Three types of resources
      1. Human
      2. Material
      3. Financial
   C. Chapter focus
      1. Budgets as planning tools
      2. Preparation of pro forma statements
      3. Break-even analysis as a profit planning tool
      4. The use of ratio analysis for financial analysis
      5. Value of decision support systems

II. The Importance of Financial Information for Entrepreneurs
   A. Key questions to be answered
      1 What is your total estimated income for the first year?
      2. What is your estimated monthly income for the first year?
      3. What will it cost you to open the business?
      4. What will be your monthly cash flow during the first year?
      5. What will your personal monthly financial needs be?
      6. What sales volume will you need in order to make a profit during the first three years?
      7. What will be your break-even point?
      8. What will be your projected assets, liabilities, and net worth on the day before you expect to open?

III. Preparing Financial Statements
   A. The operating budget
      1. Estimating the sales forecast
         a. Statistical forecasting technique
         b. Trend line analysis
      2. Estimating expenses
         a. Cost of goods sold should be first

The Dryden Press

            1. Determine the predicted number of units to be sold
            2. Figure the desired ending inventory balance
            3. Determine production requirement
        b. Determine materials requirement
        c. Determine direct labor requirement
        d. Estimate operating expenses for period
            1. Fixed costs
            2. Variable costs
            3. Mixed costs
    B. The cash-flow statement
        1. Identification and timing of cash flows
        2. Cash inflows come from three sources
            a. Cash sales
            b. Cash payments received on account
            c. Loan proceeds

IV. Pro Forma Statements
    A. Pro forma income statement
    B. Pro forma balance sheet
        1. Requires operating budget
        2. Requires cash-flow budget
        3. Requires last balance sheet prepared before budget period
        4. Verify accuracy with traditional accounting equation

V. Capital Budgeting
    A. Identify cash flows and their timing
    B. Main objective is to maximize value of firm
    C. Should answer two questions
        1. Which of several mutually exclusive projects should be selected?
        2. How many projects, in total, should be selected?
    D. Three most common methods
        1. Payback method
            a. Determining criterion is the time needed to payback investment
            b. Drawback is that it ignores cash flows beyond payback period
            c. Reasons to continue using this method
        2. Net present value
            a. Based on premise that a dollar today is worth more than a dollar tomorrow
            b. Cost of capital is the rate used to adjust future cash flows to present value
            c. Subtract present value of future cash flows from initial cost to get net present value
            d. Select project with highest net present value
        3. Internal rate of return
            a. Discount future cash flows at a rate that makes net present value equal to zero

        b. Select project with highest internal rate of return
        c. Difficulty of technique is a major drawback

VI. Break-Even Analysis
    A. Break-even analysis provides information to
        1. Price competitively
        2. Earn a fair profit

VII. Break-Even Point Computation
    A. Contribution margin approach
        1. Difference between selling price and variable cost per unit
        2. Formula is $FC = (SP - VC)S$
    B. Graphic approach
        1. Must graph at least two numbers
            a. Total revenue
            b. Total costs
        2. Intersection is the break-even point
        3. May plot two additional costs
            a. Variable costs
            b. Fixed costs
    C. Handling questionable costs
        1   Designed specifically for entrepreneurial firms
        2. Calculate break-even points
            a. Under fixed and variable costs
            b. Test if product's profitability is sensitive to cost behavior
        3. Decision rules
            a. Product should be profitable if expected sales exceed the higher break-even point
            b. Product should be unprofitable if expected sales do not exceed the lower break-even point
            c. Investigate the questionable cost's behavior further if sales fall between the two break-even points
        4. Substitute the cost as fixed, then variable
            a. For fixed cost use $0=(SP-VC)S-FC-QC$
            b. For variable cost use $0=[SP-VC-(QC/U)]S-FC$

VIII. Ratio Analysis
    A. Key relationships
        1. Return on investment (ROI)
        2. Return on assets (ROA)
        3. Net profit margin
        4. Asset turnover
        5. Return on assets
        6. Average collection period

        7. Inventory turnover
        8. Working capital
        9. Current ratio
       10. Quick ratio
    B. Measuring and interpreting

IX. Use of Decision Support Systems
    A. Technique used in managing financial resources
    B. Used to facilitate financial planning process through
        1. Integrated pro forma statements
        2. Generation of alternatives that can be quickly explored
    C. Allows entrepreneurs to
        1. Specify desired minimum cash balance
        2. Determine minimum level of sales needed to meet this requirement
        3. Calculate net income at various points to see how it compares with targeted profits
    D. Sensitivity analysis can be performed for other levels of sales and expenses
    E. Provides more complex view of
        1. Financial characteristics
        2. Interaction of the business
        3. Formulation of plan of action

SUGGESTED ANSWERS FOR DISCUSSION QUESTIONS
(END OF CHAPTER)

1. What is the importance of financial information for entrepreneurs? Briefly describe the key components.

Financial information pulls together all the information presented in the other segments of the business: marketing, distribution, manufacturing, and management. It quantifies all the assumptions and/or historical information concerning business operations.

The key components of the financial segment include the balance sheet, which represents the financial condition of a company at a certain date. It details the items owned by your company (assets) and the amount owed by the company (liabilities). It also shows the net worth of the company and its liquidity. The balance sheet must follow the traditional accounting equation: Assets=Liabilities + Equity.

Another key statement is the income statement, commonly referred to as the P & L (profit and loss) statement, which provides the owner/manager with the results of operations. It measures the success of the business.

Finally, the statement of cash flow is an analysis of the cash availability and cash needs of the business. The projected cash flow is a planning tool to allow management to make borrowing and investing decisions.

2. ***What are the benefits of the budgeting process?***
   Budgeting allows top management to determine the company's goals. This is a benefit because top management is more familiar with the goals, strategies, and available resources of the company. Another benefit can be the involvement of operating management in the budget process. This is more likely to get a commitment from them than the top-down approach is.

3. ***How is the statistical forecasting technique of simple linear regression used in making a sales forecast?***
   Simple linear regression is used to show the relationship between three variables. The equation for simple linear regression is $Y=a+bx$. $\underline{Y}$ represents expected sales, $\underline{x}$ is the factor on which sales are dependent, b is the change in Y divided by the change in $\underline{x}$, and $\underline{a}$ is a constant. The entrepreneur uses this analysis to draw conclusions about the relationship between x and Y.

4. ***Describe how an operating budget is constructed.***
   The operating budget is constructed by estimating sales, expenses, and cost of goods. These three budgets are combined to make up the operating budget.

5. ***Describe how a cash-flow budget is constructed.***
   The cash-flow budget is created by first determining the cash inflows and their timing. Then the cash outflows must be determined. These are combined to make up the cash-flow budget.

6. ***What are pro forma statements? How are they constructed? Be complete in your answer.***
   Pro forma statements are projections of a firm's financial position over a future period of time or on a future date. The pro forma income statement is created first. It is a combination of all of the pro forma income statements that were created for the preparation of the operating budget. Preparing the pro forma balance sheet requires the last balance sheet prepared before the budget period began, the operating budget, and the cash-flow budget. Projected balance sheet totals are created by adding the projected changes as shown on the budgets, starting with the beginning balance sheet balances. The accuracy of the pro forma balance sheet is checked by using the traditional accounting equation: Assets = Liabilities + Owner's Equity.

7. ***Describe how a capital budget is constructed.***
   The first step is to identify the cash flows and their timing. The formula is represented by capital budgeting. Expected Returns = $x(1-T)$ + Depreciation. x is equal to the net operating income, and T is the tax rate. The principal objective is to maximize the value of the firm. The three most common methods are the payback method, net present value method, and the internal rate of return.

8. *One of the most popular capital budgeting techniques is the payback method. How does this method work? Give an example.*

   The entrepreneur will select a maximum time frame for the payback period. Any project that requires a longer period will be rejected, and those projects that fall into the time frame will be accepted.

Year	Proposal A	Proposal B
1	500	100
2	400	200
3	300	300
4	20	400
5	10	500

   Each machine costs $1,000

   This is the payback method with a cutoff period of 3 years. Proposal A would be paid back in 2 1/3 years; $900 of the original investment will be paid back in the first 2 years and the last $100 in the third year. Proposal B will require 4 years for its payback. Proposal A should be chosen.

9. *Describe the net present value method. When would an entrepreneur use this method? Why?*

   The net present value (NPV) method is a technique that helps to minimize some of the shortcomings of the payback method by recognizing the future cash flows beyond the payback period. The concept works on the premise that a dollar today is worth more than a dollar in the future. The entrepreneur is adjusting future cash flows to determine their value in present period terms. The entrepreneur would use this method when he/she isn't satisfied with the results of the payback method.

10. *Describe the internal rate of return method. When would an entrepreneur use this method? Why?*

   Future cash flows are discounted; however, they are discounted at a rate that makes the NPV of the project equal to zero. The project with the highest IRR is selected. When using the IRR concept, the entrepreneur must begin with a NPV of zero and work backward through the tables. The entrepreneur must estimate the approximate rate. When future cash flows beyond the payback are to be considered, the NPV and the IRR are the methods to be used in determining the best proposal.

11. *When would an entrepreneur be interested in break-even analysis?*

   When the entrepreneur needs relevant, timely, and accurate information that will enable him or her to price competitively and yet be able to earn a fair profit. It helps determine how many units must be sold in order to break even at a particular selling price.

12. *If an entrepreneur wants to use break-even analysis but has trouble assigning some costs as either fixed or variable, can break-even analysis still be used? Explain.*

If the entrepreneur has trouble assigning fixed or variable costs, he can still do break-even analysis using a technique specifically designed for entrepreneurial firms. This technique is known as handling questionable costs. This technique calculates break-even points under alternative assumptions of fixed or variable costs to see if a product's profitability is sensitive to cost behavior. There are three decision rules for this cost.

(1) The product should be profitable if sales exceed the higher break-even point.
(2) The product should be unprofitable if expected sales do not exceed the lower break-even point.
(3) If expected sales fall between the two break-even points, then the questionable cost's behavior needs to be looked at further.

13. *What is Ratio Analysis? How is horizontal analysis different from vertical?*

Financial statements report both on a firm's position at a point in time and on its operations over some past period. However, the real value of financial statements lies in the fact that they can be used to help predict the firm's earnings and dividends. From an investor's standpoint, predicting the future is what financial statement analysis is all about; from an entrepreneur's standpoint, financial statement analysis is useful both as a way to anticipate conditions and, more importantly, as a starting point for planning actions that will influence the course of events.

An analysis of the firm's ratios is generally the key step in a financial analysis. The ratios are designed to show relationships between financial statement accounts.

Ratio analysis can be applied from two directions. Vertical analysis is the application of ratio analysis to one set of financial statements. Here, an analysis "up and down" the statements is done to find signs of strengths and weaknesses. Horizontal analysis looks at financial statements and ratios over time. In horizontal analysis, the trends are critical: are the numbers increasing or decreasing, and are particular components of the company's financial position getting better or worse?

14. *What is a decision support system? How can it be of value in helping entrepreneurs manage their resources?*

A decision support system is a technique that a firm can use in managing its financial resources. It can facilitate the financial planning process by using integrated pro forma financial statements and generating alternatives that can be explored quickly. By using this technique, the entrepreneur can determine the desired minimum cash balance and the minimum level of sales needed to meet this requirement for the budget period or business plan. Net income can be calculated at various points to compare it with targeted profits. The decision support system can be used for sensitivity analysis for other levels of sales and expenses. All of this information can give the entrepreneur a more complete view of the financial characteristics and interaction of the business so that he/she can make a sound plan of action.

TEACHING NOTES FOR END-OF-CHAPTER CASES

CASE: IT'S ALL GREEK TO HER

1. *What is the purpose of a cash-flow budget? What does it reveal? Of what value would it be to an entrepreneur?*

    It tells the overall cash inflows and outflows of a period. It reveals to a manager when the business may have cash problems in the future, so he or she can try to overcome the problems in an efficient way.

    The value to an entrepreneur is that this sort of budget lays out the business on a monthly basis. It pinpoints good times of sales and bad, so the entrepreneur can work on those spots of bad times.

2. *How does the payback method work? How does the net present value method work? How would you explain each of these methods to Regina?*

    The payback method determines when the project will pay for itself. The initial cost is the starting point, and then you subtract the first year's projected earnings, the second year's earnings, etc., until the initial cost has been covered. This can be measured in fractions of years.

    Net present value determines the future cash flows' worth in the present. This is done by multiplying the year's cash flows by the net present value factor from a chart or with a financial calculator.

    The payback period method is exactly what it says. It tells you how long it will take to get your initial cash outlay back, whereas the net present value method gives you an up-to-date figure of the projected cash flows. These cash flows are multiplied by a present value factor, added together, and then subtracted from the original cash outlay. The project with the most money left over is the choice to make.

3. *How does the internal rate of return method work? How would you explain this?*

    The internal rate of return is sort of an estimated percentage of capital. The net present value method is equal to zero as the expected cash flows are multiplied by a value factor, and when added they would equate to the initial cash outlay.

    This method is similar to the net present value method. The only difference is that the interest rate is unknown. When the net present value equals zero, the estimated percentage rate of return is assigned.

CASE: THE CONTRACT PROPOSAL

1. **What is the break-even point for this project?**
    Fixed cost question:
Selling price	=	$800.00
Variable cost	=	$400.00
Fixed cost	=	$35,000.00

Number of units sold = $\underline{S}$
Question cost = $\underline{QC}$

$(800 - 400)S - 35,000 - 1,000 = 0$
$400S - 36,000 = 0$
$36,000 = 400S$
$90 = \underline{S}$ = break-even point

Variable cost question:
$(\underline{S} - \underline{VC} - \underline{QC}/\underline{U}) \underline{S} - \underline{FC} = 0$
$(400 - 8.34)S - 35,000 = 0$
$391.66\underline{s} - 35,000. = 0$
$35,000 = 391.66\underline{s}$
$89.36 = \underline{S}$ = break-even point
90 units

The break-even point is 90 units; therefore, if 120 units are sold a profit will occur.

2. *If the project is profitable, will it provide Dennis the desired 20 percent? Explain.*
   This project will provide the 20 percent return that Dennis requires. Break-even point is 90 units at $800 per unit, and that equals $72,000 in sales revenue. Twenty percent is $14,400, which added to $72,000 equals $86,000. So, Dennis sells 120 units making $96,000, well above the desired return according to the project.

3. *Of what value is break-even analysis to Dennis? Be complete in your answer.*
   Dennis relies on this analysis approach to help him decide which project to undertake and which to decline. This approach also gives him a set number of units to go by when evaluating a project. If the break-even point is too many units produced, then Dennis will know quickly to stay away from that deal. This keeps him in a safe financial state.

ADDITIONAL EXPERIENTIAL EXERCISES

"Working the Financials"

Divide the class into groups of four or five students. Give each group information (financials) on a small business. Have the group do a budget, either operating or cash flow, and have them go through all of the necessary steps that are required to make these budgets work. Next, instruct the group to prepare the pro forma balance sheet and the pro forma income statement if time allows. Have the group do one of the forms of capital budgeting by putting them in a situation where these methods will be applicable. Finally, have the group perform a break-even analysis on their respective company by using either the contribution margin approach or the graphic approach.

(OR)

"Keeping a Journal"

Survey two small businesses and watch their biweekly or weekly profits and compare the two businesses profit-wise. Write down a journal of profits and/or losses and then write up a 2 to 3 page summary. For example, state how the businesses could improve or where they went wrong or how they could possibly expand, in your own viewpoint.

CHAPTER 10

DEVELOPING AN EFFECTIVE BUSINESS PLAN

CHAPTER OUTLINE

I. Critical Factors in Planning a Venture
   A. Set realistic goals
   B. Gain support and the commitment of everyone involved
   C. Set milestones as well as a time frame to complete them in
   D. Anticipate obstacles and prepare alternate plans

II. Pitfalls to Avoid in Planning
   A. No realistic goals
      1. Lack of attainable goals
      2. Lack of time frame to accomplish things
      3. Lack of priorities
      4. Lack of action steps
   B. Failure to anticipate roadblocks
      1. No recognition of future problems
      2. No admission of possible flaws or weaknesses in the plan
      3. No contingency or alternative plans
   C. No commitment or dedication
      1. Excessive procrastination
      2. Missed appointments
      3. No desire to invest personal money
      4. Appearance to make a "fast buck" from a hobby or a "whim"
   D. Lack of demonstrated experience (business or technical)
      1. No experience in business
      2. No experience in the specific area of the business
      3. Lack of understanding of the industry in which the venture fits
      4. Failure to convey a clear picture of how and why the venture will work and who will accept it
   E. No market niche (segment)
      1. Uncertainty about who will buy the basic idea(s) behind the venture
      2. No proof of need or desire for the good or product being proposed
      3. Assumption that there will be customers or clients just because the entrepreneur thinks so

III. What Is a Business Plan?
   A. Definition: The written document that details the proposed venture
   B. Uses of the business plan
      1. Used internally as a "road map" for operations
      2. Used to gain external financing

IV. Benefits of a Business Plan
   A. Benefits for the entrepreneur
      1. Forces the entrepreneur to view venture critically and objectively
      2. Subjects the entrepreneur to close scrutiny of his or her assumptions about the success of the venture
      3. Causes the entrepreneur to develop and examine operating strategies and expected results for outside evaluators
      4. Quantifies goals and objectives by providing measurable benchmarks for comparing forecasts with actual results
      5. Provides the entrepreneur with a communication tool for outside financial sources as well as an operational tool for guiding the venture toward success
   B. Benefits for financial sources
      1. Provides details of the market potential and plans for securing a share of that market
      2. Illustrates the venture's ability to service debt or provide an adequate return on investment
      3. Identifies critical risks and crucial events with a discussion of contingency plans
      4. Gives financial sources a clear, concise document that contains the necessary information for a thorough business and financial evaluation

V. Developing a Well-Conceived Business Plan
   A. Who reads the plan?
      1. The entrepreneur's viewpoint
      2. The marketplace's viewpoint
      3. The investor's point of view
   B. Putting the package together
      1. Should have a neat appearance
      2. Length should be kept to no more than forty pages
      3. Cover and title page should have name of the company, its address, and phone number, and the month and year in which the plan was issued
      4. Executive summary should be no more than two pages
      5. Should include a well-designed table of contents
   C. Guidelines to remember
      1. Keep the plan respectably short
      2. Organize and package the plan appropriately
      3. Orient the plan toward the future
      4. Avoid exaggeration
      5. Highlight critical risks
      6. Give evidence of an effective entrepreneurial team
      7. Do not overdiversify
      8. Identify the target market
      9. Keep the plan written in the third person
      10. Capture the reader's interest

VI. Elements of a Business Plan
   A. Summary
   B. Business description
   C. Marketing segment
      1. Market niche and market share
      2. Competitive analysis
      3. Pricing policy
      4. Advertising plan
      5. Market strategy
   D. Research, design, and development segment
   E. Manufacturing segment
   F. Management segment
      1. Organizational structure
      2. Management team and critical personnel
      3. Experience and technical capabilities of the personnel
      4. Ownership structure and compensation agreements
      5. Board of directors and outside consultants and advisers
   G. Critical risks segment
      1. Potential risks
         a. Effect of unfavorable trends in the industry
         b. Design or manufacturing costs that have gone over estimates
         c. Difficulties of long lead times encountered in purchasing parts or materials
         d. New competition that was not planned for
      2. Possible problems
         a. The competition cuts prices
         b. The industry slumps
         c. The market projections are wrong
         d. The sales projections are not achieved
         e. The patents do not come through
         f. The management team breaks up
   H. Financial segment
      1. Pro forma balance sheet
      2. Income statement
      3. Cash-flow statement
   I. Milestone schedule segment
   J. Appendix and/or bibliography segment

VII. Presentation of the Business Plan
   A. Suggestions for preparation
      1. Know the outline thoroughly
      2. Utilize key words in the outline that help recall examples, visual aids, or other details
      3. Rehearse the presentation in order to get a feel of its length

           4. Be familiar with any equipment to be used in the presentation
           5. The day before, practice the complete presentation using all visual aids and equipment
           6. The day of the presentation, arrive early in order to set up, test any equipment, and organize notes and visual aids
        B. What to expect
           1. Audience will be antagonistic
           2. Main objective is to succeed but it doesn't have to succeed on the first try

VIII.   Summary

CHAPTER OBJECTIVES

1. To examine the critical factors that should be addressed in planning
2. To explore the planning pitfalls that plague many new ventures
3. To outline the importance of a business plan and describe the benefits derived from it
4. To set forth the viewpoints of those who read a business plan and illustrate the six steps followed in the reading process
5. To emphasize the importance of coordinating the business plan segments
6. To review key recommendations by venture capital experts for the development of a plan
7. To present a complete outline of an effective business plan and a discussion of each segment
8. To present some helpful hints for writing an effective business plan
9. To highlight points to remember in the presentation of a business plan

CHAPTER SUMMARY

Planning entails the formulation of goals, objectives, and directions for the future of a venture. In planning, there are a number of critical factors that must be addressed: realistic goals, commitment, milestones, and flexibility. The comprehensive business plan is the major tool used in determining the essential operation of the business.

There are a number of pitfalls in the business plan process that should be avoided. Specifically, there are five pitfalls that represent the most common errors committed by the entrepreneur. They are: (1) no realistic goals, (2) failure to anticipate roadblocks, (3) no commitment or dedication, (4) lack of demonstrated experience (business or technical), and (5) no market niche (segment).

A business plan is the written document that details the proposed venture. It must illustrate current status, expected needs, and projected results of the new business. Every aspect of the venture needs to be described--the project, marketing, research and development, manufacturing, management, critical risks, financing, and milestones or timetables. A description of all these facets of the proposed venture is necessary to demonstrate a clear picture of what the venture is, where it is projected to go, and how the entrepreneur proposes it will get there. The business plan is the entrepreneur's map for a successful enterprise.

Most investors agree that only a well-conceived and well-developed business plan can gather the necessary support that will eventually lead to financing. Three main viewpoints need to be clearly understood in preparing the plan. The first viewpoint is, of course, the entrepreneur's since he or she is the one developing the plan and clearly has the most knowledge of the technology or the creativity involved. This is the most common viewpoint, and it is essential. The marketability of a new venture is also important. Referred to as "market driven," this type of enterprise convincingly demonstrates the benefit to users--the particular group of customers it is aiming for--and the existence of a substantial market. This viewpoint--that of the marketplace--is the second critical emphasis with which a business plan must be written. The third viewpoint is related to the marketing emphasis just discussed. The investor's point of view is concentrated on the financial forecast. Sound financial projections are necessary if investors are to evaluate the worth of their investment.

When presenting a business plan to potential investors, the entrepreneur must realize that the entire package is important. Below is a summary of key issues that need to be watched by the entrepreneur if the plan is going to be viewed successfully.

Investors are looking for evidence that the principals treat their own property with care--and will likewise treat the investment carefully. In other words, form as well as content is important, and investors know that good form reflects good content. The most important format issues are appearance, length, the cover and title page, the executive summary, and the table of contents.

A detailed business plan usually has 10 sections. The ideal length of a plan is 40 pages, although depending on the need for detail, the overall plan could range from 10 to 100 pages. The specific parts of the plan are as follows: the summary, the business description, the marketing segment, the research, design and development segment, the manufacturing segment, the management segment, the critical risks segment, the milestone schedule segment, and the appendix and/or bibliography segment.

Once a business plan is prepared, the next major challenge is presenting the plan to either a single financial person or, in some parts of the country, a forum where numerous financial investors are gathered. In any situation, the oral presentation is the key step to "selling" the business plan to potential investors.

The following steps are suggested for entrepreneurs in the oral presentation: (1) know the outline thoroughly, (2) utilize key words in the outline that help recall examples, visual aids, or other details, (3) rehearse the presentation in order to get a feel of the length, (4) the day of the presentation, arrive early to set up any equipment and organize notes and visual aids.

Entrepreneurs should realize that the audience viewing their business plan will be antagonistic. The venture capital sources are pressuring the entrepreneur in order to test the venture as well as the entrepreneur. Thus, the entrepreneur must expect and prepare for a critical, sometimes skeptical audience of financial sources. The entrepreneur must be prepared to handle the questions from the evaluators and learn from the criticism.

Should the entrepreneur be turned down for sources the first time, he/she must gather information to revise, rework, and improve the plan. The goal is not so much to succeed the first time as it is to succeed.

LECTURE NOTES

DEVELOPING AN EFFECTIVE BUSINESS PLAN

I. Critical Factors to Be Addressed in Planning
   A. Realistic goals: must be specific, measurable, and set within time parameters
   B. Commitment: must be supported by all those involved, including family, partners, employees, and team members
   C. Milestones: subgoals must be set for continual and timely evaluation of progress
   D. Flexibility: obstacles anticipated and alternative strategies must be formulated

II. Pitfalls to Avoid in Planning
   A. No realistic goals
      1. Indicators
         a. Lack of any attainable goals
         b. Lack of a time frame to accomplish things
         c. Lack of priorities
         d. Lack of action steps
      2. One way to avoid this pitfall is to set up a timetable with specific steps to be accomplished during a specific time period
   B. Failure to anticipate roadblocks
      1. Indicators
         a. No recognition of future problems
         b. No admission of possible flaws or weaknesses in the plan
         c. No contingency or alternative plans
      2. Best ways to avoid this pitfall
         a. List the possible obstacles that may arise
         b. List the alternatives that state what might have to be done to overcome the obstacles
   C. No commitment or dedication
      1. Indicators
         a. Excessive procrastination
         b. Missed appointments
         c. No desire to invest personal money
         d. Appearance of making a "fast buck" from a hobby or a "whim"
      2. Ways to avoid the pitfall
         a. Act quickly and be sure to follow up all professional appointments
         b. Be ready and willing to demonstrate a financial commitment to the venture

D. Lack of demonstrated experience (business or technical)
   1. Indicators
      a. No experience in the business
      b. No experience in the specific area of the venture
      c. Lack of understanding of the industry in which the venture fits
      d. Failure to convey a clear picture of how and why the venture will work and who will accept it
   2. Ways to avoid this pitfall
      a. The entrepreneur needs to give evidence of personal experience and background for this venture
      b. Demonstration of a "team" composed of those who will be helping out may also be useful
E. No market niche (segment)
   1. Indicators
      a. Uncertainty about who will buy the basic idea(s) behind the venture
      b. No proof of need or desire for the good or product being proposed
      c. Assumption that there will be customers or clients just because the entrepreneur thinks so
   2. Ways to avoid this pitfall
      a. Have a market segment specifically targeted
      b. Be able to demonstrate why and how the specific product or service will meet the needs or desires of this target market

III. What Is a Business Plan?
   A. A business plan is the written document that details the proposed venture
   B. It must illustrate current status, expected needs, and projected results of the new business
   C. The business plan is the entrepreneur's road map for a successful enterprise
   D. The business plan allows the entrepreneur entrance into the investment process
   E. The business plan describes to investors and financial sources all of the events that may affect the venture being proposed
   F. The emphasis of the business plan should always be on the final implementation of the venture

IV. Benefits of a Business Plan
   A. Benefits to the entrepreneur
      1. Forces him/her to view the venture critically and objectively
      2. Subjects him/her to close scrutiny of his/her assumptions about the success of the venture
      3. Helps him/her develop and examine operating strategies and expected results for outside evaluators
      4. The business plan quantifies goals and objectives

The Dryden Press

5. The completed business plan provides him/her with a communication tool for outside financial sources as an operational tool for guiding the venture to success
   B. Benefits to the financial source
      1. Provides details of the market potential and plans for securing a share of that market
      2. Illustrates the venture's ability to service debt or provide an adequate return on equity
      3. Identifies critical risks and crucial events
      4. Gives a clear, concise document that contains the necessary information for a thorough business and financial evaluation
      5. Provides a useful guide for assessing the individual entrepreneur's planning and managerial ability

V. Developing a Well-Conceived Business Plan
   A. Who reads the plan?
      1. Viewpoints
         a. The viewpoint of the entrepreneur
         b. The viewpoint of the marketplace
         c. The viewpoint of the investor
      2. Steps involved in reading a business plan
         a. Determine the characteristics of the venture and its industry
         b. Determine the financial structure of the plan
         c. Read the latest balance sheet
         d. Determine the quality of entrepreneurs in the venture
         e. Establish the unique feature in this venture
         f. Read the entire plan over lightly
   B. Putting the package together
      1. Appearance--must be neat but not too lavish
      2. Length--should be no more than 40 pages
      3. The cover and title page--should bear the name of the company, its location, and phone number
      4. The executive summary--should summarize the whole business plan in two pages
      5. Table of contents
   C. Guidelines to remember
      1. Keep the plan respectably short
      2. Organize and package the plan appropriately
      3. Orient the plan toward the future
      4. Avoid exaggeration
      5. Highlight critical risks
      6. Give evidence of an effective entrepreneurial team.
      7. Do not overdiversify
      8. Identify the target market

        9. Keep the plan written in the third person
     10. Capture the reader's interest

VI. Elements of a Business Plan
    A. The summary
       1. Gives a brief overview of what is to follow
       2. Helps put all of the information into perspective
       3. Should be written only after the entire business plan has been completed
       4. Must present the quality of the entire report
    B. Business description
       1. The name of the venture should be identified
       2. The industry background should be presented in terms of current status and future trends
       3. The new venture should be thoroughly described along with its proposed potential
       4. The potential advantages the new venture possesses over the competition should be discussed at length
    C. Marketing segment
       1. Must convince investors that there is a market
       2. Must convince that sales projections can be achieved
       3. Must convince that the competition can be beat
       4. Market niche and market share
          a. A "niche" is a homogeneous group with common characteristics
          b. The writer should address the bases of customer purchase decision
          c. There should be a list of potential customers who have expressed interest in the product or service, together with an explanation for their interest
       5. Competitive analysis
          a. Assess the strengths and weaknesses of the competing products or services
          b. Comparison of competing products or services
          c. Short discussion of the current advantages or disadvantages of competing products and services and why they are not meeting customers' needs
          d. Review of competing companies
       6. Pricing policy
          a. Pricing strategies should be examined
          b. One strategy should be convincingly presented
       7. Advertising plan
          a. All advertising media that is being considered should be presented
          b. The schedule and cost of promotion and advertising should be presented.
       8. Market strategy
          a. The general philosophy and strategy of the company should be outlined.
          b. Discuss the kinds of customer groups that will be targeted for initial intensive selling effort
          c. Discuss the customer groups that will be targeted for later selling efforts

- d. Discuss methods of identifying and contacting potential customers in these groups
- e. Discuss the features of the product or service that will be emphasized to generate sales
- f. Discuss an innovative or unusual marketing concept that will enhance customers' acceptance.
- D. Research, design, and development segment
  1. The extent of any research, design, and development in regard to cost, time, and special testing should be covered in this segment
  2. The entrepreneur should have technical assistance in preparing a detailed discussion
- E. The manufacturing segment
  1. Describing the location of the new venture
  2. Production needs should be discussed
  3. Other factors are the suppliers and transportation costs involved in shipping materials
  4. The cost data associated with any of the above factors should be presented
- F. The management segment
  1. Identify the key personnel, their positions and responsibilities, and the career experiences that qualify them for those roles.
  2. The entrepreneur's role in the venture should be clearly outlined.
  3. Any advisers, consultants, or members of the board should be identified and discussed.
  4. The structure of payment and ownership should be clearly outlined.
- G. Critical risks segment
  1. Potential risks
     - a. Effect of unfavorable trends in the industry
     - b. Design or manufacturing costs that have gone over estimates
     - c. Difficulties on long lead times encountered in purchasing parts or materials
     - d. New competition that was not planned for
  2. "What-ifs"
     - a. The competition cuts prices
     - b. The industry slumps
     - c. The market projections are wrong
     - d. The sales projections are not achieved
     - e. The patents do not come through
     - f. The management team breaks up.
- H. The financial segment
  1. The pro forma balance sheet
     - a. Projects what the financial condition of the venture will be at a particular point in time
     - b. Prepared at start-up, semiannually for the first years, and at the end of each of the first three years

        c. Details the assets required to support the projected level of operations
        d. Shows how these assets are to be financed
     2. The income statement
        a. The projected operating results based on profit and loss
        b. The sales forecast
        c. Production costs must be budgeted based on the level of activity needed to support the projected earnings
     3. The cash-flow statement
        a. Sets forth the amount and timing of expected cash inflows and outflows
        b. The cash-flow forecast will highlight the need for and the timing of additional financing and will indicate peak requirements for working capital
        c. Can direct the entrepreneur's attention to operating problems before serious cash crises arise
  I. Milestone schedule segment
     1. Provides investors with a timetable for various activities to be accomplished
  J. Appendix/bibliography

VII. Presentation of the Business Plan
  A. Suggestions for preparation
     1. Know the outline thoroughly
     2. Utilize key words in the outline that help recall examples, visual aids, or other details
     3. Rehearse the presentation in order to get the feel of its length
     4. Be familiar with any equipment to be used in the presentation
     5. The day before, practice the complete presentation using all visual aids and equipment
     6. The day of the presentation, arrive early in order to set up, test any equipment, and organize notes and visual aids
  B. What to expect
     1. Must expect and prepare for a critical, sometimes skeptical audience of financial sources
     2. The entrepreneur must be prepared to handle the questions and learn from the criticism

SUGGESTED ANSWERS FOR DISCUSSION QUESTIONS (END OF CHAPTER)

1. ***What are the critical factors to be considered in preparing a business plan?***
   In planning, there are a number of critical factors that must be addressed:
   (1) Realistic goals--these must be specific, measurable and set within time parameters.
   (2) Commitment--the venture must be supported by all involved: family, partners, employees, team members.

(3) Milestones--subgoals must be set for continual and timely evaluation of progress.
(4) Flexibility--obstacles must be anticipated and alternative strategies must be formulated.

2. ***Describe each of the five planning pitfalls often encountered by entrepreneurs.***
   (1) No realistic goals
   (2) Failure to anticipate roadblocks--The entrepreneur is so immersed in his or her own idea that objectivity goes out the window.
   (3) No commitment or dedication--Too many entrepreneurs appear to lack real commitment to their ventures.
   (4) Lack of demonstrated experience (business or technical)--Since many investors weight very heavily the entrepreneur's actual experience in a venture, it is important to demonstrate what background the entrepreneur possesses.
   (5) No market niche--Many entrepreneurs propose an idea without really finding out who the potential customers are going to be.

3. ***Identify an indicator of each pitfall named above. What would you do about each?***
   (1) No realistic goals: Lack of attainable goals. A way to avoid this pitfall is to set up a realistic timetable with specific steps to be accomplished during a specific time period.
   (2) Failure to anticipate roadblocks: No recognition of future problems. The best way to avoid this is to list the possible obstacles that may arise and the alternatives that state what might have to be done to overcome the obstacles.
   (3) No commitment or dedication: Excessive procrastination. Act quickly and be sure to follow up all professional appointments. Also, be ready and willing to demonstrate financial commitment to the venture.
   (4) Lack of demonstrated experience (business or technical): No experience in business. To avoid this pitfall, the entrepreneur needs to give evidence of personal experience and background for this venture. If there is a lack of specific knowledge or skills, the individual should obtain assistance from those who possess this knowledge or these skills. Demonstration of a "team" concept of those who will be helping out may be useful.
   (5) No market niche: Uncertainty about who will buy the basic ideas behind the venture. Have a market segment specifically targeted and be able to demonstrate why and how the specific product or service will meet the needs or desires of this target group.

4. ***Identify the benefits of a business plan first for an entrepreneur, then for financial sources.***
   Entrepreneur:
   (1) The time, effort, research, and discipline needed to put together a formal business plan force the entrepreneur to view the venture critically and objectively.

(2) The competitive, economic, and financial analysis that is included in the business plan subjects the entrepreneur to close scrutiny of his/her assumptions about the success of the venture.
(3) Since all the aspects of the business venture must be addressed in the plan, the entrepreneur develops and examines operating strategies and expected results for outside evaluators.
(4) The business plan quantifies goals and objectives that provide measurable benchmarks for comparing forecasts with actual results.
(5) The completed business plan provides the entrepreneur with a communication tool for outside financial sources as well as an operational tool for guiding the venture toward success.

Financial Sources:
(1) The business plan provides for financial sources the details of the market potential and plans for securing a share of that market.
(2) Through prospective financial statements, the business plan illustrates the venture's ability to service debt or provide an adequate return on equity.
(3) The plan identifies critical risks and crucial events with a discussion of contingency plans that provide opportunity for the venture's success.
(4) By providing a comprehensive overview of the entire operation, the business plan gives financial sources a clear, concise document that contains the necessary information for a thorough business and financial evaluation.
(5) For a financial source with no prior knowledge of the entrepreneur or the venture, the business plan provides a useful guide to assessing the individual entrepreneur's planning and managerial ability.

5. *What are the three major viewpoints to be considered in developing a business plan?*
The *first* viewpoint is the entrepreneur's since he or she is the one developing the venture and clearly has the most in-depth knowledge of the technology or creativity involved. This is the most common viewpoint in business plans, and it is essential.
More important than high technology or creative flair is the marketability of a new venture. Referred to as "market driven," this type of enterprise convincingly demonstrates the benefits to users, the particular group of customers it is aiming for, and the existence of a substantial market. This viewpoint, that of the marketplace, is the *second* critical emphasis with which a business plan must be written.
The *third* viewpoint is related to the marketing emphasis just discussed. The investor's point of view is concentrated on the financial forecast. Sound financial projections are necessary if investors are to evaluate the worth of their investment.

6. *Name the six-step process venture capitalists follow when reading a business plan.*
(1) Determine the characteristics of the venture and its industry.
(2) Determine the financial structure of the plan (amount of debt or equity investment required).
(3) Read the latest balance sheet (to determine liquidity, net worth, and debt/equity).

(4) Determine the quality of entrepreneurs in the venture (sometimes the most important step).
(5) Establish the unique feature in this venture (find out what is different).
(6) Read the entire plan over lightly (this is where the entire package is paged through for a casual look at graphs, charts, exhibits, etc.).

7. ***What are some components to consider in the proper packaging of a plan?***
   (1) Appearance--the binding and printing must not be sloppy, nor should the presentation be too lavish. A plastic spiral binding holding together a pair of cover sheets of a single color provides both a neat appearance and sufficient strength to withstand handling by a number of people without damage.
   (2) Length--a business plan should be no more than 40 pages long. Adherence to this length forces entrepreneurs to sharpen their ideas and results in a document likely to hold investors' attention.
   (3) The cover and the title page--the cover should bear the name of the company, its address and phone number, and the month and year in which the plan is issued. An interested investor wants to be able to contact a company easily and to request further information or express an interest either in the company or in some aspect of the plan.

   Inside the front cover should be a well-designed title page on which the cover information is repeated, and in an upper and lower corner, the legend "copy number" should be provided. Besides helping entrepreneurs keep track of plans in circulation, holding down the number of copies outstanding (usually to no more than 20) has a psychological advantage. After all, no investor likes to think that the prospective investment is shopworn.
   (4) The executive summary--the two pages immediately following the title page should concisely explain the company's current status, its products or services, the benefits to customers, the financial forecasts, the venture's objectives in three to seven years, the amount of financing needed, and how investors will benefit.

   This is a tall order for a two-page summary, but it will either sell investors on reading the rest of the plan or convince them to forget the whole thing.
   (5) The table of contents--after the executive summary, include a well-designed table of contents. List each of the business plan's sections, and mark the pages for each section.

8. ***Identify five of the ten guidelines to be used in preparing a business plan.***
   (1) Keep the plan respectably short. Readers of business plans are important people who refuse to waste time. Therefore, entrepreneurs should explain the venture not only carefully and clearly but concisely as well.
   (2) Organize and package the plan appropriately. A table of contents, an executive summary, an appendix, exhibits, graphs, proper grammar, a logical arrangement of segments, and overall neatness are critical elements in the effective presentation of a business plan.
   (3) Orient the plan toward the future. Entrepreneurs should attempt to create an air of excitement in the plan by developing trends and forecasts that describe what the

venture intends to do and what the opportunities are for the use of the product or service.
- (4) Avoid exaggeration. Sales potentials, revenue estimates, and the venture's growth should not be inflated. Many times a best-case, worst-case, and probable-case scenario should be developed for the plan. Documentation and research are vital to the credibility of the plan.
- (5) Highlight critical risks. The critical risks segment of the business plan is important in that it demonstrates the entrepreneur's ability to analyze potential problems and develop alternative courses of action.

9. *Briefly describe each of the major segments to be covered in a business plan.*
   - (1) The Summary: Many people who read business plans (bankers, venture capitalists, investors) like to see a summary of the plan that features its most important parts. Such a summary gives a brief overview of what is to follow and helps put all of the information into perspective and should be no longer than three pages.
   - (2) Business description: The name of the venture should be identified, with any special significance related (e.g., family name, technical name, etc.). The industry background should also be presented. The new venture should be thoroughly described along with its proposed potential. Also, the potential advantages the new venture possesses over the competition should be discussed at length.
   - (3) Market segment: In this segment of the report, the entrepreneur must convince investors that there is a market, that sales projections can be achieved, and that the competition can be beaten.
   - (4) Research, design, and development segment: The extent of any research, design, and development in regard to cost, time, and special testing should be covered in this segment. Investors need to know the status of the project in terms of prototypes, lab tests, and scheduling delays.
   - (5) The manufacturing segment: This segment should always begin by describing the location of the new venture. The chosen site should be appropriate in terms of labor availability, wage rate, proximity to suppliers and customers, and community support. In addition, local taxes and zoning requirements should be sorted out, and the support of area banks for new ventures should be touched upon.
   - (6) The management segment: This segment should identify the key personnel, their positions and responsibilities, and the career experiences that qualify them for those particular roles. Complete resumes should be presented for each member of the management team.
   - (7) The financial segment: The financial segment of a business plan must demonstrate the potential viability of the undertaking.
   - (8) The milestone schedule segment: This segment provides investors with a timetable for the various activities to be accomplished. It is important to demonstrate that realistic time frames have been planned and that the interrelationship of events within these time boundaries are understood.
   - (9) The appendix and/or bibliography segment: The final segment is not mandatory, but it allows for additional documentation that is not appropriate in the main parts of the

plan. Diagrams, blueprints, financial data, vitae of management team members, or bibliographical information that supports the other segments of the plan are examples of material that can be included.

10. *Why is the summary segment of a business plan written last? Why not first?*
    The summary should be written only after the entire business plan has been completed. In this way, particular phases or descriptions from each segment can be identified for inclusion in the summary. Since the summary is the first, and sometimes the only, part of a plan that is read, it must present the quality of the entire report.

11. *What are five elements included in the marketing segment of the business plan?*
    Market niche and market share, competition analysis, pricing policy, advertising plan, and market strategy

12. *What are some critical factors covered in the management segment of a business plan?*
    Organizational structure, management team and critical personnel, experience and technical capabilities of the personnel, ownership structure and compensation agreements, board of directors, and outside consultants and advisors

13. *What is the meaning of the term critical risks?*
    This means that potential risks such as the following should be identified: effect of unfavorable trends in the industry, design or manufacturing costs that have gone over estimates, difficulties on long lead times encountered in purchasing parts or materials, or new competition that was not planned for.

14. *Describe each of the three financial statements that are mandatory for the financial segment of a plan.*
    (1) The pro forma balance sheet--pro forma means projected, as opposed to actual. The pro forma balance sheet projects what the financial condition of the venture will be at a particular point in time. Pro forma balance sheets should be prepared at start-up, semiannually for the first years, and at the end of the first three years.
    (2) The income statement--the income statement illustrates the projected operating results based on profit and loss. The sales forecast, which was developed in the marketing segment, is essential to this document.
    (3) The cash-flow statement--in new-venture creation, the cash-flow statement may be the most important document since it sets forth the amount and timing of expected cash inflows and outflows. This section of the business plan should be constructed carefully.

15. *Why are milestones important to a business plan?*
    It is important to demonstrate that realistic time frames have been planned and that the interrelationship of events within these time boundaries is understood.

TEACHING NOTES FOR END-OF-CHAPTER CASES

CASE: IT'S JUST A MATTER OF TIME

1. ***In addition to financial questions, what other questions is the venture capitalist likely to ask Pedro?***

    He will likely ask questions about recognition of future problems. The few testimonies that Pedro received do not guarantee his success. Therefore, he must give consideration to potential roadblocks. Pedro needs to give evidence of personal experience and background for this venture. If he lacks specific knowledge or skills, he should seek assistance from those who possess them. The venture capitalist will probably want to know about Pedro's goals. Pedro will need to set up a timetable with specific steps to be accomplished during a specific time period. He should also be willing to demonstrate his commitment to the venture. The venture capitalist will need to see that Pedro is taking this venture seriously and not trying to make a fast buck on a whim.

2. ***Would a business plan be of any value to Pedro? Why or why not?***

    Yes, it would be especially valuable to Pedro, who seems to have an idea that could turn into something successful, but at this point in time lacks a plan to see his idea through to fruition. In his efforts preparing a business plan, he will be able to view his venture objectively. He will be able to scrutinize his assumptions about the venture through competitive, economic, and financial analysis. A business plan will also provide Pedro with a communication tool for outside financial sources who will read the plan. If he does a thorough job investigating and provides a comprehensive overview of the entire operation, it will enhance his chances of making a successful presentation to the venture capitalist.

3. ***How would you recommend that Pedro get ready for his meeting with the venture capitalist?***

    He should prepare a business plan and know it thoroughly before the meeting. He should rehearse his presentation and then be able to answer any potential questions asked by the venture capitalist. Pedro should expect and prepare for a critical and skeptical response to his business plan. He will be pressured in order to test the venture as well as his own commitment to the venture. Pedro should have a strong enough belief in his plan that even if he is turned down, his commitment will be to improve the business plan for future use. The ultimate goal is to succeed, and if his desire is strong enough he can revise, rework, and improve the business plan.

CASE: THE INCOMPLETE PLAN

1. ***What should Joan put in the marketing segment? What types of information will she need?***

    She should include a market niche and market share. The niche will define all of the people who have a need for the new monthly magazine. When describing this niche, Joan should address what these potential customers base their decisions on: price, quality, service, or a combination of these factors. Joan should include a list of people who have expressed interest in the magazine, together with an explanation for their interest. Sales projections should be made for at least three years, and there should be a review of previous market trends. She also needs to assess the strengths and weaknesses of competing magazines. A number of pricing strategies should be examined, and one should be convincingly presented. A discussion of the advertising and promotional campaign that is contemplated to introduce the product and the kind of sales aids that will be provided should be included. Finally, Joan should include the general marketing philosophy and strategy of the company. This includes the features that will be emphasized to sell the magazine as well as any unusual marketing concepts that will enhance customer acceptance.

2. *In the critical-risks assessment segment, what key areas does Joan have to address? Discuss two of these.*

One area is new competition that was not planned for. A magazine directed toward women in the workplace may be a product with a definite market. If Joan's magazine is successful, other magazines directed toward women in the workplace will hit the market. One of these magazines may be run by a publisher with unlimited resources. These magazines could afford to have larger budgets and more people on their staffs than Joan does and therefore make it difficult for her to compete. Another area that she needs to consider is an unfavorable trend in the industry. In the last few months many business magazines have devoted sections of their magazine to women in the workplace. It is possible that with the trend of magazines devoting more space to women, a magazine specifically for women in the workplace is not needed in the market.

3. *In the financial segment, what suggestions would you make to Joan regarding the kinds of information to include? Be as specific as possible.*

She should include three financial statements: the pro forma balance sheet, the income statement, and the cash-flow statement. The balance sheet details the assets required to support the projected level of operations and shows how these assets are to be financed. Investors will want to look at the projected balance sheets to determine if ratios, working capital, and inventory turnover are within the acceptable limits required to justify the future financings projected for the venture. The cash-flow statement may be the most important document since it sets forth the amount and timing of expected cash inflows and outflows. In the financial segment it is important to mention any assumptions that were used in preparing the figures. Joan should also include a break-even chart, which shows the level of sales needed to cover all costs.

ADDITIONAL EXPERIENTIAL EXERCISES

"Outlining a Plan"

The student is required to construct the outline of a business plan. This outline should contain the 10 different areas that are covered in the plan. Under each area the student is required to state no less than three items that should be covered in that particular section. The summary segment and appendix and/or bibliography segment should only be stated and not broken down into specific points.

The importance of this exercise is to show students the detail that a well-constructed business plan should contain.

(OR)

"Researching Business Plans"

Students must survey three small businesses to determine the following information:
1. Does the business possess a business plan?
2. If so, what sections does that plan contain?
3. How long has the business had the plan?
4. Has the plan ever been revised, or are there plans to revise the plan at a future date?
5. To what extent is the plan used in the day-to-day operations of the firm? In strategic planning?
6. Who compiled the plan?
7. Were any experts consulted for help in writing the plan?

These are just possible questions. The answers would be interesting as well as informative. Students would get a chance to find out, firsthand, about various types of business plans and their uses.

PART IV

Initiating Entrepreneurial Ventures

Chapter 11 - Assessment and Evaluation of Entrepreneurial Opportunities

Chapter 12 - Structuring the New Business Venture

Chapter 13 - Legal Issues Related to Emerging Ventures

Chapter 14 - Sources of Capital Formation for Entrepreneurs

CHAPTER 11

ASSESSMENT AND EVALUATION OF ENTREPRENEURIAL OPPORTUNITIES

CHAPTER OUTLINE

I. The Challenge of New-Venture Start-ups

II. Pitfalls in Selecting New Ventures
   A. Lack of objective evaluation
      1. Engineers and technically trained people fall in love with an idea before giving it careful study and investigation
   B. No real insight into the market
      1. Entrepreneurs do not realize the importance of a marketing approach
      2. Entrepreneurs do not understand the life cycle that must be considered
   C. Inadequate understanding of technical requirements
      1. Failure to anticipate technical difficulties can sink a new venture
   D. Poor financial understanding
      1. Overestimate funds required
      2. Underestimate development costs
      3. Victims of inadequate research and planning
   E. Lack of venture uniqueness
      1. A new venture ought to have special characteristics or design concepts
      2. Performance or service should be superior to competitive offerings
   F. Ignorance of legal issues
      1. Make marketplace safe for employees
      2. Provide reliable and safe products and services
      3. Necessity for patents, trademarks, and copyrights

III. Critical Factors for New-Venture Development
   A. Three phases
      1. Prestart-up
      2. Start-up
      3. Poststart-up
   B. Critical factors
      1. Uniqueness--extends from fairly routine to highly routine
      2. Investment
         a. Extent and timing of funds are a critical issue
         b. Key questions
      3. Growth of Sales - Critical through the start-up phase
         a. Key questions
         b. Three classifications
            1. Lifestyle venture

        2. Smaller profitable venture
        3. High-growth venture
    4. Product availability
    5. Customer availability
        a. Venture risk is affected by the availability of customers for start-up
        b. The customers and their buying habits must be determined

IV. Why New Ventures Fail
    A. Inadequate market knowledge
    B. Faulty product performance
    C. Ineffective marketing and sales efforts
    D. Inadequate awareness of competitive pressures
    E. Rapid product obsolescence
    F. Poor timing for the start of the new venture
    G. Undercapitalization, unforeseen operating expenses, excessive investments in fixed assets, and related financial difficulties
    H. Bruno, Leidecker, and Harder found three major categories of causes for failure:
        1. Product/market problems
        2. Financial difficulties
        3. Managerial problems
    I. More recent study of *Inc. 500*
        1. Start-up problems
            a. Sales/marketing
            b. External financing
            c. Internal financial management
        2. Growth stage
            a. Sales/marketing
            b. Internal financial management
            c. Human resource management
    J. "Failure prediciton" model
        1. Profitability and cash flow
        2. Debt
        3. Initial size
        4. Velocity of capital
        5. Control

V. The Evaluation Process
Solid analysis and evaluation of the feasibility of the product/service is a critical task
    A. Ask the right questions
        1. Is it a new product/service idea?
        2. What are its weak points?
        3. Has it been to trade shows?
    B. Profile analysis
        1. Results enable the entrepreneur to judge the potential of the business

        2. Failure can be avoided through a careful profile analysis
   C. Feasibility criteria approach
        1. Is it proprietary?
        2. Are initial production costs realistic?
        3. Are initial marketing costs realistic?
        4. Does the product have potential for very high margins?
        5. Is the time required to get to market and to reach break-even realistic?
        6. Is the potential market large?
        7. First of a growing family?
        8. Is there an initial customer?
        9. Development costs and calendar times realistic?
        10. Is this a growing industry?
        11. Can the product and the need for it be understood by the financial community?
   D. Comprehensive Feasibility Approach
        1. Incorporates external factors into the questions listed above
        2. Technical feasibility
        3. Marketability

VI. Summary

CHAPTER OBJECTIVES

1. To explain the challenge of new venture start-ups
2. To review common pitfalls in the selection of new-venture ideas
3. To present critical factors involved in new-venture assessment
4. To examine why new ventures fail
5. To study certain factors that underlie venture success
6. To analyze the evaluation process methods: profile analysis, feasibility criteria approach, and comprehensive feasibility method
7. To outline the specific activities involved in a comprehensive feasibility evaluation

CHAPTER SUMMARY

    During the last few years, the number of new venture start-ups has been consistently high. It is reported that over 600,000 new firms have emerged in the United States every year since the mid-eighties. That works out to approximately 1,500 business start-ups per day.
    The reasons for entrepreneurs starting up new ventures are numerous. One study reported seven components of new venture motivation: the need for approval, the need for independence, the need for personal development, welfare (philanthropic) considerations, perception of wealth, tax reduction and indirect benefits, and following role models. These components are similar to the characteristics discussed in Chapter 2 concerning the "entrepreneurial perspective." While it

is agreed that there are many reasons for starting a venture, the entrepreneurial motivations of individuals usually relate to the personal characteristics of the entrepreneur, the environment, and the venture itself.

There are certain pitfalls associated with selecting new ventures. Lack of objective evaluation is a pitfall entrepreneurs need to be concerned with. Many entrepreneurs lack the objectivity necessary to properly assess the feasibility of a new venture. They are prone to "falling in love" with their idea. The entrepreneur needs to rigorously study the new venture idea before implementing it.

Other pitfalls commonly encountered include: no real insight into the market, inadequate understanding of technical requirements, poor financial understanding, lack of venture uniqueness, and the ignorance of legal issues.

Within the marketing pitfalls are the facts that not only does the entrepreneur need to project the life cycle of the product, but he also needs to be concerned with the timing of bringing that product to the marketplace. Timing is a big key to success.

New techniques involved in the development of a new product need to be fully understood by the entrepreneur. This is associated with the pitfall of inadequate understanding of technical requirements. Entrepreneurs need to sufficiently study and research their project ideas. Encountering unexpected technical difficulties can lead to costly and time-consuming problems.

Entrepreneurs need to possess financial knowledge. The pitfall of poor financial understanding may lead the entrepreneur to underestimate development costs by wide margins. Financial knowledge is crucial for the entrepreneur to properly estimate development costs.

The pitfall, lack of venture uniqueness, is also something a potential entrepreneur should be aware of. A new venture should be unique. Effective product differentiation is necessary so that the entrepreneur's product is distinct from his/her competitor's. Pricing becomes less of a concern when the customer views the entrepreneur's product as better than its competitors'.

Ignorance of legal issues is a dangerous pitfall for a new venture. Since we live in a "litigation society," a business is subject to a wide array of laws and regulations that an entrepreneur needs to be aware of.

Along with these pitfalls, there are also a number of critical factors in new-venture assessment that an entrepreneur needs to be aware of. A new venture evolves through three phases: prestart-up, start-up, and poststart-up. There are five critical factors associated with the first two phases which need to be addressed.

As stated earlier, new-venture uniqueness is important. Uniqueness ranges on a continuum extending from fairly routine to highly nonroutine. The amount of innovation required during prestart-up is what separates the routine from the nonroutine. This distinction is based on the need for new-process technology to produce services or products and/or the need to service new-market segments.

Initial investment in a new venture is also an important factor. The range of money needed to start with can vary considerably. Not only is the amount of money needed important, but also the timing and extent of the funds is crucial.

The extent to which the product is available once the new venture opens its doors is another critical factor to be expected. The success of the venture is dependent upon the availability of saleable goods or services. Lack of product availability in the finished form can affect the company's image and its bottom line.

Not only is product availability important, but also equally critical is customer availability. Venture risk is affected by this availability of customers during the start-up phase. There are two extremes to this risk. One end concerns customers who are willing to pay for the products or services before delivery. The other end deals with the venture not knowing exactly who will buy its products. A key concern is how long it will take to determine who the customers are and what their buying habits are.

The last critical factor concerns sales growth. The growth pattern of sales and profits needs to be anticipated for a better assessment of the possible new venture. Most ventures can be classified by one of three classifications: (l) life-style ventures. The characteristics involved here are: independence, autonomy, and control as the primary motives for the venture. (2) smaller profitable venture. Financial considerations play a major role in this type of venture. The entrepreneur is also concerned with keeping control over the ownership of the venture. Lastly, (3) high-growth venture. Significant sales and profit growth are expected to the extent that it may be possible to attract venture capital money and funds raised through public or private placements.

Although finding an idea for a new venture is fairly easy, implementing and keeping that idea afloat is a completely different matter. So many of the newly started businesses in the United States end in failure. One major study was conducted which analyzed some of the underlying factors influencing failure. Amazingly, in most cases, these factors were within the control of the entrepreneur. One of these factors is inadequate market knowledge. The entrepreneur needs to be aware of the market he or she is trying to reach. Poor timing for the start of the new venture is also a vital concern. Selecting the wrong time to introduce a new venture often leads to failure. The entrepreneur may launch the new venture before a market actually exists. Also, inadequate awareness of competitive pressures can lead to failure. The entrepreneur needs to take into account the possible reactions of competitors, such as severe price cuts or special discounts to retailers.

A study done by Bruno, Leidecker, and Harder identified three major categories of causes for failure. Ten firms were studied in depth, and the three categories analyzed were: product/market problems (such as poor timing, unclear business definition, and overreliance on one customer), financial problems (such as assuming debt too early, initial undercapitalization, and venture capital relationship problems), and managerial problems, which focus on two areas. Concept of a team approach is a managerial problem which deals with topics such as nepotism, incompetent support professionals, and relationship problems between the parent company and venture capitalists. The other area deals with human resource problems. For example, inflated owner ego and employee-related concerns are included here. Interpersonal problems uncovered here included: kickbacks, deceit, verbal agreements not honored, and protracted lawsuits around the time of discontinuance.

In a more recent study of successful ventures (firms listed in the *Inc.* 500 group of fastest-growing privately held companies), the most significant problems encountered at start-up were researched in order to systematically sort them into a schematic. It was found that dominant problems at start-up were sales/marketing, obtaining external financing, and internal financial management problems. In the growth stage, sales/marketing remained the most dominant problem, but it was less important than in the start-up stage. Internal financial management continued to be a dominant problem as well as human resource management problems.

New ventures need to follow an evaluation process. A new venture needs to be evaluated as to the feasibility of the product/service idea getting off the ground. The idea needs to be properly analyzed to determine any fatal flaws which can destroy the new venture.

One avenue to take which is helpful in the evaluation process is asking the right questions. There are ten sets of preliminary questions which can be used to screen an idea. These questions range from the product itself through questions about the skills necessary to operate the new venture.

Evaluation through profile analysis may also be helpful to a potential entrepreneur. This checklist approach enables the entrepreneur to analyze major strengths and weaknesses in the financial, marketing, organizational, and human resource factors that are needed for the venture to progress successfully. Many of the reasons listed under "failure of new ventures" can be avoided through the use of profile analysis.

Another evaluation method is the feasibility criteria approach. This method, through the use of certain feasibility questions, allows entrepreneurs to gain insights into the viability of their venture. Some of these questions include: "Are the initial marketing costs realistic?", "Are the initial production costs realistic?", and "Is the time required to get to market and to reach break-even realistic?" to name a few. This method provides an entrepreneur with a way of analyzing the internal strengths and weaknesses that exist in a new venture by focusing on the marketing potential and industry potential that are critical to assessment. A new venture which is able to meet seven or more of the criteria involved is in a better position to attract outside funds if needed.

The last evaluation method is called the comprehensive feasibility approach. This approach incorporates external factors--technical, market, financial, organizational, and competitive--as well as the questions posed in the feasibility criteria approach. These five areas are all important, but the technical and market factors merit special attention.

Technical feasibility deals with identifying the technical requirements for producing a product or service that will satisfy the expectations of potential customers. Some important characteristics include: flexibility, product safety, and reasonable utility. The results of this analysis provide a means for assessing whether a new venture is feasible from a technical point of view.

The marketability factor is the second area which merits special attention. There are three areas to deal with, which include: investigating the full market potential and identifying customers (or users) for the goods or service, analyzing the extent to which the enterprise might exploit this potential market, and using market analysis to determine the opportunities and risks associated with the venture. To gather the information necessary to study these three areas, general sources of information are helpful. Economic trends, market data, pricing data, and competitive data are included here. This comprehensive feasibility approach is closely tied to the thorough preparation of a business plan. The need to evaluate each segment of the venture before initiating it is illustrated through the use of this approach.

LECTURE NOTES

ASSESSMENT AND EVALUATION OF NEW VENTURES

I. The Challenge of New-Venture Start-ups
   A. 600,000 new firms emerge every year
   B. Reasons for start-up are similar to chapter 3 -- The Entreprenuerial Perspective

II. Pitfalls in Selecting New Ventures
   A. Lack of objective evaluation
      1. Many entrepreneurs lack objectivity
      2. All ideas should be subject to rigorous study and investigation
   B. No real insight into the market
      1. Entrepreneurs must project the life cycle of the new product
      2. Timing of product is critical
   C. Inadequate understanding of technical requirements
      1. Entrepreneurs need to be thorough in studying a new product
      2. Unexpected technical difficulties frequently pose time-consuming and costly problems
   D. Poor financial understanding
      1. Entrepreneurs are sometimes ignorant of costs
      2. Entrepreneurs are sometimes victims of inadequate research and planning
      3. Entrepreneurs quite often underestimate development costs by wide margins
   E. Lack of venture uniqueness
      1. A new venture should be unique
      2. Product differentiation is needed to separate product from competitor's

III. Critical Factors for Venture Development
   A. Three specific phases
      1. Prestart-up
      2. Start-up
      3. Poststart-up
   B. Critical factors of prestart-up and start-up phases
      1. Uniqueness
         a. Range in a new venture can be considerable
         b. Further characterized by the length of time a nonroutine venture will remain nonroutine
      2. Investment
         a. Can vary considerably
         b. Extent and timing of funds needed
         c. Key questions to ask
            1. Will industry growth be sufficient to maintain break-even sales to cover a high fixed cost structure during the start-up period?

2. Do the principal entrepreneurs have access to substantial financial reserves to protect a large initial investment?
3. Do the entrepreneurs have the appropriate contacts to take advantage of various environmental opportunities?
4. Do the entrepreneurs have both industry and entrepreneurial track records which justify the financial risk of a large-scale start-up?
   3. Growth of sales through the start-up phase
      a. Key questions to ask
         1. What is the growth pattern anticipated for new-venture sales and profits?
         2. Are sales and profits expected to grow slowly or level off shortly after start-up?
         3. Are large profits expected at some point with only small or moderate sales growth?
         4. Are both high sales growth and high profit growth likely?
         5. Will there be limited initial profits with eventual high-profit growth over a multiyear period?
      b. Venture classification
         1. Life-style ventures
            a. Independence, autonomy, and control are the primary driving forces
            b. Sales and profits deemed to provide a sufficient and comfortable living for the entrepreneur
         2. Smaller profitable ventures
            a. Financial considerations play a major role
            b. Autonomy and ownership control are important factors
         3. High-growth ventures
            a. Significant sales and profit growth are expected
            b. May be possible to attract venture capital money
            c. May be possible to attract funds raised through public or private placements
         4. Product availability
            a. Goods or services must be available
            b. Lack of product availability can affect the company's image and its bottom line
         5. Customer availability
            a. Risk continuum (two extremes)
               1. Customers willing to pay cash before delivery
               2. Venture begun not knowing exactly who will buy the product
            b. Two critical considerations
               1. How long will it take to determine who the customers are?
               2. What are the customers' buying habits?

IV. Why New Ventures Fail
   A. Inadequate market knowledge
      1. Lack of information about the demand potential

      2. Present and future size of the market
      3. Market share that can realistically be expected
      4. Appropriate distribution methods
   B. Faulty product performance
      1. Hasty shortcuts in production development
      2. Product testing
      3. Quality control
   C. Ineffective marketing and sales efforts
      1. Inadequate or misdirected promotional efforts
      2. Lack of appreciation of the problems involved
         a. In selling to unfamiliar markets
         b. In servicing of unfamiliar markets
   D. Inadequate awareness of competitive pressures
      1. Possible reactions of competitors
         a. Price cuts
         b. Special discounts to retailers
   E. Rapid product obsolescence
   F. Poor timing for the start of the new venture
      1. Introduced too soon to the marketplace
      2. Introduced too late to the marketplace
   G. Undercapitalization, unforeseen operating expenses, excessive investments in fixed assets, and related financial difficulties

V. Three Major Categories of Causes for Failure
   A. Product/market problems
      1. Poor timing
      2. Product design problems
      3. Inappropriate distribution strategy
      4. Unclear business definition
      5. Overreliance on one customer
   B. Financial difficulties
      1. Initial undercapitalization
      2. Assuming debt too early
      3. Venture capital relationship problems
   C. Managerial problems
      1. Concept of a team approach
         a. Hirings and promotions on the basis of nepotism
         b. Poor relationship with parent companies and venture capitalists
         c. Founders who focused on their weaknesses rather than on their strengths
         d. Incompetent support professionals
      2. Human resource problems
         a. Inflated owner ego
         b. Employee-related concerns
         c. Control factors

  d. Interpersonal problems
    1. Kickbacks and subsequent firings
    2. Deceit
    3. Verbal agreements not honored
    4. Protracted lawsuits around the time of discontinuance

VI. More Recent Studies of Failure
  A. *Inc.* 500 ventures
    1. Start-up problems
     a. Sales/marketing
     b. External financing
     c. Internal financial management
    2. Growth stage
     a. Sales/marketing
     b. Internal financial management
     c. Human resource management
  B. "Failure prediction" model
    1. Profitability and cash flows
    2. Debt
    3. Initial size
    4. Velocity of capital
    5. Control

VII. The Evaluation Process
  A. Critical tasks
    1. Solid analysis of the new business enterprise
    2. Evaluation of the feasibility of the product/service idea
  B. Asking the right questions
    1. Is it a new product/service idea?
     Is it proprietary?
     Can it be patented or copyrighted?
     Can it be easily copied?
    2. Has a prototype been tested by independent testers?
     What are its weak points?
     Will it stand up?
     If it is a service, has it been tested on guinea pig customers?
    3. Has it been taken to trade shows?
     Were any sales made?
     Has it been taken to distributors?
     Have they placed any orders?
    4. Is the product or service easily understood by customers, bankers, venture capitalists, accountants, lawyers, and insurance agents?

5. What is the overall market?
      What are the market segments?
      Are there special niches that can be explored?
   6. Has market research been conducted?
      Who else is in the market?
      How fast is it growing?
      What are the trends?
      What type of advertising and promotion plan will be used?
   7. What distribution and sales methods will be used?
      How will the product be transported?
   8. How will the product be made?
      How much will it cost?
      What is the break-even point?
   9. Will the business concept be developed and licensed to others or developed and sold away?
   10. Can the company get or has it already lined up the necessary skills to operate the business venture?
       Who will be the workers?
       How much capital will be needed now?
       How much more in the future?
       Have stages in financing been developed?
C. Profile analysis
   1. Different variables need to be investigated before the new idea is put into practice
   2. Enables the entrepreneur to judge the potential of the business
   3. Internal profile analysis
      a. Checklist approach
      b. Allows the entrepreneur to identify major strengths and weaknesses
      c. Can be used for the financial, marketing, organizational, and human resources aspects of the new venture
D. Feasibility criteria approach
   1. Key questions to ask
      a. Is it proprietary?
         1. Should permit a long head start against competitors
         2. Should permit a period of extraordinary profits early to offset start-up costs
      b. Are the initial production costs realistic?
         1. Most estimates are too low
         2. Careful, detailed analysis should be made
      c. Are the initial marketing costs realistic?
         1. Identify target markets
         2. Identify market channels
         3. Identify promotion strategy

       d. Does the product have potential for very high margins?
          1. A necessity for a fledgling company
          2. Gross margins are important
       e. Is the time required to get to market and to reach break-even realistic?
          1. The faster, the better
          2. An error here can spell trouble later on
       f. Is the potential market large?
          1. Must look three to five years into the future
          2. Market needs time to emerge
       g. Is the product the first of a growing family?
       h. Is there an initial customer?
       i. Are the development costs and calendar times realistic?
          1. Preferably, they are zero
          2. A ready-to-go product gives the venture a big advantage over competitors
       j. Is this a growing industry?
       k. Can the product and the need for it be understood by the financial community?
  E. Comprehensive feasibility approach
     1. Five critical factors
        a. Technical
        b. Market
        c. Financial
        d. Organizational
        e. Competitive
     2. Two merit special attention
        a. Technical feasibility
           1. Technical requirements for producing a product or service
              a. Functional design of the product and attractiveness in appearance
              b. Flexibility for ready modification
              c. Durability of the materials from which the product is made
              d. Reliability
              e. Product safety
              f. Reasonable utility
              g. Ease and low cost of maintenance
              h. Standardization
              i. Ease of processing or manufacture
              j. Ease in handling and use
        b. Marketability
           1. Three major areas involved
              a. Investigating the full market potential and identifying customers
              b. Analyzing the extent to which the enterprise might exploit this potential market
              c. Using market analysis to determine the opportunities and risks
           2. General information sources
              a. General economic trends

          1. New orders
          2. Housing starts
          3. Inventories
          4. Customer spending
      b. Market data
          1. Customers
          2. Customer demand patterns
      c. Pricing data
          1. Ranges of prices
          2. Base prices
          3. Discount structures
      d. Competitive data
          1. Major competitors
          2. Competitive strength

SUGGESTED ANSWERS FOR DISCUSSION QUESTIONS (END OF CHAPTER)

1. ***Explain the challenges involved in new-venture development.***

    The main challenges involve the survival and growth of a new venture. These are accomplished through a complete understanding of the environment, the characteristics of the entrepreneur, and the venture itself.

2. ***Describe some of the key factors involved in new-venture performance (use fig. 11.1).***

    The key factors, as illustrated in figure 11.1, are the effect of the environment (narrow markets, scarce resources), the entrepreneur's personal goals and founding processes, and the diversity of the venture itself.

3. ***Many entrepreneurs lack objectivity and have no real insight into the market. In what way are these considered pitfalls in selecting new ventures?***

    Engineers and technically trained people are particularly prone to falling in love with an idea for a product or service. They seem unaware of the need for the careful scrutiny they would give to a design or project in the ordinary course of their professional work.

    Some entrepreneurs show a managerial shortsightedness. Also, they do not understand the life cycle that must be considered in introducing a new product or service.

4. ***Many entrepreneurs have a poor understanding of the finances associated with their new venture and/or have a venture that lacks uniqueness. In what way are these considered pitfalls in selecting new ventures?***

    Sometimes entrepreneurs are ignorant of costs or are victims of inadequate research and planning. Quite often they tend to underestimate development costs by wide margins.

    A new venture should be unique. It ought to have special characteristics and/or design concepts that draw the customer to it, and it should provide performance or service that is superior to competitive offerings.

5. ***Describe each of the five critical factors involved in the prestart-up and start-up phases of a new venture.***
   (1) Uniqueness--The range of uniqueness in a new venture can be considerable, extending from fairly routine to highly nonroutine. What separates the routine from the nonroutine venture is the amount of innovation required during prestart-up. Venture uniqueness is further characterized by the length of time a nonroutine venture will remain nonroutine.
   (2) Investment--The capital investment required to start a new venture can vary considerably. Another critical issue is the extent and timing of funds needed to move through the venture process.
   (3) Growth of sales--The growth pattern needs to be anticipated for new-venture sales and profits. Key questions to answer: Are sales and profits expected to grow slowly or level off shortly after start-up? Are large profits expected at some point with only small or moderate sales growth? Or are both high-sales growth and high-profit growth likely? It is important to remember that most ventures can be classified as: life-style ventures, smaller profitable ventures, or high-growth ventures.
   (4) Product availability--Essential to the success of any venture is the availability of a salable good or service at the time the venture opens its doors. Lack of product availability in finished form can affect the company's image and its bottom line.
   (5) Customer availability--If the product is available before the venture is started, the likelihood of venture success is considerably better than otherwise. Venture risk is affected by the availability of customers for start-up. A critical consideration is how long it will take to determine who the customers are and what their buying habits are.

6. ***Identify and discuss three examples of product market problems that can cause a venture to fail.***
   (1) Poor timing--Premature entry into the marketplace can result in failure.
   (2) Inappropriate distribution strategy--Distribution should be aimed at the product and customer.
   (3) Unclear business definition--Some firms are uncertain about the "exact" business they are in and undergo constant change and lack stabilization.

7. ***Identify and discuss two examples of financial difficulties that can cause a venture to fail.***
   (1) Assuming debt too early--Assuming debt financing too soon and in too large amounts can result in debt service problems.
   (2) Venture capital relationship problems--Entrepreneurs may have different goals and motivations which cause the venture to fail.

8. *Identify and discuss two examples of managerial problems that can cause a venture to fail. What are some examples?*
   (1) Concept of a team approach: Hiring and promoting personnel because they are family or friends, not because they are qualified. Examples: incompetent support professionals, poor relationship with parent companies, and venture capitalists.
   (2) Human resource problems: An owner who can't relate to employees or never fulfills promises can cause a venture to fail. Examples: kickbacks and subsequent firings, verbal agreements not honored, deceit by the venture capitalist or the president.

9. *List four major types of problems that new ventures confront.*
   Marketing and sales, product development, internal financial management, external financing, human resource management.

10. *Describe the proposed "Failure Prediction" model for newly founded firms.*
    Using financial dates from newly founded firms, the model was based upon an assumption that the failure process is characterized by too much initial indebtedness and too little revenue financing. Specific applications of the model include: the role of profitability and cash flows, the role of debt, the role of initial size, the velocity of capital, and role of control.

11. *How can asking the right questions help an entrepreneur evaluate a new venture? What types of questions are involved?*
    Asking the right questions can help the entrepreneur by screening an idea before implementing it and taking into account the feasibility and possible profits to be had from the idea.
    The types of questions involved include: Is it a new product/service idea? Has a prototype been tested by independent testers? Has it been taken to trade shows? Is the product or service easily understood? What is the overall market? Has market research been conducted? What distribution and sales methods will be used? How will the product be made? Will the business concept be developed and licensed to others, or developed and sold away? Can the company get or has it already lined up the necessary skills to operate the business venture?

12. *Explain how a feasibility criteria approach works.*
    This was developed as a criteria selection list from which entrepreneurs can gain insights into the viability of their venture. The criteria approach is based on the following questions: Is it proprietary? Are the initial production costs realistic? Are the initial marketing costs realistic? Does the product have potential for very high margins? Is the time required to get to market and reach break-even realistic? Is the potential market large? Is the product the first of a growing family? Is there an initial customer? Are the development costs and calendar times realistic? Is this a growing industry? Can the product and the need for it be understood by the financial community? If the new venture meets fewer than six of these criteria, it typically lacks feasibility for funding. This

approach provides a means of analyzing the internal strengths and weaknesses that exist in a new venture by focusing on the market potential and the industry potential.

13. *Explain how a comprehensive feasibility approach works.*

A comprehensive feasibility approach incorporates external factors in addition to the questions presented in question 10. The five critical areas covered include: technical, market, financial, organizational, and competitive. The two which merit special attention are the technical and marketability aspects. Some of the factors included within the technical feasibility area include: functional design of the product, flexibility of the product, durability of the materials the product is made from, reliability, product safety, reasonable utility, etc.

Under marketability the three major areas within this type of analysis include: (1) investigating the full market potential and identifying customers for the goods or services, (2) analyzing the extent to which the enterprise might exploit this potential market, (3) using market analysis to determine the opportunities and risks associated with the venture.

Other things to include in a market feasibility analysis would be general sources such as: general economic trends, market data, pricing data, and competitive data. Thus, the comprehensive feasibility analysis approach is closely related to the preparation of a thorough business plan. This approach clearly illustrates the need to evaluate each segment of the venture *before* initiating the business or presenting it to capital sources.

TEACHING NOTES FOR END-OF-CHAPTER CASES

CASE: NOTHING UNIQUE TO OFFER (Answers to Questions)

1. *Is there any truth in the potential investor's comment? Is the lack of uniqueness going to hurt George's chances of success? Explain.*

Yes, because he really doesn't have anything unique to offer to the public except "pizza." Yes, because he is competing with the three other businesses, and he is not going to have any business if he cannot be unique in his offerings with other distinguishing features to make him stand out from the other competitors. He needs to be more versatile with more varieties of products or services offered to make his business more attractive to his potential customers.

2. *If George were going to make his business venture unique, what steps might he take? Be complete in your answer.*

To make his business venture unique, he needs to become more specialized. He needs a gimmick which will make his business more attractive such as: crazy bread, bread sticks, large salad bar with fresh vegetables, a large selection of dressings, and desserts. For the college students, it might offer free delivery during college daytime class hours for students who are busy studying. For the senior citizens, he might offer free delivery at all times plus a senior citizen discount. In addition, he would be wise to offer a selective number of sandwiches for customers who may not like pizza. Also, he might have coupons printed in the local paper or college student paper for an additional savings to the community. He could hire college students to distribute fliers advertising the grand opening of the business, as well as aiding in the delivery of eatables to customers. Convenient hours would also help in making his business profitable and unique. There could be an offer of "Buy one large pizza and receive free a small pizza of the same type or a 2-liter bottle of Dr. Pepper or an additional order of bread sticks with a large pizza order."

3. ***In addition to the uniqueness feature, what other critical factors is George overlooking? Identify and describe three, and give your recommendations for what to do about them.***

   Marketing of Goods and Services - How will George go about advertising and selling his products and services? How will prices be set, and how will they compare with the competition's prices? Where will the business be located? What is his target market? Recommendations would be to advertise his business by distributing fliers for his grand opening and specials. He also needs to have coupons printed to help sell his products. He cannot undercut his competitor's prices as a new business venture or he may go under. On specials he can offer better prices, but to compete he has to offer the same prices as his competitors. He needs to be located relatively close to the college campus so he can sell to the students, but he also needs to be relatively close to others as well. He wants to appeal to all consumers, but his main target market is college students.

   Production of Goods and Services - How will he go about getting the materials for his pizza business? What equipment will he need? How long will delivery take? How will quality be controlled? How will customer complaints be handled? George needs to check out different suppliers and find the most reasonable prices for materials needed. He will need to see how these materials are going to be transported to his business. He will need to check prices on different ovens and appliances needed and see about the cost for repairs to this equipment. George needs to decide how he will go about delivering his products, such as: students driving their own vehicles to deliver or buying vehicles for delivery. Employees who are answering the phones when the customer calls to order need to tell the customer when the order will be delivered. George needs to see that adequate managers are hired to oversee the employees when George cannot be there. To insure the maintaining of customers, complaints should be handled with the customer being considered first in all cases. In other words, keep the customer happy and satisfied at all costs.

   Buyer Decisions in the Venture--Who will the customers be? Approximately how many customers will he sell to? Where are these customers located? He wants to appeal to senior citizens and students as well as other consumers. The number of customers he can sell to are those people who are in his delivery area or whoever may come into the store. The customers are located near the college campus or in the nearby area.

CASE: A PRODUCT DESIGN PROBLEM

1. ***What happened? What mistake did Bill make in terms of the new venture?***

   Bill tried to do too much too soon and did not take the time to check his basic design to see if it fit the needs of the buyers. He made a big mistake in not blueprinting these design plans and making samples of his components for his buyers first.

2. ***How could this problem have been prevented? Defend your answer.***

   Bill should have provided samples of his components for his buyers to see if they were scaled and correctly gauged to specifications of the government as well as private firms. He should have blueprinted each component part first and made up the specifications for each buyer. He should never have run all the component parts without inspecting them for possible flaws. He may have been timely in his venture, but this mistake could have been very costly to correct, if that was even possible, and he may have sent his business venture into the red due to poor design and quality errors.

3. ***What lesson about new-venture assessment does this case provide? Be complete in your answer.***

   The lesson that this case provides is that in the production of goods and services, we must consider how waste or scrap will be controlled. How will quality be controlled, and how will Bill resolve this problem with the government and private firms? Samples would have solved the quality flaw problem before contracts were signed and after specs were provided. This would have been a very important and crucial step that should have been implemented first.

ADDITIONAL EXPERIENTIAL EXERCISES

"Venture Assessment"

Have students set up interviews with *at least* two small business owners (0-50 employees). In conducting the interview, students should find out how the owner made his business a success. What strategies and type of financing did he use (did he borrow money at first or use his own cash), did he have a marketing niche, what type of advertising did he start out with, etc.?

Students should then compare the interviews to see how each differs from or is similar to the other, and if each owner used basically the same techniques for success, or if they were totally different from each other. Students could also see if the owner had previously failed in owning his own business, and if so, what did he do differently the second time to make his business successful.

(OR)

"Computer Simulation"

A computer simulation project would be a good way for students to make decisions regarding the operating of a small business. If a template could be developed which would allow students to input variables such as sales, inventory, and expenses against variables simulated by the computer, such as inflation, competitors, pricing, etc., students would be able to see how well they can manage a small business against the computer. The computer would then assign a score to the students based on their performance. The students would then write a paper on the decisions they made, analyzing their strengths and weaknesses.

CHAPTER 12

STRUCTURING THE NEW BUSINESS VENTURE

CHAPTER OUTLINE

I. Identifying Legal Structures

II. Sole Proprietorship: A Business Owned and Operated by One Person
   A. Advantages of sole proprietorship
      1. Ease of formation
      2. Sole ownership of profits
      3. Decision making and control vested in one owner
      4. Flexibility
      5. Relative freedom from governmental control
      6. Freedom from corporate business taxes
   B. Disadvantages of sole proprietorship
      1. Unlimited liability
      2. Lack of continuity
      3. Less available capital
      4. Relative difficulty in obtaining long-term financing
      5. Relatively limited viewpoint and experience

III. Partnership: An Association of Two or More Persons Acting as Co-owners of a Business for Profit
   A. Types of partners
      1. Ostensible partner
      2. Active partner
      3. Secret partner
      4. Dormant partner
      5. Silent partner
      6. Nominal partner
      7. Subpartner
      8. Limited partner
   B. Advantages of the partnership
      1. Ease of formation
      2. Direct rewards
      3. Growth and performance facilitated
      4. Flexibility
      5. Relative freedom from governmental control and regulation
      6. Possible tax advantage
   C. Disadvantages of the partnership
      1. Unlimited liability of at least one partner
      2. Lack of continuity

The Dryden Press

3. Relative difficulty in obtaining large sums of capital
4. Being bound by the acts of just one partner
5. Difficulty of disposing of partnership interest
D. Partnerships' success

IV. The Corporation: A Separate Legal Entity Apart from the Individuals Who Own It
A. Advantages of the corporation
1. Limited liability
2. Transfer of ownership
3. Unlimited life
4. Relative ease of securing capital in large amounts
5. Increased ability and expertise
B. Disadvantages of the corporation
1. Activity restriction
2. Lack of representation
3. Regulation
4. Organizing expenses
5. Double taxation

V. Specific Forms of Partnerships and Corporations
A. Limited partnership is used in situations where a form of organization is needed that permits capital investment without responsibility for management and without liability for losses beyond initial investment
B. Limited Liability Partnerships (LLP)
C. R & D limited partnership has become a popular tool for funding research and development.
D. S corporation, commonly known as a "tax option corporation," is taxed similarly to a partnership
E. Limited Liability Companies (LLC)
F. Other classifications of corporations
1. Domestic and foreign corporations
2. Public and private corporations
3. Nonprofit corporations
4. Professional corporations
5. Close corporations

VI. Costs Associated with Incorporation
A. Lawyers' fees
B. Accountants' fees
C. Fees to the state
D. Unemployment insurance taxes
E. Employer's contribution to social security
F. Annual legal and accounting fees

VII. Franchising
    A. Advantages
    B. Disadvantages
    C. Franchise law

VIII. Final Thoughts

CHAPTER OBJECTIVES

1. To examine the legal forms of organization--sole proprietorship, partnership, corporation, and franchising
2. To illustrate the advantages and disadvantages of each of these four legal forms
3. To compare the characteristics and tax considerations of a partnership with those of a corporation
4. To explain the nature of the limited partnership
5. To examine how an S corporation works
6. To define the additional classifications of corporations
7. To review the costs and benefits associated with the corporate form of organization
8. To examine the franchise structures, benefits, and drawbacks

CHAPTER SUMMARY

Before entrepreneurs decide how to organize an operation, they must first identify legal structures. There are four primary legal structures: the sole proprietorship, the partnership, the corporation, and the franchise, all of which have their own advantages and disadvantages.

The first form is the sole proprietorship, a business that is owned and operated by one person who has unlimited liability and the right to all profits. Some of the advantages of the sole proprietorship include the ease of formation, sole ownership of profits, decision making and control vested in one owner, flexibility, relative freedom from corporate business taxes, and relative freedom from government control. There are also quite a few disadvantages, such as unlimited liability, lack of control, less available capital, relative difficulty in obtaining long-term financing, and relatively limited viewpoint and experience.

The second form is the partnership, which is an association of two or more persons acting as co-owners of a business. Each partner contributes and shares in profits and losses. There are several provisions necessary for forming a partnership and several different types of partners. Among the various types of partners are the ostensible partner, the active partner, the secret partner, the nominal partner, the silent partner, the dormant partner, the subpartner, and the limited partner. There are several advantages to a partnership, including the ease of formation, direct rewards, growth and performance facilitated, flexibility, relative freedom from governmental control and regulation, and possible tax advantage. There are also several disadvantages, such as unlimited liability of at least one partner, lack of continuity, relative difficulty in obtaining large sums of capital, being bound by the acts of just one partner, and difficulty of disposing of partnership interest.

The third form is the corporation, "an artificial being, invisible, intangible, and existing only in contemplation of the law." Some of the advantages of the corporation are limited liability, transfer of ownership, unlimited life, relative ease of securing capital in large amounts, and increased ability and expertise. Some of the disadvantages include activity restrictions, lack of representation, regulation, organizing expenses, and double taxation.

There are numerous specific forms of partnerships and corporations. The first, the limited partnership, is used in situations when a form of organization is needed that permits capital investment without liability for losses beyond that of the initial investment. A second form is the Limited Liability Partnership (LLP), which is easily established by professionals normally doing business as partners yet wishing to avoid the malpractice liability of other partners. A third form is the R&D limited partnership, which has become a popular tool for funding research and development. A fourth form is the S corporation, which is known as a "tax option corporation" and is taxed like a partnership. A fifth is the Limited Liability Company (LLC), which allows members to participate fully in management activities of the firm, yet maintain the tax status of a partnership with the limited liability of a corporation. There are several other classifications of corporations, including domestic and foreign corporations, public and private corporations, nonprofit corporations, professional corporations, and close corporations. There are various costs associated with incorporation such as the lawyers' fees, accountants' fees, fees to the state, unemployment insurance taxes, employer's contribution to social security, and annual legal and accounting fees.

The fourth form of organization is the franchise. This is an arrangement in which the owner of a trademark, trade name, or copyright licenses others to use it in the selling of goods and services. A franchise is usually legally independent but economically dependent on the integrated business system of the franchise. The advantages include: training and guidance, brand-name appeal, proven track record, and financial assistance. The disadvantages are franchise fees, franchiser control, and unfulfilled promises. Franchises have outgrown the laws to regulate them; however, the states are quickly moving to stronger registration and disclosure requirements.

LECTURE NOTES

STRUCTURING THE NEW BUSINESS VENTURE

I. Identifying Legal Structures
   A. Sole proprietorship, partnership, corporation

II. The Sole Proprietorship
   A. Characteristics
      1. Owned and operated by one person
      2. Unlimited liability
      3. Most widely used

   B. Advantages
      1. Ease of formation
      2. Sole ownership of profits
      3. Decision making and control vested in one owner
      4. Flexibility
      5. Relative freedom from government control
      6. Freedom from corporate business taxes
   C. Disadvantages
      1. Unlimited liability
      2. Lack of continuity
      3. Less available capital
      4. Relative difficulty in obtaining long-term financing
      5. Relatively limited viewpoint and experience

III. The Partnership
   A. Characteristics
      1. Association of two or more persons acting as co-owners of a business for profit
      2. Articles of partnership highly recommended
         a. Name, purpose, domicile
         b. Duration of agreement
         c. Contributions by partners
         d. Any relevant information pertaining to the relationship
   B. Types of partners
      1. Ostensible
      2. Active
      3. Secret
      4. Dormant
      5. Silent
      6. Nominal
      7. Subpartner
      8. Limited partner
   C. Advantages
      1. Ease of formation
      2. Direct rewards
      3. Growth and performance facilitated
      4. Flexibility
      5. Relative freedom from governmental control and regulation
      6. Possible tax advantage

   D. Disadvantages
      1. Unlimited liability of at least one partner
      2. Lack of continuity
      3. Relative difficulty in obtaining large sums of capital

The Dryden Press

   4. Being bound by the acts of just one partner
   5. Difficulty of disposing of partnership interest
  E. Partnership success
   1. Trust
   2. Willingness to coordinate activities
   3. Ability to convey a sense of commitment
   4. Communication strategies

IV. The Corporation
  A. Characteristics
   1. "An artificial being, invisible, intangible, and existing only in the contemplation of the law"
   2. Separate legal entity apart from owners
   3. Must gain approval from secretary of state where it is formed
  B. Advantages
   1. Limited liability
   2. Transfer of ownership
   3. Unlimited life
   4. Relative ease of securing capital in large amounts
   5. Increased ability and expertise
  C. Disadvantages
   1. Activity restrictions
   2. Lack of representation
   3. Regulation
   4. Organizing expenses
   5. Double taxation

V. Specific Forms of Partnerships and Corporations
  A. Limited partnership
   1. Capital investment without managerial responsibility
   2. Limited liability to amount of investment
   3. Can share in profits
   4. Governed by Uniform Limited Partnership Act
   5. Creation is a formal proceeding
  B. Limited Liability Partnership (LLP)
   1. Tax benefits of partnership
   2. Avoids personal liability from partners' malpractice
   3. Easy to establish
  C. R&D limited partnership
   1. Not a taxable entity, taxed as personal income
   2. General partner manages operations and assumes obligations
   3. Sponsoring company retains greater control of the project
   4. Sponsoring company pays only in the event of a successful development

5. Improves debt-to-equity ratio
6. Improved ability to generate cash
D. The S corporation
   1. Avoids corporate income taxes
   2. Retains limited liability
   3. Guidelines
      a. Must be a domestic corporation
      b. Must not be member of affiliated group of corporations
      c. Corporation or partnerships cannot be stockholders
      d. Must have 75 or fewer shareholders
      e. Only one class of stock, all having voting rights
      f. Must have less than 20 percent of gross receipts from passive investment income
      g. Must have less than 80 percent of gross receipts outside the United States
      h. No shareholder can be a nonresident alien
   4. Benefits
      a. At loss, shareholders offset taxable income.
      b. If shareholders' tax bracket is lower than S corporation's, then the corporation gets a lower tax rate
      c. Taxable income is taxable only to shareholders
      d. Can defer shareholders' taxes
      e. Shareholder free to give stock to lower tax bracket family member
      f. Tax-free corporate benefits offered
E. Limited Liability Companies (LLC)
   1. Hybrid form between partnership and corporation
   2. Members participate fully in management activities
   3. Corporations and partnerships can be investors
   4. Because state statutes differ, multistate operations can be difficult
F. Other classifications of corporations
   1. Domestic and foreign corporations
      a. Classified by location
      b. Domestic = in home state
      c. Foreign = out of home state
      d. Applies only in United States
   2. Public and private corporations
      a. Classified by source of funds
      b. Public corporations are created by public agencies
      c. Private corporations are created wholly or in part for private benefit
   3. Nonprofit corporations
      a. Usually religious, charitable, or educational organizations
      b. Most are private in nature
   4. Professional corporations
      a. Relatively new
      b. Tax benefits

   5. Close corporations
     a. A "closely held" corporation is where all stock is held by one person or a small number of shareholders
     b. Shareholders manage the firm directly

VI. Costs Associated with Incorporation
  A. Lawyers' fees
  B. Accountants' fees
  C. Fees to the state
  D. Unemployment insurance taxes
  E. Employer's contribution to social security
  F. Annual legal and accounting fees

VII. Franchising
  A. Advantages of franchising
   1. Training and guidance
   2. Brand-name appeal
   3. Proven track record
   4. Financial assistance
  B. Disadvantages of franchising
   1. Franchise fees
   2. Franchisor control
   3. Unfulfilled promises
  C. Franchise law
   1. Growth of franchising has outdistanced the laws
   2. UFOC = Uniform Franchise Offering Circular

VIII. Final Thoughts
  A. Key questions
   1. What is the size of the risk? What is the amount of the investor's liability for debt and taxes?
   2. What would the continuity (life) of the firm be if something happened to the principal(s)?
   3. What legal structure would ensure the greatest administrative adaptability for the firm?
   4. What effect will federal, state, and local laws have on the operation?
   5. What are the possibilities of attracting additional capital?
   6. What are the needs for and possibilities of attracting additional expertise?
   7. What are the costs and procedures associated with starting the operation?
   8. What is the ultimate goal and purpose of the enterprise, and which legal structure can best serve this purpose?

SUGGESTED ANSWERS FOR DISCUSSION QUESTIONS
(END OF CHAPTER)

1. ***Identify the legal forms that are available for entrepreneurs in structuring their ventures.***
   Sole proprietorship, partnership, corporation

2. ***Define each of the following: sole proprietorship, partnership, corporation.***
   (1) Sole proprietorship: A business that is owned and operated by one person.
   (2) Partnership: An association of two or more persons acting as co-owners of a business for profit.
   (3) Corporation: "An artificial being, invisible, intangible, and existing only in contemplation of the law."

3. ***What are the specific advantages and disadvantages associated with each legal form of organization?***

Sole Proprietorship

Advantages	Disadvantages
Ease of formation	Unlimited liability
Sole ownership of profits	Lack of continuity
Decision making and control vested in one owner	Less available capital
Flexibility	Relative difficulty in obtaining long-term financing
Relative freedom from government control	Relatively limited viewpoint and business experience
Freedom from corporate business taxes	

Partnership

Advantages	Disadvantages
Ease of formation	Unlimited liability of at least one partner
Direct rewards	Lack of continuity
Growth and performance facilitated	Relative difficulty in obtaining large sums of capital
Flexibility	
Relative freedom from government control and regulation	Being bound by the acts of one partner
Possible tax advantages	Difficulty of disposing of partnership interest

The Dryden Press

Corporations

Advantages	Disadvantages
Limited liability	Activity restrictions
Transfer of ownership	Lack of representation
Unlimited life	Regulation
Relative ease of securing capital in large amounts	Organizing expenses
	Double taxation
Increased ability and expertise	

4. *Compare the major tax considerations of a partnership with those of a corporation.*
   Partnerships have a major tax advantage in that they pay a lower rate than corporations. Income tax is levied as personal tax.
   Corporations, on the other hand, are subject to double taxation. Income taxes are levied both on corporate profits and on individual salaries and dividends. This is a major disadvantage to corporations.

5. *What is the ULPA? Describe it.*
   ULPA is the Uniform Limited Partnership Act, which governs limited partnerships. It covers such areas as general provisions, formation, limited partners, general partners, finance, distributions and withdrawals, assignment of partnership interest, dissolution, foreign limited partnerships, derivative actions, and miscellaneous considerations. These guidelines should be examined by prospective partners.

6. *Name three specific types of partners. How do they differ?*
   (1) A secret partner is active in the business but is not disclosed or known as a partner.
   (2) A dormant partner is inactive in the business and is also unknown or undisclosed as a partner.
   (3) A silent partner, by contrast, is inactive in the business but may be known to be a partner.

7. *Explain the Limited Liability Partnership.*
   The Limited Liability Partnerships (LLP) is a relatively new form of partnership that allows professionals the tax benefits of a partnership while avoiding the personal liability for the malpractice of other partners. Normally, LLP statutes are simply amendments to a state's already existing partnership laws.

8. *What is the double taxation that corporations face?*
   The double taxation that corporations face is such that income taxes are levied both on corporate profits and on individual salaries and dividends.

9. *How does a limited partnership work? Give an example.*
   A limited partnership enables partners to associate for the purpose of creating a business for profit, but the twist is that not all partners must take part in management

procedures. A person may provide capital to the organization for investment purposes but remain free from responsibility as a manager. Also, an investor is limited in liability only equal to the amount of the initial investment.

10. *What is the nature of an S corporation? List five requirements for such a corporation.*
    The designation of S corporation enables a firm to avoid the double taxation problems of a corporation yet maintain many benefits of a corporation such as limited liability. There are some specific guidelines or requirements which must be followed to qualify for the S corporation designation. Here are some of them:
    (1) Corporation must be domestic
    (2) Corporation must not be a member of an affiliated group of corporations
    (3) Corporation must have 15 or fewer shareholders
    (4) Corporation can have only one class of stock, and all stockholders must have the same voting rights
    (5) Corporations or partnerships must not be shareholders

11. *Define each of the following: foreign corporation, nonprofit corporation, professional corporation, and close corporation.*
    (1) A foreign corporation is one that is not operating within its "home" state.
    (2) A nonprofit corporation is usually a church, school, or charitable organization whose purpose is not to make a profit, but it may be allowed to do so if the profit is left within the corporation.
    (3) A professional corporation is a private corporation usually involving doctors, lawyers, and accountants. It has several tax benefits.
    (4) A close corporation is a corporation where all the stock is held by one or a small number of shareholders who manage directly. Stock is not for public purchase.

12. **What is a Limited Liability Company?**
    A Limited Liability Company (LLC) is a hybrid form of business between a partnership (taxes) and corporation (structure). While members may fully participate in the management activities of the firms, they can retain limited liability status. In addition, there is no limit on the number of stockholders. However, since LLC's are relatively new, each state may have different requirements.

13. **What are the advantages and disadvantages of franchising?**
    The advantages of franchising include training and guidance from the franchisor, brand-name appeal, a proven track record, and some financial assistance. The disadvantages of franchising are the franchise fees--both initial fee and royalty payments each year -- control exerted by the franchisor, and the sometimes unfulfilled promises made by franchisors to franchisees.

14. **Identify the UFOC. Explain why it is important in franchising.**
    As explained in the "Contemporary Entrepreneurship" feature in the chapter, the UFOC is the Uniform Franchise Offering Circular. This was established in 1979 by the

The Dryden Press

Federal Trade Commission requiring franchisors to make full disclosure of all pertinent information to prospective franchisees. There are 23 different items, from fees to certified financial statements. It must be given to a prospective franchisee at least 10 days prior to the payment of any fees or contracts signed.

15. **What are four key questions to be considered by entrepreneurs before structuring their venture?**
    (1) What is the size of the risk?
    (2) What legal structure would ensure the greatest administrative adaptability for the firm?
    (3) What are the costs and procedures associated with starting the operation?
    (4) What effect will federal, state, and local laws have on the operation?

TEACHING NOTES FOR END-OF-CHAPTER CASES

CASE: GINA'S DECISION

1. **What are the benefits of the company becoming a corporation? Is this a better idea than the banker's proposal of taking a $200,000 loan? Why or why not?**
   One of the advantages associated with a corporation is limited liability. The stockholders' liability is limited to the individual's investment. You can lose only the amount of money that you have invested. You can also transfer ownership through the sale of stock to buyers who are interested. The company has unlimited life. It can continue operating long after the life of the owners. It is relatively easy to secure capital in large amounts. Capital can be acquired through the issuance of bonds and shares of stock and through short-term loans made against the assets of the business. The corporation will also be able to draw on the expertise and skills of a number of individuals ranging from the major stockholders to the professional managers who are brought on board. At this point they should borrow the money and see if the second business is going to work before they form a corporation. They should not think about incorporating at this point. If they were to form a corporation, there would be a lot of expenses involved. There are extensive governmental regulations and reports required by local, state, and federal agencies that often result in a great deal of paperwork and red tape.

2. **How does an S corporation work? Would this be a good idea for the firm? Why or why not?**
   This is called a subchapter S corporation. This allows a business to be able to avoid the imposition of income taxes at the corporate level, yet retain some of the benefits of a corporation. An S corporation is taxed similarly to a partnership. An information form is filed with the IRS to indicate the shareholders' income. This allows the double taxation problem to be avoided. This is very useful for small businesses, but there are strict guidelines to follow. It could be a good idea, and there are a lot of benefits that may be

useful to them. Since the first boutique has been around for six years and has grown greatly over the years, the odds of the other boutique being successful are quite good. By forming an S corporation, they would have several benefits that they could take advantage of. This would allow shareholders to offset their losses by using these losses to offset taxable income. Stockholders also are in a tax bracket lower than that of a corporation. Their entire income is taxed on the shareholders' income bracket. Taxable income of an S corporation is taxable only to those who are shareholders at the end of the corporate year when the income is distributed. They can choose a fiscal year that will permit them to defer some of the shareholders' taxes. The shareholder can give some of his or her stock to other members of the family who are in a lower tax bracket. They can also offer some tax-free corporate benefits.

3. *What would you recommend to Gina? Explain in detail.*
   For now she should continue with the partnership and see how it goes before forming a corporation or an S corporation. There will be some risk associated with her opening the second boutique, but if she is to be successful, she will need to take the risk. After both boutiques are operating well and making a profit, then she should consider making a change by forming an S corporation. This is very involved and she needs to make sure this is exactly what she wants to do. She probably would not want to do too many things at once. If she were to incorporate, there are a lot of money and legal formalities involved, and it is not something she wants to rush into unless it is the best decision for the business. With the advantages she has with a partnership, it would be in her best interest to continue with the way things are until she is sure the second boutique is operating successfully.

ADDITIONAL EXPERIENTIAL EXERCISES

"Examine the Business Structure"

The student must pick a type of business structure, then find a company that has this structure and interview its principals. Some questions to ask:
(1) Why did they pick this structure?
(2) Do they wish they were a different structure?
(3) What recent legislation has most affected their company's structure?
(4) Were they ever restricted? If yes, from what?
(5) What structure did they start as?
(6) What advantages and disadvantages of their structure have been most helpful and most harmful?

(OR)

"Personal Experience"

Have a sole proprietor, a member of a partnership, and an executive of a corporation come into class to discuss personal situations regarding legal and financial aspects of their respective organizations.

CHAPTER 13

LEGAL ISSUES RELATED TO EMERGING VENTURES

CHAPTER OUTLINE

I. Introduction
   A. Concepts that affect entrepreneurial ventures
      1. Those that relate to the inception of the venture
      2. Those that relate to the ongoing venture
      3. Those that relate to the growth and continuity of the venture
   B. Legal concepts to be discussed throughout the chapter
      1. Patents
      2. Copyrights
      3. Trademarks
      4. Bankruptcy law

II. Patents
   A. Intellectual property right that is a result of a unique discovery protecting patent holders against infringement by others
   B. Qualified items for patent protection
      1. Processes
      2. Machines
      3. Products
      4. Plants
      5. Compositions of elements (chemical compounds)
      6. Improvements on already existing items
   C. Securing a patent
      1. Recommendation made by experts in pursuing a patent effectively
         a. Research and record all steps taken for proprietary opportunities in a notebook
         b. Outline and prepare a detailed analysis of competition and technological similarities in relation to your idea
         c. Remain close in actions to the original patent plan
         d. Prepare a realistic budget for infringement
         e. Determine strategically if the patent is worth defending
      2. Two detailed parts of innovations that should be included in patent applications
         a. Specification
            1. Introductory paragraph explaining invention
            2. Cite and describe all prior art
            3. Summary of the invention
            4. Description of the invention
            5. Examples and/or experimental results
         b. Claims
            1. Series of short paragraphs one page or less long

The Dryden Press

        2. Sharply limited not to cover anything prior to art
    c. File the application with the Patent and Trademark Office of the Department of Commerce

III. Copyrights
    A. Forms of expressions concerning copyrights
        1. Books
        2. Periodicals
        3. Dramatic or musical compositions
        4. Art
        5. Motion pictures
        6. Lectures
        7. Sound recordings
        8. Computer programs
    B. Length of copyrights
        1. Works created after January 1, 1978
        2. Life of author plus 50 years
    C. Owner's rights concerning copyrights
        1. Reproduce the work
        2. Prepare derivative works, e.g., novels
        3. Distribute copies of work by sale or otherwise
        4. Perform work publicly
        5. Display work publicly
    D. Understanding the copyright protection
        1. Copyright in tangible form
        2. Author's own work
        3. Product of own skill or judgment
        4. "Fair use" doctrine of copyrights
        5. Lawyer's point of view
            a. No cost in obtaining copyright
            b. Not necessary to register
            c. Use commercial point of view
            d. Watch for trap lines
            e. Copyrighted advertisements have advantage
            f. Noncopyrightable items
                1. Government publications
                2. Statutes
                3. Cases
                4. Congressional history
                5. Congressional debates
    E. Protected ideas?

IV. Trademarks
    A. Distinctive name or symbol

            1. Name
            2. Mark
            3. Symbol
            4. Motto
        B. Types of marks
            1. Trademarks identify goods
            2. Service marks identify services
            3. Certification marks denote quality and materials
            4. Collection marks used by groups
        C. Generic words are not trademarked
        D. Advantages of being listed in Principal Register
            1. Nationwide notice
            2. Customs protection against use by importers
            3. Incontestability after five years
        E. Registration of trademark
            1. Registration lasts for a twenty-year period historically
            2. Current registrations are good for 10 years and renewable for 10 more
        F. Trademark Revision Act of 1988
            1. "Intent to use" provision
            2. 3-year period from notification to use
        G. Four ways in which a trademark may be invalidated
            1. Cancellation proceedings
            2. Cleaning-out procedure
            3. Abandonment
            4. Generic meaning
        H. Avoiding the pitfalls
            1. Trademark registration very expensive
            2. Infringement even more expensive
            3. Five rules to avoid pitfalls in selecting a trademark
                a. Never choose without trademark search
                b. Trust lawyer's judgment
                c. Seek a coined or fanciful mark
                d. Select a logotype in dictating situations
                e. Avoid abbreviations and acronyms
        I. Trade secrets

V. Bankruptcy
    A. Foreseeing impending failure
        1. New competition enters market
        2. Other firms selling advanced products
        3. R & D budget proportionately less than competition's
        4. Retailers always overstocked
    B. Early warning signs
        1. Financial management is lax

2. Company officers too busy for bookkeeping
   3. Repeated emergency loans to company from family and officers
   4. Large discounts for prompt payment
   5. Low-price contracts accepted
   6. Bank wants loans subordinated
   7. Sales and inventory ordering do not correlate
   8. Key personnel depart
   9. Inadequate supply of materials
   10. Payroll taxes not paid
C. Bankruptcy Act
   1. Specific procedures for handling insolvent debtors
   2. Purpose of act
      a. Ensure property distributed fairly among creditors
      b. Protect creditors from debtor's unreasonably diminishing assets
      c. Protect debtors from creditors
   3. Three major sections of act
      a. Straight bankruptcy
      b. Reorganization
      c. Adjustment of debts
D. Straight bankruptcy, Chapter 7
   1. Referred to as liquidation
   2. Debtor surrenders all property to court trustee
   3. Assets sold and proceeds paid to creditors
   4. Debtor relieved of obligations
   5. May be voluntary or involuntary
E. Reorganization, Chapter 11
   1. Most common form of bankruptcy
   2. Develops plan to pay a portion of debts
   3. Plan must provide several things
      a. Divide creditors into classes
      b. Set forth how each creditor will be satisfied
      c. State which claims are impaired by plan
      d. Provide same treatment to each creditor in a particular class
   4. Debtor continues operation after filing
   5. Once accepted by creditors, it is binding on the debtor
F. Adjustment of debts, Chapter 13
   1. Allows individuals to
      a. Avoid bankruptcy declaration
      b. Pay installments
      c. Be protected by federal court
   2. Eligibility requirements for Chapter 13
      a. Unsecured debts of less than $100,000
      b. Secured debts of less than $350,000
      c. Must be voluntary

3. Detailed plan for treatment of debts must
   a. Allow for turnover of future earnings
   b. Provide for full payment of priority debts
   c. Extend same treatment of debts to each class
   d. Provide for payment within three years
4. Court can discharge debt
5. Creditor benefits by recovering larger percentage than in liquidation
6. Suggestions to minimize legal costs
   a. Establish fee construction
   b. Compromise and attempt to settle rather than liquidate
   c. Have lawyer design forms
   d. Use less-expensive lawyer for small collections
   e. Suggest cost-saving methods
   f. Visit during regular business hours
   g. Consult on several matters at one time
   h. Look for legal developments in own field
   i. Handle some matters personally
   j. Shop around for your lawyer

VI. Summary

CHAPTER OBJECTIVES

1. To introduce the importance of legal issues to entrepreneurs
2. To examine patent protection, including definitions, preparation, and proper attorney selection
3. To review copyrights and their relevance to entrepreneurs
4. To study trademarks and their impact on new ventures
5. To present the major segments of the bankruptcy law that apply to business
6. To highlight some cost-saving legal tips

CHAPTER SUMMARY

This chapter starts out discussing patents, which are "intellectual property rights that were the results of a unique discovery." A vast number of products, processes, and machines are covered by this definition. The patent is the government's way to promote creativity and free enterprise for those who otherwise might not take the risk.

There are five suggestions for pursuing a patent and they are: do not limit the idea; when preparing a plan be as detailed and precise as possible; when the pursuit of the patent is in its infancy, keep your goals relevant to your original plan; and be prepared financially to protect your legal rights. Each patent typically takes three years to obtain and you must evaluate the long-range profitability of your plan. After one has determined the exact format for the potential patent, the next step is to prepare a patent application.

The patent application has two parts, the specification, which is an in-depth and detailed summation of the patent idea, and the claims, which specifically point out which feature or features of the idea are to be protected by the patent.

Copyrights is the next major section of Chapter 10. A copyright may be obtained on any physical form that is the author's own work. The copyright gives the author exclusive rights to reproduce the work and prepare derivative works based on it. Other rights are the right to distribute copies of the work and the right to perform and display the work in public.

The chapter also covers trademarks, which are any distinct name, mark, symbol, or motto identified with a company's product. Trademarks can be invalidated through four methods: cancellation proceedings, cleaning out procedure, abandonment, and generic meaning.

Just as the chapter started out strong with a discussion on patents, it ended using the same style with bankruptcy as the main topic. Bankruptcy can often be foreseen by small-business owners if they know the warning signs. Some of these signs are: key personnel depart suddenly, payroll taxes are not paid, financial management is lax, and officers and family make repeated emergency loans to the company. The Bankruptcy Act was established by the federal government to ensure fair treatment and the protection of both the debtor and the creditor. This act makes sure that the assets of the debtor are fairly distributed to all the creditors. This act also protects the creditors from any unfair reduction of assets that may be attempted by the debtor. The last part of the act protects the debtor from extreme demands by the creditors.

There are three different types of bankruptcy discussed in this chapter. The first type is called Chapter 7: straight bankruptcy, and it may be initiated by either the creditors or the debtor. This form of bankruptcy in most cases sells off all the debtor's assets and distributes them fairly among the creditors. The next type is entitled Chapter 11: reorganization. This form also may be initiated by either party, and it is the most common type of bankruptcy. The debtor attempts to formulate a plan to pay a portion of the debts, have the remaining sum discharged, and continue to stay in operation. To achieve this, a plan is formulated that will divide the creditors into different categories and establish how each creditor is going to be paid, while also establishing a guarantee of equal treatment for all the creditors in each particular class.

The final type of bankruptcy discussed is Chapter 13: adjustment of debts. In this form the individual does not have to declare bankruptcy, and only the debtor can file a Chapter 13. This form allows the debtor to pay back his or her outstanding debts in installments while still staying in business, and the debtor is protected by the federal court. The debtor is required to file a plan showing how the debts are going to be repaid, and the plan must include the following: The turnover of such future income of the debtor to the trustee as is necessary for the execution of the plan, full payment in deferred cash payments of all claims entitled to priority, and the same treatment of each claim within a particular class. The debtor is expected to make good against his/her debts within three years unless the courts declare an extension to five years. The court can also release the debtor from his/her obligations if it is satisfied that the failure is due to circumstances beyond the debtor's control.

This chapter provides a very comprehensive look at some of the benefits and difficulties of copyrights, patents, and trademarks. It also gives an in-depth look and understanding of bankruptcy and some of its various forms.

LECTURE NOTES

LEGAL ISSUES RELATED TO EMERGING VENTURES

I. Patents
   A. Definition of a patent
      1. A patent is an intellectual property right. It is the result of a unique discovery, and patent holders are provided protection against infringement by others.
      2. There are a number of items that can qualify for patent protection, among them processes, machines, products, plants, chemical compounds, and improvements on already existing items.
      3. A patent allows the owner complete control and ownership of a product or process for a number of years, and this promotes innovation.
         a. Most patents are in effect for seventeen years.
         b. Design patents are the only exception to the rule, and they last fourteen years.
   B. Securing a patent
      1. There are five suggestions for the proper pursuit of a patent
         a. Do not limit the idea; it is important that the patent be as broad and commercially feasible as possible.
         b. When preparing a plan, be as detailed and precise as possible.
         c. When the pursuit of the patent is in its infancy, keep your goals relevant to your original plan.
         d. Be prepared financially to protect your legal rights.
         e. Each patent typically takes three years to obtain, and you must evaluate the long-range profitability of your plan.
      2. To obtain a patent one must complete the two parts of a patent application
         a. The first part is the specification, and it is an in-depth and detailed summation of the patent idea.
            1. The specification has an introduction that stresses the function of the patent.
            2. It also includes any similar patented or nonpatented ideas that you are aware of.
            3. A summary of the idea is also included and stresses the innovative aspects that make it unique.
            4. A highly organized and detailed description of the idea that completely answers any technical questions should be the main part of the specification.
         b. The second part of the application is the claims section
            1. The claims specifically point out which feature or features of the idea are to be protected by the patent.
            2. The claims area also defines and limits the patented idea.
      3. Patents can be declared invalid for several reasons
         a. The holder waits too long to claim his/her patentable rights.

           b. It can be shown that the holder misused the patent rights.
           c. The patent can be shown to not meet tests of patentability.

II. Copyrights
    A. Definition of copyrights
       1. A copyright provides exclusive rights to creative individuals for the protection of their literary or artistic productions.
       2. After January 1, 1978, anyone who receives a copyright is protected by law for life and fifty years after death.
       3. Copyright owners have certain rights
           a. The right to produce the work
           b. The right to prepare derivative works based on it
           c. The right to distribute copies of the work by sale or otherwise
           d. The right to perform the work publicly
           e. The right to display the work publicly
    B. Understanding copyright protection
       1. The creative material must be in a physical form so that it can be communicated or reproduced.
       2. The creative material must be the author's own work.
       3. Anyone who violates an author's exclusive rights is liable for infringement.
       4. The "fair use" doctrine states that some uses of the author's material is not an infraction: When the material is used for criticism, comment, news reporting, teaching, scholarship, or research
       5. There are several factors that will be considered to determine the legality of the use
           a. The purpose and character of the use
           b. The nature of the copyrighted work
           c. The amount and substantiality of the portion used in relation to the work as a whole
           d. The effect of the use upon the potential market for a value of the copyrighted work
    C. Copyright protection from a lawyer's view
       1. It costs the author nothing to protect, by copyright, his/her material. Any writings that involve any great amount of time should be protected.
       2. It is not necessary to register copyrights with the Copyright Office unless and until you want to sue someone for infringement.
       3. There may be some slight advantage in copyrighting an advertisement. This is so that your competitors will not use any advertisement that took a good deal of time to develop.
       4. There are some things which cannot be copyrighted. Some examples are: United States government publications, statutes, cases, congressional history, and debates
    D. Protected ideas
       1. Ideas cannot be copyrighted. Therefore, if someone writes an article and

copyrights it, others are still free to extract the information and use it in their own material.

III. Trademarks
   A. Definition of trademarks
      1. A trademark is a distinctive name, mark, symbol, or motto that is identified with a company's product.
      2. Trademarks are used to identify and distinguish goods.
      3. Trademarks are usually not generic or descriptive words.
   B. Trademark Revision Act of 1988
      1. "Intent to use" provision
      2. 3-year period from notification to use
   C. Trademark invalidation
      1. A trademark may be invalidated through cancellation proceedings.
      2. A trademark may be invalidated through cleaning-out procedure.
      3. A trademark may be invalidated through abandonment.
      4. A trademark may be invalidated through its acquiring a generic meaning.
   D. Avoiding the pitfalls
      1. Never select a corporate name or a mark without first doing a trademark search.
      2. If your attorney says you have a potential problem with a mark, trust that judgment.
      3. Seek a coined or a fanciful name or mark before you settle for a descriptive or highly suggestive one.
      4. Whenever marketing or other considerations dictate the use of a name or a mark that is highly suggestive of the product, select a distinctive logotype of the descriptive or suggestive words.
      5. Avoid abbreviations and acronyms wherever possible, and when no alternative is acceptable, select a distinctive logotype in which the abbreviation or acronym appears.
   E. Trade secrets
      1. Competitive information (i.e. customer lists, plans, research and development, techniques)
      2. Extends coverage to both ideas and their expression
      3. Trade secrets cannot be known by competitors, the business would lose significant advantages if they were divulged, and the business has taken reasonable steps to protect the secrets

IV. Bankruptcy
   A. Some warning signs of bankruptcy
      1. There is no real record of how the company's finances are being spent.
      2. The company officers are too busy or inefficient to keep a proper eye on the books.
      3. The company is drawing emergency funds from the officer or family.
      4. Inventory is liquidated to produce rapid cash.

5. Contracts are accepted below standard price to generate cash.
   6. The bank wants loans subordinated.
B. The Bankruptcy Act
   1. It ensures that the property of the debtor is distributed fairly to the creditors.
   2. It protects creditors from having debtors unfairly reduce their actual assets.
   3. It protects the debtors from extreme demands by the creditors.
C. Chapter 7: Straight bankruptcy
   1. This requires the debtor to surrender all property to a trustee appointed by the court.
   2. The assets are sold, and the creditors are paid equally out of the proceeds, and the debtor is released from his/her obligations.
   3. The liquidation may be voluntary or involuntary
      a. Voluntary bankruptcy is achieved when the debtor files a petition with the court.
      b. An involuntary bankruptcy entails the creditors forcing the debtor into bankruptcy
         1. Must be 12 or more creditors with at least three of them having a total of $5,000 of claims
         2. Fewer than twelve creditors with one or more creditors having a claim of $5,000 against the debtor
D. Chapter 11: Reorganization
   1. This is the most common form of bankruptcy.
   2. The debtor attempts to formulate a plan to pay a portion of the debts, have the remaining sum discharged, and continue to stay in operation
      a. The plan must separate the different creditors into "urgency of payment" categories.
      b. The plan must establish how each creditor is to be paid.
      c. The plan must state which of the debtors' claims are getting slighted by the program.
      d. The plan must guarantee equal treatment for all the creditors in each particular class.
E. Chapter 13: Adjustment of debts
   1. Individuals do not have to declare bankruptcy.
   2. The debtors are allowed to pay their debts in installments.
   3. The debtors are protected by the federal court.
   4. The petition must be made voluntarily
      a. The individuals must have unsecured debts of less than $100,000 or secured debts of less than $350,000 to be eligible.
      b. The creditors are not allowed to file a Chapter 13 proceeding.
   5. The debtor files a plan describing the handling of his/her debts
      a. The plan must describe the turnover of future revenue toward the completion of the plan.
      b. The plan must describe the full payments in deferred cash payments of all claims entitled to priority.

c. The plan must show the intention of equal payment of each claim within a particular class.
   d. The plan must show payment within three years unless the courts extend it to five years.
   e. The courts can release the debtor from his or her obligations if it feels that the noncompletion of that obligation was not the debtor's fault.

SUGGESTED ANSWERS FOR DISCUSSION QUESTIONS (END OF CHAPTER)

1. In your own words, what is a patent? Of what value is a patent to an entrepreneur? What benefits does it provide?

A patent is the government's attempt to prevent the exploitation of product or concept pioneers. It is the only way to provide innovative persons a guarantee that they will receive the fruits of their labor. The patent is invaluable to the entrepreneur because it allows him/her to compete innovatively with much larger organizations. The patent also helps protect the entrepreneur from unfair manipulation by his/her larger competitors. A patent allows an innovator time to capitalize and receive a fair return on his/her investment. A patent provides a person with a chance of legal recourse against any infringements of his/her rights.

2. What are four basic rules that entrepreneurs should remember about securing a patent?

(1) Pursue patents that are broad, commercially significant, and offer a strong position.
(2) Prepare a patent plan in detail. This plan should outline the costs to develop and market the innovation as well as analyze the competition and technological similarities to your idea.
(3) Have your actions relate to your original patent plan. This does not mean a plan cannot be changed. However, it is wise to remain close to the plan during the early stages of establishing the patent. Later, the path that is prepared may change, e.g., licensing out the patent versus keeping it for yourself.
(4) Establish an infringement budget. Patent rights are effective only if potential infringers fear legal damages. Thus, it is important to prepare a realistic budget for prosecuting violations of the patent.

3. When can a patent be declared invalid? Cite two examples.

A patent can be declared invalid when it is challenged in court. An example is when the patent holder waited an unreasonable length of time before asserting his or her rights. Another example is when other parties are able to prove that the patent itself fails to meet tests of patentability.

4. If a patent is infringed upon by a competitor, what action can the patent holder take? Explain in detail.

The infringement of a patent can be a very costly ordeal. When planning of the patent is performed, the holder should account for infringement costs. These funds will be used to legally challenge the violator. The patent should first be examined to determine if it will withstand legal challenge and be worth the costs of the fight. The challenge may entail a very sizable legal fee. If the process is successful, the patent holder may collect infringement damages plus court costs. The infringer can be held liable for all profits of the infringement, plus legal fees. The court may decide to award the infringee up to three times the damages.

5. *In your own words, what is a copyright? What benefits does a copyright provide?*

    A copyright is the right of a person to hold exclusive rights to protect his/her work. These works may be literary or artistic productions. An idea may not be copyrighted, but the means by which the idea is expressed may be copyrighted. For example, books, periodicals, motion pictures, and computer programs may be copyrighted. The copyright provides the legal security that the works of the author will not be copied. Therefore, the profits from the work will, if not infringed upon, be directed toward the author.

6. *How much protection does a copyright afford the owner? Can any of the individual's work be copied without paying a fee? Explain in detail. If there is an infringement of the copyright, what legal resources does the owner have?*

    Under the copyright law, anyone who violates the rights of the author is liable for infringement, although this infringement is difficult to determine because of the "fair use" doctrine. This doctrine allows certain groups of people to reproduce the material without infringement of the author. The author's work may be reproduced for the purpose of criticism, comment, news reporting, teaching, scholarship, or research. If the author is infringed upon, the author may legally collect actual damages, plus any profits received by the violator.

7. *In your own words, what is a trademark? Why are generic or descriptive names or words not given as trademarks?*

    A trademark is a unique way of having a company identified without always having the company's name printed out. A trademark is a unique logo or symbol that goes along with a certain company. For personal names or generic words to be trademarked, they have to be suggestive or fanciful or linked to a specific design.

8. *When may a trademark be invalidated? Explain.*

    Four ways in which a trademark may be invalidated:
    (1) Cancellation proceedings: Third party's challenge to the mark's distinctiveness within five years of its issuance.
    (2) Cleaning-out procedure: Failure of a trademark owner to file an affidavit stating that it is in use or justifying its lack of use within six years of registration.
    (3) Abandonment: Nonuse of a trademark for two consecutive years without justification or a statement regarding abandonment of the trademark.
    (4) Generic meaning: Allowance of a trademark to represent a general grouping of products or services. For example, Kleenex has come to represent tissue, cellophane

has come to represent plastic wrap, and scotch tape has come to represent transparent tape. Xerox is currently seeking, through national advertising, to avoid having its name used to represent copier machines.

9. ***What are three of the pitfalls that individuals should avoid when seeking a trademark?***
Never select a corporate name or a mark without first doing a trademark search. If your attorney says you have a potential problem with a mark, trust that judgment. Seek a coined or a fanciful name or mark before you settle for a descriptive or a highly suggestive one.

10. ***How can an entrepreneur find out if the business is going bankrupt? What are three early warning signs?***
The entrepreneur should look out for new competition or competition that seems to be generations ahead. Another indicator is when retailers always seem to be overstocked. Three warning signs are:
   (1) Financial management is lax. No one knows how the company's money is spent.
   (2) Company officers are too busy to keep tabs on the bookkeeping and have trouble providing information or documentation of corporate transactions to the accountant.
   (3) Officers and family make repeated emergency loans to the company. This usually means the business cannot get credit from banks.

11. ***What type of protection does Chapter 7 offer to a bankrupt entrepreneur?***
Chapter 7 protects debtors from extreme demands by creditors. After the debtor's assets have been liquidated, the balance of the debts, except for certain exceptions, are then discharged, and the debtor is relieved of his/her obligations.

12. ***What type of protection does Chapter 11 offer to a bankrupt entrepreneur? Why do many people prefer Chapter 11 to Chapter 7?***
It allows the debtor to keep his/her business in operation while paying a portion of his/her debts and having the remaining sum discharged. People prefer Chapter 11 to Chapter 7 because they are able to keep their business and possibly recover and start to earn a profit again.

13. ***What type of protection does Chapter 13 offer to a bankrupt entrepreneur? How does Chapter 13 differ from Chapter 7 or Chapter 11?***
Chapter 13 allows people to avoid declaring bankruptcy, pay their debts in installments, and be protected by the federal court. Chapter 13 is different because bankruptcy does not have to be declared, and it is a voluntary petition only.

TEACHING NOTES FOR END-OF-CHAPTER CASES

CASE: A PATENT MATTER   (Answers to Questions)

1. ***Given the nature of the industry, how valuable will a patent be to Tom? Explain.***
    A patent would not be useful in Tom's case. Even though it is commonplace in this industry to seek a patent, Tom's resources probably aren't good enough to fight court battles. In addition, he makes the point that it will take the competition four years to catch up with him. At that time he hopes to have made further improvements, which would make a patent meaningless.

2. ***If Tom does get a patent, can he bring action against infringers? Will it be worth the time and expense? Why or why not?***
    Tom will need three years in order to obtain a patent. If a competitor meets or exceeds his invention during this time, Tom will have wasted his time and effort. Also, Tom will need the resources to fight possible court battles. He doesn't seem to be in the position to do this.

3. ***What do you think Tom should do? Why?***
    Tom should implement his new technology in whatever way is most beneficial to himself. He can sell his technology to an industry leader for money and possible employment. Or, he can begin his own business. After he is established, he will then be in a position to make improvements and seek patents.

CASE: ALL SHE NEEDS IS A LITTLE BREATHING ROOM

1. ***What type of bankruptcy agreement would you recommend? Why?***
    Recommend Chapter 13 bankruptcy. Chapter 13 would allow Debbie to reorganize her debt structure with the least amount of harm to her credit rating.

2. ***Why would you not recommend the other types of bankruptcy? Be complete in your answer.***
    Chapter 7 requires liquidation of the business. Debbie feels that the business can survive if given one more year. Chapter 11 is reorganization, and this is not necessary. Since Debbie feels the business can pay all of its bills eventually, Chapter 11 will only serve to harm Debbie's credit rating.

3. ***In selling the creditors on your recommendation, what arguments would you use?***
    In selling Debbie's creditors on Chapter 13, the main argument is Debbie's suggestion that giving her more time is the only situation in which everyone can win. But her creditors see only a failing business with their money being lost. For her to get them to accept this, she needs convincing facts on sales and why this will turn a profit. She needs this not only for her creditors, but for her own decisions. A feeling that the business will

succeed is not enough. Continuing with a losing proposition will only show arrogance and poor judgment.

ADDITIONAL EXPERIENTIAL EXERCISE

"Applying for a Patent?"

The students are to come up with their own concept or process that they would like to see patented. Then, they are to prepare a patent application for submission to the Patent and Trademark Office. The patent application should include the elements of specification and claims. Indicate within the plan how you intend to deal with infringement of the patent. Also, remember the five rules of securing a patent. The plan should accommodate adequate detail to actually apply for and be granted a patent. The idea does not necessarily have to be sent off, but the preparation of the project should enable the students to learn a good deal about patents and team work. You never know; one might come up with the idea that makes his/her fortune.

CHAPTER 14

SOURCES OF CAPITAL FOR ENTREPRENEURS

CHAPTER OUTLINE

I. Debt Versus Equity
   A. Debt
      1. Involves a payback of funds plus a fee for use of money
   B. Equity
      1. Involves the sale of some of the ownership in the venture

II. Debt Financing
   A. Short-term borrowing (one year or less)
   B. Repaid out of proceeds from sale
   C. Long-term debt (one to five years)
   D. Sources
      1. Commercial banks
         a. Advantages
            1. No relinquishment of ownership
            2. More borrowing allows for potentially greater return on investment
            3. During periods of low interest rates, opportunity cost is justified
         b. Disadvantages
            1. Regular interest payments
            2. Intensified continual cash-flow problems
            3. Heavy use of debt can inhibit growth and development
      2. Trade credit
         a. Given by suppliers who sell goods on account
         b. Must be paid in 30 to 90 days
      3. Accounts receivable financing
         a. Short-term financing
         b. Requires collateral
      4. Factoring
         a. Sale of accounts receivable
      5. Finance companies
         a. Asset-based lenders

III. Equity Financing
   A. Require sharing ownership and profit with the funding source
   B. Sources
      1. Public offerings
         a. Raising money through the sale of securities on the public market
         b. Advantages
            1. Size of capital amount

                2. Liquidity
                3. Value
                4. Image
            c. Disadvantages
                1. Cost
                2. Disclosure
                    a. History and nature of company
                    b. Capital structure
                    c. Description of any material contracts
                    d. Description of securities being registered
                    e. Audited financial statements
                3. Requirements
                4. Shareholder pressure
        2. Private placements
            a. Regulation D
                1. Eased reports required for selling stock
                    a. Rule 504a-placements of less than $500,000
                    b. Rule 504-placements up to $1 million
                    c. Rule 505-placements of up to $5 million
                    d. Rule 506-placements in excess of $5 million

IV. The Venture Capital Market
    A. Financial services
        1. Capital for start-up
        2. Market research for marketing department
        3. Management consulting
        4. Contact with prospective people
        5. Assistance in negotiating
        6. Counseling and guidance
    B. Recent developments
        1. Growth of venture capital
            a. 1991-1992 marked a resurgence to $2.55 billion
            b. By 1995, increased to $3.8 billion
        2. Trends
            a. Pension institutions are becoming the predominant investors
            b. Funds are more specialized and less homogeneous
            c. Feeder funds are emerging
            d. Smaller start-up investments are drying up
            e. No legal environment
    C. Dispelling some myths
        1. Venture capital firms want to own control of your company and tell you how to run it
            a. They want the entrepreneur and management team to run it profitably
        2. Venture capitalists are satisfied with a reasonable return on investment

          a. If there is a high degree of risk, there must be a high return on investment
      3. Venture capitalists are quick to invest
          a. It takes a long time to raise venture capital
      4. Venture capitalists are interested in backing new ideas or high-technology inventions; management is a secondary consideration
          a. Venture capitalists back only good management
      5. Venture capitalists need only basic summary information before they make an investment
          a. A detailed, organized business plan is a must
    D. Venture capitalist objectives
      1. Concerned with return on investment
      2. Measure the product, service, and management of a business

V. Criteria for Evaluating New-Venture Proposals
    A. Entrepreneur's personality
    B. Entrepreneur's experience
    C. Characteristics of the product or service
    D. Characteristics of the market
    E. Financial consideration
    F. Nature of the venture team
    G. Evaluation process
      1. Stage 1: initial screening
      2. Stage 2: evaluation of business plan
      3. Stage 3: oral presentation
      4. Stage 4: final evaluation
    H. Recent studies on venture capitalist's criteria

VI. Evaluating the Venture Capitalist
    A. Questions asked
      1. Does the venture capitalist understand the proposal?
      2. Is the individual familiar with the business?
      3. Is the person someone with whom the entrepreneur can work?

VII. Informal Risk Capital--Angel Financing
    A. Investors who have already made money now seek to support young promising ventures = "Angels"
    B. Angels invest $10 billion a year in 30,000-40,000 companies

VIII. Summary

CHAPTER OBJECTIVES

1. To differentiate between debt and equity as methods of financing.

2. To examine commercial loans and public stock offerings as sources of capital.
3. To discuss private placements as an opportunity for equity capital.
4. To study the market for venture capital and to review venture capitalists' evaluation criteria for new ventures.
5. To discuss the importance of evaluating venture capitalists for a proper selection.
6. To examine the existing informal risk-capital market.

CHAPTER SUMMARY

Every entrepreneur planning a new venture should be aware that there are numerous combinations of financial packages available for start-up capital. By knowing this and by understanding the various sources, the entrepreneur can eliminate some of the frustration involved in finding start-up capital.

Many entrepreneurs feel that debt financing is necessary. Debt financing is short-term borrowing (one year or less). There are many different sources of debt financing, including commercial banks, trade credits, accounts receivable financing, factoring, and finance companies. On the other hand, equity financing is also available, although this type of financing does require the relinquishment of partial ownership to avoid borrowing. There are two major sources of equity: financing public offerings and raising capital through the sale of securities on the public market.

Besides these equity fundings, the venture capital market is another way of raising capital. The venture capitalists are experienced professionals who provide a full range of financial services for new and growing ventures. The venture capital market grew rapidly in the 1980s. In fact, by early 1985, the total pool was about $16.5 billion. However, 1989 and 1990 brought about a decrease in available capital ($2.4 billion). However, 1991-1992 saw a resurgence in venture capital to $3.8 billion by 1995. Despite all the capital available through the venture capitalists, entrepreneurs tend to avoid this route. This is mainly due to the prevalent myths about the venture capitalist. But if entrepreneurs do decide to take this route, they should be prepared to be evaluated and answer a lot of questions concerning themselves and their business. However, they in turn have the opportunity to evaluate the venture capitalist, which would be a wise thing to do.

Still, there is another route entrepreneurs can choose to raise capital: the information risk capital. These are people who have already made their money and now seek to help promising new ventures financially.

To conclude, it can be very frustrating for new ventures to come up with start-up capital. But knowing the sources or right names available for help can make things a lot easier.

LECTURE NOTES

SOURCES OF CAPITAL FOR ENTREPRENEURS

I. Debt Versus Equity

A. Debt financing--The use of debt to finance a new venture involves a *payback* of the funds plus a fee (interest) for the use of the money.
   1. Short-term debt: one year or less is often required for working capital and is repaid out of the proceeds from sales.
   2. Long-term debt: term loans of one to five years or long-term loans maturing in more than five years. Used to finance the purchase of property or equipment with the purchased asset serving as collateral for the loans.
B. Sources of debt financing
   1. *Commercial banks*: Most common source. Most bank loans are secured by receivables, inventories, or other assets. Banks offer services such as: computerized payroll preparation, letters of credit, international services, lease financing, and money market accounts.
   2. *Trade credit*: Credit given by suppliers who sell goods on account. Most cases must be paid in 30 to 90 days.
   3. *Finance companies*: Asset-based lenders who loan money against assets such as receivables, inventory, and equipment.
   4. *Factoring*: The sale of accounts receivables at a discounted value. Under a standard agreement the factor will buy the client's receivables outright, without recourse, as soon as the client creates them by its shipment of goods to customers.
   5. *Accounts receivable financing*: Short-term financing that involves either the pledge of receivables as collateral for a loan or the sale of receivables (factoring). Either notification/nonnotification.
      a. Notification: The purchaser of goods is informed that his/her account has been assigned to the bank.
      b. Nonnotification: The borrower collects his/her accounts as usual and then pays off the bank loan.
   6. Other financial sources include equity instruments
      a. Loans with warrants provide the investor with the right to buy stock at a fixed price at some future date.
      b. Convertible debentures are unsecured loans that can be converted into stock.
      c. Preferred stock is equity that gives investors a preferred place among the creditors in the event the venture is dissolved.
      d. Common stock is the most basic form of ownership. Stock carries the right to vote for the board of directors.
C. Five common questions an entrepreneur will have to answer in securing a bank loan
   1. What do you plan to do with the money?
   2. How much do you need?
   3. When do you need it?
   4. How long will you need it?
   5. How will you repay the loan?
D. Advantages of debt financing
   1. There is no relinquishment of ownership
   2. More borrowing allows for potentially greater return on equity

The Dryden Press

3. During periods of low interest rates, the opportunity cost is justified since the cost of borrowing is low
E. Disadvantages of debt financing
1. There are regular interest payments (monthly)
2. Continual cash-flow problems can be intensified because of payback responsibility
3. Heavy use of debt can inhibit growth and development

II. Equity Financing
A. Equity financing: Equity capital is money invested in the venture with no legal obligation to repay the principal amount or pay interest on it.
B. Sources of equity capital
1. *Public offerings:* Going public is a term used to refer to a corporation's raising capital through the sale of securities on the public markets.
2. *Advantages*
   a. Size of capital amount
   b. Liquidity
   c. Value
   d. Image
3. **Disadvantages**
   a. Cost
   b. Disclosure
   c. Requirements
   d. Shareholder pressure
2. *Private placements:* SEC adopted Regulation D, which eased the regulations for reports and statements required for selling stock to private parties, friends, employees, customers, relatives, local professionals.
Regulation D's three exemptions
   a. Rule 504a: placements of less than $500,000. There are no special disclosure/information requirements and no limits on the kind or type of purchasers.
   b. Rule 504: placements up to $1 million. Again, no specific disclosure/information requirements.
   c. Rule 505: placements of up to $5 million. Sales of securities can be made to not more than 35 nonaccredited purchasers and to an unlimited number of accredited purchasers.
   d. Rule 506: there may be no more than 35 nonaccredited purchasers and an unlimited number of accredited purchasers. However, the nonaccredited purchasers must be "sophisticated" in investment matters.
3. *Securities and exchange commission* (SEC): The entrepreneur must follow the state laws pertaining to the raising of such funds and must meet the requirements set forth by the SEC. The SEC requires the filling of a registration statement that includes a complete prospectus on the company. The SEC then reviews the registration, ensuring that there is full disclosure before giving permission to proceed.

III. Venture Capital Market
　A. Financial services offered
　　1. Capital for start-ups and expansion
　　2. Market research and strategy for those businesses that do not have their own marketing departments
　　3. Management consulting functions and management audit and evaluation
　　4. Contacts with prospective customers, suppliers, and other important business people
　　5. Assistance in negotiating technical agreements
　　6. Help in establishing management and accounting controls
　　7. Help in employee recruitment and development of employee agreements
　　8. Help in risk management and the establishment of an effective insurance program
　　9. Counseling and guidance in complying with government regulations
　B. Recent developments
　　By early 1985 the total pool was about $16.5 billion. 1989 showed a decrease to $3.1 billion, and in 1990 it decreased further to $2.4 billion. However, 1991-92 witnessed a resurgence with $3.8 billion by 1995.
　C. Five major trends in venture capital field
　　1. Pension institutions are becoming the prodominant investors.
　　2. Funds are more specialized and less homogeneous.
　　2. Feeder funds are emerging.
　　3. Smaller start-up investments are drying up.
　　4. There is a new legal environment.
　D. Myths
　　1. Venture capital firms want to own control of your company and tell you how to run the business.
　　2. Venture capitalists are satisfied with a reasonable return on investments.
　　3. Venture capitalists are quick to invest.
　　4. Venture capitalists are interested in backing new ideas or high-technology inventions; management is a secondary consideration.
　　5. Venture capitalists need only basic information before they make an investment.
　E. Criteria for evaluating new-venture proposals
　　1. Entrepreneur's personality
　　2. Entrepreneur's experience
　　3. Characteristics of the product or service
　　4. Characteristics of the market
　　5. Financial considerations
　　6. Nature of the venture team
　F. Five major aspects of the business plan
　　1. Size of the proposal
　　2. Financial projections
　　3. Recovery of the investment
　　4. Competitive advantage
　　5. Management of the company

G. Four common stages of the evaluation process
   1. Initial screening
   2. Evaluation of the business plan
   3. Oral presentation
   4. Final evaluation
H. Evaluating the venture capitalist by asking the right questions
   1. Does the venture capital firm invest in your industry?
   2. What is it like to work with the venture capital firm?
   3. What experience does the partner doing your deal have, and what is his/her clout within the firm?
   4. How much time will the partner spend with your company if you run into trouble?
   5. How healthy is the venture capital fund, and how much has been invested?
   6. Are the investment goals of the venture capitalists consistent with your own?
   7. Have the venture firm and the partner championing your deal been through any economic downturn?

IV. Informal Risk Capital (Angel Financing). Someone who has already made his/her money and now seeks out promising young ventures to support financially. The pool of today's "angel capital" is five times the amount in the institutional venture capital market. Over $10 billion is invested annually.

SUGGESTED ANSWERS FOR DISCUSSION QUESTIONS
(END OF CHAPTER)

1. ***Figure 14.1 shows that entrepreneurs prefer venture capital when getting started but five years later prefer to raise capital through public offerings. What is the logic behind this strategy?***

   Entrepreneurs prefer venture capitalists when starting because they provide capital for start-ups. Venture capitalists assist them in other areas of operations. With public offerings the cost is higher than with other sources of capital. There are requirements that drain large amounts of time along with a disclosure which gives away private information.

2. ***What are the benefits and drawbacks of equity and debt financing? Briefly discuss both.***

   One major benefit of equity is that there is no legal obligation to repay the principal amount or pay interest on it. There are two types of equity financing: public offerings and private placements. By going public you can raise large sums of capital in a short time. Other advantages include liquidity, value on stock, and image. Along with advantages there are disadvantages, which include cost, disclosure requirements, and shareholder pressure. Private placements allow selling stock to private parties. Debt financing involves a payback of the funds plus a fee for the use of the money. Advantages are: no relinquishment of ownership, greater return on equity, and low interest rates.

Disadvantages include: regular interest payments, possible cash-flow problems because of payback responsibility, and heavy use of debt, which can inhibit growth and development.

3. *Identify and describe four types of debt financing.*
   (1) Commercial banks--This is the most common source. Most bank loans are secured by receivables, inventory, or other assets.
   (2) Trade credit--Credit given by suppliers.
   (3) Factoring--The sale of accounts receivable at a discounted value; under a standard agreement the factor will buy the client's receivables outright.
   (4) Finance companies--Asset-based lenders who loan money against assets such as receivables, inventories, and equipment.

4. *If a new venture has its choice between long-term debt and equity financing, which would you recommend? Why?*
   Equity financing should be recommended because it would give the entrepreneur the chance to start off the small business with a big debt. Long-term debt matures in five years, which isn't adequate time for the business to show a large profit. Also, long-term debt is used mainly to finance the purchase of property or equipment.

5. *Why would a venture capitalist be more interested in buying a convertible debenture for $50,000 than in lending the new business $50,000 at 10 percent?*
   With a convertible debenture the venture capitalist would have an opportunity to own stock in the company, whereas the loan would not offer that opportunity.

6. *What are some of the advantages of going public? What are some of the disadvantages?*

Advantages	Disadvantages
Size of capital amount	Cost
Liquidity	Disclosure
Value	Requirements
Image	Shareholder pressure

7. *Why do entrepreneurs look forward to the day when they can take their company public?*
   By going public, the entrepreneur will be able to raise large sums of capital in a short period of time. It will provide liquidity for owners since they can readily sell their stock. Also, it allows value to be placed on the corporation. Lastly, the image of going public is stronger in the eyes of suppliers, financiers, and customers.

8. *What is the objective of Regulation D?*
   Regulation D eases the regulations for reports and statements required for selling stock to private parties.

The Dryden Press

9. *If a person inherited $100,000 and decided to buy stock in a new venture through a private placement, how would Regulation D affect this investor?*

There are no special disclosure/information requirements and no limits on the kind or type of purchasers.

10. *How large is the venture capital pool today? Is it growing or shrinking?*

The venture capital pool had about $16.5 billion in 1985. The venture capital pool decreased to $2.4 billion in 1990; however, 1992 witnessed a resurgence with $3.8 billion by 1995.

11. *Is it easier or more difficult to get new-venture financing today? Why?*

It is more difficult to get new-venture financing because smaller start-up investments are drying up. More money is being allocated to salvaging or turning around problem ventures. Also, venture capital funds lack professionals who have experience with start-ups and first-stage ventures.

12. *Some entrepreneurs do not like to seek new-venture financing because they feel venture capitalists are greedy. In your opinion, is this true? Do these capitalists want too much?*

No, when venture capitalists invest in a business they are taking a very high risk, and they should be compensated for the risk.

13. *Identify and describe three objectives of venture capitalists.*

Security and payback; return on investment; large returns on investments.

14. *How would a venture capitalist use Figure 14.2 to evaluate an investment? Use an illustration in your answer.*

A venture capitalist would realize the decrease in venture capital by the fifth year and thus seek out investments that produce high returns in the first few years.

15. *Identify and describe four of the most common criteria used by venture capitalists in evaluating a proposal.*
    1. Capable of sustained intense effort--Will the entrepreneur be able to cope with bad times of the business?
    2. Thoroughly familiar with the market--Does the entrepreneur know enough about the market to operate in it?
    3. At least ten times return in 5-10 years--Will the business profits show a return 10 times the amount it started showing?
    4. Demonstrated leadership in past--Has the owner held any leadership roles?

16. *Of what practical value is Table 14.5 to new-venture entrepreneurs?*

Table 14.5 would allow the new-venture capitalist and the owner to see how much return on investment the venture capitalist would get from the business.

17. **In evaluating a new venture, what are the four stages through which a proposal typically goes? Describe each in detail.**
    (1) Initial screening--This is a quick review of the basic venture to see if it meets the venture capitalist's particular interest.
    (2) Evaluation of the business plan--This is a detailed reading of the plan done in order to evaluate the factors mentioned earlier.
    (3) Oral presentation--The entrepreneur will verbally present the plan to the venture capitalist.
    (4) Final evaluation--After analyzing the plan and visiting with suppliers, customers, consultants, and others, the venture capitalist will make a final decision.

18. **An entrepreneur is in the process of contacting three different venture capitalists and asking each to evaluate her new business proposal. What questions should she be able to answer about each of the three?**
    1. Does the venture capital firm invest in your industry?
    2. What is it like to work with this venture capital firm?
    3. What experience does the partner doing your deal have, and what is his/her clout within the firm?
    4. How much time will the partner spend with your company if you run into trouble?
    5. How healthy is the venture capital fund, and how much has been invested?
    6. Are the investment goals of the venture capitalist consistent with your own?
    7. Have the venture firm and the partner championing your deal been through any economic downturns?

19. **An entrepreneur of a new venture has had no success in getting financing from formal venture capitalists. He has now decided to turn to the informal risk-capital market. Who is in this market? How would you recommend the entrepreneur contact these individuals?**
    This type of investor is someone who has already made his/her money and now seeks out promising young entrepreneurs to support financially. They contact these individuals through a network of friends. Also, many states are formulating venture capital networks, which attempt to link informal investors with entrepreneurs and their new or growing ventures.

20. **How likely is it that the informal risk-capital market will grow during the next five years? Defend your answer.**
    The informal risk-capital market will continue to grow and expand especially since various states are making serious efforts to establish networks that bring together potential entrepreneurs and informal investors.

21. **Of all the sources of capital formation, which is ideal? Why?**
    The most ideal source of capital formation is informal risk capital. They are more concerned with nonfinancial returns such as creation of jobs in areas of high

unemployment, development of technology for social needs, urban revitalization, minority or disadvantaged assistance, and personal satisfaction in assisting entrepreneurs.

TEACHING NOTES FOR END-OF-CHAPTER CASES

CASE: LOOKING FOR CAPITAL   (Answers to Questions)

1. *Would a commercial banker be willing to lend money to the Abrams? How much? On what do you base your answer?*

    A commercial bank would not loan the Abrams the total amount. It would loan only a portion. The most it would loan would be $4,000 in addition to the already available $6,000. This is based on the fact that banks tend to loan conservatively, even to existing firms. Since the Abrams mention no collateral other than inventory, the bank must assume that at liquidation the books may only bring 5 to 10 cents on the dollar, $14,000 to $28,000. The Abrams are also asking for a medium-term loan for an expanded product line. Banks prefer short-term, highly secure loans. Since the Abrams' sales are increasing steadily, the bank would probably consider this small loan because there is collateral, but a large, long-term loan would be seen as out of the question.

2. *Would this venture have any appeal for a venture capitalist? Why?*

    Most venture capitalists would not be interested in the Abrams' venture. Their business does not yield the return on investment sought by most capitalists. Venture capitalists generally target a 30 to 60 percent annual return for second stage developments. The Abrams have not even reached break-even after a year in business.

3. *If you were advising the Abrams, how would you recommend they go about seeking additional capital? Be complete in your answer.*

    Make a dual recommendation to the Abrams. They should draw from their existing line of bank credit to meet immediate needs only. By not borrowing more than absolutely necessary, they will not put the added burden of repayment on an already fragile financial situation.

    Secondly, they should seek the additional capital needed for expansion from the informal risk-capital pool. Since the Abrams are in a business that has very loyal, involved customers, they probably could find an individual to invest. The capital needed is not an amount that would be prohibitive to a wealthy person.

CASE: THE $3 MILLION VENTURE

1. *What would be the benefits of raising the $3 million through a private placement? What would be the benefits of raising the money through a venture capitalist?*

    The sale of stock can be made to 35 nonaccredited purchasers and to an unlimited number of accredited purchasers. Thus, the benefit of using a private placement is to gain equity investment from a larger number of people.

A venture capitalist offers the advantage of securing the entire amount ($3 million) from one source. This guarantees the needed capital without the great deal of paperwork that a private placement would require.

2. *Of the two above approaches, which would be best for Charles? Why?*

Due to the number of interested customers that would purchase stock in the new ventures, Charles should pursue the private placement instead of a venture capitalist. The amount of ownership given up to a venture capitalist may be too great, and there is a question of investment by a venture capital firm in Charles' type of business.

3. **What would you recommend that Charles do now? Briefly outline a plan of action he can use in getting the financing process started.**

Charles could pursue a private placement for a portion of the money needed ($2 million, for example). Then, he could secure a loan from the bank for the remaining amount ($1 million). Thus, he would keep the venture balanced between equity and debt; however, the equity side would be stronger.

ADDITIONAL EXPERIENTIAL EXERCISE

"Seeking the Sources"

This project is designed to let students experience how hard it is for entrepreneurs to come up with start-up capital. Various qualified professionals in the financial areas should be sought out for students to experience the different sources of raising capital. The student is required to come up with an outline of a basic business plan and present it to each professional until the student is able to come up with what he/she needs to get started. This might seem simple, but you have to realize that these financial sources know exactly what to look for when evaluating the entrepreneurs. So be precise!

The Dryden Press

PART V

Growth and Development of Entrepreneurial Ventures

Chapter 15 - Strategic Planning for Emerging Ventures

Chapter 16 - Managing Entrepreneurial Growth

Chapter 17 - Global Opportunities for Entrepreneurs

CHAPTER 15

STRATEGIC PLANNING FOR EMERGING VENTURES

CHAPTER OUTLINE

I. The Nature of Planning in Emerging Firms
   A. Understand the venture
   B. Long- and short-range objectives
   C. Alternative courses
   D. Implementation
   E. Analyze and follow up

II. Strategic Planning

III. Key Dimensions Influencing a Firm's Strategic Planning Activities
   A. Demand on strategic manager's time
   B. Speed of decision making
   C. Problems of internal politics
   D. Environmental uncertainty
   E. The entrepreneur's vision
      1. Commitment to an open planning process
      2. Accountability to a corporate conscience
      3. Establishment of a pattern of subordinate participation in the development of the strategic plan

IV. The Lack of Strategic Planning
   A. Reasons
      1. Time scarcity
      2. Lack of knowledge
      3. Lack of expertise
      4. Lack of trust and openness

V. The Value of Strategic Planning
   A. A five-level planning classification
      1. Strategy Level 0 (SL0)
      2. Strategy Level 1 (SL1)
      3. Strategy Level 2 (SL2)
      4. Strategy Level 3 (SL3)
      5. Strategy Level 4 (SL4)
   B. A scarce, fragile commodity in small-business environment
      1. Improved performance is often the result of better planning

VI. Fatal Vision in Strategic Planning
   A. Misunderstanding industry attractiveness
   B. No real competitive advantage
   C. Pursuing an unattainable competitive position
   D. Compromising strategy for growth

VII. Implementing a Strategic Plan
   A. Opportunity management approach
      1. Strategic profile
         a. An evaluation of internal resources
         b. A forecast of external market conditions
         c. An evaluation of company strengths and weaknesses
         d. A formulation of business objectives
      2. Opportunity profile
         a. Action programs are designed
         b. Resources are allocated
         c. Expected results are identified
         d. Implementation and control steps followed
      3. Easy to understand
      4. Adjustable to meet changing conditions
   B. Milestone planning approach
      1. Takes new venture from start-up through strategy reformulation
      2. Three advantages
         a. The use of logical and practical milestones
         b. Avoidance of mistakes caused by failure to consider key parts
         c. A methodology for replanning
      3. Popular with new ventures that are
         a. Technical in nature
         b. Have multiple phases
         c. Involve large sums of money
   C. Strategic model approach
      1. Tends to be more idealistic than realistic
      2. Many find it not flexible enough for their needs
      3. Steps
         a. The decision to plan
         b. Situational analysis
         c. Personal and company objectives
         d. Issue specification
         e. Option generation
         f. Evaluation and selection
         g. Implementation
         h. Control and feedback loop
   D. Multistaged contingency approach
      1. Critical variables

          a. Individual
          b. Venture
          c. Environment
      2. Stages of venture
          a. Pre-venture
          b. Start-up
          c. Early growth
          d. Harvest
      3. Career perspective
          a. Early
          b. Middle
          c. Late

VIII. The Nature of Operational Planning
    A. Incorporates all factors in strategic planning and the implementation tools
    B. Tools most widely used
      1. Budgets
          a. Used to establish future plans in financial terms
      2. Policies
          a. Fundamental guides for the venture
      3. Procedures
          a. Policies standardized as a continuing method

IX. Summary

CHAPTER OBJECTIVES

1. To introduce the importance of planning to an entrepreneurial venture
2. To discuss the nature of strategic planning
3. To examine the key dimensions that influence a firm's planning process
4. To discuss some of the reasons why entrepreneurs do not carry out strategic planning
5. To relate some of the benefits of strategic planning
6. To examine four of the most common approaches used by entrepreneurs in implementing a strategic plan
7. To review the nature of operational planning for a venture

CHAPTER SUMMARY

This chapter deals primarily with strategic planning for emerging ventures. Some of the important topics this chapter discusses are the importance of planning to the entrepreneur, the entrepreneur's personality and the way it affects his or her business, problems that entrepreneurs have when trying to plan, and benefits of strategic planning. It also examines some approaches used, and the chapter discusses a related topic known as operational planning for a venture.

The major way for a new venture to direct its business is strategic planning. The complexity of the business will determine how much of a systematic approach the firm must assume.

There are five basic steps that should be followed when a firm starts the planning process: (1) understand the venture, (2) establish long- and short-range objectives, (3) outline alternative courses of actions, (4) implement a plan of action, and (5) take follow-up action.

The key dimensions influencing a firm's strategic planning activities include: the increased demand on a manager's time; the expected speed of decision making; problems with internal politics; increased environmental uncertainty; and an entrepreneur's vision or ego. The understanding of the entrepreneur's vision will help determine the look or form of the venture plan. By the use of strategic planning, ideas can be put into action. The process of transforming these visions into actions reflects three basic steps. Because of many entrepreneurs' suspicions of planning, the first step should be a commitment to an open planning process. The second step should utilize a corporate conscience, and this is very effectively done with an advisory board. Lastly, the full use of key subordinates should be of primary concern to the new-venture operation.

Lack of strategic planning has a great impact on some new ventures that are just starting up. Reasons for lack of planning can sometimes be attributed to lack of time, lack of knowledge, lack of expertise, and lack of trust.

Strategic planning is thought by many entrepreneurs not to be worth their while, but studies show that it really is. In one study, five levels of planning were established. Twenty percent of the firms that used the lowest level of planning failed, whereas only 8 percent of the firms that used the highest level of planning failed.

The actual execution of a strategy is extremely important, and four fatal flaws need to be pointed out. These are: misunderstanding industry attractiveness; no real competitive advantage; unattainable competitive pursuit; and compromising strategy for growth.

Four approaches can be used when formulating a strategic plan: opportunity management, milestone planning, the strategic model approach, and a multistaged contingency approach.

Opportunity management uses a formal worksheet that can point out the company's strong and weak points on a year-to-year basis. The milestone planning approach uses goals throughout the plan that can be linked together and performed in line one before the other. The strategic model approach uses expert theory as to how the plan should be made and performed. Finally, the contingency model is based on three stages: critical variables; stage of venture; and a career perspective.

The last area that this chapter covers is the nature of operational planning. Because the operational plan takes all of the factors and theories of the strategic plan and puts them to use for the company, it is often viewed as an extension of the strategic plan.

Many areas such as finance, marketing, production, and management should be part of the planning in order to maintain the policies of the strategy. Tools that aid in the operational planning process are planning devices such as budgets. Policies should be used throughout the process as guides, and procedures should be utilized over and over again to maintain a strict planning philosophy.

LECTURE NOTES

STRATEGIC PLANNING FOR EMERGING VENTURES

I. The Nature of Planning in Emerging Firms
   A. There are two major types of planning
      1. Long range planning--Strategic planning is the primary step in determining the future direction of a business.
      2. Operational planning consists of the specific practices that are established to carry out the objectives set forth in the strategic plan.
   B. Influences of planning
      1. The degree of uncertainty
      2. The strength of competition
      3. The experience of the entrepreneur

II. Strategic Planning
   A. There are five basic steps that must be followed in strategic planning
      1. Understand the venture
      2. Establish short-range objectives
      3. Outline alternative courses of action
      4. Implement a plan of action
      5. Analyze the results and take follow-up action

III. Key Dimensions Influencing a Firm's Strategic Planning Activities
   A. The demand on a strategic manager's time increases with the complexity brought about by entrepreneurial growth.
   B. The speed of decision making needs to be improved through better delegation.
   C. The problems of internal politics can be controlled by strategic planning.
   D. The presence of environmental uncertainty increases the need for strategic planning.
   E. Entrepreneur's vision
      1. Planning is the process of transforming entrepreneurial vision and ideas into action. This involves three basic steps
         a. Commitment to an open planning process. Most entrepreneurs are afraid of planning; they fear loss of control and/or flexibility. This, in turn, blocks out other input from knowledgeable people.
         b. Accountability to a corporate conscience. This is often in the form of an advisory board. This committee differs from a board of directors by its lack of legal standing. Its primary objectives are to increase the owner's sensitivity to larger issues of direction and make the owner accountable, although it may be on a voluntary basis.
         c. Establishment of a pattern of subordinate participation in development of the strategic plan. The plan can create energy in the organization, especially when key members in the organization are instrumental in creating the plan.

The Dryden Press

IV. Lack of Strategic Planning
   A. Research has shown a distinct lack of planning on the part of new ventures. There are four basic reasons for the lack of planning.
      1. Time scarcity--Managers have a hard time setting aside time for planning. They are caught up in day-to-day operating problems.
      2. Lack of knowledge--Not many managers have the experience of planning. Many entrepreneurs are also unfamiliar with any planning information sources and how they can be used.
      3. Lack of expertise--Most managers are generalists. They lack the specialized expertise necessary in the planning process.
      4. Lack of trust and openness--Small-business owners are afraid and sensitive about decisions concerning their business. Because of this they are hesitant to formulate a strategic plan that requires employee input or outside consultants.

V. The Value of Strategic Planning
   A. In a research study it was found that the firms that used strategic planning were financially better off than those that did not. These firms were broken down into five levels of planning.
      1. Strategy level 0: No knowledge of next year's sales profitability or profit implementation plans
      2. Strategy level 1: Knowledge of only next year's sales, but no knowledge of upcoming industry sales, company profits, or profit implementation
      3. Strategy level 2: Knowledge of next year's company and industry sales, but no knowledge of company profits or profit implementation plans
      4. Strategy level 3: Knowledge of company and industry sales and anticipated profit, but no profit implementation plans
      5. Strategy level 4: Knowledge of next year's company and industry sales, anticipated company profits, and profit implementation plans
   B. Benefits of long-range planning
      1. Cost savings
      2. Accurate forecasting
      3. Faster decision making
      4. Resource allocation
      5. Improved competition position
      6. Thorough exploration of alternatives

VI. Fatal Vision in Strategic Planning
   A. Misunderstanding industry attractiveness
   B. No real competitive advantage
   C. Pursuing an unattainable competitive position
   D. Compromising strategy for growth

VII. Implementing a Strategic Plan
   A. There are many approaches to implementing a strategic plan. The choice depends on

the entrepreneur's personality and the environment in which the firm operates. There are four basic approaches.
1. Opportunity management is based most heavily on environmental analysis. This process constructs a strategic profile that considers
   a. An evaluation of internal resources that enables the firm to gain maximum advantage from its resources
   b. A forecast of external market conditions
   c. Evaluation of company strengths and weaknesses--Lead from strength, and do what one does best
   d. A formulation of business objectives, including organizing personnel, establishing budgets, formulating schedules, and analyzing financial statements
2. Milestone planning is based on the use of incremental goal attainment that takes a new venture from start-up through strategy reformation. This is popular with new ventures that are technical in nature
   a. Milestone planning advantages are the use of logical and practical milestones
   b. The avoidance of costly mistakes caused by failure to consider key parts of the plan.
   c. A methodology for replanning, based on continuous feedback from the environment
3. A strategic model is sometimes regarded as normative because it represents the order in which strategy experts recommend strategy planning be conducted. One problem with this method is it tends to give an idealistic rather than a realistic outlook
   a. The decision to plan and commit time and money to strategic planning--The decision plan is always based on anticipated positive results.
   b. Situational analysis--This step enables the entrepreneur to gain an understanding of the venture, its current strategy, and potential thrusts or opportunities.
   c. Personal and company objectives are often the entrepreneur's personal objectives for the company. The primary consideration typically is given to objectives such as return on investments, sales growth, productivity, cost containment, and personal acquisition and development.
   d. Issue specification--The entrepreneur reviews the findings of the situational analysis in the context of both personal and company objectives in order to determine problem areas. This review will determine whether or not to continue the strategy.
   e. Option generation identifies those alternatives that might provide a solution to current major problems. Considerations are competencies, resources, values, and financial capabilities.
   f. Evaluation and selection take the alternatives generated in the opinion stage and compare them in terms of relative effectiveness in dealing with key strategic issues.

g. Implementation in setting timetables determines who will be doing what and by what time.
h. Control and feedback loop assures that everything is being done according to plan.
4. Multistaged contingency approach is based on three stages of variables that need to be considered before attempting any strategic plan.
   a. Critical variables
      1. Individual
      2. Venture
      3. Environment
   b. Venture stages
      1. Pre-venture
      2. Start-up
      3. Early growth
      4. Harvest
   c. Career perspective
      1. Early
      2. Middle
      3. Late

VIII. The Nature of Operational Planning
   A. Operational planning refers to short-range planning and establishes procedures to carry out the objectives set forth in the strategic planning in the areas of
      1. Finance
      2. Marketing
      3. Production
      4. Management
      5. Functional policies to attain these goals
   B. Operational planning process--This incorporates all of the factors involved in strategic planning. Some of the tools used in operational planning are
      1. Budgets are planning devices used to establish future plans in financial terms.
      2. Policies are the fundamental guides for ventures as a whole. These are used as guides on day-to-day problems.
      3. Procedures are policies that have been standardized as a continuing method for problems that arise.

SUGGESTED ANSWERS FOR DISCUSSION QUESTIONS
(END OF CHAPTER)

1. ***In what way does an entrepreneur's vision affect the company's strategic plan?***
   To a large degree, venture planning is an extension of the entrepreneur's ego. Planning is the process of transforming entrepreneurial vision and ideas into action. This is done through three basic steps:

(1) Commitment to an open planning process
(2) Accountability to a corporate conscience
(3) Establishment of a pattern of subordinate participation in the development of the strategic plan

2. ***How is the strategy plan of an engineer/scientist entrepreneur likely to be different from that of an entrepreneur whose primary strength is in the manufacturing area?***
In smaller companies, the owner's personal objectives will influence company objectives. The engineer/scientist entrepreneur will tend to develop a strong technological edge, while the entrepreneur whose primary strength is in the manufacturing area will use these skills in determining the company's objectives. Company objectives are chosen to exploit the strengths of the business and sidestep its weaknesses. Primary consideration is usually given to objectives such as return on investment, sales growth, productivity, cost containment, and personal acquisition and development.

3. ***What are the three basic steps involved in transforming entrepreneurial vision and ideas into action?***
    (1) Commitment to an open planning process--Due to suspicions about planning, many entrepreneurs fear the loss of control and/or flexibility. This fear can be the chief obstacle to future success by blocking the ideas of other knowledgeable people.
    (2) Accountability to a corporate conscience--Often this occurs in the form of an advisory board that lacks legal status. Its primary objectives are to increase the owner's sensitivity to larger issues of direction and make the owner accountable, even though it's on a voluntary basis.
    (3) Establishment of a pattern of subordinate participation in the development of the strategic plan--This participation enhances the support for the plan.

4. ***Give three reasons why many entrepreneurs do not like to formulate strategic plans.***
    (1) Time scarcity--Some feel they do not have the time to allocate to planning.
    (2) Lack of knowledge--This may be due to minimal exposure to and knowledge of the planning process.
    (3) Lack of expertise--Many of those who do have the knowledge of the planning process still lack the specialized expertise necessary in the planning process.

5. ***Describe five difficulties that entrepreneurs face in long-range planning.***
    (1) Lack of time available for planning--Many entrepreneurs feel after dealing with the day-to-day needs of a firm that there are not enough hours in a day for long-range planning.
    (2) The cost in time and dollars to do long-range planning properly is often felt to be too expensive.
    (3) Managers who lack experience in and knowledge of planning are a problem.
    (4) The ever-changing political policies create uncertainties for long-range planning.

(5) The difficulty of obtaining accurate and timely data needed for planning will always be with the entrepreneur.

6. *Does strategic planning really pay off for small ventures? Why or why not?*

Yes. Improved performance is often the result of planning. A recent study showed firms recognized cost savings, accurate forecasting, and faster decision making as a result of long-range planning.

7. *A new venture entrepreneur is considering formulation of a strategic plan. However, he is concerned that this effort will have little value for him. Is he right or wrong? Explain.*

Wrong, most of the studies in the last 20 years imply, if not directly state, that planning influences the chances of survival for a venture.

8. *How can an entrepreneur use an opportunity management approach in formulating and implementing a strategic plan? Discuss the process.*

The construction of a strategic profile considers:
(1) an evaluation of internal resources,
(2) a forecast of external market conditions,
(3) an evaluation of company strengths and weaknesses, and
(4) a formulation of business objectives.

On the basis of this strategic profile, an opportunity profile will be constructed. Action programs are designed, resources are allocated, and expected results are identified. Implementation and control steps are next. They include organizing personnel, establishing budgets, formulating schedules, and analyzing financial statements. On the basis of the results, a new strategic profile and/or opportunity profile is constructed, and the process starts over.

9. *What are the advantages of an opportunity management approach to strategic planning?*

The advantages of an opportunity management approach are that it is easy to understand and that implementation can be adjusted to meet changing conditions.

10. *What types of ventures are most likely to profit from an opportunity management approach to strategic planning?*

The types of ventures that are most likely to profit from an opportunity management approach are less technical ventures that must be able to adjust to changing conditions. These ventures lead from strength, by doing what they do best.

11. *How does the milestone planning approach to strategic planning work?*

This approach is based on the use of incremental goal attainment, which takes a new venture from start-up through strategy reformulation. Each step is completed before going to the next step, and all are linked together in an overall strategic plan.

12.   What type of venture might profit from the use of a milestone planning approach? Defend your answer.

The milestone planning approach works well with new ventures that are technical in nature, have multiple phases, and/or involve large sums of money. It is also used when close linkage between milestones or major objectives is needed. Milestone planning is more comprehensive and typically involves a greater investment of time and money than would opportunity management.

13.   Why is the strategic model approach to planning not as popular as the opportunity management or milestone planning approach?

Many ventures find the strategic approach is not flexible enough for their needs. Plus, it tends to be of more value in large rather than in small undertakings.

14.   What benefits does the multi-staged contingency approach offer to new-venture entrepreneurs?

Because the model is based upon the different variables--individual, venture, and environment--the different stages of ventures, and the different career perspectives of entrepreneurs, it allows for a flexible or contingency approach to planning. It helps define strengths and weaknesses. Company objectives are able to be selected so as to exploit the strengths of the business, venture stage, environment, etc. Alternatives can be identified and used when needed.

15.   What is operational planning? What specific tools are used?

Operational planning consists of the specific practices that are established to carry out the objectives set forth in the strategic plan. It is an outgrowth or expansion of the strategic planning process. Some of the tools most widely used are budgets, policies, and procedures.

16.   How does operational planning fit with strategic planning?

The overall planning process incorporates all of the factors involved in strategic planning and the implementation tools of operational planning.

TEACHING NOTES FOR END-OF-CHAPTER CASES

CASE: THE BANKER'S REQUEST   (Answers to Questions)

1.   In Elizabeth's case, what approach would you recommend she use in writing her plan? Why?

She should transform her vision into action steps. Her commitment to an open planning process will help her understand the entire business better. Thus, she needs to analyze all of her previous operations in order to project the addition of a fourth restaurant. The milestone planning approach is based upon the use of incremental goal attainment and would be the most appropriate approach for Elizabeth.

2. *What specific steps should Elizabeth take in writing her plan? Will her current idea of what to include in the plan be of any value?*

After analyzing her environment, Elizabeth needs to set out her long-range and short-range objectives with alternative courses of action listed. Then she can examine each factor of her operation--marketing, finances, location, employees, etc.--and measure its strengths and weaknesses. Figure 13.2 in the text would be an excellent chart to use. Elizabeth's current idea needs to be expanded, but the financials would be valuable to use.

3. *What benefits would a strategic plan have for Elizabeth's firm? Be complete in your answer.*

The benefits of a strategic plan would include: cost savings, accurate forecasting, faster decision making, better allocation of resources, improved competitive position, and a thorough exploration of alternatives.

CASE: A TWO-PHASED APPROACH

1. *If you were advising Diego, what approach would you recommend he use in putting together his strategic plans? Why?*

An opportunity management approach would be ideal for Diego. Although any one of the approaches presented in the chapter could be used by Diego (and a case could be made for each one), the opportunity management approach would allow him to construct a strategic profile and an opportunity profile.

2. *What advantages would your proposed approach have over other approaches? Compare and contrast at least three approaches.*

As mentioned in question 1, the opportunity management approach will allow Diego the chance to create a strategic profile and then an opportunity profile. However, a comparison of the approaches could produce advantages for each one. Students should present a chart comparing the strategic planning approaches and list the distinct advantages of each alternative for Diego.

3. *How would your approach allow Diego to incorporate expansion planning into the overall plan?*

In the opportunity profile, there is a section for "action programs." These could always be expanded.

ADDITIONAL EXPERIENTIAL EXERCISE

"Focus on Strategic Planning"

Create a survey for small business. Ask key questions such as: Do you use strategic planning? If so, what type: opportunity management, milestone approach, or a strategic model approach? Add questions that you feel are appropriate. Then administer the survey to at least seven small businesses that have been in existence by the same owner for three years or more to find out their strategic planning and/or lack of planning. Compare your findings (1 to 2 pages). Include your perceptions as to what the future holds for these firms and why. Focus more on the growing firms.

CHAPTER 16

MANAGING ENTREPRENEURIAL GROWTH

CHAPTER OUTLINE

I. Introduction

II. Stages of Development
   A. New-venture development
   B. Start-up activities
   C. Growth
   D. Stabilization of the business
   E. Innovation or decline

III. Understanding the Entrepreneurial Company
   A. The entrepreneurial mind
   B. Building the adaptive firm
      1. Share the entrepreneur's vision
      2. Increase the perception of opportunity
      3. Institutionalize change as the venture's goals
      4. Instill the desire to be innovative
         a. Reward system
         b. An environment that allows for failure

IV. The Transition: From an Entrepreneurial Style to a Managerial Approach
   A. Hofer and Charan seven-step process
   B. Balancing the focus
   C. The self-management concept
      1. Self-observation
      2. Self-established goals
      3. Cueing strategies
      4. Rehearsal
      5. Self-applied consequences

V. Understanding the Growth Stage
   A. Key factors during the growth stage
      1. Control
      2. Responsibility
      3. Tolerance of failure
         a. Moral failure
         b. Personal failure
         c. Uncontrollable failure

      B. Managing paradox and contradiction
         1. Bureaucratization vs. decentralization
         2. Environment vs. strategy
         3. Strategic emphases on quality vs. cost vs. innovation
      C. Confronting the growth wall
         1. Get the facts
         2. Create a growth task force
         3. Plan for growth
         4. Staff for growth
         5. Maintain a growth culture
         6. Use an advisory board
      D. Growth and decision making
         1. Use of external resources
         2. Responsibility charting
VI. Effective delegation
      A. View thinking as a strategy
      B. Schedule large blocks of uninterrupted time
      C. Stay focused on relevant topics
      D. Record, sort, and save thoughts

VII. Summary

CHAPTER OBJECTIVES

1. To discuss the five stages of a typical venture life cycle: development, start-up, growth, stabilization, and innovation or decline
2. To explore the elements involved with an entrepreneurial firm
3. To survey the ways in which entrepreneurs build adaptive firms
4. To examine the transition that occurs in the movement from an entrepreneurial style to a managerial approach
5. To explain the importance of the self-management concept in managing the growth stage
6. To identify the key factors that play a major role during the growth stage
7. To discuss the complex management of paradox and contradiction
8. To introduce useful steps for breaking through the growth wall

CHAPTER SUMMARY

The first major area of this chapter is the discussion of the five stages of development that a venture goes through. These stages are:
(1) New-venture development
(2) Start-up activities
(3) Growth

(4) Stabilization of the business
(5) Innovation or decline

All of these stages are important, but this chapter examines closely the growth stage.

The second major area of discussion is understanding the entrepreneurial company. The entrepreneurial mind is one that is willing to change, and one should avoid a bureaucratic environment. The entrepreneur directly affects the growth orientation of the venture. It is desirable for the entrepreneur to maintain a creative climate through this way of thinking. To help him or her do this, certain steps can be taken in order to build an adaptive firm. First, increase the perception of opportunity through job designing and job objectives. Second, make change a goal of the firm. Third, instill the desire to be innovative by use of a reward system for being innovative, by allowing for failure, and by being a flexible operation. These steps will help with maintaining the entrepreneurial frame of mind that makes a venture innovative and creative. But as the company changes, some other ways of the entrepreneur will need to change.

The transition from an entrepreneurial style to a managerial approach occurs during the growth stage and is important and difficult. The success of the venture depends on the ability of the entrepreneur to change styles. This is an important change during the growth stage. Hofer and Charan describe a seven-step process to make the transition successful. It is critical to maintain a balance between the entrepreneurial characteristics that create a climate of innovativeness and creativity and the personal transition from an entrepreneurial style to a managerial approach. There are five major factors to consider:

(1) Strategic orientation
(2) Commitment to seize opportunities
(3) Commitment of resources
(4) Control of resources
(5) Management structure

Next, the chapter considers the self-management concept. The key steps to this are self-observation, self-established goals, cueing strategies, rehearsal, and self-applied consequences.

The third major area discussed is called understanding the growth stage. The four key factors during the growth stage are:

(1) Control
(2) Responsibility
(3) Tolerance of failures: moral, personal, and uncontrollable
(4) Change

When a venture experiences surges in growth, a number of multiple challenges begin to evolve. Therefore, managing paradox and contradiction becomes important. Some of the contradictory forces at work include: bureaucratization vs. decentralization, environment vs. strategy, and strategic emphasis on quality vs. cost vs. innovation.

Growth brings about more complex concerns in decision making. Understanding the stages of the firm (early, growth, later stage) can help to focus on the decision-making characteristics of each stage. The use of external resources may help in decision making during the growth stage. Another method of assistance to entrepreneurs in decision making during the growth stage is responsibility charting. This involves decision, roles, and types of participation in the decision-making process. Effective delegation is a major consideration during the growth stage. There are three steps to this process:

(1) Assignment of specific duties
(2) Granting authority to carry out these duties
(3) Creating the obligation of responsibility for necessary action

Two related responsibilities are to hire the best employees and to use delegation to free up time for thinking.

LECTURE NOTES

MANAGING ENTREPRENEURIAL GROWTH

I. Introduction

II. Stages of Development
    A. New-venture development
        1. Accumulation and expansion of resources
        2. Initial entrepreneurial strategy formulation
    B. Start-up activities
        1. Creating a formal business plan
        2. Searching for capital
        3. Carrying out marketing activities
        4. Developing an effective entrepreneurial team
    C. Growth
        1. Reformulation of strategies
        2. Transition: entrepreneurial, one-person leadership to managerial, team management leadership
    D. Stabilization of the business
        1. Long-term planning
        2. "Swing" stage
        3. Innovation
    E. Innovation or decline
        1. Acquire other innovative firms.
        2. Work on new product/service development.

III. Understanding the Entrepreneurial Company
    A. The entrepreneurial mind
        1. Is willing to change and innovate
        2. Affects the firm's growth orientation
    B. Building the adaptive firm
        1. Share the entrepreneur's vision.
        2. Increase the perception of opportunity.
            a. "Staying close to the customer"
            b. Coordination and integration of the functional areas
        3. Institutionalize change as the venture's goal.
            a. Resources are made available.

            b. Departmental barriers are reduced.
        4. Instill the desire to be innovative.
            a. A reward system
            b. An environment that allows for failure
            c. Flexible operations
    C. The transition from an entrepreneurial style to a managerial approach
        1. Threats preventing the transition
            a. A highly centralized decision-making system
            b. An overdependence on one or two key individuals
            c. An inadequate repertoire of managerial skills and training
            d. A paternalistic atmosphere
        2. Carefully planning and gradually implementing the process
            a. Wanting the change.
            b. Day-to-day procedures changed.
            c. Institutionalize key operating tasks.
            d. Develop middle management.
            e. Evaluate and modify the firm's strategy.
            f. Modify organizational structure.
            g. Develop a professional board of directors.
        3. Balancing the focus (entrepreneur and manager)
            a. Vital for success
            b. Entrepreneurial focus versus administrative focus
        4. The self-management concept
            a. Self-observation
            b. Self-established goals
            c. Cueing strategies
            d. Rehearsal
            e. Self-applied consequences

IV. Understanding the Growth Stage
    A. Key factors during the growth stage
        1. Control
            a. Does the control system imply trust?
            b. Does the resource allocation system imply trust?
            c. Is it easier to ask permission than to ask forgiveness?
        2. Responsibility
            a. Authority
            b. Delegation
        3. Tolerance of failure
            a. Moral failure
            b. Personal failure
            c. Uncontrollable failure
        4. Change
    B. Managing paradox and change

The Dryden Press

1. Rigid, bureaucratic procedures are always in conflict with the flexible, organic designs needed for entrepreneurial companies
2. Specific contradictory forces
    a. Bureaucratization vs. decentralization
    b. Environment vs. strategy
    c. Strategic emphasis on quality vs. cost vs. innovation
- C. Confronting the growth wall
    1. Get the facts
    2. Create a growth task force
    3. Plan for growth
    4. Staff for growth
    5. Maintain a growth culture
    6. Use an advisory board
- D. Growth and decision making
    1. Focus and style of decision making differ in the growth stage.
    2. "External resources" (networking) involves using resources outside of the venture's ownership or control to assist in decisions.
    3. "Responsibility charting" assumes that decision making involves multiple roles that participate in various ways at different points over time.

V. Effective Delegation
- A. The process
    1. Assignment of specific duties
    2. Granting authority to carry out these duties
    3. Creating the obligation of responsibility for necessary action
- B. Additional steps
    1. Hire the best employees
    2. Use delegation to free up time for thinking effectively
- C. Extra suggestions
    1. View thinking as a strategy
    2. Schedule large blocks of uninterrupted time
    3. Stay focused on relevant topics
    4. Record, sort, and save thoughts

VI. Summary

SUGGESTED ANSWERS FOR DISCUSSION QUESTIONS (END OF CHAPTER)

1. ***Briefly identify and describe the stages of development for a new venture.***
    (1) New-venture development: Includes accumulation and expansion of resources and initial entrepreneurial strategy formulation
    (2) Start-up activities: Includes creating a formal business plan, searching for capital,

carrying out marketing activities, developing an effective entrepreneurial team
   (3) Growth: Includes reformulation of strategies and a transition from one-person leadership to team leadership
   (4) Stabilization of the business: Includes long-term planning and innovation
   (5) Innovation or decline: Includes acquiring other innovative firms and working on new product/service development

2. *Firms that fail to innovate will die. What does this statement mean in the context of new ventures?*
   When a firm leaves the fourth stage of development, it will either have to swing into higher gear and greater profitability or swing toward decline and failure ("swing" stage). This is done by innovation.

3. *What are the dangers of an entrepreneur evolving into a bureaucrat?*
   No one in the venture is willing (or encouraged) to become innovative or entrepreneurial because the owner/founder stifles such activity. The firm will not be adaptive.

4. *How can entrepreneurs build an adaptive firm? Be complete in your answer.*
   By increasing the perception of opportunity through the use of careful job design. The work should have defined objectives and responsibilities. Change as a goal of the venture rather than preservation of status quo. Instill the desire to innovate by using a reward system for innovative attempts, allowance for failure by recognizing that many attempts are needed, and by a flexible operation where change can take place.

5. *Successful ventures balance entrepreneurial characteristics with managerial style. What does this statement mean?*
   Entrepreneurial characteristics such as innovation, creativity, and a willingness to change help to promote growth in a venture, but as the firm grows, more of a managerial approach must be taken by the entrepreneur in delegating authority and tasks to free up time for thinking.

6. *When comparing the entrepreneurial focus with the administrative focus, there are five major areas of consideration. What are these areas?*
   Strategic orientation, commitment to seize opportunities, commitment of resources, control of resources, and management structure.

7. *How can the self-management concept be of value to entrepreneurs in managing the growth stage?*
   The concept identifies management behavior requiring change and assists in making those changes. It is a way for entrepreneurs to analyze their style, realign their behavior and time allotments, and reinforce effective management techniques.

8. **Identify and describe the four key factors that need to be considered during the growth stage.**
   (1) Control--Three critical questions. Does the control system imply trust? Does the resource allocation system imply trust? Is it easier to ask permission than to ask forgiveness?
   (2) Responsibility--Authority can be delegated, but a sense of responsibility must be created.
   (3) Tolerance of failure--Moral failure is a violation of internal trust; personal failure is a lack of skill or application; uncontrollable failure is caused by external factors.
   (4) Change--Planning, operations, and implementation are all subject to change.

9. **What is meant by managing paradox and contradiction?**
   In the growth stage the more flexible factors needed for an innovative firm will be in conflict with the more structural factors of an established firm. Therefore, some of the specific contradictory forces include: bureaucratization vs. decentralization, environment vs. strategy, and the strategic emphasis on quality vs. cost vs. innovation.

10. **Identify some examples of conflicting designs of structural factors. (Use Table 16.2)**
    Some examples of conflicting designs of structural factors would be under flexible or bureaucratic designs such as:

	Flexible	Bureaucratic
Culture	Autonomous	Formalized
	Risk Taking	Risk Averse
Staffing	External Hiring	Internal Hiring
Appraisal	Subjective	Objective
	Participative	Formalized

11. **Describe the concepts of networking and responsibility charting, and explain their potential for improving an entrepreneur's decision-making abilities.**
    Decision making is critical during the growth stage, and it differs from the processes used during other stages of a firm's development. Therefore, two methods of assistance for entrepreneurs are networking and responsibility charting. Networking involves the use of external resources that are not owned by the entrepreneur. Thus, the entrepreneur can gain assistance in the administrative areas or day-to-day operating problems. Responsibility charting combines the major components of decision making--decisions, roles, and types of participation--formed into a matrix so that an entrepreneur can assign a type of participation to each role for a specific decision. Both of these methods help entrepreneurs clarify the complexities of decision making and improve their ability to delegate.

12. Why is delegation so important to entrepreneurs in making the transition from an entrepreneurial venture to the diversified operations of the growth stage? Explain in detail.

It gives you the opportunity to free up time for effective thinking and problem solving. Effective thinking leads to innovation and creativity so the venture can grow. The entrepreneur needs to rely on others to carry out day-to-day activities.

TEACHING NOTES FOR END-OF-CHAPTER CASES

VIDEO CASE: BABY BOOMERS AND BEYOND: CENTEX LOOKS FORWARD

1. *How would Centex Corporation fit into the life cycle of a venture?*

   Centex would illustrate a business that has stabilized and is now seeking to innovate rather than decline. Looking to the new markets of senior housing and Centex Home Services are examples of innovation.

2. *Describe the elements of building an adaptive firm that apply to Centex.*

   Increasing the perception of opportunity, institutionalizing change as the venture's goal, and instilling a desire to be innovative (rewards and flexible operations) would be some of the elements that Centex appears to exhibit.

3. *What indications are there that Centex's management team balances the focus of entrepreneurial and administrative?*

   Based upon the openness to new ideas and the formation of a task force to evaluate Centex's core competencies, Centex's management team exhibits the entrepreneurial point of view:
   - Where is the opportunity?
   - How do I capitalize on it?
   - What resources do I need?
   - How do I gain control over them?
   - What structure is best?

   However, the team still balances some administrative factors such as which opportunity is appropriate? and what structure determines our organization's relationship to its market?

CASE: HENDRICK'S WAY (Answers to Questions)

1. *What is the danger in Hendrick's thinking? Explain in detail.*

   The danger in Hendrick's thinking is that he is ignoring the signs that the marketplace is giving him. He is assuming that if he makes a few changes, the demand for his product will come back. His company has reached the stabilization of the business phase in the

The Dryden Press

business venture life cycle. His product started out as a one-of-a-kind product. Now the market is being invaded with a host of look-alikes at cheaper prices. Since this is Hendrick's only product, his company stands a great chance of going under. Hendrick's company needs to innovate into a company that can produce what the consumer wants and needs so his company will once again be profitable and continue to grow.

2. *Could the self-management concept be of any value to Hendrick? Why or why not?*
   Yes, because the time when the self-management concept is very useful is during the growth stage. Hendrick's company has been growing very fast for the last two years. The techniques used in the self-management concept are designed to help identify the management behavioral changes the entrepreneur needs to make. An example of this would be using the techniques of self-established goals. Here Hendrick would set goals that could be directed. One of these goals might be to expand the market in which the drill is sold and to do it in a period of six months.

3. *Using Table 16.1 as your point of reference, how would you describe Hendrick's focus? Based on your evaluation, what recommendations would you make to him?*
   Hendrick's focus is very closed minded. In the chapter, it says that an adaptive firm needs to retain certain entrepreneurial characteristics in order to encourage innovation and creativity. It also says entrepreneurs need to translate this spirit of innovation and creativity to their personality while personally making a transition toward a more managerial style. Hendrick is not doing this because there is no indication of his encouraging innovation and creativity. Some of the pressures listed in the table that he is ignoring are: diminishing opportunities, narrow decision windows, lack of control over the environment, demands for more efficient use, risk of obsolescence, etc. Hendrick seems to want to hold on to the past and not worry about the future.

CASE: KEEPING THINGS GOING

1. *In what phase of the venture life cycle is Jan's firm currently operating? Defend your answer.*
   Jan's company is at the innovation or decline phase. For the last three years, her company has been very successful. The company's use of work teams show that it has made the transition from entrepreneurial leadership to team management leadership. Jan seems to realize the importance of keeping the customer satisfied and staying ahead of the competition. Her hiring practices show that she wants people with innovative ideas and good hard workers. All this points to the innovation or decline phase.

2. *How are Jan's actions helping to build an adaptive firm? Give three specific examples.*
   (1) She has instituted a bonus system that is tied to sales. These bonuses are shared by all of the personnel.
   (2) She gives quarterly salary increases with the greatest percentages going to the

employees who are most active in developing new programs and procedures for handling client problems.

(3) Every six months she has retreats where the entire staff goes away for a long weekend in the mountains. Here they spend three days discussing current work-related problems and ways of dealing with them. Time is also devoted to developing an esprit de corps among the personnel.

3. ***If Jan's firm continues to grow, what recommendations would you make for future action? What else should Jan be thinking about doing in order to keep things going along smoothly? Be specific in your answer.***

Jan's company seems to be on the right track. It is important for Jan to realize that as the company grows, more delegation of authority will be necessary to keep operations running smoothly. She should continue her reward system to keep people innovated. She should also prepare an environment that allows for failure. One of the most important things Jan will have to do is to keep the company operations flexible. Flexibility creates the possibility of change taking place, and that has a positive effect. Finally, the business may come to a point where it is so financially successful that Jan may want to try to acquire other innovative firms to ensure the company's future growth.

ADDITIONAL EXPERIENTIAL EXERCISE

"Examining the Stages of Development"

Students should research several businesses of their choice. They should figure out the current stage of development for these businesses. What are they doing wrong? What are they doing right? How could they improve? What do they have directly ahead of them in the future?

The students should compare the businesses and then look for significant trends or similarities in the stages.

CHAPTER 17

GLOBAL OPPORTUNITIES FOR ENTREPRENEURS

CHAPTER OUTLINE

I. The International Environment
   A. The World Trade Organization and GATT
   B. North American Free Trade Agreement (NAFTA)
   C. The European Union (EU)
   D. Japan and Asia

II. Methods of Going International
   A. Importing
   B. Exporting
      1. Management company
         a. Participation
         b. Questions to ask
         c. Dangers
      2. Freight forwarder
         a. Services provided
         b. Advantages
         c. Guidelines in selecting
      3. Foreign sales corporation
      4. Other ideas
   C. Joint Venture
      1. Advantages
      2. Disadvantages
   D. Direct foreign investment
      1. Methods
         a. Acquire interest
         b. Establish subsidiary
         c. Purchase assets
         d. Build
      2. Reasons to invest
         a. Trade restrictions
         b. Tax incentives
   E. Licensing
      1. Programs
         a. Patents
         b. Trademarks
         c. Technical know-how
      2. Steps to take

        3. Advantages
        4. Disadvantages

III. Entering the International Marketplace
    A. Conduct research
        1. Federal Depository
        2. Publications
        3. TOP
    B. Prepare a feasibility study
    C. Secure adequate financing
        1. Letter of credit
        2. Financial guarantee
        3. Local banks
    D. File proper documents
    E. Draw up and implement the plan
        1. Define the firm's policy
        2. Ensure efficient organization
        3. Implement the plan

IV. Summary

CHAPTER OBJECTIVES

1. To introduce the new international developments that have expanded opportunities for the global market
2. To examine how entrepreneurs can take advantage of importing opportunities
3. To explore the entrepreneurial benefits of exporting
4. To discuss the advantages and disadvantages of entrepreneurial joint ventures
5. To examine the benefits of direct foreign investment by entrepreneurs
6. To explain how licensing arrangements work and to review their advantages and disadvantages
7. To set forth the five key steps for entering the international marketplace

CHAPTER SUMMARY

    This chapter introduces the international opportunities emerging for entrepreneurs to capitalize upon. Beginning with an examination of the current international environment, the chapter highlights the World Trade Organization and GATT (General Agreement on Tariffs and Trade) and their effect on expanding international markets. The chapter then focuses on the North American Free Trade Agreement (NAFTA) that has been developed to remove trade barriers between Canada, Mexico, and the U.S. The European Union (EU) is then highlighted along with the growing markets in Japan and Asia that created a single market throughout

Europe. The chapter then talks about the five ways in which an entrepreneur can actively engage in the international market, which are: importing, exporting, joint ventures, direct foreign investment, and licensing. The choice that a particular entrepreneur makes will depend on his/her organization's needs. The second half of the chapter deals with a procedural outline for centering on the international marketplace. Each of the alternatives available and the procedural outline will be discussed briefly.

Importing, which is the shipping of foreign-made goods into this country, is the first alternative. Each year the United States has imported an increasing amount of goods. The year 1984 marked the first time that this country became a net debtor nation since World War II. An entrepreneur becomes aware of import opportunities by attending trade shows and fairs and by monitoring trade publications. Exporting is the shipping of domestically produced goods to a foreign destination for consumption. Exporting should be important for entrepreneurs because it often means increased market potential with a broader sales market. However, it usually takes time to learn of all the tricks of the trade. Participation in the export market basically has three alternative forms, which are: an export management company, a freight forwarder, and a foreign sales corporation. In addition to the selections available for exporting, the chapter lists the most common mistakes that potential exporters make. These mistakes include the following:

(1) Failure to obtain qualified export counseling and to develop a master international marketing plan
(2) Insufficient commitment by top management
(3) Insufficient care in selecting overseas distributors
(4) Chasing orders from around the world instead of establishing a basis for profitable operations
(5) Neglecting export business when the market booms
(6) Failure to treat international distributors on an equal basis
(7) Unwillingness to modify products
(8) Failure to print services, sales, and warranty messages
(9) Failure to consider use of an export management company
(10) Failure to consider joint venture agreements

This list is designed to prevent the entrepreneur from making the mistakes that have plagued other entrepreneurs.

The third alternative is a joint venture, which is a company owned by more than two companies and is sometimes referred to as a consortium. The fourth alternative is a direct foreign investment, which is a domestically controlled foreign production facility. This does not mean that the firm owns a majority of the operation, but the typical direct foreign investment involves ownership of 10 percent to 25 percent of the voting stock in a foreign enterprise. The three methods used to make a direct foreign investment are: by acquiring interest in an ongoing business, by obtaining a majority interest in a foreign company, and by purchasing part of the assets of a foreign concern. The final way an entrepreneur can actively engage in the international market is through a licensing agreement, which is a business arrangement in which the manufacturer of a product grants permission to some other group or individual to manufacture that product in return for specified royalties or other payments. The three basic types of international licensing programs available are patents, trademarks, and technical know-how. Licensing requires minimum capital and can generate savings in tariffs and transportation costs, but there are also disadvantages that are involved, like the possibility that the licensee will become a competitor after the contract expires.

The next part of the chapter discusses the procedural outline used for entering the international marketplace. The first step is to conduct research. Research can be done at the Federal Depository in a major library and with Overseas Business Reports (OBR) and the Foreign Economic Trends (FET). Step two is to prepare a feasibility study, which should be undertaken to determine if the proposed project is capable of being carried out. Step three is to prepare a feasibility study and secure adequate financing. Two ways that such financing can be obtained are through an irrevocable letter of credit and a financial guarantee. Step four entails filing the proper documents. One of the most effective ways to file is to use the *Exporter's Encyclopedia*, which is available in the reference section of many local libraries. The final step is to draw up and implement the plan. The first step in implementing an international strategy is to define the firm's policy. The next step is to ensure that the firm is efficiently organized for international operations. Finally, after the plan has been drawn up, it must be put into effect.

LECTURE NOTES

GLOBAL OPPORTUNITIES FOR ENTREPRENEURS

I. The International Environment
   A. The World Trade Organization and GATT
      1. Trade liberalization organization
      2. GATT = General Agreement on Tariffs and Trade
      3. Changes on tariffs, import quotas, intellectual property rights, and overseas manufacturing
   B. North American Free Trade Agreement (NAFTA)
      1. Bilateral trade agreement between Canada, Mexico, and the United States
   C. European Union (EU)
      1. Created a single continental-scale market in Europe
      2. The term "Euroconsumer" has developed to illustrate the potential consumer base
   D. Japan and Asia

II. Methods of Going International
   A. Importing
      1. Factors causing a change of trade status to importing
         a. Rising cost of energy
         b. Low labor costs in other countries
         c. Some products are not produced domestically
      2. How to become aware of import opportunities
         a. Trade shows and fairs
         b. Trade publications

B. Exporting
   1. New product ideas
      a. Indoor golf
      b. Choose your seat
      c. Keeping time
   2. Export management company
      a. Private firm
      b. Be cautious when approaching an E.M.C.
      c. One of the dangers is losing control of the export function
   3. Freight forwarder
      a. Services provided by a freight forwarder
         1. Quoting shipping costs
         2. Arranging inland shipping and reserving space
         3. Advice about international packing
         4. Preparing the necessary documentation
         5. Seeing that the goods reach the port
      b. Guidelines that should be followed
         1. Be licensed by the Federal Maritime Commission
         2. Obtain references from past customers
         3. Services and costs should be provided
         4. Talk with experienced exporters
         5. Check with current shippers
   4. Foreign sales corporation--Tax-exempt treatment for FSCs if conditions are met
      a. It must have a foreign presence
      b. It must have economic substance
      c. It must perform activities outside the United States
   5. Common mistakes that potential exporters make
      a. Failure to obtain qualified export counseling
      b. Insufficient commitment by top management
      c. Insufficient care in selecting overseas distributors
      d. No basis for profitable operations
      e. Neglecting business when the market booms
      f. Failure to treat international distributors on an equal basis with domestic counterparts
      g. Unwillingness to modify products
      h. Failure to print services, sales, and warranty messages in understood languages
      i. Failure to consider an export management company
      j. Failure to consider joint-venture agreements
C. Joint ventures
   1. Joint ventures are more popular in the auto industry
   2. Advantages
      a. An intimate knowledge of the local conditions
      b. Use of the other firm's resources

The Dryden Press

   c. Initial capital outlay and the overall risk will both be lower
   d. Strategic fit of domestic firm (D-type) with the third world (TW-type) firm
  3. Disadvantages
   a. Fragmented control
   b. Significant control can be exerted by one party
 D. Direct foreign investment
  1. Methods of making a direct foreign investment
   a. Acquire an interest in an ongoing business
   b. Obtain a majority interest in a foreign company
   c. Purchase part of the assets of a foreign concern
  2. Reasons for making the direct investment
   a. Possibility of trade restrictions
   b. Tax incentives
   c. An exciting venture
 E. Licensing
  1. Three types of licensing programs available
   a. Patents
   b. Trademarks
   c. Technical know-how
  2. Advantages of licensing
   a. Minimum capital outlay
   b. Generation of savings in tariffs
   c. More realistic means of expansion
   d. Access to the market is easier
   e. Potential for the licensees to become partners
  3. Disadvantages of licensing
   a. Possibility that the licensee will become a competitor after the contract expires
   b. Contractual obligations
   c. Must resolve conflicts or misunderstandings
   d. Integrity and independence must be maintained

III. Entering the International Marketplace: A Procedural Outline
 A. Conduct research
  1. Federal Depository at a major library
  2. Overseas Business Reports (OBR)
  3. Foreign Economic Trends (FET)
  4. Trade Opportunities Program (TOP)
 B. Prepare a feasibility study
 C. Secure adequate financing
  1. Irrevocable letter of credit
  2. The financial guarantee
  3. Overseas Private Investment Corporation (OPIC)
  4. Export-Import Bank (Eximbank)
  5. Small Business Administration (SBA)

D. File proper documents
   1. The *Exporter's Encyclopedia*
   2. The federal and state departments
   3. Some banks
E. Draw up and implement plan
   1. Define the firm's policy
   2. Ensure the firm is efficiently organized
   3. Put the plan into effect

SUGGESTED ANSWERS FOR DISCUSSION QUESTIONS (END OF CHAPTER)

1. ***Describe some of the powerful economic forces that are creating global opportunities for entrepreneurs.***

   There are two specific economic developments that are creating new global opportunities for entrepreneurs. First, the World Trade Organization and GATT (General Agreement on Tariffs and Trade) and their effect on expanding international markets. Secondly, the North American Free Trade Agreement (NAFTA) that has been developed to remove trade barriers between Canada, Mexico, and the U.S. Also, the European Union (EU) has created a single market throughout Europe. The trade barriers between countries are removed, and the entire continent of Europe will operate as one large market. The term "Euroconsumer" is now being used to illustrate this development.

2. ***How can an entrepreneur become aware of import opportunities?***

   One way is by attending trade shows and fairs in which firms gather to display their products and/or services. Another way is by monitoring trade publications.

3. ***Of what value are an export management company and a freight forwarder to entrepreneurs who are seeking to export goods?***

   Export management companies will purchase the product and sell it themselves to foreign customers. In addition, export management companies facilitate the export process by handling all of the details, from making the shipping arrangements to locating the customers. Freight forwarders provide the following services:
   1. Quoting shipping costs for inland, ocean, and air
   2. Arranging inland shipping and necessary reserve space aboard an ocean vessel
   3. Advising on the requirements of international packing
   4. Preparing the necessary export documentation
   5. Seeing to it that the goods reach the port and tracing lost shipments

4. ***Before engaging the services of an export management company, what questions should an entrepreneur ask?***
   1. What is the reputation of the firm? Is it financially sound?
   2. How long has the company been in business?

3. What is the track record as an export management company?
4. Is it a full-time or part-time operation?
5. Will it accept a nonexclusive contract?
6. What is the minimum term of contract it will accept?
7. Does it have representatives overseas?

5. **What is a foreign sales corporation? Of what value is it to entrepreneurs in the export business?**

    A foreign sales corporation is the replacement created by Congress for the controversial domestic international sales corporation. A foreign sales corporation allows tax-exempt treatment to a portion of export income. To qualify for this treatment, the exporter must meet the following three conditions: it must have a foreign presence, it must have economic substance, and it must perform activities relating to its exporting income outside the United States.

6. **What are five of the most common mistakes made by potential exporters?**
    1. Failure to obtain qualified export counseling and to develop a master international marketing plan
    2. Insufficient care in selecting overseas distributors
    3. Neglecting export business when the U.S. market booms
    4. Failure to treat international distributors on an equal basis with domestic counterparts
    5. Failure to consider use of an export management company

7. **How does a joint venture work? What are the advantages of this arrangement? What are the disadvantages?**

    A joint venture is a company owned by more than one organization. When it is owned by more than two companies, it is sometimes referred to as a consortium. One advantage of a joint venture is that the firm will be able to gain an intimate knowledge of the local conditions and government. Another advantage is that each participant will be able to use the resources of the other firms involved in the venture. A disadvantage of a joint venture is the problem of fragmented control. A joint venture can be a very effective tool in the international marketplace.

8. **How can a firm make a direct foreign investment?**

    A firm can make a direct investment in a variety of ways. One is to acquire an interest in an ongoing foreign operation. Another is to obtain a majority interest in a foreign company. Finally, the acquiring firm may simply purchase part of the assets of a foreign concern in order to establish a direct investment.

9. *How does a licensing arrangement work? What are the advantages and disadvantages of such an arrangement?*

Licensing is a business arrangement in which the manufacturer of a product grants permission to some other group or individual to manufacture that product in return for specified royalties or other payments. One advantage of licensing is it requires a minimum capital outlay and can generate savings in tariffs and transportation costs. Another advantage is that it is a more realistic means of expansion. Finally, there is a potential for the licensees to become partners and contributors in improving the "learning curve" of technology. There are also some disadvantages to licensing. First, there is the possibility that the licensee will become a competitor. Second, the licenser must get the licensee to meet contractual obligations and adjust products or services. Finally, the integrity and independence of both the licenser and licensee must be maintained.

10. *When entering the international marketplace, what are the five specific steps that should be followed?*
    (1) Conduct research
    (2) Prepare a feasibility study
    (3) Secure adequate financing
    (4) File proper documents
    (5) Draw up and implement the plan

TEACHING NOTES FOR END-OF-CHAPTER CASES

VIDEO CASE: PIER 1 IMPORTS: MANAGING WORLDWIDE GROWTH (Answers to Questions)

1. *As Pier 1 shifts from importing to exporting, what are some key points to remember?*

According to the learning curve concept, increased sales will lead to greater efficiencies along the cost curve, which in turn will lead to increased profits. (The learning curve essentially states that as more and more units are produced, the firm becomes more efficient, thereby lowering the cost per unit. The lower unit cost thus enables the firm to compete more effectively in the marketplace.) It should be pointed out, however, that exporting normally will take three to five years to become profitable. Even if the firm is producing more units efficiently, it will take time to learn the intricacies and efficiencies of international business.

2. *What are the emerging global markets that Pier 1 should be seeking?*

According to Table 17.1, Canada, Japan, and Mexico are the three largest export markets. In addition, the European Union represents a huge market for U.S. products as well as the entire Pacific rim (Asia).

3. *Discuss the advantages and disadvantages of a joint venture since it is Pier 1's strategy for expansion.*

   A firm may decide to participate in a joint venture for several reasons. One is that the firm would be able to gain an intimate knowledge of the local conditions and government where the facility is located. Another is that each participant would be able to use the resources of the other firms involved in the venture. This allows participating firms a chance to compensate for weaknesses they may possess. Finally, both the initial capital outlay and the overall risk would be lower than if the firm were setting up the operation alone.

   Additional advantages of a joint venture relate to the strategic fit of the domestic firm with the foreign firm. One study examined the strategic fit of domestic firms (D-type) with third world firms (TW-type) in a joint venture. The dimensions of corporate-level advantages, operational-level advantages, and environmental advantages were all compared to the strategic fit of the partners in the joint venture.

   One of the disadvantages associated with joint ventures is the problem of fragmented control. For example, a carefully planned logistics flow may be hampered if one of the firms decides to block the acquisition of new equipment. This type of problem can be avoided or diminished in a number of ways: (1) One party can control more than 50 percent of the voting rights. This will normally give formal control; however, even a minority opposing view can carry considerable influence. This can be particularly true if the differences of opinion reflect different nationalities. (2) Only one of the parties is made responsible for the actual management of the venture. This may be complemented by a buyout clause. In case of a disagreement among the owners, one party can purchase the equity of the other. (3) One of the parties can control either the input or the output, exerting significant control over the venture decision, despite voting and ownership rights.

CASE: A FOREIGN PROPOSAL

1. *What type of arrangement is Edgar using in his business dealings with the European firms?*

   Edgar is using the exporting arrangement. He is producing his computer chips in the United States and then selling 50 percent of his output to the European firms and selling the rest to U.S. firms.

2. *Is the Japanese business proposal a joint venture? Why or why not? Would you recommend that Edgar accept it? Why or why not?*

   The Japanese business proposal is not a joint venture because they will not own part of Bruning Computer at any time. In the beginning, Bruning is exporting only his output to the Japanese: after 90 days, Bruning would be licensing his computer chips to the Japanese so they could make them there.

   Recommend to Bruning not to accept the Japanese offer, and try to work out a licensing agreement. It seems with the Japanese approach that Bruning will not have much control over the product and would be better off finding firms to deal with the European firms.

3. ***If Edgar were looking for an alternative approach to doing business with the Japanese, what would you suggest?***

   Bruning should license the computer chips. Because of the program's technical know-how and without product protection after five years, it will more than likely be out of date, since it deals with computers.

ADDITIONAL EXPERIENTIAL EXERCISE

"Preparing a Feasibility Study"

A creative exercise for students would be to work through the procedural outline for entering the international marketplace. Each student could work through each of the five steps and be able to see what it would really be like to go international. It would be similar to building and creating a business plan, only the student would be finding out about another aspect of business, the international phase.

PART VI

Contemporary Challenges in Entrepreneurship

Chapter 18 - Valuation of Business Ventures

Chapter 19 - Management Succession and Continuity: A Family Business Perspective

Chapter 20 - Total Quality and the Human Factor: Continuous Challenges for Entrepreneurs

CHAPTER 18

VALUATION OF BUSINESS VENTURES

CHAPTER OUTLINE

I. Buying a Business Venture
   A. Personal references
   B. Examination of opportunities
      1. Business brokers
      2. Newspaper ads
      3. Trade sources
      4. Professional sources
   C. Evaluation of the selected venture
      1. The business environment
      2. Profits, sales, and operating ratios
      3. The business assets
   D. Key questions to ask
      1. Why is the business being sold?
      2. What is the physical condition of the business?
      3. How many key personnel will remain?
      4. What is the degree of competition?
      5. What are the conditions of the lease?
      6. Are there any liens against the business?
      7. Will the owner sign a covenant not to compete?
      8. Are there any special licenses required?
      9. What are the future trends of the business?
      10. How much capital is needed to buy?

II. The Importance of Business Valuation
   A. Buying or selling a business
   B. Raising growth capital
   C. Determine inheritance tax
   D. Structuring a buy/sell agreement

III. Underlying Issues
   A. Goals of the buyer and seller
   B. Emotional bias
   C. Reasons for acquisition

IV. Analyzing the Business
   A. Lack of management depth
   B. Undercapitalization

  C. Insufficient controls
  D. Divergent goals

V. Establishing the Value of a Firm
  A. Methods of valuation
    1. Adjusted tangible book value
    2. Price/earnings ratio (multiple of earnings) method
    3. Discounted earnings method

VI. Other Factors to Consider
  A. Avoiding start-up costs
  B. Accuracy of projections
  C. Control factor

VII. The Leveraged Buyout: An Alternative for Smaller Ventures
  A. Issues involved with LBOs
    1. Entrepreneurial leveraged buyout (E-LBO)
    2. Cash-flow LBO
  B. Tax considerations of the LBO
    1. Top corporate tax rates are now lower than top individual tax rates
    2. Capital gains are now treated the same as ordinary income and taxed at the ordinary tax rate

VIII. Summary

CHAPTER OBJECTIVES

1. To describe four basic steps to follow in buying a business.
2. To outline ten key questions to ask when buying an ongoing venture.
3. To explain the importance of valuation.
4. To examine the underlying issues involved in the process of valuation.
5. To outline the various aspects of analyzing a business.
6. To present the major points to consider in establishing the value of a firm.
7. To highlight the available methods of valuing a venture.
8. To examine the three principal methods currently used in business valuations.
9. To consider additional factors affecting the valuation of a venture.
10. To discuss the leveraged buyout (LBO) as a method for purchasing a business.

CHAPTER SUMMARY

  When thinking of going into business, one way that may help to save money is buying an existing business. An entrepreneur may find this successful, but there are many factors that must be considered. First of all, personal preferences play a part in the decision. If someone has a perfect place and size in mind for the business, the entrepreneur should try to accomplish his or her goals. When searching for a venture, the entrepreneur should examine the available opportunities through sources such as business brokers, newspaper ads, trade sources, and professional sources. The next step is to evaluate specific factors of the venture being offered for sale. These can include the business environment, profit, sales, and operating ratios, and the business's assets, such as inventory, goodwill, and accounts receivable. The entrepreneur should also ask key questions pertaining to the business. Some of them are: Why is the business being sold? What is the physical condition of the business? How many key personnel will remain? What is the degree of competition?

Next, the entrepreneur should be able to calculate the value of the business and of competitors' businesses. This is essential in buying or selling a business, division, or major asset, attempting to buy out a partner, and giving a gift of stock to a family member. The entrepreneur must next consider some underlying issues of the valuation of the business. The first of these are goals of the buyer and seller. It is important to realize that they will generally be opposite. The second issue is the emotional bias of the seller. After he/she has developed the whole business, he/she may think it is worth more than it actually is. The last issue is the reasons for acquisition. Some of the more common reasons are increasing market share by acquiring a firm in the company's industry and using idle or excess plant capacity by acquiring a firm that can operate in the company's current plant facilities.

The next step is to analyze the business. The important thing to remember is not to compare the small business with larger corporations. Many closely held ventures have shortcomings such as lack of managerial depth, undercapitalization, insufficient controls, and divergent goals. Since these weaknesses exist, careful analysis is needed.

The entrepreneur must now establish the value of the firm. There are three principal methods to use in establishing the value. The first is the adjusted tangible book value. This is where goodwill, patents, deferred financing costs, and other intangible assets are considered with the other assets and deducted from or added to net worth. The second method is the price/earnings ratio (multiple of earnings) method. It is determined by dividing the market price of the common stock by the earnings per share. The last method is the discounted earnings method. The idea of this is that dollars earned in the future (based on projections) are worth less than dollars earned today (due to the loss of purchasing power).

The entrepreneur must now realize that there are other factors to consider in the valuation process. Among these are avoiding start-up costs, accuracy of projections, and control factors. Finally, an entrepreneur may use a leveraged buyout to secure a business. This is where he/she finances the transaction by borrowing on the target company's assets. Usually, a company that is a target of a leveraged buyout has dependable cash flow from operations, a high ratio of fully depreciated fixed assets, an established product line, and low current and long-term debt.

Finally, an entrepreneur should closely evaluate the business to make sure the transaction is feasible. If he/she reacts solely on emotions and not on facts, he/she may wish later on that he/she had never bought the business.

LECTURE NOTES

VALUATION OF BUSINESS VENTURES

I. Buying a Business Venture
   A. Personal preferences
      1. Background
      2. Skills
      3. Interests
      4. Experiences
   B. Examination of opportunities
      1. Business brokers--Professionals who specialize in business opportunities often can provide leads or at least assist in finding a business venture.
      2. Newspaper ads--The classified ads are a good place to find businesses for sale.
      3. Trade sources--Suppliers, distributors, manufacturers, trade publications, trade associations, and trade schools may have information on a business to purchase.
      4. Professional sources--Management consultants, attorneys, and accountants sometimes hear of businesses to buy.
   C. Evaluation of the selected venture
      1. The business environment--Analyze the local environment of the business to establish the potential of the company.
      2. Profits, sales, and operating ratio--The key to a business is its profit potential.
      3. The business assets -- Analyze the tangible and intangible assets of the business.
   D. Key questions to ask
      1. Why is this business being sold? Find out the owner's reason for selling.
      2. What is the physical condition of the business? The overall condition of the company needs to be examined in order to prevent major expenses after purchase.
      3. How many key personnel will remain? Key personnel may be valuable to keep the company running smoothly.

II. The Importance of Business Valuation--Keeping Track of Value
   A. The owner becomes disabled: The company can still be sold at a fair price.
   B. Dissolution of a partnership: The other partner knows what it will cost to buy the other out.
   C. Death of one owner: How much will remaining owners have to pay to buy out the deceased?

III. Underlying Issues
   A. Goals of the buyer and the seller
      1. To establish an agreeable price settlement
   B. Emotional bias--The seller feels his/her company is worth more that it actually is
   C. Reasons for the acquisition
      1. Developing more growth-phase products--Acquire a firm that has developed new products in the company's market.
      2. Increase number of customers--Buy a firm whose customers will substantially increase the company's customer base.
      3. Increase market share--Purchase a firm in the company's market.

IV. Analyzing the Business--Factors that distinguish the corporation and valuation of the establishment.
   A. Lack of management depth--The amount of skills, versatility, and competence is limited.
   B. Undercapitalization--The business is lacking in money investment.
   C. Insufficient controls--Monitoring and controlling operations are limited because of lack of management.
   D. Divergent goals--The entrepreneurs and the stockholders have different goals.

V. Establishing the Value of the Firm
   A. Methods used in valuing a business
      1. Estimations
      2. Assumptions
      3. Projections
   B. Hidden values and costs
      1. Goodwill
      2. Personal expense
      3. Family members on payroll
      4. Planned losses

VI. Methods of Valuation
   A. Adjusted tangible book value--Determines the difference between total assets and total liabilities when considering net worth.
   B. Price/earnings ratio--Divide the market price of the common stock by the earnings per share.
   C. Discounted earnings method--Determines true value of the firm.

VII. Other Factors to Consider
   A. Avoiding start-up costs
      1. Buyers are willing to pay more for an existing business than deal with start-up costs.
      2. Buying an old business avoids the need to establish a clientele for the company.

B. Accuracy of projections
     1. Sales and earnings are projected in historical, financial, and economic data.
     2. Examine trends, fluctuations, and patterns of the company.
     3. Analyze the market and earning potential of the firm.
  C. Control factor--If the owner of the firm has the control, then the value increases.

VIII. The Leveraged Buyout
  A. Alternative for small ventures
     1. The entrepreneur borrows liquidity on the target company's assets.
     2. The owner borrows on the company's accounts receivable, inventory, and equipment.
  B. Issues involved with LBOs
     1. Entrepreneurial leveraged buyout (E-LBO) is characterized as having at least 2/3 of the purchase price from borrowed funds; more than 50 percent of stock owned by a single family; and the majority investor is actively managing the company.
     2. Cash-flow LBO relies heavily on the target company's cash receipts with indicators of continued positive cash flow.
  C. Tax considerations of the LBO
     1. The top individual tax rates are higher than top corporate tax rates at this time.
     2. Capital gains are now treated the same as ordinary income and taxed at the ordinary income tax rate.

SUGGESTED ANSWERS FOR DISCUSSION QUESTIONS
(END OF CHAPTER)

1. ***What are the four basic steps to follow in buying a business?***

In buying a business venture there are numerous options open to a prospective entrepreneur. Prospective entrepreneurs may seek to purchase a business venture rather than start up an enterprise from scratch. There are basic steps to take and some key questions to ask. Stipulated below are some of those steps:

(1) Personal preferences--An entrepreneur's personal background, skill, and experience are all important factors a prospective entrepreneur should ponder in his/her mind before making a decision regarding what he/she wants.

(2) Examination of opportunities--The sources where available opportunities can be examined are business brokers, newspaper ads, trade sources, professional sources.

(3) Evaluation of the selected venture--This is the evaluation of factors that will affect the venture being offered for sale. These factors are business environment, profit-sales-operating ratios, and the business assets.

(4) And finally, asking some key questions about why the business is being sold, the physical condition of the business, the retention of key personnel, who the competitors are, lease conditions, any liens against the business, etc.

2. ***Identify five (out of ten) key questions to ask when buying an ongoing venture.***
   (1) Why is this business being sold? It is important to find out if the owner has a genuine reason for selling the business or if he/she is trying to get rid of a venture that is in trouble.
   (2) What is the physical condition of the business? This question is important in order to avoid major expenses after purchasing.
   (3) How many key personnel will remain? Certain key personnel may be extremely valuable to the continuity of the business.
   (4) What is the degree of competition? The quantity and quality of competitors is vital. That is, how many competitors are out there, and what are their strengths and weaknesses?
   (5) Are there any special licenses required? It is important for the buyer to verify the federal, state, or local requirements that pertain to the type of business being purchased.

3. ***Identify and discuss the three underlying issues in the evaluation of a business.***
   Three underlying issues in the evaluation of a business are the differing goals of buyer and seller, the emotional bias of the seller, and the reasons for acquisition.
   (1) Goals of the buyer and seller--The buyer and the seller always assign different values to the enterprise because of their basic objectives. There is always a tendency for the seller to establish the highest possible value for the business regardless of the true market condition, the environment, or the economy. The buyer will always seek the lowest possible price to be paid. To the buyer, the enterprise is an investment, and it is normal to assess the profit potential.
   (2) Emotional bias--The seller sees the enterprise as something that has matured and is ready to bring in profits, and as a result there is a tendency for the seller to see the venture as worth more than outsiders believe it is really worth.
   (3) Reasons for the acquisition--Reasons might be: increasing market share, vertical integration, expansion of product line, using idle or excess plant capacity.

4. ***Taxes will affect the purchase or sale of an enterprise. What does this statement mean? Include a discussion of Table 18.2 in your answer.***
   When buying or selling a business, both the buyer and the seller are affected by taxes. For the buyer it is the deductibles and nondeductibles that affect outcome or profit. For the seller, it is the cash and noncash incomes that affect the profit outcome.

The Dryden Press

5. **To analyze a business, what types of questions or concerns should the entrepreneur address in the following areas: history of the business, market and competition, sales and distribution, manufacturing?**
   (1) History of the business: date company was founded, state in which company was incorporated, and company's original line of business and any subsequent changes.
   (2) Market and compensation: company's major business and market, description of major projects, and sales literature on projects.
   (3) Sales and distribution: compensation of salesmen, are any sales made on consignment, and details on branch office sales, if any.
   (4) Manufacturing: are facilities owned or leased, are any licenses needed to manufacture product, and how is quality control handled in the factory?

6. **To analyze a business, what types of questions or concerns should the entrepreneur address in the following areas: employees, physical facilities, ownership?**
   (1) Employees: total number of employees by function, any strikes or work stoppages, and fringe benefits, vacation time, sick leave, etc.
   (2) Physical facilities: which facilities are owned or leased, are facilities easily accessible to required transportation?
   (3) Ownership: do the shares carry an investment letter, are the shares fully paid for, is there cumulative voting?

7. **To analyze a business, what types of questions or concerns should the entrepreneur address in the following areas: financial, management?**
   Financial--Obtain details on franchise, lease, and royalty agreements, determine if company has subsidiaries (or divisions), review consolidating statements of profit and loss, and verify the cash balance and determine maximum and minimum cash balances needed throughout the year.
   Management--Organization chart, what is management's reputation in its industry, and does key management devote 100 percent of its time to the business?

8. **One of the most popular methods of business valuation is the adjusted tangible book value method. Describe how this method works.**
   Goodwill, patents, deferred financing costs, and other tangible assets are considered with the other assets and deducted from or added to the net worth. This upward or downward adjustment reflects the excess of the fair market value of each asset above or below the value reported on the balance sheet.

9. **Explain how the price/earnings ratio method of valuation works. Give an example.**
   The valuation is determined by dividing the market price of the common stock by the earnings per share. If a company has 200,000 shares of common stock and a net income of $100,000, the earnings per share are $2. Since the company has 200,000 shares of common stock, the valuation of the enterprise would be $400,000.

10. **What are the steps involved in using the discounted earnings method? Give an example.**

There are basically four steps to this method:
(1) Expected cash flow is estimated.
(2) An appropriate discount rate is determined.
(3) A reasonable life expectancy of the business must be determined.
(4) The firm's value is determined by discounting the estimated cash flow over the expected life of the business.

(A good example would be Table 18.5, or substitute new figures.)

11. **How do the following methods of valuation of a venture work: fixed price, multiple of earnings, return on investment, replacement value, liquidation value, excess earnings, market value?**

Table 18.4 in the chapter provides a complete description of each method with key points to remember.

12. **Explain why the following are important factors to consider in valuing a business: start-up costs, accuracy of projections, degree of control.**

The following factors may intervene in the valuation process of a business. Start-up costs are extensive, and a buyer may be willing to pay more for an ongoing business in order to avoid these costs. Sales revenues, market potential, and earnings potential should all be examined carefully for their accuracy because they are subject to economic data, fluctuating trends, and uncertain environments. The degree of control that the seller has in his or her business is equal to his or her actual interest. Therefore, the seller should control 51 percent of the company, or the buyer will *not* be purchasing full control of the company.

TEACHING NOTES FOR END-OF-CHAPTER CASES

CASE: WHICH WILL IT BE? (Answers to Questions)

1. **If the owner reduces the earnings estimates from seven to five years, what effect will this have on the final valuation? If the individual increases the discount factor from 15 percent to 20-22 percent, what effect will this have on the final valuation?**

If the owner reduces the earnings estimate from seven to five years, it would increase the final valuation. At 15 percent the PVIF is .3759, but at five years the PVIF is .4972. If the discount factor increases from 15 percent to 20-22 percent, the final valuation will decrease. At 15 percent for seven years the PVIFA is 4.1604, and for 20 percent at seven years the PVIFA is 3.6046, so using different amounts of years and discount rates will change the final valuation.

The Dryden Press

2. *How do the replacement value and liquidation value methods work? Why would the Isaacsons want to examine these methods?*

The replacement value works based on the value that each asset is replaced at current costs. The firm's worth is calculated as if the company is starting from the beginning. You use inflation and annual depreciation of assets in raising the value above the reported book value. Replacement value doesn't reflect earnings power or intangible assets and doesn't consider earning potential. It's best used when a company is breaking into a new line of business. When using the liquidation value method, you have to assume the business stops operation. You have to sell all assets and pay off liabilities. The amount left over is distributed to the shareholders. This amount reflects the bottom value of a firm and also indicates the amount of money that could be borrowed on a secured basis. The liquidation value is effective in giving absolute bottom value, which a firm should liquidate rather than sell. The Isaacsons would want to use the replacement value because some of the assets in the company may be old, and in a few years the Isaacsons might have to replace those assets. The assets would increase in price due to inflation. If the Isaacsons used the replacement value and the company had older assets, the Isaacsons could acquire the company at a lower price. The Isaacsons would want to use the liquidation value because it represents the bottom value of the firm. The liquidation value eliminates all assets and liabilities the company has. Using the liquidation value would tell the Isaacsons what the company is worth if it ceases to operate.

3. *If the Isaacsons conclude that the business is worth $410,000, what will be the final selling price, assuming a sale is made? Defend your answer.*

The final selling price would be $455,000. Compute this cost by adding what the seller wants to sell for $500,000 and adding what the buyer wants to buy for $410,000 and dividing it by two. This is a 50-50 split on the remaining differences in the two prices between the seller and the buyer.

CASE: A VALUATION MATTER

1. *Under the adjusted tangible book value method, what is Charles's business worth? Show your calculations.*

Charles's business is worth $400,000.

(1) Adjusted value of tangible net worth. $400,000

(2) Earning power at 10 percent of an amount equal to the adjustable tangible net worth.   40,000   (400,000 X .10)

(3) Reasonable salary for owner/
operator in the business   48,000   (40,000 + 8,000)

(4) Net earnings of the business
over recent years   30,000   (150,000/5)

(5) Extra earning power of the
business (line 4 minus lines
2 and 3)   (58,000)   [30,000-(40,000
                                             +48,000)]

(6) Value of intangibles   none

(7) Final price, add
lines 1 and 6 $400,000

2. **Under the discounted earning method, what is Charles's business worth? Show your calculations.**

Charles's business is worth $410,300.

Year	Estimated Earnings	Present Value	Estimated Earnings X Present Value
1	100,000	.806	80,600
2	125,000	.650	81,250
3	150,000	.524	78,600
4	200,000	.423	84,600
5	250,000	.341	82,250
			410,300

3. **Which of the two methods is most accurate? Why?**
The discounted earnings method is more accurate because it uses the value of money over time. Using the discounted earnings method lets you use the present value factor so you can calculate the increase in inflation.

ADDITIONAL EXPERIENTIAL EXERCISES

"Researching a Business for Sale"

The students should be placed into groups of four or five in order to conduct research in the field. They should do a report on their research findings.

The groups should go to a business which is presently being offered for sale.

They should proceed as if they were actually going to buy the business. This should include setting up interviews with the realtor, the owner of the business, and anyone else they may feel it is necessary to interview.

The students should follow the chapter using each section of the chapter and applying it.

Once the leg work is done, the groups should prepare oral and written reports for a grade. This exercise should excite interest, as well as give practical experience, by showing how each group went about their research and what they found.

Who knows? Maybe this information would be valuable to the seller or a potential buyer of the business.

(OR)

"Analyzing the Ratios"

From a computer program, students will be given the ideal ratios for adjusted tangible book value, price/earnings ratio method, and discounted earnings method. Students will then be given information that will be used to make vital changes in the ratios. These changes will both increase and decrease the ratios. Students will then be instructed to evaluate the changes and determine whether the changes help or hinder the firm. This exercise is intended to help students understand what will happen to the ratios when changes are made.

CHAPTER 19

MANAGEMENT SUCCESSION AND CONTINUITY: A FAMILY BUSINESS PERSPECTIVE

CHAPTER OUTLINE

I. Family-Owned Business
   A. Family businesses grow in spite of complex challenges
   B. Family values and influences
      1. Preserving humanity in the workplace
      2. Focusing on the long run
      3. Emphasizing quality
   C. Key advantages
      1. Greater flexibility
      2. Stability
      3. Resilience
   D. Key disadvantages
      1. Family disputes
      2. Nepotism
      3. Succession dramas

II. The Management Succession Issue
   A. Transition of managerial decision making in a firm
   B. Myriad of problems
      1. The owner
      2. Death-negative conotation
      3. Sibling rivalry

III. Key Factors in Succession
   A. Pressures and interests inside the firm
      1. Family members
         a. Pressure for family management
         b. Pressure to designate an heir
         c. Rivalry among branches of family
      2. Nonfamily employees
         a. Effort to protect interest
         b. Accommodation critical for survival
   B. Pressures and interest from outside the firm
      1. Family members
         a. Pressure to inherit part of operation
         b. Pressure to get involved in business
         c. Pressure to hire family member
      2. Nonfamily elements

        a. Competition changing its strategy
        b. Other factors
    C. Forcing events
        1. Death
        2. Illness or nonterminal physical incapacitation
        3. Mental or psychological breakdown
        4. Abrupt departure to retire immediately
        5. Legal problems
        6. Severe business decline
        7. Financial difficulties
    D. Sources of succession
        1. Entrepreneurial successor
        2. Managerial successor
        3. Early entry vs. delayed entry strategies
    E. Legal restrictions
        1. Oakland Scavenger Company case
        2. Be aware when preparing succession plan

IV. Developing the Succession Strategy
    A. Understanding the contextual aspects
        1. Time
        2. Type of venture
        3. Capabilities of manager
        4. Entrepreneur's vision
        5. Environmental factors
    B. Identifying successor qualities
        1. Qualities and characteristics depend on situation
    C. Understanding influencing forces
        1. Family and business culture issues
        2. Owner's concerns
        3. Family member concerns
        4. Written policy strategies
        5. Additional actions to consider
    D. Carrying out the succession plan
        1. Identify a successor
        2. Groom an heir
        3. Agree on a plan
            a. Detailed person-to-person discussion
            b. Attention to day-to-day operations
        4. Consider outside help

V. The Harvest Strategy: Selling Out
    A. Step 1: Prepare a financial analysis
    B. Step 2: Segregate assets

    C. Step 3: Value the business
    D. Step 4: Appropriate timing
    E. Step 5: Publicize the offer to sell
    F. Step 6: Finalize the prospective buyers
    G. Step 7: Remain involved through the closing
    H. Step 8: Communicate after the sale

VI. Summary

CHAPTER OBJECTIVES

1. To describe the importance of family businesses and their unique problems
2. To examine the key factors in family business succession
3. To identify and describe some of the most important sources of succession
4. To discuss the potential impact of recent legislation on family business succession
5. To relate the ways to develop a succession strategy
6. To explain the steps involved in carrying out a succession plan
7. To present a "harvest strategy" for selling out as a final alternative

CHAPTER SUMMARY

    This chapter introduces the importance of family business to the U.S. economy. After highlighting some of the values and influences of family firms, the key advantages and disadvantages are presented.

    The management succession issue is a critical concern since the average life expectancy of a family business is 24 years. The transition of decision making in a firm is challenged by many problems including the owner, death anxiety, and sibling rivalry.

    The chapter then discusses some of the key factors that can affect the succession issue. Pressures and interest from inside and outside the firm need to be addressed by the entrepreneur. Employees, both family and nonfamily members, may have an interest in the succession of the owner's business. Even nonemployed family members may want a stake in the business. Other nonfamily elements such as competition, technology, tax laws, management trends, etc., can cause pressure on the entrepreneur.

    Another key factor is family feuding. Family feuding can often result in a business going bankrupt, being sold, or being terminated. Family feuding can also be critically important to the economy. When small and large family-dominated firms are combined, they account for over 50 percent of the gross national product.

    The easiest way to avoid these problems is by grooming a successor. However, the founder may be reluctant to give up his/her power and may consider his/her children to be too young to run the business. An interpretation problem may also occur among family members that may cause the entrepreneur to avoid the succession issue.

The Dryden Press

Other situations that one may encounter is threat of the founder, who may be unwilling to share his/her authority; the children who may not want the business; a group of heirs who may want to play a role in the business; or the transaction may be made in a logical, businesslike manner.

The last factor the chapter describes as being key in succession issues is that of forcing events. These events require the owner to step down and let somebody else direct the operation. These events include death, illness or nonterminal physical incapacitation, mental or psychological breakdown, legal problems, severe business decline, and financial difficulties.

Next, the chapter discusses succession in further topics such as sources of succession and legal restrictions. Under sources of succession, one way of determining a successor is to consider an entrepreneurial successor, who would be high in ingenuity and creativity, or a managerial successor, who is interested in efficiency and internal control. Another way of determining a successor is to look inside the family for a leader such as a son or daughter or a nephew or a niece. One important factor is that the successor and the owner get along. The founder may also train a team of executive managers consisting of family and nonfamily members in hopes of producing a successor.

Other sources of successors may be family members outside the firm and nonfamily outsiders. The owner may not see an immediate successor and hire a professional manager temporarily. The owner may also hire a specialist to help rejuvenate a business with financial difficulties. Lastly, the owner may hire an assistant who has the right talents and who will eventually own the business.

Another topic is that of legal restrictions. The Oakland Scavenger Company case has had a major effect on the management succession plan in that a family-dominated business can be sued by an employee of a different ethnic origin based upon not being provided with the same treatment as a son or daughter. Family businesses will have to be aware of this challenge when preparing a succession plan.

The third major topic Chapter 19 addresses is that of developing a succession strategy. There are three steps in developing a strategy: (1) understanding the contextual aspects, (2) identifying successor qualities, and (3) carrying out the succession plan.

There are five key conceptual aspects to developing a succession plan. These are the aspects of time, type of venture, capabilities of the manager, entrepreneur's vision, and environmental factors. Unless the individual and the environment fit well together, the successor will be less than maximally effective.

When identifying a successor's qualities and characteristics, you must remember that they may be different depending on the situation. Also, there are some influencing forces that may affect what qualities are needed in a successor. These are family and business culture issues, owner's concerns, family member concerns, written policy strategies, and any additional concerns the owner may find pertinent.

The last step is carrying out the succession plan. There are four steps which one should follow when carrying out the plan. First, the owner should identify the successor or at least the characteristics and experience needed. Next, the owner should groom an heir. Then, the successor and owner must agree on a plan. This requires a detailed person-to-person discussion and attention to day-to-day operations. Lastly, the owner should consider outside help in order to back up any of his or her weaknesses.

The last section of the chapter deals with the harvest strategy. This is the method that an entrepreneur should follow when selling out his/her business. There are eight steps for the proper preparation, development, and realization of the sale. These are: (1) prepare a financial analysis, (2) segregate assets, (3) value the business, (4) utilize appropriate timing, (5) publicize the offer to sell, (6) finalize the prospective buyers, (7) remain involved through the closing, and (8) communicate after the sale. In addition, the entrepreneur must be aware of the tax implications arising from the sale of a business.

LECTURE NOTES

MANAGEMENT SUCCESSION AND CONTINUITY: A FAMILY BUSINESS PERSPECTIVE

I. Family-Owned Business
   A. Family businesses do grow despite the complex challenges that they face.
   B. There are values and influences apparent in family business such as long-run focus, quality emphasis, and humane values.
   C. Some of the key advantages involved with family businesses are
      1. Greater flexibility
      2. Stability
      3. Resilience
   D. Some of the disadvantages of family firms are
      1. Family disputes
      2. Nepotism
      3. Succession dramas

II. The Management Succession Issue--Family management succession poses one of the greatest challenges for entrepreneurs. One of the major problems is the owner. The owner is the business. The individual's personality and talents make the operation what it is. If this person were to be removed from the picture, the company might be unable to continue.

III. Key Factors in Succession--There are a number of considerations that affect the succession issue. One way of examining them is in terms of pressures and interests inside the firm and outside the firm. Another way is by examining the topic of family feuding. A third is in terms of forcing events.
   A. Pressures and interests inside the firm. There are two types of pressures that originate within the firm.
      1. Rivalry among the family members
      2. Nonfamily employees
   B. Pressures and interests from outside the firm. Outside the firm there are pressures and interests from both family members and nonfamily elements.
      1. Family members: They are interested in ensuring that they inherit part of the

operation or are allowed to get involved in the business.
2. Nonfamily elements: Competition that continually changes its strategies. Other factors include: customers, technology, and new-product development. Tax laws, regulatory agencies, and trends in management practices constitute still other elements with which the owner must contend.
C. Forcing events--Those happenings that cause the replacement of the owner-manager. The following are typical examples
1. Death
2. Illness
3. Mental or psychological breakdown
4. Abrupt departure
5. Legal problems
6. Severe business decline
7. Financial difficulties

IV. Succession: Further Topics
A. Who should be the next company president? In answering this question, in addition to what has already been discussed, there are two aspects of the problem that merit attention
1. Sources of succession--One way of determining a successor is through consideration of an entrepreneurial successor or a managerial successor. When the entrepreneur is looking for an insider, he or she usually looks for a son or daughter, nephew or niece. The entrepreneur can also train a team of executives and choose a successor from this team.
2. Legal restrictions--The traditions of succession practices in family businesses recently have been challenged in the Oakland Scavenger Company case. This suit was brought by a group of black and Hispanic workers in the California-based Oakland Scavenger Company who complained of employment discrimination because of their race. The Oakland Scavenger case has started a movement that is sure to result in new guidelines and limitations for family employment, and family businesses will have to be aware of this challenge when preparing succession plans.

V. Developing a Succession Strategy--There are several important steps in developing a succession plan
A. Understanding the contextual aspects
1. Time
2. Type of venture
3. Capabilities of managers
4. Entrepreneur's vision
5. Environmental factors
B. Identifying successor qualities--There are many qualities or characteristics that successors should possess
C. Understanding influencing forces

1. Family and business culture issues
    a. Business environment
    b. Stage of firm's development
    c. Business traditions and norms
    d. Family culture strength and influence
    e. Owner's personal motivations and values
2. Owner's concerns
    a. Relinquishing power and leadership
    b. Keeping the family functioning as a unit
    c. Defining family members' future roles in the business
    d. Assuring competent future leadership in the firm
    e. Educating family and nonfamily members about key roles
    f. Keeping nonfamily resources in the firm
3. Family member concerns
    a. Gaining and losing control of family assets
    b. Having control over decisions made by business leadership
    c. Protecting interest when ownership is dispersed among family members
    d. How to get money out of the business if necessary
    e. Assurance that the business will continue
4. These forces and concerns prepare the legal adviser for establishing a management continuity, strategy, or policy. A written policy can be established in one of the following strategies
    a. The owner controls the management continuity strategy entirely
    b. The owner consults with selected family members
    c. The owner works with professional advisers
    d. The owner works with family involvement
5. If the owner is still reasonably healthy and the firm is in a viable condition, the following additional actions should be considered
    a. Formulate buy-sell agreements
    b. Consider employee stock ownership plans
    c. Sell or liquidate the business when the owner loses enthusiasm
    d. Sell or liquidate when the owner discovers a terminal illness

D. Carrying out the succession plan--History reveals that while succession can be a problem, there are effective ways of dealing with it. The following are four important steps in doing so
1. Identify a successor
2. Groom an heir
3. Agree on a plan
4. Consider outside help

VI. The Harvest Strategy: Selling Out
   A. Prepare a financial analysis
   B. Segregate assets

C. Value the business
D. Utilize appropriate timing
E. Publicize the offer to sell
F. Finalize the prospective buyers
G. Remain involved through the closing
H. Communicate after the sale

SUGGESTED ANSWERS FOR DISCUSSION QUESTIONS (END OF CHAPTER)

1. *Describe the importance of family business in our economy.*

    Family businesses account for the largest percentage of our nation's businesses, according to expert estimates at the federal level. These family businesses also account for nearly 50 percent of the gross domestic product (GDP) product and employ about half of the private sector workforce. During the last decade, there were more than 600,000 new business start-ups yearly in this country. Many of these were family firms that will help increase GDP and employment. However, small business survival is becoming more difficult each year.

2. *What are some of the advantages and disadvantages of family firms?*

    Psychologist Manfred Kets de Vries examined the advantages and disadvantages associated with family businesses. Table 19.1 provides an overview of his particular items. Some of the key advantages have already been touched upon (greater flexibility of action, long-term orientation, stability, resilience, and less bureaucracy). The disadvantages include family disputes, paternalistic (or maternalistic) rule, confusing organization (no clear division of tasks), nepotism (promoting inept family members), and succession dramas.

3. *There are a number of barriers to succession in family firms. Using Table 19.2, identify some of the key barriers.*

    One of the major ones is the owner. To a large degree, the owner **is** the business. Any attempts by the family to get the person to step aside are often viewed by the owner as efforts by greedy family members who want to plunder the operation for personal gain. More significantly, there may be anxiety over death, since raising the topic of death conjures up a negative image in everyone's mind.

    Other barriers to succession may be sibling rivalry, family members' fear of losing status, or a complete aversion to death for fear of loss or abandonment.

4. *What pressures do entrepreneurs sometimes face from inside the family? (Use Figure 19.1 in your answer.)*

    The entrepreneur will face the pressure of a family member wanting to manage the business, the pressure of the family members wanting an heir to be declared, and also rivalry among the different branches of the family. Also, from family members outside the firm, the entrepreneur will face the pressure to inherit part of the operation, to become involved in the business, and the pressure to be hired.

5. ***What pressures do entrepreneurs sometimes face from outside the family? (Use Figure 19.1 in your answer.)***

   From outside the family and within a firm, an employee may pressure the entrepreneur to give the employee an opportunity to buy a stake in the business or be given a percentage of the business in the owner's will. Also, from outside the firm the entrepreneur may feel pressure from competitors and customers along with technological pressure, new-product development, tax laws, regulatory agencies, and trends in management.

6. ***There are a number of choices that an entrepreneur can make regarding a successor. Using Table 19.3 as a guide, what are these choices? Discuss each.***

   The entrepreneur can look for an entrepreneurial successor. This is someone who often provides critical ideas for new-product development and future ventures. This person has high ingenuity, creativity, and drive. The entrepreneur can look for a managerial successor. This person would be interested in efficiency, internal control, and the effective use of resources and often provides the stability and day-to-day direction needed to keep the enterprise going.

   The entrepreneur could also look inside or outside his/her family for a successor. Looking inside, he or she would look for a son or daughter, nephew or niece with whom he or she gets along well. Looking outside, the entrepreneur would look for a professional manager, a specialist, or a person with the right talents to be an assistant. The entrepreneur might also be training a team of both family and nonfamily members in hopes that a successor will arise from there.

7. ***How might the Oakland Scavenger case affect succession decisions in small business?***

   The Oakland Scavenger case may affect succession decisions in small businesses in that a small business may be sued by an employee of a different ethnic origin than the owner, based upon not being accorded the same treatment as a son or daughter.

8. ***What are three of the contextual aspects that must be considered in an effective succession plan?***

   Three of the contextual aspects that must be considered in an effective succession plan are type of venture, capabilities of managers, and environmental factors.

9. ***In what way can forcing events cause the replacement of an owner-manager? Cite three examples.***

   A forcing event will require the entrepreneur to step aside and let somebody else direct the operation. Three examples would be death, an abrupt departure with no advance warning, and illness or a nonterminal physical incapacitation.

10. **What are five qualities or characteristics successors should possess?**

Five qualities or characteristics a successor should possess are enthusiasm about the enterprise, a high degree of perseverance, a reasonable amount of aggressiveness, problem-solving ability, and talent to develop people.

11. **What are four steps that should be taken in carrying out a succession plan? Describe each of these steps.**

The first step in carrying out a succession plan is to identify a successor. The owner-manager should name a successor, or at least the characteristics and experience needed by the individual should be stated. The next step is to groom an heir. The heir must be allowed to learn the practice and take on some of the authority before becoming the owner-manager. Next, the owner and the heir agree on a plan. In a small firm it is wise to have a detailed person-to-person discussion of how responsibilities will be transferred to the successor. Afterwards, it will be wise to have those who are affected help in making the final plans. The last step is to consider outside help. Some owner-managers do not realize or refuse to admit that the business has outgrown them. An outsider may be able to make this clear and enhance the business.

12. **When harvesting a business, what eight steps should be followed? Discuss each of these steps.**

The eight steps to harvesting a business start with preparing a financial analysis. The purpose of an analysis is to define priorities and to focus the next few years of business. The second step is to segregate assets. There are four points that tax accountants and lawyers may suggest to follow to reduce your taxes. The third step is to value the business. This part constitutes a most important step in its sale. The fourth step is appropriate timing. Knowing when to sell your business is critical. The fifth step is to publicize the offer to sell. This should consist of a short prospectus with enough information to interest investors. Step six is finalizing the prospective buyers. You should assess characters and managerial reputation in order to find the best buyer. Step seven is to remain involved through the closing. Meet with the buyer to help eliminate misunderstandings and negotiate major requirements. The final step, eight, is to communicate after the sale. Problems between new managers and remaining employees need to be resolved for a smooth transition.

TEACHING NOTES FOR END-OF-CHAPTER CASES

CASE: JUST AS GOOD AS EVER (Answers to Questions)

1. **Why is Pablo reluctant to turn over the reins to Jose? Include a discussion of Figure 19.1 in your answer.**

Pablo's business has been in operation for 22 years. It has taken him that long to get his business where he wants it. Now he must turn it over to someone, and Pablo does not want his life's work to go down the drain. Pablo also knows his business inside and out. He is probably capable of doing any job that there is in his company. It would be hard for Pablo to turn over his company to an untrained person.

2. ***Cite and discuss two reasons Pablo should begin thinking about succession planning.***

   Recently Pablo suffered a heart attack. Obviously his health is not good. Pablo must come up with a succession plan before his health fails again. If Pablo died there would be nobody capable of running his company. The sooner Pablo starts grooming an heir, the better off his family would be.

3. ***What would you recommend Rebecca and Jose do to convince Pablo they are right? Offer at least three operative recommendations.***

   Jose and Rebecca should try to convince Pablo that he needs help with the company. They should look within the company for a competent manager that could do Pablo's job. Another place to find a replacement for Pablo is outside the company. Pablo could start looking for a person with his skills and experience and bring him into the company. Also, Pablo could start training his son for the president's chair, although, as was stated, it will take ten to fifteen years. Pablo has enough time to train his son as long as his son is interested. Another alternative to the problem is to sell the company. The company is very successful, and Pablo would have no problem finding a buyer.

CASE: NEEDING SOME HELP ON THIS ONE

1. ***Identify and explain four characteristics you would expect to find in a successful manager in this type of venture.***

   To work in an auto repair shop, a person must be familiar with that kind of work. It would be unlikely that a person with no automotive experience could manage a repair shop. Also, a manager must be able to plan and organize. This would be important to Jack's repair shop because of the number of cars that are backed up waiting to be worked on. Enthusiasm also would be a good managerial quality. If the manager is bored and unmotivated, business will tend to stagnate. Also, a manager's work should be thorough.

2. ***What steps does Jack need to follow in successfully identifying and grooming a successor?***

   To successfully determine an heir, Jack must learn to delegate authority and decentralize his operations. By doing this, Jack will let others do his job. Jack must also look at all his possible successors. In his case, he has three possible successors. Jack can plan for more than just one successor. He could do this by developing the successor's skills at running a company. Jack could also do this by encouraging the successor to find work outside the company. Jack should also keep his successors updated on what is going on within the company. By letting them know important business situations, Jack's successors could find insight in the business. Jack should also plan with his successors for the future of his business. By doing this, Jack would get an idea of what his heirs intend to do with the company and if he agrees with them.

3. *If you were going to advise Jack, what would you recommend he do first? How should he get started with his succession plan? What should he do next? Offer him some general guidance on how to handle this problem.*

Jack should look toward the most competent individual to run his company. If his sons and nephew are all equally qualified and interested in his business, he should also consider dividing it among the three. But if the three do not get along, he should consider an alternative division of the company. Jack should definitely figure out who he wants to head his company before any other plans are made. Jack's decision should be based on a person's motivation, knowledge of the business, qualifications, honesty, and if he has good social skills. After being chosen for that position, a person must be trained. Jack must delegate his authority and decentralize his operations to his heirs. By doing this, it will give his heirs the experience they need. When Jack feels his heir or heirs are competent to take over the business, the only thing left to do is to step aside.

ADDITIONAL EXPERIENTIAL EXERCISES

"Creating a Successor"

Develop a business of your own using outstanding qualities and characteristics that you possess as key factors to the efficiency of the business.

Now, assume you have been running this business all your life and it has been a great success. From your family members, determine who would be the most effective person to install in your business if you were retiring. Remember key factors such as growth of the business, whether the business needs an entrepreneurial or a managerial leader, and any other factors that would be pertinent for a successor.

Now compare the qualities and characteristics you see your assigned successor possess and the qualities and characteristics you possess that you used when starting your business. How similar are the qualities and characteristics? How different are they? Give reasons for your findings. Discuss your comparisons in class.

(OR)

"Making the Choice--A Role Play"

Studying and learning about succession is important, but to actually make the decisions concerning succession is quite difficult. This exercise is designed to familiarize students with the problems of succession, firsthand. Organize into groups of four. Choose three of the group members to be children of the owner and one to be the owner of a family business. The students should be given packets of information concerning all the children's qualifications, weaknesses, and perhaps education. Additional information may be put into the packets by the teacher. Each of the three children is to put together a five-minute presentation on why he or she should be the successor or why someone else should not. After role playing, the owner must make a decision as to who will be the successor and why.

CHAPTER 20

TOTAL QUALITY AND THE HUMAN FACTOR: CONTINUOUS CHALLENGES FOR ENTREPRENEURS

CHAPTER OUTLINE

I. Introduction

II. Nature of Total Quality Management
   A. Core values and concepts
   B. Vision formulation
   C. Top management support
   D. Planning and organizing
   E. Implementing and controlling

III. TQM Tools and Techniques
   A. Data collection sheets
   B. Pareto charts
   C. Cause-and-effect diagrams
   D. Scatter diagrams
   E. Tool box

IV. Customer Service Focus
   A. Beliefs and values
   B. Data gathering
   C. Data analysis

V. Cycle Time Focus
   A. Paring time

VI. Employee Focus
   A. Training
   B. Empowerment
   C. Recognition

VII. Continuous Improvement
   A. Benefits and characteristics
   B. Guidelines and principles

VIII. Summary

CHAPTER OBJECTIVES

1. To define the term *total quality management* (TQM).
2. To review the core values and concepts of TQM.
3. To examine some of the most commonly used TQM tools and techniques that are employed by entrepreneurial firms in increasing the quality of goods and services.
4. To present some of the ways that total quality management firms focus on meeting customer needs.
5. To study some of the ways in which cutting-edge firms use employee focus and continuous improvement concepts to remain highly competitive.

LECTURE NOTES
Total Quality and the Human Factor: Continuous Challenges for Entrepreneurs

I. Introduction
   A. Total quality management is a people-focused management system that aims at continual increases in customer service at continually lower real costs. There are three ways in which this is typically done. One way is by finding out what customers want and designing goods and services to meet these needs. A second is by learning how to provide this output as efficiently as possible by eliminating both time and cost. A third is by continuing to improve the process by looking for improvements.

II. Nature of Total Quality Management
   A. The nature of total quality management encompasses a series of ten TQM values and concepts.
      1. Customer-driven quality
      2. Leadership
      3. Continuous improvement
      4. Full participation
      5. Rapid response
      6. Prevention, not detection
      7. Long-range outlook
      8. Management by fact
      9. Partnership development
      10. Public responsibility

   B. Vision formulation is needed in order to determine how TQM will be merged with the operating philosophy of the business.
   C. Top management support is critical to the formulation and implementation of TQM because managers need to know how the process works if they are to lead it, and the

rest of the personnel want to know that the managers both know and support the TQM program.
   D. After top management gives its support to the program, the next step is to plan and organize the effort. This involves setting quality objectives, forming quality teams, and determining how the overall effort will be supervised.
   E. The next step is to implement and control the TQM plan. This involves such steps as focusing on key result areas and ensuring that adequate progress continues to be made.

III. Tools and Techniques
   A. Data collection sheets are used to gather information on performance so that problems can be identified and corrected. These sheets are designed so that the information can be easily recorded, tabulated, and analyzed.
   B. A Pareto chart is a special form of vertical bar graph that helps identify which problems are to be solved and in what order. The basic concepts behind this chart is explained by the Pareto principle, which holds that 80 percent of all outcomes can be attributed to 20 percent of all causes. Since a small number of problems account for a large percentage of what goes wrong, entrepreneurs can increase the quality of their output by correcting these handful of problems.
   C. Cause-and-effect diagrams are often used as a follow-up to Pareto analysis. The Pareto chart identifies the problems; the cause-and-effect diagram helps explain the reasons and points the way toward solutions or improvements. This TQM tool typically begins with a brainstorming session designed to identify some of the causes of the problem. Then the reasons are put into categories which are used to construct a cause-and-effect diagram.
   D. Another widely used TQM tool is the scatter diagram, which illustrates the relationship between two variables.
   E. Depending on the problem under investigation, some tools and techniques will be of more value than others. If the personnel choose the right tool, they can accurately investigate the problem and arrive at an action plan that is likely to resolve the matter.

IV. Customer Service Focus
   A. The primary focus of all TQM efforts is the customer. For this reason, every total quality management strategy must be designed to find out what the customer wants, how well the firm is currently providing this output, and what the company needs to do to improve its performance and at least match, if not stay ahead of, customer expectations. This is typically done by placing attention on three areas: beliefs and values, data gathering, and data analysis.
   B. Total quality firms clearly think through their beliefs and values about customer service and then communicate these to the personnel.
   C. There are a number of ways that customer-related information can be gathered. These include questionnaire surveys, customer panel surveys, and interviews.

D. After gathering the data, the next step is to analyze the information and draw conclusions for action. One of the simplest, most direct ways that this is done is by determining the frequency of responses to the various questions and then constructing a Pareto chart.

V. Cycle Time Focus
A. Cycle time is the time needed to complete a task. This time is critical to quality improvement because of its impact on productivity.
B. One of the most common approaches to improving cycle time is to examine how the work is currently done and then identify and eliminate extraneous steps. An example is provided by flow charting, in which all the steps in a job or process are identified and written out in the form of a flow diagram. Then the diagram is examined for the purpose of identifying those steps which can be eliminated or combined with others, thus reducing the cycle time for the job. A related approach is to eliminate nonvalue-added tasks and activities. Another approach to paring time is by breaking down walls between departments and getting everyone to cooperate. Another is to establish close relations with suppliers and thus reduce the time needed in getting materials from them.

VI. Employee Focus
A. Effective TQM firms always spend a great deal of attention on employee training, empowerment, and recognition.
B. Training is critical to total quality management efforts because many times the personnel have to be taught how to do things somewhat differently from the way they did them in the past. Training typically involves both mandatory and optional courses, and while inside personnel are used for most training, outside trainers are often used to supplement this process.
C. Empowerment is the authority to take control and make decisions. This process typically involves two critical elements: delegation of authority and assignment of resources for completing the work.
D. Total quality management firms maintain their quality-driven momentum through the effective use of rewards. These rewards come in a variety of different forms. Table 20.4 provides some examples.
E. Continuous improvement is the process of increasing the quality of goods and services through small incremental gains accompanied by occasional innovation. There are a number of benefits that entrepreneurially driven firms can achieve from continuous improvement. One is increased quality of output since there are ongoing improvements in the way goods and services are delivered. A second is increased competitiveness since the company is continually getting better and thus keeping up with (or surpassing) the competition. A third is higher profitability because increased quality brings about greater market demand and reduces costs caused by the need to correct mistakes. A fourth and accompanying benefit is a lower operating break-even point that is a result of lower cost per unit.

F. In achieving continuous improvement there are a number of steps that organizations will implement. Examples include: (a) keep the workplace clean so that it is easy to find things, and machinery and equipment is maintained in proper working order; (b) develop procedures for getting things done quickly and correctly, and follow these procedures each time so that it takes less time to complete work assignments; and (c) communicate openly and honestly with other employees so that information is shared and ideas that will result in continuous improvement are known to everyone.

SUGGESTED ANSWERS FOR DISCUSSION QUESTIONS (END OF CHAPTER)

1. ***What is meant by the term total quality management? How does the primary rule of total quality tie into this definition? Explain.***

    The term total quality management refers to a people-focused management system that aims at continual increases in customer service at continually lower real costs. The primary rule of total quality ties into this definition because the rule says that things should be done right the first time. This not only helps improve customer service but ensures that costs will remain low because the company will not have to spend time and money correcting mistakes.

2. ***In what way do each of the ten core values and concepts of TQM help ensure that goods and services are provided in highly cost-effective ways?***

    Each of the core values and concepts helps the company focus its efforts and ensures that buyers are getting what they want at a competitive price. Examples include: (a) customer-driven quality ensures that the company knows what the customer wants; (b) leadership helps the firm focus all of its efforts on achieving its customer-driven goal; (c) continuous improvement helps ensure that the company keeps working to improve its output; (d) full participation is useful in getting everyone to play an active role in the process; (e) rapid response ensures that the output is provided on time or earlier; (f) prevention, not detection, helps the company work on avoiding mistakes rather than correcting them later on; (g) a long-range outlook ensures that the firm focuses on the goods and services that the customer wants today and will want in the future; (h) management by fact ensures that the company documents what it is doing rather than relying on anecdotal references; (i) partnership developments help the firm get all important groups involved in the TQM process, including suppliers and customers; and (j) a public responsibility focus helps ensure that the firm remains a good corporate citizen.

3. *Why is top management support critical to all TQM efforts?*

Top management support is critical because much of what is going to happen will require changes in both thinking and work processes. Without senior-level support these changes will not come about, and the company will resort back to its pre-TQM days. Top management support ensures that management "stays the course."

4. *How is a data collection sheet used in the TQM process?*

A data collection sheet is used to gather information performance so that problems can be identified and corrected. These sheets are designed so that the information can be easily recorded, tabulated, analyzed, and acted upon. In particular, a well-designed data collection sheet can help the firm quickly and easily pinpoint problems.

5. *How does a Pareto chart work, and of what value is it in the TQM process?*

A Pareto chart is a special form of vertical bar graph that helps identify which problems are to be solved and in what order. The logic behind Pareto charts is found in the Pareto principle: 80% of all outcomes can be attributed to 20% of all causes. So by focusing on those few factors that cause most of the problems, a company can direct its TQM effort with a minimum waste of time.

6. *How does a cause-and-effect diagram work?*

A cause-and-effect diagram is used to identify the reasons for a particular outcome such as the causes of employee tardiness. These reasons are then grouped into major categories and used as a basis for following action.

7. *A company would like to know if there is any relationship between the amount of training that is being given to its salespeople and the effectiveness of these people out in the field. How could a scatter diagram be of any value in this process?*

A scatter diagram could be very useful in helping the firm correlate the relationship between sales training and sales results in the field. What the company could do is to plot the amount of training that has been given to each salesperson on the vertical axis of a graph and plot the sales of each person on the horizontal axis of the graph. Then an analysis of the dots could be made to see if there is any relationship. Hopefully, it would show that the best salespeople are those who have had the most training and vice versa. If it did, then the firm would schedule the poorest salespeople for more training. Of course, if the data showed just the opposite, the firm would stop doing sales training because the training is of no value.

8. *How does the concept of "tool box" help personnel in applying TQM tools and techniques?*

The concept of tool box holds that individuals should choose those TQM tools and techniques that will be of most value in increasing quality and ignore the other tools and techniques. Personnel are taught to choose only the right tools.

9. *Why is a customer service focus so important to all TQM efforts?*

A customer service focus is important because the objective of all TQM efforts is to provide continual increases in customer service at continually lower real costs. The customer is the focus of all efforts. Everything that is done is either directly or indirectly aimed at increasing service and keeping price as low as possible.

10. *How is cycle time related to quality? Why does a reduction in cycle time increase quality? Explain.*

Cycle time is the time needed to complete a task. If a company can provide the same amount of quality but at a faster rate, quality goes up because the firm can increase the amount of goods that it is providing to a customer without spending any more time doing so.

11. *In what way do employee training, empowerment, and recognition help an organization maintain an employee focus during its TQM effort?*

Employee training helps ensure that the personnel know how to apply TQM tools and techniques. Empowerment ensures that the personnel have both the authority and the resources to implement the suggestions and recommendations that they believe will be most effective in increasing the quality of goods and services. Recognition ensures that the employees do not lost their interest in continually increasing the quality of the goods and services they are providing.

12. *What is meant by continuous improvement? Why is this idea so important to every total quality management effort?*

Continuous improvement is the process of increasing the quality of goods and services through small incremental gains accompanied by occasional innovation. Continuous improvement is important because it ensures that the TQM effort continues to move forward every day. Rather than trying to hit a couple of home runs now and then, the organization focuses on hitting singles every day. As a result, the firm gets better and better, one small step at a time.

TEACHING NOTES FOR END-OF-CHAPTER CASES

VIDEO CASE: J.C. PENNEY: VALUING DIVERSITY

1. *How is J.C. Penney exemplifying the human side of total quality management?*

Penney's original philosophy followed some of the core values of TQM such as customer-driven quality, full participation, and leadership. J.C. Penney's newest programs on diversity demonstrate their commitment to an employee focus: training, empowerment, involvement, and recognition.

2. *Compare the efforts of the Henry Lee Company with J.C. Penney's efforts.*

   Henry Lee instituted the "shining star" program where any employee who submits a quality-related idea receives a reward. The awards are scaled upward to increase with the ideas and to keep employees suggesting new ideas. J.C. Penney's goes further by instituting specific programs on topics such as diversity and then sets up mentor committees to measure the progress and help associates advance and improve.

3. *Discuss continuous improvement as it applies to J.C. Penney.*

   Continuous improvement is the process of increasing the quality of goals and services through incremental gains accompanied by occasional innovation. Part of the guidelines include continuous communications with employees. J.C. Penney is doing this by way of the diversity program and the support areas that go with it.

IT'S ALL A MATTER OF QUALITY   (Answers to Questions)

1. *How can the ten core values and concepts of TQM be of value to Harry?*

   The ten core values and concepts of TQM are important to Harry because they can help guide and lead him in implementing total quality management. For example: (a) a customer-driven approach will ensure that he knows what the customer wants; (b) leadership will help him focus the organization's efforts; (c) continuous improvement will help his company get continually better; (d) full participation will ensure that everyone plays an active role; (e) rapid response will help ensure that jobs are completed on time or earlier; (f) a focus on prevention, not detection, will help ensure that the company works on avoiding mistakes rather than correcting them later on; (g) a long-range outlook will ensure that the firm focuses on the goods and services that the customer wants today and will want in the future; (h) management by fact will help the company document what it is doing rather than relying on anecdotal references; (i) partnership developments will help the firm get all important groups involved in the TQM process, especially customers; and (j) a public responsibility focus will help ensure that the firm remains a good corporate citizen.

2. *How can Harry ensure that he is providing the best service to his customers? Give two examples.*

   One way that Harry can ensure that he is providing the best service to his customers is by asking each of them to fill out a questionnaire on how well the work has been done, thus providing him with feedback on what he is doing well and poorly. A second way he can ensure he is providing the best service is to take the information from this questionnaire and act on it appropriately. A third way is by looking at the amount of repeat business he receives. If customers give his name to their friends and more and more people call up Harry and ask for his services, he will know that he is providing the best service.

3. *What type of TQM training should Harry provide to his people? Give two examples.*

There are a couple of types of training that Harry could provide to his people. One is how to gather information so they will know how to get feedback on performance. Another is how to analyze the data. This could take the form of Pareto charts and/or the fishbone technique. The first would give the company information on which it could act. The second would help point the way to action.

CLARA'S PLAN

1. *What steps should Mary take first if she wants to introduce a TQM approach in her organization? Identify and describe two.*

There are a number of steps that Mary could take. One is to decide what she means by quality, i.e., define her objectives. The second is organize her operation so that it can deal with the results of the questionnaire. A third is to train her people to use TQM tools and techniques. A fourth is to get the personnel to accept a continuous improvement philosophy and keep looking for new ways to improve overall service.

2. *Which two total quality management tools would you suggest she use in analyzing the data and deciding what to do as a result? Explain how this process should be carried out.*

The first tool she should use is Pareto analysis. This would quickly indicate that faster service is needed and there should be an increase in the selection of menu items. From here she could have her people fishbone the respective problems, identify possible reasons for them, and develop an action plan for resolving them.

3. *What role should training play in Mary's TQM effort? Explain your reasoning.*

Training is going to be important in Mary's TQM effort because her people probably do not know very much (if anything) about TQM tools and concepts. She should start by discussing with them her reasons for wanting to introduce a total quality management approach and get them involved in helping define quality and identify ways of improving it. Then she could have them trained in those TQM tools that would be of most value. Finally, she could get them to accept continuous improvement. These would be some excellent objectives with which Mary could start her TQM effort.

Instructor's Teaching Notes

for Comprehensive Case Studies

COMPREHENSIVE CASE FOR PART 1

ODYSSEUM: AN INTRAPRENEUR'S VISION AT POLAROID

Teaching Notes

SUMMARY OF THE CASE

This case deals with the actual experiences of a woman employed at the Polaroid Corporation who developed a new idea for possible venture development. Several aspects of her story are highlighted in order to determine the fate of her idea.

Odysseum (a name taken from Odysseus, the great explorer in Greek mythology, and Lyceum, a place of entertainment) is the new venture idea that Joline Godfrey created. It is a visual experience game that allows participants to take pictures that solve a puzzle or riddle. In so doing they "experience" more of what they see.

The major challenge for Joline is presenting her idea to the executive board at Polaroid and convincing them to keep the concept alive as a separate business entity even though it is a service concept in a products company.

TEACHING OBJECTIVES

1. To illustrate new concept development within an existing corporation.
2. To develop a service idea in a products company.
3. To show the challenge of pushing a new idea through the executive board of a corporation when they're unsure of the concept's future.
4. To discuss the ramifications of a Fortune 500 company's flexibility in allowing employees to develop new ideas.
5. To explain the importance of a corporation's strategy in the acceptance of new ventures within the corporate environment.

This teaching note was prepared by Dr. Donald F. Kuratko, College of Business, Ball State University. Presented and accepted by the refereed Midwest Society for Case Research Workshop, 1985. All rights reserved to the author and to the Midwest Society for Case Research. Copyright (c) 1985 by Donald F. Kuratko.

APPROPRIATE APPLICATIONS OF THE CASE

    Entrepreneurship
    Strategic management
    Business policy
    Management (innovation and development)

ISSUES IN THE CASE

A number of prominent issues surface for consideration in this case. They include:

(1) The concept of intrapreneurship--How far should companies let employees go in developing new ideas? Can intrapreneurship really take place?
(2) Odysseum as an idea--Could this concept really become a venture of its own at Polaroid? What are the major problems for the executives to consider?
(3) The culture at Polaroid--What type of culture is being developed at Polaroid in allowing Joline to test this idea? Is it healthy or harmful?
(4) Strategic direction--How should the executive board react to Joline's presentation? Does it fit their strategic direction or would it create a new strategic direction?
(5) Joline Godfrey as an intrapreneur--What characteristics are evident in Joline that seem entrepreneurial? Does she illustrate what is needed to be a corporate intrapreneur?

QUESTIONS FOR CLASS DISCUSSION

1. ***As a member of Polaroid's executive board, what decision would you make concerning Odysseum? Why?***

This decision is difficult, and this could be a leading question. With the limited information provided, an executive decision would definitely be to stop further development of the idea unless it becomes a marketing tool for selling products. Specifically, more detailed financial projections would have to be presented for an executive board to analyze the strategic decision.

However, encourage students to react with this limited information and analyze their decisions. In other words, this is a perfect "setup" for typical corporate decision making that rejects creative thoughts and seeks logical, analytical thinking. Thus, a strong discussion can take place concerning the desire for corporations to become innovative despite their inability to allow creative development since that requires free thinking, brainstorming, and little structure.

2. *If you were Joline Godfrey, what would you do if Polaroid did not accept your idea?*

   In the actual outcome of the case provided for the instructor, Joline Godfrey did leave Polaroid and start her own company. However, it is interesting to let students discuss what they would do if they were in Joline's position. This can lead to the benefits vs. costs of leaving the corporate structure to begin a new venture. The difficulties of entrepreneurship that differ from intrapreneurship can be brought out here.

3. *What major problems do you see for this venture to succeed at Polaroid?*

   There are a number of major problems for this venture to continue and succeed at Polaroid. First, it is a service idea within a products firm. That, of course, can be a totally different strategy for a corporation to follow. Second, there needs to be a more distinct projection of the financial success of this idea. What is being charged per customer, and how many customers are needed to break even? Sales, expenses, overhead, etc., all need to be delineated. Finally, what exactly will this venture do for Polaroid's image? How will customers perceive this new type of venture evolving from Polaroid's established operations? In other words, could this idea backfire and cause Polaroid to lose customers in their traditional markets?

4. *What benefits can be realized by Polaroid in accepting the idea?*

   At this point specific benefits are only speculation, yet, there are a few possible ones to mention. Listed below are possible benefits that could be discussed in class:
   (1) Development of a new venture
   (2) Development of a service venture, thus, expanding from the products market
   (3) Fostering of a creative, innovative culture at Polaroid
   (4) Encouragement for other employees to develop new ideas
   (5) Opportunity for executives to work through the different strategies needed in an intrapreneurial venture.

5. *Has Joline developed a feasible venture idea? Why or why not? Be specific.*

   From a strict business point of view, no. From a more creative point of view, yes. Therefore, the answer may go either way depending upon the student's research and information provided to support his or her position. If the student says no, then the strategic processes must be explained, and it must be demonstrated how Odysseum has not fulfilled that process. If the student says yes, then material or creative thinking and new product innovation needs to be presented. (Recommend researching 3-M's development of Post-It Notes as an example.)

The Dryden Press

ACTUAL OUTCOME OF THE CASE

Joline Godfrey left Polaroid and developed Odysseum into an independent firm. Located in Boston, Massachusetts, Odysseum raised more than $1 million in start-up capital from private investors (Polaroid being one of them) and two venture capital firms. Joline partnered with Jane Lytle, an MBA, in order to have business acumen brought into the venture. The two developed a complete business plan that outlined a 5-year plan projecting $25 million in revenues.

Today, Odysseum has over 50 corporate clients (including Walt Disney, American Airlines, AT&T, Apple, and Citibank), $1 million in revenues, and 14 full-time and 15 part-time employees with a $40,000 monthly payroll.

This latest strategy is to expand into the college market. Specifically Odysseum will aim at the "freshman orientation week" environment where administrators are searching for experiential exercises that acclimate the new students to each other and the campus.

COMPREHENSIVE CASE STUDY FOR PART 2

"SPORTIN' LIFE": A MINORITY ENTREPRENEUR'S CREATION

Teaching Notes

SUMMARY OF THE CASE

This case deals with a creative artist/entrepreneur, George Huggins, in his attempt to develop a cartoon character, "Sportin' Life," into a viable business venture.

A number of distinct possibilities are examined in the case including the manufacture of a *doll* and the development of *posters*. These ideas are all analyzed for a possible profitable venture. Portions of the business plan are presented including the marketing research, manufacturing and cost data, pricing, pro forma financials, and critical risks.

The case attempts to illustrate the difficulty of establishing a "creative idea" into a viable business venture. In addition, the need for a comprehensive and clear business plan from the perspective of researching the needed material is presented. "Sportin' Life" allows students the opportunity to critically assess the direction of this new venture idea.

Therefore, the segments of information and research in the case need to be analyzed by the students in reference to opportunity, feasibility, and profitability. "Sportin' Life" presents a unique entrepreneurial start-up that illustrates the challenges and frustrations of venture development.

TEACHING OBJECTIVES

1. To demonstrate the immense amount of work involved in preparing a business plan.
2. To illustrate the development and research of a new venture.
3. To provide an interesting example of a creative concept being analyzed for a profitable venture.
4. To present portions of the research needed for a business plan required for new ventures.
5. To analyze the opportunities and feasibility of a new venture.
6. To stress the importance of in-depth research for every phase of a proposed business idea.

This teaching note was prepared by Dr. Donald F. Kuratko, College of Business, Ball State University. Presented and accepted by the refereed Midwest Society for Case Research Workshop, 1985. All rights reserved to the author and to the Midwest Society for Case Research. Copyright (c) 1985 by Donald F. Kuratko.

APPROPRIATE APPLICATIONS OF THE CASE

Entrepreneurship
Small business management
Marketing
Business policy (start-up strategies)

ISSUES IN THE CASE

A number of critical issues surface in this case for consideration. They include:

(1) The immense frustration that entrepreneurs experience when confronted with so many facets of business plan development.
(2) The feasibility of the opportunities presented for "Sportin' Life" dolls, posters, or sponsorship.
(3) The examination of other opportunities for "Sportin' Life" that are not brought out in the case to develop creativity in students.
(4) Would the information presented in the case provide a solid foundation for a complete business plan?
(5) The type of financing George could pursue. Would investors be interested in this idea? Why or why not?

QUESTIONS FOR CLASS DISCUSSION

1. **As a consultant to George Huggins, what exactly would you recommend as the most viable opportunity and why?**

    The most viable opportunity for George is the development and promotion of posters. It's the quickest and most inexpensive beginning for "Sportin' Life" to emerge as a character. This is validated in the case. However, students should be encouraged to work in teams to analyze and propose various options for "Sportin' Life." (See question 2.)

2. **Are there entrepreneurial opportunities that George has not considered? What are they?**

    There are a number of entrepreneurial opportunities that George has not considered. Of course, this answer is limited only by the student's creativity and viable analysis of new avenues, but a few suggestions are provided below:
    (1)   A children's storybook series featuring "Sportin' Life"
    (2)   A cartoon strip with ongoing episodes of "Sportin' Life" in the current sports season

(3) A celebration/party supply store selling paper goods with "Sportin' Life" featured as a party theme

(4) A full-sized costume of "Sportin' Life" that could be rented for appearances at promotional events.

3. In developing a complete business plan, what information is needed or should be expanded for this concept?

In developing the complete business plan, a few more segments need to be expanded. For example, more detailed financial information will have to be developed, a more solid strategy of tangible outcomes needs to be developed, an organizational development section is needed, and contingency plans need to be covered for investors to see the alternative strategies for this character.

4. What other sources of capital should be pursued by George?

There are a number of sources within each state that should be pursued. Students should be encouraged to research the sources carefully in order to discuss the specific requirements of these sources and whether a concept like George's would qualify. Some examples of sources to be examined are: local banks, SBA guaranteed loans, SBA minority programs, venture capitalists, informal investors, and economic development agencies.

ACTUAL OUTCOME OF THE CASE

As of the writing of this case (August, 1989) George had developed a complete business plan and submitted it to a variety of sources. The Minority Business division of Indiana's Department of Commerce and the Small Business Administration have agreed that the idea is excellent but too risky for their financial support. Other sources such as drug abuse agencies and informal investors had not responded yet.

George has donated the use of his character to the Delaware County Sheriff's Office and Police Department for a bumper sticker campaign that used "Sportin' Life" in an Uncle Sam outfit, saying, "I want you to turn in a dope dealer."

In addition, George invested his own money to have large posters (8 1/2 x 11) made and offered them to school districts for their anti-drug education programs. To date, two school districts have placed orders for 50 posters each. George is currently selling the posters for $5.50 each.

Finally, as a note of interest, George was invited to the White House by Nancy Reagan in the spring of 1988 for a conference on the "Say No To Drugs" campaign. George attended, and "Sportin' Life" was very well received by Mrs. Reagan and other campaign officials. However, everyone wanted the character donated to the campaign and offered no financial support to further develop the concept. Fearing the loss of his idea before it became commercialized, George refused. Since then, none of the national campaign people have contacted George.

George is currently putting together a children's book featuring "Sportin' Life." His idea is still his passion.

COMPREHENSIVE CASE STUDY FOR PART 3

THE ROARING '20s MUSEUM—A BUSINESS PLAN

Teaching Notes

SUMMARY OF THE CASE

Michael Graham has developed a business plan on a Roaring '20s Museum. In fact, this plan won the international award at the University of Miami International Business Plan Competition. The primary objective of the Roaring '20s Museum is to attract customers to step back in time and relive Chicago's era of gangsters and rowdiness. In short, the museum will chronologically organize political and social characters and events of the 1920s era so that the customers will be able to easily follow the events in a historical fashion. The Roaring '20s Museum's three primary goals are to entertain visitors during their stay in Chicago, educate them on Chicago's and the nation's history, and meet or exceed the projected return on investment for the limited partnership.

CRITICAL ANALYSIS OF THE BUSINESS PLAN SEGMENTS

Business Description

The Roaring '20s Museum is the first and only prohibition/gangster museum located in Chicago. This museum will offer a service to the public, which is to step back in time and relive the prohibition/gangster era during the 1920s. The visitors will participate and interact with the museum's displays and multimedia presentations, and they will participate in a raid led by Elliot Ness. Thus, the customers will understand not only what it is like to live and die as gangsters but also as a crime fighter. Michael Graham has thus far described an interesting idea to attract customers that want to learn more about the "Al Capone" days as well as being entertained on past historical events.

One of Michael Graham's strengths is that he has a collection of memorabilia on the prohibition era, which was used in the movie "The Untouchables." Moreover, he has set up a national network of antique dealers for collecting memorabilia for his museum. He is considered an expert on Chicago and the nation's history during the prohibition era. However, in his business description, he did not clearly explain the growth potential for the Roaring '20s Museum. The uniqueness of his museum is that the historical collection of prohibition memorabilia can never be duplicated. He has the doors from Al Capone's

---

This teaching note is comprised of analyses by David (Jeff) McLaughlin and Kelli M. Hurley, both 1994 graduates of the Entrepreneurship Program at Ball State University. Their critical insights provide a framework for other students to emulate.

bedroom and some other 2,000 authentic pieces from the 1920s era. Thus, with the use of multimedia technology, visitors will be able to experience a historical event with the use of technological advancements.

This description does state short- and long-term objectives but does not state exactly how these will be met. The statement of purpose and description of the business were well done, for they stated the type of business, financial information, and the opportunity it will serve. The only service it failed to mention in that section is the souvenir shop. A shuttle bus was also mentioned in this section with cooperation with Sieben's Brewing Company, but the expense was not mentioned in the financial section. Competition was also a segment in this section; however, it is supposed to be positioned in the marketing section. A promotional campaign was also a segment in this section; however, it is supposed to be positioned in the marketing section. A promotional campaign was also wrongly mentioned in this section but gave no explanation of what it is or where in the plan it can be located.

Marketing

The Roaring '20s Museum's potential customers are foreign tourists, conventioneers, out-of-state visitors, and the Chicagoland metropolitan market visitors. The size of the market for the museum is 2.8 million conventioneers, 900,000 foreign tourists, 3.1 million out-of-state tourists, and 3.5 million Chicagoland residents. He has even broken down each segment of the market into a geographical analysis of where each customer comes from. Moreover, he has identified his competitors in the business description instead of the marketing section. Also, he does not identify how the competitor's businesses are prospering. Graham gives a detailed description on how he will promote sales through his effective advertising methods. Furthermore, he gives a breakdown of expected market share versus time for each market segment. Finally, he does not indicate how he will determine the price for admission.

Graham's biggest strength in this section is his advertising methods. His advertising focuses on attracting the customer through radio, print, billboards, and brochure distribution. Furthermore, he identifies a projected market through market research. In his research, he conducted a market survey that authenticates his actual customer base. On the other hand, Graham located the identification of his potential competitors in another section. Finally, he does not give any indication of how the price for admission will be determined.

Although there is said to be a market survey that shows that foreign visitors show the greatest interest in Chicago's gangster era, no evidence to back it up can be found. There is no identification of industry analysis in this field. In the section on channel of distribution, it says 50,000 to 67,000 cars pass over the Ohio/Ontario corridor each day according to a survey. Unfortunately, it does not mention what survey, and if their market share is geared toward primarily visitors, then only the number of visitors in those cars are relevant to this point. It is also mentioned that 165,000 annual patrons to the brewery restaurant next door are regarded as potential visitors. What proof is behind this assumption? He does have some potential customers mentioned in this section who commented on the feasibility of the museum; however, not one of them out of six are foreign. Although the section does mention the market share very briefly with no proof, it does not mention at all the position it will hold or the pricing of the expected service. There are also no foreseen cost estimates to validate proposed strategies or costs for brochures in the financial section. This section also mentions doing 48 radio ads that will be aired on Friday mornings during the peak tourist seasons of June, July, and August. This is wonderful, but the two radio stations that were picked do not have any foreign announcements or shows. Therefore, if their biggest audience is foreign, how will foreigners who do not speak English learn about the museum besides word of mouth?

Research, Design, and Development

Graham has clearly defined the technical description and purpose of the Roaring '20s Museum. However, he does not explain how he will set up the multimedia presentations or what the costs will be for the technical assistance. He also does not illustrate what the anticipated research needs are going to be or the cost involved in the research and design process. This segment of his business plan is lacking vital parts of information that is relevant to research, design, and development of his business idea. For example, he uses past feasibility tests to help determine what admission customers would be willing to pay. Thus, he needs to determine what price should be charged for admission so that he is able to cover his expenses and run a profitable business. Finally, he needs to develop future surveys that address issues on market research, promotion, and exhibition material or events.

This section gave a good description of the technical service and floor plan. However, there are some incongruities within the section. The feasibility tests should have been located in the marketing section as well as the survey located in an appropriate appendix. Nevertheless, there were no indications of how the surveys were distributed. There were only five questions mentioned in the survey, and there was not one question that asked for ethical background or geographic location. Because of this how did they know 750 foreign visitors, 600 out-of-state visitors, and 1,600 Chicago-area residents were surveyed? There is also a segment concerning future tests; however, there are no specific methods given. Surveys are the only method mentioned but only to find out customers' likes and dislikes. It is also mentioned in this section that modifications of exhibits will be made after certain trends have developed. What trends are they expecting, and when? Another incongruity is that there is an additional 1,500 square feet that will be used for ticket and souvenir sales, office and research facilities, and public restrooms. However, the footnote below the floor plan indicates that there is 1,620 square feet for these facilities. There is also no cost structure defined on the materials that will be needed.

It is apparent that Graham has not identified all of the technical aspects of his business. He has not identified the costs associated with his research and design or how much it will be to operate a multimedia presentation tool. He was vague in describing technical help, if any, that was needed for operating his museum--i.e. fire and burglar alarm systems, construction costs, special lighting, climate controls, and preservation methods. As a result, this portion of his business plan is lacking significant information that is pertinent to the development and research needs of his business.

Management

Graham clearly identifies who will manage the business and produces their qualifications. Also, he gives a detailed description of each of the employee duties and their responsibilities. However, there is no mention of employee salaries, wages, or benefits. Graham also requires the services of a consultant who will serve as the museum's liaison with city hall. This liaison will help expedite any city licenses or deal with any zoning problems that could arise. Furthermore, Graham has chosen a limited partnership for the Roaring '20s Museum but does not state why he chose this type of partnership. He also does not indicate what types of permits or licenses he will need or what regulations will effect his business.

Graham's strengths in this section include who will manage the firm, a detailed description of what each person is required to do, and the services of the consultant who will help aid in the license and zoning process. However, Graham's weaknesses in this section are: no mention of salaries, wages, and benefits. He did not list the types of permits or licenses needed for his business. Moreover, he did not indicate why he chose this type of partnership. Finally, he did not include any regulations that would affect his business.

This section mentions that the Board of Directors is all inside the organization. This is not healthy for an organization and in some places is illegal. The above issue should be examined more thoroughly. Management expertise should be incorporated into this section but is mislocated in the critical risk section. The number of employees is not clearly stated, and there is no indication of the paying procedures. Consultants consisting of lawyers, accountants, public relations, and commercial bankers are represented in the organizational chart, but it is not mentioned how they will be utilized within the business.

Critical Risks

Graham has identified six problems that could adversely affect his business. First, there could be a time delay in raising capital, improving the premise, acquiring the movie rights for multimedia presentations, or obtaining permits and licenses. Second, the faulty design of the multimedia equipment may result in delays and substandard performances, and the cost for environmental controls designed to protect historic material may be higher than anticipated. Third, the management lacks experience in the operation of a commercial museum. Fourth, the public could change its acceptance due to the violent subject matter. Fifth, there is a possibility that other museums may open sections dealing with Chicago's history during this period. Finally, the limited partner's return on investment by income distribution and sale is uncertain. On the other hand, there was no mention of how many obstacles he anticipated, what the calculated risks were, or what the alternative courses of action were.

Thus, Graham identified six critical risks that could affect his business. However, he did not mention how many obstacles he could foresee or what the calculated risks were for the business. Finally, he did not submit any alternative courses of action. As a result, Graham's business could face unfavorable results.

For example, the political-legal and economic risks should have been considered as well as changes in sociocultural events. In the public acceptance segment, it says "all indications" show a positive public response to the museum concept, but those indications are not stated, and there is no proof of this statement. Because there are so many museum competitors in the Chicago area, there need to be more critical risks considered as well as the way in which they will be handled if they occur.

Financial

The total estimated income for the first year is not stated clearly. Furthermore, the monthly income for the first year is not indicated in his financial report. Finally, the quarterly income for the first year is not clearly stated. He also did not include the initial cost of opening the business. However, the monthly cash flow during the first year can be obtained from the first year's monthly cash flow projection. Furthermore, Graham does not indicate what his personal financial needs are each month. He also does not explain what sales volume will be needed to make a profit for the first year, and there is no sign of a break-even point. Next, he does not give what his projected assets, liabilities, and net worth are on the day before he is expected to open. However, he does explain his total financial needs and how he will allocate the funds acquired from lenders. He clearly explains a detailed use of capital funds obtained from the sale of twenty-five limited partnership units. Thus, the financial portion of the business plan needs improvements and clarity.

Four hundred twenty thousand dollars is the anticipated sales for the first year, but it is not clear what these sales are based on. There is no specific price of museum entrance given. All that is understandable is that there are no expected souvenir sales the first year, which does not make sense. The anticipated salaries seem unacceptable for the mere fact that there are not too many people that will take on a full-time job in the city of Chicago for only $10,000. This of course could be done, but he/she could not afford a roof over his/her head nor a vehicle to get to work. Even if he does find people who will work for that kind of money, turnover will probably be great when they find better jobs. Besides the limited partnerships of $26,000 each, there are no funding sources given in the case of lack of sales of these. The cash flow projections are also laid out in an unorganized fashion, and the explanations to each of the projections refer to line numbers, but the projections are not numbered. A professional support section is also included in this section, whereas it should be included in the management section. There are also no personal monthly financial needs given.

It is apparent that Graham's financials are missing an abundant amount of vital information. In fact, his financial segment should be considered the weakest part of his business plan. For example, he did not have any financial ratios that would project liquidity, solvency, or financial risks. These ratios can help determine if the firm is headed in the wrong direction or even bankruptcy. Thus, Graham not only needs to improve his financial section, but he also needs to supply more information pertaining to his validation of financial data.

Milestone Schedule

Graham has set a timetable for starting the business. It lists a detailed schedule for the first eight months of operations. He has not set any objectives or deadlines for each stage of his business. Moreover, there was not a section for a milestone schedule. The timetable was listed in the summary and conclusion. Thus, Graham needs to implement a milestone section in his plan and show his objectives.

Appendix

The business plan does not have an appendix. It should include any documents, drawings, or agreements to support the information in the business plan. For example, there were not limited partner agreements or legal letters that confirm contributions of $200,000, but there was a lack of industry analysis compiles or sample surveys. The names of references, advisers, or technical sources are located in the financial section of the business plan instead of the appendix. Therefore, Graham should incorporate an appendix into his business plan.

Concluding Comments

Overall, this business plan was clearly thought out, but its organization needs to be reevaluated. The idea is brilliant and seems to have a specific niche in the marketplace. The physical location of the facility seems ideal for this service, and it is obvious there has been a lot of research done on the positioning of the museum. The analysis focused mainly on the weaknesses because the strengths spoke for themselves.

COMPREHENSIVE CASE STUDY FOR PART 4

THE PLAYBOY EMBLEM: A CASE OF TRADEMARK INFRINGEMENT

Teaching Notes

SUMMARY OF THE CASE

This case deals with a small business (a tavern) that has used a rabbit head emblem on its establishment for almost 30 years. In 1982, Playboy Enterprises, Inc., sent a letter to John P. Browne, who owned and operated the tavern, threatening legal action for violation of a registered trademark that Playboy has had since 1953.

The legal environment of small business as well as the particular issues of unfair competition by a small firm are illustrated in this actual case.

While alternative courses of action are desired from students, the actual outcome of the case is provided for professors to utilize in discussion.

TEACHING OBJECTIVES

1. To illustrate trademark infringement by a small business.
2. To offer a classic example of problems smaller firms can encounter.
3. To describe the dangers of careless planning by small business--even in the case of the business's name and logo.
4. To discuss the ramifications of larger corporations reacting to small business's infringements and protecting their property rights.
5. To emphasize the importance of understanding the legal environment for today's entrepreneurial start-ups.

ISSUES IN THE CASE

Five prominent questions surface in this case as issues for consideration.

1. Is this *trademark infringement*?
The first question arises as to whether Bunny's rabbit head is indeed a replica of Playboy's and thus *infringes the trademark*. (Compare the pictures.)

This teaching note was prepared by Dr. Donald F. Kuratko, College of Business, Ball State University. Presented and accepted by the refereed Midwest Society for Case Research Workshop, 1985. All rights reserved to the author and to the Midwest Society for Case Research. Copyright (c) 1985 by Donald F. Kuratko.

2. **Does the use of any "similar" rabbit head design constitute infringement on the basis of *unfair competition*?**

    The second question is whether or not the use of *any* similar rabbit head design constitutes infringement on the basis of unfair competition to Playboy Enterprises. This questions the definition of "unfair competition" and indicates that other factors should be considered in deciding the case.

3. **What was Bunny Browne's *intent*?**

    What was Bunny Browne's intention in having the rabbit head design on his establishment? Did he intend to confuse the public, replicate Playboy, or hope to aggrandize himself through the use of someone else's design?

4. **If the use of the rabbit head design is trademark infringement, what are the *damages* caused to Playboy?**

    If Bunny's emblem is proved to be too similar, what damages are caused to Playboy Enterprises, Inc., from the use of this rabbit head design?

5. **What about the *timing* involved when Playboy contests the design?**

    Why, after almost 30 years, has Playboy now decided to "crash down" on Bunny Browne's tavern? Why wasn't Playboy carefully policing their protected design 30 years ago? And, if Playboy would claim the rebuttal of not knowing about the use of their emblem until now, then apparently the design caused no interference for almost 30 years. Why, therefore, is Playboy so concerned at this time?

QUESTIONS FOR CLASS DISCUSSION

1. *If you were Bunny Browne, what exactly would you do? Why?*

    This question should provoke students to put themselves "in the shoes" of a small-business person and justify what course of action they would pursue against Playboy Enterprises--if any.

2. *Explain what a trademark is and what rights it provides the owner.*

    The Lanham Act of 1946, Sections 2, 3, and 4, provides for the registration on the Principal Register of Trademarks, Servicemarks, Collective and Certification Marks. A trademark is defined as any word, name, symbol, or device or any combination thereof adopted and used to identify goods and distinguish them from those manufactured or sold by others. (Adapted from *Patent Law* by Choate & Francis, West Publishing Co., 1981.)

    Today a trademark provides three functions: (1) to indicate origin, (2) to guarantee certain quality, and (3) to advertise and sell.

3. *What exactly would a court evaluate in determining the similarity of a trademark?*
   According to Choate & Francis, *Patent Law* (1981), the generally accepted factors in determining whether a designation is confusing to another's are:
   (1) The degree of similarity in appearance, pronunciation of words, verbal translation of designs, suggestion.
   (2) The intent of the actor in adopting the designation.
   (3) The relation in use and services marketed by the actor and those marketed by the other
   (4) The degree of care likely to be exercised by purchasers.

4. *What are the alternative solutions available to Bunny Browne? Discuss.*
   The students should be encouraged to be creative and attempt to figure various alternatives including:
   (1) Get legal counsel.
   (2) Take the case to court (consider facts of financial costs).
   (3) Comply with Playboy's demands and remove the rabbit head design.
   (4) Paint a new design to replace the old one.
   (5) Seek community support and generate a local protest.
   (6) Establish a contest to find a new design.
   (7) Continue media coverage in hopes of pressuring Playboy to either drop their case or help pay for removal of the emblem.

   These are suggestions. Encourage students to think of solutions that are inexpensive for a small-business person and still beneficial.

5. *What lessons can be learned from the Bunny Browne situation?*
   Various aspects could be proposed on this case; however, the most viable is the legal environment of small business. Entrepreneurs must understand the diverse laws and regulations that encompass doing business. Even a sole proprietor is subject to the laws, restrictions, and regulations that govern all aspects of business.
   In addition, thoughts and attention can be turned to the protective position of Playboy Enterprises. Their emblem has stood for an "image" or "way of life," and any promotions using this symbol that have no connection to Playboy could begin a substantial dilution of the symbol's representation. (References could be cited concerning Kleenex and Xerox in being protective of their trade names.)
   Thus, the position of the small entrepreneur and the large business are considered for analysis of this situation.
   Finally, the creative problem solving of entrepreneurs should surface: How can I turn an impending problem into an opportunity? This is a good test of the student's ability to creatively adapt and think through a problem situation when there are few resources at his/her disposal.

ACTUAL OUTCOME OF THE CASE

The actual course of action taken by Bunny Browne was one of compliance to Playboy's demand. However, a creative and profitable approach was taken. Bunny thought of turning this dilemma into an opportunity.

In the spring of 1983, the removal of the emblem began as a high school project after a contest was conducted to determine a winning entry for a "new" design.

The idea of creating a contest and seeking a new artistic design was an alternative to fighting back against Playboy Enterprises. Bunny Browne decided that his emblem was old and peeling. Therefore, to stand up against Playboy's threat was more of a question of principle and could prove very costly.

Since a new design would be ideal, the thought of a contest became the answer. In this manner a new rabbit design could be completed inexpensively, and media interest could easily be generated.

So in 1983, a new rabbit design was painted by commercial artist Margo Rife, the winner of the media contest.

The unveiling of the new design brought attention, advertising, and customers.

COMPREHENSIVE CASE FOR PART 5

ACORDIA'S "LITTLE GIANTS"

Teaching Notes

SUMMARY OF THE CASE

This case deals with the restructuring attempt by The Associated Group (formerly known as Blue Cross/Blue Shield of Indiana) as it shifted from a large bureaucratic corporation into a network of small entrepreneurial companies.

During the late 1970s and early 1980s, the health care industry experienced permanent changes on both the market and product sides of the business. The Associated Group realized, as costs and competition increased rapidly, that major strategic changes would need to be implemented to ensure long-term success. Their solution was to decentralize operations and develop a more aggressive, entrepreneurial corporate culture. The new strategy would focus on becoming more diversified and serving more markets by building businesses, known as Acordia companies, from its core competencies.

This case describes some of the objectives and structures that led to the successful restructuring of The Associated Group. While the case also discusses many of the specific issues facing The Associated Group in the near future, one general observation can be made: They will likely continue their commitment to growth and diversification.

TEACHING OBJECTIVES
1. To illustrate the need for change and innovativeness within a growing firm.
2. To provide an interesting example of an entrepreneurial restructuring strategy.
3. To discuss the ramifications of implementing a new strategy within an existing business.
4. To demonstrate the importance of strategy-focused objectives and structures.
5. To present an actual example of a company that successfully managed entrepreneurial growth.

APPROPRIATE APPLICATIONS OF THE CASE

Entrepreneurship
Corporate entrepreneurship
Strategic management
Management (innovation and development)

This teaching note was prepared by Melissa A. Ewen, Midwest Entrepreneurial Education Center, Ball State University

ISSUES IN THE CASE

1. Identification of the positive and negative implications of decentralizing.
2. Identification of the positive and negative implications of diversifying.
3. The internal changes that facilitate the implementation of an entrepreneurial strategy.
4. In managing entrepreneurial growth, are other entrepreneurial changes apparent or missing that could have fostered the strategy's success?
5. A new compensation plan that supported the entrepreneurial development.

QUESTIONS FOR CLASS DISCUSSION

1.   Describe the significant changes that The Associated Group went through.

The Associated Group underwent many significant changes. The actual physical reconstruction transformed the organization from a centralized structure into a network of 50 decentralized, diversified companies. Other changes included the elimination of multiple levels of management, expansion of workweek hours, addition of Employee Profit Sharing Plan, dress code, Employee Advisory Committee, etc. The organization's culture also underwent major changes as the company tried to instill a more aggressive and entrepreneurial environment. The cultural change affected most procedures, policies, systems, and structures within the organization, the compensation plan being one example. Other specific changes included the increase of direct responsibility, development of small work teams, and focus on service

2.   What exactly is the Acordia strategy?

Acordia's vision is to become the nation's largest supplier of insurance products to mid-market clients. This would be implemented by targeting cities of 100,000 to 1,000,000 in population as well as by targeting employers with less than 5,000 employees and with $200,000 annually in property and casualty commissions and individuals with incomes greater than $50,000 and net worth greater than $500,000. Acordia seeks to become the "Wal-Mart" of insurance and brokerage administration.

3.   Describe The Acordia Compensation Plan and how it helped the innovative strategy.

The Acordia Compensation Plan was made of three major segments: cash wages, long-term incentives, and benefits. Cash wages include a below-average base salary combined with above-average incentives. The incentives are determined by the individual Acordia company's performance for the year, the individual Acordia company's board-of-directors assessment, and Acordia, Inc.'s discretionary input. Each area of compensation is clearly tied directly to the firm's performance. This approach to compensation helps the innovative strategy by fostering and supporting an ownership perspective among the officers in all Acordia companies. See Figure 2 and Table 2 for a complete breakdown.

ACTUAL OUTCOME OF THE CASE

In 1997, the network of Acordia companies was folded back into the original corporate structure that existed prior to 1986 under the new name of Anthem. All of Acordia's stock was purchased by Anthem and was then taken off the market.

Anthem's major goal now is to become one of the top five health care providers in the United States. Anthem currently boasts revenues exceeding $14 billion. The entrepreneurial concept was very successful for over ten years; however, size and economy of scale now appear to be the strategy for Anthem in the health care industry.

COMPREHENSIVE CASE STUDY FOR PART 6

EMGE PACKING COMPANY, INCORPORATED

Teaching Notes

SUMMARY OF THE CASE

This case deals with a family-owned firm which has gradually grown from a very small operation to a moderate-sized player in the industry. Walter Emge, the key decision maker, is currently in an awkward position with regard to the firm's strategic direction. Mr. Emge feels loyalty toward both the employees of the firm as well as the shareholders. He was, additionally, largely responsible for the development of the firm through the years. All of these factors make strategic planning difficult when environmental pressures plague the firm.

Emge Packing Company, a regional meat processing firm faced numerous problems in 1988: (1) The industry was rapidly becoming dominated by three or four major players; (2) The second generation Emge family managers were aging, and succession was inevitable; (3) Nonmanagement family members feared that their investment in the company was at great risk, as they had little confidence in current management; (4) Increasing health concerns on the part of consumers constantly decreased red meat consumption and placed pressure on the industry as a whole.

The case illustrates the difficulty a firm has in exiting an industry. It is often difficult for those involved to make decisions--especially when they feel an obligation toward both employees and shareholders. This case should effectively illustrate how various parties involved place pressure on the firm's decision makers to implement policy which reflects their own best interest.

TEACHING OBJECTIVES

1. To illustrate the development of a firm from start-up through maturity.
2. To develop a strategy for a firm which is still a family business.
3. To present problems of managerial succession.
4. To develop a plan of action for a firm competing in a difficult industry.
5. To demonstrate corporate level decision making which minimizes negative impact on all parties involved.

This teaching note was prepared by Mr. Michael E. Busing, College of Business, Clemson University. All rights reserved to the author. Copyright (c) 1985 by Michael E. Busing.

APPROPRIATE APPLICATIONS OF THE CASE

   Small business management
   Marketing
   Business policy (mature industries)

ISSUES IN THE CASE

   A number of critical issues surface in this case for consideration. They include:

   (1) Competition--Emge is competing in a difficult industry made up of a few dominant competitors. As a result, smaller firms such as Emge are constantly exiting.
   (2) Stockholder discontent--Emge stockholders are not satisfied with current dividend practices. Constant pressure is being placed on the board of directors to liquidate some of the cash surplus.
   (3) Managerial resources--It is pointed out in the case that some concern exists about younger manager capability.
   (4) Decision to exit--Students should realize that a firm does not need to be in financial distress to exit an industry. Emge may be able to operate for several years but may be able to maximize shareholder value either by finding a buyer for their firm now or by liquidating the assets of the organization.

QUESTIONS FOR CLASS DISCUSSION

1. *What problems does Emge currently face? Rank the problems from most to least important.*
    The problems at hand for Emge seem to be internal in nature. First of all, it is mandatory that they determine who will be the successor to Mr. Emge when he retires. Secondly, the company needs to assess their current management pool and to recruit outside members if necessary. Finally, stockholder support needs to be gained.
    Long-term problems involve Emge, a relatively small firm, competing against a few very large firms. Emge should develop a plan which maximizes the utility of their retained earnings (approximately $30 million). Students should be aware that Emge has both short- and long-term problems.

2. *What plan of action would you recommend that Mr. Emge take to deal with the company's problems? Defend your recommendation.*
    Students will most likely develop one of two plans for Emge.
    1. Remain in business: This could consist of a variety of alternatives such as using a portion of the cash surplus to fund a modernization effort, maintaining status quo, hiring an outside management team, or any combination of the above.

2. Exit the industry: Students will likely suggest that Emge either find a buyer for the company or discontinue operations (i.e., go out of business). Students should be prepared to defend their positions financially as well as qualitatively. Students should be encouraged to develop other innovative plans for Emge.

3. ***Does the plan of action in question 2 minimize negative impact on all parties involved (i.e., stockholders, managers, employees, and consumers)?***

In answering this question, students should become aware that any "pure" strategy will not satisfy the best interest of all parties involved. For example, many stockholders would not be satisfied with the plan to use surplus cash to fund a modernization effort. At the same time, however, employees and the community can be severely affected by Emge's exit from the industry.

4. ***Is Emge in the position to remain in the industry and compete? What steps are necessary in order for Emge to be effective?***

Given the environmental pressures which Emge faces, it would be necessary to invest at least a portion of the cash surplus toward modernization in order to effectively compete. Before this could even be considered, however, it would be wise, albeit difficult, to gain stockholder support. It should also be noted that the revenue which the cash surplus generates has been used in the past (1989) to offset operating losses. This would no longer be available to help the company weather a storm.

ACTUAL OUTCOME OF THE CASE

Since this case was written in May 1990, Emge Packing Company has been sold to Excel Corporation, a division of Cargill, Inc. Excel is one of the "big three" meat processors in the United States. Most of the Emge family are no longer part of the organization. While some hourly employees have been terminated, a great deal of the original workforce has been retained.

Although Excel has begun renovating the two existing Emge Plants, the specific plan for Emge is not known. Speculation suggests that Emge will one day become a nationally known brand name.

ADDITIONAL CASES

(Not Available in Text)

Chapter 1:   Entrepreneurship from Several Angles

Chapter 2:   Creativity Continued

Chapter 4:   Changing the Climate
             A Hiring Decision

Chapter 5:   Jesse's Environmental Assessment Challenge

Chapter 7:   Now What?

Chapter 17: Going International?

CASE: ENTREPRENEURSHIP FROM SEVERAL ANGLES

Roberta Flinch is a student in a basic entrepreneurship course. As part of her class assignment, she is in the process of gathering information on the topic "How Entrepreneurs See Their World." She lined up interviews with three people whom she feels are entrepreneurial and received the following information from each.

Interviewee No. 1: "I spend most of my time looking for seed capital for new ventures. I bring together the people who need the money with those who are willing to lend it. My job is sort of that of a broker, but at the same time I see myself as an entrepreneur. I talk to hundreds of bankers and investors every month in an effort to find out what types of ventures they are willing to fund. To me, entrepreneurship begins with the finance function. I'm the entrepreneurial type that opens the door for the others."

Interviewee No. 2: "I've had my own business for six years. The key to my success can be found in two words: market awareness. I look for ideas and concepts that can be developed and presented in a different fashion. For example, I found out that one of the local high schools was looking for a catering service to provide lunches to the students. I put together the necessary people and bid on the contract. I lost, but in the process, I learned what catering is all about. As a result, when the local jail put out bids for a food service, I was in a good position to win the contract. Sometimes failing at something gives you the experience you need to succeed."

Interviewee No. 3: "To me entrepreneurial success is the result of effective planning. In particular, this means formulating a unique approach to operations: unique markets, unique products, unique resources. If you can't be unique, you won't win. On the other hand, if you can figure out how to be 'one of a kind,' you can't lose. It's all a result of how you plan."

CASE DISCUSSION QUESTIONS AND ANSWERS

1. **To which school of entrepreneurial thought does the first interviewee belong? Defend your answer.**

    The first interviewee is an illustration of the financial capital school of entrepreneurial thought. This school is based upon the venture-seeking process at every stage of a new, growing, or maturing enterprise. Thus, the first interviewee exhibits the belief that the venture capital process is *the key element* in the entrepreneurial process.

2. **To which school of entrepreneurial thought does the second interviewee belong? Defend your answer.**

    The second interviewee illustrates the venture opportunity school of entrepreneurial thought. The search for ideas, development of concepts, and implementation of a venture opportunity are the major areas of focus for this school of thought. According to this school's emphasis, developing the right idea at the right time for the right niche is the key to entrepreneurial success. This is exactly what the second interviewee was demonstrating with the catering idea; however, in finding the contract for the local job, the "corridor principle" is revealed. The "corridor principle" occurs when new pathways and opportunities arise and lead entrepreneurs in different directions.

3. **To which school of entrepreneurial thought does the third interviewee belong? Defend your answer.**

    The third interviewee reflects the strategy formulation school of entrepreneurial thought. Identifying unique elements -- markets, people, products, or resources -- is the major focus of this school. Once identified, the effective planning process of organization, management, environment, production, processes, and purpose all need to be coordinated for a clear strategy. Thus, the strategy school encompasses critical elements and managerial functions.

CASE: CREATIVITY CONTINUED

While the Polaroid Corporation has been doing extremely well with its Spectra camera, the company also is expanding its horizons and looking for new markets where its expertise can help it capture a niche. The product the firm is betting on for the 1990s is the electronic still camera, the first new variety of instant photography. Management believes that this camera will revolutionize photography in the 1990s. The major current problem is that the firm does not yet have a prototype. All that has been developed thus far is some of the components. Additionally, the first version will carry a very high price tag, perhaps as much as $2,500, and will be aimed at professionals and those who want to be the first to have the latest gadget. It will be well into the 1990s before an electronic camera hits the mass market. Nevertheless, Polaroid is determined to produce one.

The electronic camera will look just like an ordinary 35mm model. However, it will work differently. A computer chip, called the image sensor, will be used instead of film to record pictures. Light will pass through a lens and hit the image sensor, which in turn will convert it into an electronic signal. Another chip, called an image processor, will adjust the picture for sharpness and color. The electronic information will then be stored on a two-inch magnetic disk that will be able to hold as many as 30 pictures. These disks will be much cheaper than film, and the user will be able to look at what was snapped on a television screen before making instant prints of the shots.

While it is working on the electronic camera, Polaroid also is expanding its current product line. For example, the commercial division, which makes cameras for instant passport and driver's license photos, is now offering a new product: FreezeFrame. This black box transforms video pictures into instant photographic prints or slides. Additionally, the company is working on a high-density floppy disk for personal computers. Most floppy disks can hold about 360,000 characters of information. Polaroid's high-density floppy is being designed to handle up to 50 million characters of information. The company hopes to make $50 million a year on this product.

CASE DISCUSSION QUESTIONS AND ANSWERS

1. *In developing new products, how would the four phases of the creative thinking process be used? Explain.*

    Each of the four phases in the creative thinking process are important in developing new products such as Polaroid's. *Knowledge accumulation* through investigation and information gathering is a key step in understanding all of the basics involved in the development of Polaroid's new products. The *incubator process* allows individuals to mull over the large amount of information that was gathered in the first phase. This phase lets the creative person see things in a different light. The *idea experience* is the actual formulation of a solution. It is usually the result of the first two phases. This is probably true for Polaroid's new products being developed. *Evaluation and implementation* is exactly the phase Polaroid is currently in. It is carefully evaluating each new product by testing and modifying until a final product emerges for implementation.

2. *What type of people would you expect to be working in new-product development at Polaroid? Would these people be highly creative?*

    According to Table 2.1 in the chapter, the people at Polaroid working on new-product development would resemble "innovators." Their problem-solving style would include:
    (1) Approaches tasks from unusual angles.
    (2) Discovers problems and avenues of solutions.
    (3) Questions basic assumptions related to current practices.
    (4) Has little regard for means; is more interested in ends.
    (5) Has little or no need for consensus; often is insensitive to others.

    In addition, if these people were highly creative, the following characteristics would be apparent in them:
    (1) Bright but not necessarily brilliant. Creativity is not directly related to extraordinarily high intelligence.
    (2) Good at generating a high degree of different ideas in a short period of time.
    (3) Have a positive image of themselves. They like who they are.
    (4) Sensitive to the world around them and the feelings of others.
    (5) Motivated by challenging problems.
    (6) Able to withhold the decision on a problem until sufficient facts have been collected.
    (7) Value their independence and do not have strong needs for group approval.
    (8) Lead a rich, almost bizarre, fantasy life.
    (9) Flexible as opposed to rigid or dogmatic.
    (10) More concerned with the meanings and implications of a problem than with small details.

The Dryden Press

3. ***Which sources of innovation (of the seven described in the chapter) would be useful in creating an electronic camera? Explain.***

In creating an electronic camera as Polaroid has done, a number of innovative sources may be cited. For example, industry and market changes are a source since technological developments have opened the door for Polaroid to develop this new type of camera. In addition, the knowledge-based source is also very applicable to this new camera. Since it is a new invention, there is a great amount of knowledge that is being brought together. Thus, the two best sources of this innovation are industry/market changes and knowledge-based concepts.

As far as a 50-million-character floppy disk is concerned, the "process need" innovative source may apply since it's an extension of existing disks. Also the industry and market changes are a factor since the idea of such a floppy disk arises from the consumer demand for more and more storage capability of disks.

CASE: CHANGING THE CLIMATE

The Liga Corporation was founded 25 years ago and was soon able to land a major government contract. Its performance on the project was so highly rated (and continues to be) that the firm has been able to secure additional government contracts every year. By 1987 over 75 percent of Liga's business was government related. By this time, however, management had become convinced that increased nongovernmental work would be needed if it hoped to achieve annual sales of $100 million by 1990. The company also is concerned that it is too reliant on government contracts and needs to diversify its customer base.

There are two primary areas where the company believes it can develop markets. One is in the area of robotics. The firm has had a great deal of experience building cybernetic-control equipment for the government. This technological/manufacturing experience could serve as the basis for a new product line to be produced and sold to firms in the auto-making, computer-manufacturing, and warehousing industries. There would also, of course, be a governmental market including the military and the postal service.

The other area is in the manufacture of lightweight material for use in a variety of products. The company believes that this market could have many different niches, including parts for airplanes, computers, household appliances, and sports equipment.

Although these ideas are only in the thinking stage, Liga believes their potential could account for 75 percent of all sales by 1995. However, one of the major problems is that the firm is not yet prepared to make the transition from government to private sector manufacturing. Liga has so long been organized along bureaucratic lines designed to help it comply with governmental regulations and procedures that the firm lacks the internal entrepreneurial drive to create and champion in-house product development. "We've been dependent on others to provide us our business," notes the president, Sandra Liga. "If we start developing our own product lines, we'll have to become more entrepreneurial and self-reliant. This means the creation of a different work climate, one that is much more conducive to market conditions."

CASE DISCUSSION QUESTIONS AND ANSWERS

1. *What type of manager works at Liga? Describe the individual.*

    The manager at Liga must deal with strict policies and procedures. He or she is a person who must go through the "chain of command" to get results. One could also assume that the managers are very "title" oriented and use their titles to give a push to or a stop to any ideas that may be profitable for the company. These good ideas could very well go to waste.

2. *What type of manager does Liga need to be successful if it moves into the areas of robotics and lightweight materials? Explain in detail.*

    Both areas or endeavors are sure to fail unless Liga changes its corporate climate. It does not matter what type of manager Liga hires. Liga should not hire one specific manager for each area. They should get individuals together to work as a team to work on ideas and innovations. These individuals must be innovative and not be pressured by failure. The team of managers for the robotics project should have a more technical background, and the lightweight materials project needs managers who are more creative.

3. *How should Liga go about changing its current climate? What initial steps would you recommend to the firm?*

    One thing that Liga should avoid is a "fast forward" approach to implementing an intrapreneurial climate. This would surely lead to failure. A nice, steady pace starting at the top level of management would be better. Top management does not understand how this type of individual works, and he or she must be trained on how to deal with them. Develop and emphasize the basics: explicit goals, feedback and positive reinforcement, individual responsibility, and rewards based upon results.

CASE: A HIRING DECISION

For the last two months Albert Rodriquez has been slowly increasing the intrapreneurship climate in his company. During this period Albert has created four project teams for developing and selling new products and services. One of these teams is working on a new liquid crystal display (LCD) screen to use with laptop portable computers. Annual sales for laptops have been increasing for the last three years, and an improved LCD could be a major technological breakthrough in the industry.

Another of the project teams is developing a software package for use in a high school physics class. If the package is found to be effective, there is an excellent chance that the state will buy the program for use in all school districts. This could result in sales of over $600,000 in an 18-month period. The cost of developing the package will be approximately $18,000.

A third project team is working on a local area network (LAN) system for linking together organizational computers and allowing the personnel to operate more efficiently. While this segment of the computer industry is highly competitive, Albert's firm believes that it has developed state-of-the-art technology that will revolutionize the current LAN system.

Albert is presently in the process of hiring an additional manager to head an in-house project. He has narrowed the list to two people: Paul Dandridge and Monica Wheatley. Paul is now a production manager with a medium-sized manufacturing firm. He has been in this position for five years, having worked his way up the ranks from machinist. He supervises a department of 117 people and has been responsible for increasing productivity in the department by 37 percent over the past two years. He is considered a very capable manager who works extremely well with others. Monica is a product manager with a large consumer goods firm. She has personally developed and brought to market a very successful consumer product that currently accounts for over 1 percent of her corporation's gross sales. Monica directly supervises a marketing group of 27 people who are responsible for covering the entire U.S. market including Alaska and Hawaii.

CASE DISCUSSION QUESTIONS AND ANSWERS

1. *In your own words, how would you describe Paul? Is he a traditional, an entrepreneurial, or an intrapreneurial manager? (Use Table 4.2 to help formulate your answer.)*

    Paul is a more traditional manager in nature. He worked his way up through the ranks, working out problems within the system, and sees the hierarchy as something that has to be dealt with instead of bypassing it when a problem occurs. In Paul's background, status symbols and titles are very important to him. Paul has his main focus of attention directed primarily on the dealings within the company he is working for.

2. *What type of manager is Monica? (Again, use Table 4.2 to help you in describing her.)*

    Monica is more intrapreneurial in nature. She is the type of person who wants her freedom and access to corporate resources as displayed by the facts presented in the case. She uses market research to base her business decisions since her area is concentrated more in the consumer area. Her focus of attention and attitude toward risk fit the intrapreneur characteristics.

3. *Based on the information provided about Albert's firm and the direction in which it is headed, which of the two persons would you recommend he hire? Why? Be complete in your answer.*

    At first glance, one might hire Monica for the job because she comes from a more intrapreneurial background. However, Paul would be the better choice. Albert's project is an in-house project, and a good technical background would be most desirable. Paul has this background; however, he does need to be developed in the intrapreneurial ways and understand that now he does have freedom to experiment and try new things. Monica, on the other hand, has experience as a project manager. As a project manager, she more than likely headed up a team, and she let those with the technical knowledge present their ideas and work accordingly. Her background--being more marketing and consumer products oriented--does not seem to fit Albert's needs at the present time.

CASE: JESSE'S ENVIRONMENTAL ASSESSMENT CHALLENGE

According to the Yellow Pages, there are three outlets in town that offer a "quicky lube and oil change." These outlets, all tied to the same national franchise, guarantee that they can lubricate a car and change the oil in 15 minutes. No appointment is necessary. The car owner need simply drive in and wait. Typically, it takes no more than 30 minutes to be back on the road.

Jesse Forsythe has been thinking about opening up a "quicky lube" unit in town. He believes that there is more than enough business to support another unit. Additionally, he intends to set it up in an area of town where there currently is no competition. The town has a population of 125,000, and there are approximately another 50,000 people who live within 10 minutes' driving time of the town.

Jesse believes that he can make this venture a profitable one. However, he does not want to jump into the business too quickly and lose his investment. He feels that franchise units would not have been set up if the idea were not a profitable one. On the other hand, there is little doubt that this business can be a very competitive one. Anyone with the right equipment can get started, and location and reputation undoubtedly play an important role.

Jesse feels that the place to start is with an environmental assessment. He is not sure exactly how he should go about conducting one, but he feels that careful consideration should be given to both economic and local factors. He has decided to begin by putting together a plan of action for evaluating the new venture. If things look good, he intends to push forward. If the venture appears to be highly competitive or does not promise good profits, he intends to go no further.

CASE DISCUSSION QUESTIONS AND ANSWERS

1. **What type of macro economic environmental assessment would you recommend that Jesse conduct?**

   Important questions from the text:
   (1) How many firms are in this industry?
   (2) Do the firms vary in size and general characteristics?
   (3) What is the geographic concentration?
   (4) What is the competitive nature of the business?
   (5) What federal, state, and local government regulations affect this type of business?
   Competitive Analysis--Analyze quality and quantity of the competition. What drives the competition?
   1. Clearly define the industry for the new venture.
   2. Analyze the competition, number, size, traditions, and cost structures of direct competitors.
   3. Will competition become more intense?
   4. Project the market size for the particular industry.

   Ask several questions such as: what is the competitive nature of the business, the geographic concentration, what regulations must I comply with, and do the other firms vary in these characteristics?

The Dryden Press

A competitive analysis would tell a lot about the competition. It is important to know if the market will become more competitive or less. The size of the market is important. It would be easy to understate or overstate production if you didn't know the market size.

2. *Could a competitive profile analysis such as that presented in Figure 5.4 in Chapter 5 be of any value? Why or why not?*

   A competitive profile analysis could be of benefit. A quick lube center is not that unique; therefore price and service will be most important. The location will be a very important aspect for availability and convenience. Since there are other quick lube centers in town, advertising will be important, especially in the grand-opening stage. It will be important to have brand-name oil to show the customer that the new venture is concerned about quality.

   The competitive profile analysis will be of value when planning for the new business venture. It will show that if you have an edge over the competition, that can be taken advantage of. It will also show where the competition has you beat. It is better to find out now and figure out how to counteract it than to wait and let the competition put you out of business.

3. *How would you recommend Jesse carry out a micro environmental assessment? On what areas should he focus his attention?*

   Count the number of entrepreneurs in the community, examine their types of business ventures, and establish their track records.

   Population trends are important in order to identify expanding communities. It would not be wise to start a new venture in a declining population.

   It might be wise to consider the use of a business incubator for keeping business records and hiring new employees. Since the quick lube must be sold and performed at the location of the business, an incubator may be of little use.

   Community demographics, the economic base, population trends, and the business climate are the most important items microanalysis can view.

CASE: NOW WHAT?

Andy Philder, Margaret Hanks, and Paul O'Donnell are thinking about going into business. They intend to open a sandwich shop just across the street from a large office building. They estimate that the walk-in traffic during the noon hour will be more than enough for them to break even. There are a number of competitors in the local area. Besides a smaller diner, there are six restaurants and three fast food units nearby. Most people who go out to lunch eat at one of these establishments. A small number drive to a restaurant located six blocks away.

The three partners intend to offer both hot and cold sandwiches. Many of these orders, they estimate, will be called in by office workers and then picked up. There also will be delivery on all orders placed before 11 A.M.

The group's current plans call for each person to contribute $5,000 to get the business started and to share equally in all profits and losses. If more funds are required, Andy has stock worth $27,000 that could be liquidated and used to support the venture.

The work arrangement calls for Andy to run the shop and to answer the phone. Margaret will be in charge of making the sandwiches. Paul, who is a vice president of a large bank, will not be involved in the day-to-day affairs of the business. Other workers in the concern will be hired as employees and will be salaried. These will include one or two persons to help make the sandwiches and a third person to handle deliveries. Initial plans call for the group to hire one full-time person and one or two part-timers, depending on the amount of business.

CASE DISCUSSION QUESTIONS AND ANSWERS

1. *In this operation, who will be a general partner? Why?*

    Andy will be the general partner. They must have one person out of the three who is responsible for the debt of the entire enterprise. This person is the general partner and has unlimited liability. Andy is the one who is most active in the business and the day-to-day running of the business.

2. *What type of partner will Paul be? Be complete in your answer.*

    He would be a silent partner, one not involved in the day-to-day operation of the business. One assumes from the case he is going to be a known partner. If he was not a known partner, he would be a dormant partner.

3. *Would you recommend that the partnership be an S corporation? Why or why not?*

    No. In their situation they should take one step at a time. They have little experience in operating a business, and they are not quite sure how the business venture is going to work out. They may consider forming an S corporation if everything works out for them and they want to expand some day. With a partnership they can form with very few legal formalities and much less expense. By being a partnership, the partners will be more motivated to put forth their best efforts. The partnership offers a great deal of flexibility, and they have very little governmental interference in the operation of the partnership. They would pay taxes as individuals. Granted, there are benefits to S corporations, such as being taxed similarly to a partnership, while having some of the benefits of a corporation such as limited liability. It can be very beneficial for a small business, but there are strict guidelines to follow. They are not quite ready for all of this right now. With the partnership they can form relatively easily, and if everything works out then they may consider expanding. They will have to take the risk and hope it will pay off for them.

The Dryden Press

CASE: GOING INTERNATIONAL?

When Laura Larsen started her designer sportswear company, she had no idea that business would be so brisk. Her first line of clothing was a series of summer outfits for boating, tennis, and golf. The outfits were advertised in the local paper and sold through her small clothing store. Business was so good that Laura had to reorder within three weeks.

Since opening her store two years ago, Laura's sales have reached the $500,000 mark. She has become one of the most popular designer-manufacturers in the area. Most of her outfits are sold locally. However, a careful analysis of her customer list reveals that 22 percent of all sales are being made to sales agents for overseas firms. Laura has been thinking about the possibility of expanding her operation into the international arena.

From what Laura can glean from the sales records, most of her international sales are in France and Italy, although there have been some small purchases made by firms in Switzerland, Austria, and Spain. Laura would very much like to tap this international market, but she feels she does not know enough about how to go international. She would prefer to have someone overseas handle all of the business for her rather than get involved in setting up operations, establishing a sales force, and conducting business the way she does here in the United States. Laura is prepared to take whatever steps are in the best interest of the firm, but for the moment she has made only one decision: She is going to look into foreign expansion and evaluate the pros and cons of the various alternatives that are available to her.

CASE DISCUSSION QUESTIONS AND ANSWERS

1. *Based on what you know about Laura's intentions to go international, which approach would you recommend: exporting, joint venture, direct foreign investment, or licensing?*

    Recommend that Laura should use the exporting approach, like freight forwarding. Since she is new to the business, with only two years' experience, and has little knowledge of the international market, the freight forwarder would advise her on cost, prepare documents, and take away the burden of shipping. Since only 22 percent of her sales now are international, she should not try a joint venture or licensing approach yet.

2. *What steps would you recommend Laura take in going international?*

    Laura should first research her options as well as the countries she is considering. She needs to project her costs and how long it will take her before she makes a profit. Laura needs to look at her financing options and see if any suit her needs. She needs to gain some knowledge of the country and of all the documents and preparations that will be required. She will need to set her company's objectives and decide if she is ready to go international.

3. If Laura were successful in her efforts to enter the European market, would she be able to use the same basic approach in entering the Far East market?

If Laura would enter the Far East market, she might be able to use the same approach, but she would have to redo her entire strategy and look at the Far East market more closely since it is different from Europe, and her past international sales were not with the Far East.

Instructor's Test Bank

for

Entrepreneurship: A Contemporary Approach (4th Edition)

True/False Questions
Multiple Choice Questions
Essay Questions

CHAPTER 1

THE ENTREPRENEURIAL REVOLUTION

True/False

Entrepreneurs: Challenging the Unknown

T   1.   Entrepreneurs are aggressive catalysts for change within the marketplace.

F   2.   Entrepreneurs are not heroes in today's marketplace.

Entrepreneurship: A Perspective

T   3.   Entrepreneurship is more than mere creation of business.

F   4.   The most dominant force in today's economic revolution is marketing.

The Environment of Entrepreneurship

T   5.   Small enterprises are the most common form of establishment, regardless of the industry.

T   6.   Venture financing emerged in the 1990s in more abundance.

T   7.   NFIB stands for National Federation of Independent Business.

T   8.   During the past ten years, new business incorporations averaged 600,000 per year.

T   9.   The all-time record for new business incorporations was 807,000 in 1995.

F   10.   Small enterprises are defined as having fewer than 1,000 employees.

F   11.   Today there are entrepreneurship courses offered at only a handful of schools.

Age of the Gazelles

T   12.   A "gazelle" is a business establishment with at least 20 percent sales growth every year.

F   13.   Gazelles produce only one half the innovations per employee that larger firms do.

The Dryden Press

Women-Owned Businesses

T   14. Women represent 34 percent of all business owners in the United States.

F   15. The Women's Business Ownership Act has failed twice to be signed into law by the president.

T   16. Women-owned businesses increased from 2.6 million in 1982 to 6.4 million in 1997.

F   17. From 1990 to 2005 the participation of women in the labor force will rise only 11 percent.

T   18. By 2005 women will account for 26 percent of the entire U.S. workforce net growth.

F   19. Women-owned companies are experiencing their most significant growth in retail businesses.

F   20. Women business owners do not recognize work-home role conflict as a major problem area.

T   21. The future will bring about a closing of the funding gap between men and women entrepreneurs.

Minority-Owned Business

T   22. Asian-American-owned businesses have increased 394 percent.

T   23. Cumulatively, minority-owned businesses generated over $78 billion in gross receipts.

F   24. From 1982 through 1987, minority-owned businesses declined in every category.

T   25. The two most frequently cited areas of improvement for minority entrepreneurs are education in business skills and access to capital.

Multiple Choice

Entrepreneurs: Challenging the Unknown

D   26.   Entrepreneurs are best characterized as:
- a. aggressive catalysts for change
- b heroes of today's marketplace
- c. creating jobs at a breathtaking pace
- d. all of the above

B   27.   Entrepreneurs have been compared to which of the following?
- a. couch potatoes
- b. top gun pilots
- c. corporate managers
- d. none of the above

Entrepreneurship: A Perspective

A   28.   The most dominant force in today's economic revolution would be:
- a. the entrepreneurial perspective
- b. the marketing wave
- c. the economic resurgence
- d. the legal barriers

The Environment of Entrepreneurship

A   29.   During the past ten years, there were approximately how many business incorporations per year?
- a. 600,000
- b. 500,000
- c. 700,000
- d. none of the above

D   30.   An enterprise could be
- a. a company
- b. a firm
- c. a business
- d. all of the above

D   31. To determine the overall number of business enterprises, you could check with which of the following sources of data?
   a. Statistics of Income
   b. Dunn & Bradstreet
   c. Small Business Data Base
   d. All of the above

C   32. SBA stands for the
   a. Student Business Association
   b. Small Business Association
   c. Small Business Administration
   d. Student Business Administration

A   33. A large enterprise has
   a. more than 100 employees
   b. fewer than 100 employees
   c. more than 50 but fewer than 100
   d. none of the above

C   34. NFIB stands for
   a. National Formation of Institute's Business
   b. National Fraternity of Innovative Business
   c. National Federation of Independent Business
   d. none of the above

B   35. Which is not a major area of study at most university centers for entrepreneurship?
   a. entrepreneurship education
   b. management of the entrepreneur
   c. outreach activities with entrepreneurs
   d. entrepreneurship research

D   36. Categories of small business establishments identified by the Small Business Administration include:
   a. apparent small
   b. small
   c. large
   d. all of the above

C 37. Which of the following statements depicts a development discovered in research and education concerning entrepreneurship?
a. Entrepreneurship and management are mutually exclusive domains
b. Venture financing has been reduced in the amounts available for entrepreneurs
c. Entrepreneurship education has become one of the fastest growing topics in business schools
d. Women entrepreneurs are not emerging in very large numbers

B 38. Today, entrepreneurship courses are offered at over _____ schools with that number _____.
a. 25; decreasing
b. 500; increasing
c. 1500; increasing
d. 125; stable

D 39. Most University Centers of Entrepreneurship focus on which of the following:
a. entrepreneurship education
b. outreach activities
c. entrepreneurship research
d. all of the above

Age of the Gazelles

A 40. Which of the following statements best describes a "gazelle"?
a. a business with at least 20 percent sales growth every year.
b. a business with no sales growth
c. a business that has acquired numerous firms
d. none of the above

D 41. Gazelles have been responsible for which of the following:
a. 5 million jobs
b. 55 percent of innovations
c. 95 percent of all radical innovations
d. all of the above

Women-Owned Business

A 42. Women entrepreneurs now represent
a. 34 percent of all business ownership
b. more business ownerships than men
c. more than half of all business ownership
d. almost 90 percent of all entrepreneurs

C 43. The number of businesses owned by women increased from 1982 to 1997 from _____ to _____.
a. 100,000 to 2 million
b. 1 million to 25 million
c. 2.6 million to 6.4 million
d. 50 million to 100 million

D 44. By 1997 there were approximately _____ million businesses owned by women.
a. 1.5
b. 2.9
c. 4.6
d. 6.4

C 45. Women-owned businesses have approximately _____ percent in the service sector.
a. 16
b. 10
c. 29
d. 75

D 46. In which of the following areas are women entrepreneurs dominating with 50 percent of all companies?
a. mining, manufacturing, and construction
b. transporation
c. finance, insurance, and real estate
d. retail business

C 47. From 1990 to 2005 the net growth of the workforce by women will be:
a. 18 percent
b. 22 percent
c. 62 percent
d. 54.7 percent

C 48. By 2005 women will account for _____ of the entire workforce net growth.
a. 62
b. 33
c. 47
d. 75

A 49. Which is a perceived weakness in women entrepreneurs?
a. financing
b. training
c. planning
d. establishing policies

The Dryden Press

B 50. The concept of dual income families and professional women in the workforce has created tension for women known as
   a. professional career conflict
   b. interrole conflict
   c. role assertion tension
   d. role tension syndrome

D 51. Work-home role conflict for women entrepreneurs is associated with
   a. level of business satisfaction
   b. level of self-esteem
   c. spouse's career choice
   d. a and b only

C 52. Women believe their highest management skills include
   a. budgeting
   b. forecasting
   c. ability to deal with people
   d. none of the above

C 53. One study found women entrepreneurs experienced less role conflict due to
   a. higher level of family life satisfaction
   b. greater autonomy from self-employment
   c. both a and b
   d. none of the above

C 54. The two major types of problems for women entrepreneurs are
   a. start-up problems and financing problems
   b. ongoing problems and mental problems
   c. start-up problems and ongoing problems
   d. ongoing problems and finishing problems

Future Challenges for Women Entrepreneurs

D 55. The future for women entrepreneurs holds
   a. an increase in their numbers
   b. an expansion to virtually every industry
   c. an increase in the number of women as service-industry owners
   d. all of the above

A 56. Why will the service industry be so popular with women entrepreneurs?
   a. It is less capital intensive
   b. It requires less hard work
   c. There is little competition there
   d. The returns on investment are phenomenal

The Dryden Press

B   57.   Developments affecting women entrepreneurs will include all of the following *except*:
a. a closing of the funding gap
b. more research on male entrepreneurs
c. more preparedness for entrepreneurial activity
d. growth of the service labor

B   58.   Which one of the following statements is true regarding the funding gap for women entrepreneurs?
a. The funding gap will continue to grow
b. As women gain more knowledge, the gap will decrease
c. Venture capitalists will not recognize women as capable entrepreneurs
d. Women will always use personal loans

A   59.   What area of research on women entrepreneurs will receive the greatest attention in the future?
a. personal and family-related variables
b. comparisons to men
c. motivation
d. money studies

A   60.   Ongoing research of entrepreneurship is likely to provide greater insights into
a. women's goals and motivation
b. time and motion studies
c. job satisfaction statistically analyzed
d. the future meanings of work-related activities

A   61.   The future will bring
a. a greater attention to research on women entrepreneurs
b. more attention to research on women entrepreneurs
c. no attention to research on women entrepreneurs
d. less attention to research on women entrepreneurs

Minority-Owned Business

A   62.   Asian-American-owned businesses have increased _____ in recent years.
a. 394 percent
b. 56 percent
c. 88 percent
d. 100 percent

B   63. Hispanic-owned businesses have increased _____ in recent years.
          a. 371 percent
          b. 55 percent
          c. 93 percent
          d. 10 percent

C   64. Between 1982 and 1987, the number of minority-owned businesses _____ in every category.
          a. decreased
          b. increased
          c. stabilized
          d. none of the above

D   65. Black-owned businesses increased _____ percent between 1982 and 1987.
          a. 394
          b. 161
          c. 90
          d. 38

A   66. Hispanic-owned businesses increased _____ percent between 1982 and 1987.
          a. 80.5
          b. 161
          c. 364.8
          d. 57.4

B   67. Which of the following minority groups account for the largest share of businesses?
          a. Asian-American
          b. Black Americans
          c. Pacific Islanders
          d. none of the above

D   68. Which of the following problem areas is/are associated with minority entrepreneurs?
          a. access to capital
          b. business training
          c. idea generation
          d. a and b only

D   69. Which of the following problem areas is/are associated with minority entrepreneurs?
          a. lack of management experience
          b. lack of business training
          c. perceived lack of experience
          d. all of the above

The Dryden Press

A   70. All of the following areas are considered problems for minority entrepreneurs *except:*
- a. product innovation
- b. lack of business training
- c. access to capital
- d. obtaining lines of credit

A   71. How do minority entrepreneurs deal with their perceived problem areas?
- a. a support system of family, friends, and business associates
- b. education in business skills
- c. perseverance
- d. all of the above

D   72. Increasing skills through business education can be accomplished by:
- a. college campuses
- b. seminars
- c. trade publications
- d. all of the above

Future Challenges for Minority Entrepreneurs

A   73. The "staying power" of minority-owned businesses is considered
- a. strong
- b. weak
- c. stable
- d. nonexistent

A   74. The two most frequently cited areas that need improvement for minority entrepreneurs are:
- a. product innovation and dealing with people
- b. business education and access to people
- c. support systems and idea generation
- d. none of the above

D   75. In the years to come, better initial capital opportunities may be provided by:
- a. "angel" financing
- b. minority-owned banks
- c. minority enterprise small business investment companies
- d. all of the above

Essays

76. *Describe entrepreneurs and entrepreneurship in today's marketplace.*

Entrepreneurs are individuals who recognize opportunities where others see chaos or confusion. They are aggressive catalysts for change within the marketplace. They have been compared to Olympic athletes challenging themselves to break new barriers, to long-distance runners dealing with the agony of the miles, to symphony orchestra conductors who balance the different skills and sounds into a cohesive whole, or to top-gun pilots who continually push the envelope of speed and daring. Whatever the passion, because they all fit in some way, entrepreneurs are the heroes of today's marketplace. They start and create jobs at a breathtaking pace.

Entrepreneurship is an integrated concept that permeates an individual's business in an innovative manner. It is this perspective that has revolutionized the way business is conducted at every level and in every country. *Inc.* magazine reported on the cover of one issue some time ago that "America is once again becoming a nation of risk takers and the way we do business will never be the same." So it is. The revolution has begun in an economic sense, and the entrepreneurial perspective is the dominant force.

77. *How dominant have new and small ventures been in the economy?*

The past decade has demonstrated the powerful emergence of entrepreneurial activity in the United States. Many statistics illustrate this fact. For example, during the past ten years new business incorporations averaged 600,000 *per year*. Although many of these incorporations may have been sole proprietorships or partnerships previously, it still demonstrates venture activity, whether it was through start-ups, expansion, or development. More specifically, 807,000 new smaller firms were established in 1995, an all-time record. Let's examine some of the latest tabulated numbers.

Smaller firms constitute more than 90 percent of the entire business population. Granted, this figure depends on the definition of the term "small"; however, the Internal Revenue Service (IRS) reports that 21 million businesses exist based on business tax returns. Figure 1.1 was developed by the National Federation of Independent Business (NFIB) in order to demonstrate the breakdown. Approximately 12 million businesses have owners whose *principal* occupation is owning and operating them.. Approximately 7 million (out of 12 million) have owners who work for themselves without employing anyone else. Of the 5 million remaining firms, only 15,000 employ 500 or more people.

78. *Define a "gazelle" and discuss some of the impact that gazelles have on the economy.*

New and smaller firms create the most jobs in the U.S. economy. The facts speak for themselves. The vast majority of these job-creating companies are fast-growing businesses. David Birch of Cognetics, Inc., has named these firms "gazelles." A gazelle, by Birch's definition, is a business establishment with at least 20 percent sales growth every year from 1990 to 1994 (the last year for which Cognetics has complete numbers), starting with a base of at least $100,000.

Despite the continual downsizing in major corporations, the gazelles produced 5 million jobs and brought the net employment growth to 4.2 million jobs.

Gazelles are leaders in innovation, as shown by the following:

- New and smaller firms have been responsible for 55 percent of the innovation in 362 different industries and 95 percent of all radical innovations.

- Gazelles produce twice as many product innovations per employee as do larger firms.

- New and smaller firms obtain more patients per sales dollar than do larger firms.

79. *What are some of the recent trends that are changing the nature of women entrepreneurs?*

Women are entering into fields that were once considered male roles. More women are studying business and science in school. Also, more women are choosing to put off having a family or choosing not to have a family at all. The economy is becoming more service-oriented, which is well suited to the women entrepreneurs' strengths. In correlation with family decisions, women are considered equals in personal relationships today and are more independent. These trends make it easier for women to start their own business.

80. *Describe the increasing trend of minority-owned businesses.*

In recent years, the number of minority-owned firms increased dramatically. Asian-American-owned firms increased 394 percent, Native American-owned firms 40 percent, Hispanic-owned firms 93 percent, and Black-owned firms increased 87 percent. Cumulatively, these firms generated over $78 billion in gross receipts. These statistics correspond to over 1,213,570 minority-owned businesses that, in addition to providing salaries for over 300,000 proprietorships, provided paid employment for 836,000 people.

These figures represent 8.9 percent of all businesses within the scope of the Bureau of Census and 3.9 percent of the receipts of those businesses. Black-owned businesses accounted for the largest share of minority-owned businesses (34.9 percent), and the businesses owned by Asian-Americans and Pacific Islanders accounted for the largest share of minority-owned business receipts (42.6 percent). Businesses owned by Asian-Americans and Pacific Islanders were also the largest among minority-owned businesses in terms of average receipts, with receipts per firm of $93,221, compared to an average of $64,131 for minority-owned businesses overall.

CHAPTER 2

ENTREPRENEURSHIP: AN EVOLVING CONCEPT

True/False

The Evolution of Entrepreneurship

T   1.   Three characteristics of an entrepreneur are personal initiative, management skills, and a desire for autonomy.

T   2.   Two characteristics of an entrepreneur are aggressiveness and competitiveness.

F   3.   The word entrepreneur is derived from the Spanish word *entreprendre,* meaning "to undertake."

T   4.   There is no single definition of an entrepreneur; however, research is providing a sharper focus on the subject.

T   5.   Recognition of entrepreneurs dates back to the French economist Richard Cantillon.

F   6.   In the past century, entrepreneurship has become closely linked with socialism and regulated business.

The Myths of Entrepreneurship

F   7.   Most entrepreneurs are inventors.

T   8.   An entrepreneur does not need a lot of money or luck.

T   9.   Prepared entrepreneurs who seize opportunities when they arise often appear to be lucky.

F   10.   Entrepreneurs are high risk takers.

T   11.   The myths of entrepreneurship are present because of lack of research.

F   12.   Characteristics of entrepreneurs cannot be taught or learned.

F   13.   Entrepreneurs are born, not made.

The Dryden Press

F 14. Entrepreneurs are doers, not thinkers.

F 15. Entrepreneurs must fit the "profile."

Approaches to Entrepreneurship

T 16. The macro view includes external processes that are sometimes beyond the control of the entrepreneur.

T 17. The displacement school of thought focuses on group phenomena.

T 18. The strategic formulation school of thought emphasizes the planning process in successful venture development.

F 19. In the environmental school of thought, external factors affect a potential entrepreneur's lifestyle.

T 20. Venture capital availability is a part of the environment in the multidimensional approach.

Process Approaches

F 21. Entrepreneurship is a series of isolated activities or undertakings.

T 22. The entrepreneurial events approach focuses on such factors as initiative, organization, autonomy, and risk taking.

T 23. The entrepreneur is a catalyst for economic change who uses purposeful searching, careful planning, and sound judgment in carrying out the entrepreneurial process.

T 24. The four major dimensions considered in the multidimensional approach are the individual, the environment, the organization, and the process.

F 25. Intrapreneurship is the same as entrepreneurship.

Multiple Choice

The Evolution of Entrepreneurship

C   26.   The word entrepreneur is derived from the French *entreprendre*, which is translated as
- a. to apprehend.
- b. to enter and dare.
- c. to undertake.
- d. to compete.

D   27.   The entrepreneur is one who
- a. organizes.
- b. manages.
- c. assumes the risks.
- d. does all of the above.

A   28.   Which of the following characteristics is most important to an entrepreneur?
- a. management skills
- b. neatness
- c. friendliness
- d. all of the above

D   29.   Who coined the word entrepreneur?
- a. Joseph Schumpeter
- b. Jean Baptiste Say
- c. Richard Cantillon
- d. none of the above

D   30.   Today an entrepreneur is which of the following?
- a. an innovator
- b. a developer
- c. a risk taker
- d. all of the above

A   31.   Which economist associated the "risk bearing" activity in the economy with the entrepreneur?
- a. Richard Cantillon
- b. Robert C. Ronstadt
- c. Peter F. Drucker
- d. Jean Baptiste Say

The Dryden Press

D   32. Which is *not* one of the chief characteristics of an entrepreneur?
   a. personal initiative
   b. ability to consolidate resources
   c. risk taking
   d. desire for monogamy

D   33. Which is a key factor in successful entrepreneurship?
   a. identifying the strengths and weaknesses of a venture
   b. setting up clear timetables with contingencies for handling problems
   c. minimizing problems through careful strategy formulation
   d. all of the above

B   34. Entrepreneurial traits include which of the following?
   a. salesmanship
   b. initiative
   c. wealth
   d. all of the above

B   35. Robert C. Ronstadt put together a summary definition of entrepreneur that included which of the following key phrases?
   a. ...the acceptance of risk of failure
   b. ...the dynamic process of creating incremental wealth
   c. ...take advantage of economic endowments
   d. ...a phenomenon that comes under the wider aspect of leadership

A   36. In the present century, which of the following is entrepreneurship considered synonymous with:
   a. free enterprise.
   b. socialism.
   c. multimillion-dollar enterprises.
   d. partnership.

The Myths of Entrepreneurship

D   37. Which is a true statement about entrepreneurs?
   a. Entrepreneurs are doers, not thinkers.
   b. All you need is money to be an entrepreneur.
   c. Ignorance is bliss for an entrepreneur.
   d. None of the above is true.

A 38. Throughout the years, many myths have arisen about entrepreneurship as a result of?
  a. a lack of research about entrepreneurship
  b. a lack of interest in the field
  c. a total disregard for the truth
  d. a destructive attitude by government

C 39. The "corridor principle" is best described by which of the following statements?
  a. If at first you don't succeed, try, try, again.
  b. The right place at the right time.
  c. With every new venture launched, new and unintended opportunities arise.
  d. Luck happens when preparation meets opportunity.

D 40. Which of the following is a common cause of failure of a small business?
  a. poor investments
  b. poor planning
  c. lack of financial understanding
  d. all of the above

D 41. Most new ventures fail within
  a. 5 years.
  b. 10 years.
  c. 20 years.
  d. None of the above is correct.

B 42. Which of the following traits is *not* that of an entrepreneur?
  a. drive
  b. shyness
  c. willingness to take risks
  d. human relations skills

D 43. Which one of the statements below is correct?
  a. Entrepreneurs are doers, not thinkers.
  b. Entrepreneurs are born, not made.
  c. All you need is money to be an entrepreneur.
  d. None of the above is correct.

C 44. Which of the following is *not* a common myth about entrepreneurs?
  a. Entrepreneurs are academic and social misfits.
  b. Entrepreneurs are doers, not thinkers.
  c. Entrepreneurs today are considered heroes.
  d. All you need is money to be an entrepreneur.

The Dryden Press

B 45. Which statement is *not* true?
   a. Luck happens when preparation meets opportunity.
   b. Entrepreneurs do not hold up in today's competitive market.
   c. Failure due to lack of proper financing often is an indicator of other problems.
   d. It takes more than just money to be a successful entrepreneur.

D 46. Most entrepreneurs should be categorized as
   a. inventors.
   b. innovators.
   c. lucky.
   d. none of the above.

A 47. Which of the following statements is true?
   a. Entrepreneurship is the ability to create and build a vision from practically nothing
   b. Entrepreneurship is pure luck
   c. Entrepreneurship is simply obtaining financing and starting a business
   d. Entrepreneurship has nothing to do with creating incremental wealth

B 48. Which of the following economists wrote about entrepreneurship and its impact on economic development?
   a. Richard Dailey
   b. Joseph Schumpeter
   c. Paul Samuelson
   d. Robert McConnell

E 49. In our present century entrepreneurship has become synonymous or closely linked with:
   a. failure
   b. socialism and monopolies
   c. multimillion-dollar enterprises
   d. free enterprise and capitalism

C 50. Michael Gerber has written a book titled "The E-Myth," where he contends:
   a. the entire field of study in entrepreneurship is a myth
   b. there is no such thing as entrepreneurship
   c. today's business owners are not true entrepreneurs
   d. everybody in business is an entrepreneur

A 51. Michael Gerber's book "The E-Myth" explains the failure of most small businesses is due to:
   a. owners being more technicians rather than entrepreneurs
   b. owners being more managerial rather than technical
   c. owners being more entrepreneurial rather than managerial
   d. owners being more customers rather than businesspeople

C 52. Entrepreneurs had been historically considered academic misfits because:
   a. educational institutions refused to admit them
   b. they were always bored with school
   c. they never studied their course material
   d. educational institutions did not recognize entrepreneurship

B 53. When referring to "luck" and an entrepreneur, which of the following statements is an appropriate adage?
   a. always wait for luck to happen
   b. luck happens when preparation meets opportunity
   c. luck happens to everyone
   d. luck is the key to entrepreneurship

C 54. The statement, "with every new venture launched, new and unintended opportunities often arise," would be associated with:
   a. the entrepreneurial principle
   b. the opportunity principle
   c. the corridor principle
   d. the Dilbert principle

A 55. Entrepreneurs themselves perceive the concept of risk in which of the following ways:
   a. calculated risk taking
   b. gambling risk
   c. distorted risk taking
   d. social risk

D 56. In the study of contemporary entrepreneurship, one concept reoccurs:
   a. no one understands the field
   b. folklore dominates the studies
   c. there is no theoretical base
   d. entrepreneurship is interdisciplinary

B 57. The macro view of entrepreneurship presents factors exhibiting a strong _____.
   a. internal locus of control
   b. external locus of control
   c. environmental locus of control
   d. contemporary locus of control

The Dryden Press

Approaches to Entrepreneurship

C   58. Which of the following schools of thought is *not* a micro view school of thought?
   a. the entrepreneurial trait school of thought
   b. the venture opportunity school of thought
   c. the displacement school of thought
   d. none of the above

A   59. Which of the following are characteristic elements in the strategic formulation school of thought?
   a. unique markets and unique ideas
   b. unique angles and unique elements
   c. opportunities and traits
   d. all of the above

A   60. The macro view can be broken down into which three areas?
   a. the environmental, financial, and displacement
   b. the financial/capital, strategic, and opportunity
   c. the displacement, trait, and financial
   d. the entrepreneurial trait, opportunity, and strategic

D   61. The displacement school of thought can be divided into which three groups?
   a. political, cultural, environmental
   b. cultural, environmental, and financial
   c. environmental, financial, and economic
   d. economic, cultural, and political

B   62. The micro view is divided into which three theories?
   a. the entrepreneurial, financial, displacement
   b. the venture opportunity theory, entrepreneurial, strategic
   c. the strategic, environmental, and opportunity
   d. the environmental, financial, and displacement

B   63. Which of the following is not a form of displacement in the displacement school of thought?
   a. political
   b. racial
   c. economical
   d. cultural

C   64. Creativity and market awareness are viewed as essential elements for which of the following?
   a. strategic formulation school of thought
   b. displacement school of thought
   c. venture opportunity school of thought
   d. financial school of thought

B   65. Which of the following does not apply to the strategic formulation school of thought?
   a. unique people
   b. unique places
   c. unique markets
   d. unique products

Process Approaches

C   66. The Entrepreneurial Assessment Approach stressed that assessments must be made _____ in regard to the entrepreneur, the venture, and the environment.
   a. qualitatively and quantitatively
   b. strategically and ethically
   c. all of the above
   d. none of the above

C   67. Which of the following is a process of innovation and new venture creation through four major dimensions: individual, organization, environment, and process?
   a. entrepreneur process
   b. entrepreneurial management
   c. entrepreneurship
   d. none of the above

A   68. The entrepreneurial events approach is a process by which individuals _____, _____, and _____ their entrepreneurial activities.
   a. plan, implement, control
   b. plan, implement, divide
   c. plan, organize, control
   d. research, implement, control

The Dryden Press

B 69. The multidimensional approach has four specific factors which are ___, ___, ___, and ___.
   a. initiative, organization, risk taking, planning
   b. individual, environment, organization, process
   c. plan, implement, control, divide
   d. plan, organize, control, research

B 70. In the multidimensional approach, the environment deals with ___.
   a. the need for achievement
   b. venture capital availability
   c. job satisfaction
   d. type of firm

B 71. The *need for achievement* would be under which dimension of the multidimensional approach?
   a. environment
   b. individual
   c. organization
   d. process

B 72. How many major dimensions are in the multidimensional approach?
   a. 6
   b. 4
   c. 10
   d. 3

A 73. Entrepreneurship is a process of innovation and new venture creation that includes which of the following dimensions?
   a. individual, environment, and organization
   b. government, organization, and individual
   c. environment, process, and groups
   d. individual, groups, and government

B 74. Intrapreneurship is a popular concept that refers to
   a. corporate accountants.
   b. entrepreneurs within a corporate setting.
   c. uniquely optimistic executives.
   d. planners in a government position.

B 75. Since entrepreneurship is based upon a discipline of principles involving innovation, the underlying theme of the textbook is
   a. environmental assessment.
   b. entrepreneurial management.
   c. intrapreneurship.
   d. opportunistic venturing.

Essays

76. *Name and describe four of the ten major myths of management.*

   One of the myths of management says that entrepreneurs are born, not made. This myth implies that entrepreneurs cannot be taught how to be successful. It says that they must be born with certain traits, such as aggressiveness, initiative, drive, and skill in human relations. However, recent recognition of entrepreneurship as a discipline is helping to dispel this myth. Another myth is the "all you need is money" myth, which says businesses fail because of inadequate financing. Actually, poor financing usually indicates other problems such as managerial incompetence, poor investments, and poor planning. A third myth says that entrepreneurs are either inventors or innovators. While many inventors and innovators are entrepreneurs, many entrepreneurs excel at other profit-seeking activities. A final myth is that all you need is luck. "Luck happens when preparation meets opportunity" means that being prepared for situations can lead to success when the time is right.

77. *List and categorize the schools of entrepreneurial thought.*

   The schools of entrepreneurial thought can be grouped into two major headings, macro and micro. The macro view of entrepreneurship presents a broad array of factors. These include external factors, which sometimes cannot be controlled. In the macro view, the environmental school of thought deals with external factors that affect the possible lifestyle of the entrepreneur. Also under macro, the financial/capital school looks for seed and growth capital to develop the entrepreneur. The displacement school is the final macro view. It holds that the group affects or eliminates certain factors that project the individual into an entrepreneurial venture. The micro view examines factors specific to entrepreneurship and part of the "internal" locus of control. The entrepreneurial trait school says that successful entrepreneurs *usually* exhibit similar characteristics. The venture opportunity school focuses on opportunities in directions other than where the entrepreneur is presently headed. The final school, the strategic formulation school, emphasizes the planning process in successful venture development.

78. *Describe the three process approaches that also examine the activities involved in entrepreneurship.*

   The first process approach is the entrepreneurial events approach. This approach combines the activities and undertakings of entrepreneurship. It focuses on the process of entrepreneurial activities from someone taking the initiative to begin, to organizing the resources, to managing and administering, to disposing and distributing resources, to sharing in the risks of success or failure. The second approach is the entrepreneurial assessment approach. It stresses that assessments must be made qualitatively, quantitatively, strategically, and ethically, in regard to the entrepreneur, the venture, and the environment. This approach, when compared to the stage of an entrepreneur's career, develops the "entrepreneurial perspective." The third approach is the multidimensional approach. It is a more complex and detailed approach that emphasizes the individual, the environment, the organization, and the venture process. Some of the individual factors related to this approach include a need for achievement, locus of control, age, education, job satisfaction, and experience. The environmental factors surrounding it include venture capital availability, accessibility of suppliers, governmental influences, and living conditions. The organizational factors related to this approach include the type of firm, strategic variables, and competitive entry wedges. The venture process deals with location, resources, marketing products, producing the product, building the organization, and responding to government and society. All of these factors overlap to some degree and relate to each other to combine all aspects into entrepreneurship.

79. *Trace the evolution of entrepreneurship, list the men who wrote about it, and describe its impact on economic development.*

Entrepreneurship was first recognized by Richard Cantillon in eighteenth-century France. He described an entrepreneur as someone who bears the risks of business. During the same time period, the Industrial Revolution was taking form in England, and the entrepreneur was seen taking risks and transforming resources into products. Entrepreneurship has long been associated with economic development. Many definitions of entrepreneurship prior to 1950 came from economists such as Cantillon, Jean Baptiste Say (1803), and Joseph Schumpeter (1934). In the twentieth century, entrepreneurship has been associated with free enterprise and capitalism. Entrepreneurs generally are seen as people who provide creative and innovative ideas for businesses and help them grow and become profitable. Now, entrepreneurship is regarded as "pioneer ship" on the frontier of business.

80. *Describe the increasing trend of women- and minority-owned businesses.*

Women-owned businesses are the fastest-growing segment of small business in the nation, with an increase from 2.6 million businesses in 1982 to 6.4 million in 1997. Before 1970, women owned 5 percent of all U.S. businesses. Today women own nearly 34 percent of all businesses, 50 percent of all retail businesses, and 29 percent of all service companies.

In recent years the number of minority-owned firms has increased dramatically. Asian-American-owned firms increased 394 percent; Native American-owned firms, 40 percent; Hispanic-owned firms, 93 percent; and African American-owned firms, 87 percent. Cumulatively, these firms generated more than $78 billion in gross receipts. These statistics correspond to more than 1,213,570 minority-owned businesses that, in addition to providing salaries for more than 300,000 proprietorships, provided paid employment for 836,000 people.

CHAPTER 3

INTRAPRENEURSHIP:

DEVELOPING ENTREPRENEURSHIP IN THE CORPORATION

True/False

F 1. Intrapreneurial activity occurs outside the firm.

T 2. Polaroid and 3M have had successful intrapreneurial ventures.

T 3. One reason that intrapreneurship has become popular is because it allows corporations to tap the innovative talents of the personnel.

The Nature of Intrapreneurship

T 4. As part of creating an innovative climate, a firm should base rewards given upon results achieved.

F 5. Most people understand what intrapreneurship is all about.

T 6. A corporation can encourage intrapreneurship activities if top management sponsors intrapreneurial projects.

F 7. Few firms today realize the need for intrapreneurship.

T 8. The need for intrapreneurship has risen in response to the increasing number of competitors.

T 9. Clever bootlegging of ideas refers to secretly working on new ideas on company time as well as on personal time.

T 10. Individuals may avoid corporate entrepreneurial behavior due to the impact of traditional management techniques.

F 11. Skunkworks are project groups that work within the traditional lines of authority.

Specific Elements of a Corporate Intrapreneurial Strategy

T 12. Corporations that promote personal growth will attract the best people.

F 13. When an intrapreneurial environment is created, a company does not usually set aside traditions of the company.

F 14. Every businessperson feels comfortable operating in an intrapreneurial environment.

T 15. The first step in planning a strategy of intrapreneurship is sharing the vision of innovation that executives wish to achieve.

F 16. Systematic evolution of a product or service into newer or larger markets is referred to as radical innovation.

F 17. Intrapreneurs should be restricted to the resources of their own divisions of the corporation.

T 18. Researchers have identified specific factors that organizations can concentrate on in helping individuals develop more entrepreneurial behavior.

T 19. Venture teams have been recognized as the productivity breakthrough of the 1990s.

The Interactive Process of Intrapreneurship

T 20. Most intrapreneurs begin their "intraprise" in what is termed the "daydream phase."

T 21. Intrapreneurs are people who are action oriented and self-determined.

F 22. One of the ten commandments intrapreneurs follow is to remember it is easier to ask for permission than for forgiveness.

F 23. There is a great deal of similarity between the myths surrounding both intrapreneurs and entrepreneurs.

F 24. Intrapreneurs generally are power oriented or power hungry.

T 25. The Interactive Process is a result of individuals and organizational characteristics interacting with some precipitating event.

Multiple Choice

Introduction

D   26.   Intrapreneurial activity takes place _____ the firm.
- a. only with outside suppliers to
- b. with anyone outside
- c. both inside and outside
- d. inside

C   27.   Which of the following has *not* been reported to have had a successful corporate venture?
- a. Polaroid
- b. 3M
- c. Systems Analog
- d. Bell Atlantic

D   28.   One reason why intrapreneurship has done so well is that it allows organizations to
- a. increase salaries.
- b. fire the dead wood.
- c. encourage high risk taking.
- d. tap the innovative talents of their people.

The Nature of Intrapreneurship

D   29.   _____ people thoroughly understand the concept of intrapreneuring.
- a. Just about all
- b. Most
- c. Many
- d. Few

C   30.   The major thrust of intrapreneuring is to
- a. encourage greater risk taking.
- b. raise profitability.
- c. encourage innovation.
- d. increase morale.

A   31.   All of the following are reasons for the growth of intrapreneurship except
- a. a desire to dramatically increase profitability.
- b. a rapidly growing number of new and sophisticated competitors.
- c. a sense of distrust in the traditional methods of corporate management.
- d. an exodus of some of the best people out of corporations.

D 32. Which of the following helps account for the rise of interest in intrapreneurship?
   a. There is an increase in the number of sophisticated competitors.
   b. There is a distrust in traditional methods of corporate management.
   c. Corporations are now losing some of their best people.
   d. All of the above.

C 33. Which of the following is *not* one of the four characteristics in establishing an innovative climate?
   a. the presence of explicit goals
   b. a system of feedback and positive reinforcement
   c. an emphasis on corporate responsibility
   d. rewards based upon results

C 34. In following the rules for innovation, a manager should do all of the following *except*
   a. encourage action.
   b. use formal meetings whenever possible.
   c. punish failure.
   d. reward performance.

C 35. In restructuring corporate thinking, top management should
   a. identify potential intrapreneurs after an innovation program is in operation.
   b. make the intrapreneur follow strict corporate guidelines.
   c. promote intrapreneurship through experimentation.
   d. create diversity and order in strategic activities.

D 36. Intrapreneurship is on the rise in terms of all of the following except
   a. status.
   b. publicity.
   c. economic development.
   d. stress attrition.

C 37. Secretly working on new ideas on company time as well as on personal time is referred to as
   a. skunkworks.
   b. champion.
   c. bootlegging.
   d. interactive learning.

A   38. The adverse impact of _____ can be so destructive that individuals within the enterprise will tend to avoid entrepreneurial behavior.
   a. traditional management techniques
   b. innovative climate rules
   c. specific intrapreneurial strategies
   d. informal meetings

B   39. Innovative factors identified by James Brian Quinn that exist in large organizations experienced in successful innovation include all of the following *except:*
   a. interactive learning.
   b. uniform compensation.
   c. multiple approaches.
   d. skunkworks.

A   40. Groups that function outside traditional lines of authority permitting rapid turnaround of new ideas as well as instilling a high level of group loyalty are called:
   a. skunkworks.
   b. multiple approaches.
   c. champions.
   d. strategic innovators.

C   41. Which of the following would *not* be considered an obstacle to corporate venturing?
   a. compensate uniformly
   b. manage functionally
   c. interactive learning
   d. promote compatible individuals

B   42. In an innovative climate, failure is viewed as
   a. the end of the world.
   b. a learning experience.
   c. O.K., inevitable since the employee is probably not capable of further innovative thought.
   d. a basis for firing.

A   43. One step an organization can take to make its corporate environment more innovative is to
   a. gain top management support of an intrapreneuring program.
   b. fire top management and hire young executives.
   c. change the dress code to "casual attire."
   d. give across-the-board raises.

The Dryden Press

A   44. Which of the following will help to foster an innovative climate?
   a. encourage action from employees
   b. punish mistakes
   c. eliminate coffee breaks to encourage employees to work harder
   d. do away with dress codes

Specific Elements of a Corporate Intrapreneurial Strategy

A   45. Authoritarian management is being replaced by
   a. networking.
   b. independent contractors.
   c. Japanese managers.
   d. benevolent managers.

C   46. Which of the following will help to foster an innovative climate?
   a. fire malcontented employees
   b. demand high profitability
   c. reward innovative thought
   d. punish malingerers

D   47. In attempting to create an intrapreneurial climate, the organization should consider that
   a. the corporations that promote personal growth will attract the best people.
   b. the best people seek ownership in a corporation.
   c. third-party contractors of labor will be used increasingly.
   d. all of the above are true.

D   48. All of the following are important characteristics for establishing an intrapreneurial climate *except*
   a. the presence of explicit goals.
   b. feedback.
   c. positive reinforcement.
   d. punishment of mistakes.

B   49. Rewards should be based upon _____ to encourage the desired behavior.
   a. seniority
   b. results
   c. attitude
   d. morale

The Dryden Press

D   50. Key features in the success of any innovative program include all of the following *except*
   a. confidence.
   b. trust.
   c. accountability.
   d. high profitability.

B   51. Intrapreneurship within the corporate structure allows employees to develop their ideas without
   a. losing their jobs to more loyal subordinates.
   b. the risk associated with leaving the company.
   c. making their spouses so angry that they quit their jobs.
   d. fear of being promoted.

B   52. The first step in planning a strategy of intrapreneurship for enterprise is
   a. identifying specific objectives.
   b. sharing the vision of innovation.
   c. applying the exact tools of the entrepreneur.
   d. developing radical innovation.

D   53. The second step in planning a strategy of intrapreneurship for the enterprise is
   a. identifying specific objectives.
   b. sharing the vision of innovation.
   c. applying the exact tools of the entrepreneur.
   d. developing and encouraging innovation.

B   54. Which of the following terms represents the systematic evolution of a product or service into newer or larger markets?
   a. radical innovation
   b. incremental innovation
   c. collective entrepreneurship
   d. strategic management

A   55. Which of the following terms represents the inaugural breakthroughs launched from experimentation and determined vision?
   a. radical innovation
   b. incremental innovation
   c. collective entrepreneurship
   d. strategic management

The Dryden Press

C   56. Which of the following are specific factors identified by researchers that organizations can concentrate on in structuring an intrapreneurial climate?
a. radical innovation, incremental innovation, and vision
b. skunkworks, multiple approaches, and vision
c. top management support, time, resources, rewards, and organizational boundaries
d. rewards, resources, innovation, and vision

A   57. Internal venture capital that is set aside for special intrapreneurial projects is termed:
a. intracapital.
b. project capital.
c. intrapreneurial seed money.
d. collective capital.

D   58. Which of the following are innovative rules that the 3M Corporation uses to encourage its employees to foster ideas?
a. tolerate failure
b. motivate champions
c. don't kill a project
d. all of the above

D   59. When entrepreneurship is diffused throughout a company and experimentation goes on continuously by all workers seeking to improve the organization, it is referred to as
a. incremental innovation.
b. multiple approaches.
c. interactive learning.
d. collective entrepreneurship.

D   60. Which of the following is an advantage to developing an intrapreneurial environment?
a. development of new products
b. helps to retain and motivate the best employees
c. creation of a work force that can help the enterprise maintain a competitive posture
d. all of the above

C   61. Which of the following is *not* a strategy for corporate intrapreneuring?
a. promote personal growth
b. use people-style management
c. decrease the use of third-party contracts
d. allow intrapreneur to develop ideas

D   62. Which of the following modules were included in the Intrapreneurship Training Program (ITP) described in the chapter?
   a. personal creativity
   b. resource allocation
   c. intrapreneuring
   d. a and c only

D   63. In order to develop an intrapreneurial environment, factors that organizations need to be aware of include:
   a. management support and rewards
   b. autonomy and time
   c. business plans and inventions
   d. a and b should be considered

B   64. Which of the following internal factors were *not* identified as key elements for firms seeking to develop an intrapreneurial environment?
   a. autonomy/work discretion
   b. venture plans
   c. organizational boundaries
   d. time availability

A   65. A small group of people who operate as a semi-autonomous unit to create and develop new ideas is referred to as a:
   a. venture team
   b. innovation hub
   c. transformation group
   d. none of the above

B   66. What is the first thing a corporation can do to foster the intrapreneurship process?
   a. hire traditional managers
   b. examine and/or revise its philosophy of management
   c. give across-the-board raises
   d. keep doing things as usual

The Interactive Process of Intrapreneurship

C   67. Most intrapreneurs begin their "intraprise" with
   a. the copycat suspect phase.
   b. the decreased loyalty phase.
   c. the daydreaming phase.
   d. a desire to become wealthy.

A   68.   Intrapreneurial characteristics include
           a. a strong drive to succeed.
           b. superior intelligence.
           c. high risk taking.
           d. low morals.

A   69.   Typically, when faced with setbacks or failure, intrapreneurs
           a. remain optimistic and view it as a learning experience.
           b. become outraged and take a short vacation.
           c. blame top management.
           d. resign.

B   70.   Concerning ethics and morals, intrapreneurs
           a. have no morals and ethics.
           b. have high morals and ethics.
           c. view morals and ethics as hurdles to success.
           d. never consider the subject.

B   71.   Concerning risk taking, intrapreneurs are
           a. high risk takers.
           b. moderate risk takers.
           c. low risk takers.
           d. not risk takers.

A   72.   Which is *not* a characteristic of the "ten commandments" of intrapreneurship?
           a. Do only what is written in the job description.
           b. Come to work willing to be fired.
           c. Keep your vision strong.
           d. Be loyal and truthful to your sponsors.

C   73.   Which of the following statements is *not* a myth about intrapreneurship?
           a. Their primary motivation is money.
           b. They are high risk takers.
           c. They are extremely analytical.
           d. They lack morals and ethics.

A   74.   One research model illustrated the process of intrapreneurship as an interaction of which elements?
           a. organization, individual, precipitating event
           b. intrapreneur, entrepreneur, manager
           c. myths, realities, perceptions
           d. none of the above

D 75. Precipitating events in the corporate entrepreneurship process could include:
   a. merger or acquisition.
   b. development of new technologies.
   c. change in company management.
   d. all of the above.

Essays

76. *Describe the steps necessary to take an individual from a climate that is very hierarchical in nature to an intrapreneurial setting.*

    As a quote from the text states, "To establish corporate entrepreneuring, companies need to provide the freedom and encouragement that intrapreneurs require to develop their ideas." This statement is very true, but it could be developed further. For example, managers coming from a traditional style of management believe in keeping ideas bottled up in their heads because they actually believe that it will serve no purpose to present them to upper management. Often, shop floor personnel are overlooked in terms of being innovative. Secondly, a more horizontal way of communication and delegation would be better. This way no one person could stop a project completely, and everyone could work as a team providing input. Lastly, develop and practice the basics as mentioned in the text.

77. *Compare and contrast vertical integration and horizontal integration as they relate to the traditional style of management and intrapreneurial management.*

    In using table 3.4 as reference, one will notice that the traditional manager works in an environment that is primarily vertical in nature, and the intrapreneur manager works in an environment that is more horizontal in nature. For example, the traditional manager has an attitude that others are in charge of his or her destiny and is also very cautious. On the other hand, the intrapreneur tries to outwit the system and likes the risk associated with the job. The horizontal nature that the intrapreneur works in allows him or her to bypass and outwit certain things because the system is so flexible. However, if the traditional manager would try something like that, he could possibly be fired because of the hierarchy and channels that must be used. Also, the traditional manager cares very much about his/her title, because this is related to his/her position in the hierarchy. The intrapreneur does not care about titles and would rather have freedom.

78. *Discuss the manner in which the intrapreneur goes through the basic process of planning, organizing, and controlling.*

    The intrapreneur deals with the same basic functions that most other managers deal with: planning, organizing, and controlling. For the intrapreneur, planning for a specific project entails setting the objective that he or she wants to accomplish by the end of the investigation stage and going from there. Organizing is the stage at which jobs and other specific duties are assigned to the workers on the project. Lastly, controlling is probably the most difficult stage for the intrapreneur. Because it is a new project, it is more difficult to set standards and measure the standards against the actual result.

79. *Using the Signode's V-Teams example from the text, explain how some programs may succeed or fail using this approach.*

Signode is using an aggressive strategy to pursue new products. Success will be tough for some products, but the stringent rules placed on the new products will help to keep the basic use of technology that Signode has and possibly develop new technologies instead of branching out into some area that the company has never pursued, i.e., the clothing industry. The failure may come from the fact that Signode wants to be worth $1 billion-plus by 1990. It may not be enough time for them to accomplish this task. If the push is big enough, the company may find itself in bad shape financially and have to rethink the primary purpose of the company.

80. *Explain some of the disadvantages that may occur in firms that are trying to incorporate intrapreneurship into their organizations.*

One disadvantage may be that there is resistance to change by some managers. Also, if a company jumps into intrapreneuring too quickly without proper training, there may be some managers left not knowing what to do. If the corporate climate is not right for intrapreneuring, there is almost no chance for success.

CHAPTER 4

UNDERSTANDING THE ENTREPRENEURIAL PERSPECTIVE IN INDIVIDUALS

True/False

The Entrepreneurial Perspective

T   1.   Each and every person has the potential and free choice to pursue a career as an entrepreneur.

F   2.   The "entrepreneurial perspective" within individuals is established through scientific methods.

Who are the Entrepreneurs?

F   3.   Entrepreneurs are pessimists who see the cup half empty rather than half full.

T   4.   The *Harvard Business Review* is an example of a journal used in entrepreneurial research.

T   5.   Government publications are used in researching small business.

T   6.   Inexperience and incompetent management are the main reasons for failure.

T   7.   Good entrepreneurs seek feedback from others.

T   8.   A good trait for an entrepreneur is to be a calculated risk taker.

T   9.   Most successful entrepreneurs have failed at one time or another.

F   10.   Entrepreneurs do not need foresight.

Sources of Research for Entrepreneurs

T   11.   Publications, direct observation, speeches, and presentations are all major sources of information that supply data related to the entrepreneurial perspective.

Characteristics of Entrepreneurs

F   12.   Commitment, determination, and perseverance are the only characteristics one needs to become a successful entrepreneur.

T   13.   Creativity was once regarded as an exclusively inherited trait.

The Dark Side of Entrepreneurship

Risk Analysis

T   14.   There are many risks in entrepreneurship.

T   15.   There can be great financial risk in small business.

T   16.   The higher the rewards, the greater the risk that entrepreneurs face.

Stress and the Entrepreneur

T   17.   There are four causes of entrepreneurial stress.

F   18.   Immersion in business can be cured by networking.

T   19.   The need to achieve can be a source of stress for entrepreneurs.

The Entrepreneurial Ego

F   20.   The entrepreneur's ego is not involved in the desire for success.

F   21.   The "dark side" of entrepreneurship refers to the stress that entrepreneurs experience.

F   22.   Entrepreneurs never experience the negative effects of an inflated ego.

T   23.   Entrepreneurs like to remain alert to competition, customers, and government regulations, but this continual scanning of the environment can lead to a negative sense of distrust.

Entrepreneurial Motivation

T   24.   Lanny Harron and Harry Sapienza stated, "Because motivation plays an important part in the creation of new organizations, theories of organization creation that fail to address this notion are incomplete."

F   25.   According to the Model of Entrepreneurship Motivation, the entrepreneur's expectations are not compared with the actual or perceived outcomes of the firm.

Multiple Choice

The Entrepreneurial Perspective

B   26.   Every person has the _____ and _____ to pursue a career as an entrepreneur
               a. stubbornness; stupidity
               b. potential; free choice
               c. rights; regulations
               d. obligation; duty

A   27.   Examining characteristics associated with entrepreneurs allows us to look at the entrepreneurial potential in everyone. This is referred to as the:
               a. "Entrepreneurial Perspective"
               b. Discipline of Entrepreneurship
               c. Self-Renewing Agents
               d. None of the above

Who are the Entrepreneurs?

C   28.   Sources of information available to entrepreneurs include
               a. journals.
               b. textbooks.
               c. all of the above.
               d. none of the above.

A   29.   Government publications can
               a. supply information.
               b. increase cash flow.
               c. be wasted.
               d. do none of the above.

E 30. Which source of information about entrepreneurial characteristics is direct observation?
   a. biographies of entrepreneurs
   b. autobiographies of entrepreneurs
   c. books about entrepreneurs
   d. all of the above
   e. none of the above

Characteristics of Entrepreneurs

E 31. Characteristics often attributed to the entrepreneur include:
   a. commitment, determination, and perseverance
   b. egotism
   c. power hungry
   d. ability to be indecisive
   e. a and b only

D 32. Which are traits of a successful entrepreneur?
   a. desire to achieve
   b. initiative
   c. innovation
   d. all of the above

A 33. Entrepreneurs with a drive to achieve want to
   a. compete.
   b. watch.
   c. do none of the above.
   d. do a and b.

B 34. Which of the following is *not* a trait of successful entrepreneurs?
   a. initiative
   b. frustration
   c. perseverance
   d. all of the above

D 35. With persistent problem solving, entrepreneurs
   a. are not intimidated.
   b. are not aimless.
   c. think anything is possible.
   d. all of the above.

D 36. One could correlate _____ with a high energy level.
        a. creativity
        b. innovativeness
        c. all of the above
        d. none of the above

A 37. For entrepreneurs, vision describes
        a. where the entrepreneur wants to go.
        b. eyesight.
        c. people.
        d. none of the above.

D 38. Team building
        a. is good.
        b. will be highly qualified.
        c. does nothing.
        d. is both a and b.

C 39. An innovative product
        a. is usually an invention.
        b. won't ensure success.
        c. does all of the above.
        d. does none of the above.

C 40. Which of the following is a *false* statement about entrepreneurs?
        a. They burn with the competitive desire to excel.
        b. They see the cup half full rather than half empty.
        c. They do not use failure as a tool for learning.
        d. None of the above is false.

A. 41. Which of the following publications deal with research methodology and are tightly structured?
        a. technical and professional journals
        b. textbooks on entrepreneurs
        c. news periodicals
        d. all of the above

C 42. Which is *not* a source of information in an entrepreneurial profile?
        a. publications
        b. direct observation of practicing entrepreneurs
        c. word of mouth
        d. speeches and presentations

The Dryden Press

B   43. One factor *not* found in high achievers is
   a. responsibility.
   b. lack of feedback.
   c. moderate risk taking.
   d. high risk taking.

C   44. Which of the following is *not* a common characteristic of entrepreneurs?
   a. vision
   b. team building
   c. lack of motivational drive
   d. independence

A   45. Which of the following statements is false?
   a. Entrepreneurs are born with the skills necessary to manage a business.
   b. Their belief in their ability seldom wavers.
   c. Independence is a driving force behind contemporary entrepreneurs.
   d. Entrepreneurs know where they want to go.

D   46. Which of the following is *not* a true statement about team building?
   a. Most successful entrepreneurs have highly qualified teams that handle the growth and development of the venture.
   b. Compared to the owner, personnel are often more qualified to handle day-to-day implementation challenges.
   c. The entrepreneur has the clearest vision in the firm.
   d. All of the above are untrue statements.

B   47. Which of the following statements is false?
   a. Entrepreneurs want the authority to make important decisions.
   b. Management skills are not important characteristics for entrepreneurs to possess.
   c. Successful entrepreneurs strive to build a successful team around them.
   d. An entrepreneur can develop the vision of the company over time.

B   48. When entrepreneurs believe that their accomplishments and setbacks are within their own control and influence, they are exhibiting
   a. persistent problem-solving.
   b. internal locus of control.
   c. external locus of control.
   d. opportunity orientation.

B 49. If entrepreneurs believe in themselves and that their accomplishments and setbacks are within their own control, they possess a (n) _____ .
   a. confidence level higher than most entrepreneurs
   b. internal locus of control
   c. cockiness level too high to be an entrepreneur
   d. high energy level
   e. none of the above

The Dark Side of Entrepreneurship

E 50. What characteristic(s) that propel entrepreneurs into success can be exhibited to the "extreme"?
   a. overbearing need for control
   b. unrealistic optimism
   c. sense of distrust
   d. overriding desire for success
   e. all of the above

Risk Analysis

A 51. Areas of risk to the entrepreneur include
   a. career, family, psychic.
   b. family, business, social.
   c. psychic, social, physical.
   d. all of the above.

B 52. With psychic risk you fear
   a. losing your sanity
   b. failure.
   c. money
   d. adapting.

C 53. Which of the statements below is *not* a risk faced by entrepreneurs?
   a. financial risk
   b. career risk
   c. business risk
   d. none of the above

The Dryden Press

B 54. Small business owners face many day-to-day risks. Which statement is related to risk?
   a. The slightest risk may be to the well-being of an entrepreneur.
   b. Entrepreneurs run the risk of having an incomplete family experience.
   c. The psychological impact of failure has never been proven severe.
   d. All of the above.

B 55. In starting or buying a new business, the higher the rewards, the
   a. risk is then minimized.
   b. greater the risk.
   c. greater the size of a business.
   d. smaller the enjoyment.

C 56. Which of the following may be the greatest risk to the well-being of the entrepreneur?
   a. social risk
   b. financial risk
   c. psychic risk
   d. family risk

A 57. In the Monroy-Folger Model of Risk Typology, profit-seeking activity is associated with:
   a. strong desire to maximize profit
   b. weaker desire to maximize profit
   c. strong desire to minimize profit
   d. none of the above

Stress and the Entrepreneur

C 58. Loneliness is most likely to cause which of the following:
   a. business success.
   b. old people's excitement.
   c. entrepreneurial stress.
   d. migraines.

C 59. Stress can be dealt with by:
   a. networking.
   b. delegating.
   c. both a and b.
   d. doing none of the above.

A 60. Which of the following is *not* a source of stress?
a. success in business
b. immersion in business
c. people problems
d. none of the above

B 61. Which of the following is *not* a way to combat stress?
a. acknowledging its existence
b. ignoring coping mechanisms
c. probing personal unacknowledged needs
d. none of the above

A 62. The four major causes of entrepreneurial stress are
a. loneliness, immersion in business, people, need to achieve.
b. people, size of business, need to achieve, fear.
c. fear, failure, pressure, competition.
d. drive for success, loneliness, fear, competition.

B 63. The best antidote for relieving the stress involved with total immersion in business is
a. networking.
b. getting away from it all.
c. finding satisfaction outside the company.
d. delegating.

B 64. Which of the following is *not* a way in which entrepreneurs can cope with stress?
a. networking
b. drinking alcohol
c. getting away from business
d. delegating

The Entrepreneurial Ego

B 65. Traits of the "dark side" of entrepreneurship include
a. invincibility and pessimism.
b. distrust and external optimism.
c. control and pursuit.
d. none of the above.

The Dryden Press

A   66. Entrepreneurs with a sense of distrust
   a. scan the environment.
   b. examine the business.
   c. ignore everything.
   d. do none of the above.

C   67. Which of the following is an aspect of the "dark side" of entrepreneurship?
   a. a need for control
   b. a sense of distrust
   c. both a and b
   d. none of the above

C   68. Which of the following is *not* one of the four major traits that characterize the "dark side" of entrepreneurs?
   a. an external optimism
   b. a desire for success
   c. a need to frustrate
   d. a sense of distrust

A   69. The "dark side" of entrepreneurship refers to
   a. a destructive force within the energetic drive of entrepreneurs.
   b. the part of entrepreneurship that is most exciting.
   c. a misunderstanding about the results of entrepreneurship.
   d. another myth of entrepreneurship.

Entrepreneurial Motivation

E   70. The decision to behave entrepreneurially is the result of the interaction of:
   a. the individual's personal environment
   b. the existence of a viable business idea
   c. the relevant business environment
   d. individual's personal goal set
   e. all of the above

Essays

71. *Name the three sources of research on entrepreneurs, and explain five entrepreneurial characteristics that you feel are important.*
    The three sources of research are publications, direct observations, and speeches or presentations. Publications include both research-based and popular sources. Direct observation is done through interviews, surveys, and case studies. Speeches and

presentations are given by practicing entrepreneurs. Characteristics that are important to one individual may not be the same characteristics that are important to another. One characteristic is the drive to achieve.

72. *Explain and discuss the "dark side" of entrepreneurship.*
The entrepreneurial profile has its destructive side. First, the need for control can become an obsession. The need for control can cause problems in networking and in an entrepreneurial team. A sense of distrust can cause the entrepreneur to lose sight of reality or focus on trivial things. An entrepreneur's desire for success can also be destructive if the individual becomes more important than the venture itself. The last "dark side" trait is external optimism. When the entrepreneur takes optimism to the extreme, he or she may begin using a fantasy approach to the business. Trends, facts, and reports are ignored because the entrepreneur thinks everything will turn out fine.

73. *Discuss the specific areas of entrepreneurial risk.*
The four areas of risk are financial risk, career risk, family and social risk, and psychic risk. First, financial risk deals with the amount of savings or resources that the entrepreneur puts into the venture. If the venture is not successful, the money or resources will most likely be lost. The entrepreneur will probably sign obligations that exceed his or her personal wealth. The second risk is career. The would-be entrepreneur frequently asks if he or she will be able to find a job or go back to a previous job. The new venture has no guarantees about career security. Family and social risk are also to be considered.

74. *Name the sources of entrepreneurial stress, and discuss the ways of dealing with stress.*
Entrepreneurs experience four types of stress. The first is loneliness. Although there are many people around the entrepreneur, there are few in whom he/she can confide. Another stress is immersion in business. A successful entrepreneur may make enough money for vacations but never have the time to go because the business would not allow it. People problems are another type of stress. The entrepreneur may get frustrated, disappointed, and aggravated by employees or other individuals upon whom the venture's work depends. Usually this happens when the entrepreneur's expectations of a high performance are not met. The last source of stress is the need to achieve. The entrepreneur usually attempts to accomplish too much and sometimes cannot manage to control the need for achievement. The three steps an entrepreneur can take to reduce stress are acknowledging its existence, developing coping mechanisms, and probing for personal unacknowledged needs. There are five ways in which an entrepreneur can cope with stress. First is networking. Networking involves sharing experiences with other business owners. Another coping mechanism is to get away from it all. These interludes help combat immersion in business. Communicating with subordinates may help to cope with stress. The entrepreneur can be aware of the concerns employees have about their jobs. Finding satisfaction outside of the company is also important. The entrepreneur needs to get away and enjoy life. The last way an entrepreneur can deal with stress is by

The Dryden Press

delegating. Appropriate delegates need to be found and trained so the entrepreneur can gain time away from the business.

CHAPTER 5

DEVELOPING CREATIVITY AND UNDERSTANDING INNOVATION

True/False

Innovation and the Entrepreneur

F　1.　Peter Drucker has stated that innovation is *not* the specific function of entrepreneurship.

T　2.　Innovation is the process by which entrepreneurs convert opportunities into marketable ideas.

F　3.　The innovation process involves *only* the development of a good idea.

T　4.　In analyzing a problem, it is important to know what the problem is, whom it affects, and whether or not it can be solved.

T　5.　Entrepreneurs are always looking for unique opportunities to fill needs or wants.

The Role of Creativity

T　6.　Creativity is the generation of ideas that result in the improved efficiency or effectiveness of a system.

F　7.　Creativity cannot be developed or improved.

T　8.　A creative person tends to view things and people in terms of how they can be used to satisfy his or her needs.

F　9.　The evaluation and implementation phase of the creative process is the easiest phase.

F　10.　Complete ideas emerge from the idea experience.

T　11.　Many inventions and innovations are a result of the inventors seeing new and different relationships among objects, processes, materials, technologies, and people.

T　12.　Two important aspects of creativity are processes and people.

T   13. Creative people are motivated by challenge.

F   14. Creative people *always* exhibit a strong need for group approval.

T   15. The four phases of the creative process are knowledge accumulation, incubation, idea experience, and evaluation.

F   16. Eliminating muddling mindsets means that entrepreneurs should develop a functional perspective.

T   17. The left hemisphere of the brain produces logical and analytical skills.

F   18. The creative climate can be established through a rigid atmosphere that rejects changes or mistakes.

The Innovation Process

F   19. Innovation is planned and predictable.

T   20. Most innovations result from a conscious, purposeful search for new opportunities.

F   21. Most successful innovations are complex and focused.

T   22. Incongruities are gaps or differences between expectations and reality.

F   23. Big projects will develop better innovations than smaller ones.

T   24. Innovators must always search for new ideas, opportunities, or sources of innovation.

F   25. Extension is the combination of existing concepts and factors into a new formulation.

Multiple Choice

Innovation and the Entrepreneur

D   26. Which of the following questions concerning innovation is *not* relevant?
a. "What is the problem?"
b. "Whom does it affect?"
c. "What costs are involved?"
d. "When does the product go to market?"

A   27. Which of the following statements is true?
   a. Innovation is the specific function of entrepreneurship.
   b. Innovation is the process by which entrepreneurs consume marketable ideas.
   c. Innovation does not involve change.
   d. None of the above is true.

B   28. Which of the following are keys to understanding opportunity and its development for entrepreneurs?
   a. creativity and capital
   b. innovation and creativity
   c. background and knowledge
   d. incubation and experience

C   29. Entrepreneurs are able to blend _____ and _____ with a systematic, logical process ability.
   a. responsive, procedural thinking
   b. reciprocal, rational thinking
   c. imaginative, creative thinking
   d. far-fetched, unimaginative thinking

The Role of Creativity

C   30. The two most important aspects of creativity are
   a. design and solution.
   b. intelligence and technical competence.
   c. process and people.
   d. capital and opportunity.

B   31. Which of the following statements is true?
   a. People are born with creativity and can do nothing to change their level of creativity.
   b. People can learn to be creative.
   c. Creativity has nothing to do with learning.
   d. The creative mind cannot be developed.

D   32. Some ways to develop a creative mind include
   a. reading in a variety of fields.
   b. traveling to new places.
   c. becoming curious about everything.
   d. all of the above.

D   33. The incubation process involves which of the following?
- a. engaging in "mindless" activities
- b. exercising regularly
- c. meditating
- d. all of the above

B   34. Which of the following statements is true?
- a. The right brain helps people analyze and verbalize.
- b. The right brain helps people understand analogies and imagine things.
- c. The left brain helps people understand analogies and imagine things.
- d. Right and left brain concepts are meaningless.

D   35. Which of the following can help speed up the creative process?
- a. daydreaming regularly
- b. practicing hobbies
- c. taking breaks while working
- d. all of the above

A   36. Which of the following can help carry out the evaluation and implementation stage?
- a. increasing your energy level
- b. hide your ideas from knowledgeable people
- c. avoid advice from others
- d. ignore hunches and feelings

D   37. Some important characteristics of the creative climate include
- a. open channels of communication.
- b. sufficient resources for accomplishing goals.
- c. enjoyment in experimenting with new ideas.
- d. all of the above.

A   38. Which of the following is a characteristic of creative people?
- a. bright but not necessarily brilliant
- b. poor image of themselves
- c. rigid and dogmatic
- d. unmotivated by challenging problems

C   39. Which of the following statements is true?
- a. The right brain is more important in the creative process than the left brain.
- b. The left brain is more important in the creative process than the right brain.
- c. Both sides of the brain are important to the creative process.
- d. None of the above statements is true.

A   40. Which of the following mental habits inhibit creativity and innovation?
   a. either/or thinking, stereotyping
   b. functional perspective, mindsets
   c. security hunting, risks
   d. stereotyping, incubation

D   41. Which of the following help eliminate muddling mindsets?
   a. taking small risks in professional life
   b. going out of your way to talk to people whom you think conform to some stereotype
   c. making some decisions in the present
   d. all of the above

A   42. Which of the following statements is *not* true?
   a. Creative ideas never come out of the blue.
   b. Ideas often emerge during activities unrelated to the enterprise.
   c. Answers usually come to an individual incrementally.
   d. Creative individuals allow their subconscious to mull over information.

D   43. Which one is *not* one of the phases in the creative process?
   a. background or knowledge accumulation
   b. evaluation and implementation
   c. the incubation process
   d. preliminary investigation

D   44. In the incubation process, ways of getting away from a problem include
   a. sleeping.
   b. working on something else.
   c. playing sports or board games.
   d. all of the above.

A   45. Successful entrepreneurs are able to identify
   a. those ideas that are workable and that they have skills to implement.
   b. those ideas that will make money.
   c. those ideas that are not feasible.
   d. none of the above.

B   46. Security hunting is
   a. looking for a safe place to sleep.
   b. trying to make the right decision or take the correct action.
   c. taking no action that involves risk.
   d. none of the above.

The Dryden Press

C 47. Creativity is most likely to occur when the "climate" is right. What is a characteristic of that climate?
   a. willingness to avoid change
   b. fear of consequences
   c. trustful management
   d. none of the above

A 48. Relying on abstractions can
   a. limit one's perception of reality.
   b. do nothing detrimental.
   c. help in making correct choices.
   d. do all of the above.

A 49. Logical, analytical skills are developed by the
   a. left hemisphere of the brain.
   b. right hemisphere of the brain.
   c. central hemisphere of the brain.
   d. anterior hemisphere of the brain.

B 50. Which of the following terms would *not* be associated with the right hemisphere of the brain?
   a. synthesizing
   b. linear
   c. spatial
   d. intuitive

C 51. Which of the following terms would be associated with the left hemisphere of the brain?
   a. nonrational
   b. nonverbal
   c. abstract
   d. imagining

C 52. All of the following are characteristics of a creative climate *except*
   a. a large variety of personality types.
   b. an enjoyment in experimenting with new ideas.
   c. restricted communication with outsiders.
   d. a willingness to accept change.

A   53. The four phases in the creative process *in order* are
   a. background or knowledge accumulation, incubation, idea experience, and evaluation and implementation.
   b. idea experience, background or knowledge accumulation, incubation, and evaluation and implementation.
   c. incubation, background or knowledge accumulation, idea experience, and evaluation and implementation.
   d. evaluation and implementation, idea experience, incubation, and background or knowledge accumulation.

The Innovation Process

A   54. Which of the following statements is true?
   a. Successful innovations are clear and focused.
   b. Successful innovations are directed toward unclear applications.
   c. Most successful innovations are detailed and ambiguous.
   d. They are never directed at specified designs.

A   55. The four types of innovation include which of the following?
   a. invention, extension, synthesis, duplication
   b. extension, retention, analysis, duplication
   c. synthesis, extension, retention, analysis
   d. analysis, synthesis, duplication, retention

B   56. Which of the following statements is true?
   a. A good innovator should be a genius.
   b. Innovators rarely work in more than one field.
   c. Innovators are poor workers.
   d. A good innovator uses only the left side of the brain.

A   57. Which of the following are sources of innovation?
   a. unexpected occurrences and incongruities
   b. duplication and processes
   c. synthesis and technology
   d. industry changes and extension

B   58. Which of the following are causes of industry and market changes?
   a. process needs
   b. advancements in technology
   c. unexpected occurrences
   d. all of the above

The Dryden Press

B　　59.　Most innovations result from
　　　　　a. the total genius of inventors.
　　　　　b. a conscious and purposeful search for new opportunities.
　　　　　c. lucky guesses.
　　　　　d. the subconscious adaptation to reality.

A　　60.　The combination of existing concepts and factors into a new formulation would define which of the following terms?
　　　　　a. synthesis
　　　　　b. extension
　　　　　c. invention
　　　　　d. analysis

B　　61.　Ray Kroc's development of McDonald's would be a good illustration of which form of innovation?
　　　　　a. invention
　　　　　b. extension
　　　　　c. duplication
　　　　　d. synthesis

B　　62.　A potential entrepreneur needs to realize that
　　　　　a. there are no principles of innovation.
　　　　　b. principles of innovation can be learned.
　　　　　c. monetary gain is the principal motivator in all innovation.
　　　　　d. all of the above are true.

A　　63.　Most successful innovations are
　　　　　a. simple and focused.
　　　　　b. complex and focused.
　　　　　c. focused and extensive.
　　　　　d. complex and extensive.

C　　64.　Which of the following is *not* a type of innovation?
　　　　　a. invention
　　　　　b. duplication
　　　　　c. adaptation
　　　　　d. synthesis

B　　65.　A gap or difference between expectations and reality defines
　　　　　a. process needs.
　　　　　b. incongruities.
　　　　　c. demographic changes.
　　　　　d. changes in perception.

B   66. The try-test-revise approach is the truthful side of what myth?
   a. Innovation is planned and predictable.
   b. Technical specifications should be thoroughly prepared.
   c. Big projects will develop better innovations than smaller ones.
   d. None of the above.

C   67. The phase of the creative process when the idea or solution the individual is seeking is discovered is the
   a. background or knowledge accumulation.
   b. incubation process.
   c. idea experience.
   d. evaluation and implementation.

B   68. SBIR stands for
   a. Small Business Invention Research.
   b. Small Business Innovation Research.
   c. Standard Board for Invention Regulations.
   d. Student Business Investment Research.

A   69. Overnight package delivery can be an illustration for which source of innovation?
   a. incongruities
   b. unexpected occurrences
   c. process needs
   d. change in perception

B   70. Retirement centers for older people reflect which source of innovation?
   a. industry changes
   b. demographic changes
   c. perception changes
   d. unexpected occurrences

A   71. Which of the following is considered a myth of innovation?
   a. Creativity relies on blue sky ideas.
   b. Small projects develop into successful innovations.
   c. Innovations are unpredictable.
   d. None of the above are myths.

C   72. Which of the following is *not* considered a principle of innovation?
   a. Be action oriented.
   b. Start small.
   c. Invest in securities.
   d. Reward heroic activity.

C   73. From the Chapter material, the two major sources of financial backing for innovations are
         a. banks and savings and loans.
         b. family and friends.
         c. venture capital and government support.
         d. major corporations and the media.

A   74. Government programs that support innovation have been
         a. on the rise over the last few years.
         b. on the decline over the last few years.
         c. on a budget restriction.
         d. abolished.

C   75. In Phase I of the SBIR program, financial awards are given for research projects up to a maximum of
         a. $200,000.
         b. $500,000.
         c. $100,000
         d. $25,000.

Essays

76. *List and briefly explain each of the phases in the creative process.*
     The first phase is known as background or knowledge accumulation. This is the process of reading, conversations with others working in the field, and general absorption of information relative to the problem or issue under study. The second phase is the incubation process. This involves the subconscious, which processes information gathered previously. The third phase is idea experience. This is when the idea being sought is discovered. Sometimes the idea comes while performing unrelated tasks. The final phase is known as evaluation and implementation. This phase requires courage, self-discipline, and perseverance. Ideas are often reworked to obtain a final form. Most importantly, the entrepreneur doesn't give up.

77. *Creative talents can be improved through practice and awareness of habits that can cause problems. However, there are ways to increase creativity; one area is to recognize relationships. Explain what is meant by this.*
     Many inventions and innovations are a result of the inventor seeing new and different relationships between objects, processes, materials, technologies, and people.

78. *Creativity is most likely to occur when the "climate" is right. The text listed several important characteristics of this climate. What is the right climate?*

It is a climate where communication flows between a variety of people and fear of management is rare or nonexistent. This environment displays a willingness to change and rewards innovation.

79. *Describe the innovation process.*

The process begins with a conscious, purposeful search for new opportunities, followed by an analysis of the sources of new opportunities.

80. *The Small Business Innovation Development Act directs that small firms get at least a fixed minimum percentage of research and development awards made by federal agencies with sizable R&D budgets. What are the implications of this act?*

This means that small high-technology firms will receive more federal R&D awards than before. This will help small businesses remain competitive with larger companies. Under this Act, the SBIR (Small Business Innovation Research) program was established. Proposals are solicited from small high-technology firms by eleven federal agencies. There are three phases of an R&D award in the SBIR programs. In Phase I, awards are made for research projects intended to evaluate the scientific and technical merit and feasibility of an idea. These awards generally are $100,000 or less, and the phase lasts about six months. Funding for those projects with the most potential are continued. In Phase 2, awards of $750,000 or less are made for further development of the innovation. This phase usually lasts about two years. Phase 3 is characterized by private-sector investment and support that will bring the innovation to the marketplace.

CHAPTER 6

ETHICAL AND SOCIAL RESPONSIBILITY CHALLENGES FOR ENTREPRENEURS

True/False

Introduction

T   1.   The Greek thinker, Chilon, felt that a merchant does better to take a loss than to make a dishonest profit.

F   2.   Today's entrepreneurs are faced with few ethical decisions.

F   3.   "Ethos" means morality.

Defining Ethics

T   4.   Ethics provides the basic rules or parameters for conducting any activity in an "acceptable" manner.

F   5.   Ethics represents a set of principles prescribing a behavioral code that does not include moral duty and obligations.

F   6.   The definition of ethics is "based on universal principles on which society agrees."

T   7.   Society operates in a dynamic and ever-changing environment.

T   8.   Ethics deals with right and wrong behavior.

Ethics and Law

F   9.   Nonrole acts are those acts against a firm in which the person fails to perform his or her managerial role.

T   10.   Role distortion deals with morally questionable acts that are committed "for the firm."

T   11.   The law provides the boundaries for what is illegal (even though the laws are subject to constant interpretation).

The Dryden Press

T   12.   Morals and law are not synonymous but may be viewed as two circles that are partially superimposed upon each other.

T   13.   Qualities such as innovation and risk taking are qualities that have produced complex trade-offs between economic profits and social welfare.

T   14.   A code of conduct is a statement of ethical practices or guidelines to which an enterprise adheres.

Establishing Strategy for Ethical Responsibility

F   15.   Entrepreneurs need not be concerned with establishing strategy for ethical responsibility.

F   16.   Amoral and immoral management are the same thing.

T   17.   One of the most important principles for ethical management is to hire the right people.

T   18.   The holistic management approach is an aesthetic, philosophical perspective, but the understanding of it "reminds the administrator that there exists complementary forms of acquiring managerial knowledge."

F   19.   The most important principle for ethical management is setting standards more than rules.

F   20.   Institutionalization is a deliberate step to incorporate the ethical objectives of society with the economic objectives of the venture.

Ethics and Business Decisions

F   21.   Ethical decisions have extended consequences, but others outside of the venture are never affected.

T   22.   An entrepreneur can never be certain what actual consequences a decision will have.

T   23.   Venture success, financial opportunity, and new-product development are all areas that may be impacted by decisions having ethical consequences.

F   24.   Social responsibility consists of those obligations that society has to businesses.

T   25.   The range of intensity in corporate obligations to society range from social obligation to social responsiveness.

Multiple Choice

Introduction

A   26.   The Greek word *ethos* means
              a. mode of conduct.
              b. morale.
              c. elan.
              d. esprit de corps.

B   27.   The topic of ethics has been important in philosophical thought since the time of
              a. Virgo.
              b. Socrates.
              c. Kennedy.
              d. Schumpeter.

A   28.   Today's entrepreneurs are faced with many ethical decisions, especially during the _____ stages of their new venture.
              a. early
              b. middle
              c. late
              d. closing

C   29.   A decision to sell pharmaceuticals that have not been cleared with the Federal Drug Administration is an example of a(n)
              a. illegal and ethical decision.
              b. legal and unethical decision.
              c. illegal and unethical decision.
              d. legal and ethical decision.

B   30.   Many medical researchers believe that the sale of cigarettes is a(n)
              a. illegal and ethical decision.
              b. legal and unethical decision.
              c. illegal and unethical decision.
              d. legal and ethical decision.

B   31. A decision to sell toys that pass minimum safety standards but can often result in minor accidents to children is an example of a(n)
   a. illegal and ethical decision.
   b. legal and unethical decision.
   c. illegal and unethical decision.
   d. legal and ethical decision.

Defining Ethics

B   32. In the _____ sense, ethics provides the basic rules or parameters for conducting any activity in an "acceptable manner."
   a. abstract
   b. broadest
   c. narrowest
   d. most concrete

C   33. Ethics represents a set of principles prescribing a behavioral code that explains what is
   a. good and right.
   b. bad and wrong.
   c. both a and b.
   d. none of the above.

B   34. A definition of ethics in such a rapidly changing environment must be based more on _____ than on a static code.
   a. a luxury
   b. a process
   c. deterministic rule
   d. policy

A   35. Instead of relying on a set of fixed ethical principles, it is important to develop
   a. an ethical process.
   b. a luxury process.
   c. a concerned process.
   d. a vacillating process.

D   36. Which of the following causes conflict over the ethical nature of decisions?
   a. multiple alternatives
   b. society undergoing dramatic change
   c. personal implications
   d. all of the above cause conflict

D 37. A change in society may result in a change in
   a. mores.
   b. values.
   c. norms.
   d. all of the above.

Ethics and Laws

D 38. One study developed a typology of morally questionable acts that included which of the following distinctions?
   a. nonrole acts
   b. role failure
   c. role distortion
   d. all of the above

C 39. Morally questionable acts committed on behalf of the firm are termed
   a. non-role.
   b. role failure.
   c. role distortion.
   d. all of the above.

B 40. Morally questionable acts committed against the firm are termed
   a. role distortion.
   b. role failure.
   c. role assertion.
   d. none of the above.

A 41. For the entrepreneur the dilemma of _____ versus ethical is a vital one.
   a. legal
   b. conceptual
   c. relative
   d. acceptable

C 42. Which of the following statements is one of the four rationalizations that managers use in justifying questionable conduct?
   a. The company will not condone it.
   b. It does not help the company.
   c. It is in the individual's or corporation's best interest.
   d. It will result in our losing money.

D   43. Rationalizations for unethical behavior often appear _____, given the behavior of many business enterprises today.
   a. logical
   b. fake
   c. cosmopolitan
   d. realistic

C   44. Ethical conduct may reach beyond the _____ of the law.
   a. mentality
   b. concept
   c. limits
   d. philosophy

B   45. Morals and law are not synonymous but may be viewed as _____ circles that are partially superimposed upon each other.
   a. one
   b. two
   c. three
   d. four

D   46. _____ is/are the backbone of the free enterprise system.
   a. Innovation
   b. Risk taking
   c. Venture creation
   d. All of the above

A   47. Qualities such as innovation have produced complex trade-offs between _____ and social welfare.
   a. economic profits
   b. businesses
   c. government
   d. none of the above

B   48. The requirements of law may overlap at times, but they do not duplicate the moral standards of society because
   a. legal requirements tend to be negative.
   b. some laws have no moral content whatsoever.
   c. morality tends to be negative.
   d. the two have totally different objectives.

The Dryden Press

D   49.   The dilemma of legal versus ethical is due to
          a. a lack of information on issues.
          b. misrepresentation of values or laws.
          c. an imprecise judicial system.
          d. all of the above.

D   50.   Legal behavior represents
          a. belief that an action is not actually illegal.
          b. belief that an action that aids the firm will be condoned.
          c. belief that the action is in the firm's best interest.
          d. none of the above.

C   51.   There are conflicting needs in the free enterprise system between
          a. honesty and social respect.
          b. jobs and efficiency.
          c. generation of profits and integrity.
          d. revenues and costs.

A   52.   Legal requirements as set by the law, often _____ acceptable moral standards of society.
          a. lag behind
          b. lead
          c. serve as guides for
          d. discourage

D   53.   Legal requirements tend to be _____; morality tends to be _____.
          a. positive because they regulate behavior; positive because it regulates morals
          b. positive because they regulate behavior; negative because it limits personal behavior
          c. negative because they forbid certain acts; negative because it discourages certain acts
          d. negative because they forbid certain acts; positive because it encourages certain acts

C   54.   Moral and ethical standards
          a. are the same.
          b. greatly overlap.
          c. overlap somewhat.
          d. are totally different.

The Dryden Press

Establishing Strategy for Ethical Responsibility

A 55. A recent survey found that _____ of executives had a code of conduct for their company.
   a. 75 percent
   b. 85 percent
   c. 90 percent
   d. 99 percent

A 56. A statement of ethical practices or guidelines to which an enterprise adheres is termed a(n)
   a. code of conduct.
   b. personnel guideline.
   c. ethical practice statement.
   d. moral principle.

B 57. In focusing on an ethical position for entrepreneurs, various _____ should be analyzed.
   a. employees
   b. organizational characteristics
   c. institutional characteristics
   d. profit motives

B 58. Before setting forth any strategy, it is imperative that entrepreneurs analyze their _____ reactions to organizational characteristics.
   a. employees'
   b. own
   c. board of directors'
   d. customers'

D 59. All of the following are managerial approaches to ethics *except*
   a. immoral.
   b. amoral.
   c. moral.
   d. quasi-moral.

A 60. The holistic approach is
   a. a dual-focused approach.
   b. a single-focused approach.
   c. a multi-faceted approach.
   d. an approach for holy people.

C   61.   Moving from an immoral or amoral position to a moral position requires a great deal of _____ effort.
            a. attentive
            b. inactive
            c. personal
            d. group

C   62.   Which of the following best describes the strategy of moral management?
            a. Exploit opportunities for corporate gain.
            b. Give managers free rein.
            c. Live by sound ethical standards.
            d. Forget profit.

C   63.   What is a holistic management approach?
            a. A triple-focused approach that includes "knowing how," "knowing that," and "knowing why."
            b. A technique used to set codes of conduct.
            c. An aesthetic, philosophical perspective, but the understanding of it reminds the administrator that there exist complementary forms of acquiring managerial knowledge.
            d. An approach that balances profit and ethical considerations.

D   64.   What principle can be applied to the holistic approach?
            a. Set standards more than rules.
            b. Don't let yourself get isolated.
            c. Hire the right people.
            d. All the above can be applied to the holistic approach.

B   65.   Which of the following best describes immoral management in terms of ethical norms?
            a. Management is neither moral nor immoral, but decisions lie outside the sphere to which moral judgments apply.
            b. Management decisions are discordant with accepted ethical principles.
            c. Ethical leadership is commonplace on the part of management.
            d. Management may imply a lack of ethical perception and moral awareness.

B   66.   _____ is a deliberate step to incorporate the ethical objectives of the entrepreneur with the economic objectives of the venture.
            a. Integration
            b. Moral management
            c. Ethical consciousness
            d Venture integration

D 67. Ethical consciousness is developed
  a. through an open exchange of issues and processes within the venture.
  b. by establishing codes of ethics for the company.
  c. by examples of the entrepreneur.
  d. all of the above.

A 68. Ethical process and structure refer to _____ that are designed to avoid ambiguity.
  a. the procedures
  b. the codes
  c. the conscripts
  d. the interrelationships
  e. none of the above

Ethics and Business Decisions

C 69. Business decisions are complex for all of the following reasons *except*
  a. ethical decisions have extended consequences.
  b ethical questions have multiple alternatives.
  c. ethical decisions have certain ethical consequences.
  d. ethical business decisions often have mixed outcomes.

A 70. Ethical business decisions often have _____ outcomes.
  a. mixed
  b. finite
  c. conceptual
  d. integrative

B 71. The consequences of ethical decisions may affect all of the following *except*
  a. financial opportunities.
  b. industry climate.
  c. venture success.
  d. new-product development.
  e. all of the above.

D 72. One researcher established a framework that classified social actions of corporations into distinct categories that included
  a. social obligation.
  b. social responsiveness.
  c. social action.
  d. a and b only.

C 73. The most proactive position for a corporation to take in regard to social responsibility would be termed
   a. social obligation.
   b. social intensity.
   c. social responsiveness.
   d. social decisiveness.

D 74. One study revealed a strong ethical stance of small business owners regarding specific issues such as
   a. misleading advertising.
   b. misleading financial reporting.
   c. favoritism in promotions.
   d. all of the above.

A 75. One study revealed a greater ethical tolerance by entrepreneurs regarding specific issues such as
   a. copying computer software.
   b. misleading advertising.
   c. faulty investment advice.
   d. all of the above.

Essays

76. *Define ethics, and discuss some conflicts over the ethical nature of decisions.*
   In a broad sense, ethics is the rules or parameters for conduct in any activity as long as it is done in an "acceptable" manner. Ethics can also be described as a set of principles prescribing a behavioral code that explains what is good and right or bad and wrong. Even though society is in an ever-changing state, this definition implies that universal principles remain intact. An entrepreneur faces many conflicts for many reasons. One conflict arises as a business is faced with outside as well as inside interests. Some examples are stockholders, the community, the government, employees, and unions. Also, as society changes, the values and mores of society must change.

77. *Give some in-depth examples of the dilemmas entrepreneurs face with ethics and laws.*
   One dilemma entrepreneurs face is managerial rationalization. Managers may use rationalizations to justify questionable conduct. Some examples are: believing that the activity is not "really" illegal or immoral, the act is in the company's best interest, the behavior will not be found out, and the company will condone the act. The questionable act may seem all right to the manager using these rationalizations and yet is against the laws of the business world and society.
   Another dilemma concerns the matter of morality. Using LaRue Hosmer's conclusions concerning legal requirements and moral judgments, the requirements might overlap but not duplicate the moral standards of society. First, this results from laws not

having any moral content, laws being morally unjust, and moral standards having no legal basis. Second, legal requirements tend to be negative, whereas morality tends to be positive. Third, legal requirements can lag behind the acceptable moral standards of society.

Another dilemma entrepreneurs are often faced with concerns economic trade-offs. Economic trade-offs occur when innovations, risk taking, or venture creation are used to stimulate the economic system to create new jobs and new growth. These qualities produce the trade-off between economic and social welfare. Some examples are: advertising for cigarettes with death as a possible result; toxic waste dumps invading lakes, streams, and eventually drinking water; minorities being laid off only because they were the last to be hired; and capital gains realized through the advance information of mergers.

78. *How can an entrepreneur establish strategies for ethical responsibility? Fully explain your answer.*

The entrepreneur needs to establish a strategy for ethical responsibility within the free enterprise system. To do this he or she must focus on an ethical position or on an organizational characteristic and analyze it. To do this, the entrepreneur has four approaches to use, which include the holistic approach, ethical consciousness, ethical process and structure, and institutionalization. The holistic approach requires the entrepreneur to develop specific principles that will help in taking the right external steps as the venture evolves. Under this approach there are four principles: hire the right people, set standards more than rules, avoid isolation, and set an absolutely impeccable ethical example. With time, these principles will establish a strategy for ethical responsibility. Ethical consciousness is the development of an open exchange of processes within the venture, establishing codes of ethics for the company, and setting examples by the entrepreneur. This must be accomplished by the entrepreneur so that his or her vision can stay intact.

To keep the ethical goals designed to avoid ambiguity and to position statements or codes, the entrepreneur must have an ethical process and structure. As an example of this approach, affidavits can be used to ensure the willingness of employees to adhere to the venture's specific goals. Institutionalization is a means to combine the ethical objectives of the entrepreneur with the economic objectives of the venture. Even so, there are times when the policies or operations that infringe on ethical values may need to be adjusted, thus testing the entrepreneur's commitment to his or her values. By using feedback and by reviewing the procedures, institutionalized ethical responsibility can be achieved.

79. *Discuss the five reasons the business decisions of entrepreneurs are complex. Fully explain your answer.*

The first reason is that decisions can have a ripple effect that can extend beyond the venture. An example would be how unsafe products could harm both the workers and the consumers. The next reason involves ethical questions having multiple alternatives. These decisions have a wide range of outcomes that may allow a mixture of less important decisions. The third reason involves a mixed set of outcomes. This could include social benefits versus costs as well as revenues versus expenses. Another reason may be that the ethical outcome of the decision is unknown. As with all decisions, this one includes risk. The final reason decisions can be complex is that decisions involve the entrepreneur personally. Because the entrepreneur is involved in the success, the financial opportunity, and the ethical operation of the venture, it is difficult to be impartial and to follow the ethics of the business when making decisions.

80. *Describe the five major problems in laws reflecting ethical standards.*

Members of society make moral standards based upon the information that is available to them. If the public is misinformed or not informed at all, the judgments they create will not be based on the truth. Therefore, it is not possible for society to make personal moral standards to influence or to establish laws if relevant information is missing. People of society assemble into small groups with similar norms, beliefs, and values. Within these groups, they formulate standards that are similar among all the members and act from motives instead of morality. The problem lies in the fact that the personal moral standards that should influence the laws are replaced with the standards of the small group. Just as there are problems with the moral standards of the smaller groups, there are problems with the misrepresentation of moral standards of larger groups. As large organizations share the same norms, beliefs, and values, the individuals and the groups within the organization do not share equal weight and influence with regard to the consensus. An example of this would include hospitals where the norms, beliefs, and values of the doctors and staff set the majority of the visible standards. Looking at the larger picture, not all organizations have equal influence or equal influence weighted by size to determine the law. This is another example of misrepresentation of moral standards. The meaning and application of some laws need to be clarified. Under the condition of product liability and equal employment issues, incomplete or imprecise legal requirements must be supplemented by judicial court decisions or by administrative agency actions. As a result of this, personal moral standards cannot influence the laws directly, if at all, in two of the means of formulating the law.

CHAPTER 7

ENVIRONMENTAL ASSESSMENT: PREPARATION FOR A NEW VENTURE

True/False

The Environment for New Ventures

T   1. Environmental scanning is the effort used in examining the internal and external environments.

T   2. The external environment has two parts: task and societal.

F   3. Strengths and weaknesses refer to the external environment.

T   4. The internal environment includes a venture's environment.

F   5. In assessing the environment, government regulations, at the local level, do *not* have to be considered.

T   6. The economic environment plays a vital role in the success or failure of any new venture.

T   7. The two major macro areas that entrepreneurs should consider are the overall economic environment and the specific industry environment.

F   8. The number of firms in an industry is irrelevant to the small business environment.

T   9. Over the last decade, the federal government has become a partner to small business.

T   10. Government regulations affect smaller ventures in a variety of ways including prices and mental burden.

F   11. The Regulatory Flexibility Act has five stipulations that help ensure justice for small businesses.

T   12. The Prompt Payments Act was enacted to help small businesses collect their money after doing work for the federal government.

T   13. Short-time horizons are a common characteristic of new and emerging industries.

F   14.   It is not important to examine the historical progression of a given market when establishing a new business.

F   15.   Determining the strength and characteristics of suppliers is not part of a competitive analysis.

A Micro View: The Community Perspective

T   16.   Assessing the local community environment is as vital to the success of a new venture as is the assessment of the regulatory economy and the industry.

F   17.   Three important factors of a small business to consider when researching a location are community demographics, economic base, and overall business climate.

T   18.   If there is a lot of entrepreneurial activity, the community will be more receptive to new ventures.

T   19.   Community growth usually indicates solid, aggressive civic leadership.

T   20.   One view of the community, in considering new ventures from the business perspective, is consideration of transportation.

F   21.   One way in which the entrepreneur can gain exceptional community support for his or her venture is by willingness to make a commitment to the community.

T   22.   People in a community generally identify with those businesses they think deserve support.

T   23.   Incubators are targeted toward providing benefits to small business and subsequently to the community.

F   24.   The four major types of incubators are publicly sponsored, nonprofit sponsored, profit sponsored, and privately sponsored.

T   25.   The basic purpose of an incubator is to increase the survival chances for new start-up businesses.

Multiple Choice

The Environment for New Ventures

D   26.   An owner's-entrepreneur's efforts to examine the external and internal environments before making decisions is referred to as:
        a. industry analysis
        b. task situation
        c. environmental realization
        d. environmental scanning

B   27.   The external environment consists of which two distinct parts?
        a. culture and structure
        b. task and societal
        c. social and economic
        d. customers and supplies

C   28.   The internal environment of a venture includes all of the following <u>except</u>:
        a. structure
        b. culture
        c. competitors
        d. resources

A   29.   The two major macro areas that warrant consideration in the environmental assessment of new ventures are
        a. economic and industry.
        b. community and state.
        c. competitive and personal.
        d. regulatory and local.

D   30.   Which question is among the most important in the assessment of the economic environment?
        a. How many firms are in the industry?
        b. What is the competitive nature of this business?
        c. Do the firms vary in size and general characteristics, or are they all similar?
        d. All of the above are correct.

D   31.   Which of the following is *not* a certain skill needed for proper assessment of the economic environment?
        a. the development of political skills
        b. the need for communication skills
        c. the development of motor skills
        d. all of the above

B 32. A new network to advocate the interests of smaller firms and new ventures includes
- a. trade and professional associations only.
- b. the Small Business Administration, universities, and others.
- c. the Federal Regulation Administration.
- d. none of the above.

A 33. Government regulations affect smaller ventures in terms of
- a. prices.
- b. trade relations.
- c. capital expenditures.
- d. all of the above.

B 34. A major goal of the Regulatory Flexibility Act is to
- a. encourage businesses to provide regulatory relief to customers.
- b. increase agency awareness and understanding of the impact of their regulations on small business.
- c. require agencies to explain their findings to the public.
- d. do all of the above.

B 35. Which of the following is considered a "milestone" law for small businesses?
- a. Federal Pollution Regulation Act
- b. Equal Access to Justice Act
- c. Equal Employment Opportunity Act
- d. Anti-Discrimination Registration Act

A 36. Which of the following statements is *not* a stipulation under the Equal Access to Justice Act?
- a. There is a dollar limit to the award.
- b. The government or the small business may initiate litigation.
- c. Bad faith on the part of the governmental agency does not have to be proven.
- d. Substantially justified actions must be demonstrated by the agency.

A 37. The White House has convened three special conferences on small business in which of the following years?
- a. 1980, 1986, and 1995
- b. 1987, 1988, and 1990
- c. 1985, 1988, and 1989
- d. 1980, 1984, and 1992

D 38. A common industry characteristic would be
   a. technology uncertainty.
   b. strategic uncertainty.
   c. short-time horizons.
   d. all of the above.

C 39. Barriers to entry may include
   a. risk and advantages in time horizon.
   b. cost advantages and bargaining power.
   c. proprietary technology and risk.
   d. a and c only.

A 40. A useful step that can assist an entrepreneur in examining the industry is
   a. determining the strength and characteristics of suppliers.
   b. analyzing the customers.
   c. projecting the manufacturing size for the particular industry.
   d. all of the above.

A 41. A critical step in the overall economic assessment of a new venture is
   a. the evaluation of the industry environment.
   b. the evaluation of the surrounding environment.
   c. evaluation of the integrated environment.
   d. evaluation of the basic environment.

D 42. There are certain characteristics that are common to new and emerging industries. The most important of these is
   a. technological uncertainty.
   b. strategic uncertainty.
   c. first-time buyers.
   d. all of the above.

B 43. The concept of contribution analysis in which sales minus raw materials costs is calculated would be the
   a. competitive analysis.
   b. value-added measure.
   c. demographic variable.
   d. market value.

C 44. A major macro area that warrants consideration is
   a. the overall academic environment.
   b. the personnel department.
   c. the specific industry environment.
   d. a and c only.

The Dryden Press

C 45. The _____ environment plays a vital role in the success or failure of any new venture.
a. host
b. surrounding
c. economic
d. cultural

C 46. Entrepreneurs with emerging ventures must realize that certain _____ and skills are needed for proper assessment of the environment.
a. criteria
b. facts
c. attitudes
d. none of the above

C 47. Which of the following is *not* a barrier to entry?
a. proprietary technology
b. access to distribution channels
c. experience of technology
d. risk

A 48. In competitive analysis the competition must be carefully scrutinized in terms of
a. quality and quantity.
b. quantity and ability.
c. quality and stability.
d. elementary and ability.

A Micro View: The Community Perspective

D 49. Which is a factor in researching the new venture's location?
a. community demographics
b. community economic base
c. community population trends
d. all of the above

D 50. In community demographics, analysis of which factor is helpful in evaluating the new venture's potential?
a. sales
b. growth
c. employment
d. all of the above

A   51. Favorable signs of a growing community typically include
   a. a good school system.
   b. vacant buildings.
   c. a regressive chamber of commerce.
   d. isolated industrial activities.

D   52. A summary view of the community from the business perspective includes
   a. consideration of transportation.
   b. consideration of banking activities.
   c. consideration of professional services.
   d. all of the above.

C   53. The question, "How familiar is the entrepreneur with the community in which the venture will be located?" refers to
   a. population trends.
   b. community demographics.
   c. determining reliance and deservedness.
   d. examination of business incubators.

B   54. Which of the following is a major way in which entrepreneurs can gain community support for a new venture?
   a. through charitable contributions
   b. through the existence of a community perception as to the deservedness of the entrepreneur
   c. by the government's need for the new venture
   d. all of the above

D   55. Which of the following is *not* a major type of incubator?
   a. nonprofit sponsored
   b. privately sponsored
   c. publicly sponsored
   d. business affiliated

B   56. The major goal of incubators that are organized and managed by private corporations is
   a. to translate research into new products.
   b. to make a profit.
   c. to redevelop an area.
   d. to create jobs.

A 57. The major goal of incubators that are organized through city economic development programs or development commissions is
  a. job creation.
  b. area development.
  c. profit.
  d. transfer of research.

C 58. Regardless of type, most incubators provide which of the following services?
  a. increased visibility and tax breaks.
  b. tax benefits and conference rooms.
  c. below-market rate rent and sharing of equipment.
  d. free rent and elimination of taxes.

A 59. The phrase, "An increase in business tenants' visibility to the community" refers to
  a. examining the use of business incubators.
  b. population trends.
  c. community demographics.
  d. determining reliance and deservedness.

C 60. Which of the following is *not* an important community benefit of incubators?
  a. increased employment opportunities
  b. diversification of the local economic base
  c. enhancement of government agencies
  d. transformation of underutilized property into a center of productivity

D 61. Which of the following is a constraint to industry development?
  a. erratic product quality
  b. absence of infrastructure
  c. inability to obtain raw materials and components
  d. all of the above

B 62. Which is *not* a selected source of environmental data?
  a. the Census of Population
  b. the Census of Disposable Income
  c. the Census of Business
  d. the Department of Commerce

C 63. Which of the following agencies existed before 1970?
  a. the Occupational Safety and Health Administration
  b. the Office of Employee Benefits Security
  c. the Equal Employment Opportunity Commission
  d. the Environmental Protection Agency

D 64. Which of the following is a comparison characteristic between public and private sponsored incubators?
  a. rent
  b. staff
  c. financial services
  d. all of the above

A 65. In comparing privately sponsored and publicly sponsored incubators, which of the following is true about exit policies?
  a. Public facilities have a time limit while private ones do not.
  b. Private facilities have a time limit while public ones do not.
  c. Neither type of facilities have time limits.
  d. Both facilities have time limits.

A 66. After analyzing the macro environment of the economy and the industry, the entrepreneur needs to focus on
  a. micro environmental assessment.
  b. macro environmental assessment.
  c. cultural factors.
  d. all of the above.

A 67. Which of the following major community facets would *not* be considered in researching the location?
  a. community volunteers
  b. community demographics
  c. community economic base
  d. community population trends

C 68. When dealing with community demographics, a few factors may be of special concern. Which of the following is *not* a factor?
  a. size of the new venture relative to the community itself
  b. the amount of entrepreneurial activity in the community
  c. statistics on young adults living in the area
  d. residents' purchasing power

D 69. Favorable signs of community growth typically include all of the following *except*
  a. chain or department store branches throughout the area.
  b. branch plants of large industrial firms.
  c. a good school system.
  d. a growing population in the urban area.

The Dryden Press

C 70. The entrepreneur can gain exceptional community support in which way?
   a. the strength of the community's reliance on or need for the entrepreneur's venture
   b. the entrepreneur's willingness to make a commitment to the community
   c. both a and b
   d. none of the above

A 71. What is the definition of a business incubator?
   a. a facility with adaptable space leased to small businesses on flexible terms and at reduced rents
   b. a storage place for trash
   c. a type of business automation system
   d. none of the above

A 72. In assessing new ventures, entrepreneurs typically focus on the following considerations:
   a. analyze the macro environment, then move to the micro.
   b. analyze the micro environment, then move to the macro.
   c. analyze both environments at the same time.
   d. ignore both environments equally.

A 73. A micro view of the environment concentrates on
   a. the community perspective.
   b. the personal perspective.
   c. the competitive perspective.
   d. the industry perspective.

B 74. The basic purpose of an incubator is to
   a. make more room for storage space.
   b. increase the chances of survival for new businesses.
   c. increase management techniques.
   d. do all of the above.

C 75. The major types of incubators do *not* include
   a. publicly sponsored.
   b. nonprofit sponsored.
   c. provisionally sponsored.
   d. university related.

Essays

76. *What is the Regulatory Flexibility Act?*

This act is a law that recognizes that not all businesses are equal when it comes to their ability to comply with federal regulations. The purpose of the law is to ensure that legislation is not unfair to small business. The major goals of this act were to increase awareness of regulation of small businesses, to provide regulatory relief, and to require agencies to explain their findings to the public. The law puts on the government the burden of making sure that regulation is not unfair to small businesses.

77. *Why is it important to determine whether or not a new business venture will have community support?*

If the new business must depend on local purchases and regulation, community support is very important. If there is a strong need for the product or service, community support will be there. The support from the community is greater if the entrepreneur is willing to commit to the community. The commitment from the entrepreneur could come from club memberships, volunteer work, backing children's programs, and many other activities. Deservedness is another test of community support. People want a business to succeed if they think it deserves to. Deservedness may be affected in several ways. If there are negative impacts on the community, the new venture will have to take active steps to reduce the problems. If this is not done, there will be little community support. The entrepreneur should become familiar with the community before starting a new venture.

78. *Why is it important to examine the competition before starting a new business venture?*

By looking at the competition, the entrepreneur can see advantages and disadvantages in relation to the competitors. He/she may find that his/her product is of much better quality or that he/she can give faster service. These would be the things he/she would promote to encourage customers to do business with his/her company. A very important reason to look at the competition is to see if competition is possible at any level. The competition may have better prices or offer faster delivery with better product quality. In this case, the entrepreneur may decide not to go into business at all. Such a decision would be less costly than starting a business and then going out of business because of inability to compete.

79. *Explain the need for a small business to assess the economic environment before starting up.*

It will benefit a new small business to assess the economic environment. Some of the factors the new venture must assess are competition, regulation, market, geographic concentration, and the number of firms already in the industry. The information from the assessment will give the owner a good idea of the business climate in which he or she must operate. This climate is the external environment that will affect the new venture and its owners. Often businesses fail because the owners haven't taken the time to assess the environment in which the business must operate.

80. **Why is it important to review the regulatory environment in which a new venture must operate?**

The regulatory environment is important to a small business venture. Rules and regulations can cause expenses to be much higher than expected. Other ways that government regulation affects business are prices, cost inequities, competitive restriction, managerial restriction, and mental burden. Because of extensive governmental regulations, there is now the burden of large amounts of required paperwork. The burden of completing the required paperwork in a small business often falls on the owner. This robs the owner of valuable time that he or she could use in other areas of the business.

CHAPTER 8

MARKETING RESEARCH FOR NEW VENTURES

True/False

Introduction

T 1. A market is a group of consumers who have purchasing power and unsatisfied needs.

Marketing Research

T 2. Marketing research involves the gathering of information about a particular market, followed by analysis of the information.

F 3. The first step in marketing research is to gather primary data.

T 4. Information that has already been compiled is known as secondary data.

T 5. It is usually less expensive to gather secondary data than primary data.

F 6. Most firms generally gather primary data and then see if there is secondary data to supplement it.

F 7. Mail surveys are less expensive than telephone surveys.

F 8. Mail surveys generally have much higher response rates than telephone surveys.

T 9. The need for marketing research will depend on the type of venture.

Inhibitors to Marketing Research

F 10. There are no inexpensive marketing techniques for entrepreneurs to use; therefore these techniques are not used at all.

F 11. Only major strategic decisions need to be supported through marketing research.

T 12. Marketing research is sometimes irrelevant to a problem; however, it sometimes provides useful information.

Developing the Market Concept

T   13.   There are three distinct types of marketing philosophies that exist among new ventures.

F   14.   There are two main types of consumers--those who buy with cash and those who buy with credit.

T   15.   Shopping goods are products that consumers will take time to examine carefully and compare for quality and price.

Marketing Stages for Growing Ventures

T   16.   There are four distinct marketing stages in a growing venture.

F   17.   Entrepreneurial marketing deals with marketing products toward entrepreneurs.

Marketing Planning

T   18.   Marketing planning is the process of determining a clear, comprehensive approach to the creation of customers.

F   19.   A marketing information system compiles and organizes data according to a customer's sex, age, and geographic location.

F   20.   Sales forecasting is a process of projecting future sales through educated guesses.

Telemarketing

T   21.   Telemarketing is the use of telephone communications to sell merchandise directly to customers.

F   22.   Telemarketing is an outdated technique which few modern firms use.

Pricing Strategies

T   23.   One of the problems of telemarketing is rapid turnover of telephone staff.

T 24. Even after marketing research is done, many entrepreneurs are unsure of how to price their products or services.

F 25. Pricing procedures are the same for all types of ventures.

Multiple Choice

Introduction

A 26. A market is
   a. a group of consumers who have purchasing power and unsatisfied needs.
   b. a way of gaining consumer data.
   c. a segment of the economy.
   d. a group of known purchasers.

C 27. The key to marketing analysis is
   a. secondary data.
   b. psychographic information.
   c. marketing research.
   d. marketing response data.

Marketing Research

B 28. All of the following techniques are used in gathering primary data *except*
   a. observational methods.
   b. analysis of company records.
   c. surveys.
   d. experimentation.

B 29. Which of the following is a way of summarizing and simplifying information for users?
   a. monthly written reports
   b. charts
   c. spreadsheets
   d. computer correlations

D 30. Surveys include contact by
   a. mail.
   b. telephone.
   c. personal interviews.
   d. all of the above.

C   31. Secondary data consists of
   a. internal data only.
   b. external data only.
   c. existing information.
   d. newly developed primary research.

A   32. Which of the following is *not* a method of collecting primary data?
   a. review of government publications
   b. telephone
   c. mail survey
   d. observation

A   33. The primary reason many entrepreneurs fail to use marketing research is
   a. high cost.
   b. ignorance.
   c. lack of time.
   d. lack of sophistication.

C   34. Which of the following is a complex marketing research technique?
   a. observation
   b. telemarketing
   c. statistical analysis
   d. survey

D   35. Which one of these typically has the lowest response rate?
   a. direct face-to-face contact
   b. interviews
   c. phone survey
   d. mail survey

Developing the Marketing Concept

B   36. Which of these is the most expensive to conduct?
   a. phone surveys
   b. interviews
   c. mail surveys
   d. all are of equal cost

A   37. Which of the following is least expensive to conduct?
   a. mail survey
   b. interview
   c. phone survey
   d. telegram survey

D   38. Effective marketing is based on all of the following *except*
- a. marketing philosophy.
- b. market segmentation.
- c. consumer behavior.
- d. psychographic determination.

C   39. Which of the following is a marketing philosophy?
- a. computer-driven philosophy
- b. wholesale-driven philosophy
- c. consumer-driven philosophy
- d. cost-driven philosophy

C   40. The sales-driven philosophy
- a. is based on the belief "produce efficiently and worry about sales later."
- b. relies on research to discover consumer preferences before production begins.
- c. focuses on personal selling and advertising to persuade customers to buy the company's output.
- d. is strictly cost driven.

A   41. Which of the following influences the choice of marketing philosophy?
- a. competitive pressure
- b. economic outlook
- c. Dow Jones Industrial averages
- d. cost of living index

B   42. Market segmentation is
- a. the process of categorizing products into different segments.
- b. the process of identifying a specific set of characteristics that differentiate one group of consumers from the rest.
- c. the process of segmenting the sales force.
- d. heavily psychographic in nature.

A   43. Marketing segmentation focuses on which variable?
- a. demographic
- b. market share
- c. cyclographic
- d. profitability

C   44. Which of the following would be first to adopt a new product?
- a. early majority
- b. early adopters
- c. innovators
- d. laggards

The Dryden Press

A   45. Which of the following would adopt a new product before the others?
   a. early adopters
   b. laggards
   c. late majority
   d. early majority

D   46. Which of the following would be last to adopt a new product?
   a. early majority
   b. early adopters
   c. innovators
   d. laggards

A   47. Which of the following is *not* a demographic variable?
   a. height
   b. education
   c. age
   d. sex

D   48. Which of the following is a demographic variable?
   a. weight
   b. hair color
   c. attitude
   d. income

B   49. Products that consumers will take time to examine carefully and compare for quality and price are
   a. convenience goods.
   b. shopping goods.
   c. specialty goods.
   d. generic goods.

C   50. Products or services that consumers make a special effort to find and purchase are
   a. convenience goods.
   b. shopping goods.
   c. specialty goods.
   d. generic goods.

B   51. Encyclopedias and cemetery plots are
   a. convenience goods.
   b. unsought goods.
   c. shopping goods.
   d. specialty goods.

The Dryden Press

Marketing Stages for Growing Ventures

D   52.   Which of the following are marketing stages for growing ventures?
   a. entrepreneurial marketing
   b. opportunistic marketing
   c. responsible marketing
   d. all of the above

B   53.   Entrepreneurial marketing
   a. attempts to market toward entrepreneurs.
   b. has a strategy of developing a market niche and a goal of obtaining credibility in the marketplace.
   c. has a strategy of marketing products to new ventures.
   d. has a strategy of marketing goods to old ventures.

Marketing Planning

C   54.   Which of the following is part of the marketing planning process?
   a. market niche
   b. market segmentation
   c. marketing research
   d. marketing myopia

B   55.   The purpose of marketing research
   a. is to gain customers.
   b. is to identify customers' target markets and to fulfill their desires.
   c. to keep costs low.
   d. to develop new products.

D   56.   A marketing information system compiles and organizes data according to
   a. cost revenue.
   b. profit from the customer base.
   c. myopic potential.
   d. market niche potential.

A   57.   Which of the following is *not* a key factor affecting a marketing information system?
   a. size of the system
   b. usefulness or understandability of data
   c. timeliness of the reporting system
   d. relevancy of data

B 58. Sales forecasting is
 a. 100 percent accurate.
 b. the process of projecting future sales through historical sales figures.
 c. a useless technique since it relies on historical data.
 d. almost always qualitative in nature.

C 59. What element promotes and distributes products according to market research findings?
 a. marketing research
 b. marketing plans
 c. sales research
 d. cost analysis

D 60. What area best identifies where marketing research performs the important task of keeping management abreast of significant changes in government rates, standards, and tax laws?
 a. outside factors
 b. market profile
 c. consumer profile
 d. legal changes

A 61. What part of the marketing plan emphasizes the factors that contribute to a firm's competitive edge?
 a. appraisal of marketing strengths and weaknesses
 b. development of marketing strategies
 c. determining pricing structures
 d. conducting market research

A 62. What part of the marketing plan strategies begins with identifying the end users, wholesalers, and retailers, as well as their needs and specifications?
 a. product/service
 b. marketing
 c. pricing structure
 d. competitive focus

D 63. The final critical factor in the marketing-planning process is
 a. analysis.
 b. cost projection.
 c. sales forecasting.
 d. evaluation.

Telemarketing

A   64.   Telemarketing
- a. is the use of telephone communications to sell merchandise directly to customers.
- b. is a marketing strategy for telephone companies.
- c. is the oldest marketing technique.
- d. is proving unworkable.

D   65.   Which of the following is a disadvantage of telemarketing?
- a. increased sales
- b. high phone bills
- c. angry customers
- d. rapid turnover of telephone staff

B   66.   Which of the following is an advantage of telemarketing?
- a. easier communication
- b. cost effectiveness
- c. larger sales staff
- d. employee loyalty

A   67.   Telephone sales are growing at an annual rate of
- a. 25-35 percent.
- b. 35-45 percent.
- c. 45-55 percent.
- d. 55-65 percent.

C   68.   The major reason for the dramatic growth in telemarketing is
- a. immediate feedback.
- b. time management.
- c. cost effectiveness.
- d. flexibility.

D   69.   Which advantage of telemarketing can be attributed to salespeople penetrating markets anywhere in the world where telephones are available?
- a. receptiveness
- b. more presentations
- c. impressions
- d. unlimited geographic coverage

A   70. Which advantage of telemarketing can be attributed to the sales force being supervised more easily than a field staff?
      a. better control
      b. immediate feedback
      c. perceptiveness
      d. less "piracy"

Pricing Strategies

D   71. Which of the following factors affects pricing strategies?
      a. degree of competitive pressure
      b. availability of sufficient supply
      c. seasonal or cyclical changes in demand
      d. all of the above

A   72. Which of the following are psychological factors affecting pricing?
      a. even-numbered prices for prestigious items and odd-numbered prices for commonly available goods
      b. inflationary pressures
      c. schizophrenia
      d. myopic quantitativeness

D   73. Which of the following types of ventures needs different pricing strategies?
      a. retail ventures
      b. manufacturing ventures
      c. service ventures
      d. all of the above

A   74. Which of the following is *not* a step in price determination?
      a. Research one's own product offerings.
      b. Estimate the total market demand.
      c. Calculate the available sales potential.
      d. Determine the volume objectives.

A   75. The two elements in pricing strategies are
      a. environmental and psychological.
      b. environmental and marketing.
      c. feedback and expenses.
      d. cost and revenues.

Essays

76. *How would you characterize your markets?*

Applying criteria to your best customers makes sense for the smallest of businesses and asks how each one can be more thoroughly characterized for the individual and the business. Examples of individual characteristics include age, gender, race and ethnic group, hobbies, lifestyle, education, social class, occupation, and income level. Business definitions include the kind or type of business (manufacturing, wholesale, service, or retail), location, structure, sales level, distribution patterns, and number of employees.

77. *How can an entrepreneur find more people (businesses/buyers) like the ones he or she already has?*

This question is a key to future business strategies. An entrepreneur must continually look for more customers to replace those lost through normal attrition and focus on becoming acquainted with new potential customers who are candidates for frequent returns.

78. *How will you attract and keep these markets?*

The initial response to this question comes from the answer the question reveals; however, the basis should have already been thought of in the initial business plan. The development of the answer should involve such questions as how and where to advertise, the stability of the business's location, the attractiveness and accessibility of the store, and the fit between your business and your chosen markets.

79. *How can an entrepreneur expand his or her markets?*

Because it is difficult to expand before you attract, the entrepreneur must not only focus on new customers but realize when his or her market has become large enough to bring in new merchandise or other services to satisfy new and returning customers. Continual research is effective in this area. Many times customers find new products or ideas that are innovative and hence, potential profit makers.

80. *Why do they buy from one entrepreneur and not from the competition?*

Strategy is probably one of the most difficult things to determine for an entrepreneur. One must always keep the investor/customer in mind when beginning a business. The more sacrifice customers see or receive from a business the more often they will return. There are many benefits a business can pass along to its customers that other competitors may or may not be willing to risk.

CHAPTER 9

FINANCIAL PREPARATION FOR ENTREPRENEURIAL VENTURES

True/False

The Importance of Financial Information for Entrepreneurs

T   1.   Financial information pulls together all the information presented in the other segments of the business.

F   2.   The set of assumptions on which financial projections are based has little meaning.

Preparing Financial Statements

F   3.   It is typical for a firm to prepare an operating budget but *not* a cash budget.

T   4.   A budget is one of the most powerful tools that the entrepreneur can use in planning business operations.

T   5.   The cash-flow budget provides an overview of cash inflows and outflows for the budget period.

The Operating Budget

F   6.   The first step in preparing the operating budget is estimating expenses.

T   7.   The first type of expense to be estimated when preparing an operating budget is cost of goods sold.

T   8.   The first step in creating an operating budget is to prepare the sales forecast.

F   9.   The last step in preparing the operating budget is to estimate the current sales.

T   10. A firm using only a bottom-up approach may find that it is losing control of the budget process due to management being concerned only with the goals, strategies, and available resources for their individual departments.

The Cash-Flow Budget

T   11. After the operating budget has been prepared, the entrepreneur can proceed to the next phase of the budget process, the cash-flow budget.

F   12. The first step in the preparation of the cash-flow budget is the identification and timing of cash outflows.

T   13. The typical business will have cash inflows from three sources: cash sales, cash payments received on account, and loan proceeds.

Pro Forma Statements

F   14. Pro forma statements show the firm's present financial position.

T   15. The pro forma income statement is prepared before the pro forma balance sheet.

F   16. The traditional accounting equation is: **assets + liabilities = owner's equity**.

Capital Budgeting

T   17. Capital investments or capital expenditures are expected to last beyond one year.

T   18. Capital budgeting is used to help the entrepreneur plan for capital expenditures.

T   19. The principal objective of capital budgeting is to maximize the value of the firm.

Break-Even Analysis

T   20. Break-even analysis is used to tell how many units must be sold in order to break even at a particular selling price.

F   21. Contribution margin is the difference between the selling price and the fixed cost per unit.

F   22. The entrepreneur must graph at least two numbers, total sales and total expenses, when using the graphic approach for break-even analysis.

T   23. The handling questionable costs approach of break-even analysis was specifically designed for entrepreneurship firms.

Use of Decision Support Systems

T   24.   A DSS is used to help a firm manage its financial resources.

F   25.   DSS stands for Disc Systems Support.

Multiple Choice

The Importance of Financial Information for Entrepreneurs

D   26.   Financial information is important to entrepreneurs because:
    a. it pulls together all the information presented in other segments of the business.
    b. it quantifies all the assumptions concerning business operations.
    c. it answers all questions about the business and the entrepreneur.
    d. a and b are both correct.

D   27.   Which of the following is *not* true about financial *assumptions*.
    a. They explain how the numbers are derived.
    b. They should be clear and precise.
    c. They are the most integral part of the financial segment.
    d. They do not necessarily correlate with information from other parts of the business.

Preparing Financial Statements

D   28.   One type of budget used by the entrepreneur is
    a. an operating budget.
    b. a cash budget.
    c. a capital budget.
    d. all of the above.

B   29.   A budget that is a statement of estimated income and expenses over a specified period of time is referred to as an
    a. anticipated budget.
    b. operating budget.
    c. entrepreneurial budget.
    d. expected results budget.

The Operating Budget

A   30. The way of constructing an operating budget is
  a. the bottom-up approach.
  b. the horizontal approach.
  c. the matrix approach.
  d. all of the above.
  e. a and c only.

B   31. In the simple linear regression analysis equation, **Y = a + bx, x** represents
  a. expected sales.
  b. the factor on which sales are dependent.
  c. the slope of the line.
  d. none of the above.

D   32. A manufacturing firm needs to establish which of the following budgets?
  a. a production budget
  b. a material purchases budget
  c. a direct labor budget
  d. all of the above

C   33. A variable cost
  a. changes in the same direction and in inverse proportion to changes in operating activity.
  b. changes in the opposite direction and in direct proportion to changes in operating activity.
  c. changes in the same direction and in direct proportion to changes in operating activity.
  d. does none of the above.

C   34. For a manufacturing firm, the production budget represents
  a. the number of units that must be produced to break even.
  b. the number of units that must be produced to achieve the desired profit level.
  c. the number of units that must be produced in order to meet the sales forecast.
  d. none of the above.

A   35. In the simple linear regression analysis equation, **Y = a + bx, b** represents
  a. the slope of the line.
  b. expected sales.
  c. the constant.
  d. the factor on which sales are dependent.

B　36. In the production budget for a manufacturing firm, the number of units needed in inventory is determined by
   a. the sum of beginning inventory and expected sales.
   b. the sum of the desired ending inventory and the number of units to be sold.
   c. the sum of beginning inventory and the desired ending inventory.
   d. none of the above.

B　37. The last step in preparing the operating budget is to
   a. estimate current sales.
   b. estimate operating expenses.
   c. estimate variable costs.
   d. do none of the above.

B　38. Production requirements are figured by subtracting the period's beginning inventory from
   a. inventory from the previous period.
   b. inventory needed for that period.
   c. both of the above.
   d. none of the above.

D　39. A key concept in developing an expense budget is that of
   a. fixed costs.
   b. variable costs.
   c. mixed costs.
   d. all of the above.

B　40. After the firm has forecast its sales for the budget period
   a. net income is figured.
   b. expenses are estimated.
   c. ending inventory is figured.
   d. none of the above.

D　41. When using trend line analysis, how many periods are required?
   a. three
   b. two
   c. one
   d. five

C   42. More established ventures will use a sales forecast where the estimation of current sales will increase a certain percentage over the prior period's sales. This percentage is based upon
   a. newly established sales only.
   b. an inventory analysis.
   c. a trend line analysis.
   d. all of the above.

The Cash-Flow Budget

D   43. Cash inflows come from
   a. cash sales.
   b. cash payments.
   c. loan proceeds.
   d. all of the above.

A   44. The cash-flow budget describes
   a. cash inflows/cash outflows.
   b. cash outflows/accounts receivables.
   c. interest income/interest expense.
   d. all of the above.

B   45. A fixed cost
   a. changes in response to changes in activity for a given period of time.
   b. does not change in response to changes in activity for a given period of time.
   c. changes inversely to changes in activity for a given period of time.
   d. does none of the above.

C   46. The first step in the preparation of the cash-flow budget is the
   a. identification of cash inflows.
   b. identification of cash outflows.
   c. identification and timing of cash inflows.
   d. identification and timing of cash outflows.

Pro Forma Statements

D   47. Which of the following is needed in preparing a pro forma balance sheet?
   a. the last balance sheet prepared before the budget period began
   b. the operating budget
   c. the cash-flow budget
   d. all of the above

A 48. The traditional accounting equation that verifies the accuracy of the entrepreneur's balance sheet is
  a. **assets = liabilities + owner's equity.**
  b. **assets + liabilities = owner's equity.**
  c. **assets + owner's equity = liabilities.**
  d. **assets = liabilities - owner's equity.**

D 49. Which of the following are forms of pro forma statements?
  a. income statements
  b. balance sheet
  c. cost of goods sold
  d. a and b

D 50. How many months of the year should be illustrated in the first pro forma income statement?
  a. three
  b. eight
  c. six
  d. twelve

D 51. Contained in the pro forma balance sheet is
  a. the last balance sheet prepared before the budget began.
  b. the operating budget.
  c. the cash-flow budget.
  d. all of the above.

Capital Budgeting

D 52. When using the internal rate of return method, the future cash flows are discounted at a rate that makes the net present value equal to
  a. assets minus liabilities.
  b. assets minus owner's equity.
  c. assets minus (liabilities plus owner's equity).
  d. none of the above.

B 53. The principle objective of capital budgeting is to
  a. minimize the value of the firm.
  b. maximize the value of the firm.
  c. maximize the costs to the firm.
  d. minimize the number of project requests.

C   54. Net present value method is a capital budgeting technique that helps to minimize some of the shortcomings of the payback method by
   a. discounting all future projects.
   b. recognizing past cash flows of projects.
   c. recognizing future cash flows beyond the payback period.
   d. recognizing the payback dollars over again.

A   55. A method that discounts future cash flows at a rate that makes the net present value of the project equal to zero is known as
   a. internal rate of return.
   b. net present value.
   c. payback method.
   d. break-even point.

A   56. Capital budgeting is designed to show
   a. how many projects, in total, should be selected.
   b. which project is most profitable.
   c. which of several mutually exclusive projects should be selected.
   d. all of the above.

D   57. Despite the drawbacks of the payback method, the entrepreneur should continue to use it because
   a. it is very simple to use in comparison to other methods.
   b. projects with a faster payback period normally have more favorable short-term effects on earnings.
   c. it provides a faster return of funds.
   d. none of the above.

B   58. The rate used to adjust future cash flows to determine their value in present period terms is the
   a. current interest rate.
   b. cost of capital.
   c. rate determined by the ratio of assets to liabilities.
   d. none of the above.

A   59. Investments in which returns are expected to extend beyond one year are referred to as
   a. capital investments.
   b. stocks.
   c. bonds.
   d. mutual funds.

C 60. One of the easiest capital budgeting methods to understand is the
- a. net present value.
- b. internal rate of return.
- c. payback method.
- d. strategic analysis approach.

D 61. Many companies continue to use the payback method. It is
- a. very simple to use.
- b. more favorable in its short-term effects on earnings.
- c. a faster return of funds.
- d. all of the above.

C 62. The concept of the net present value method works on the premise that
- a. a dollar today is worth less than a dollar in the future.
- b. a dollar today is worth the same in the future.
- c. a dollar today is worth more than a dollar in the future.
- d. a dollar today cannot be measured in future dollars.

C 63. Allowing members of top management to determine overall goals is an example of what kind of approach?
- a. bottom-up
- b. bottom-down
- c. top-down
- d. none of the above

A 64. Loan proceeds are *not* directly tied to
- a. sales revenue.
- b. expenses.
- c. meeting cash flow problems.
- d. planned expansion of a firm.

Break-Even Analysis

C 65. Break-even analysis is used to assess
- a. expected capital expenditures.
- b. revenue.
- c. expected product profitability.
- d. all of the above.

C 66. Contribution margin is the difference between
   a. selling price and fixed cost per unit.
   b. purchase price and variable cost per unit.
   c. selling price and variable cost per unit.
   d. purchase price and fixed cost per unit.

D 67. The contribution margin approach formula is
   a. CM = SP (VC - FC) S
   b. S = SP (FC - VC)
   c. SP = (FC - VC) S
   d. FC = (SP - VC) S

A 68. When using the graphic approach to break-even analysis, the entrepreneur must plot which of the following?
   a. total revenue and total costs
   b. total expenses and total revenue
   c. total costs and total income
   d. total income and total expenses

D 69. Which of the following is a decision rule for handling questionable costs?
   a. If expected sales are between the two break-even points, the questionable costs behavior needs further investigation.
   b. If expected sales exceed the higher break-even point, the product should be profitable.
   c. The product should not be profitable if expected sales do not exceed the lower break-even point.
   d. None of the above is correct.

B 70. Break-even analysis is a technique commonly used to assess the
   a. rate of return on investment.
   b. expected product profitability.
   c. net present value.
   d. none of the above.

A 71. In handling questionable costs, the cost in question is substituted first as a _____ and then as a _____.
   a. fixed cost; variable cost
   b. mixed cost; fixed cost
   c. variable cost; total cost
   d. total cost; fixed cost

Ratio Analysis

A   72.   The key steps in comparing financial numbers in order to make decisions is referred to as:
- a. ratio analysis.
- b. debt reduction.
- c. comparable fractions.
- d. none of the above.

B   73.   Ratio analysis can be applied from which of the following directions?
- a. vertical only
- b. vertical and horizontal
- c. horizontal only
- d. external and internal

Use of Decision Support Systems

B   74.   DSS stands for
- a. decision standing systems.
- b. decision support systems.
- c. disc system support.
- d. disc support standards.

D   75.   What can a DSS be used for?
- a. To facilitate the financial planning process through the use of integrated pro forma financial statements
- b. To calculate net income at various points
- c. To perform a sensitivity analysis for other level of sales and expenses
- d. To do all of the above

Essays

76.   *What is included in a operating budget, and how is this helpful?*
    The operating budget includes a sales forecast. A forecast can be acquired from a linear regression analysis or a trend line analysis. This is a good place to start because a manager must look at past months' sales figures. It usually gives an idea of what to expect in the upcoming year. This type of budget also includes an estimation of expenses. A layout of the groundwork helps the manager to get a clear picture of the costs involved in keeping up the business. The layout will also help estimate the number of sales needed each month.

77. *Explain what a cash-flow budget tells a manager/owner.*
    This type of budget keeps accurate records of all cash coming into the business and going out of the business. It indicates where a cash problem may occur. Cash comes from essentially three forms in a business. These include cash sales, cash payments, and loan proceeds.

78. *Name and describe the final phase of the budget process.*
    The third phase is the pro forma statements. They include a pro forma balance sheet and a pro forma income statement. The pro forma income statement tells the manager the outlook for income and expenses in a month-by-month format. The pro forma balance sheet uses the operating budget and the cash budget. The intended changes are then carried through to produce new totals.

79. *List the elements of a capital budget, and define its main objective.*
    A capital budget is used to help plan for investments and expenditures. It also helps to decide which investment or purchase to make. Three methods help make this decision, and they include: payback method, net present value method, and internal rate of return. Capital budgeting is used to maximize the worth of the firm.

80. *Define break-even analysis, and name some useful methods for finding the break-even point.*
    Break-even analysis is the point in production when the firm has no losses or gains. You make or sell enough of your product to break even. Some popular applications include graphing total costs and total revenues. The point at which these two lines cross is your break-even point. Another is the contribution margin approach or the unknown-cost approach. Each method uses the selling price, variable cost, fixed costs, and the unknown cost (number of units to sell).

CHAPTER 10

DEVELOPING AN EFFECTIVE BUSINESS PLAN

True/False

Introduction

F   1.   The major tool used in determining the essential operation of a venture is the pro forma balance sheet.

T   2.   Four critical factors that must be addressed when planning a new venture include setting realistic goals, determining milestones, making a commitment, and having flexibility.

Pitfalls to Avoid in Planning

F   3.   One of the indicators of the failure to anticipate roadblocks is a lack of priorities.

T   4.   A lack of demonstrated experience, no clear market niche, a failure to anticipate roadblocks, no realistic goals set, and a lack of commitment are pitfalls or common points of failure that occur *before* an entrepreneur ever gets his/her plan reviewed.

T   5.   Lack of any time frame to accomplish things is an indicator of the pitfall known as no realistic goals.

F   6.   The easiest way to avoid the pitfall of no commitment or dedication is to make the appearance that the venture is a hobby or a whim.

What Is a Business Plan?

T   7.   An investment prospectus is the same as a business plan.

F   8.   The major purpose of a business plan is that it is to be utilized as a working document.

F   9.   A business plan must illustrate the current status of the venture but *not* the projected results.

T   10.   The business plan is the entrepreneur's road map for a successful enterprise.

F   11. The emphasis of the business plan should never be the final implementation of the venture.

Benefits of a Business Plan

F   12. One of the benefits of a business plan for a financial source is that it forces the source to view the plan critically and objectively.

T   13. An entrepreneur is much better off preparing his or her own business plan rather than hiring someone else, even if more experienced, to prepare it.

F   14. A business plan should be no more than 150 pages.

T   15. Because of the competition for funding, an entrepreneur's business plan needs to capture the reader's interest right away by stating the uniqueness of the venture.

F   16. There are only two viewpoints from which a business plan should be written, the entrepreneur's and the financial source's.

T   17. An entrepreneur should include a three-to five-year financial projection so that the financial source can adequately evaluate the venture.

Elements of a Business Plan

F   18. A summary gives a brief overview of what is to follow, helps put all of the information into perspective, and should be no longer than ten pages.

T   19. A "niche" is a homogeneous group with common characteristics, i.e., all the people who have a need for the newly proposed product or service.

F   20. The manufacturing segment of the business plan should identify key personnel, their responsibilities and their positions, and career experience that qualifies them for those particular roles.

F   21. The pro forma balance sheet is used in the critical-risk segment of the business plan.

Presentation of the Business Plan

T   22. One suggestion for helping to recall key examples, visual aids, and other details when presenting the business plan is to utilize key words in the outline.

F   23. The entrepreneur should expect to encounter a friendly and supportive audience when presenting the business plan to potential financial sources.

F   24. The entrepreneur's professionalism and how well he or she handles the venture capitalist is far more important than being well organized and prepared.

F   25. In preparing a business plan for oral presentation, the entrepreneur should scan the outline once or twice.

Multiple Choice

Introduction

B   26. Which of the following is one of the critical factors that an entrepreneur may face in planning?
   a. lack of time to make the plan
   b. lack of realistic goals
   c. too much time in the daily operations of the business
   d. none of the above

C   27. In planning, there are a number of critical factors that must be addressed. One is
   a. having a calendar.
   b. the timetable involved.
   c. commitment.
   d. a firm plan.

C   28. Which of the following is *not* a critical factor that should be addressed in planning a venture?
   a. milestones
   b. flexibility
   c. undertaking
   d. realistic goals

A   29. The comprehensive business plan should be the result of
   a. meetings and reflections on the direction of the venture.
   b. continuous operations of the venture.
   c. investors' promises for large amounts of capital.
   d. all of the above.

The Dryden Press   445

Pitfalls to Avoid in Planning

A   30. Which of the following is a pitfall to avoid in planning?
   a. lack of priorities
   b. lack of profit
   c. no admission of possible success in the plan
   d. refusal to write items down

C   31. What is one possible way to avoid the pitfall of no market niche (segment)?
   a. conduct a market analysis
   b. check market niches in marketing journals to determine which one the venture falls into
   c. clearly specify which market niche the venture plans to target
   d. none of the above

B   32. A business plan should illustrate
   a. the current status of the entrepreneur.
   b. the projected needs of the new business.
   c. the desires of the competitors.
   d. none of the above.

D   33. An indicator of the planning pitfall of failure to anticipate roadblocks is
   a. no recognition of future problems.
   b. no admission of possible flaws in the plan.
   c. no contingency or alternative plans.
   d. all of the above.

B   34. An indicator of the planning pitfall "no commitment or dedication" is
   a. no experience in the business.
   b. excessive procrastination.
   c. no recognition of future problems.
   d. lack of understanding about the industry.

A   35. An indicator of the planning pitfalls of no realistic goals is
   a. lack of timetable to accomplish things.
   b. missed appointments.
   c. excessive procrastination.
   d. lack of desire to invest personal money.

What Is a Business Plan?

A   36. Sometimes a business plan is referred to as
       a. a loan proposal.
       b. the book.
       c. the master plan.
       d. none of the above.

B   37. The major thrust of the business plan is
       a. to provide a working document for the venture.
       b. to encapsulate the strategic development of the project in a comprehensive document.
       c. to serve as a communication tool for the entrepreneur.
       d. none of the above.

D   38. A business plan is
       a. a written document that details the proposed venture.
       b. an illustration of current status and expected needs.
       c. the projected results of the new business.
       d. all of the above.

B   39. In some professional areas the business plan is referred to as
       a. a proposal for economic development.
       b. an investment prospectus.
       c. a strategic development project.
       d. a and b only.

D   40. Which of the following statements about a business plan is (are) true?
       a. It is the entrepreneur's road map for success.
       b. It is the minimum document required by financial sources.
       c. It allows the entrepreneur entrance into the investment process.
       d. All of the above are true.

Benefits of a Business Plan

C   41. A business plan
       a. forces the venture capitalist to prepare an effective strategy to use in case of trouble.
       b. provides a foolproof "blueprint" for a small business.
       c. may help an entrepreneur avoid a project which is "doomed" from the start.
       d. does none of the above.

C 42. To the entrepreneur, one of the benefits of a business plan is
  a. the development of operating strategies for outside evaluators.
  b. benchmarks for comparing forecasts with actual results.
  c. both a and b.
  d. neither a nor b.

C 43. It is important that an entrepreneur
  a. seek the assistance of outside professionals to prepare a business plan.
  b. develop an entrepreneurial team to organize the plan.
  c. prepare his or her own plan.
  d. do a and b only.

A 44. The completed business plan provides the entrepreneur with
  a. a communication tool for outside financial sources.
  b. a sense of well-being for the firm's venture.
  c. a timetable.
  d. a nicely designed booklet.

C 45. Which of the following is *not* an important aspect of the venture?
  a. current status
  b. expected needs
  c. family support
  d. marketing

A 46. Which of the following would be a benefit gained by financial sources from a business plan?
  a. The venture's ability to service debt or provide an adequate return on equity is illustrated.
  b. Particular amounts of funds are promised to the evaluators.
  c. The proper grammar of the plan is effective reading.
  d. all of the above

Developing a Well-Conceived Business Plan

A 47. Which of the following is the most common viewpoint in business plans?
  a. the entrepreneur's viewpoint
  b. the marketplace's viewpoint
  c. the financial source's viewpoint
  d. all of the above

C 48. Which of the following is *not* one of the six steps in reading a business plan?
a. Establish the unique feature in this venture.
b. Read the latest balance sheet.
c. Thoroughly read each section.
d. none of the above

C 49. When a venture capital firm believes that successful new ventures usually reach approximately 50 percent of their projected financial goals, it is applying what is known as a
a. discounted capital element.
b. reduced forecast theory.
c. projection discount factor.
d. five minute reading.

A 50. Which of the following describes advantages of the business plan for financial sources?
a. The plan identifies critical risks.
b. The plan helps assess the entrepreneur's family.
c. all of the above
d. none of the above

B 51. The final copy of the business plan should be
a. paperclipped so that the financial sources can easily look through it.
b. put in a plastic folder.
c. professionally bound and typeset.
d. none of the above.

A 52. The cover page should bear
a. the name of the company.
b. the phone number of each supplier.
c. the month and year.
d. all of the above.

C 53. An important guideline in putting the plan together is
a. overdiversity.
b. do not highlight critical risks.
c. identify the target market.
d. long plans always look impressive.

The Dryden Press

B   54. Entrepreneurs orient the plan toward the future
- a. by informing the capitalists of how wealthy they will be.
- b. by developing trends and forecasts that describe what the venture intends to do.
- c. by showing what the opportunities are for the investors.
- d. by planning 20 years ahead.

B   55. Which of the following statements is *not* part of the "five-minute reading" by venture capitalists?
- a. Determine the characteristics of the venture and industry.
- b. Determine the strengths and weaknesses of the entrepreneur.
- c. Determine the financial structure of the plan.
- d. Read the latest balance sheet.

B   56. The recommended length of a business plan is
- a. 100 pages.
- b. 40 pages.
- c. 150 pages.
- d. 10 pages.

B   57. Which of the following statements would *not* be an appropriate guideline for successful business plan development?
- a. Avoid exaggeration.
- b. Orient the plan to the present.
- c. Highlight critical risks.
- d. Do not overdiversify.

Elements of a Business Plan

B   58. One thing that should be included in the business description is
- a. the name of each investor.
- b. the industry background.
- c. potential disadvantages of the venture.
- d. all of the above.

D   59. Which of the following is a "what if"?
- a. the sales projections are not achieved
- b. the industry slumps
- c. key personnel leave the company
- d. all of the above

B   60. The second section of the business plan is called
- a. the summary.
- b. the business description.
- c. the purpose and goals.
- d. none of the above.

D   61. Which of the following is part of the marketing segment?
- a. the advertising plan
- b. the competitive analysis
- c. the market strategy
- d. all of the above

C   62. Which of the following is a critical factor to be considered in the management segment?
- a. the suppliers
- b. the location of the plant
- c. the organizational structure
- d. all of the above

B   63. Which of the following ratios are analyzed using a pro forma balance sheet?
- a. sales to revenue
- b. inventory turnover
- c. stockholders' equity to owners' equity
- d. none of the above

C   64. Which of the following statements may be the most important in new venture creation?
- a. the pro forma balance sheet
- b. the income statement
- c. the cash-flow statement
- d. all of the above

A   65. Blueprints, sketches, drawings, and models are often important features to be placed in what section of the business plan?
- a. research, design, and development
- b. marketing
- c. manufacturing
- d. critical risks

C   66. The appendix and/or bibliography segment is not mandatory, but it allows for
- a. incorporation of the venture.
- b. additional capital funding.
- c. additional documentation not appropriate in the main parts of the plan.
- d. completion of design and development.

D   67. The financial segment presents
  a. the pro forma balance sheet.
  b. the income statement.
  c. the cash-flow statement.
  d. all of the above.

B   68. Competitive analysis, advertising plan, and pricing policy are all part of the
  a. research, design, and development segment.
  b. marketing segment.
  c. milestone schedule segment.
  d. financial plan segment.

B   69. Which of the following is a critical factor that should be discussed in the management segment?
  a. unfavorable trends in the industry
  b. board of directors and consultants
  c. competitive analysis
  d. size of manufacturing operation

Presentation of the Business Plan

D   70. Which of the following is suggested for helping in the oral presentation of a business plan?
  a. the use of mnemonic devices
  b. the use of 3" X 5" index cards
  c. rote memorization
  d. utilization of key words on an outline

C   71. Which of the following is something an entrepreneur should *not* do when preparing for the oral presentation of the business plan?
  a. Organize the presentation.
  b. Develop an outline of the plan.
  c. Make the presentation very rigid.
  d. all of the above

C   72. Which of the following is a key question that might be asked when a business plan is turned down?
  a. "That means you do not know how to evaluate a good plan?"
  b. "Can you name your friends who would like this kind of deal?"
  c. "If you were in my position, how would you proceed?"
  d. none of the above

A   73. The entrepreneur must be
- a. able to handle questions from the evaluators.
- b. interesting and humorous.
- c. able to criticize the evaluators.
- d. all of the above.

B   74. Should a business plan/venture be turned down the first time, the entrepreneur should
- a. feel defeated.
- b. revise, rework, and improve the plan.
- c. take it personally.
- d. change careers.

D   75. The day of the presentation, the entrepreneur should arrive early to
- a. greet all the venture capitalists.
- b. have breakfast and coffee.
- c. read the paper to relieve nervousness.
- d. set up, test any equipment, and organize notes and visual aids.

Essays

76. *What are some of the errors made in the preparation of a business plan that minimize an entrepreneur's chance for success?*

There are five pitfalls that represent the most common errors made by entrepreneurs when preparing a business plan. The first pitfall is the lack of realistic goals. One way to avoid this pitfall is to set up a timetable with specific steps to be accomplished during a specific time period. Another error made in the planning stage is the failure to anticipate roadblocks. The best way to avoid this pitfall is to list the possible obstacles that may arise and the alternatives that state what might be done to overcome the obstacles. The third pitfall is an entrepreneur's lack of commitment or dedication. One way to avoid this problem is for the entrepreneur to be ready to demonstrate a financial commitment to the venture. A lack of demonstrated experience is the next pitfall. In this situation the entrepreneur should provide evidence of his or her background for this venture or at least the willingness to obtain assistance from those who possess the knowledge and skills needed. The last pitfall is the omission of a market niche. The best way to avoid this is to have a market segment specifically targeted and to demonstrate why and how this product or service will meet the needs and desires of this target group.

77. *How does a business plan benefit the entrepreneur?*

A business plan allows the entrepreneur entrance into the investment process. It is the minimum document that is required by any financial source. The business plan describes to investors and financial sources all of the events that may affect the venture being proposed. Besides being a comprehensive document for outside investors to read and understand, a business plan is the entrepreneur's road map for a successful enterprise. It is the entrepreneur's description and prediction for the venture; thus, it is essential that the entrepreneur prepare his or her own business plan. It is during this preparation that it may become evident that the business is ill-fated and should not be started. The time, effort, research, and discipline needed to put the plan together will force the entrepreneur to view the venture critically and objectively.

78. *What is the basic structure of a business plan?*

A business plan usually has 10 sections, and the ideal length is 50 pages. The beginning section is the summary. The summary gives a brief overview of what is to follow and helps put all the information into perspective. The summary is followed by the business description segment, which identifies any special significance of the venture. The marketing segment follows with its market niche and market share projections, competitive analysis, pricing policy, advertising plan, and market strategy. The fourth section is the research, design, and development segment. The entrepreneur should have technical assistance in preparing a detailed discussion. The next segment, the manufacturing segment, should always begin by describing the location of the new venture. The management segment should identify the key personnel, their positions and responsibilities, and the career experiences that qualify them for those particular roles. The critical-risks segment identifies potential risks that are usually outside factors. The financial segment contains a pro forma balance sheet along with an income statement and a cash-flow statement. The milestone schedule segment provides investors with a timetable for the various activities to be accomplished. The last section is the bibliography segment. The bibliography segment is not mandatory, but it allows for additional documentation that is not appropriate in the main parts of the plan.

79. *How should an entrepreneur prepare to present his or her business plan?*

An entrepreneur is likely to present the business plan to either a single financial person or numerous financial investors. The entrepreneur must be able to sell the plan to potential investors. The entrepreneur should outline the significant highlights of the plan that will capture the audience's interest. In preparation for the presentation, the entrepreneur should know the outline thoroughly and rehearse the presentation in order to get the feel of its length without memorizing it. Entrepreneurs should realize that the audience reviewing their business plan is antagonistic. The entrepreneur must be prepared to handle questions from the evaluators and learn from their criticism. If a venture capitalist turns down the entrepreneur, he or she must feel confident enough in the plan not to give up the effort to succeed.

80. *Should an entrepreneur attempt to make a business plan sound too good for an investor to turn down?*

Potential investors expect the plan to look good, but not too good. Sales potentials, revenue estimates, and the venture's potential growth should not be inflated. Many times a best-case, worst-case, and a probable-case scenario should be developed for the plan. Documentation and research are vital to the credibility of the plan. The business plan must describe the new venture with enthusiasm and yet with complete accuracy. There are numerous professionals who may be involved with reading the business plan, such as venture capitalists, bankers, investors, potential large customers, lawyers, consultants, and suppliers. Any erroneous statements or figures would be spotted, and all credibility would be lost.

CHAPTER 11

ASSESSMENT AND EVALUATION OF ENTREPRENEURIAL OPPORTUNITIES

True/False

The Challenge of New-Venture Start-ups

T   1. During the last few years, the number of new start-up ventures is approximately 1500 per day.

T   2. The entrepreneurial motivations of individuals relate to the entrepreneur, the environment, and the venture.

F   3. There is a great abundance of reliable data concerning the start-up, performance, and failure of new ventures.

Pitfalls in Selecting New Ventures

T   4. Many entrepreneurs do not understand the marketing life cycle of a new product.

F   5. Most entrepreneurs are objective when they evaluate their new idea.

T   6. A common pitfall in selecting a new venture is the lack of venture uniqueness.

T   7. Pricing becomes less of a concern when customers become aware of a product's unique characteristics that are superior to the competitions'.

T   8. Essential to the success of any venture is the availability of a salable good at the time the venture opens its doors.

Critical Factors for New-Venture Development

F   9. There are five specific phases a new venture goes through.

F   10. The extent and timing of funds needed to move through the venture process is *not* a critical issue.

T   11. In the lifestyle venture, independence, autonomy, and control are the primary driving forces.

The Dryden Press

F   12. The decision of an entrepreneur to ignore the market is a safe one if he or she is sure that the idea will be a success.

T   13. The range of uniqueness in a new venture can extend from fairly routine to highly nonroutine.

Why New Ventures Fail

F   14. There are seven major categories of causes for new-venture failure.

F   15. Timing has little to do with the success or failure of a new venture.

T   16. Obtaining external financing is considered one of the major types of problems for a new venture during its first year.

T   17. Two important factors classified by Bruno as managerial that could be a cause for failure include resource problems and a team approach.

T   18. Proper understanding of the market will help an entrepreneur avoid failure with a new venture.

T   19. "Intensity of competition" changes the dominance of problem areas.

The Evaluation Process

T   20. Solid analysis and evaluation of the feasibility of the product/service idea are critical tasks in starting a new business.

T   21. A product does not have to be patented in order to be introduced into the marketplace.

F   22. The evaluation process must be done by a research firm.

T   23. Asking feasibility questions is important in the evaluation process.

F   24. A feasibility criteria approach would not assist the entrepreneur in judging the potential of the business.

T   25. Feasibility analyses include the technical, market, financial, organizational, and competitive analyses.

Multiple Choice

The Challenges of New-Venture Start-ups

A   26. It is reported that _____ new firms have emerged in the United States every year since the mid-eighties.
   a. 500,000
   b. 100,000
   c. 22,000
   d. 230,000

D   27. The entrepreneurial motivations of individuals usually relate to which of the following factors?
   a. the environment
   b. the entrepreneur
   c. the venture
   d. all of the above

D   28. Researchers have described a "fully developed new firm" with a number of characteristics including:
   a. requires a full-time commitment
   b. has formal financial support
   c. has not hired any individuals
   d. a and b both apply

Pitfalls in Selecting New Ventures

C   29. Many entrepreneurs lack _____ for their new venture.
   a. innovation
   b. intelligence
   c. objectivity
   d. both a and b

D   30. Which of the following is critical to a product's success?
   a. timing
   b. marketing approach
   c. objectivity
   d. all of the above

The Dryden Press

D   31. When a customer sees a product that is superior to its competitors', _____ becomes less important.
   a. size
   b. color
   c. quantity
   d. price

B   32. A new venture should be
   a. cheap.
   b. unique.
   c. easy to copy.
   d. inferior to its competitors.

A   33. A common pitfall in selecting a new venture is
   a. poor financial understanding.
   b. proper objective evaluation.
   c. real insight into the market.
   d. none of the above.

B   34. Timing is especially critical in which area?
   a. the new venture profitability method
   b. marketing
   c. accounting
   d. none of the above

D   35. Many entrepreneurs lack
   a. objectivity.
   b. venture uniqueness.
   c. real insight into the market.
   d. all of the above.

D   36. Name the pitfall described by the statement "Engineers and technically trained people are particularly prone to falling in love with an idea for a product or service."
   a. inadequate understanding of technical requirements
   b. lack of venture uniqueness
   c. no real insight into the market
   d. lack of objective evaluation

B 37. Poor financial understanding for an entrepreneur would be characterized by which of the following?
   a. failure to anticipate technical difficulties
   b. overly optimistic estimates of funds
   c. failure to realize the life cycle of a product
   d. lack of product differentiation

Critical Factors for New-Venture Development

C 38. A new venture must go through _____ phases.
   a. five
   b. two
   c. three
   d. seven

A 39. The uniqueness of a new venture can range from:
   a. fairly routine to highly nonroutine.
   b. fairly unique to highly unique.
   c. fairly original to highly original.
   d. none of the above.

C 40. Sales growth is a critical factor in the
   a. pre-start-up phase.
   b. post-start-up phase.
   c. start-up phase.
   d. none of the above.

D 41. Most ventures fit into which of the following classifications?
   a. lifestyle ventures
   b. smaller profitable ventures
   c. high-growth ventures
   d. all of the above

A 42. Three specific phases that a new venture goes through are
   a. pre-start-up, start-up, post-start-up.
   b. start-up, post-start-up, evaluation.
   c. beginning start-up, start-up, ending start-up.
   d. none of the above.

C   43. Lack of finished product availability can affect
   a. the company's image.
   b. the success of any venture.
   c. both a and b.
   d. none of the above.

C   44. Ronstadt notes that the decision to ignore the market is
   a. a smart one.
   b. a fairly risky one.
   c. an extremely risky one.
   d. a critical one.

B   45. Financial considerations play a major role in
   a. lifestyle ventures.
   b. smaller profitable ventures.
   c. high-growth ventures.
   d. corporate debentures.

A   46. The amount of capital required to start a new venture _____.
   a. can vary considerably depending upon the industry
   b. is generally the same for all start-ups
   c. is never available
   d. will always be a small number

C   47. Independence and autonomy are the major driving forces behind which of the following types of ventures?
   a. small unprofitable ventures
   b. corporate ventures
   c. lifestyle ventures
   d. high-growth ventures

B   48. The type of venture that is expected to attract venture capital would most likely be a
   a. corporate venture.
   b. high-growth venture.
   c. lifestyle venture.
   d. smaller venture.

B   49. What is a critical consideration when assessing customer availability?
   a. amount of products sold
   b. length of time needed to determine who the customers are and what their buying habits are
   c. the exact profitability of the venture
   d. all of the above

A   50. Venture risk is affected by
  a. availability of customers for start-up.
  b. venture capitalists.
  c. uniqueness.
  d. none of the above.

D   51. Which of the following is considered a critical factor in new-venture assessment?
  a. profile analysis
  b. marketability
  c. venture capitalists
  d. product availability

B   52. In recent studies of new-venture problems, the *most* dominant problems at start-up were:
  a. regulatory environment
  b. sales/marketing
  c. production/operations
  d. none of the above

A   53. In recent studies of new-venture problems, the *most* dominant problems during the growth stage were:
  a. sales/marketing
  b. organization design
  c. regulatory environment
  d. none of the above

A   54. Using the "Failure Prediction Model" illustrated in the chapter, the risk of failure can be reduced by:
  a. using less debt as initial financing and generating revenue in the initial stages.
  b. using more debt as initial financing and generating less revenue in the initial stages.
  c. using more revenue to enhance more debt in the initial stage.
  d. all of the above.

A   55. Which of the following are major reasons for the failure of a new venture?
  a. inadequate market knowledge
  b. good product performance
  c. none of the above
  d. a and b

The Dryden Press

B   56. Product/market problems include which of the following?
- a. venture capital relationship problems
- b. unclear business definition
- c. concept of a team approach
- d. assuming debt too early

B   57. Hirings and promotions on the bases of nepotism rather than qualification fall under the managerial problem of
- a. human resource problem.
- b. the concept of a team approach.
- c. unclear business definition.
- d. all of the above.

C   58. A common human resource problem is
- a. poor relationships with parent companies and venture capitalists.
- b. incompetent support professionals.
- c. inflated owner ego.
- d. all of the above.

B   59. Rapid technological advances in many industries cause a concern for _____ in new-venture development.
- a. faulty product performance
- b. rapid product obsolescence
- c. inadequate awareness of competitive pressures
- d. undercapitalization

A   60. When premature entry into the marketplace causes the failure of a new venture, it can be termed
- a. poor timing.
- b. good timing.
- c. a design problem.
- d. a distribution problem.

The Evaluation Process

A   61. A solid analysis is
- a. a critical task in starting a new business.
- b. of no importance.
- c. no way to discover flaws in the new-venture idea.
- d. both a and c.

A	62.	Which of the following are key questions to ask when screening an idea?
	a. Is it proprietary?
	b. Can it easily make money?
	c. What are its points of discussion?
	d. All of the above are correct.

C	63.	The results of a profile analysis enable the entrepreneur to judge
	a. himself or herself.
	b. the competition.
	c. the potential of the business.
	d. all of the above.

D	64.	A checklist approach allows the entrepreneur to identify major strengths and weaknesses in _____ factors of a new venture.
	a. the financial
	b. the marketing
	c. the organizational
	d. all of the above

B	65.	Failure of a new venture can be avoided
	a. by being a high risk taker.
	b. through a careful profile analysis.
	c. through both a and c.
	d. through none of the above.

B	66.	In determining the potential market, one must look _____ into the future.
	a. one year
	b. three to five years
	c. ten years
	d. three months

D	67.	Which of the following are questions an entrepreneur can ask to gain insight into the viability of a venture?
	a. Is it proprietary?
	b. Are the initial production costs realistic?
	c. Is the potential market large?
	d. All of the above are correct.

A	68.	Of the five areas in a critical feasibility study, the two most important are
	a. technical and market.
	b. financial and competitive.
	c. market and financial.
	d. organizational and competitive.

The Dryden Press

A   69. The comprehensive feasibility approach takes into account which factor?
   a. financial
   b. initial customers
   c. calendar times
   d. none of the above

D   70. What two factors merit special attention under the comprehensive feasibility approach?
   a. timing and design
   b. undercapitalization and financial
   c. venture capital and competitive
   d. market and technical

C   71. General sources for a market feasibility analysis include
   a. reliability studies.
   b. statistical analyses.
   c. pricing data.
   d. all of the above.

B   72. In shaping the ultimate success or failure of a new venture, which of the following statements applies the best?
   a. A single strategic variable is usually responsible.
   b. A single strategic variable is seldom responsible.
   c. A single strategic variable will change.
   d. A single strategic variable influences the entire outcome.

A   73. The comprehensive feasibility analysis approach is closely related to which of the following?
   a. preparation of a business plan
   b. dissemination of marketing results
   c. assessment of the entrepreneurial profile
   d. none of the above

C   74. Which evaluation method enables an entrepreneur to judge the potential of the business?
   a. the entrepreneurial analysis method
   b. the venture analysis method
   c. the profile analysis
   d. the net out-of-pocket cost method

A 75. An approach developed as a criteria selection list from which entrepreneurs can gain insights into the viability of their venture is the
   a. feasibility criteria approach.
   b. time-essence of a venture approach.
   c. marketability feasibility approach.
   d. comprehensive feasibility approach.

Essays

76. Explain three major reasons why new ventures fail.

The first reason new ventures often fail is poor timing for the start of a new venture. A new product might be put on the market before a real need for the item exists, or it may be introduced too late, when there is little demand for the product. The second reason is rapid product obsolescence. The life of a product needs to be assessed as important discoveries are always being made in updating the product's usefulness. The third reason is faulty product performance. Tests have not been conducted appropriately for the product, or quality has not been adequately controlled.

77. List and describe three pitfalls in selecting a new venture.

The first pitfall in selecting a new venture is lack of objective evaluation. Ideas for products or services lack the careful planning measures to bring them up to their proper potential. The second pitfall is the lack of real insight into the market; a failure on the part of managerial staff to realize the full potential and life cycle of the product from the beginning. The third pitfall concerns the lack of venture uniqueness. There is no specific characteristic to set the business apart from competitors in the same field.

78. What are three critical factors in a new-venture assessment?

One of the critical factors in a new-venture assessment is the basic feasibility of the venture. A venture has to operate within the realm of reality, and it must also be a legitimate business venture. A second critical factor is the buyer decisions in the venture. Decisions as to customer identification in terms of location and specific classification of customers will be served by this venture. The third critical factor is the competitive advantages of the venture. Basically, this is comparing a venture with the competitors'. The venture must have advantages that are not available to the competition's realm of business.

79. *What are the five specific feasibility phases that a new venture will go through?*

The first phase is finding out technical feasibility. The feasibility measured is whether the product or service will meet all technical criteria and tests for serviceability that are measurable. The second phase concerns marketability. Different tests are used to assure the success of the product or service rendered. This product must be salable and marketable to the public with a plan for promoting, pricing, and distributing the product to consumers or customers. The third phase is financial feasibility. Required finances are compared to available financial resources. The fourth phase deals with organizational capabilities as far as the personnel needs and requirements. The final phase is the competitive analysis of existing, as well as potential, competitors.

CHAPTER 12

STRUCTURING THE NEW BUSINESS VENTURE

True/False

Identifying Legal Structures

F   1.   Legal structure has very little to do with the organization of an operation.

T   2.   There are three primary legal forms of organization.

The Sole Proprietorship

F   3.   An individual in a sole proprietorship has limited liability in the operation.

T   4.   Sole proprietorships are the most common forms of organization.

T   5.   If the proprietor chooses to use a fictitious or assumed name, he or she must also file a certificate of assumed business name.

F   6.   Sole proprietorships suffer from huge taxes levied by the IRS.

The Partnership

F   7.   Written articles of partnership are required through the Uniform Partnership Act.

T   8.   Each member of a partnership shares in the profits and losses incurred in the operation of a partnership.

T   9.   The articles of partnership typically define the name, purpose, and domicile of the firm and the duration of the agreement.

F   10.   Silent partners are active in the business but are not recognized as such by the public.

F   11.   Because a partnership involves two or more people, it is relatively easy to obtain large sums of capital.

T   12.   A limited partner risks only his or her agreed-upon investment in the business.

The Dryden Press

The Corporation

T 13. A corporation is an artificial being, invisible, intangible, and existing only in contemplation of the law.

F 14. Provided the corporation is chartered properly in its home state, it may operate freely from state to state.

T 15. A corporation exists in perpetuity.

T 16. Limited liability is an advantage associated with corporations.

T 17. The creation of a corporation involves many organizational and licensing fees.

Specific Forms of Partnership and Corporations

F 18. An S corporation is commonly referred to as a foreign corporation.

T 19. Limited liability partnership allows professionals the tax benefits of a partnership while avoiding personal liability for the malpractice of other partners.

T 20. Limited partnership permits capital investment without responsibility for management.

F 21. A limited partnership creates an unlimited liability situation for investors.

T 22. Limited liability companies (LLCs) differ from state to state in the statutory requirements.

Franchising

T 23. Franchising allows a franchiser to operate as an independent businessperson but still obtain the advantages of a regional or national organization.

F 24. Franchisors generally do not exercise a great degree of control over franchisees.

T 25. The UFOC stands for the Uniform Franchise Offering Circular.

Multiple Choice

Identifying Legal Structures

A   26. Which of the following represents a reason for carefully identifying the legal structure that best fits a venture?
   a. liability situations
   b. desire for profit
   c. concerns of government
   d. all of the above

D   27. Which of the following are primary forms of legal organization?
   a. sole proprietorships
   b. partnerships
   c. corporations
   d. all of the above

The Sole Proprietorship

A   28. The following are all advantages of a sole proprietorship *except*:
   a. less available capital.
   b. flexibility.
   c. ease of formation.
   d. sole ownership of profits.

D   29. Most people don't want to go into business for themselves because
   a. there is unlimited liability.
   b. there is a lack of continuity in the business.
   c. it is difficult to raise capital.
   d. all of the above.

B   30. When one or more persons involved in a business are personally responsible for the debts of that business, the legal term description is
   a. limited liability.
   b. unlimited liability.
   c. routine liability.
   d. specific business liability.

A   31. Which of the following has the most difficulty raising capital?
   a. a sole proprietorship
   b. a partnership
   c. a corporation
   d. both a and b

The Dryden Press

D   32. Which is *not* a disadvantage of a sole proprietorship?
   a. liability
   b. continuity
   c. available capital
   d. governmental control

A   33. Lack of continuity as a disadvantage of a sole proprietorship refers to
   a. the termination of an enterprise due to death or illness of the owner.
   b. the destruction of continuous documentation.
   c. the obstruction of continual decisions by one party.
   d. the elevation of more than one person to management.

The Partnership

C   34. Which form of organization can outlive the owner?
   a. a sole proprietorship
   b. a partnership
   c. a corporation
   d. both b and c

D   35. Which form of organization may lack continuity?
   a. a sole proprietorship
   b. a partnership
   c. a corporation
   d. both a and b

B   36. Owners are taxed on accumulated as well as distributed earnings in
   a. a sole proprietorship.
   b. a partnership.
   c. a corporation.
   d. both a and b.

B   37. In many states, which form of organization is *not* subject to state income taxes?
   a. sole proprietorship
   b. partnership
   c. corporation
   d. none of the above

B   38. A partner who is active but not known to the general public is
   a. an ostensible partner.
   b. a secret partner.
   c. a dormant partner.
   d. a silent partner.

C 39. An association of two or more persons acting as co-owners of a business for profit defines a
   a. corporation.
   b. R&D investment.
   c. partnership.
   d. sole proprietorship.

C 40. A person who is not a partner but who contracts with one of the partners is
   a. a secret partner.
   b. an active partner.
   c. a subpartner.
   d. a limited partner.

B 41. Which one of the following can be held accountable for the partnership's actions even though he/she participated in the partnership?
   a. a subpartner
   b. a nominal partner
   c. a silent partner
   d. an ostensible partner

C 42. Which is *not* an advantage of a partnership?
   a. ease of formation
   b. flexibility
   c. continuity
   d. both a and c

D 43. All partners are expected to contribute
   a. money.
   b. labor.
   c. skills.
   d. all of the above.

D 44. The articles of partnership clearly define and outline the financial and managerial contributions of the partners. This information typically includes
   a. name, purpose, and domicile.
   b. the extent of each partner's responsibility.
   c. separate debts.
   d. all of the above.

E 45. One type of partner is
   a. an ostensible partner.
   b. a silent partner.
   c. a private partner.
   d. a dormant partner.
   e. all of the above are types of partners.

D 46. Partnerships have advantages similar to those of sole proprietorships *except*
   a. ease of formation.
   b. flexibility.
   c. relative freedom from government regulation.
   d. all of the above.

B 47. A person who is inactive in the business and is not known or disclosed as a partner would be known as a
   a. silent partner.
   b. dormant partner.
   c. ostensible partner.
   d. secret partner.

D 48. The UPA is
   a. the Uniform Partnership Act.
   b. followed by most states.
   c. an act that requires the use of articles of partnership.
   d. all of the above.

C 49. Which of the following statements is false?
   a. Ostensible partners are also general partners.
   b. Active partners may also be ostensible.
   c. Silent partners are active but unknown.
   d. None of the above is false.

The Corporation

D 50. Corporations are
   a. created by the authority of state laws.
   b. formed with transfer of money or property by prospective shareholders.
   c. artificial beings, invisible, intangible, and existing only in contemplation of the law.
   d. all of the above.

D 51. Corporations offer
- a. limited liability.
- b. unlimited life.
- c. increased ability and expertise.
- d. all of the above.

A 52. Corporations, like sole proprietorships and partnerships, have several drawbacks. Which is *not* a drawback?
- a. difficulty in raising capital
- b. organizing expenses
- c. double taxation
- d. lack of representation

A 53. One of the advantages associated with a corporation is unlimited life, which means
- a. the company has a distinct existence from its owners.
- b. the company limits the life of its owners.
- c. the company recognizes the life of its owners.
- d. the company associates unlimited life to its owners.

C 54. Transfer of ownership in a corporation is accomplished by
- a. securing a fixed number of bonds.
- b. filing an affidavit of ownership.
- c. selling stock to interested buyers.
- d. establishing particular property rights.

A 55. One disadvantage of a corporation is the income tax that is levied both on corporate profits and on individual dividends. This is known as
- a. double taxation.
- b. regulation D.
- c. subchapter S.
- d. Rule 10-6-5.

Specific Forms of Partnerships and Corporations

A 56. The ULPA is
- a. the Uniform Limited Partnership Act.
- b. the United Liability Partnership Act.
- c. Uniforms Liability Practitioners Association.
- d. a and b.
- e. a and c.

A   57.   R&D limited partnerships are
- a. subject to tax shelter restrictions.
- b. products of the Risk & Development Partnership Act.
- c. both a and b.
- d. none of the above.

D   58.   The number of R&D partnerships has been growing in recent years. Which of the following is *not* a disadvantage?
- a. cost of funds
- b. use of invested funds is restricted to R&D expenses
- c. R&Ds are expensive to establish
- d. the sponsoring company pays only in the event of a successful development

B   59.   Which of the statements below are *not* true?
- a. Domestic corporations operate within their home state.
- b. Foreign corporations are from outside the United States.
- c. Nonprofit corporations usually involve churches and schools.
- d. All of the statements are true.

D   60.   Closed corporations
- a. are "closely held."
- b. have a single shareholder or a small number of shareholders.
- c. have no stock available to the public.
- d. do all of the above.

D   61.   Which of the following is a cost of incorporation?
- a. lawyers' fees
- b. accountants' fees
- c. fees to the state
- d. all of the above

D   62.   Within the legal structures
- a. all partners are responsible for the other partners' acts.
- b. corporations are separate legal entities.
- c. sole proprietorships offer unlimited liability.
- d. all of the above are correct.

D   63.   One advantage of a corporation is
- a. regulation.
- b. organizing expenses.
- c. taxation.
- d. liability.

B 64. To qualify to be an S corporation, a company does not have to
   a. be domestic.
   b. sell common and preferred stock.
   c. have less than 16 shareholders.
   d. have no shareholders that are partnerships or corporations.

B 65. Common stock
   a. represents ownership.
   b. has a fixed dividend rate.
   c. elects a board of directors.
   d. has claims against the property and income.

D 66. Limited liability partnerships are:
   a. a form of partnership
   b. relatively new
   c. structured to allow partners to avoid liability of other partners' malpractice
   d. all of the above

A 67. LLC stands for:
   a. limited liability company
   b. legal limited corporation
   c. limited legal certification
   d. none of the above

C 68. Limited liability companies include which of the following factors:
   a. limited liability of a corporation
   b. profits "passed through" to individuals for taxes
   c. state statutes differ
   d. all of the above

A 69. Which type of corporation is incorporated out of state?
   a. foreign corporations
   b. public corporations
   c. nonprofit corporations
   d. closed corporations

B 70. When a form of organization is needed that permits capital investment without responsibility for management and without liability for losses beyond the initial investment, which of the following could be used?
   a. foreign corporation
   b. limited partnership
   c. sole proprietorship
   d. S corporation

C   71.   The "tax-option corporation" refers to which of the following?
           a. closed corporation
           b. privately-held corporation
           c. S corporation
           d. none of the above

Franchising

B   72.   An arrangement in which the owner of a trademark, tradename, or copyright licenses others to use it in selling goods and services is known as a:
           a. partnership.
           b. franchise.
           c. close corporation.
           d. none of the above.

D   73.   Which of the following would *not* be considered an advantaged associated with franchising?
           a. training and guidance
           b. proven track record
           c. brand-name appeal
           d. franchise fees

C   74.   Which of the following would *not* be considered a disadvantage associated with franchising?
           a. franchise fees
           b. franchise control
           c. proven track record
           d. unfulfilled promises

D   75.   Which of the following statements best describes the situation of Franchise Law?
           a. Growth in franchising has outdistanced the law of franchising.
           b. Franchising does not fit the traditional business relationships governed by business law.
           c. There has yet to be developed a solid body of franchise decisions to establish "case law."
           d. all of the above

Essays

76. *How does a sole proprietorship work? Explain the advantages and disadvantages of a sole proprietorship.*

A sole proprietorship is a business that is owned and operated by one person. The enterprise has no existence apart from its owner. The individual has a right to all of the profits and bears all of the liability for the debts and obligations of the business. To establish a sole proprietorship, a person merely obtains whatever local and state licenses are necessary to begin operations. One advantage is ease of formation. There is less formality and fewer restrictions associated with establishing a sole proprietorship than with any other legal organization. It needs little or no governmental approval, and it is usually less expensive than a partnership or corporation. There are no co-owners or partners who must be consulted in the running of the operation. Management is able to respond quickly to business needs in the form of day-to-day management decisions as governed by various laws and good sense. There is relative freedom from governmental control. Sole proprietors are taxed as individual taxpayers and not as businesses. Disadvantages include unlimited liability, meaning the owner has personal responsibility for all business debts, including assets. Upon death of the owner, the business may be crippled or terminated. Capital is less available than with partnerships and corporations.

77. *What are the characteristics of a partnership? List various types of partners.*

A partnership is an association of two or more persons acting as co-owners of a business for profit. Each partner contributes money, property, labor, and/or skills, and each shares in the profits as well as the losses of the business. There are various types of partners, and at least one partner must be a general partner. The general partner is responsible for the debts of the enterprise and has unlimited liability. Another partner, also known as a general partner, is an ostensible partner. An ostensible partner is active in the business and is known as a partner. An active partner is active in the business and may be ostensible. A secret partner is active in the business but is not known or disclosed as a partner. A dormant partner is inactive and is not known as a partner. A silent partner is inactive but may be known as a partner. There are other types of partners, but the above are the most common.

78. *What are some of the tax considerations when comparing partnerships and corporations?*

In a partnership federal income tax is charged to each individual on his/her share of the partnership's income, even if this income is not distributed. Income of the corporation is taxed; shareholders are also taxed on distributed dividends. Partners are taxed on accumulated as well as distributed earnings, whereas corporate stockholders are not taxed on accumulated earnings. All partners are taxed on their proportionate share of capital gains and losses. Partners are not taxed on exempt interest received from the firm, whereas any exempt interest distributed by a corporation is fully taxable income to the stockholders. Partners are not eligible for an exempt pension trust, whereas employees who are also stockholders can be beneficiaries of a pension trust. Partners do not match social security payments but often must pay a self-employment tax. All compensation to employee stockholders is subject to social security taxation. For partners there is no exemption from payments to their beneficiaries. Benefits up to $5,000 can be received tax free by stockholders and employee beneficiaries. In many states the partnership is not subject to state income taxes. The corporation is subject to state income taxes even though these taxes can be deducted on federal returns.

79. *What are some of the costs associated with incorporation?*

Most people can start a corporation, but numerous expenses are associated with starting and running a business. First you must consider lawyers' fees. These can range from $250 to $3,000. Accountants' fees can range from $200 to $500 for the establishment of a bookkeeping system. The state can require an annual corporate fee ranging from a few dollars to several hundred dollars. Even if a corporation has only one employee, it must still pay unemployment insurance taxes, either to the state in which it is located or to the federal government. If a person is a salaried employee of some other company in addition to being an employee of his or her own corporation, he or she must pay an employer's contribution to social security, and this is non-refundable. A variety of forms must be filed for corporations in different states. You must also maintain corporate records and minute books. Usually a lawyer or accountant will do this for you. Annual fees for such a service can run into many hundreds of dollars.

80. *How do bonds and common stock differ?*

First, bonds represent debt, whereas stocks represent ownership. Interest on bonds must be paid, whether or not any profit is earned. Stocks do not have a fixed dividend rate. Bondholders usually have no voice in or control over management of the corporation. Stockholders can elect a board of directors that controls the corporation. Bonds have a maturity date when the bondholder must repay the face value of the bond. Stocks do not have a maturity date; the corporation does not usually repay the stockholder. Corporations do not have to issue bonds, whereas all corporations issue or offer to sell stock. Bondholders have a claim against the property and income of a corporation that must be met before claims of stockholders. Stockholders have a claim against the property and income of a corporation after all creditors' claims have been met.

CHAPTER 13

LEGAL ISSUES RELATED TO EMERGING VENTURES

True/False

Introduction

T   1. Entrepreneurs should be knowledgeable about certain legal concepts that affect their business venture.

F   2. Laws governing intellectual property rights include copyrights, trademarks, and leases.

Patents

T   3. A patent is an intellectual property right.

F   4. Design patents last for 20 years.

T   5. Patents eventually expire.

F   6. The patent process is not complex and does not require careful planning.

T   7. The two parts of a patent application are specification and claims.

T   8. The object of a patent is to provide the holder with a temporary monopoly on his or her innovation.

Copyrights

T   9. A copyright provides exclusive rights to creative individuals for the protection of their artistic productions.

T   10. Works created and copyrighted after January 1, 1978, are protected for the life of the author plus 50 years.

T   11. Anyone who violates an author's exclusive rights under a copyright is liable for infringement.

T   12. Because of the "fair use" doctrine, it is sometimes difficult to establish infringement.

F   13. Copyrights have to be registered with the Copyright Office.

The Dryden Press

Trademarks

T 14. A trademark is a distinctive name, mark, or symbol that is identified with a company's product.

T 15. An example of a trademark is a logo.

T 16. Once issued, the trademark is listed in the Principal Register of the Patent and Trademark Office.

F 17. The registration of a trademark is for 40 years.

F 18. Trademark registration and search is not costly.

T 19. If infringement can be proven in court, an award may be given to the trademark holder.

Bankruptcy

T 20. Every business at some point needs the services of an attorney.

T 21. The Bankruptcy Act was set up in order to provide assistance to both debtors and creditors.

F 22. Chapter 7, Chapter 9, and Chapter 11 are the most common forms of bankruptcy.

T 23. Straight bankruptcy is often called liquidation.

F 24. Chapter 13 bankruptcy involves a reorganization of the enterprise.

F 25. Business owners normally prefer Chapter 7 bankruptcy over any other form of bankruptcy.

Multiple Choice

Patents

D 26. Items that can qualify for patent protection include all of the following *except*
    a. machines.
    b. products.
    c. processes.
    d. ideas.

C   27. Design patent protection lasts for _____ years.
- a. 10
- b. 12
- c. 14
- d. 20

B   28. Patents that are not design patents have _____ years protection.
- a. 15
- b. 17
- c. 22
- d. 25

C   29. A patent gives the holder a temporary
- a. profit.
- b. oligopoly.
- c. monopoly.
- d. specification.

B   30. There are two parts to a patent application, claims and _____.
- a. percentage
- b. specification
- c. value
- d. integration

A   31. The two parts to a patent application are specification and _____.
- a. claims
- b. percentage
- c. value
- d. perception

A   32. The text of a patent application is known as the
- a. specification.
- b. particulars.
- c. concept.
- d. value.

D   33. The text of a patent application is known as the
- a. presentable data.
- b. claim.
- c. context.
- d. specification.

The Dryden Press

B 34. That part of a patent application which identifies the features that are protected is known as the
- a. particular.
- b. claim.
- c. identification.
- d. essence.

B 35. If an entrepreneur concludes that the innovation will withstand any legal challenge, a patent should be
- a. dropped.
- b. pursued.
- c. integrated.
- d. obfuscated.

B 36. To effectively pursue a patent, experts recommend that the entrepreneur
- a. handle all matters personally.
- b. prepare a realistic budget for infringement.
- c. fill out a preprinted form obtained from a patent office.
- d. sue as quickly as possible.

D 37. The specification section of a patent application should include all of the following *except*
- a. an introduction.
- b. examples and/or experimental results.
- c. a summary of invention.
- d. a budget for handling infringement.

C 38. In order to obtain a patent, an application should be filed with
- a. the Office of Government Publications.
- b. the Patent and Trademark Office of the Department of Commerce.
- c. Government Accounting Office.
- d. the United States Patent Office.

A 39. What percentage of issued patents are commercially valuable?
- a. a very small percentage
- b. around 20 percent
- c. 40 percent
- d. 75 percent

D 40. A person who loses an infringement battle in court may have to pay
- a. extra legal fees.
- b. damages of up to three times the actual amount.
- c. lost profits due to the infringement.
- d. all of the above.

A   41. An infringement budget deals with
   a. legal battles.
   b. government bribes.
   c. the outside molding of a building.
   d. advertising expenditures.

Copyrights

B   42. The owner of the copyright may do all of the following *except*
   a. reproduce the work.
   b. sell the rights for a period of 200 years.
   c. perform the work publicly.
   d. display the work publicly.

B   43. Anyone who violates an author's exclusive rights under a copyright is liable for:
   a. a prison term.
   b. infringement.
   c. a monetary payment equal to proven damages.
   d. two times annual sales.

C   44. For the author of creative material to obtain a copyright, the material must be in _____ form.
   a. nontangible
   b. technical
   c. tangible
   d. commercial

A   45. Because of the _____ doctrine, it is sometimes difficult to establish infringement.
   a. fair use
   b. acquisition
   c. freedom of information
   d. right to publish

A   46. The determination of fair use of copyrights is based on
   a. the effect of use on potential markets.
   b. the time period involved.
   c. specific legal guidelines set forth by OSHA.
   d. the GAD doctrine.

D   47. Under copyright law, which of the following is the right of the owner?
   a. the right to reproduce work
   b. the right to display work publicly
   c. the right to perform work publicly
   d. all of the above

A 48. Works created after January 1, 1978, have a copyright for the life of the author plus
   a. 50 years.
   b. 25 years.
   c. 14 years.
   d. 10 months.

D 49. Copyrights may be expressed in
   a. books.
   b. periodicals.
   c. motion pictures.
   d. all of the above.

C 50. The form of legal protection that computer programs fall under is
   a. patents.
   b. trademarks.
   c. copyrights.
   d. service marks.

A 51. Copyrights can be placed on all of the following *except*
   a. ideas.
   b. lectures.
   c. books.
   d. music.

B 52. Often companies put _____ into their catalogs to snag the unwary plagiarizer.
   a. hidden meanings
   b. trap lines
   c. misquoted prices
   d. hero sandwiches

C 53. None of the following can be copyrighted *except*
   a. Congressional debates.
   b. U.S. government publications.
   c. presidential bibliographies.
   d. Congressional history.

Trademarks

D 54. A trademark is a distinctive _____ that is identified with a company's product.
   a. name
   b. mark
   c. symbol
   d. all of the above

A   55. Which of the following is *not* a trademark?
   a. a sales price
   b. a logo
   c. a symbol
   d. a name

A   56. Which of the following are *not* trademarks?
   a. generic words
   b. symbols
   c. mottos
   d. names

D   57. Which of the following is a useful rule used to avoid pitfalls in selecting a trademark?
   a. Trust a lawyer's judgment.
   b. Copy a competitor's trademark.
   c. Avoid abbreviations and acronyms.
   d. Never choose a trademark without first conducting a trademark search.

C   58. The registration of a trademark has a lifetime of
   a. 20 years plus a 5-year renewable period.
   b. 25 years.
   c. 10 years plus a 10-year renewable period.
   d. the lifetime of the author.

D   59. Which of the following is a way in which a trademark may be invalidated?
   a. cancellation proceedings
   b. cleaning-out procedure
   c. generic meaning
   d. all of the above

A   60. The process of trademark registration is
   a. expensive.
   b. impossible.
   c. one that must be handled by a lawyer.
   d. inexpensive.

B   61. All of the following are ways of invalidating a trademark *except*
   a. cleaning-out proceedings.
   b. clearing-out proceedings.
   c. abandonment.
   d. generic meaning.

The Dryden Press

B   62. When seeking to invalidate a trademark, if a third party challenges the mark's distinctiveness within 5 years of issuance, this is known as
   a. abandonment.
   b. cancellation proceedings.
   c. cleaning-out procedure.
   d. generic meaning.

C   63. When trying to invalidate a trademark, if a party seeks to prove that the trademark has not been used within six years of registration, this is known as
   a. abandonment.
   b. cancellation proceedings.
   c. cleaning-out procedure.
   d. generic meaning.

A   64. When a party seeks to invalidate a trademark by showing that it has not been used for two consecutive years, the party is making use of a legal approach known as
   a. abandonment.
   b. cancellation proceedings.
   c. cleaning-out procedure.
   d. generic meaning.

D   65. When a trademark becomes the name of a general group of products or services, the trademark protection may be lost because of
   a. abandonment.
   b. cancellation proceedings.
   c. cleaning-out procedure.
   d. generic meaning.

B   66. The Patent and Trademark Office will accept
   a. signatures.
   b. initials.
   c. portraits.
   d. flag symbols.

Bankruptcy

C   67. Which of the following is an indicator that an entrepreneur's business is failing?
   a. other firms selling advanced products
   b. retailer overstocked
   c. liquidation
   d. R&D budget proportionally less than competitions'.

D 68. Which is *not* one of the major sections of the bankruptcy act?
   a. straight bankruptcy
   b. reorganization
   c. adjustments of debts
   d. liquidation

D 69. Which of the following is a suggestion to minimize legal costs?
   a. visit the lawyer during normal hours
   b. have the lawyer design forms
   c. handle some matters personally
   d. all of the above

C 70. Which of the following falls under Chapter 7 bankruptcy?
   a. The debtor surrenders most property to a court trustee.
   b. The debtor fails to file income taxes.
   c. The debtor is relieved of obligations.
   d. The debtor is arrested.

D 71. A typical symptom of impending bankruptcy is when
   a. new competition enters the market.
   b. other firms seem to be selling products that are a generation ahead.
   c. retailers always seem to be overstocked.
   d. all the above are true.

A 72. There are specific financial _____ that can be of assistance in detecting impending bankruptcy.
   a. ratios
   b. payrolls
   c. cash flows
   d. overflows

B 73. In 1986 there were _____ federal bankruptcy cases.
   a. 50,000
   b. 70,000
   c. 100,000
   d. 200,000

D 74. When considering bankruptcy, entrepreneurs normally prefer
   a. Chapter 5.
   b. Chapter 7.
   c. Chapter 11.
   d. Chapter 13.

Essays

75. Define a patent, and describe its limitations.

A patent is a right, granted by the government, of an inventor to protect an idea against infringement. Patents can cover products, machines, and improvements on already patented things. A patent allows the holder to have a temporary monopoly on his or her new creation. Design patents last for 14 years; all others last 17 years. But patents are expensive and time consuming to secure. Also, if a patent is infringed upon, a court battle decides its validity. A patent can be invalidated for three reasons: A patent holder may wait too long before asserting his or her rights, a patent may be misused, or a patent may be proven not to meet patentability requirements.

76. What does a copyright protect, and what are the guidelines for copyright protection?

A copyright protects a person's literary and artistic creations. Since 1978, a copyright gives protection for the life of the creator plus 50 years. A copyright allows the holder to reproduce the work, prepare copies, perform the work, and display the work. There are certain important guidelines for copyright protection. It isn't necessary to register copyrights unless you need to sue someone. Needless registration only adds unnecessary time and effort. When buying material for internal use, it would be reasonable to duplicate certain parts on occasion. But duplicating entire pieces on a regular basis would clearly violate a copyright holder's rights. Care should be taken in using materials such as catalogs. Materials that require a lot of expense to compile many times contain fictitious items to trap people who merely copy material. It may be useful to copyright advertisements that may be of use to competitors. Government documents cannot be copyrighted, but their format can. Therefore, you can't simply duplicate a page of text. And finally, use common sense in using copyrighted material. It is illegal to rephrase another person's material and call it your own.

77. What are the uses of trademarks, and how can they be invalidated?

A trademark is a distinctive symbol of a company. A trademark can be used to distinguish goods, services, quality, and materials used. A trademark must be in some way unique to the object. A trademark can be invalidated in any of four ways. A third party may challenge a trademark's distinctiveness within five years. A trademark owner may fail to file an affidavit stating a trademark's use or lack of use within six years of registration. An owner may fail to use a trademark for two consecutive years without justification. And finally, a trademark may become synonymous with the product itself.

78. What are the rules for avoiding pitfalls in selecting trademarks?

Trademark registration and research is expensive. Trademark infringement is even more expensive. There are five basic rules to avoid difficulties with trademarks. A corporate name or mark should never be selected without a trademark search. If your attorney recommends against a trademark for legal reasons, trust his/her judgment. Try to find a unique name or mark. Use a distinctive logotype when using a descriptive name for a product. When an abbreviation or acronym must be used, use a distinctive logotype.

79. *Name the three forms of bankruptcy, and describe their functions.*

Bankruptcy was designed for three major reasons. One is to guarantee that assets will be fairly divided among creditors. The second is to protect debtors from losing too many of their assets. And debtors are protected from unreasonable demands of creditors. There are three major sections of bankruptcy for small business. Chapter 7 is straight bankruptcy, or liquidation. In Chapter 7, the debtor forfeits all assets of a business, which a court-appointed trustee then sells. All receipts are then divided among the creditors. Chapter 7 allows the debtor to be relieved of all obligations. Chapter 11 is known as reorganization. In this proceeding, the debtor pays a portion of the debt, and the remainder is relinquished. The debtor is then allowed to continue his or her venture.

Chapter 13 allows the debtor to repay the debt over a longer period of time. Chapter 13 avoids declaration of bankruptcy and allows payment in installments and protection by the court.

CHAPTER 14

SOURCES OF CAPITAL FOR ENTREPRENEURS

True/False

Debt Financing

T 1. Use of debt to finance a new venture involves a payback of funds plus an interest fee for the use of the money.

T 2. The most common sources of debt financing are commercial banks.

T 3. Sources of debt financing include trade credit, accounts receivable, factoring, and finance companies.

Equity Financing

F 4. Equity financing is money invested in the venture with legal obligations to repay the principal amount of interest or interest rate on it.

F 5. Public offerings is a term used to refer to corporations taking public donations to raise capital.

F 6. Because the advantages of going public outweigh the disadvantages, it is in a corporation's best interest to go public.

T 7. History and nature of the company, capital structure, and description of any material contracts are just a few examples of the specific detailed information that must be presented about a firm that is going public.

T 8. Private placement is a method of raising capital through the private placement of securities.

F 9. Regulation D strengthened the regulations for reports and statements required for selling stock to private parties, friends, employees, customers, relatives, and local professionals.

T 10. Sophisticated investors are wealthy individuals who invest more or less regularly in new and/or early- and late-stage ventures.

The Venture Capital Market

T   11.   Venture capitalists are a valuable source of equity funding for new ventures.

F   12.   The venture capital pool is rapidly declining due to overfunding.

F   13.   Venture capitalists are quick to invest.

F   14.   Venture capitalists need little information before they make an investment.

T   15.   The business plan is a critical element in the new-venture proposal.

F   16.   There is no way for the venture capitalist to evaluate the new venture.

T   17.   To find the right venture capitalist, it is important for the entrepreneur to know what working with his or her venture will be like.

F   18.   Venture capital firms want to own control of the firms in which they invest.

F   19.   Venture capitalists are usually satisfied with a reasonable return on investments.

T   20.   Venture capitalists are slow to invest.

F   21.   Venture capitalists need only basic summary information before they make a decision.

T   22.   One of the most frequently used criterion in evaluating new ventures is the ability of the entrepreneur to sustain intense effort.

Informal Risk Capital

F   23.   There is a small number of informal risk capitalists in the market today.

T   24.   Informal risk capitalists are those who have already made their money and now seek to help new ventures.

T   25.   Informal risk capitalists are often referred to as "business angels."

Multiple Choice

Introduction

C   26. At start-up time, the most desired form of financing typically is
   a. public offering.
   b. private placement.
   c. venture capital.
   d. banks.

A   27. Five years after start-up, the most preferred source of financing typically is
   a. public offering.
   b. private placement.
   c. venture capital.
   d. banks.

Debt Financing

A   28. Many new ventures find that debt financing is
   a. necessary.
   b. a waste of time.
   c. not an important consideration.
   d. their major source of funds.

B   29. Approximately how many commercial banks are there in this country?
   a. 40,000
   b. 11,000
   c. 17,500
   d. 20,500

C   30. Which of the following is not a question commonly asked by banks of entrepreneurs?
   a. What do you plan to do with the money?
   b. How much do you need?
   c. What interest rate did you have in mind?
   d. How will you repay the loan?

D   31. When starting a business, which of the following sources of financing are least likely to be used?
   a. trade credit
   b. factoring
   c. leasing companies
   d. insurance companies

The Dryden Press

A 32. When starting a business, which of the following sources of financing is most likely to be used?
  a. trade credit
  b. factoring
  c. leasing companies
  d. insurance companies

B 33. Which of the following would be most commonly used for short-term financing?
  a. insurance companies
  b. trade credit
  c. finance companies
  d. leasing companies

C 34. Which of the following would be most commonly used for medium-term financing?
  a. insurance companies
  b. trade credit
  c. finance companies
  d. leasing companies

A 35. Which of the following would be most commonly used for long-term financing?
  a. insurance companies
  b. trade credit
  c. finance companies
  d. leasing companies

D 36. When accounts receivable are bought from a company for capital funding, it is called
  a. trade credit.
  b. financing.
  c. leasing.
  d. factoring.

A 37. Which of the following is *not* a type of debt financing?
  a. private placement
  b. trade credit
  c. finance companies
  d. accounts receivables

A 38. A disadvantage of debt financing is
  a. regular interest payments.
  b. possible cash-flow enhancement.
  c. inhibition of growth and development due to equity investments.
  d. relinquishment of ownership.

The Dryden Press

B   39. Short-term debt is
- a. paid back in six months.
- b. paid back in one year.
- c. paid back after sales.
- d. all of the above.

B   40. Which of the following is a type of equity financing?
- a. convertible debentures
- b. common stock
- c. loan with warrants
- d. loan without warrants

C   41. The most common source of debt financing is
- a. trade credit.
- b. factoring.
- c. commercial banks.
- d. finance companies.

B   42. Advantages of debt financing include all of the following *except*:
- a. low interest rates can justify the opportunity cost.
- b. regular interest payments.
- c. allows potential greater return on equity.
- d. no relinquishment of ownership.

D   43. Long-term debt is used for
- a. start-up capital.
- b. funding for purchase of property or equipment.
- c. payment of payroll.
- d. both a and b.

D   44. When securing a bank loan, an entrepreneur should be prepared to answer which of the following questions?
- a. When do you need it?
- b. How do you need it?
- c. What do you need it for?
- d. All of the above questions are correct.

Equity Financing

B   45. SEC stands for the
- a. Stock Exchange Corporation.
- b. Security and Exchange Commission.
- c. Standard Equity Commission.
- d. Source of Equity Company.

D 46. When going public with public offerings, an advantage might be
- a. size of the company's capital amount.
- b. the company's liquidity.
- c. the company's value.
- d. all of the above.

C. 47. SBIC stands for the
- a. Small Business in Capital.
- b. Securities Bonds Investment Co.
- c. Small Business Investment Co.
- d. Sources Business Investment Co.

C 48. Equity capital is
- a. paid back within one year.
- b. paid back after five years.
- c. not a loan but a form of stock.
- d. all of the above.

D 49. Evaluation of new-venture proposals includes what processes?
- a. oral presentation
- b. initial screening
- c. evaluation of the business plan
- d. all of the above

A 50. One of the advantages of public offerings is
- a. liquidity.
- b. disclosure.
- c. requirements.
- d. cost.
- e. all of the above.

C 51. Which of these forms are *not* required by SEC?
- a. proxy statements
- b. form 8-K
- c. form 4-V
- d. form 10-Q

D 52. The SEC regulation D exemptions include all of the following *except*:
- a. placements of up to $5 million.
- b. placements of less than $500,000.
- c. placements in excess of $5 million.
- d. placements in excess of $10 million.

C 53. The main objective of regulation D is to
   a. increase the investment in private placement.
   b. regulate new small business investment.
   c. make it easier and less expensive for small ventures to sell stock.
   d. reduce debt financing by small enterprises.

D 54. Which of the following is *not* one of the most common questions typically required to be answered by entrepreneurs?
   a. What do you plan to do with the money?
   b. How much money do you need?
   c. When do you need the money?
   d. What exact date will you repay the money?

A 55. Equity capital is often raised through:
   a. public stock offerings.
   b. option sales.
   c. donations.
   d. preferred issues.

D 56. When going public some specific detailed information that must be presented includes
   a. the history and nature of the company.
   b. the capital structure of the company.
   c. a description of any material contracts of the company.
   d. all of the above.

A 57. Regulation D defines three separate exemptions which are based on the amount of money being raised. Which is not a rule that accompanies these exemptions?
   a. rule 503
   b. rule 504
   c. rule 505
   d. rule 506

B 58. Regulation D replaces the term "sophisticated investor" with the term "accredited purchaser." Included in this second category is/are
   a. anyone buying at least $100,000 of the offered security.
   b. institutional investors.
   c. all tax-exempt organizations with at least $100,000 in assets.
   d. general partners of any company.

The Dryden Press

The Venture Capital Market

D   59. Venture capitalists are experienced professionals who provide a full range of services for new ventures including
   a. capital for start-up.
   b. market research and strategy for marketing departments.
   c. management consulting.
   d. all of the above.

C   60. Which of the following statements is *not* true of the recent developments in the venture capital market?
   a. In 1995 the total pool of venture capital was $3.8 billion.
   b. By 1992 the total pool had decreased to $2.5 billion.
   c. The venture capital market has been steadily increasing from 1985 to 1996.
   d. The venture capital industry has a slump that began in 1989.

A   61. There are four major trends in the venture capital field today. They include all of the following *except*
   a. funds are less specialized and more homogenous.
   b. emerging feeder funds.
   c. a decrease in smaller start-up investment.
   d. a new legal environment.

C   62. Which of the following statements is *not* true about venture capitalists?
   a. They want the entrepreneur and the management to run the company.
   b. They expect high return on investments.
   c. They are more interested in trying to manage the firm themselves than in ideas or products.
   d. They take a long time to raise venture capital.

D   63. Criteria that venture capitalists use in evaluating new venture proposals include:
   a. the entrepreneur's personality.
   b. the entrepreneur's experience.
   c. the characteristics of the product or service.
   d. all of the above.
   e. none of the above.

D   64. Venture proposals are often rejected due to significant deficiencies in
   a. the size of the proposal.
   b. financial projection.
   c. available funds.
   d. both a and b.

B 65. Which is *not* a stage of the evaluation process?
    a. initial screening
    b. evaluation of the business plan
    c. group discussion
    d. management integration

A 66. Which is an important question for the entrepreneur to ask when evaluating the venture capitalist?
    a. Is the person someone with whom the entrepreneur can work?
    b. Is the person a close relative?
    c. Is the person wealthy?
    d. Is the person a college graduate?

C 67. The entrepreneur should ask the venture capitalist _____ questions.
    a. at most ten
    b. exactly twenty
    c. an unlimited number of
    d. no

A 68. Which is one of the seven most important questions for entrepreneurs regarding venture capitalists?
    a. What is it like to work with this firm?
    b. Is he or she a good communicator?
    c. Is he or she wealthy?
    d. Is he or she good at financial computation?

B 69. Criteria for evaluating new-venture proposals include all of the following *except*
    a. the entrepreneur's personality.
    b. the entrepreneur's age.
    c. the entrepreneur's experience.
    d. financial considerations.

Informal Risk Capital

D 70. Which of the following is a true statement about raising capital?
    a. All capital is raised through formal sources.
    b. All capital is raised through debt sources.
    c. Capital is easy to get.
    d. It often takes a great deal of time.

C 71. How many people in America have a net worth in excess of $1 million?
  a. 100,000
  b. 200,000
  c. 500,000
  d. 1,000,000

C 72. If 40 percent of the individuals with a net worth in excess of $1 million were interested in venture financing, how many millionaires would be available?
  a. 120,000
  b. 150,000
  c. 200,000
  d. 400,000

B 73. An informal risk capitalist is referred to as:
  a. your neighbor.
  b. a business angel.
  c. a retiree.
  d. none of the above.

B 74. Informal investors find projects through
  a. newspapers.
  b. a network of friends.
  c. commercials.
  d. all of the above.

C 75. What percentage of "angel capital" is devoted to seed a start-up venture versus growth financing?
  a. 60 percent
  b. 25 percent
  c. 5 percent
  d. 100 percent

Essays

76. *What are the major types and uses of debt financing?*
  Commercial bank loans are the most common source of debt. Banks typically loan for short to intermediate terms and require security or collateral for the loan. Banks generally prefer to loan to already existing firms rather than new start-up firms. Trade credit is given by the firm's suppliers and seen in the form of accounts payable. It is usually granted easily and is very short term. Accounts receivable financing uses the firm's receivables as either collateral or as a product for sale. Factoring is short term and offered mainly to existing firms. Finance companies make short- to intermediate-term asset guaranteed loans. They deal mainly with existing firms and often make loans that a

bank would not. They also charge a hefty premium for this by having interest rates that are at least 2 percent over bank rates.

77. *How does a public offering differ from a private placement?*
A public offering involves entering the stock exchange. Once the stock is publicly offered, anyone can buy shares and, in turn, ownership. Public offerings are very expensive and highly regulated. These disadvantages are offset by the large amounts of capital and liquidity the offerings can provide. A private placement is used more often by small ventures. It allows the sale of the stock to private, personally selected individuals. The Securities and Exchange Commission has enacted special rules to make private placement easier and less expensive for small businesses. Both of these equity financing plans differ from debt financing. They require a relinquishment of ownership but don't demand a fixed payback of the invested principal.

78. *As the venture capital market has experienced rapid growth, several market trends have emerged. What are the major trends of today?*
One trend is specialized funds. As more firms are founded, their interests and focus become more specialized. Another market trend concerns the emergence of feeder funds. These are funds that are usually focused on seed-stage and start-ups. As these businesses grow, their business is fed back to the large firms. There are also fewer start-up investments. Those partners with start-up knowledge are spending their time trying to fix the numerous troubled ventures they already have. This doesn't allow them to devote the time needed in start-ups. The final trend concerns legal issues. Competition and our "lawsuit" culture have forced highly legalized agreements.

79. *Should entrepreneurs accept proposals from the first venture capitalist that offers?*
Entrepreneurs must evaluate their capitalist just as their capitalist evaluates them. Not every capitalist is right for every entrepreneur, even if he or she does have the money needed. The entrepreneur must look at the capitalist's skills and knowledge and decide how well they can work together, while keeping in mind that venture capital is hard to come by.

80. *Are formal firms the only source of venture capital?*
There are many individuals willing to invest where venture capitalists will not. These are usually wealthy people looking for investments and are referred to as "business angels." These people are generally well off. They don't need the high, immediate rate of return required by the venture capital firms. They often seek social rather than purely financial returns on their investments.

The Dryden Press

CHAPTER 15

STRATEGIC PLANNING FOR EMERGING VENTURES

True/False

The Nature of Planning in Emerging Firms

T 1. The actual need for systematic planning will vary with the nature, size, and structure of the business.

F 2. Formal planning can be divided into strategic and nonstrategic.

T 3. A "SWOT" analysis refers to analyzing the strengths, weaknesses, opportunities, and threats.

T 4. The "best" strategic plan will be influenced by the abilities of the entrepreneur, the complexity of the venture, and the nature of the industry.

Key Dimensions Influencing a Firm's Strategic Planning Activities

T 5. Demand on a strategic manager's time is a key factor in shaping the strategic management activities of growing companies.

T 6. To a large degree, venture planning is an extension of the entrepreneurial ego.

T 7. An advisory board can enhance the functioning of the entrepreneurial ego.

F 8. Participation by subordinates in a strategic plan is never appropriate.

Lack of Strategic Planning

T 9. Most entrepreneurs are unfamiliar with many planning information sources.

T 10. Strategic planning is not an easy task for new ventures.

T 11. Research has shown a distinct lack of planning on the part of new ventures.

F 12. Small firm owner/managers are usually very open and trusting about their businesses and the decisions that affect them.

F   13. Lack of expertise has never been considered a reason for the lack of strategic planning in new ventures.

The Value of Strategic Planning

T   14. Many studies during the past 20 years imply, if they do not directly state, that planning influences a venture's survival.

T   15. Improved performance is often the result of better planning.

T   16. Both high- and low-performing firms have many similarities and differences in their long-range planning efforts.

T   17. Misunderstanding the industry attractiveness can be a fatal flaw in strategic planning.

Implementing a Strategic Plan

T   18. An evaluation of internal resources is a step in beginning the opportunity management approach.

F   19. The strategic plan is popular because it is easy to understand.

T   20. Each important step must be completed before moving to the next in the milestone planning approach.

T   21. A multistaged contingency considers the individual, the venture, and the environment.

The Nature of Operational Planning

F   22. Operational planning is also referred to as long-range planning.

T   23. The operational plan is an outgrowth or extension of the strategic planning process.

T   24. Budgets are planning devices used to establish future plans in financial terms.

F   25. Procedures are the fundamental guides for the venture as a whole.

Multiple Choice

The Nature of Planning in Emerging Firms

C 26. Formal planning is usually divided into which two major types?
  a. strategic and future
  b. organizing and implementing
  c. strategic and operational
  d. organizing and future

B 27. Planning is the process of transforming entrepreneurial vision and ideas into action. This process involves _____ basic steps.
  a. four
  b. three
  c. five
  d. two

B 28. Emerging ventures that are rapidly expanding with constantly increasing personnel size and market operations will need
  a. less formal planning because of constant changes.
  b. to formalize planning because there is a great deal of complexity.
  c. to establish a pattern of subordinate participation.
  d. to evaluate company strengths and weaknesses.

C 29. Venture planning is an extension of the
  a. rapid changes that occur.
  b. personal involvement needed.
  c. entrepreneurial ego.
  d. entrepreneur's vision.

D 30. In many new small ventures planning is too often
  a. well accomplished.
  b. overdone.
  c. overused.
  d. lacking.

D 31. What are the reasons for an entrepreneur to switch his/her planning from informal to formal systematic style?
  a. the degree of uncertainty
  b. the amount and type of experience
  c. the strength of the competition
  d. all of the above

The Dryden Press

A   32.   A "SWOT" analysis refers to
  a. strength, weaknesses, opportunities, threats
  b. small, weak, ordinary, tact
  c. sound warnings of takeovers
  d. none of the above

Key Dimensions Influencing a Firm's Strategic Planning Activities

D   33.   Which of the following factors would *not* be considered a key dimension that shapes the strategic management activities of a growing firm?
  a. speed of decision making
  b. problems of internal politics
  c. environmental uncertainty
  d. lack of knowledge

D   34.   The key dimensions influencing a firm's strategic planning activities include which of the following factors?
  a. the entrepreneur's vision
  b. demand on strategic manager's time
  c. environmental uncertainty
  d. all of the above

A   35.   The basic aspect of the entrepreneur's vision is
  a. establishment of a pattern of subordinate participation in the development of the strategic plan.
  b. commitment to private planning sessions.
  c. accountability to making a profit.
  d. all of the above.

C   36.   Which of the following aspects depicts a reason for entrepreneurs being suspicious of planning?
  a. intimidation of employees
  b. frustration with daily activities
  c. fear of loss of control
  d. belief that planning is useless

B   37.   Which is *not* a primary objective of corporate conscience?
  a. to make the owner accountable, albeit on a voluntary basis
  b. to improve the benefit package
  c. to increase the owner's sensitivity to larger issues.
  d. a and c

Lack of Strategic Planning

C   38. A reason for lack of strategic planning has been found to be
      a. lack of preference.
      b. time sharing.
      c. lack of expertise.
      d. lack of dominance.

D   39. The reason many small business managers lack expertise is that they are
      a. optimists.
      b. specialists.
      c. subordinates.
      d. generalists.

A   40. Both high-performing and low-performing small ventures have problems with
      a. long-range planning.
      b. a poor planning climate.
      c. unfavorable economic conditions.
      d. both a and c.

A   41. Which is not perceived as a difficulty in long-range planning?
      a. arranging vacation time
      b. inadequately defined objectives
      c. poor planning climate
      d. inexperienced managers

D   42. New ventures are important to the economy in terms of
      a. innovation.
      b. employment.
      c. sales.
      d. all of the above.

C   43. Which of the following is *not* a reason for the lack of planning in new ventures?
      a. time scarcity
      b. lack of trust
      c. lack of dominance
      d. lack of knowledge

B   44. A reason new venture managers lack knowledge in the strategic planning process is because
   a. they refuse to learn new things.
   b. they have minimal exposure to the planning process.
   c. they attempt to implement too quickly.
   d. they are too confident of the planning components.

C   45. Unfavorable economic situations represent what percent of the difficulty involved in long-range firms?
   a. 18
   b. 57
   c. 31
   d. 25

The Value of Strategic Planning

B   46. Researchers have been able to establish a _____ level planning classification.
   a. four
   b. five
   c. six
   d. seven

A   47. Both high-performing and low-performing firms are able to benefit from long-range planning in the area of
   a. cost savings.
   b. better resource allocation.
   c. increased sales.
   d. both a and c.

A   48. Knowledge of next year's company and industry sales but no knowledge of company profit or profit implementation plans is which planning classification?
   a. strategy level 2
   b. strategy level 4
   c. strategy level 5
   d. strategy level 1

D   49. When it comes to strategic planning, most small firms
   a. do quite well.
   b. survive and prosper.
   c. recognize cost savings, accurate forecasting, and increased sales.
   d. do not engage in true strategic planning at all.

D   50. High-performing firms report
   a. better resource allocation.
   b. improved competitive position.
   c. increased sales.
   d. all of the above.

B   51. Knowledge of only next year's sales but no knowledge of upcoming industry sales, company profit, or profit implementation plans is which of the following planning classifications?
   a. strategy level 4
   b. strategy level 1
   c. strategy level 0
   d. strategy level 3

A   52. Knowledge of next year's company and industry sales, anticipated company profits, and profit implementation plans is which of the following planning classifications?
   a. strategy level 4
   b. strategy level 1
   c. strategy level 0
   d. strategy level 2

D   53. Bracker and Pearson characterized the planning levels of small firms into categories that include
   a. structured strategic plans.
   b. intuitive plans.
   c. structured operational plans.
   d. all of the above.

A   54. When there is no measurable structured planning in a firm, the term used to categorize or describe such a level of planning would be:
   a. unstructured plans (UP).
   b. intuitive plans (IP).
   c. duration plans (DP).
   d. focused plan (FP).

D   55. Which of the following would be considered fatal mistakes in strategic planning, according to researcher Michael E. Porter?
   a. no real competitive advantage
   b. pursuing a solid competitive position
   c. compromising strategy for growth
   d. a and c only

The Dryden Press

Implementing a Strategic Plan

A   56. Three basic approaches to implementing a strategic plan are
   a. the strategic model, opportunity management, and milestone planning approaches.
   b. the opportunity management, milestone planning, and standard operation approaches.
   c. the management succession, strategic model, and milestone management approaches.
   d. none of the above.

D   57. The opportunity management approach is
   a. technical in nature.
   b. popular because it is easy to understand.
   c. adjustable to meet changing conditions.
   d. both b and c.

C   58. The milestone planning approach is based on
   a. flexibility.
   b. small undertakings rather than large ones.
   c. use of incremental goal attainment.
   d. normative strategic planning.

B   59. The basic approaches used by new ventures to implement a strategic plan include all of the following *except*
   a. opportunity management approach.
   b. comprehensive planning focus.
   c. milestone planning.
   d. strategic model approach.

C   60. The first step in normative strategic planning is to
   a. seek professional help where needed.
   b. gain an understanding of the venture.
   c. commit time and money to formulating a strategic plan.
   d. review the findings of situation analysis.

B   61. The decision to plan is always based on
   a. knowledge.
   b. anticipated positive results.
   c. potential opportunities.
   d. personal objectives.

A 62. The control and feedback loop is used to
a. ensure that everything is done according to plan.
b. compare terms of relative effectiveness.
c. influence company objectives.
d. match the company's competency and resources.

D 63. What happens in the strategic profile?
a. Action programs are designed.
b. Resources are allocated.
c. Expected results are identified.
d. all of the above

B 64. Which is *not* an advantage to the milestone planning approach?
a. the use of logical and practical milestones
b. the ability to determine strengths and weaknesses
c. the methodology for replanning
d. the avoidance of costly mistakes

D 65. The milestone planning approach is popular with which new ventures?
a. those that are technical in nature
b. those that have multiple phases
c. those that involve large sums of money
d. all of the above

B 66. Which of the following is *not* an important step in the control and feedback loop?
a. begin the loop again
b. figure out another planning area
c. take steps to correct a problem
d. none of the above

B 67. The opportunity management approach is popular as a strategic implementation approach because
a. it has multiple phases.
b. it is easy to understand and easy to adjust.
c. it saves money.
d. it uses practical milestones.

C 68. The multistaged contingency approach includes which of the following elements?
a. the individual, environment, and venture
b. stages of the venture
c. the entrepreneur's career stage
d. all of the above

The Dryden Press

The Nature of Operational Planning

D 69. Which of the following is *not* one of the tools applied in the functional areas?
- a. budgets
- b. policies
- c. procedures
- d. marketing

B 70. Procedures are usually policies that have been
- a. revised and updated.
- b. standardized as a continuing method.
- c. evaluated for effectiveness.
- d. none of the above

C 71. Budgets are planning devices used to
- a. acquire operating loans.
- b. guide operation on a day-to-day basis.
- c. establish future plans in financial terms.
- d. follow specific credit policies.

B 72. Procedures are often referred to as
- a. outdated.
- b. standard operating procedures.
- c. policies for specific functional problems.
- d. established policies.

D 73. Operational planning is also referred to as
- a. short-range planning.
- b. functional planning.
- c. long-range planning.
- d. both a and b.

B 74. Established policies allow the entrepreneur the freedom to
- a. expand his or her market.
- b. work more on strategy.
- c. establish future plans.
- d. improve competitive position.

A 75. The operational plan is an outgrowth or extension of the
- a. strategic planning process.
- b. milestone planning process.
- c. opportunity planning process.
- d. none of the above.

Essays

76. Define strategic planning, and describe the five basic steps that must be followed in establishing a strategic plan.

Strategic planning is the primary step in determining the future direction of a business. It is a formal, systematic plan to guide a firm through the uncertainty of the environment as well as newer and stronger competition.

The five basic steps to be followed in establishing a strategic plan are: (1) understand the venture; (2) establish long-range and short-range objectives; (3) outline alternative courses of action; (4) implement a plan of action; (5) analyze the results and take follow-up action.

77. Identify the key dimensions influencing a firm's strategic planning activities.

There are five factors that shape the strategic management activities of growing companies. These factors are: demand on strategic manager's time; speed of decision making; problems of internal politics; environmental uncertainty; the entrepreneur's vision.

78. Research has shown that there is a distinct lack of strategic planning in new ventures. Relate some of the reasons for this lack of planning.

There are five reasons for the lack of strategic planning. The first reason is time scarcity on the part of a manager due to the time spent on day-to-day operations. The second reason is lack of knowledge about the process of planning by small business managers. Third, small business managers perceive a lack of expertise or skill necessary to perform planning activities. Fourth, there is a lack of trust and openness by small business owners to outside consultants who may be of assistance in planning. Finally, the perception of high cost associated with planning is a reason that planning may be avoided.

79. Describe the value of strategic planning as evidenced by research studies.

All of the current research indicates that firms that engage in strategic planning are more effective than those which do not. In one study of 357 Texas ventures, there was evidence of less failure in the firms that did planning over a two-year period (Sexton and Van Auken, 1985). Another study of 9,000 firms established the lack of planning as a major cause of failure (Dun & Bradstreet, 1987). Finally, the Bracker & Pearson study in 1988 demonstrated that small firms using structured strategic planning outperformed all other firms in the study.

80. Identify the approaches that can be used to implement a strategic plan.

There are four approaches described in Chapter 15 that can be used to implement a strategic plan. These approaches are: the opportunity management approach; milestone planning approach; the strategic model approach; and the multistaged contingency approach.

CHAPTER 16

MANAGING ENTREPRENEURIAL GROWTH

True/False

Stages of Development

F   1.   Increased competition and consumer indifference to the entrepreneur's goods or services are two characteristics of the innovation stage.

T   2.   Firms working on new product/service development in order to complement current offerings are characteristic of the decline stage.

F   3.   Growth is the first stage of development in the life cycle of a venture.

Understanding the Entrepreneurial Company

F   4.   Start-up activities consist of creativity and assessment of the venture.

T   5.   Start-up activities constitute the second stage of a typical new venture life cycle.

T   6.   The general philosophy and mission of a venture are often determined during the first life-cycle stage.

T   7.   The growth stage often requires major changes in entrepreneurial strategy.

F   8.   Steve Jobs was forced out of Apple during the company's "stabilization of business" phase.

T   9.   An environment that allows for failure is essential for a firm to survive the growth stage.

T   10.   If a venture is too rigidly tied to plans or strategies, it will not be responsive to new technologies, customer changes, or environmental shifts.

T   11.   An increase in the perception of opportunity can be accomplished through careful job design.

F   12.   The second step in building an adaptive firm is to instill the desire for innovation.

The Dryden Press

T 13. The transition from an entrepreneurial style to a managerial approach occurs during the growth stage.

T 14. One important step in building an adaptive firm is to expand the entrepreneur's vision.

Understanding the Growth Stage

T 15. Control is one of the key factors during the growth stage.

F 16. Tolerance of failure is not one of the key factors during the growth stage.

T 17. Effective delegation is important in making the transition from owner dominance to a diversity of operations during the growth stage.

T 18. When a venture experiences surges in growth, rigid bureaucratic designs are in conflict with flexible organic designs.

T 19. Rapidly growing firms strive to simultaneously control costs, enhance product quality, and improve product offerings.

T 20. The focus and style of decision making is distinctive from the earlier to the later stages that a venture goes through.

F 21. The use of external resources through networking is not a successful method for decision making during the growth stage of a venture.

T 22. The growth stage often requires managing paradox and contradiction.

F 23. Most venture owners confront a "growth wall" that is relatively easy to overcome.

T 24. Breaking through the growth wall may require the use of an advisory board.

T 25. Assignment of specific duties is part of effective delegation.

Multiple Choice

Introduction

D   26.   The survival and growth of a new venture require that the entrepreneur possess
- a. stabilization skills.
- b. survival abilities.
- c. developmental changes.
- d. tactical abilities.

B   27.   The requirements listed above depend in part on
- a. the venture's future development.
- b. the venture's current development.
- c. both a and b.
- d. neither a nor b.

Stages of Development

D   28.   Which of the following life-cycle stages of a new venture occurs first?
- a. growth of the venture
- b. innovation or decline
- c. stabilization of business
- d. new-venture development

B   29.   Which of the following life-cycle stages of a new venture occurs last?
- a. growth of the venture
- b. innovation or decline
- c. stabilization of business
- d. new-venture development

A   30.   Steve Jobs was forced out of Apple Computer during which one of these stages?
- a. growth of the venture
- b. innovation or decline
- c. stabilization of business
- d. new-venture development

C   31.   Which one of these phases occurs directly after new-venture development?
- a. stabilization of business
- b. innovation or decline
- c. start-up activities
- d. growth

B 32. Creativity, assessment of the venture, and formulation of the mission and direction of the enterprise are all important during which one of these stages of development?
   a. growth
   b. new-venture development
   c. decline
   d. stabilization of business

A 33. Reformulation of strategy is a critical phase during which one of these stages of development?
   a. growth
   b. new-venture development
   c. decline
   d. stabilization of business

D 34. Consumer indifference and the emergence of "me too" products often occur during which one of these stages of development?
   a. growth
   b. new-venture development
   c. decline
   d. stabilization of business

C 35. Many firms will work on new product/service development in order to prevent which one of these stages from occurring?
   a. growth
   b. new-venture development
   c. decline
   d. stabilization of business

D 36. The need for a formal business plan is often of primary importance during the _____ stage of development.
   a. new-venture development
   b. stabilization of business
   c. growth
   d. start-up activities

B 37. The development of an effective entrepreneurial team often occurs during which one of these stages of development?
   a. growth
   b. start-up activities
   c. new-venture development
   d. stabilization of business

A   38. Which of the following is the *most* true statement about the venture life cycle?
          a. Firms that fail to innovate will die.
          b. Not all of the stages of a venture life cycle are important.
          c. The growth stage is the most talked about stage.
          d. One strategy should be used for all of the stages.

D   39. Which of the following is *not* one of the five stages of venture growth?
          a. new-venture development
          b. start-up activities
          c. growth
          d. building adaptability

B   40. Which of the following is the third stage of a venture life cycle?
          a. stabilization
          b. growth
          c. new-venture development
          d. none of the above

D   41. Alfred Chandler's stages of development include all but which one of the following?
          a. initial expansion and accumulation of resources
          b. expansion into new markets to ensure the continued use of resources
          c. development of new structures to ensure mobilization of resources
          d. expiration of resources in the market

C   42. Which of the following statements is *most* true about the growth of a venture's life cycle?
          a. It is the first stage of development.
          b. The foundation work for creating a formal business plan is developed.
          c. It often requires changes in entrepreneurial strategy.
          d. Competition increases, consumer indifference grows, look-alikes saturate the market.

D   43. Carrying out marketing activities is part of which stage of development?
          a. new-venture development
          b. growth
          c. rationalization
          d. start-up activities

C   44. The stages of development in order are
        a. new-venture development, start-up activities, growth, innovation or decline.
        b. start-up activities, new-venture development, growth, stabilization of the business, innovation or decline.
        c. new-venture development, start-up activities, growth, stabilization of the business, innovation or decline.
        d. none of the above.

A   45. During the start-up stage an entrepreneur
        a. creates a formal business plan.
        b. does an assessment of the venture.
        c. searches for partners.
        d. reformulates strategies.

C   46. The stabilization of the business stage is often called the
        a. "switch" stage.
        b. "up or down" stage.
        c. "swing" stage.
        d. "flow" stage.

D   47. Which stage of the venture's life cycle is most important?
        a. decline
        b. rationalization
        c. growth
        d. all stages of development

B   48. One characteristic of new-venture development is
        a. operational planning.
        b. the networking stage.
        c. growing out.
        d. sale stabilization.

Understanding the Entrepreneurial Company

C   49. In understanding the entrepreneurial mind, if the perceived capability is *blocked* and the future goals are *change*, then the result is
        a. entrepreneur.
        b. satisfied manager.
        c. frustrated manager.
        d. classic bureaucrat.

The Dryden Press

A   50. In understanding the entrepreneurial mind, if the perceived capability is *possible* and the future goals are *change*, then the result is
   a. entrepreneur.
   b. satisfied manager.
   c. frustrated manager.
   d. classic bureaucrat.

D   51. Building an adaptive firm requires which of the following elements?
   a. expand the entrepreneur's vision
   b. institutionalize change
   c. increase the perception of opportunity
   d. all of the above

C   52. When instilling the desire to be innovative, one should
   a. start a reward system.
   b. make the environment one which allows for failure.
   c. develop flexible operations.
   d. do all of the above.

B   53. Entrepreneurs can build an adaptive firm by doing all of the following *except*
   a. increasing the perception of opportunity.
   b. reducing the desire to be innovative.
   c. instituting change as a ventures goal.
   d. balancing the focus.

D   54. Which is *not* a problem in making the transition in the growth stage?
   a. a paternalistic atmosphere
   b. an overdependence on one or two key individuals
   c. a highly centralized decision making system
   d. all are problems

C   55. A firm that increases opportunity for its employees, initiates change, and instills a desire to be innovative would be considered
   a. bureaucratic
   b. visionary
   c. adaptive
   d. traditional

D   56. Increasing the perception of opportunity can be done by
   a. defined weak objectives.
   b. staying close to the customer.
   c. careful coordination and integration.
   d. all of the above.

The Dryden Press

B   57. Which of the following is an administrative question?
          a. Where is the opportunity?
          b. What sources do I control?
          c. What structure is best?
          d. What resources do I need?

C   58. A balance of focus must be maintained between:
          a. specialist and general managers.
          b. entrepreneur and board of directors.
          c. entrepreneur and management.
          d. upper management and lower management.

B   59. Of the following, which is the *least* true statement about entrepreneurs?
          a. Entrepreneurs perceive opportunity.
          b. Entrepreneurs study opportunity in detail.
          c. Entrepreneurs pursue opportunity.
          d. Entrepreneurs believe that the venture can be successful.

A   60. Which of the following is a true statement about the entrepreneurial mind?
          a. Success may affect an entrepreneur's willingness to change and innovate.
          b. Entrepreneurs never create bureaucratic environments.
          c. The entrepreneur does not affect the growth orientation of the firm.
          d. To maintain the creative climate that launched the venture, the entrepreneur should continue as always.

Understanding the Growth Stage

D   61. A key factor in the growth stage is
          a. change.
          b. control.
          c. responsibility.
          d. all of the above.

A   62. A form of failure that is brought about by a lack of skill or application is
          a. personal failure.
          b. moral failure.
          c. uncontrollable failure.
          d. financial failure.

C   63. The key component to managerial growth success is
          a. control.
          b. change.
          c. delegation.
          d. responsibility.

B   64. When firms experience surges in growth, there is a constant struggle between rigid, bureaucratic designs and
          a. administrative style.
          b. flexible, organic designs.
          c. mature, stabilized designs.
          d. static, resourceful designs.

A   65. Which of the following factors are considered cultural elements in a flexible design?
          a. autonomous and entrepreneurial
          b. formalized and objective
          c. generalist and risk averse
          d. subjective and participative

D   66. In designing a flexible structure for high growth, which of the following forces are examples of contradictory forces?
          a. bureaucratization vs. formality
          b. innovation vs. risk taking
          c. equity vs. compensation
          d. environment vs. strategy

C   67. The system of using external resources to assist in making decisions during the growth stage is referred to as
          a. resourcing.
          b. rationalizing.
          c. networking.
          d. externalizing.

A   68. The process for assisting decision making during the growth stage that assumes decision making involves multiple roles that participate in various ways at different points over time is referred to as
          a. responsibility charting.
          b. networking.
          c. decision model.
          d. decision dynamics.

B 69. Which form of failure is a violation of internal trust?
- a. personal
- b. moral
- c. uncontrollable
- d. residual

D 70. Which of the following steps would be recommended for breaking through the "growth wall"?
- a. plan for growth
- b. create a growth task force
- c. use an advisory board
- d. all of the above

A 71. A key step to delegation is
- a. creating the obligation of responsibility for necessary action.
- b. view thinking.
- c. innovative activity.
- d. descriptive analysis.

A 72. Which of the following pressures does an entrepreneur face in his or her efforts to control resources?
- a. risk of obsolescence
- b. coordination of activity
- c. risk reduction
- d. action orientation

B 73. Which of the following is *not* subject to continual change during the growth stage?
- a. planning
- b. strategies
- c. operations
- d. implementations

B 74. Which is a step in the effective delegation process?
- a. assignment of generalized duties
- b. granting authority to carry out duties
- c. granting responsibility
- d. institutionalizing key operating tasks

D 75. Which of the following is *not* a way of viewing the thinking process?
- a. View thinking as a strategy.
- b. Record, sort, and save thoughts.
- c. Focus on relevant thoughts.
- d. Schedule small blocks of uninterrupted time.

Essays

76. *During the growth stage of the life cycle of a venture, major changes in the entrepreneurial strategy are required. Explain why this is true.*

Competition and other market forces will require the reformulation of business strategies. Some firms will outgrow the business because they can't cope with the growth of their ventures. Some entrepreneurs are unable to meet administrative challenges that accompany this stage of growth. During this stage a transition from entrepreneurial, one-person leadership to managerial, team management leadership should occur.

77. *List and describe the factors involved in instilling the desire to be innovative.*

One factor is a reward system. Recognition should be given to individuals who attempt innovative opportunities. These rewards should be in the form of bonuses, awards, salary advances, and promotions. The second factor is an environment that allows for failure. The fear of failure needs to be minimized through the general recognition that often many attempts are needed before a success is achieved. When this type of environment exists, people become willing to accept the challenge of change and innovation. The third factor is flexible operations. Flexibility creates the possibility of change, and that has a positive effect. If a venture remains too rigidly tied to plans, it will not respond to new technology, customer changes, or environmental shifts. A fourth factor is the development of venture teams to foster team innovation.

78. *List and describe the three forms of failure that should be distinguished under the key factor "tolerance of failure."*

One distinct form is moral failure. This form of failure is a violation of internal trust. This violation is a serious failure which can result in negative consequences. The second form is personal failure. This form of failure is caused by lack of skill or application. This form of failure is usually shared by the firm and the individual. The third form is uncontrollable failure. This form of failure is caused by external factors and is hard to prepare for and deal with. Examples of uncontrollable failure would be resource limitations, strategic direction, and market changes.

79. *Describe what is meant by managing paradox and contradiction.*

Research has shown that new venture managers experiencing growth--particularly in emerging industries--need to adopt flexible, organic structures; however, this comes into constant conflict with rigid, bureaucratic designs. Cultural elements, staffing and development factors, and appraisal and reward elements are all structural factors that conflict between flexible and bureaucratic. Rapidly growing firms are challenged to strike a balance between these multiple pulls when designing their managerial systems.

80. ***Explain why delegation is important to growth-oriented ventures.***
    In order to continue the growth and innovation of the venture, the entrepreneur needs to free up his or her time and rely on others in the business to carry out the day-to-day business activities. As the business becomes larger, the entrepreneur cannot possibly be in all the places at all the times he or she is needed.

CHAPTER 17

GLOBAL OPPORTUNITIES FOR ENTREPRENEURS

True/False

T   1.   GATT stands for the General Agreement on Tariffs and Trade.

F   2.   The international organization that has over 100 nations as members and implements the GATT rules is known as the World Exporting Association.

T   3.   Japan and Asia offer promising opportunities for entrepreneurs.

T   4.   The North American Free Trade Agreement (NAFTA) between Mexico, Canada, and the United States has created export opportunities for small firms.

T   5.   The term "Euroconsumer" has developed to illustrate the potential consumer base from the European Union.

Methods of Going International

F   6.   An export operation can expect immediate profits from the beginning.

F   7.   The United States exports more goods than it imports.

F   8.   An export management company and a freight forwarder are the same thing.

F   9.   All sales through a foreign sales corporation are tax exempt.

F   10.   A joint venture can have no more than one company involved.

T   11.   A joint venture by more than two companies is sometimes called a consortium.

F   12.   A company cannot form a joint venture with the state.

F   13.   One of the disadvantages of a joint venture is the lack of strategic fit between a domestic firm and a third-world firm (D-Type).

F   14.   Foreign governments always stay out of direct foreign investments.

T   15.   A direct foreign investment is domestically controlled.

T   16. In a direct foreign investment, the parent firm does not necessarily own a majority of the operation.

T   17. Direct foreign investment is a popular way of going international.

F   18. Direct investment is a good idea for all firms.

T   19. Trademarks can be licensed.

F   20. Patents cannot be licensed.

F   21. Licensing requires a large capital outlay for the licensor.

T   22. A licensee of a product could become a competitor for the company providing the license.

Entering the International Marketplace: A Procedural Outline

T   23. The first step in entering the international marketplace is to conduct research.

T   24. Researching the international market can be very difficult.

F   25. Exporting documentation is usually an easy task.

Multiple Choice

The International Environment

A   26. According to the Small Business Administration, _____ percent of all firms that export goods and services have fewer than 100 employees.
    a. 25
    b. 60
    c. 99
    d. 3

A   27. A major trade liberalization organization whose objectives are to create a basic set of rules under which trade negotiations can take place is called:
    a. General Agreement on Tariffs and Trade (GATT)
    b. NAFTA
    c. export association
    d. none of the above

B   28. What is the organization established to implement the GATT rules and has over 100 nations as members?
   a. NAFTA
   b. World Trade Organization
   c. United Nations
   d. Export Association

Methods of Going International

A   29. Most companies that export to foreign markets are _____ businesses.
   a. small
   b. medium-size
   c. moderately large
   d. large

D   30. Most companies that export to foreign markets have _____ employees.
   a. 1,000 to 2,000
   b. 500 to 1,000
   c. 100 to 500
   d. less than 100

B   31. Exporting normally becomes profitable
   a. in one to two years.
   b. in three to five years.
   c. in five to eight years.
   d. immediately.

B   32. _____ is the shipping of a domestically produced good to a foreign destination for consumption.
   a. Importing
   b. Exporting
   c. Joint venturing
   d. Licensing

C   33. An export management company is
   a. a parent firm subsidiary.
   b. a lobbyist group.
   c. a private firm to help with exporting.
   d. a private firm dealing exclusively with shipping.

The Dryden Press

C 34. Which of the following is *not* a question to ask about a potential export management company?
  a. What is the reputation of the firm?
  b. Is the firm financially sound?
  c. Does the firm put out a weekly newsletter?
  d. Does the firm have representatives overseas?

D 35. Services provided by a freight forwarder can include
  a. quoting shipping costs.
  b. preparing necessary report documentation.
  c. advising on international packing requirements.
  d. all the above.

B 36. When exporting, which of the following would be of *least* value to a small business?
  a. freight forwarder
  b. direct foreign investment
  c. export management company
  d. foreign sales corporation

D 37. DISC is designed to
  a. promote joint ventures.
  b. eliminate trade barriers.
  c. increase import sales.
  d. increase export sales.

A 38. Some of the United States' trading partners object to DISC because they feel it violates
  a. GATT.
  b. GART.
  c. EXIM Bank regulations.
  d. Securities and Exchange regulations.

D 39. The foreign sales corporation was created to replace
  a. direct foreign investment.
  b. joint ventures.
  c. GATT.
  d. DISC.

D 40. GATT stands for
  a. General Association for Trade and Tariff.
  b. General Association of Taxes and Trade.
  c. Generally Agreement on Taxes and Transnationals.
  d. General Agreement on Tariffs and Trade.

A 41. A joint venture is
   a. an organization owned by more than one company.
   b. only existent in eastern Europe.
   c. controlled by one company.
   d. controlled by a minimum of five companies.

B 42. A consortium is
   a. a joint venture with the government.
   b. a joint venture with more than two companies.
   c. an international export tax.
   d. a new contraceptive.

B 43. In a joint venture
   a. overall risk will be higher than operating alone.
   b. overall risk will be lower than operating alone.
   c. overall risk will be the same.
   d. overall risk will be eliminated.

C 44. In examining the strategic fit of the firms in a joint venture, a D-Type refers to _____ while a TW-Type refers to _____.
   a. decision firms; transnational firms
   b. defense firms; target firms
   c. domestic firms; third-world firms
   d. direct investment firms; traditional world firms

D 45. Some governments dictate all of the following *except*
   a. hiring practices.
   b. pricing structure.
   c. earnings distribution.
   d. risk.

A 46. Methods of making a direct foreign investment include
   a. purchasing assets of a foreign concern.
   b. use of fragmented control.
   c. exporting of all excess production.
   d. sale of stock options.

C 47. A reason to make a direct foreign investment could be
   a. low trade restrictions.
   b. depreciation expenses.
   c. high trade restrictions.
   d. divine inspiration.

The Dryden Press

A 48. Trade barriers make exporting costs
- a. increase.
- b. decrease greatly.
- c. remain the same.
- d. decrease slightly.

B 49. To be attractive, the anticipated rate of return from a foreign location should be
- a. lower than at home.
- b. higher than at home.
- c. nonexistent.
- d. trivial.

C 50. Which of the following is provided to the licensee by the licensor?
- a. extensive capital
- b. daily production management
- c. expertise and advice
- d. only a and b

D 51. To arrange for licensing, one should obtain
- a. a secured patent.
- b. a trademark.
- c. a know-how position.
- d. all of the above.

B 52. Which of the following involves the greatest amount of investment on the part of a firm going international?
- a. foreign sales corporation
- b. direct foreign investment
- c. export management company
- d. freight forwarder

C 53. A disadvantage to licensing is
- a. a smaller market.
- b. a minimum capital outlay.
- c. the possibility that the licensee will become a competitor.
- d. the possibility that the licensee could become a partner.

C 54. All of the following are basic types of licensing programs *except*
- a. patents.
- b. trademarks.
- c. feasibility transfer.
- d. technical know-how.

A 55. All of the following would be useful in participating in the export market *except*
   a. an import management company.
   b. freight forwarder.
   c. a foreign sales corporation.
   d. export management company.

A 56. Which of the following is *not* a condition necessary for a foreign sales corporation to qualify for tax exempt treatment?
   a. It must be a qualified domestic organization.
   b. It must have foreign presence.
   c. It must perform activities relating to its exporting income outside the United States.
   d. It must have economic substance.

B 57. Which of the following is an independent business that handles export shipments in return for compensation?
   a. An export management company
   b. A freight forwarder
   c. A foreign sales corporation
   d. A licensing organization

D 58. Which of the following is a common mistake made by potential exporters?
   a. insufficient care in selecting overseas distributors
   b. neglecting export business when the U.S. market booms
   c. failure to consider joint-venture agreements
   d. all of the above

C 59. Which of the following approaches has the advantage of being able to gain an intimate knowledge of local conditions and government?
   a. exporting
   b. direct foreign investment
   c. joint venture
   d. licensing

A 60. Which of the following statements is true of a direct foreign investment?
   a. It typically involves ownership of 10 to 25 percent.
   b. It always involves ownership of 20 to 25 percent.
   c. It always involves ownership of more than 15 percent.
   d. It typically involves ownership of over 50 percent.

The Dryden Press

B   61.   The three basic types of programs available in an international licensing program are
        a. patents, trademarks, and goodwill.
        b. patents, trademarks, and technical know-how.
        c. trademarks, technical know-how, and goodwill.
        d. patents, trademarks, and copyrights.

D   62.   Which type of licensing is the hardest to enforce since it depends on the security of secrecy agreements?
        a. trademarks
        b. patents
        c. goodwill
        d. technical know-how

A   63.   Which is often the most realistic means of expansion, particularly for high-tech firms?
        a. licensing
        b. importing
        c. exporting
        d. direct financial investment

D   64.   Which of the following provides a quote of the shipping costs for inland, ocean, and air?
        a. a foreign sales corporation
        b. a export management company
        c. a licensing arrangement
        d. a freight forwarder

D   65.   What guideline should be followed when selecting a freight forwarder?
        a. Check with current shippers about domestic products.
        b. Obtain references from past customers.
        c. The freight forwarder should be licensed by the Federal Maritime Commission.
        d. All of the above are correct.

Entering the International Marketplace: A Procedural Outline

C   66.   The first step in implementing an international strategy is to
        a. implement the plan.
        b. draw up a timetable.
        c. define the firm's policy.
        d. provide export training.

A   67. A main objective of entrepreneurs when conducting research is to
   a. identify markets.
   b. increase revenues.
   c. increase capital outlay.
   d. reduce costs.

C   68. The Exporter's Encyclopedia contains
   a. loan applications.
   b. information about domestic issues.
   c. lists of all necessary documentation.
   d. lists of national bids.

B   69. All of the following are sources of international financing *except*
   a. local banks.
   b. the Small Business Administration.
   c. the Overseas Private Investment Corporation.
   d. the export-import bank.

C   70. What does FET stand for?
   a. federal economic trade
   b. foreign economic trade
   c. foreign economic trends
   d. federal evaluation trends

B   71. What does TOP stand for?
   a. the Trade Overseas Program
   b. the Trade Opportunities Program
   c. the Trend Opportunities Program
   d. Trading Overseas Possibilities

C   72. The second step in the procedural outline for going into the international marketplace is to
   a. secure adequate financing.
   b. prepare a research program.
   c. prepare a feasibility study.
   d. file the proper documents.

D   73. What is another name for the export-import bank which helps secure adequate financing?
   a. Expibank
   b. Expobank
   c. Exmobank
   d. Eximbank

A 74. The final step in the procedural outline for entering the international marketplace is
   a. filing proper documents.
   b. presenting a plan to the proper authorities.
   c. paying for the necessary license.
   d. none of the above.

C 75. Which of the following is the best place an owner can conduct international market research?
   a. the Small Business Administration (SBA)
   b. the Overseas Investment Company
   c. the Federal Depository
   d. the Exporter's Encyclopedia

Essays

76. *One method of going international is by exporting. List two ways of exporting, and describe a few advantages or disadvantages.*
   One method of exporting utilizes the exporting management company, a private firm that serves as an export department for manufacturers. The company transacts export business for the client in return for a commission. The disadvantage to an export management company is that the client may lose control of the export function. The client may become too dependent on the export management company. An advantage is that the company can provide the client with overseas marketing data. The company may have access to countries and firms the client could not otherwise get. Another method of exporting is freight forwarder, an independent business that handles export shipments in return for compensation. The advantage is that the freight forwarder costs less than the export management company because the freight forwarder only handles shipment. It can also take care of any shipping problems like documents and payments.

77. *What are the advantages of a joint venture?*
   A firm can gain knowledge of the local conditions and government of the foreign market it is dealing with. It can use the resources of the other firms; this participation allows compensation for each firm's weaknesses. Other advantages are that initial capital outlay is lowered and overall risk is lowered.

78. *Describe direct foreign investment thoroughly.*
   A direct foreign investment is a domestically controlled foreign production facility. The firm does not have to own a majority of the operation. A direct foreign investment normally involves ownership of 10 to 25 percent of the voting stock. Often the government may determine prices and earning distributions. One way to accomplish this is to acquire an interest in a foreign company. It can also purchase part of the assets of the company. One of the reasons for this approach is to limit trade restrictions on the

product so that there is no import fee. There may also be government incentives to set up operation in the country.

79. *What are some of the advantages and disadvantages of licensing?*
One of the advantages to licensing is that it requires minimum capital outlay. It generates savings in tariffs and transportation costs, and it is a more realistic method of expansion. It is also a potential way for firms to join and improve technology. Some of the disadvantages are that the firms may become competitors after the contract expires. They have to adjust products or services to fit the foreign company's needs. The firms must be able to resolve conflicts and misunderstandings. Integrity and independence of both firms must be maintained as well.

80. *List and describe the five mentioned steps to accomplish before entering the international market.*
The first step is to conduct research. Research the foreign company, the country's market needs, the import laws, and the opportunities available. The second step is to prepare a feasibility study to determine how realistic the project is in both the long-term and short-term prospects. Next it is necessary to secure adequate financing. A company must decide upon the financing available and what meets its needs. Following this, the firm must file proper documents. This requires researching the documents needed, preparing the forms, and filling them out. The final step is to draw up and implement the plan, establish overall objectives, make sure the firm is organized and ready for international operations, and put the plan into effect.

CHAPTER 18

VALUATION OF BUSINESS VENTURES

True/False

Buying A Business Venture

T   1.   Personal preference is one of the four basic considerations in buying a business.

F   2.   When examining opportunities, an entrepreneur should not use newspaper ads as a source.

F   3.   When evaluating the selected venture, the business environment need not be considered.

T   4.   One of the key questions when considering buying a business is whether any special licenses are required.

T   5.   Tangible assets as well as intangible assets of a business need to be assessed for proper venture evaluation.

F   6.   "Why is the business being sold?" is *not* an important question to ask when analyzing the viability of buying a business.

The Importance of Business Valuation

F   7.   An entrepreneur does not need to know how to calculate the value of a competitor's operation.

T   8.   Business valuation is essential when attempting to buy out a partner.

Underlying Issues

T   9.   Buyers and sellers assign different values to a business.

F   10.   Emotional bias is not an underlying issue in valuating a business.

T   11.   Entrepreneurs should try to be as objective as possible in determining the fair market value for their enterprise.

T   12.   Increasing market share by acquiring a firm in the company's industry is one reason for the acquisition.

T   13.   One of the most common reasons for acquiring a business is developing more growth-phase products.

Analyzing the Business

F   14.   Insufficient goals are a strength in analyzing the business being valuated.

T   15.   Weaknesses in small businesses call for careful analysis of the business being valuated.

Establishing the Value of the Firm

T   16.   Adjusted tangible book value is a popular method of valuation.

F   17.   The price/earnings ratio (multiple of earnings) method is determined by dividing the market price of common stock by retained earnings.

T   18.   The real value of any venture is its potential earning power.

F   19.   The timing of projected income or cash flows is not a critical factor in establishing the value of a firm.

T   20.   Replacement value of a business is based upon the value of each asset if it had to be replaced at a certain cost.

Other Factors to Consider

T   21.   Avoiding start-up costs is a factor to consider when valuating a business.

T   22.   The sales and earnings of a venture are always projected on the basis of historical, financial, and economic data.

The Leveraged Buyout: An Alternative for Smaller Firms

T   23.   A leveraged buyout is when the entrepreneur finances the transaction by borrowing on the target company's assets.

F 24. A firm with no established product line is a good target for a leveraged buyout.

T 25. There now exists a relatively new form of buyout called a "cash-flow LBO."

Multiple Choice

Buying A Business Venture

D 26. A basic step in buying a business is
   a. personal preference.
   b. examination of opportunities.
   c. evaluation of the selected venture.
   d. all of the above.

D 27. Examining available opportunities can be done through
   a. business brokers.
   b. newspaper ads.
   c. trade sources.
   d. all of the above.

C 28. Which of the following would *not* be a good source for entrepreneurs in search of a possible venture to buy?
   a. business opportunity ads
   b. management consultants
   c. university professors
   d. business brokers

A 29. Business assets include
   a. inventory.
   b. accounts payable.
   c. sales.
   d. all of the above.

C 30. Which of the following is a key question to ask when analyzing a business venture?
   a. Who owns the business?
   b. Is this a family-owned business?
   c. What are the conditions of the lease?
   d. None of the above.

B   31.   Specific factors of a venture being offered for sale that should be examined include
           a. age, trends, and future.
           b. profits, sales, and operating ratios.
           c. employees, suppliers, and competitors.
           d. none of the above.

The Importance of Business Valuation

D   32.   Valuation of a business is important when
           a. giving a gift of stock to family members.
           b. attempting to buy out a partner.
           c. structuring a buy/sell agreement.
           d. doing all of the above.

D   33.   Business valuation is important for the entrepreneur because a person needs to know when to
           a. buy or sell a business, division, or major asset.
           b. establish an employee stock option plan.
           c. raise growth capital through stock warrants or convertible loans.
           d. do all of the above.

B   34.   Knowing the value of a business is important in case
           a. of divorce between owner and spouse.
           b. of a dissolution of a partnership.
           c. the owner's son wants to buy in.
           d. of none of the above.

Underlying Issues

A   35.   Underlying issues to consider when valuating a firm include
           a. the goals of the buyer and seller.
           b. the goals of the lawyers.
           c. the reasons for raising capital stock.
           d. all of the above.

C   36.   Which of the following is not an underlying issue in the value of a business?
           a. emotional bias of the seller
           b. reasons for acquisition
           c. attempting to buy out a partner
           d. none of the above

D   37. The seller will attempt to establish the highest possible value for his/her business. He/she will *not* consider which of the following factors?
   a. the market
   b. the economy
   c. the environment
   d. the transportation

A   38. When valuating a business, the reason an entrepreneur's business is being acquired is
   a. to develop more growth-phase products by acquiring a firm that has developed new products in the company's industry.
   b. because of differing goals of the buyer and the seller.
   c. to determine the possible lowest price.
   d. the emotional bias of the seller.

D   39. Which of the following can assist in evaluating the importance of a firm?
   a. the firm's potential to pay for itself during a reasonable time period
   b. the difficulties a new owner may face during the transition period
   c. whether current managers intend to remain with the firm
   d. all of the above

Analyzing the Business

A   40. Closely held ventures suffer from which of the following shortcomings?
   a. a lack of management depth
   b. overcapitalization
   c. insufficient controls
   d. all of the above

D   41. When considering the history of a business, the entrepreneur should be concerned about
   a. the date the company was founded.
   b. the original name of the business and any changes.
   c. the state in which the company became incorporated.
   d. none of the above.

C   42. Which of the following is *not* a shortcoming that many closely held ventures possess?
   a. insufficient controls
   b. lack of management depth
   c. high equity and low debt
   d. divergent goals

The Dryden Press

C 43. When considering market and compensation, the entrepreneur should be concerned about
  a. the name of the competitor's CEO.
  b. the name of the competitor's janitor.
  c. the sales literature on products.
  d. all of the above.

A 44. When considering sales and distribution, the entrepreneur should be concerned about
  a. whether any sales are made on consignment.
  b. how many sales are internal.
  c. how many sales are at Indiana University.
  d. all of the above.

C 45. When considering employees, the entrepreneur should be concerned about
  a. total number of single employees.
  b. total number of female employees.
  c. total number of employees by function.
  d. all of the above.

A 46. When considering physical facilities, the entrepreneur should be concerned about
  a. which facilities are owned versus leased.
  b. which facilities are used for production.
  c. whether adequate capital is maintained.
  d. all of the above.

A 47. When considering management, the entrepreneur should be concerned about
  a. ownership positions.
  b. pension and profit sharing.
  c. total number of employees.
  d. none of the above.

Establishing the Value of a Firm

A 48. In establishing the value of the firm, part of the process is
  a. estimations.
  b. management details.
  c. project completions.
  d. all of the above.

A   49. Return on investment
   a. is net profit divided by investment.
   b. provides a replacement value.
   c. will establish a value for the business.
   d. is all of the above.

D   50. Liquidation value
   a. reflects "top value" of the firm.
   b. pays off assets and sells liabilities.
   c. assumes business begins operations.
   d. does none of the above.

A   51. The discounted earnings method establishes
   a. potential earning power.
   b. an appropriate rate for replacement.
   c. expectancy of the business expenses.
   d. all of the above.

A   52. Price/earnings ratio is
   a. most common with public corporations.
   b. not affected by market conditions.
   c. not sensitive to market conditions.
   d. all of the above.

B   53. Market value
   a. needs an unknown price paid for a similar business.
   b. is valuable only as a reference point.
   c. is easy to find in recent comparisons.
   d. is all of the above.

B   54. A drawback to the price/earnings ratio method is that
   a. the stock of a private company is publicly traded.
   b. the stated net income of a private company may not truly reflect its actual earning power.
   c. it is relatively easy to find a truly comparable publicly held company, even in the same industry.
   d. all of the above.

C   55. What hidden costs are involved when establishing the value of a firm?
   a. insufficient controls and costs
   b. divergent expenses
   c. personal expenses
   d. none of the above

The Dryden Press

D   56. Goodwill, family members on the payroll, and planned losses are examples of
   a. analyzing the business.
   b. underlying issues.
   c. emotional bias.
   d. establishing the value of a firm.

D   57. When buying a business one should
   a. get a lawyer.
   b. consider hidden risks.
   c. have the former owner sign a noncompete clause.
   d. do all of the above.

D   58. Which of the following are considered methods for valuation of a venture?
   a. return on investment
   b. stock market method
   c. multiple of earnings
   d. a and c are correct

A   59. Book value of a firm is also known as
   a. balance sheet method.
   b. income statement method.
   c. capitalized earnings approach.
   d. fixed price method.

C   60. Which of the following methods of valuation was developed by the United States Treasury to determine a firm's intangible assets?
   a. market value
   b. replacement value
   c. excess earnings
   d. multiple of earnings

A   61. When closing a deal the final thing an entrepreneur should do is
   a. check out the seller.
   b. hire a certified public accountant.
   c. get a lawyer.
   d. both a and b.

D   62. An adjusted tangible book value method includes
   a. goodwill.
   b. patents.
   c. dividing market price by common price.
   d. both a and b.
   e. none of the above.

B   63.   The price/earnings ratio is determined by
- a. patents.
- b. dividing market price of common stock by earnings per share.
- c. goodwill.
- d. deferred financing costs.

C   64.   Potential earning power, which determines the true value of the firm, is
- a. the price/earnings ratio method.
- b. the adjusted tangible book value method.
- c. the discounted earnings method.
- d. all of the above.

Other Factors to Consider

B   65.   One reason to keep projections in perspective is
- a. long histories.
- b. fluctuating markets.
- c. certain environments.
- d. a and b.

A   66.   A company is selected for a leveraged buyout when
- a. it has a dependable cash flow from operations.
- b. it has a new product line.
- c. it has high current and long-term debt.
- d. it has a low ratio of fully depreciated fixed assets.

D   67.   Due to lower individual tax rates, which of the following may become more popular?
- a. proprietorships
- b. partnerships
- c. S corporations
- d. all of the above

A   68.   Some buyers are willing to pay more for a business than what the valuation methods illustrate its worth do be. This is because buyers are often
- a. trying to avoid start-up costs.
- b. seeking to recoup earlier losses.
- c. attempting to disperse previous profits.
- d. trying to do all of the above.

B 69. When an entrepreneur finances the purchase of a business by borrowing on the target company's assets, this procedure is known as
   a. a limited partnership.
   b. a leveraged buyout.
   c. a privately held company.
   d. a power of purchase.

A 70. As an example of tax complexities, the 1986 tax reform act changed a number of business items including
   a. capital gains are now treated the same as ordinary income and taxed at ordinary tax rates.
   b. top corporate taxes are now lower than top individual rates.
   c. the General Utilities Doctrine is now in effect.
   d. all of the above.

D 71. Which factors listed below influence the final valuation of the venture?
   a. avoiding start-up costs
   b. accuracy of projections
   c. control factor
   d. all of the above

B 72. Sales and earnings of a venture are projected from
   a. historical projections
   b. historical financials
   c. data on start-ups
   d. none of the above

C 73. Top individual tax rates, capital gains, and general utilities are examples of
   a. leveraged buyout.
   b. accuracy of projection.
   c. tax considerations.
   d. avoiding start-up costs.

B 74. Taxes in large firms are handled by
   a. bookkeepers.
   b. tax accountants.
   c. the president.
   d. financial advisers.

B 75. In most cases, tax considerations have
   a. a minimal impact on a company.
   b. a large impact on a company.
   c. no impact on a company.
   d. not been necessary for a company.

Essays

76. *List and describe the sources an entrepreneur should examine to find available business buying opportunities.*

The first source is a business broker. The broker can provide leads and assistance in finding a venture for sale. The buyer should remember that a broker usually receives a commission on the sale, so it is important to check out the broker's reputation, services, and contacts. Newspaper ads under business opportunities are another source. Sometimes an ad is under one classified section of one newspaper and not another, so you should check the classified sections in all papers in the area. Trade sources are another source. You can check with some suppliers, distributors, and manufacturers in the area. Some trade publications and associations may have information about businesses for sale. Professional sources can also be used. Professionals such as management consultants, attorneys, and accountants often know of businesses available for sale.

77. *List some of the questions to ask before making a potential purchase, and explain why each is important.*

Why is the business being sold? It is important to know the reason the owners are selling the business. If the explanation given doesn't seem to be the prime motivation, then more research needs to be done. What is the physical condition of the business? This must be examined to avoid major expenses after the purchase of the business. How many key personnel will remain? Certain key personnel may be needed for a smooth transition. What is the degree of competition? It is important to know the quality and quantity of the competitors in order to compete on any level. What are the conditions of the lease? Find out who the landlord is, and discuss any future leases. Are there any liens against the business? This should be checked so no surprise costs arise. Will the owner sign a covenant not to compete? This is important to avoid losing customers to the old owner. Are any special licenses required? The buyer needs to make sure that all requirements for the purchase of this business are intact. What are the future trends of business? How will the buyer's business fit into the future trends of the business? How much capital is needed to buy the business? It is important to figure out the excess cost besides the purchase price, like inventory, working capital, and opening expenses.

78. *What should be considered in analyzing a business, and what are some weaknesses of small business?*

When analyzing a small closely held corporation, comparisons with larger corporations should be avoided. Larger corporations are run differently than small companies. Some small businesses have a lack of management depth. Their degrees of skill, versatility, and compensation are limited. Many small corporations are undercapitalized, so their amount of equity is low. They also have insufficient controls due to lack of available management and extra capital, and there are usually limited measures in place for monitoring and controlling operations. Another factor is divergent goals. The entrepreneur often has a vision for the venture that differs from the investor's goals or stockholders' desires, thus causing internal conflicts in the firm.

79. *List and briefly explain the three methods utilized for business evaluation.*

The first method is the adjusted tangible assets, which is the balance sheet value. The first thing to do is evaluate the net worth of the business. This means finding the difference between total assets and total liabilities. Depreciation and appreciation should also be used in determining assets. When computing the book value, goodwill, patents, deferred financial cost, and other intangible assets are considered with tangible assets and deducted from or added to net worth. The next is the price earnings ratio, which is also known as the multiple earnings ratio. This method is used for the valuation of publicly held corporations. The valuation is determined by dividing the market price of common stock by the company's earnings. The benefit of this approach is its simplicity. But only publicly held companies can use this valuating process. Last is the discounted earning method. This method shows the venture's potential earning power and the true value of the firm. First the expected cash flow is estimated and an appropriate discount rate is determined. Then the company's life expectancy must be determined. The firm's value is determined by discounting the estimated cash flow by the discount rate over the expected life of the business.

80. *Explain what leveraged buyout is and how it is used.*

The leveraged buyout plan allows an entrepreneur to finance transactions by borrowing on the target company's assets. This is used to help privately held firms acquire needed funds by borrowing against assets, inventory, and equipment. A company that is selected for leveraged buyout has dependable cash flow from operations, a high ratio of fully depreciated fixed assets, an established product line, and a low current and long-term debt. These statistics are used to see if there are enough assets to loan against and to see if the company can take on additional debt. Asset based LBOs have lower interest rates and allow the entrepreneur control instead of using cash-flow LBOs. Cash-flow LBOs have higher interest rates, and their use may result in some loss of a company's equity.

CHAPTER 19

MANAGEMENT SUCCESSION AND CONTINUITY:

A FAMILY BUSINESS PERSPECTIVE

True/False

Family-Owned Business

T   1.   Family businesses account for the largest percentage of our nation's businesses.

F   2.   One of the advantages of a family business is paternalistic rule.

T   3.   Nepotism is considered one of the key disadvantages to family business.

The Management Succession Issues

T   4.   Only one-third of all enterprises makes it to a second generation.

F   5.   Only one percent of all enterprises makes it to a third generation.

T   6.   The average life expectancy of a family business is 24 years.

Key Factors in Succession

T   7.   There are two types of succession pressures: family and nonfamily.

F   8.   External environmental factors do not have any effect on the succession issue.

T   9.   Nonfamily members sometimes bring pressure on the owner-manager in an effort to protect their personal interests.

T   10.   Although family members may not play an active role in the business, they still may want to inherit part of the business.

F   11.   When the founder of a business is willing to share authority, succession problems can be maximized.

T   12.   The forcing events that require an entrepreneur to step aside and let someone direct the operation are usually unforeseen and create major problems for the business.

The Dryden Press

F 13. An entrepreneurial successor is someone who is interested in efficiency and the effective use of resources.

T 14. When looking ahead in choosing a successor from inside the organization, the founder often trains a team of executive managers consisting of both family and nonfamily members.

T 15. The Oakland Scavenger case may have a major effect on the management succession plans of family business.

F 16. An important issue in the Oakland Scavenger case is that of whether nonfamily members should be allowed to be successors in family businesses.

Developing A Succession Strategy

T 17. The steps in developing a succession strategy are understanding the contextual aspects, identifying successor qualities, and carrying out the succession plan.

T 18. Some entrepreneurs are easy to replace, and some cannot be replaced.

F 19. If the successor and the business environment have a "right fit," the successor will be less than maximally effective.

T 20. Depending on the situation, some qualities or characteristics a successor should possess are more important than others.

F 21. The successor of a small business should not be identified until the last possible moment when the business is being turned over.

T 22. Especially in small firms, when a succession plan is being put into effect, attention should be given to day-to-day operations.

The Harvest Strategy: Selling Out

T 23. The idea of "selling out" should be viewed in the positive sense of "harvesting the investment."

T 24. One of the primary reasons business owners sell out is because they are burned out.

F 25. The purpose of preparing a financial analysis is to forecast the next few months of the business.

Multiple Choice

Family-Owned Business

B   26.   Family businesses account for the _____ percentage of our nation's businesses.
- a. smallest
- b. largest
- c. worst
- d. simplest

D   27.   Advantages of a family business would include:
- a. long-term orientation.
- b. preserving humanity in the workplace.
- c. emphasizing quality.
- d. all of the above.

D   28.   Disadvantages of a family business would include:
- a. nepotism
- b. paternalistic rule
- c. resilience
- d. a and b only

D   29.   Family-owned companies succeed and grow in spite of the complex challenges they face because
- a. family members sacrifice short-term profits.
- b. flexibility is a special trait in family firms.
- c. the firms thrive on ignorance.
- d. a and b only.

The Management Succession Issue

A   30.   Research on family firms demonstrates which of the following facts?
- a. only 16% make it to a third generation
- b. many family firms cease to exist after one month
- c. only nine out of ten make it to a second generation
- d. all of the above

D   31.   Barriers to successful succession planning include which of the following?
- a. sibling rivalry
- b. aversion to death
- c. dilemma of choice
- d. all of the above

The Dryden Press

A   32. The average life expectancy for a family business is
  a. 24 years.
  b. 40 years.
  c. 5 years.
  d. 68 years.

Key Factors in Succession

B   33. Which of the following is *not* an example of pressures or interests from within a firm that are considered in the succession issue?
  a. rivalry among various branches of the family
  b. pressure from a family member to start his/her own business
  c. employee wanting a percentage of the business in the owner's will
  d. pressure on the owner-manager to designate an heir

D   34. Which of the following is an event that would require the entrepreneur to step aside and let someone else direct the operation?
  a. nonterminal physical incapacitation
  b. legal problems
  c. death
  d. all of the above

B   35. When considering financial difficulties, which of the following statements constitutes a forcing event?
  a. The business has a loss for one quarter.
  b. A lender demands the removal of the owner-manager before lending the necessary funds.
  c. The business does not make a substantial profit for the first year of business.
  d. None of the above is correct.

B   36. An owner may *not* groom a successor for any of the following reasons *except*
  a. reluctance to give up power/authority.
  b. may consider one's children to be too young.
  c. poor interpretations from family members.
  d. competition-changing strategy.

A   37. Each of the following are nonfamily elements under pressure and interest from outside the firm *except*
  a. increased insurance rates.
  b. the competition-changing strategy.
  c. regulatory agencies.
  d. customers.

B   38.   Happenings that cause the replacement of the owner-manager of a family business are called
           a. abrupt happenings.
           b. forcing events.
           c. legal events.
           d. unforeseen difficulties.

B   39.   The Oakland Scavenger case is profound to owners of family businesses in that
           a. conceivably, the owner can be sued for not giving equal treatment to a son as to a daughter.
           b. conceivably, the owner can be sued by an employee of a different ethnic origin based upon not being accorded the same treatment as a son or daughter.
           c. conceivably, the owner can be sued for not declaring a family member his or her successor.
           d. the owner can be fined for not declaring his or her first son the heir to the business.

C   40.   One of the most recent legal challenges to management succession has come from the
           a. Anderson Manufacturing Corporation case.
           b. Johnson Brothers case.
           c. Oakland Scavenger Company case.
           d. Willy & Willy Inc. case.

A   41.   One of the most recent legal challenges to management succession has charged
           a. employment discrimination.
           b. retirement income discrimination.
           c. racial discrimination.
           d. minimum wage discrimination.

B   42.   A type of successor who is high in ingenuity, creativity, and drive would be considered a(n)
           a. managerial successor.
           b. entrepreneurial successor.
           c. opportunistic successor.
           d. all of the above.

A   43.   A type of successor who is interested in efficiency, internal control, and effective use of resources would be considered a(n)
           a. managerial successor.
           b. entrepreneurial successor.
           c. opportunistic successor.
           d. all of the above.

The Dryden Press

D 44. One advantage of an early entry strategy for the younger generation succeeding the older generation of a family business is
   a. normal mistakes are viewed as incompetence.
   b. perspective of the environment is broadened.
   c. successor's skills are judged with more objectivity.
   d. skills specifically required by the business are developed.

A 45. One advantage of the delayed entry strategy for the younger generation succeeding the older generation of a family business is
   a. successor's skills are judged with greater objectivity.
   b. strong relationships are readily established.
   c. normal mistakes are viewed as incompetence.
   d. knowledge of the environment is limited.

C 46. The first source of succession often is
   a. nonfamily outsiders.
   b. professional managers.
   c. family and in-house personnel.
   d. friends of the family.

C 47. One good way of choosing a successor is to
   a. pick the older child.
   b. always choose an insider.
   c. use a decision tree.
   d. flip a coin.

D 48. An entrepreneurial successor is someone who is high in
   a. ingenuity.
   b. creativity.
   c. drive.
   d. all of the above.

D 49. The managerial successor typically is *not* interested in
   a. efficiency.
   b. internal control.
   c. effective use of resources.
   d. creativity.

C 50. The Oakland Scavenger Company case resulted in
   a. a favorable ruling by the court for the plaintiffs.
   b. a favorable ruling by the court for the defendants.
   c. an $8 million out-of-court settlement.
   d. an appeal to be heard by the Supreme Court.

Developing a Succession Strategy

D   51. Which of the following is *not* a contextual aspect to be considered in an effective succession plan?
   a. time
   b. managerial ability
   c. entrepreneurial vision
   d. cost

C   52. Which of the following is *not* a step in developing a succession strategy?
   a. identifying successor qualities
   b. carrying out the succession plan
   c. forcing events
   d. understanding the contextual aspects

A   53. Which of the following is a key aspect to be considered in an effective succession?
   a. the entrepreneur's vision
   b. the family's wants and needs
   c. the profitability of the venture
   d. the marital status of the replacement

A   54. There are four strategies that can be used in preparing a management succession policy. Which of the following is *not* one of these strategies?
   a. The owner has the family control the management continuity strategy entirely.
   b. The owner controls the management continuity strategy entirely.
   c. The owner works with a professional adviser.
   d. The owner works with family involvement.

D   55. The entrepreneur may have to choose a successor with potential in developing attributes necessary to run the business. Which of the following should be taken into account?
   a. the owner's concerns
   b. the family and business culture issues
   c. the family member concerns
   d. all of the above

B   56. The correct order of steps in carrying out the succession plan is
   a. groom an heir, consider outside help, agree on a plan, and identify a successor.
   b. identify a successor, groom an heir, agree on a plan, and consider outside help.
   c. identify a successor, agree on a plan, groom an heir, and consider outside help.
   d. groom an heir, agree on a plan, organize the financial plan, and consider outside help.

The Dryden Press

D   57. Which of the following is a true statement about the characteristics that successors should possess?
   a. There are only a few characteristics needed.
   b. Situation does not matter.
   c. Knowledge of the firm is not a characteristic or quality.
   d. Some characteristics will be more important than others, depending on the situation.

C   58. Which of the following is a true statement about legal advice?
   a. Legal advice is seldom beneficial.
   b. There is great benefit to having an adviser who understands the succession issue.
   c. It is seldom crucial for legal advisers to design a plan for succession.
   d. The more you pay, the better the advice.

B   59. Which of the following is *not* a true statement about a small firm when agreeing on a succession plan?
   a. Detailed person-to-person discussion is necessary.
   b. Procedure is fairly routine.
   c. Attention to day-to-day operations is advisable.
   d. Bringing into the plan those who will be most affected is advisable.

C   60. Promotion from within is
   a. seldom effective.
   b. usually a bad idea.
   c. a morale-building philosophy.
   d. a sure way to measure profitability.

D   61. A typical example of a forcing event is
   a. death.
   b. illness.
   c. severe business decline.
   d. all of the above.

C   62. Which is not a common characteristic to entrepreneur parents and children?
   a. security
   b. love of hard work
   c. dislike of taking risks
   d. love of what they do

D   63. Which is an influencing factor in succession?
   a. family and business cultural issues
   b. owner's concerns
   c. family members' concerns
   d. all of the above

The Harvest Strategy: Selling Out

A   64. Which of the following is *not* considered a step in the harvest strategy?
   a. Look for new venture to open up.
   b. Publicize the offer to sell.
   c. Value the business.
   d. Segregate assets.

A   65. Besides the eight steps in the harvest strategy, the other implications the entrepreneur should be aware of when selling out are
   a. tax implications arising from the sale of a business.
   b. interest implications arising from the sale of a business.
   c. security interests arising from the sale of a business.
   d. home improvement implications arising from the sale of a business.

C   66. The idea of selling out should be viewed in
   a. a destructive sense.
   b. a negative sense.
   c. a positive sense.
   d. a last resort sense.

D   67. A reason for an entrepreneur to sell a venture is
   a. boredom.
   b. lack of capital.
   c. age and health.
   d. all of the above.

B   68. Which of the following is *not* a suggestion a tax accountant or lawyer might make concerning tax reduction?
   a. Place real estate in a separate corporation.
   b. Increase management's salaries and fringe benefits.
   c. Establish a leasing subsidiary.
   d. Give some or all of the owner's shares to heirs.

The Dryden Press

C 69. When selling a business all of the following is good advice *except*:
   a. timing is everything.
   b. sell during the peak sales season.
   c. the owner should sell when profits are low.
   d. sell when inventory is high.

B 70. Meeting with the potential buyers
   a. often leads to a lower selling price.
   b. helps to negotiate the major requirements.
   c. often reduces buyer confidence.
   d. often reduces seller confidence.

D 71. Which of the following steps should be carried out *first* when deciding to sell a business?
   a. Segregate the assets.
   b. Time the sale appropriately.
   c. Publicize the offer to sell.
   d. Prepare a financial analysis.

C 72. Which of the following steps should be carried out *second* when deciding to sell a business?
   a. Publicize the offer to sell.
   b. Finalize the prospective buyers.
   c. Segregate the assets.
   d. Value the business.

B 73. Which of the following steps should be carried out *third* when deciding to sell a business?
   a. Publicize the offer to sell.
   b. Value the business.
   c. Finalize the prospective buyers.
   d. Time the sale appropriately.

A 74. Which of the following steps should be carried out *last* when deciding to sell a business?
   a. Publicize the offer to sell.
   b. Segregate the assets.
   c. Time the sale appropriately.
   d. Prepare a financial analysis.

Essays

75. *Bill and James Raymond have worked for their father's company for 15 years. Their father, who is president and now wants to retire, wants his sons to take over the company. Bill and James have never agreed on anything. Should their father try another succession plan?*

    For the sake of the company, another succession plan would be needed. The sons disagree already on nonbusiness topics. When Bill and James take over the company, arguments will only get worse. The performance of the firm will probably decline. This may send the company into bankruptcy. The best thing for the father to do would be to hire an outsider to take the place of president. The father can still maintain control of the company, and at a later date he can give control to one of the sons.

76. *The employees at Donnely and Associates have noticed a case of favoritism toward the president's son Jim. Jim constantly breaks company policy. The president is planning to retire in a few years. What should be done about the growing unrest in the company?*

    Before the president retires he must discipline his son. If the son was to take over the company now, the business would surely fail. The employees feel mistreated because Jim gets more privileges than they do. Jim must go along with company policy, or else the employees might do as Jim does. The company could also lose employees if they feel they are not treated fairly.

77. *Describe the legal concerns over family business succession, citing the actual case that took place regarding this topic.*

    "Nepotistic concerns cannot supersede the nation's paramount goal of equal opportunity for all," was a decision from the appeals court in the Oakland Scavenger Case. Eventually an $8 million out-of-court settlement was made between Oakland Scavenger and the plaintiffs (over 400 employees); however, the legal concern over family business employment policies still exists. Thus, family business owners need to be careful in the policies and practices used in personnel matters.

78. *The president of a successful lumberyard has decided to retire in a year. There are two relatives working in the lumberyard who want to take over but have little business knowledge. The president wants to keep the company in family hands. What should be done so the company stays in the family?*

    The best thing the president could do to keep the company in family hands would be to hire someone. A person could be brought in to run the business side of the company while the relatives work the technical side. Until the relatives are capable of running the company completely, this would be the best possible method of succession.

79. *What are the four critical steps to consider in developing a succession strategy in a family business?*

The four critical steps to consider are (1) understand the contextual forces of time, type of venture, capabilities of managers, entrepreneur's vision, and environmental factors; (2) identify successor qualities such as energy, enthusiasm, perseverance, maturity, resourcefulness, etc.; (3) understand the influencing forces: the family and business culture issues, the owner's concerns, and family members' concerns; (4) carrying out the succession plan by identifying a successor, grooming an heir, agreeing on a plan, and using outside help.

CHAPTER 20

TOTAL QUALITY AND THE HUMAN FACTOR:

CONTINUOUS CHALLENGES FOR ENTREPRENEURS

True/False

The Nature of Total Quality Management

F   1.   Total quality management focuses on increasing customer service regardless of the cost to the company or the customer.

T   2.   The primary rule of quality is: Do it right the first time.

F   3.   One of the key rules of total quality management is: It is more important to detect and solve problems than it is to prevent them.

T   4.   TQM places a strong emphasis on management by fact.

F   5.   While top management support is desirable in TQM efforts, research reveals that it is not critical to the total quality effort.

F   6.   Lee Iacocca said, "Successful companies have to change from leveraging muscle power to leveraging intellectual power."

F   7.   TQM firms do not have to worry about becoming a "good corporate citizen."

TQM Tools and Techniques

T   8.   One step in setting up a total quality management program is to plan and organize the effort.

T   9.   Data collection sheets are useful in gathering information on performance so that problems can be identified and corrected.

F   10.   A Pareto chart helps identify and correlate the relationship between two variables such as training and worker performance.

T   11.   The first step in constructing a Pareto chart is to gather information on the problem to be studied.

T   12. Cause-and-effect diagrams help explain the reasons for a problem and point the way toward solutions or improvements.

T   13. A cause-and-effect diagram can have such factors as environment, resources/people, and procedures (i.e., agendas).

T   14. A scatter diagram illustrates the relationship between two variables.

F   15. "Tool box" is a TQM idea which holds that tools are more important than principles.

Customer Service Focus

T   16. The primary focus of all TQM efforts is the customer.

T   17. One of the most common ways of gathering information on customer service is through the use of surveys.

Cycle Time Focus

F   18. If a company can increase its cycle time, quality will also increase.

T   19. One way of reducing cycle time is through the use of flow charting.

Employee Focus

F   20. Training is critical to TQM, but remember that outside trainers should never be used to supplement this process; it should always consist of internal expertise because they know the organization best.

T   21. Empowerment is the authority to take control and make decisions.

T   22. Many total quality management firms maintain their quality-driven momentum through the effective use of rewards.

Continuous Improvement

F   23. Continuous improvement is a process that relies very heavily on a small number of very large improvements as opposed to a large number of very small improvements.

T   24.   One of the principles of continuous improvement is to keep the workplace clean so that it is easy to find things.

T   25.   One of the principles of continuous improvement is to develop procedures for getting things done quickly and correctly.

Multiple Choice

The Nature of Total Quality Management

B   26.   Entrepreneurial ability is important in running both small and large firms, and many companies spend a great deal of time trying to keep the "_____" alive.
a. authoritative management style
b. entrepreneurial fire
c. participative management style
d. employees
e. entrepreneurial creativeness

C   27.   The core values and concepts of TQM-driven firms include:
a. Short-range outlook.
b. Management by fiction.
c. Public responsibility.
d. Competitive-driven quality.
e. None of the above.

D   28.   The implementation and controlling steps are often determined when the firm formulates its total quality plan. The focus is on key results that can be measured and charted; hence, an example of results that can be measured is SQI, which stands for:
a. Several Quality Indicators
b. Seven Quality Initiatives
c. Sequential Quality Indicators
d. Service Quality Indicators
e. None of the above

A   29.   Total quality management is a _____ management system that aims at continual increases in customer service at continually lower real costs.
a. people-focused
b. profit-focused
c. time-focused
d. efficiency-focused

The Dryden Press   567

D 30. The primary rule of total quality is:
   a. do it with less materials.
   b. do it cheaper.
   c. do it faster.
   d. do it right the first time.

C 31. Giving the customer more than he or she wants or expects is known as providing:
   a. ongoing Pareto analysis.
   b. increased cycle time.
   c. customer delight.
   d. continuous improvement.

B 32. Which of the following is a core value of TQM?
   a. small not large
   b. prevention not detection
   c. cost not quality
   d. effort not time

B 33. Management by fact, a TQM core value, means that the company should avoid using or give least attention to:
   a. data collection.
   b. opinions.
   c. analysis.
   d. information.

D 34. In a TQM effort, top management support is:
   a. not always necessary.
   b. usually helpful.
   c. a good idea.
   d. critical.

C 35. Today Motorola is so effective in producing high quality products that the company measures its error rate in errors per:
   a. thousand.
   b. million.
   c. billion.
   d. trillion.

TQM Tools and Techniques

B   36. The first step in constructing a Pareto chart is to _____ .
   a. analyze Data Collection Sheets
   b. gather information
   c. discuss goals of chart
   d. identify problems
   e. all of the above

A   37. The Pareto chart identifies the _____ and the cause-and-effect diagram helps to explain the _____ .
   a. problems; reasons
   b. reasons; problems
   c. environment; procedures
   d. procedures; environment
   e. none of the above

A   38. _____ are used to gather information on performance so that problems can be identified and corrected.
   a. Data collection sheets
   b. Pareto charts
   c. Cause-and-effect diagrams
   d. Scatter diagrams

A   39. A _____ is a special form of vertical bar graph that helps identify which problems are to be solved and in what order.
   a. Pareto chart
   b. data collection sheet
   c. scatter diagram
   d. cause-and-effect diagram

C   40. The Pareto principle holds that _____ percent of all outcomes can be attributed to _____ percent of all causes.
   a. 50; 50
   b. 60; 40
   c. 80; 20
   d. 90; 10

B   41. Pareto charts are based on the principle that _____ of causes accounts for a _____ of problems or mistakes.
   a. a small number; small number
   b. a small number; large number
   c. a large number; small number

The Dryden Press

D   42. _____ are often used as a follow-up to Pareto analysis.
   a. Scatter diagrams
   b. Flow chart analyses
   c. Data collection sheets
   d. Cause-and-effect diagrams

D   43. In which of the following is brainstorming most commonly used?
   a. scatter diagrams
   b. flow charts
   c. data collection sheets
   d. cause-and-effect diagrams

C   44. _____ are used to illustrate the relationship between two variables.
   a. Data collection sheets
   b. Flow charts
   c. Scatter diagrams
   d. Cause-and-effect diagrams

B   45. A company would like to examine the effect of training on its sales force. Which one of the following TQM tools would be of most value in this process?
   a. data collection sheets
   b. cause-and-effect diagrams
   c. scatter diagrams
   d. flow charts

A   46. Individuals who are trained in TQM often learn about a concept called tool box. What does tool box encourage people to do?
   a. choose the TQM tools that are of most value and ignore the rest
   b. use mechanical approaches to improving quality
   c. think of total quality as a machine that needs to be kept finely tuned
   d. choose technical TQM tools before opting for conceptual TQM tools

E   47. TQM tools include:
   a. control charts.
   b. frequency histograms.
   c. statistical process controls.
   d. none of the above.
   e. all of the above.

Customer Service Focus

E   48.   The primary focus of TQM is typically done by placing attention on which areas?
   a. data analysis
   b. opinions and morals
   c. data emulation
   d. beliefs and values
   e. a and d only

C   49.   The primary focus of all TQM efforts is:
   a. time.
   b. cost.
   c. the customer.
   d. profits.

D   50.   Customer-related information is often gathered through the use of:
   a. questionnaire surveys.
   b. customer panel surveys.
   c. interviews.
   d. all of the above.

B   51.   Information of industry trends and developments, market segmentation practices, and newly developing markets are provided by _____ surveys.
   a. customer panel
   b. demographic
   c. questionnaire
   d. psychographic
   e. none of the above

D   52.   Ways in which one can pare time include:
   a. getting everyone to cooperate.
   b. improve cycle time.
   c. breaking down walls between departments.
   d. all of the above.
   e. none of the above.

B   53.   _____ time is the time needed to complete a task.
   a. Pareto
   b. Cycle
   c. Paring
   d. Break-even

A 54. _____ is a procedure in which all steps in a job or process are identified and written out in the form of a flow diagram.
  a. Flow charting
  b. Pareto analysis
  c. Cause-and-effect diagraming
  d. Data collection analysis

Employee Focus

B 55. Because TQM depends so heavily on employee contribution and cooperation, effective total quality management firms spend a great deal of time on all of the following *except*:
  a. empowerment.
  b. profits.
  c. training.
  d. recognition.

A 56. _____ is the authority to take control and make decisions.
  a. Empowerment
  b. Ishikawa analysis
  c. Pareto focus
  d. Flow charting

C 57. Approaches such as the Implemented Improvement System, which has been drawn from the Japanese, are designed to encourage employees to:
  a. reduce cycle time.
  b. Pareto their problem.
  c. make suggestions.
  d. build cause-and-effect diagrams.

E 58. Which is *not* a typical reward used by TQM companies?
  a. Certificates
  b. Honor roll
  c. Picture in company paper
  d. Plaques
  e. All are typical rewards

Continuous Improvement

D   59. Continuous improvement places a strong emphasis on _____ gains accompanied by _____ innovation.
   a. small; continual
   b. large; continual
   c. large; occasional
   d. small; occasional

A   60. Which of the following is most characteristic of constant improvement?
   a. long-term and long-lasting, but not dramatic, changes in quality
   b. short-term, dramatic increases in quality
   c. abrupt and volatile increases in quality
   d. heavily technologically-driven changes in quality

B   61. _____ is the process of increasing the quality of goods and services through incremental gains accompanied by occasional innovation.
   a. Customer-driven quality
   b. Continuous improvement
   c. Pareto Charts analysis
   d. TQM
   e. None of the above

E.   62. Entrepreneurially driven firms can achieve a number of benefits from continuous improvement. The benefits could include:
   a. increased competitiveness.
   b. increased quality of output.
   c. higher profitability.
   d. lower operating break-even point.
   e. all of the above.

Essay

63. *Why is Pareto analysis so popular as a TQM tool? Explain.*
   Pareto analysis is popular for two reasons. First, it is easy to Pareto problems once the data have been collected, and the bar graphs help clearly pinpoint those problems that need to be given priority. Second, since a few causes often account for a large number of problems, by focusing on just the first couple of major causes, Pareto analysis helps organizations achieve major improvements in quality without expending a great deal of time and effort.

64. ***What are three of the most common ways that organizations gather information on how the customers feel about their service and what they can do to improve this service?***

One of the most common ways that organizations gather information on how the customers feel about their service is through the use of questionnaire surveys that are distributed to the customers. The latter are asked to fill them out and send them back to the company, where they are analyzed, often put in the form of a Pareto chart, and used for deciding the type of action that will now be taken to improve the service. A second common way of gathering information is the panel survey in which customers are brought together and asked to provide face-to-face feedback to the organization. A third is through the use of interviews in which people provide one-on-one feedback to the company. All three of these methods are useful because they give the firm information that can be used in designing and streamlining the services that it provides.

Transparency Masters

TM No.

1-1	The Employee Size of U.S. Businesses
1-2	The Smallest Businesses Create the Most New Jobs
1-3	Growth by Gazelles, 1990–1994
1-4	Minority-Owned Businesses
2-1	Entrepreneurial Schools-of-Thought Approach
2-2	Entrepreneurial Events Formation Process
2-3	Entrepreneurial Assessment Approach
2-4	Variables in New-Venture Creation
3-1	Shared Vision
3-2	Radical versus Incremental Innovation
3-3	Intrapreneurial Development: Joint Function of Individual and Organizational Factors
3-4	The Ten Commandments of An Intrapreneur
3-5	An Interactive Model of Corporate Entrepreneuring
4-1	Typology of Entrepreneurial Styles
4-2	A Model of Entrepreneurial Motivation
5-1	Two Approaches to Creative Problem Solving
5-2	The Most Common Idea Stoppers
5-3	The Creative Thinking Process
5-4	Processes Associated with the Two Brain Hemispheres
5-5	Ways to Develop Left- and Right-Hemisphere Skills
6-1	Classifying Decisions Using a Conceptual Framework
6-2	Types of Morally Questionable Acts
6-3	Overlap between Moral Standards and Legal Requirements
6-4	Classifying Corporate Social Behavior
6-5	A Social Responsibility Scale
6-6	Issues Viewed by Small-Business Owners
7-1	Environmental Variables
7-2	An Entrepreneur's Contingency Decision Model for Public Policy
7-3	Elements of Industry Structure
7-4	Competitive Profile Analysis
7-5	Components of a Competitive Analysis
7-6	Reliance versus Commitment: Development of Exceptional Community Support
7-7	Deservedness versus Identification: Development of Exceptional Community Support
7-8	How Does the Incubator Work?
8-1	Using Classification of Goods to Select Channel Intermediaries
8-2	The Evolution of the Marketing Function
9-1	Summary of Account Changes for Pro Forma Balance Sheet
9-2	Financial Ratios
10-1	Helpful Hints for Writing the Business Plan
10-2	Business Plan Checklist: A Personal Step-by-Step Evaluation
11-1	The Elements Affecting New-Venture Performance
11-2	Internal and External Problems Entrepreneurs Experience
11-3	Key Areas for Assessing the Feasibility of a New Venture
12-1	Factors Associated with Partnership Success
12-2	The Costs of Franchising

The Dryden Press

13-1	Major Legal Concepts and Entrepreneurial Ventures
13-2	Trademarks: Protected and Unprotected
13-3	Business Failures through the Years (1927–1995)
13-4	Bankruptcy: A Comparison of Chapters 7,11,12, and 13
13-5	Entrepreneurs' Preferred Financial Sources
14-1	Venture Capital Disbursements by Stage, 1992
14-2	Venture Capitalist System of Evaluating Product/Service and Management
14-3	Returns on Investment Venture Capitalists Typically Seek
14-4	Key Results from Entrepreneurs Successful in Obtaining Venture Capital
14-5	"Angel Stats"
15-1	Strategic Management Model
15-2	The Opportunity Management Approach
15-3	Normative Planning Model
15-4	Entrepreneurial Strategy: A Contingency Multi-stage Approach
15-5	A Venture's Typical Life Cycle
15-6	The Entrepreneurial Mind
16-1	The Entrepreneurial Culture versus The Administrative Culture
16-2	Role of Self-Management in the Functioning and Survival of Entrepreneurs
16-3	Conflicting Designs of Structural Factors
16-4	Decision-Making Characteristics and Growth Stages
17-1	The Ten Largest U.S. Export Markets
17-2	The Ten Largest U.S. Import Markets
17-3	Risk of Entering Global Markets
17-4	Analysis of Global Expansion Decisions
18-1	Total Amount Needed to Buy a Business
19-1	Barriers to Succession Planning in Family Firms
19-2	Pressures and Interests in a Family Business
19-3	A Checklist for Succession: Some Important Steps
20-1	A Cause-and-Effect Diagram for Dealing with Unproductive Meetings
20-2	Typical Rewards Total Quality Management Companies Use
20-3	A Comparison of Constant Improvement and Innovation

TM 1-1 The Employee Size of U.S. Businesses

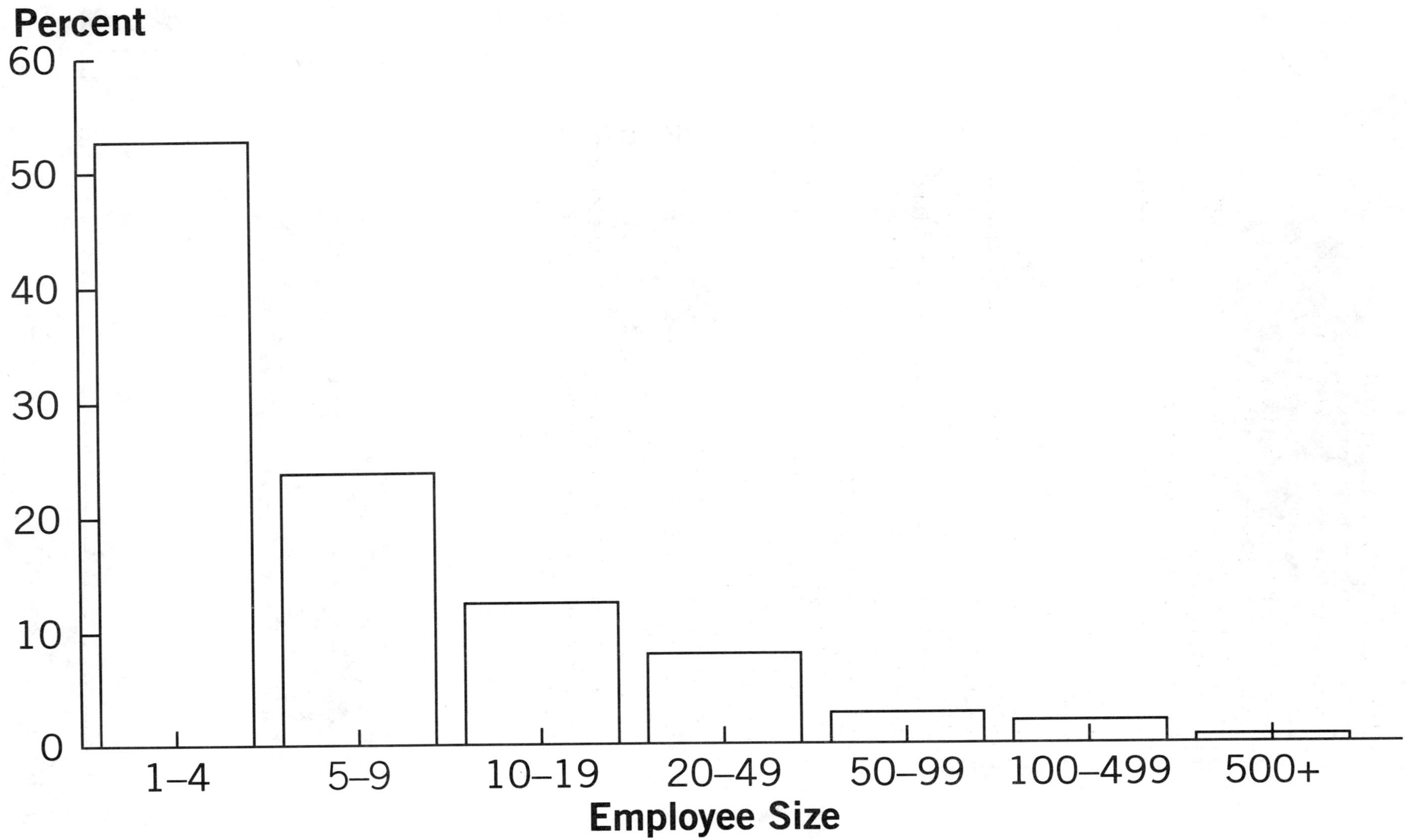

Percent

Employee Size	
1–4	~54
5–9	~23
10–19	~12
20–49	~8
50–99	~2
100–499	~2
500+	~0

The Dryden Press

TM 1-2 The Smallest Businesses Create the Most New Jobs

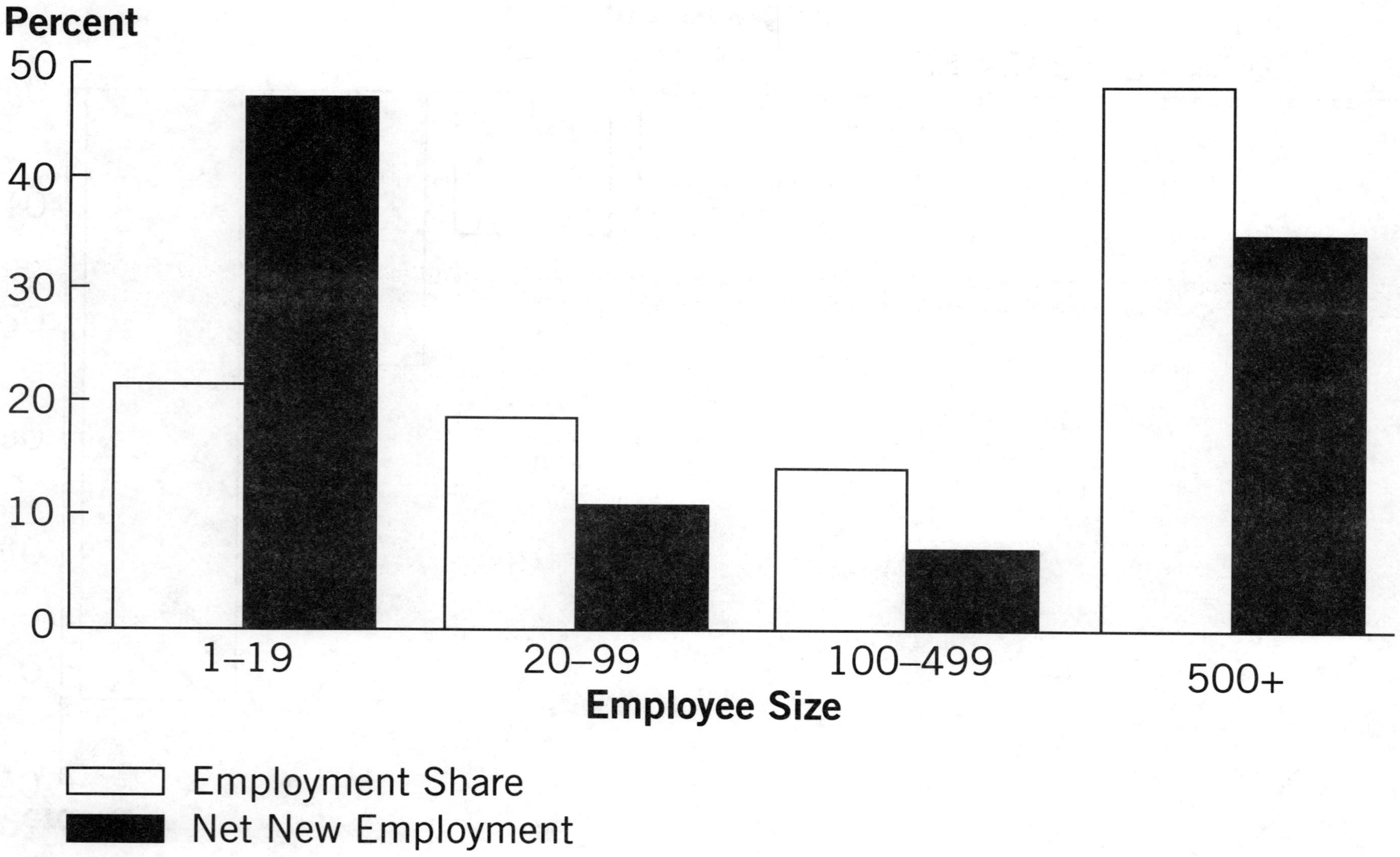

Percent

Employee Size	1–19	20–99	100–499	500+
Employment Share	~21	~18	~16	~45
Net New Employment	~47	~14	~7	~32

☐ Employment Share
■ Net New Employment

The Dryden Press

TM 1-3 Growth by Gazelles, 1990–1994

GROWTH BY GAZELLES, 1990–1994

Jobs created by gazelles	5.0 million
Jobs lost by other companies	−0.8
Net employment growth	4.2 million

The Dryden Press

TM 1-4 Minority-Owned Businesses

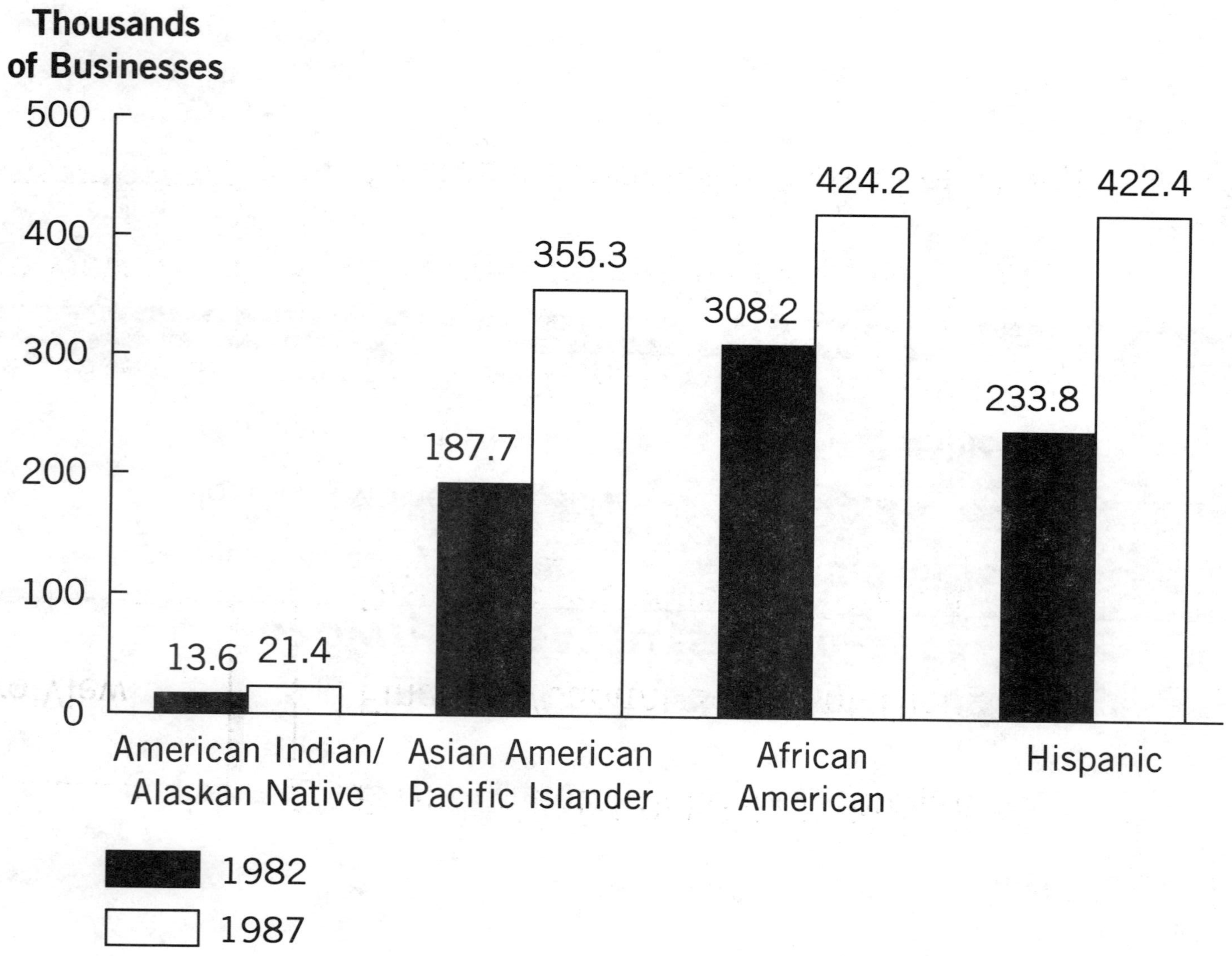

Thousands of Businesses

Group	1982	1987
American Indian/Alaskan Native	13.6	21.4
Asian American Pacific Islander	187.7	355.3
African American	308.2	424.2
Hispanic	233.8	422.4

TM 2-1 Entrepreneurial Schools-of-Thought Approach

Macro View
- Environmental School of Thought
- Financial/Capital School of Thought
- Displacement School of Thought

Micro View
- Entrepreneurial Trait School of Thought (People School)
- Venture Opportunity School of Thought
- Strategic Formulation School of Thought

The Dryden Press

TM 2-2 Entrepreneurial Events Formation Process

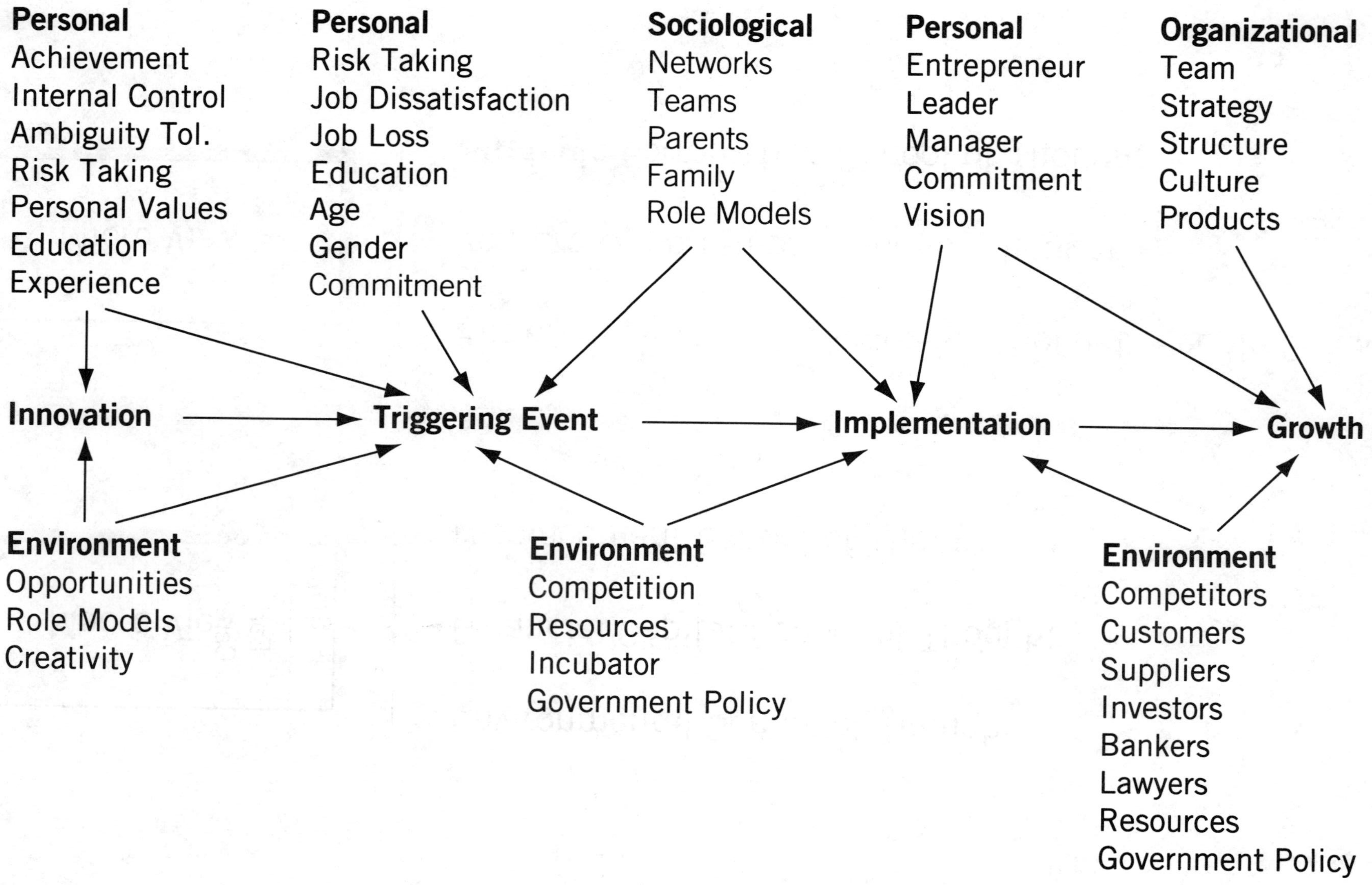

Personal	**Personal**	**Sociological**	**Personal**	**Organizational**
Achievement	Risk Taking	Networks	Entrepreneur	Team
Internal Control	Job Dissatisfaction	Teams	Leader	Strategy
Ambiguity Tol.	Job Loss	Parents	Manager	Structure
Risk Taking	Education	Family	Commitment	Culture
Personal Values	Age	Role Models	Vision	Products
Education	Gender			
Experience	Commitment			

Innovation → Triggering Event → Implementation → Growth

Environment
Opportunities
Role Models
Creativity

Environment
Competition
Resources
Incubator
Government Policy

Environment
Competitors
Customers
Suppliers
Investors
Bankers
Lawyers
Resources
Government Policy

The Dryden Press

TM 2-3 Entrepreneurial Assessment Approach

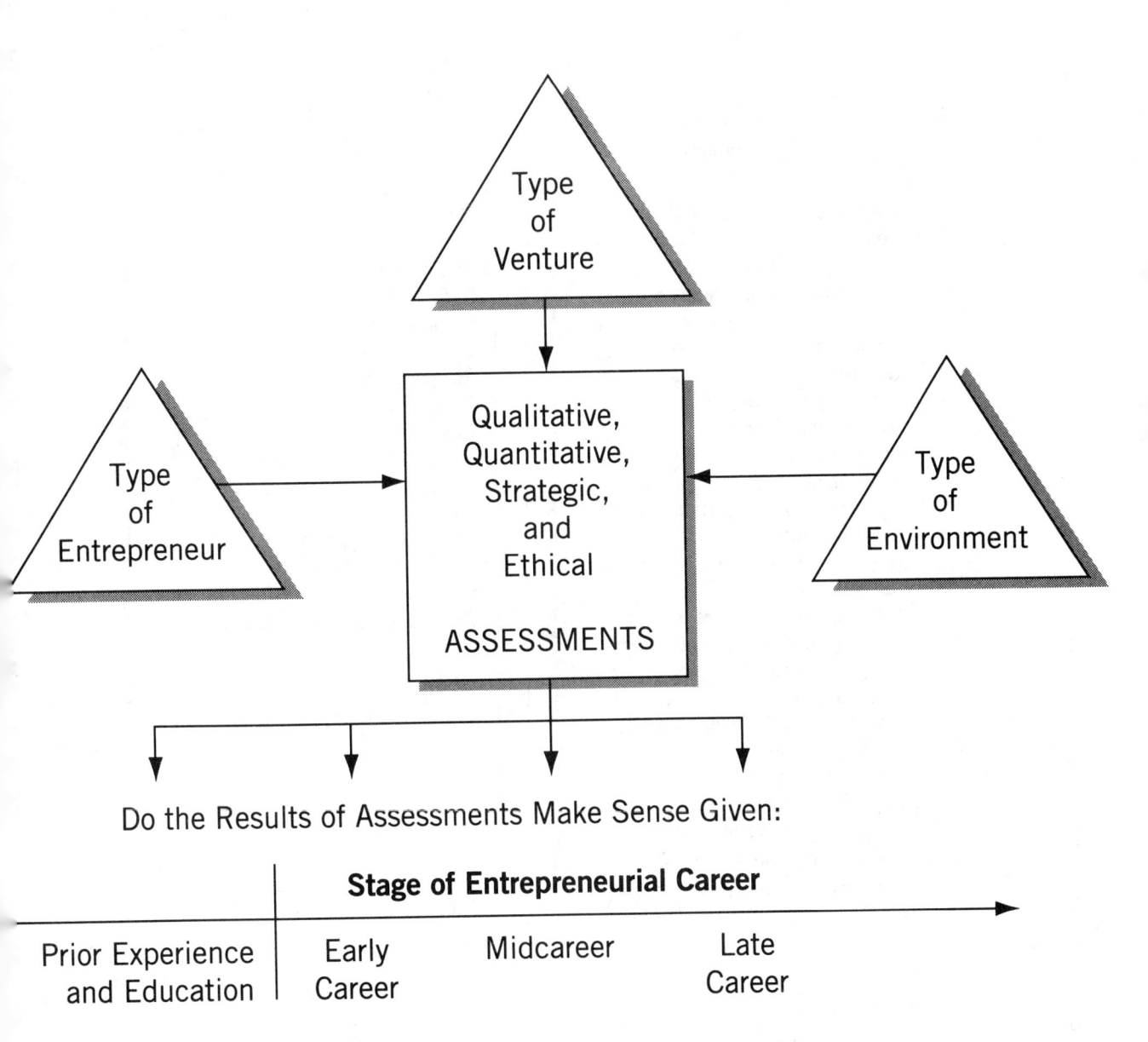

```
                    ┌─────────────┐
                    │    Type     │
                    │     of      │
                    │   Venture   │
                    └──────┬──────┘
                           │
                           ▼
  ┌──────────┐      ┌─────────────┐      ┌──────────────┐
  │   Type   │      │ Qualitative,│      │     Type     │
  │    of    │─────▶│Quantitative,│◀─────│      of      │
  │Entrepre- │      │  Strategic, │      │ Environment  │
  │   neur   │      │     and     │      │              │
  └──────────┘      │   Ethical   │      └──────────────┘
                    │ ASSESSMENTS │
                    └──────┬──────┘
                  ┌────┬───┴───┬────┐
                  ▼    ▼       ▼    ▼
```

Do the Results of Assessments Make Sense Given:

Stage of Entrepreneurial Career ──────────────▶

| Prior Experience and Education | Early Career | Midcareer | Late Career |

The Dryden Press

TM 2-4 Variables in New-Venture Creation

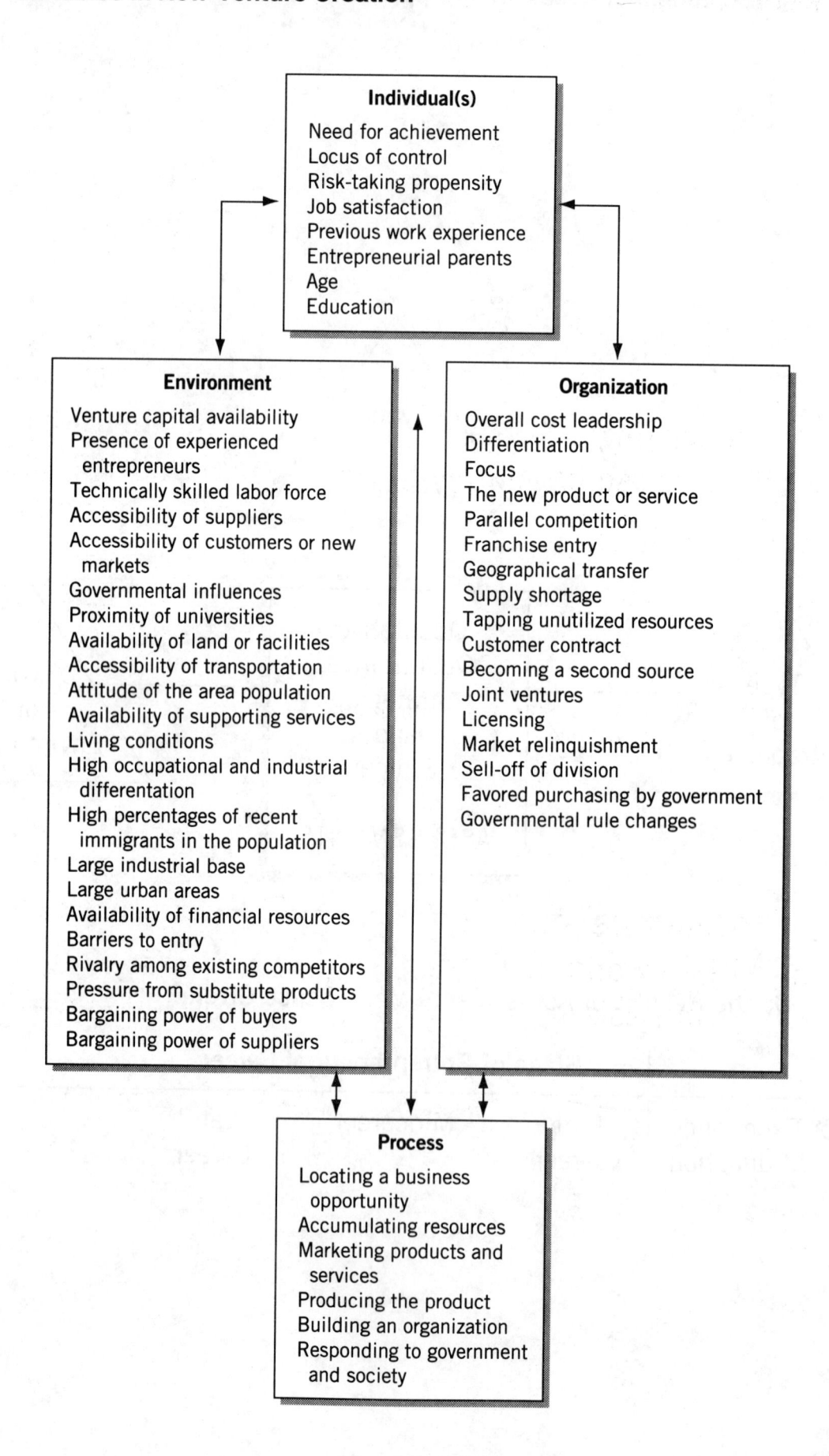

Individual(s)
- Need for achievement
- Locus of control
- Risk-taking propensity
- Job satisfaction
- Previous work experience
- Entrepreneurial parents
- Age
- Education

Environment
- Venture capital availability
- Presence of experienced entrepreneurs
- Technically skilled labor force
- Accessibility of suppliers
- Accessibility of customers or new markets
- Governmental influences
- Proximity of universities
- Availability of land or facilities
- Accessibility of transportation
- Attitude of the area population
- Availability of supporting services
- Living conditions
- High occupational and industrial differentation
- High percentages of recent immigrants in the population
- Large industrial base
- Large urban areas
- Availability of financial resources
- Barriers to entry
- Rivalry among existing competitors
- Pressure from substitute products
- Bargaining power of buyers
- Bargaining power of suppliers

Organization
- Overall cost leadership
- Differentiation
- Focus
- The new product or service
- Parallel competition
- Franchise entry
- Geographical transfer
- Supply shortage
- Tapping unutilized resources
- Customer contract
- Becoming a second source
- Joint ventures
- Licensing
- Market relinquishment
- Sell-off of division
- Favored purchasing by government
- Governmental rule changes

Process
- Locating a business opportunity
- Accumulating resources
- Marketing products and services
- Producing the product
- Building an organization
- Responding to government and society

The Dryden Press

M 3-1   Shared Vision

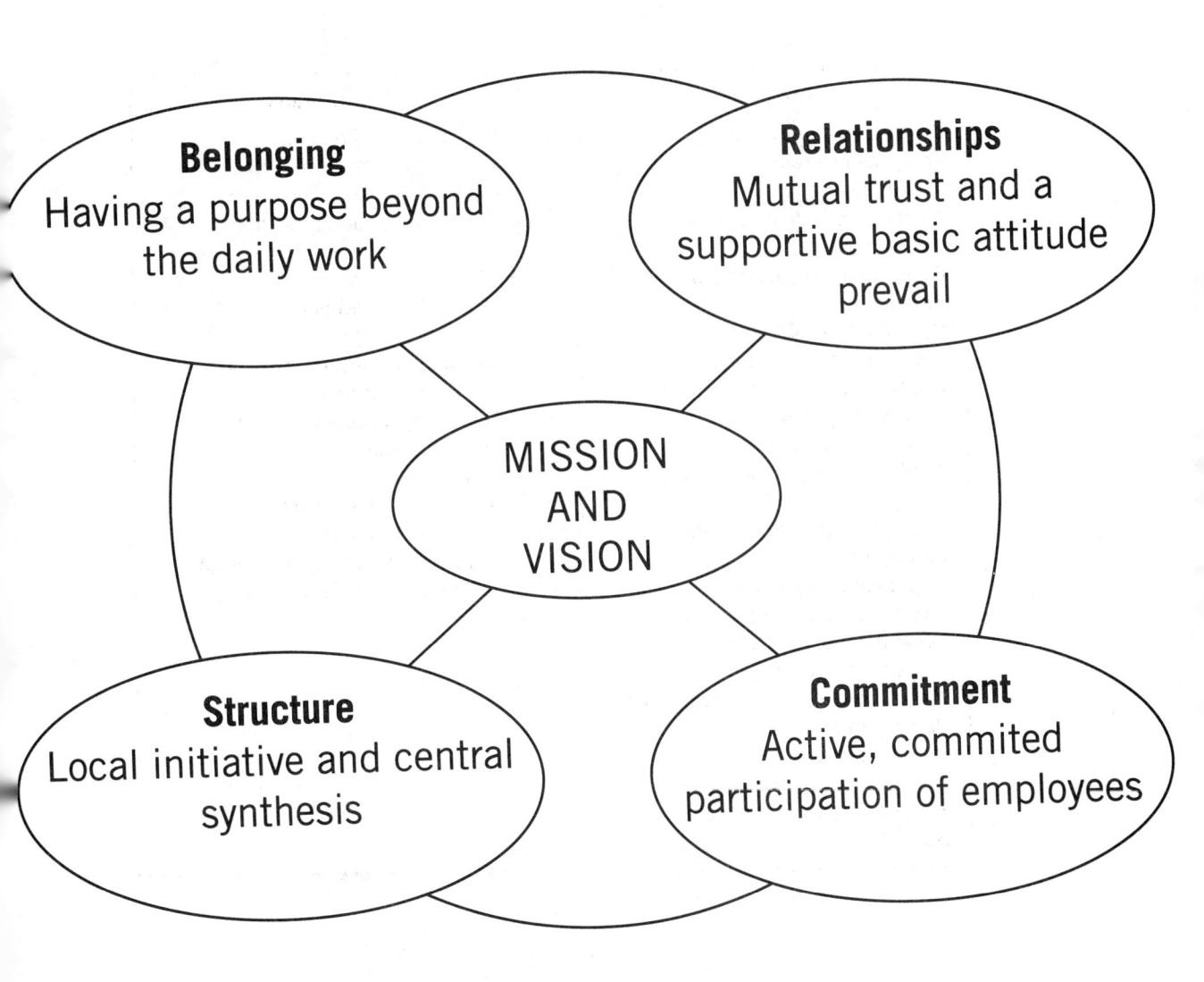

- **Belonging**: Having a purpose beyond the daily work
- **Relationships**: Mutual trust and a supportive basic attitude prevail
- **MISSION AND VISION**
- **Structure**: Local initiative and central synthesis
- **Commitment**: Active, commited participation of employees

The Dryden Press

TM 3-2 Radical versus Incremental Innovation

Dollars

Radical Innovation			Incremental Innovation		
New Products			Product Improvements and Extensions		
Creates New Markets			Better Ways of Doing Business		
Highly Experimental			More Systematic and Predictable		

| Prototype | Market Test | Rapid Growth | Industry Shake-Out | Industry Maturity | Industry Decline |

The Dryden Press

TM 3-3   Intrapreneurial Development: Joint Function of Individual and Organizational Factors

Job Attitudes

- Organizational Commitment
- Job Satisfaction

Behavioral Intentions

- Propensity to Leave

Individual Factors

- Attributes and Role Requirements
- Values
- Behavioral Orientations

Organizational Factors

- Structure
- Reward System

"Noise"

Includes stability of product, economic conditions

The Dryden Press

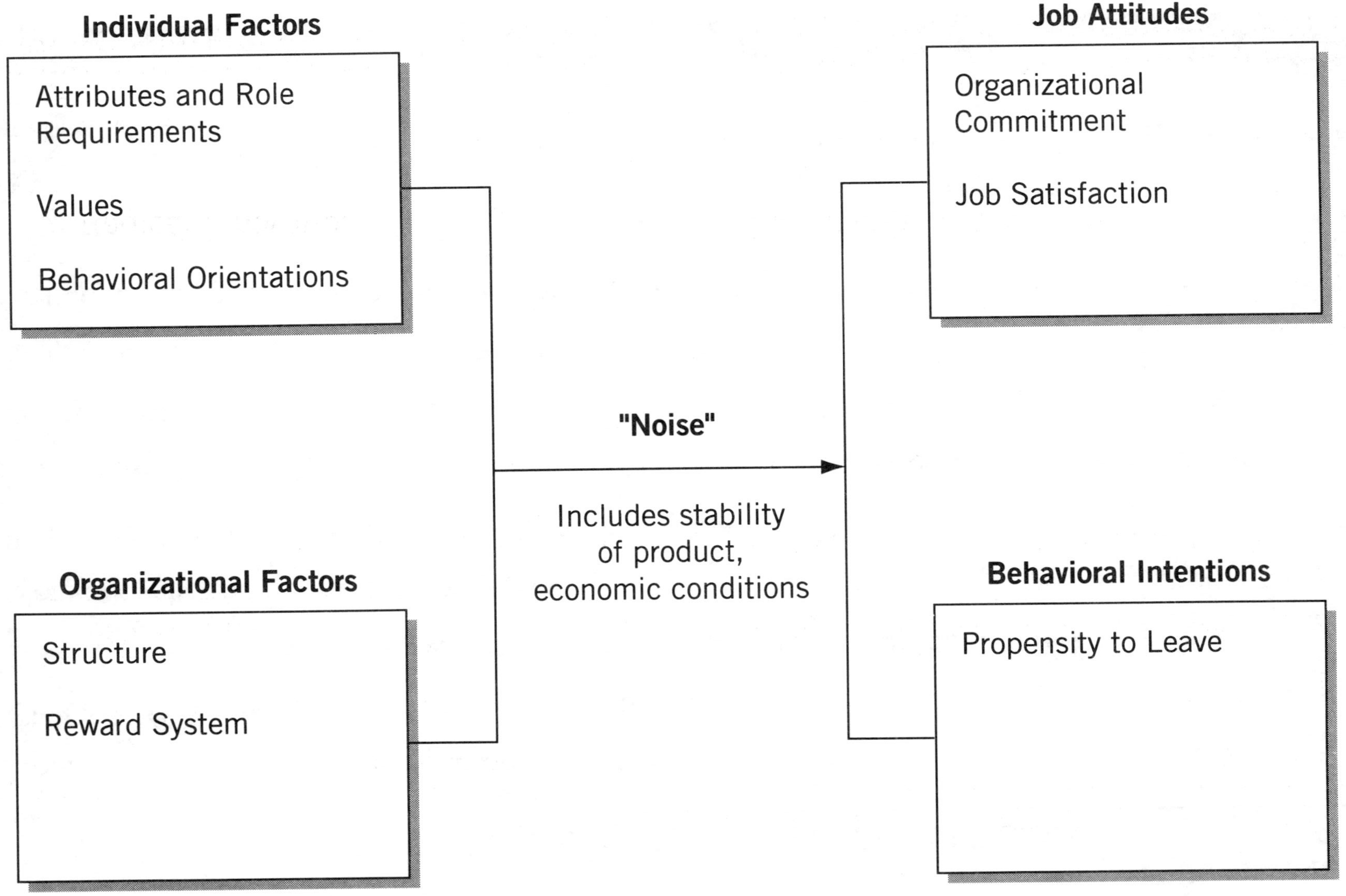

TM 3-4 The Ten Commandments of an Intrapreneur

THE TEN COMMANDMENTS OF AN INTRAPRENEUR

1. Come to work each day willing to be fired.
2. Circumvent any orders aimed at stopping your dream.
3. Do any job needed to make your project work, regardless of your job description.
4. Network with good people to assist you.
5. Build a spirited team: Choose and work with only the best.
6. Work underground as long as you can—publicity triggers the corporate immune mechanism.
7. Be loyal and truthful to your sponsors.
8. Remember it is easier to ask forgiveness than for permission.
9. Be true to your goals, but be realistic about the ways to achieve them.
10. Keep the vision strong.

SOURCE: Adapted from *Intrapreneuring* by Gifford Pinchot III, 1985, 22. Copyright © 1985 by Gifford Pinchot III. Adapted by permission of HarperCollins Publishers.

The Dryden Press

TM 3-5 An Interactive Model of Corporate Entrepreneuring

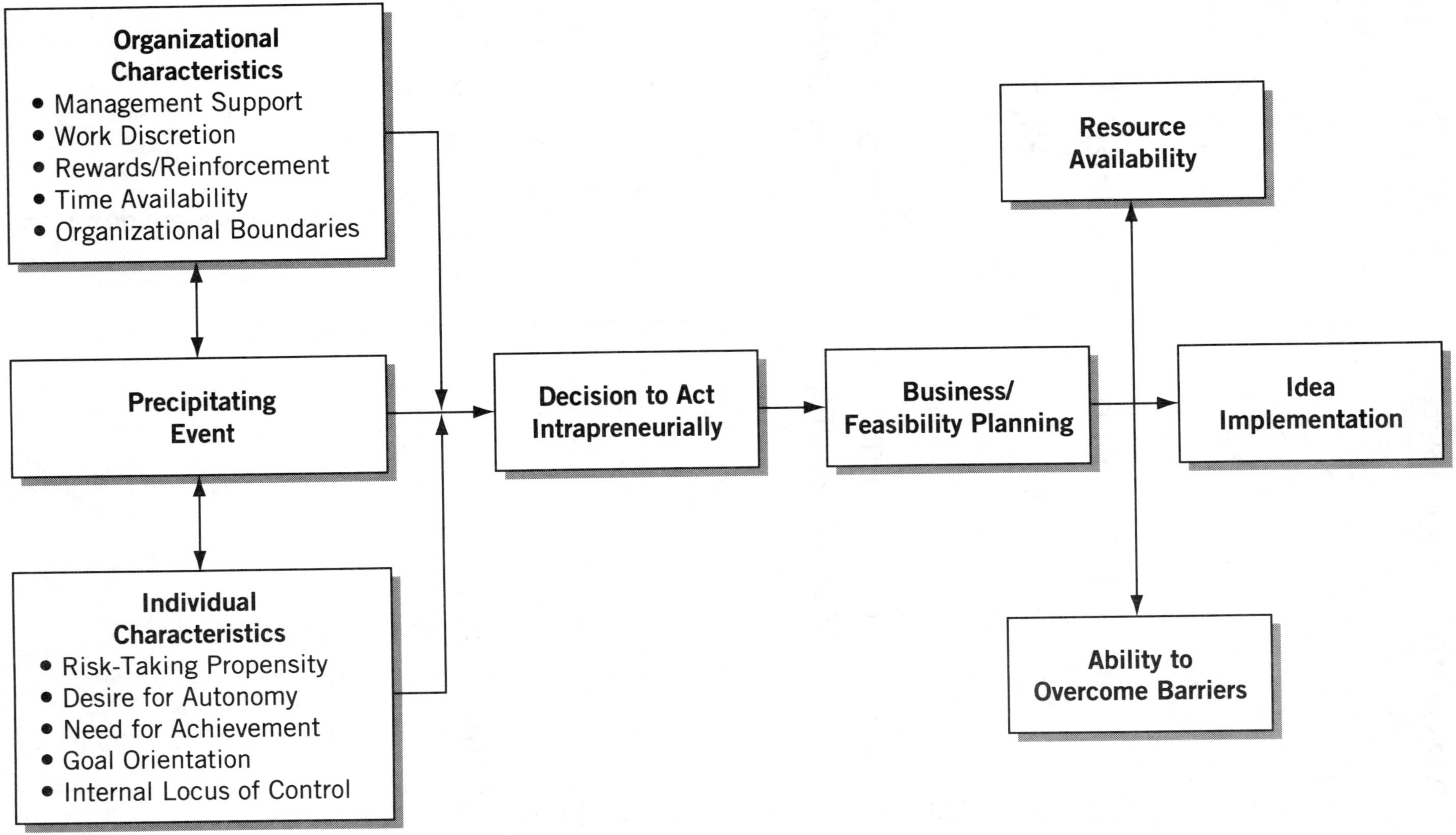

Organizational Characteristics
- Management Support
- Work Discretion
- Rewards/Reinforcement
- Time Availability
- Organizational Boundaries

Precipitating Event

Individual Characteristics
- Risk-Taking Propensity
- Desire for Autonomy
- Need for Achievement
- Goal Orientation
- Internal Locus of Control

Decision to Act Intrapreneurially

Business/Feasibility Planning

Resource Availability

Ability to Overcome Barriers

Idea Implementation

The Dryden Press

TM 4-1　Typology of Entrepreneurial Styles

	Level of Personal Financial Risk	
	Low	**High**
Low	Risk avoiding Activity seeking	Risk accepting Activity seeking
High	Risk avoiding Profit seeking	Risk accepting Profit seeking

Level of Profit Motive (row axis)

TM 4-2 A Model of Entrepreneurial Motivation

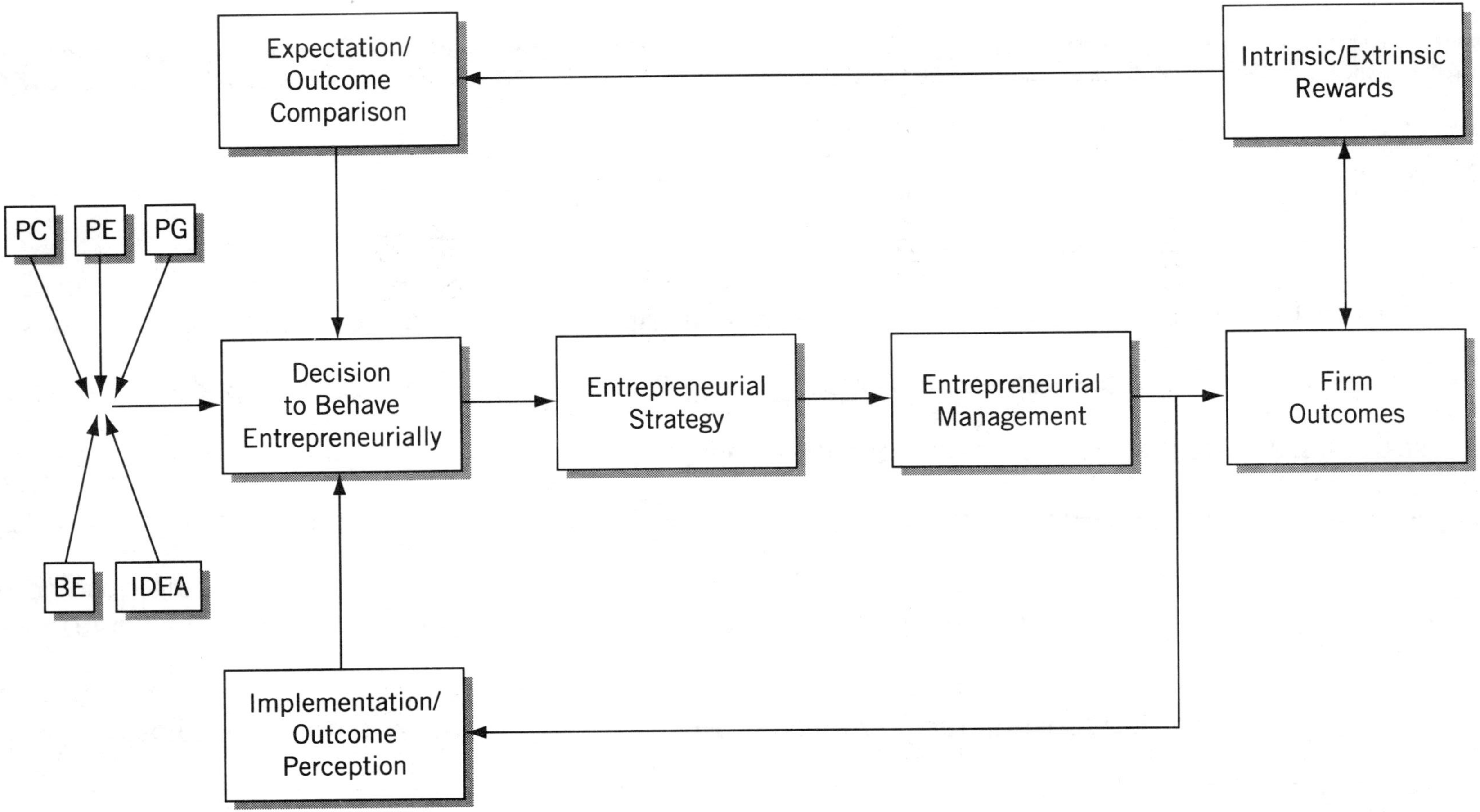

PC = Personal Characteristics
PE = Personal Environment
PG = Personal Goals
BE = Business Environment

The Dryden Press

TM 5-1 Two Approaches to Creative Problem Solving

TWO APPROACHES TO CREATIVE PROBLEM SOLVING

Adaptor	**Innovator**
Employs a disciplined, precise, methodical approach	Approaches tasks from unusual angles
Is concerned with solving, rather than finding, problems	Discovers problems and avenues of solutions
Attempts to refine current practices	Questions basic assumptions related to current practices
Tends to be means oriented	Has little regard for means; is more interested in ends
Is capable of extended detail work	Has little tolerance for routine work
Is sensitive to group cohesion and cooperation	Has little or no need for consensus; often is insensitive to others

SOURCE: Michael Kirton, "Adaptors and Innovators: A Description and Measure," *Journal of Applied Psychology* (October 1976): 623. Copyright 1976 by The American Psychological Association.

The Dryden Press

TM 5-2 The Most Common Idea Stoppers

THE MOST COMMON IDEA STOPPERS

1. "Naah."
2. "Can't" (said with a shake of the head and an air of finality).
3. "That's the dumbest thing I've ever heard."
4. "Yeah, but if you did that . . ." (poses an extreme or unlikely disaster case).
5. "We already tried that—years ago."
6. "We've done all right so far; why do we need that?"
7. "I don't see anything wrong with the way we're doing it now."
8. "That doesn't sound too practical."
9. "We've never done anything like that before."
10. "Let's get back to reality."
11. "We've got deadlines to meet—we don't have time to consider that."
12. "It's not in the budget."
13. "Are you kidding?"
14. "Let's not go off on a tangent."
15. "Where do you get these weird ideas?"

SOURCE: Adapted from *The Creative Process*, ed. Angela M. Biondi, The Creative Education Foundation, 1986.

The Dryden Press

TM 5-3 The Creative Thinking Process

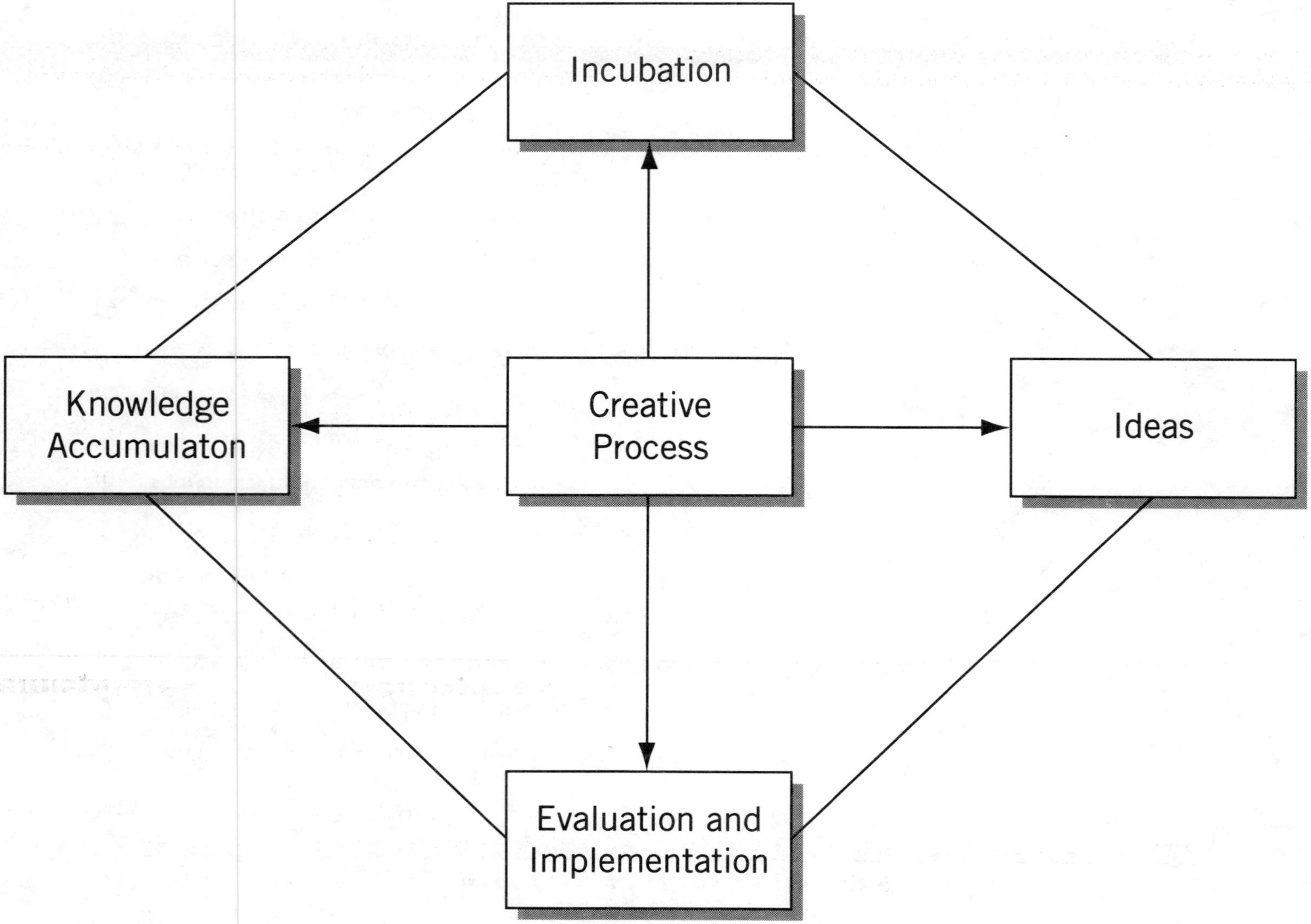

```
                    ┌──────────┐
                    │  Ideas   │
                    └──────────┘
                    ↑         ↖
                   ╱           ╲
                  ╱             ╲
    ┌────────────┐  ┌──────────┐  ┌──────────────┐
    │ Incubation │←─│ Creative │─→│ Evaluation and│
    │            │  │ Process  │  │Implementation │
    └────────────┘  └──────────┘  └──────────────┘
                  ╲       ↓      ╱
                   ╲             ╱
                    ┌──────────┐
                    │Knowledge │
                    │Accumulaton│
                    └──────────┘
```

The Dryden Press

TM 5-4 Processes Associated with the Two Brain Hemispheres

PROCESSES ASSOCIATED WITH THE TWO BRAIN HEMISPHERES

Left Hemisphere	Right Hemisphere
Verbal	Nonverbal
Analytical	Synthesizing
Abstract	Seeing analogies
Rational	Nonrational
Logical	Spatial
Linear	Intuitive
	Imaginitive

SOURCE: Betty Edwards, *Drawing on the Right Side of the Brain* (Los Angeles: Tarcher, 1979).

The Dryden Press

TM 5-5 Ways to Develop Left- and Right-Hemisphere Skills

WAYS TO DEVELOP LEFT- AND RIGHT-HEMISPHERE SKILLS

Left-Hemisphere Skills

1. Step-by-step planning of your work and life activities
2. Reading ancient, medieval, and scholastic philosophy, legal cases, and books on logic
3. Establishing timetables for all of your activities
4. Using and working with a computer program

Right-Hemisphere Skills

1. Using metaphors and analogies to describe things and people in your conversations and writing
2. Taking off your watch when you are not working
3. Suspending your initial judgment of ideas, new acquaintances, movies, TV programs, etc.
4. Recording your hunches, feelings, and intuitions and calculating their accuracy
5. Detailed fantasizing and visualizing things and situations in the future
6. Drawing faces, caricatures, and landscapes

The Dryden Press

TM 6-1   Classifying Decisions Using a Conceptual Framework

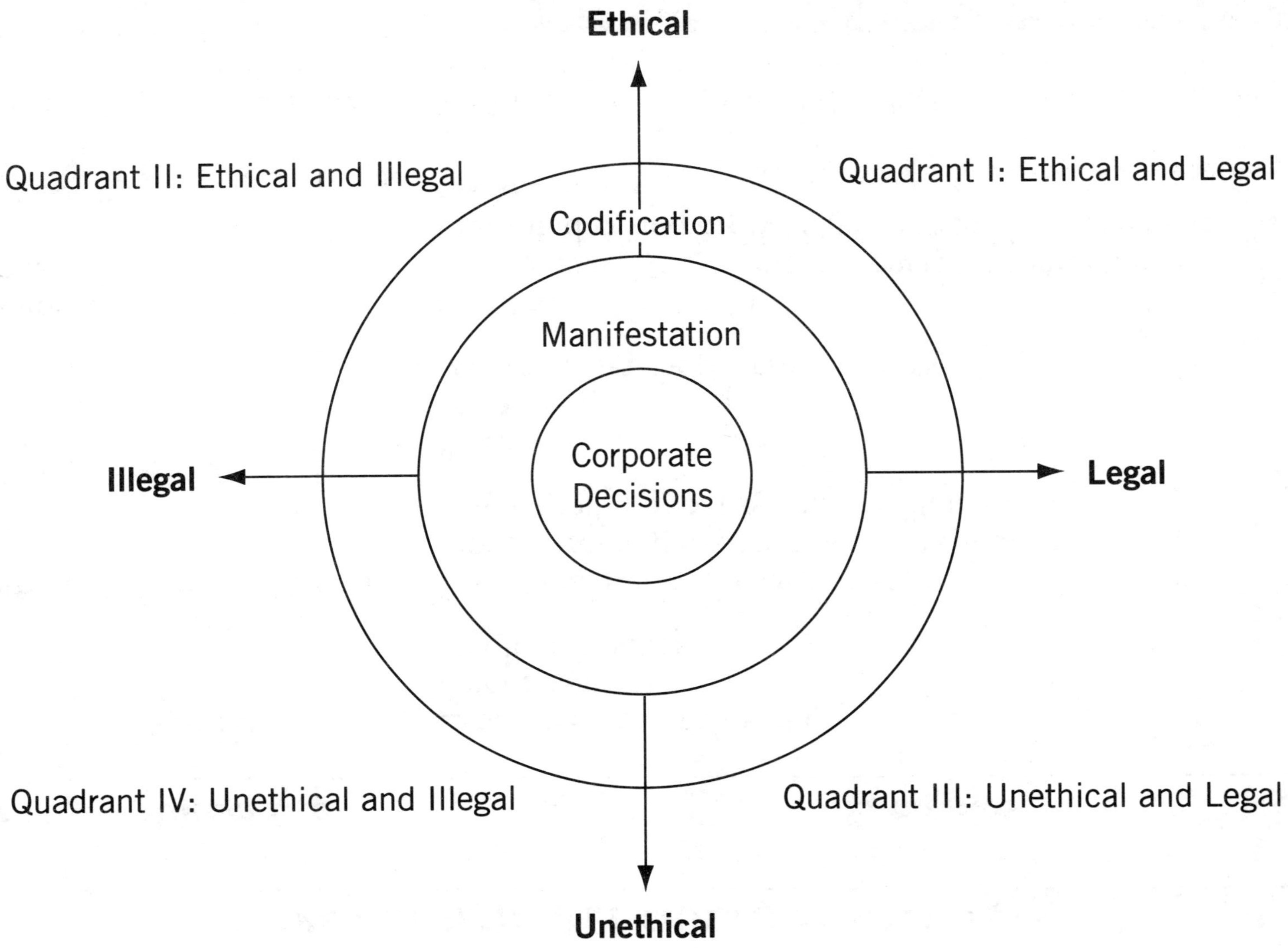

Ethical

Quadrant I: Ethical and Legal

Legal

Quadrant II: Ethical and Illegal

Codification

Manifestation

Corporate Decisions

Quadrant III: Unethical and Legal

Unethical

Quadrant IV: Unethical and Illegal

Illegal

The Dryden Press

TM 6-2 Types of Morally Questionable Acts

TYPES OF MORALLY QUESTIONABLE ACTS

Type	Direct Effect	Examples
Nonrole	Against the firm	Expense account cheating Embezzlement Stealing supplies
Role failure	Against the firm	Superficial performance appraisal Not confronting expense account cheating Palming off a poor performer with inflated praise
Role distortion	For the firm	Bribery Price fixing Manipulating suppliers
Role assertion	For the firm	Investing in South Africa Using nuclear technology for energy generation Not withdrawing product line in face of initial allegations of inadequate safety

SOURCE: James A. Waters and Frederick Bird, "Attending to Ethics in Management," *Journal of Business Ethics* 5 (1989): 494.

The Dryden Press

TM 6-3 Overlap between Moral Standards and Legal Requirements

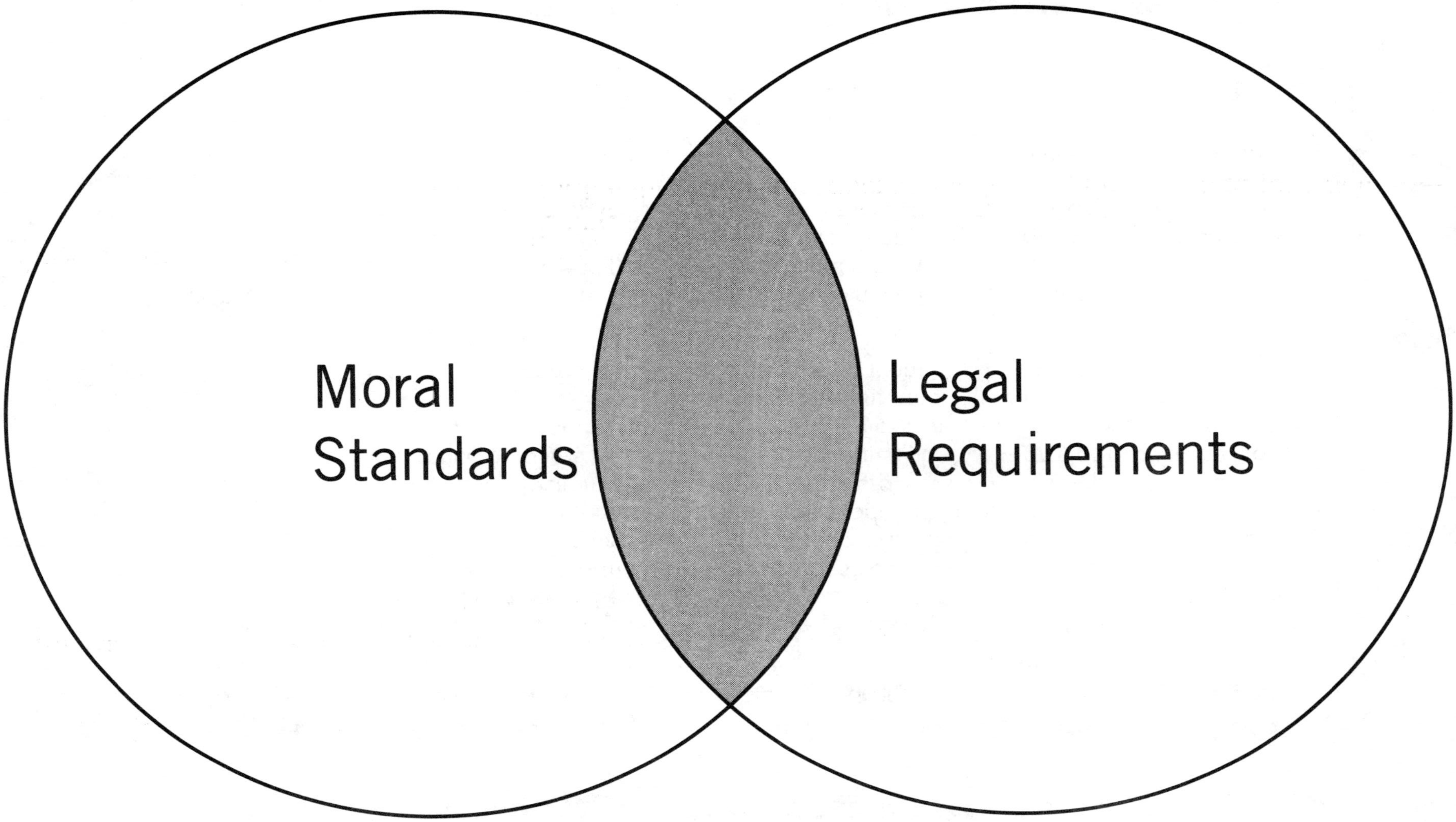

Legal Requirements

Moral Standards

The Dryden Press

TM 6-4 Classifying Corporate Social Behavior

CLASSIFYING CORPORATE SOCIAL BEHAVIOR

Dimension of Behavior	Stage One: Social Obligation	Stage Two: Social Responsibility	Stage Three: Social Responsiveness
Response to social pressures	Maintains low public profile, but if attacked, uses PR methods to upgrade its public image; denies any deficiencies; blames public dissatisfaction on ignorance or failure to understand corporate functions; discloses information only where legally required	Accepts responsibility for solving current problems; will admit deficiencies in former practices and attempt to persuade public that its current practices meet social norms; attitude toward critics conciliatory; freer information disclosures than stage one	Willingly discusses activities with outside groups; makes information freely available to public; accepts formal and informal inputs from outside groups in decision making; is willing to be publicly evaluated for its various activities
Philanthropy	Contributes only when direct benefit to it clearly shown; otherwise, views contributions as responsibility of individual employees	Contributes to noncontroversial and established causes; matches employee contributions	Activities of stage two, *plus* support and contributions to new, controversial groups whose needs it sees as unfulfilled and increasingly important

SOURCE: Excerpted from S. Prakash Sethi, "A Conceptual Framework for Environmental Analysis of Social Issues and Evaluation of Business Response Patterns," *Academy of Management Journal* (January 1979): 68.

The Dryden Press

TM 6-5 A Social Responsibility Scale

A SOCIAL RESPONSIBILITY SCALE

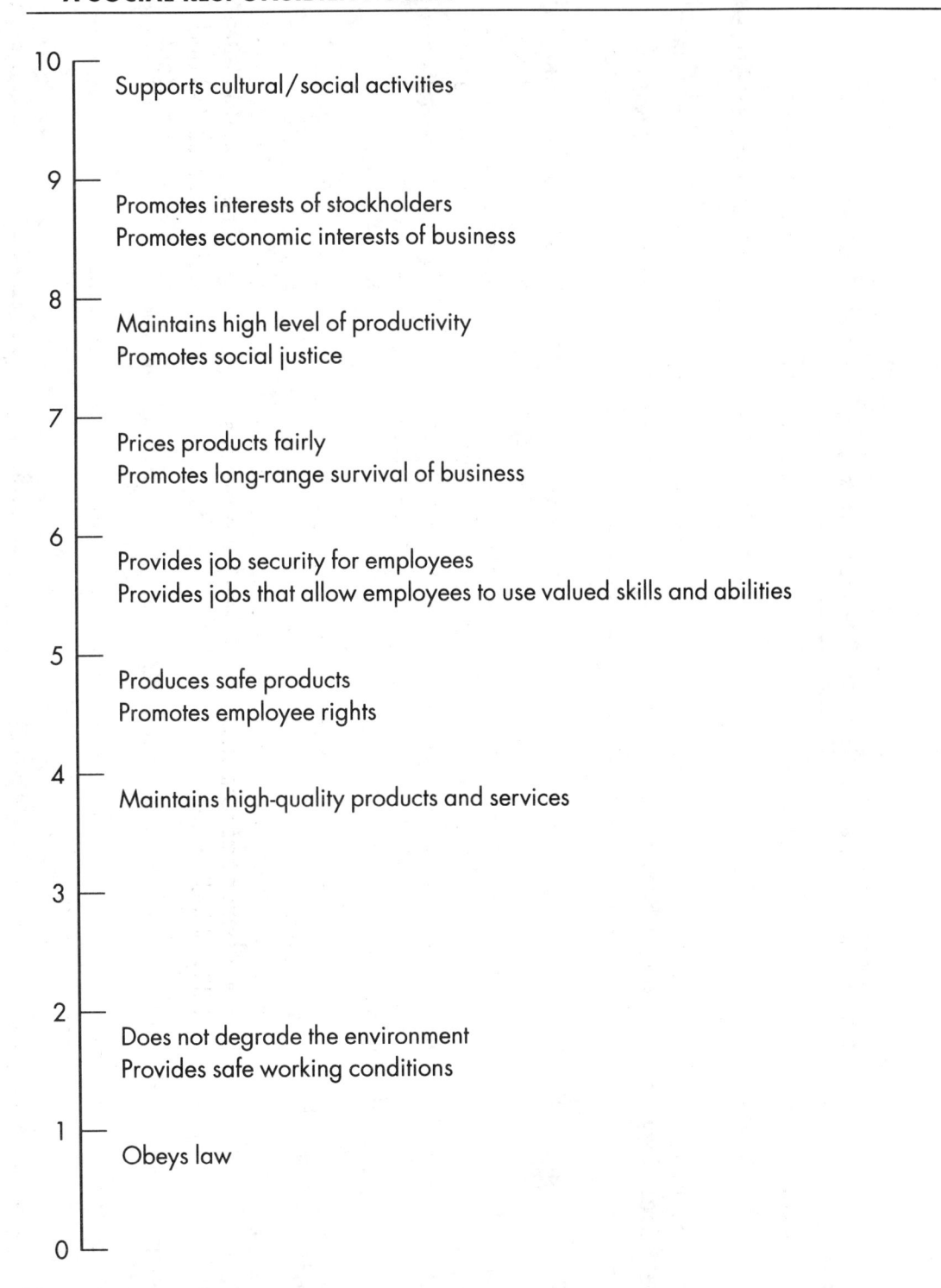

- 10 — Supports cultural/social activities
- 9 — Promotes interests of stockholders
  Promotes economic interests of business
- 8 — Maintains high level of productivity
  Promotes social justice
- 7 — Prices products fairly
  Promotes long-range survival of business
- 6 — Provides job security for employees
  Provides jobs that allow employees to use valued skills and abilities
- 5 — Produces safe products
  Promotes employee rights
- 4 — Maintains high-quality products and services
- 3 —
- 2 — Does not degrade the environment
  Provides safe working conditions
- 1 — Obeys law
- 0 —

SOURCE: Adapted from Kimberly B. Boal and Newman Peery, "The Cognitive Structure of Corporate Social Responsibility," *Journal of Management* (fall/winter 1985): 71–82.

The Dryden Press

TM 6-6 Issues Viewed by Small-Business Owners

ISSUES VIEWED BY SMALL-BUSINESS OWNERS

Demands Strong Ethical Stance	Greater Tolerance Regarding Ethical Position
Faulty investment advice	Padded expense account
Favoritism in promotion	Tax evasion
Acquiescing in dangerous design flaw	Collusion in bidding
Misleading financial reporting	Insider trading
Misleading advertising	Discrimination against women
Defending healthfulness of cigarette smoking	Copying computer software

SOURCE: Justin G. Longenecker, Joseph A. McKinney, and Carlos W. Moore, "Ethics in Small Business," *Journal of Small Business Management* (January 1989): 30.

The Dryden Press

TM 7-1　Environmental Variables

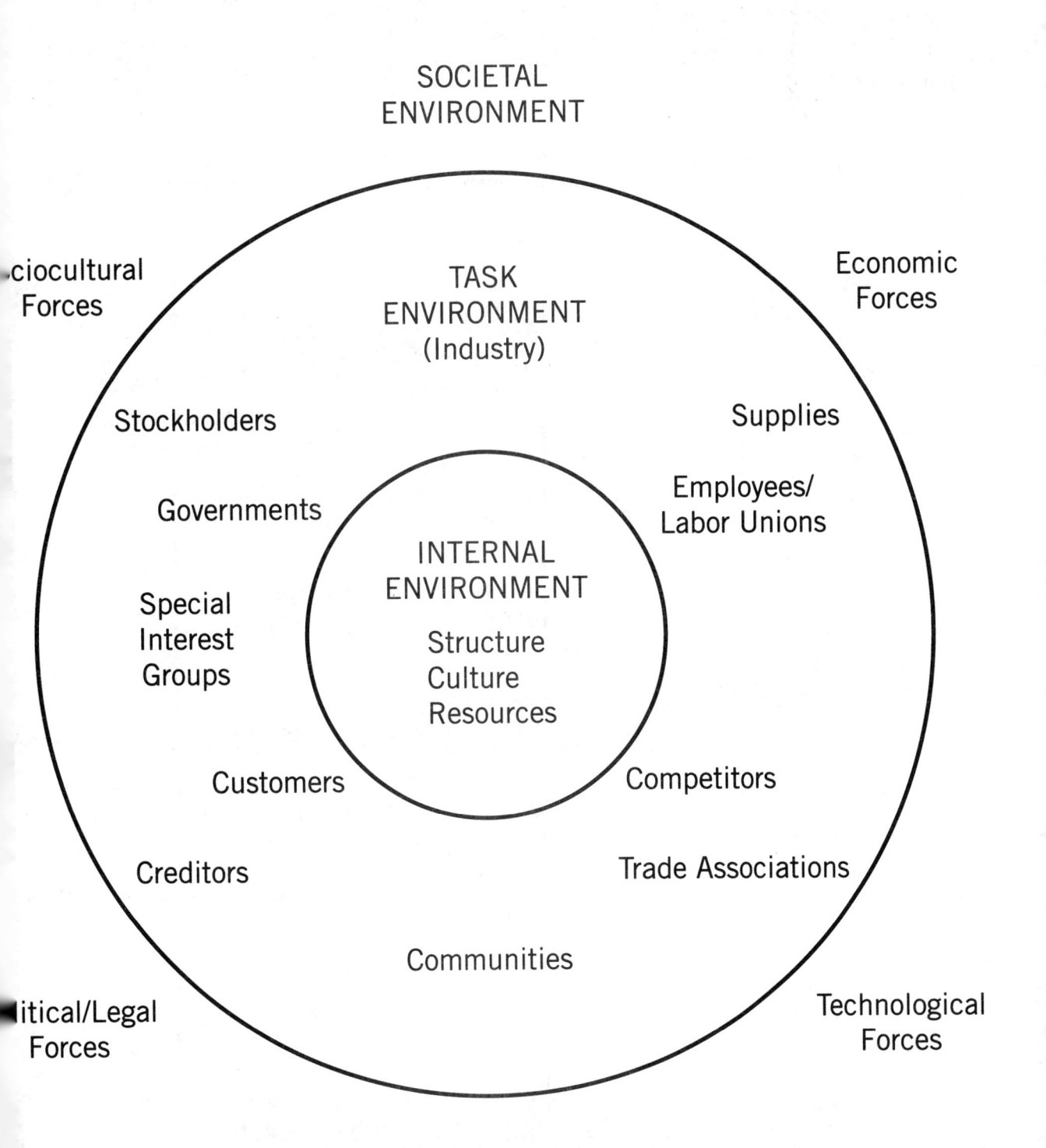

SOCIETAL ENVIRONMENT

TASK ENVIRONMENT (Industry)

INTERNAL ENVIRONMENT
Structure
Culture
Resources

- Sociocultural Forces
- Economic Forces
- Political/Legal Forces
- Technological Forces

- Stockholders
- Supplies
- Governments
- Employees/Labor Unions
- Special Interest Groups
- Customers
- Competitors
- Creditors
- Trade Associations
- Communities

The Dryden Press

TM 7-2 An Entrepreneur's Contingency Decision Model for Public Policy

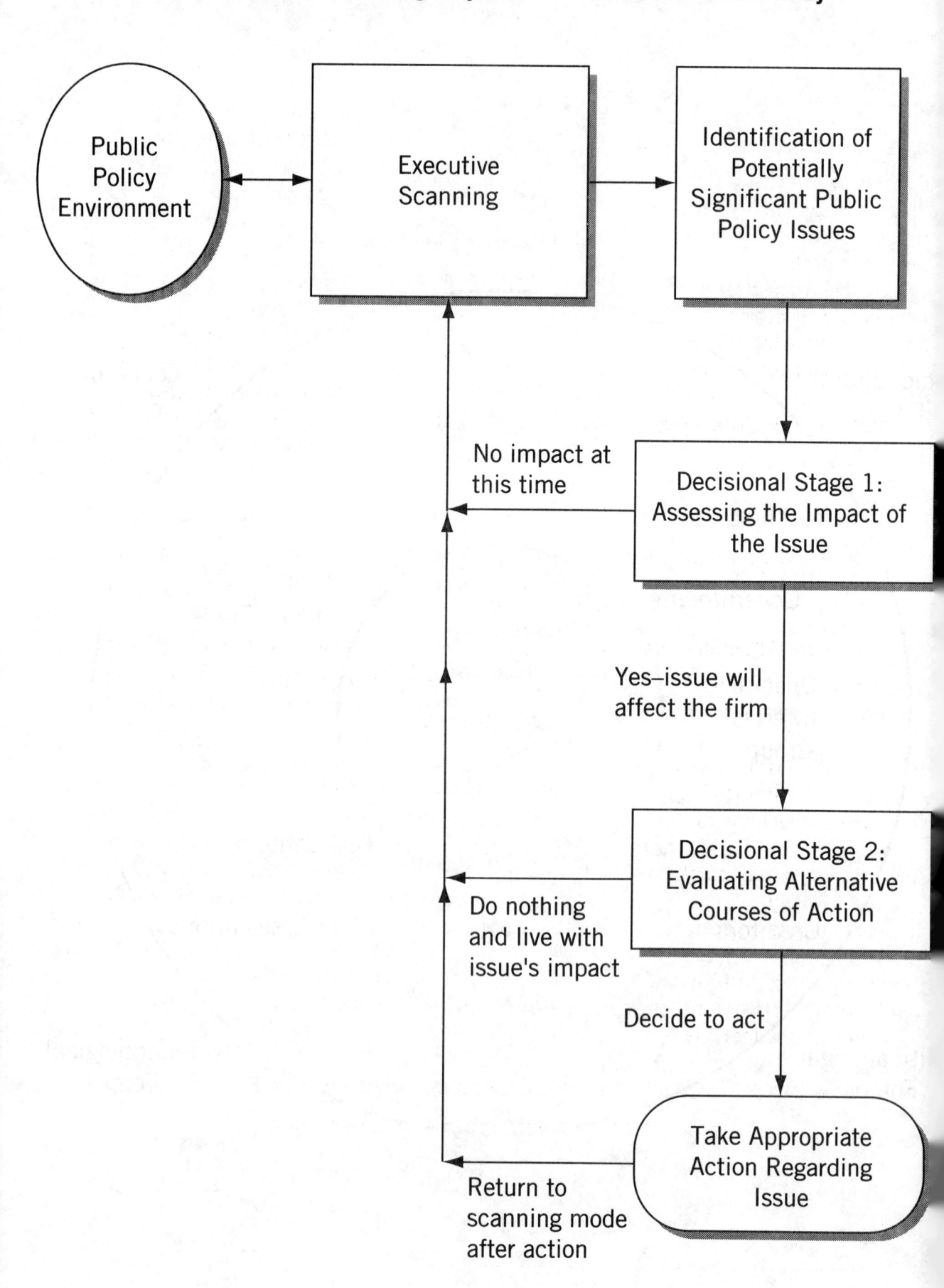

```
Public Policy          Executive                Identification of
Environment   <---->   Scanning       ----->    Potentially
                                                Significant Public
                                                Policy Issues
                           ^                          |
                           |                          v
                           |  No impact at     Decisional Stage 1:
                           |<---- this time    Assessing the Impact of
                           |                   the Issue
                           |                          |
                           |                   Yes–issue will
                           |                   affect the firm
                           |                          |
                           |                          v
                           |                   Decisional Stage 2:
                           |<---- Do nothing   Evaluating Alternative
                           |      and live with Courses of Action
                           |      issue's impact      |
                           |                   Decide to act
                           |                          |
                           |                          v
                           |<---- Return to    Take Appropriate
                                  scanning mode Action Regarding
                                  after action  Issue
```

The Dryden Press

TM 7-3 Elements of Industry Structure

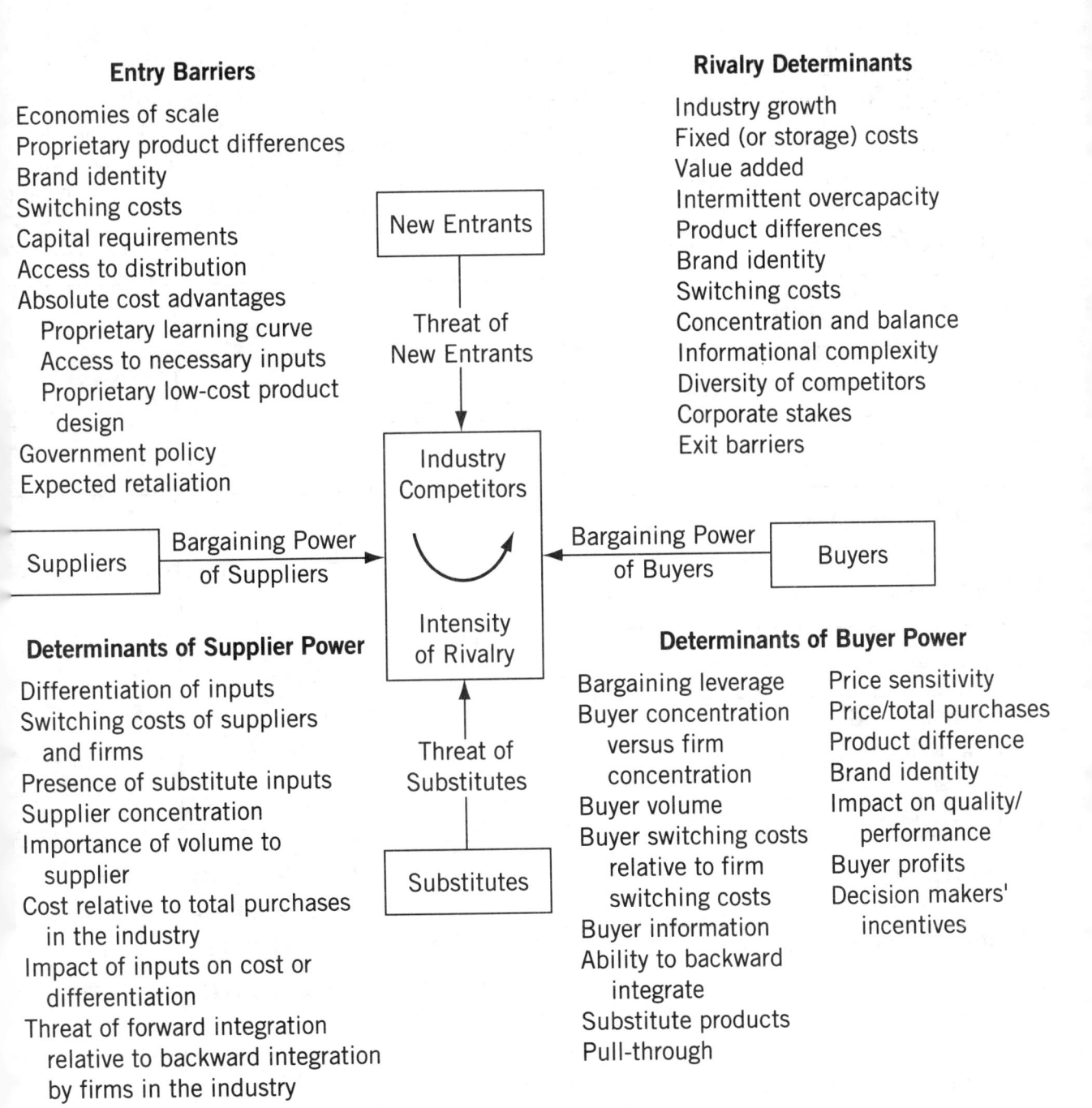

Entry Barriers

Economies of scale
Proprietary product differences
Brand identity
Switching costs
Capital requirements
Access to distribution
Absolute cost advantages
   Proprietary learning curve
   Access to necessary inputs
   Proprietary low-cost product
   design
Government policy
Expected retaliation

Rivalry Determinants

Industry growth
Fixed (or storage) costs
Value added
Intermittent overcapacity
Product differences
Brand identity
Switching costs
Concentration and balance
Informational complexity
Diversity of competitors
Corporate stakes
Exit barriers

[Diagram: New Entrants → (Threat of New Entrants) → Industry Competitors / Intensity of Rivalry; Suppliers → (Bargaining Power of Suppliers) → Industry Competitors; Buyers → (Bargaining Power of Buyers) → Industry Competitors; Substitutes → (Threat of Substitutes) → Industry Competitors]

Determinants of Supplier Power

Differentiation of inputs
Switching costs of suppliers
   and firms
Presence of substitute inputs
Supplier concentration
Importance of volume to
   supplier
Cost relative to total purchases
   in the industry
Impact of inputs on cost or
   differentiation
Threat of forward integration
   relative to backward integration
   by firms in the industry

Determinants of Buyer Power

Bargaining leverage   Price sensitivity
Buyer concentration   Price/total purchases
   versus firm   Product difference
   concentration   Brand identity
Buyer volume   Impact on quality/
Buyer switching costs   performance
   relative to firm   Buyer profits
   switching costs   Decision makers'
Buyer information   incentives
Ability to backward
   integrate
Substitute products
Pull-through

Determinants of Substitution Threat

Relative price performance of substitutes
Switching cost
Buyer propensity to substitute

The Dryden Press

TM 7-4 Competitive Profile Analysis

Instructions
Place an *X* to denote any competitive factor that a competitor has or can provide/perform better than you.

Competitive Factor	Competitive Firms			
	Company A	Company B	Company C	Your Company
Product uniqueness				
Relative product quality				
Price				
Service				
Availability/convenience				
Reputation/image				
Location				
Advertising and promotional policies/effectiveness				
Product design				
Caliber of personnel				
Raw material cost				
Financial condition				
Production capability				
R&D position				
Variety/selection				

The Dryden Press

TM 7-5 Components of a Competitive Analysis

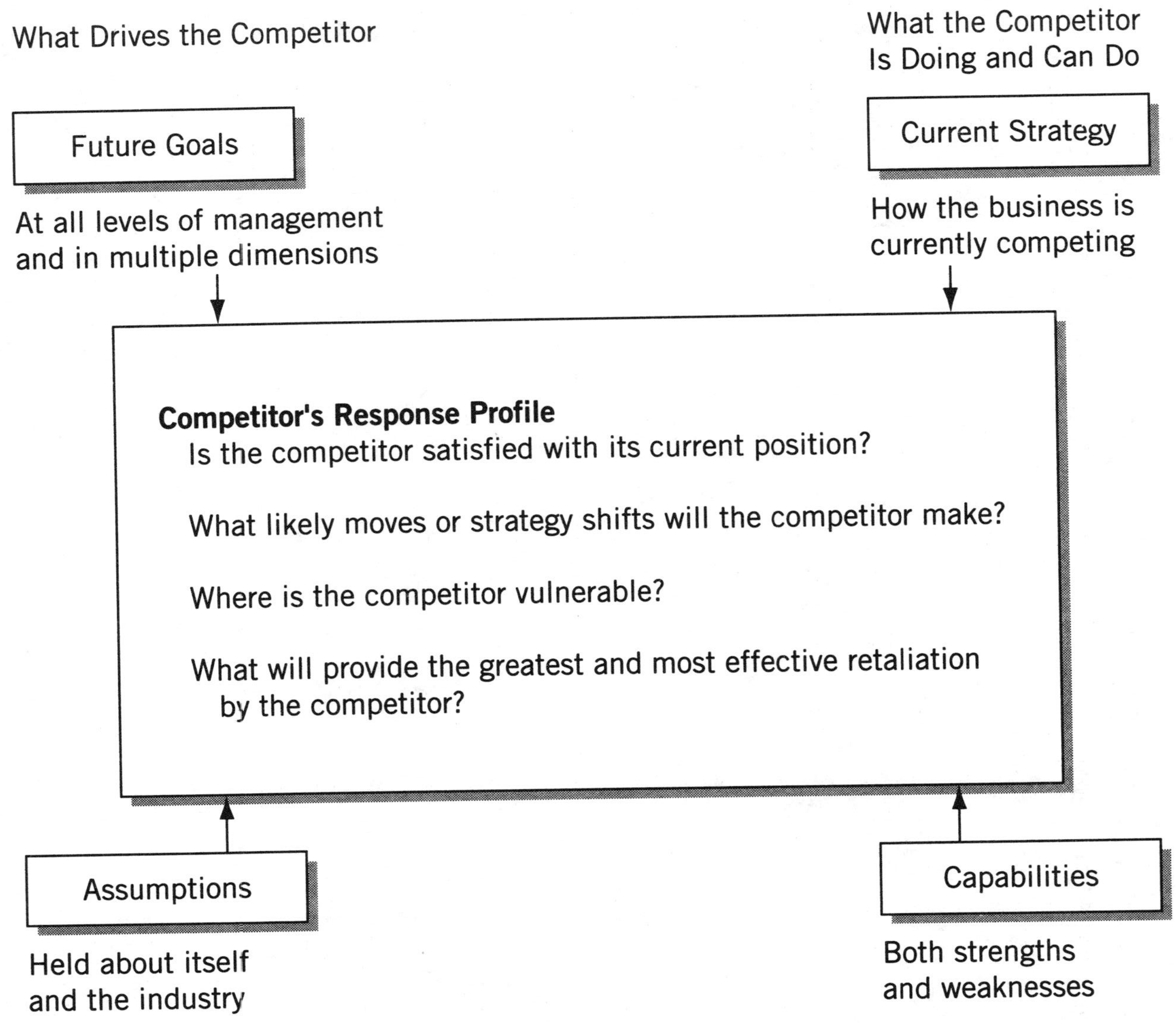

What Drives the Competitor

Future Goals
At all levels of management and in multiple dimensions

What the Competitor Is Doing and Can Do

Current Strategy
How the business is currently competing

Competitor's Response Profile
Is the competitor satisfied with its current position?

What likely moves or strategy shifts will the competitor make?

Where is the competitor vulnerable?

What will provide the greatest and most effective retaliation by the competitor?

Capabilities
Both strengths and weaknesses

Assumptions
Held about itself and the industry

The Dryden Press

TM 7-6 Reliance versus Commitment: Development of Exceptional Community Support

Community's "Reliance" (or Need) for the Venture

High ↑

Exceptional Support Likely

Some Support Likely

Exceptional Support Unlikely

Low → High

Entrepreneur's Willingness to Commit to Local Community (Loyalty)

The Dryden Press

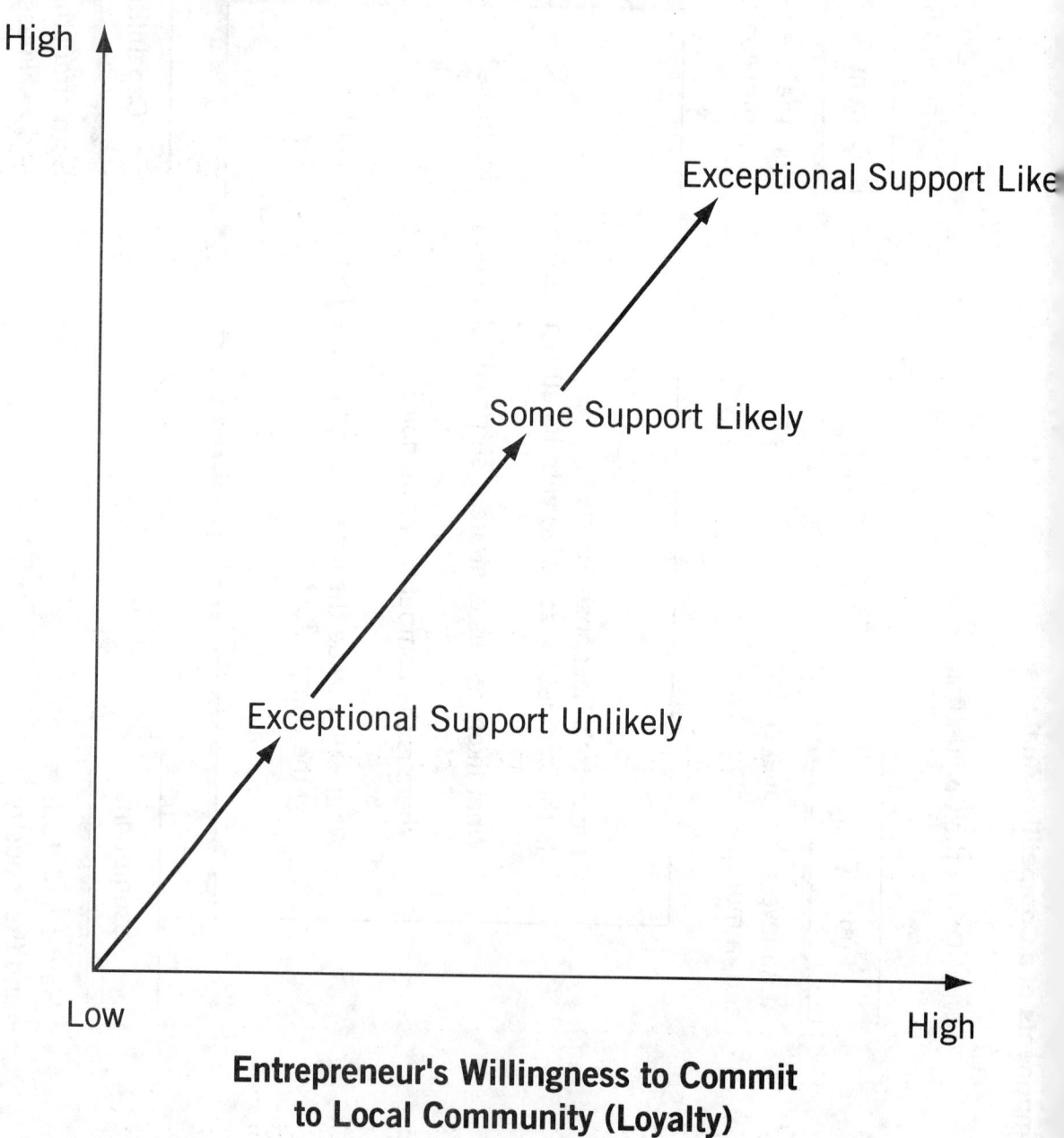

TM 7-7 Deservedness versus Identification: Development of Exceptional Community Support

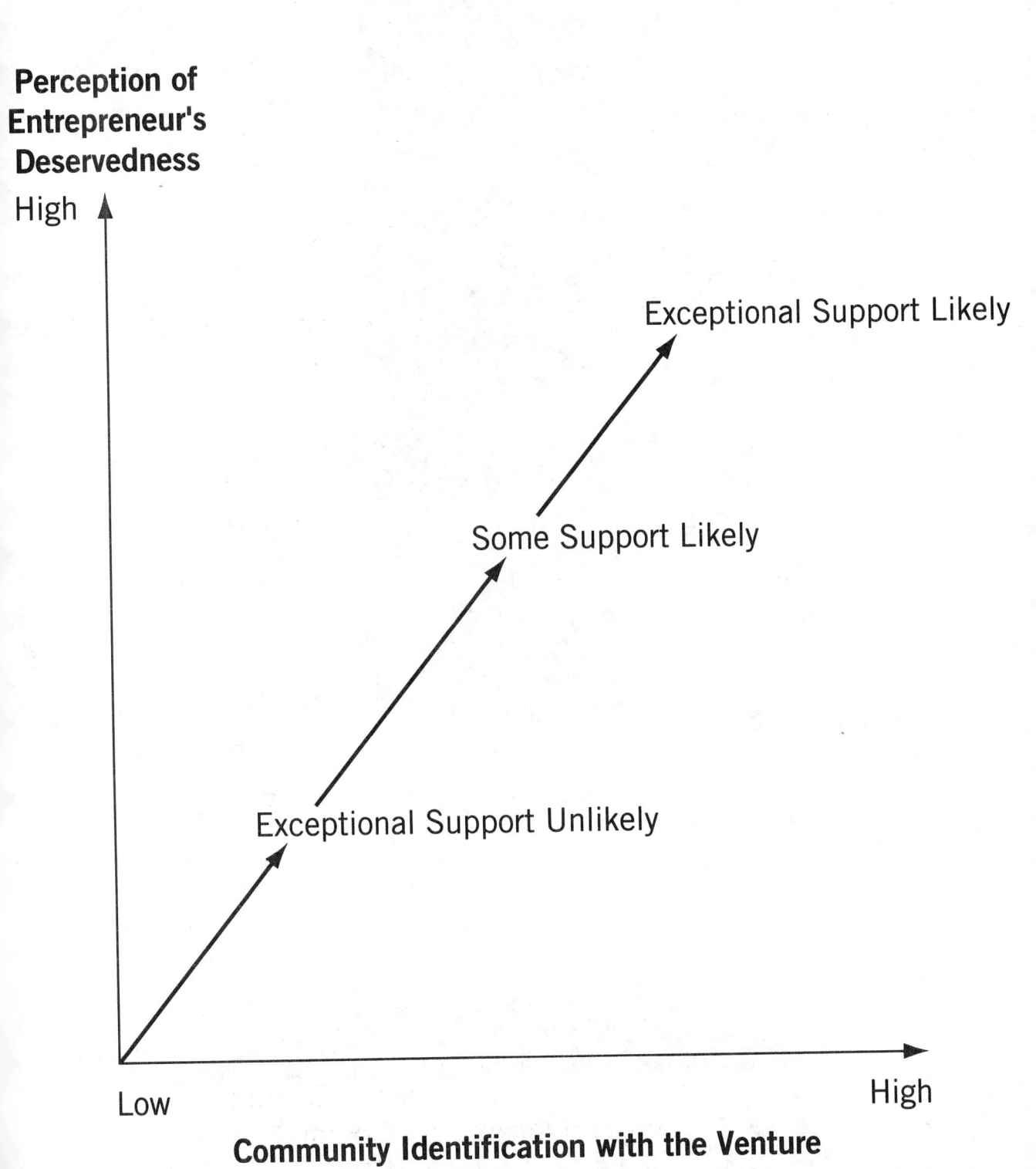

Perception of Entrepreneur's Deservedness

High

- Exceptional Support Likely
- Some Support Likely
- Exceptional Support Unlikely

Low — High

Community Identification with the Venture

The Dryden Press

TM 7-8 How Does the Incubator Work?

Types of Businesses (entering incubator):
- Commercial High Tech
- Research and Development
- Service Business
- Light Manufacturing
- Wholesaler
- Retailer
- Mail Order
- Import/Export
- Nonprofit

Entry Criteria:
- Potential to Grow
- Ability to Create Jobs
- Ability to Pay Operating Expenses
- Business Plan
- Market Analysis
- Cash-Flow Statement

Facilities/Services Provided:
- Centrex Phone System
- Staffed Reception Area
- Business Reference Library
- Mailroom
- Federal Express/UPS
- Shipping/Receiving
- Facsimile
- Typing and Secretarial
- Data and Word Processing
- Photocopying
- Notary Public
- Translation Services
- Mass Mailing Service
- Conference Rooms
- Child Day-Care Center
- Coffee Shop
- Affordable Space
- Flexible Space
- Flexible Leases

Stages:
- Business Entering the Incubator
- Business Developing
- Well-Established Business
- Business Growth Requires Move out of Incubator

Professional Services:
- Accounting Services
- Business and Financial Planning
- Marketing and Advertising
- Loan Packaging
- Legal Services
- Tax and Financial Services
- Seminars
- SBA
- SCORE
- Chambers of Commerce

The Dryden Press

TM 8-1 Using Classification of Goods to Select Channel Intermediaries

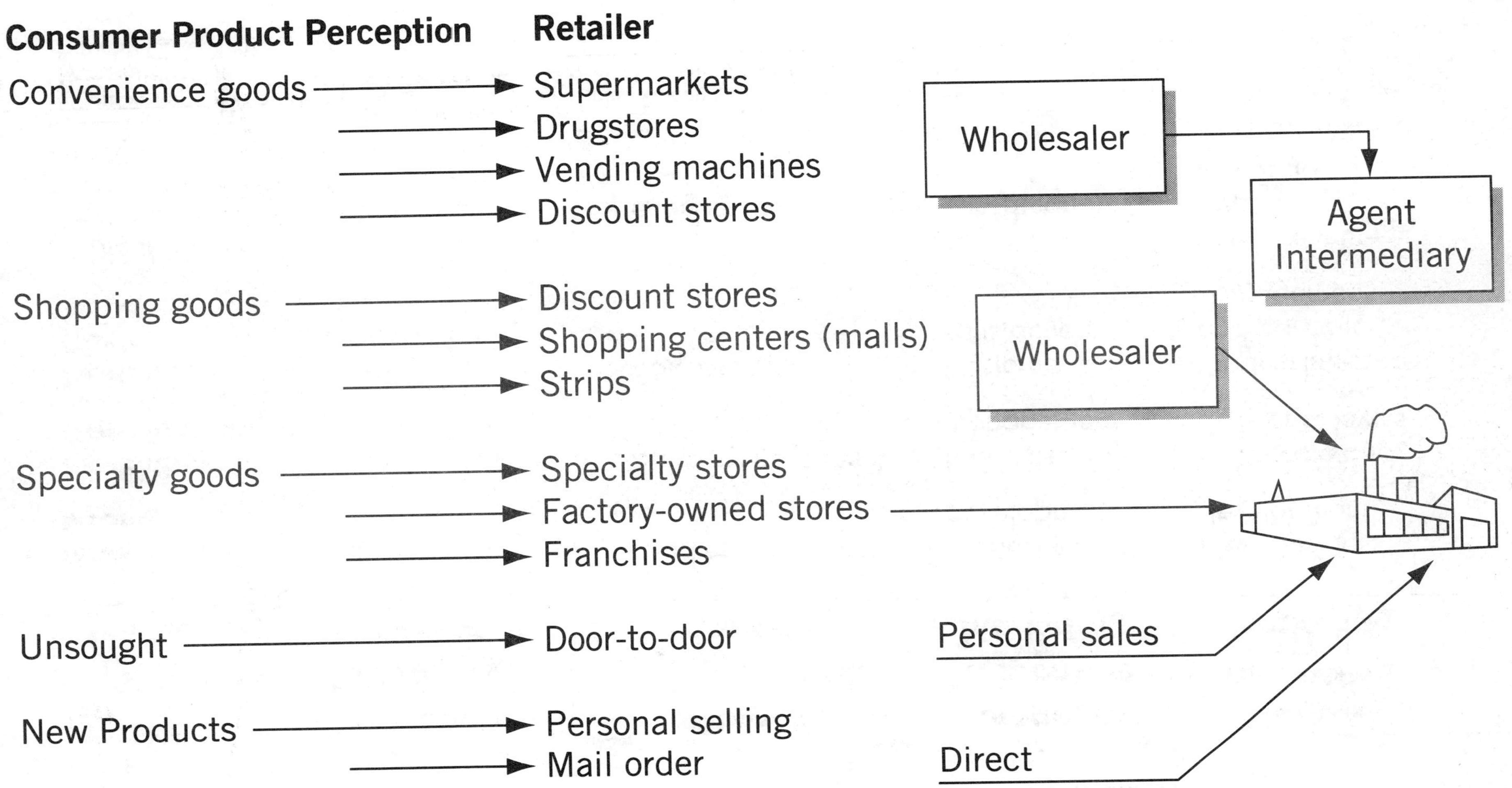

Consumer Product Perception   Retailer

Convenience goods ——→ Supermarkets
               ——→ Drugstores
               ——→ Vending machines
               ——→ Discount stores

Shopping goods ——→ Discount stores
              ——→ Shopping centers (malls)
              ——→ Strips

Specialty goods ——→ Specialty stores
               ——→ Factory-owned stores
               ——→ Franchises

Unsought ——→ Door-to-door

New Products ——→ Personal selling
            ——→ Mail order

Wholesaler → Agent Intermediary

Wholesaler

Personal sales

Direct

The Dryden Press

TM 8-2 The Evolution of the Marketing Function

THE EVOLUTION OF THE MARKETING FUNCTION

	Stage 1: Entrepreneurial Marketing	Stage 2: Opportunistic Marketing	Stage 3: Responsive Marketing	Stage 4: Diversified Marketing
Marketing Strategy	Market niche	Market penetration	Product-market development	New-business development
Marketing Organization	Informal, flexible	Sales management	Product-market management	Corporate and divisional levels
Marketing Goals	Credibility in the marketplace	Sales volume	Customer satisfaction	Product life-cycle and portfolio management
Critical Success Factors	A little help from your friends	Production economies	Functional coordination	Entrepreneurship and innovation

SOURCE: Reprinted by permission of the *Harvard Business Review* (exhibit 1) from "Growing Ventures Can Anticipate Marketing Stages," by Tyzoon T. Tyebjee, Albert V. Bruno, and Shelby H. McIntyre, January/February 1983, 64. Copyright © 1983 by the President and Fellows of Harvard College; all rights reserved.

The Dryden Press

TM 9-1 Summary of Account Changes for Pro Forma Balance Sheet

SUMMARY OF ACCOUNT CHANGES FOR PRO FORMA BALANCE SHEET

Cash. Begin with the original cash balance, and add (or subtract) the change in cash as depicted on the cash-flow budget.

Accounts receivable. Examine the last couple of months on the cash-flow budget to determine what charges will be included in the accounts receivable. Also, be sure all of the original receivables have been accounted for.

Inventory. This figure can be picked up from the cost-of-goods budget.

Fixed assets. This number will probably remain the same; however, any changes can be picked up on the cash-flow budget from an analysis of the loan proceeds.

Accounts payable. Again, examine the last couple of months on the cash-flow budget, this time analyzing the purchases to determine what purchases will not have been paid for.

Loans/notes payable. Analyze the loan proceeds. In addition, interest will have to be accrued in a separate interest-payable account.

Capital. The major item to be included here is the projected net income for the budget period.

The Dryden Press

TM 9-2 Financial Ratios

FINANCIAL RATIOS

Ratio	Formula	What It Measures	What It Tells You
Owners			
Return on investment (ROI)	$\dfrac{\text{Net income}}{\text{Average Owner's Equity}}$	Return on owner's capital; when compared with return on assets, it measures the extent financial leverage is being used for or against the owner.	How well is this company doing as an investment?
Return on assets (ROA)	$\dfrac{\text{Net Income}}{\text{Average Total Assets}}$	How well assets have been employed by management	How well has management employed company assets? Does it pay to borrow?
Managers			
Net profit margin	$\dfrac{\text{Net Income}}{\text{Sales}}$	Operating efficiency; the ability to create sufficient profits from operating activities	Are profits high enough, given the level of sales?
Asset turnover	$\dfrac{\text{Sales}}{\text{Average Total Assets}}$	Relative efficiency in using total resources to produce output	How well are assets being used to generate sales revenue?
Return on assets	$\dfrac{\text{Net Income}}{\text{Sales}} \times \dfrac{\text{Sales}}{\text{Total Assets}}$	Earning power on all assets; ROA ratio broken into its logical parts; turnover and margin	How well has management employed company assets?
Average collection period	$\dfrac{\text{Average Accounts Receivable}}{\text{Annual Credit Sales}} \times 365$	Liquidity of receivables in terms of average number of days receivables are outstanding	Are receivables coming in too slowly?
Inventory turnover	$\dfrac{\text{Cost of Goods Sold Expense}}{\text{Average Inventory}}$	Liquidity of inventory; the number of times it turns over per year	Is too much cash tied up in inventories?
Average age of payables	$\dfrac{\text{Average Accounts Payable}}{\text{Net Purchases}} \times 365$	Approximate length of time a firm takes to pay its bills for trade purchases	How quickly does a prospective customer pay its bills?

The Dryden Press

TM 10-1   Helpful Hints for Writing the Business Plan

HELPFUL HINTS FOR WRITING THE BUSINESS PLAN

The Summary

No more than three pages
This is the most crucial part of your plan because it must capture the reader's interest.
What, how, why, where, etc., must be summarized.
Complete this part *after* the finished business plan has been written.

The Business Description Segment

The name of the business
A background of the industry with history of the company (if any) should be covered here.
The potential of the new venture should be described clearly.
Any unique or distinctive features of the venture should be spelled out.

The Marketing Segment

Convince investors that sales projections and competition can be met.
Market studies should be used and disclosed.
Identify target market, market position, and market share.
Evaluate *all* competition and specifically cover why and how you will be better than the competitors.
Identify all market sources and assistance used for this segment.
Demonstrate pricing strategy, since your price must penetrate and maintain a market share to *produce profits*. Thus the lowest price is *not* necessarily the "best" price.
Identify your advertising plans with cost estimates to validate the proposed strategy.

The Research, Design, and Development Segment

Cover the *extent* of and *costs* involved in needed research, testing, or development.
Explain carefully what has been accomplished *already* (prototype, lab testing, early development).
Mention any research or technical assistance provided for you.

The Manufacturing Segment

Provide the advantages of your location (zoning, tax laws, wage rates).
List the production needs in terms of facilities (plant, storage, office space) and equipment (machinery, furnishings, supplies).
Describe the access to transportation (for shipping and receiving).
Explain proximity to your suppliers.
Mention the availability of labor in your location.
Provide estimates of manufacturing costs—be careful; too many entrepreneurs underestimate their costs.

The Management Segment

Provide résumés of all key people in the management of the venture.
Carefully describe the legal structure of the venture (sole proprietorship, partnership, or corporation).
Cover the added assistance (if any) of advisers, consultants, and directors.
Provide information on how everyone is to be compensated (how much, also).

The Dryden Press

TM 10-2 Business Plan Checklist: A Personal Step-by-Step Evaluation

BUSINESS PLAN CHECKLIST: A PERSONAL STEP-BY-STEP EVALUATION

	Have You Covered This in the Plan?	Is the Answer Clear? (Yes/No)	Is the Answer Complete (Yes/No)

Business Description Segment

1. What type of business are you planning?
2. What products or services will you sell?
3. What type of opportunity is it (new, part-time, expansion, seasonal, year-round)?
4. Why does it promise to be successful?
5. What is the growth potential?
6. What uniqueness exists?

(Discuss strengths and weaknesses in this segment.)

Marketing Segment

1. Who are your potential customers?
2. How big is the market?
3. Who are your competitors? How are their businesses prospering?
4. How will you promote sales?
5. What market share do you anticipate?
6. How will you price your product or service?
7. What advertising and promotional strategy are you using?

(Discuss strengths and weaknesses in this segment.)

Research, Design, and Development Segment

1. Have you carefully described your design or development?
2. Have you received any technical assistance?
3. What research needs do you anticipate?
4. Are the costs involved in research and design reasonable?

(Discuss strengths and weaknesses in this segment.)

Manufacturing Segment

1. Where will the business be located?
2. What factors have influenced the choice of location?
3. Have you described the needs for production facilities and equipment?
4. Who will be your suppliers?
5. What type of transportation is available?
6. What is the supply of available labor?

(Discuss strengths and weaknesses in this segment.)

Management Segment

1. Who will manage the business?
2. What qualifications do you have?
3. How many employees will you need? What will they do?
4. What are your plans for employee salaries, wages, benefits?
5. What consultants or specialists will you need? Why will you need them?
6. What legal form of ownership will you choose? Why?
7. What licenses and permits will you need?
8. What regulations will affect your business?

(Discuss strengths and weaknesses in this segment.)

The Dryden Press

TM 11-1 The Elements Affecting New-Venture Performance

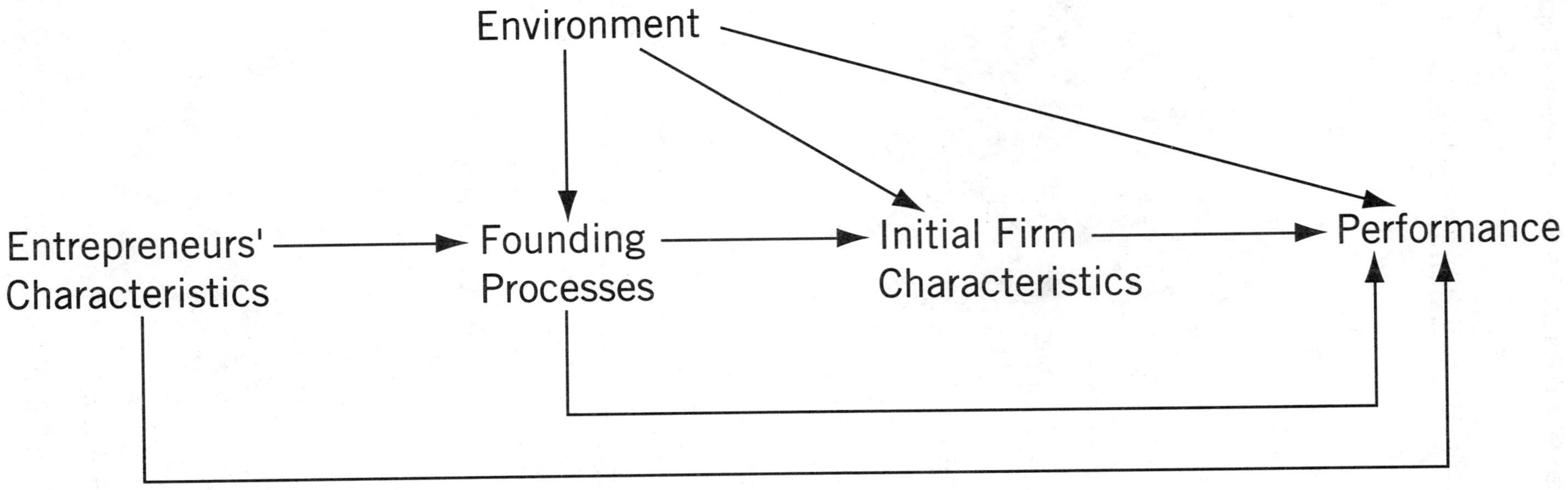

The Dryden Press

TM 11-2 Internal and External Problems Entrepreneurs Experience

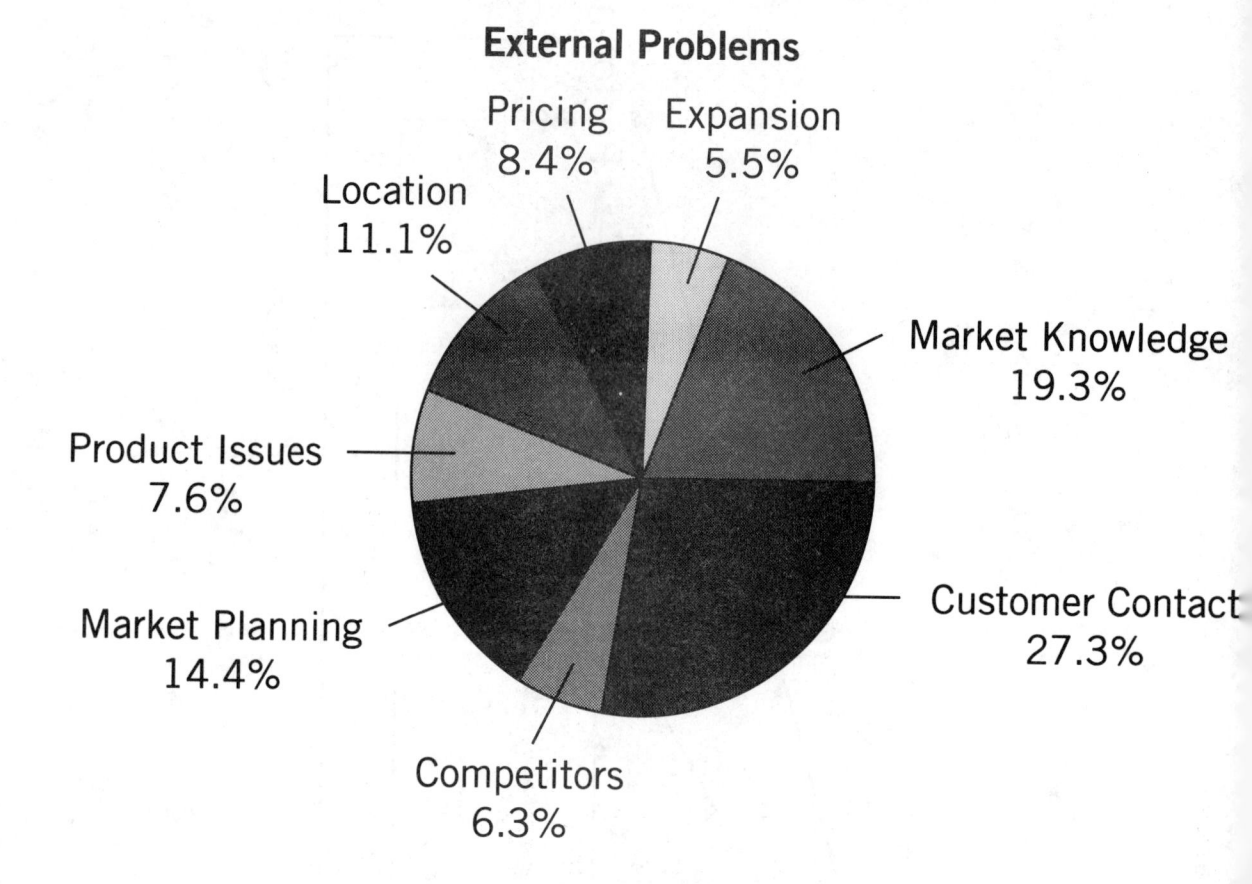

External Problems

- Pricing 8.4%
- Expansion 5.5%
- Location 11.1%
- Market Knowledge 19.3%
- Product Issues 7.6%
- Customer Contact 27.3%
- Market Planning 14.4%
- Competitors 6.3%

Internal Problems

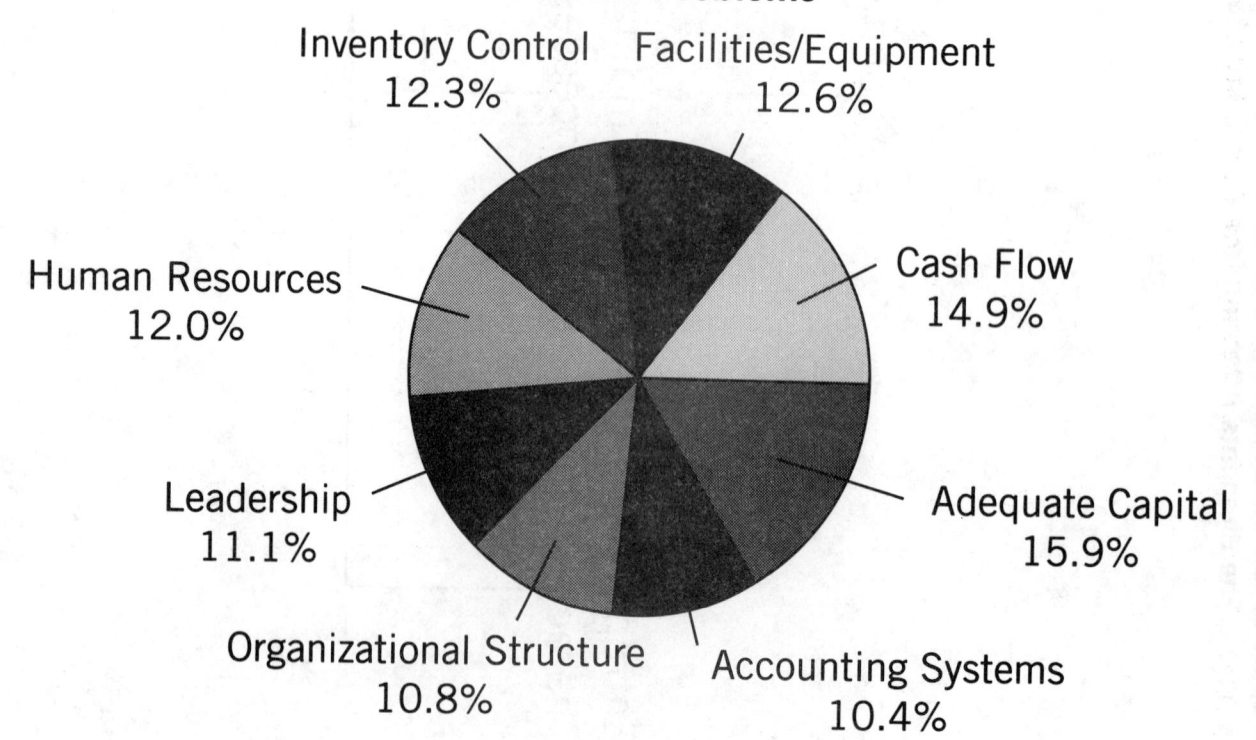

- Inventory Control 12.3%
- Facilities/Equipment 12.6%
- Human Resources 12.0%
- Cash Flow 14.9%
- Leadership 11.1%
- Adequate Capital 15.9%
- Organizational Structure 10.8%
- Accounting Systems 10.4%

The Dryden Press

TM 11-3 Key Areas for Assessing the Feasibility of a New Venture

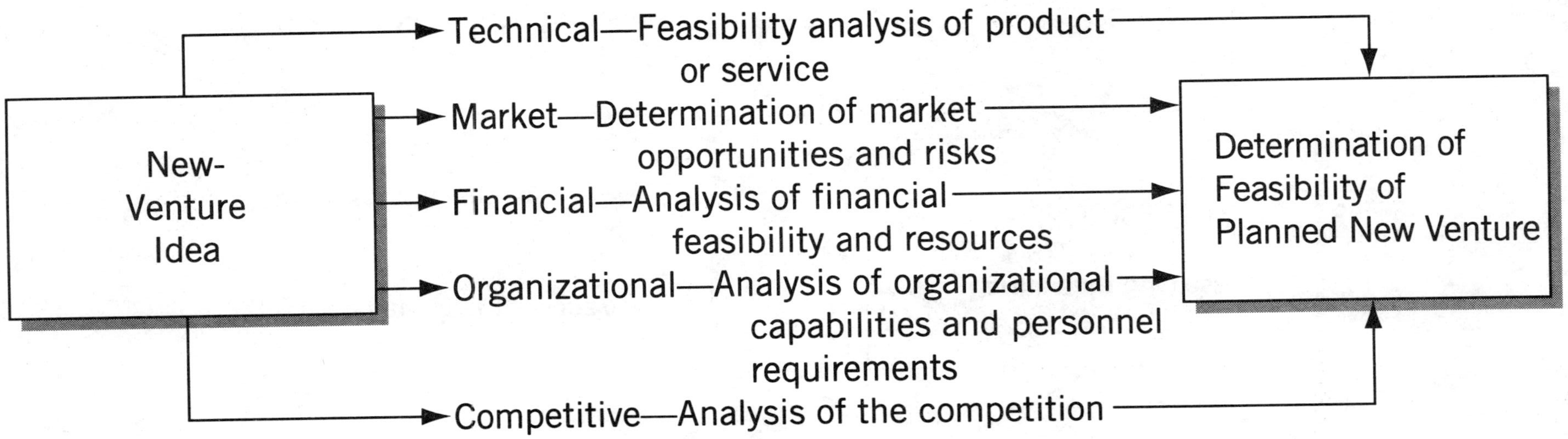

New-Venture Idea

- Technical—Feasibility analysis of product or service
- Market—Determination of market opportunities and risks
- Financial—Analysis of financial feasibility and resources
- Organizational—Analysis of organizational capabilities and personnel requirements
- Competitive—Analysis of the competition

Determination of Feasibility of Planned New Venture

The Dryden Press

TM 12-1 Factors Associated with Partnership Success

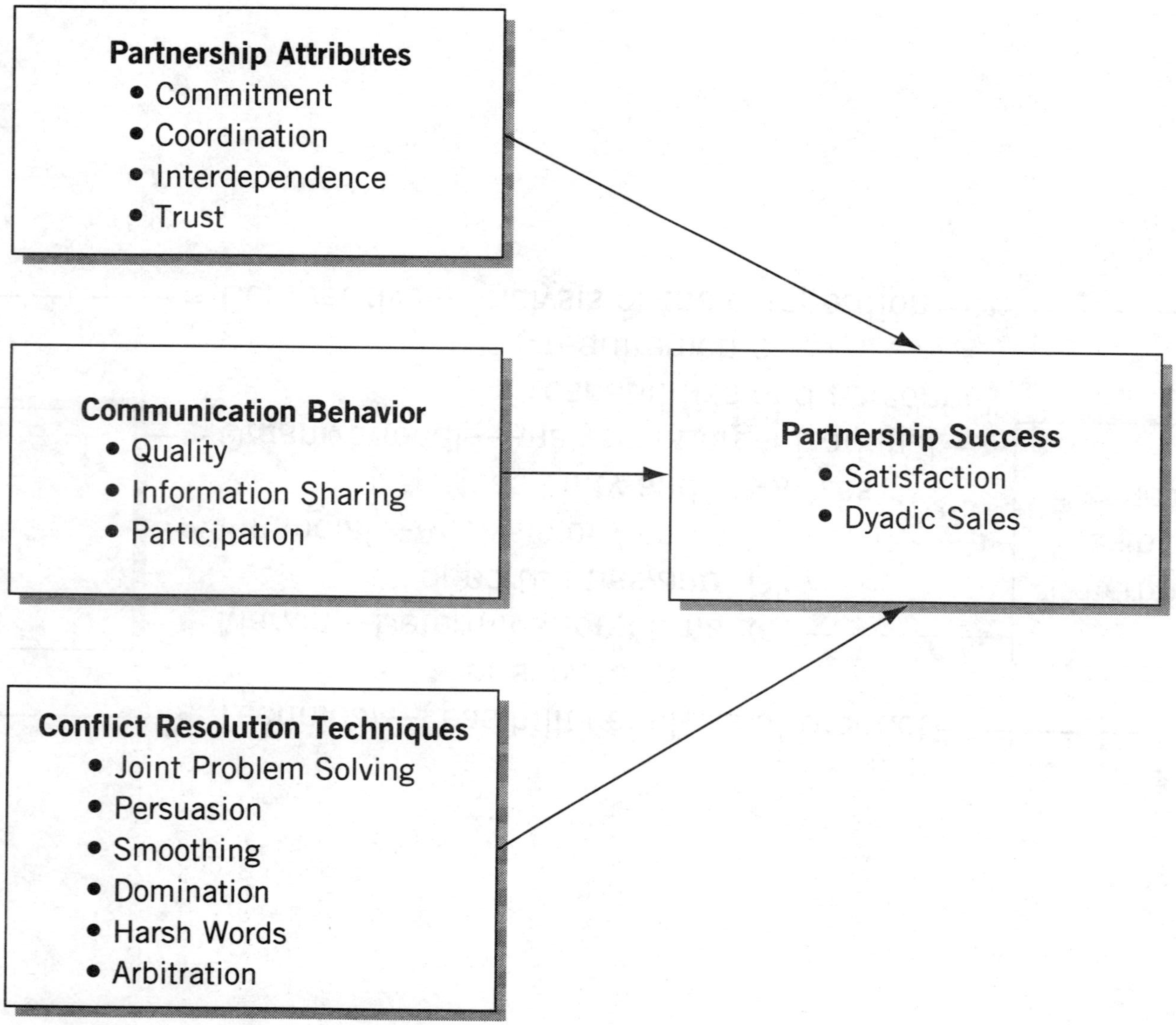

Partnership Success
- Satisfaction
- Dyadic Sales

Partnership Attributes
- Commitment
- Coordination
- Interdependence
- Trust

Communication Behavior
- Quality
- Information Sharing
- Participation

Conflict Resolution Techniques
- Joint Problem Solving
- Persuasion
- Smoothing
- Domination
- Harsh Words
- Arbitration

The Dryden Press

TM 13-2 Trademarks: Protected and Unprotected

TRADEMARKS: PROTECTED AND UNPROTECTED

Suggestive (Protected)	Descriptive (Unprotected)
Arch Rest (shoes)	After Tan (suntan lotion)
Holeproof (hosiery)	Breakfast Bread (bread)
Hour After Hour (deodorant)	Brilliant (flour)
Mr. Clean (cleaner)	Driverless (car rental)
Roach Motel (insect trap)	Faultless (bread)
Rusticide (rust remover)	5 Minute (glue setting in five minutes)
Soft Smoke (smoking tobacco)	Homemaker (calendar)
U-Drive-It (car rental)	Security (tires)
Wearever (cooking utensils)	Snap (ginger ale)

SOURCE: Reprinted by permission of *Harvard Business Review*. An excerpt from "How Can You Find a Safe Trademark?" by Thomas M. S. Hemnes, March/April 1985, 40–48. Copyright © 1985 by the President and Fellows of Harvard College; all rights reserved.

The Dryden Press

TM 13-3 Business Failures through the Years (1927–1995)

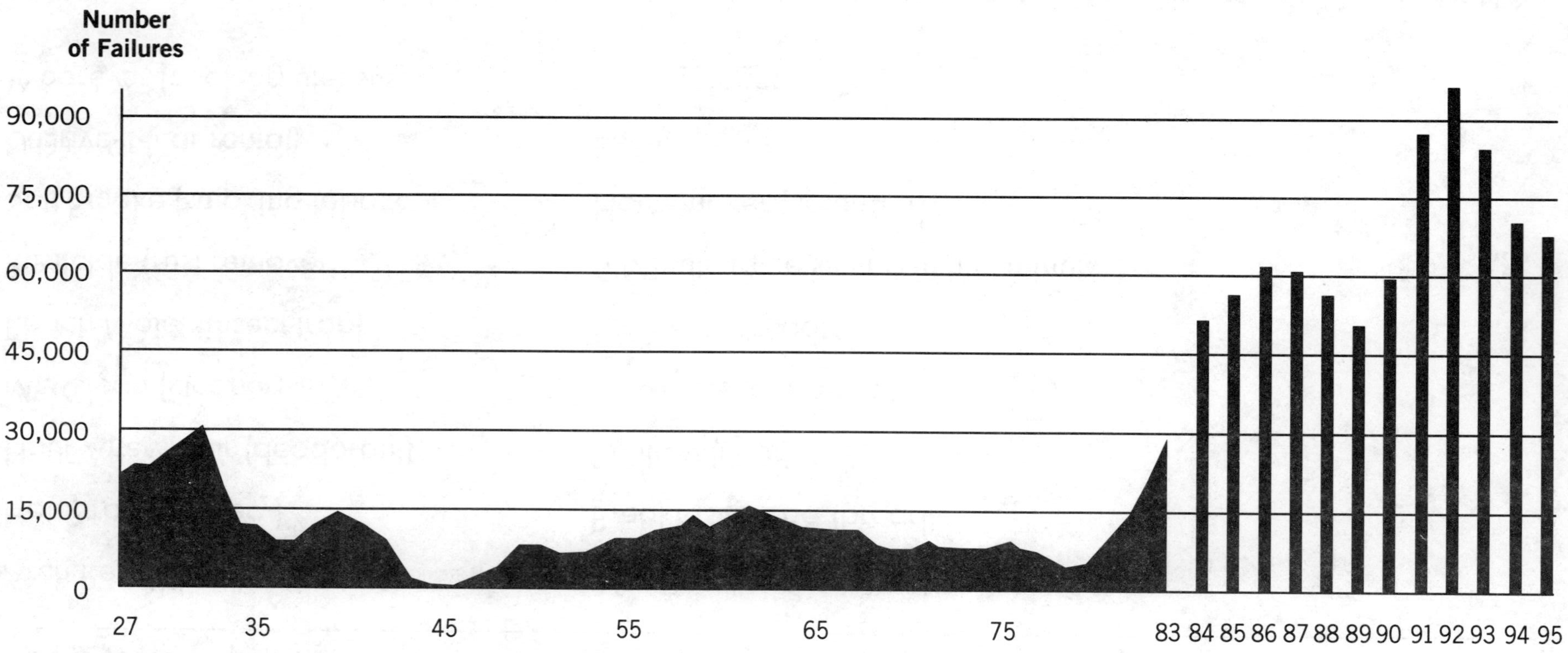

Number of Failures

The Dryden Press

TM 13-4 Bankruptcy: A Comparison of Chapters 7, 11, 12, and 13

BANKRUPTCY: A COMPARISON OF CHAPTERS 7, 11, 12, AND 13

Issue	Chapter 7	Chapter 11	Chapters 12 and 13
Purpose	Liquidation	Reorganization	Adjustment
Who can petition	Debtor (voluntary) or creditors (involuntary)	Debtor (voluntary) or creditors (involuntary)	Debtor (voluntary) only
Who can be a debtor	Any "person" (including partnerships and corporations) except railroads, insurance companies, banks, savings and loan institutions, and credit unions; farmers and charitable institutions cannot be involuntarily petitioned	Any debtor eligible for Chapter 7 relief; railroads are also eligible	*Chapter 12:* any family farmer whose gross income is at least 50 percent farm dependent and whose debts are at least 80 percent farm related or any partnership or closely held corporation at least 50 percent owned by a farm family, when total debt does not exceed $1,500,000 *Chapter 13:* any individual (not partnerships or corporations) with regular income who owes fixed unsecured debt of less than $100,000 or secured debt of less than $350,000
Procedure leading to discharge	Nonexempt property is sold with proceeds to be distributed (in order) to priority groups; dischargeable debts are terminated	Plan is submitted; if it is approved and followed, debts are discharged	Plan is submitted (must be approved if debtor turns over disposable income for three-year period); if it is approved and followed, debts are discharged
Advantages	Upon liquidation and distribution, most debts are discharged, and debtor has opportunity for fresh start	Debtor continues in business; creditors can accept plan, or it can be "crammed down" on them; plan allows for reorganization and liquidation of debts over plan period	Debtor continues in business or possession of assets; if plan is approved, most debts are discharged after a three-year period

SOURCE: Kenneth W. Clarkson, Roger L. Miller, Gaylord A. Jentz, and Frank B. Cross, *West's Business Law*, 6th ed. (St. Paul, MN: West, 1995), 650.

The Dryden Press

TM 13-5 Entrepreneurs Preferred Financial Sources

Following Year:
- SBA 1.3%
- Corporations 4%
- No Financing Needed 20%
- Public Offering 8%
- Private Offering 8%
- Individuals 12%
- Banks 18.7%
- Venture Capital 28%

Total 100%

Following 5 Years:
- No Financing Needed 12.1%
- Corporations 8.6%
- Public Offering 43.1%
- Private Placement 5.2%
- Individuals 1.7%
- Banks 19%
- Venture Capital 10.3%

The Dryden Press

TM 14-1 Venture Capital Disbursements by Stage, 1992

VENTURE CAPITAL DISBURSEMENTS BY STAGE, 1992

Item	Dollars[a] Invested	Number of Companies	Number of Financings	Number of Investments
Total	$2,542	1,087	1,566	3,218
Expansion	1,400	600	806	1,718
LBO/acquisition	176	55	73	112
Other[b]	347	191	252	530
Other early stage	336	185	226	426
Seed	74	68	78	145
Start-up	209	108	131	287

[a] In millions of dollars.
[b] Bridge loans and the public purchases.

SOURCE: Michael F. Hinds, "Venture Capital," *U.S. Industrial Outlook, 1994* (Washington, DC: Department of Commerce), 46–49.

The Dryden Press

TM 14-2 Venture Capitalist System of Evaluating Product/Service and Management

VENTURE CAPITALIST SYSTEM OF EVALUATING PRODUCT/SERVICE AND MANAGEMENT

Riskiest ↓

Level 4 Fully developed product/service; Established market; Satisfied users	4/1	4/2	4/3	4/4
Level 3 Fully developed product/service; Few users as of yet; Market assumed	3/1	3/2	3/3	3/4
Level 2 Operable pilot or prototype; Not yet developed for production; Market assumed	2/1	2/2	2/3	2/4
Level 1 Product/service idea; Not yet operable; Market assumed	1/1	1/2	1/3	1/4

Level 1	**Level 2**	**Level 3**	**Level 4**
Individual founder/ entrepreneur	Two founders; Other personnel not yet identified	Partial management team; Members identified to join company when funding is received	Fully staffed, experienced management team

← **Riskiest**

Status of Management

SOURCE: Stanley Rich and David Gumpert, *Business Plans That Win $$$*, 169. Reprinted by permission of Sterling Lord Literistic, Inc. Copyright © 1985 by Stanley Rich and David Gumpert.

The Dryden Press

TM 14-3 Returns on Investment Venture Capitalists Typically Seek

RETURNS ON INVESTMENT VENTURE CAPITALISTS TYPICALLY SEEK

Stage of Business	Expected Annual Return on Investment	Expected Increase on Initial Investment
Start-up business (idea stage)	60%+	10–15 × investment
First-stage financing (new business)	40%–60%	6–12 × investment
Second-stage financing (development stage)	30%–50%	4–8 × investment
Third-stage financing (expansion stage)	25%–40%	3–6 × investment
Turnaround situation	50%+	8–15 × investment

SOURCE: W. Keith Schilit, "How to Obtain Venture Capital," *Business Horizons* (May/June 1987): 78. Copyright © 1987 by the Foundation for the School of Business at Indiana University. Reprinted by permission.

The Dryden Press

TM 14-4 Key Results from Entrepreneurs Successful in Obtaining Venture Capital

KEY RESULTS FROM ENTREPRENEURS SUCCESSFUL IN OBTAINING VENTURE CAPITAL

	Characteristic (% of successful seekers)
I. Business stage	
Seed	
Start-up	65
Expansion	38
Bridge financing	10
Other	12
II. Amount of dollars sought	44% have sought more than $1 million
III. Written business plan	98
Balance sheet	95
List of product competition	94
Marketing plan	98
Cash-flow projections for 3 years	94
IV. Where firms seek equity capital	
In-state venture capitalists	85
Out-of-state venture capitalists	58
In-state corporations	40
Out-of-state corporations	34
In-state private investors	79
Out-of-state private investors	47
In-state consultants/investment bankers	57
Out-of-state consultants/investment bankers	31

SOURCE: Ronald J. Hustedde and Glen C. Pulver, "Factors Affecting Equity Capital Acquisition: The Demand Side," *Journal of Business Venturing* (September 1992): 369–70.

The Dryden Press

TM 14-5 "Angel Stats"

"ANGEL STATS"

Typical deal size	:	$250,000
Typical recipient	:	Start-up firms
Cash-out time frame	:	5 to 7 years
Expected return	:	35% to 50% a year
Ownership stake	:	Less than 50%

SOURCE: William E. Wetzel, University of New Hampshire's Center for Venture Research, as reported in *Small Business Reports* (April 1993): 39.

TM 15-1 Strategic Management Model

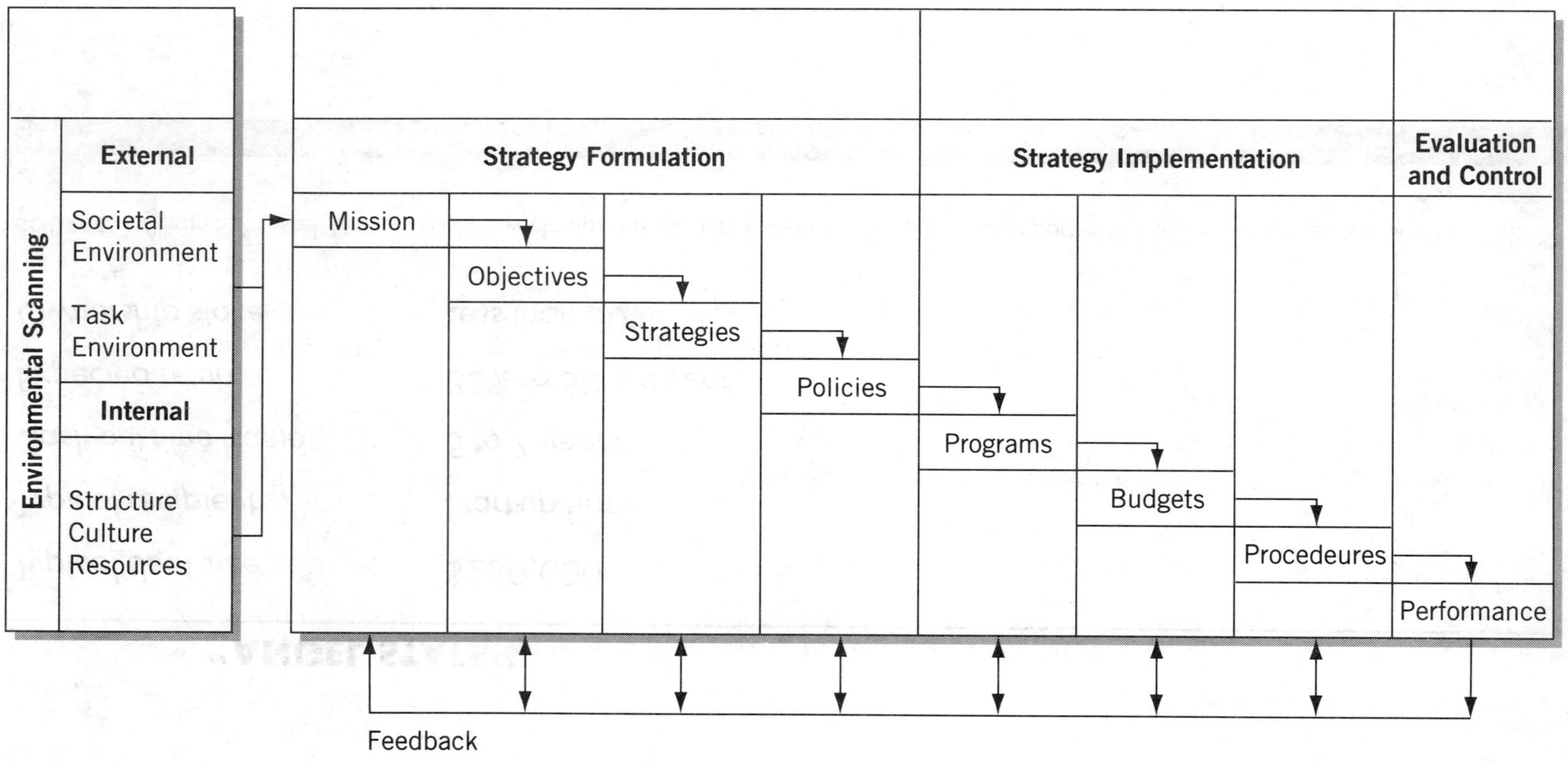

Environmental Scanning

External
- Societal Environment
- Task Environment

Internal
- Structure
- Culture
- Resources

Strategy Formulation
- Mission
- Objectives
- Strategies
- Policies

Strategy Implementation
- Programs
- Budgets
- Procedeures

Evaluation and Control
- Performance

Feedback

The Dryden Press

TM 15-2 The Opportunity Management Approach

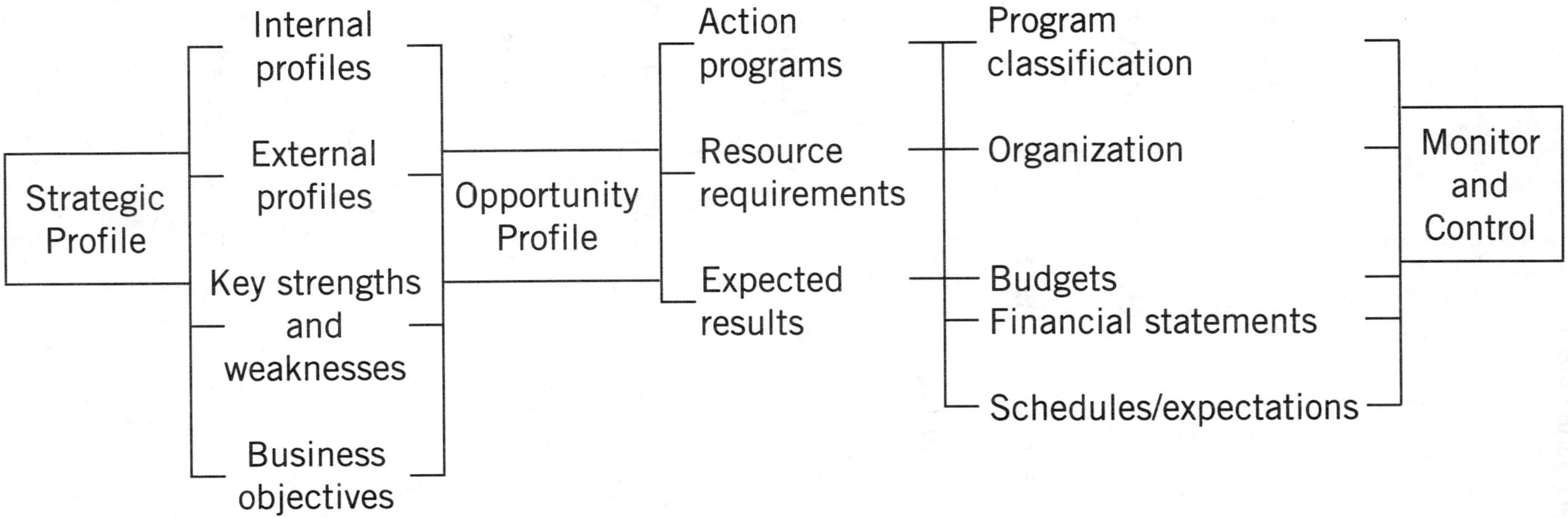

- Strategic Profile
  - Internal profiles
  - External profiles
  - Key strengths and weaknesses
  - Business objectives

- Opportunity Profile
  - Action programs
  - Resource requirements
  - Expected results

- Monitor and Control
  - Program classification
  - Organization
  - Budgets
  - Financial statements
  - Schedules/expectations

The Dryden Press

TM 15-3 Normative Planning Model

Decision to Plan
↓
Situational Analysis
↓
Personal Objectives
Company Objectives
↓
Issue Specification
↓
Option Generation
↓
Evaluation and Selection
↓
Implementation
↓
Control and Feedback

The Dryden Press

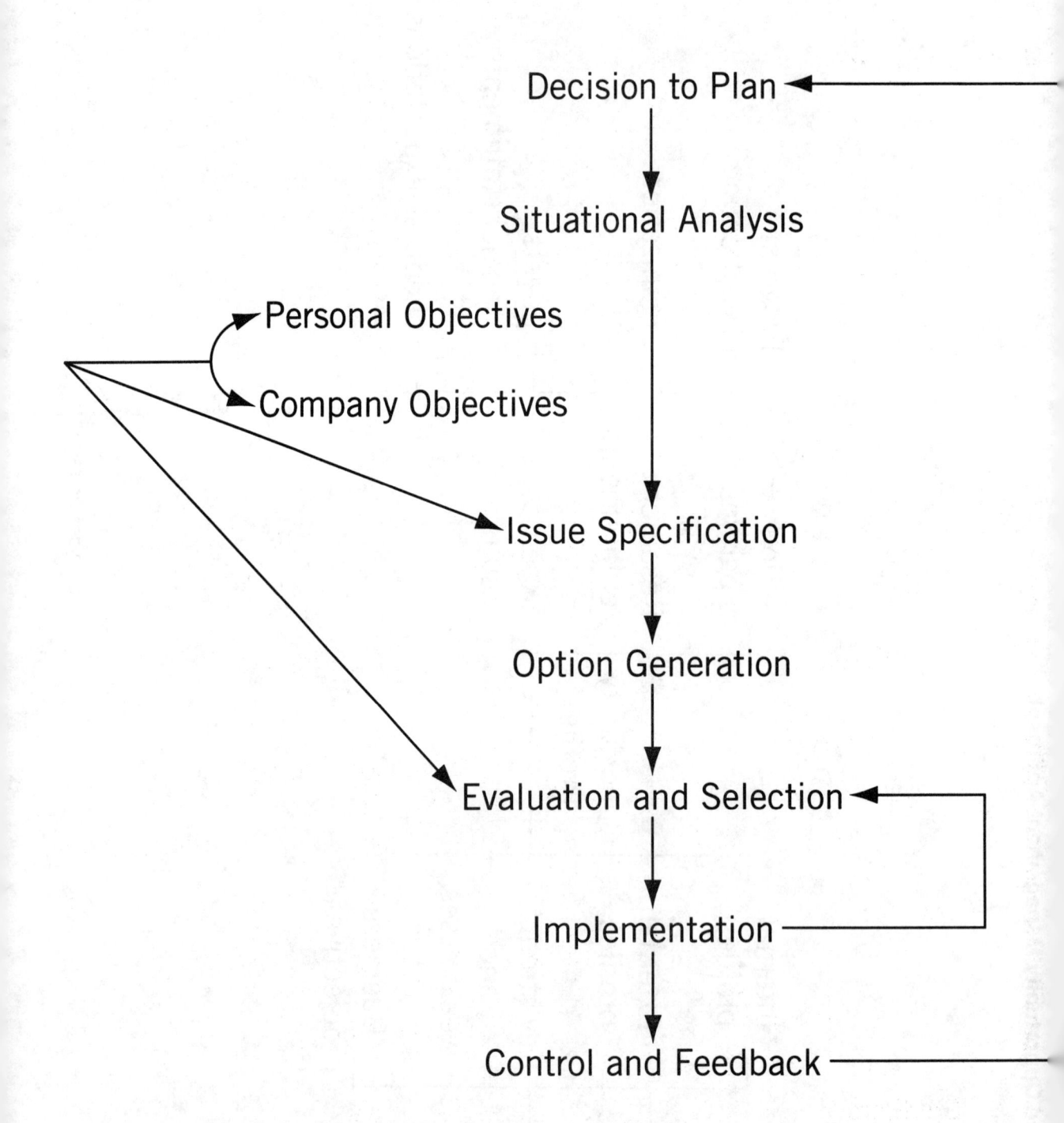

TM 15-4 Entrepreneurial Strategy: A Contingency Multistage Approach

Strategic Entrepreneurial Assessment	New-Venture Initiation	Entrepreneurial Development and Continuation	Emerging Entrepreneurial Issues
Opportunity Evaluation	New-Venture Initiation • Creativity • Assessment Evaluation • Feasibility	Entrepreneurial Growth and Development • Understanding the Entrepreneurial Company	Corporate Entrepreneurship
SWOT Analysis (Strengths/Weaknesses Opportunities/Threats)	The Business Plan Process • Definition • Benefits • Business Plan Development	Managing Paradox and Contradiction Acquisition of a Venture	International: The Global Expansion Women Entrepreneurs Family Business
		Valuation and Succession of Entrepreneurial Ventures • Methods of Valuation • Succession Strategy	Entrepreneurial Careers

The Dryden Press

TM 15-5 A Venture's Typical Life Cycle

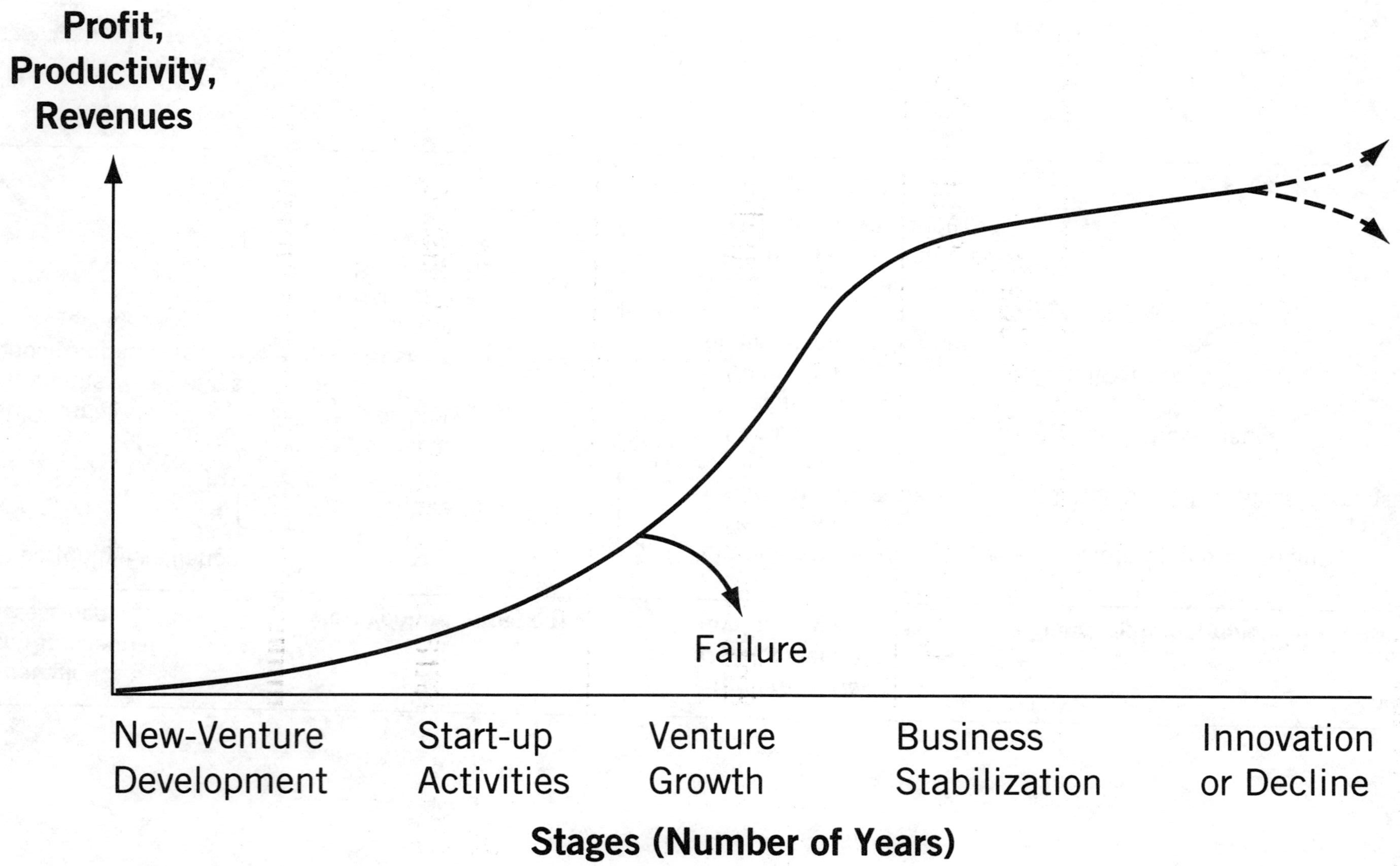

Profit, Productivity, Revenues

Stages (Number of Years):
- New-Venture Development
- Start-up Activities
- Venture Growth
- Business Stabilization
- Innovation or Decline

Failure

The Dryden Press

TM 15-6   The Entrepreneurial Mind

Future Goals

	Change	Status Quo
Possible	Entrepreneur	Satisfied manager
Blocked	Frustrated manager	Classic bureaucrat

Perceived Capability

The Dryden Press

TM 16-1 The Entrepreneurial Culture versus the Administrative Culture

THE ENTREPRENEURIAL CULTURE VERSUS THE ADMINISTRATIVE CULTURE

	Entrepreneurial Focus		Administrative Focus	
	Characteristics	**Pressures**	**Characteristics**	**Pressures**
Strategic Orientation	Driven by perception of opportunity	Diminishing opportunities Rapidly changing technology, consumer economics, social values, and political rules	Driven by controlled resources	Social contracts Performance measurement criteria Planning systems and cycles
Commitment to Seize Opportunities	Revolutionary, with short duration	Action orientation Narrow decision windows Acceptance of reasonable risks Few decision constituencies	Evolutionary, with long duration	Acknowledgment of multiple constituencies Negotiation about strategic course Risk reduction Coordination with existing resource base
Commitment of Resources	Many stages, with minimal exposure at each stage	Lack of predictable resource needs Lack of control over the environment Social demands for appropriate use of resources Foreign competition Demands for more efficient use	A single stage, with complete commitment out of decision	Need to reduce risk Incentive compensation Turnover in managers Capital budgeting systems Formal planning systems
Control of Resources	Episodic use or rent of required resources	Increased resource specialization Long resource life compared with need Risk of obsolescence Risk inherent in the identified opportunity Inflexibility of permanent commitment to resources	Ownership or employment of required resources	Power, status, and financial rewards Coordination of activity Efficiency measures Inertia and cost of change Industry structures
Management Structure	Flat, with multiple informal networks	Coordination of key noncontrolled resources Challenge to hierarchy Employees' desire for independence	Hierarchy	Need for clearly defined authority and responsibility Organizational culture Reward systems Management theory

SOURCE: Reprinted by permission of the *Harvard Business Review*. An exhibit from "The Heart of Entrepreneurship," by Howard H. Stevenson and David E. Gumpert, March/April 1985, 89. Copyright © 1985 by the President and Fellows of Harvard College; all rights reserved.

The Dryden Press

TM 16-2 Role of Self-Management in the Functioning and Survival of Entrepreneurs

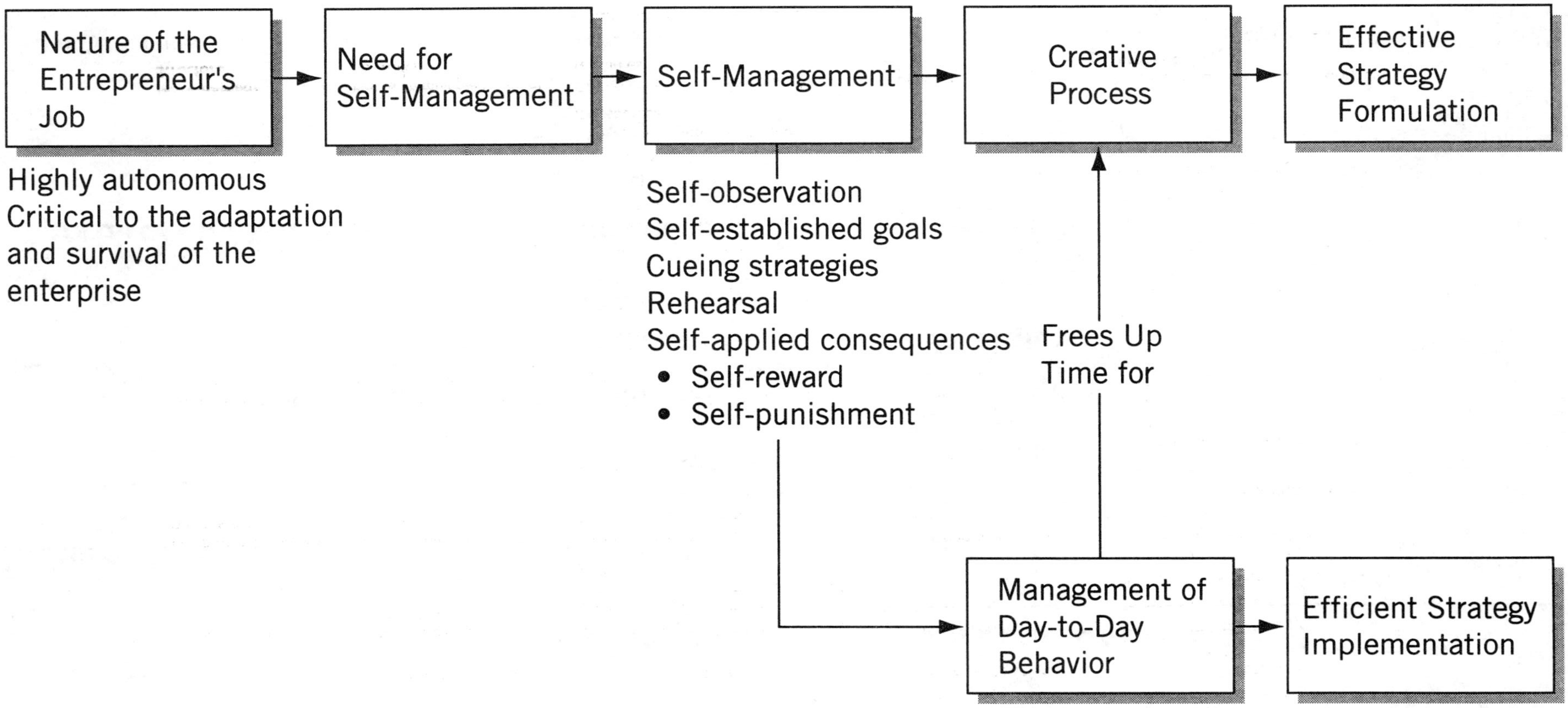

```
┌──────────────┐     ┌──────────────┐     ┌──────────────┐     ┌──────────────┐     ┌──────────────┐
│ Nature of the│ ──▶ │   Need for   │ ──▶ │    Self-     │ ──▶ │   Creative   │ ──▶ │  Effective   │
│Entrepreneur's│     │    Self-     │     │  Management  │     │   Process    │     │   Strategy   │
│     Job      │     │  Management  │     │              │     │              │     │ Formulation  │
└──────────────┘     └──────────────┘     └──────────────┘     └──────────────┘     └──────────────┘
                                                                      ▲
Highly autonomous                         Self-observation            │
Critical to the adaptation                Self-established goals      │ Frees Up
and survival of the                       Cueing strategies           │ Time for
enterprise                                Rehearsal                   │
                                          Self-applied consequences   │
                                           • Self-reward      ┌──────────────┐     ┌──────────────┐
                                           • Self-punishment  │ Management of│ ──▶ │   Efficient  │
                                                          ──▶ │  Day-to-Day  │     │   Strategy   │
                                                              │   Behavior   │     │Implementation│
                                                              └──────────────┘     └──────────────┘
```

The Dryden Press

TM 16-3 Conflicting Designs of Structural Factors

CONFLICTING DESIGNS OF STRUCTURAL FACTORS

	Flexible Design	**Bureaucratic Design**
Cultural Elements	Autonomous	Formalized
	Risk taking	Risk averse
	Entrepreneurial	Bureaucratic
Staffing and Development	Technical skills	Administrative skills
	Specialists	Generalists
	External hiring	Internal hiring
Appraisal and Rewards	Participative	Formalized
	Subjective	Objective
	Equity based	Incentive based

SOURCE: Charles J. Fombrun and Stefan Wally, "Structuring Small Firms for Rapid Growth," *Journal of Business Venturing* (March 1989): 109.

The Dryden Press

TM 16-4 Decision-Making Characteristics and Growth Stages

DECISION-MAKING CHARACTERISTICS AND GROWTH STAGES

	Early Stage(s)	Growth Stage	Later Stage(s)
Primary Focus	Product business Definition Acquisition of resources Development of market position	Volume production Market share Viability	Cost control Profitability Future growth opportunity
Decision-Making Characteristics	Informal Centralized Nonspecialized Short time horizon	Transitional	Formal Decentralized Specialized Long and short time horizon

SOURCE: Thomas N. Gilmore and Robert K. Kazanjian, "Clarifying Decision Making in High Growth Ventures: The Use of Responsibility Charting," *Journal of Business Venturing* (January 1989): 71.

The Dryden Press

TM 17-1   The Ten Largest U.S. Export Markets

THE TEN LARGEST U.S. EXPORT MARKETS

Country/Region	Value (billions of $)	Percent of World Trade
Canada	$133.7	11.6
Japan	67.5	9.7
Mexico	56.8	5.3
United Kingdom	30.9	4.6
South Korea	26.6	4.0
Germany	23.5	3.2
Taiwan	18.4	2.9
Singapore	16.7	2.8
Netherlands	16.6	2.5
France	14.4	
Subtotal	$405.1	
World	$583.9	

SOURCE: Reported in the *New York Times*, 2 March 1997, 8.

The Dryden Press

TM 17-2 The Ten Largest U.S. Import Markets

THE TEN LARGEST U.S. IMPORT MARKETS

Country/Region	Value (billions of $)	Percent of World Trade
Canada	$156.5	15.0
Japan	115.2	9.5
Mexico	73.0	6.7
China	51.5	5.1
Germany	38.9	3.9
Taiwan	29.9	3.8
United Kingdom	28.9	3.0
South Korea	22.7	2.6
Singapore	20.3	2.4
France	18.8	
Subtotal	$555.5	
World	$770.6	

SOURCE: Reported in the *New York Times*, 2 March 1997, 8.

The Dryden Press

TM 17-3 Risk of Entering Global Markets

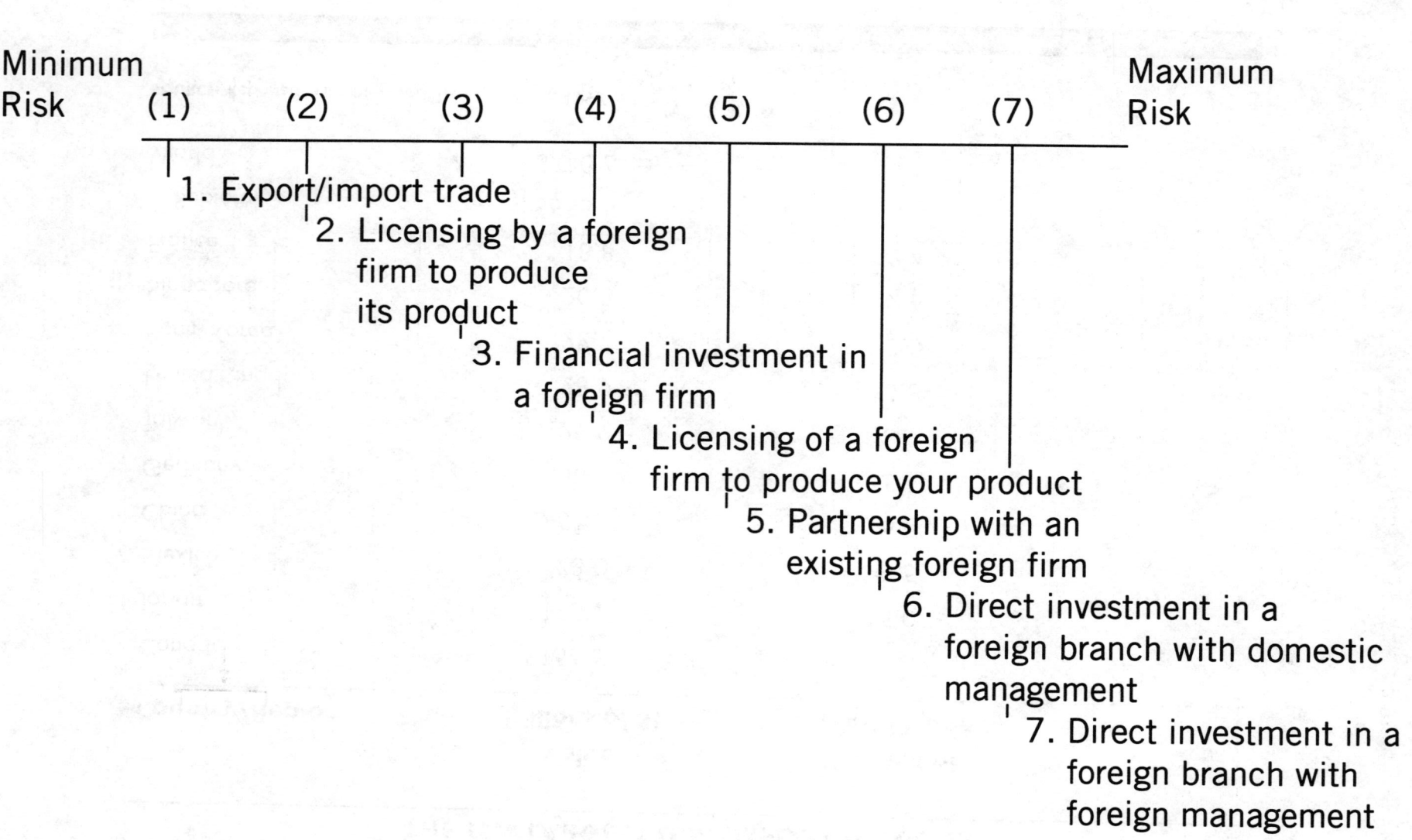

Minimum Maximum
Risk (1) (2) (3) (4) (5) (6) (7) Risk

1. Export/import trade
2. Licensing by a foreign firm to produce its product
3. Financial investment in a foreign firm
4. Licensing of a foreign firm to produce your product
5. Partnership with an existing foreign firm
6. Direct investment in a foreign branch with domestic management
7. Direct investment in a foreign branch with foreign management

The Dryden Press

TM 17-4 Analysis of Global Expansion Decisions

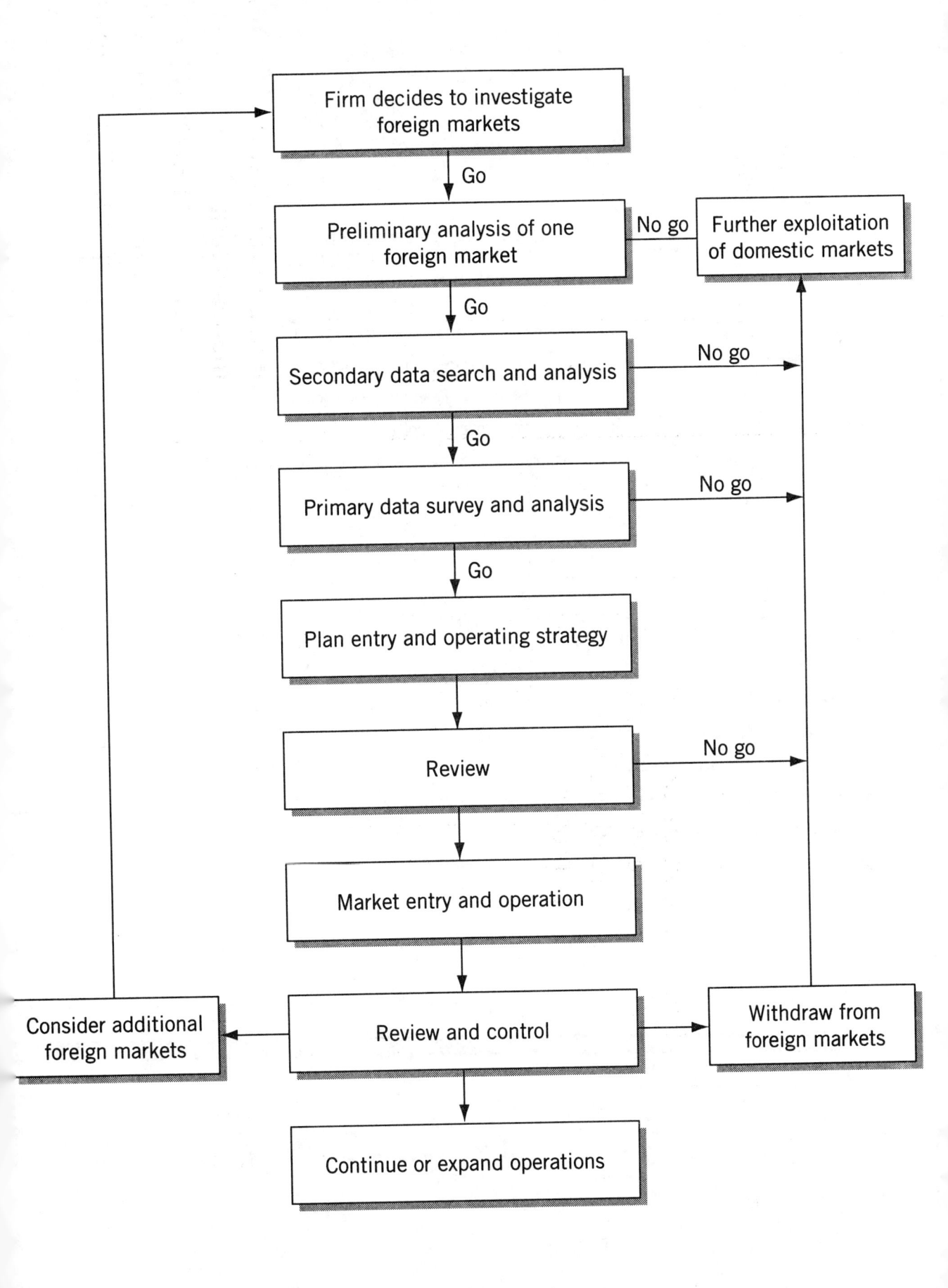

```
                    ┌──────────────────────────┐
          ┌────────▶│ Firm decides to investigate│
          │         │     foreign markets        │
          │         └─────────────┬──────────────┘
          │                       │ Go
          │                       ▼
          │         ┌──────────────────────────┐  No go  ┌──────────────────────┐
          │         │ Preliminary analysis of one│───────▶│ Further exploitation │
          │         │      foreign market        │        │  of domestic markets │
          │         └─────────────┬──────────────┘        └──────────────────────┘
          │                       │ Go                              ▲
          │                       ▼                                 │
          │         ┌──────────────────────────┐  No go             │
          │         │ Secondary data search and │────────────────────┤
          │         │         analysis          │                    │
          │         └─────────────┬──────────────┘                   │
          │                       │ Go                               │
          │                       ▼                                  │
          │         ┌──────────────────────────┐  No go              │
          │         │ Primary data survey and   │────────────────────┤
          │         │         analysis          │                    │
          │         └─────────────┬──────────────┘                   │
          │                       │ Go                               │
          │                       ▼                                  │
          │         ┌──────────────────────────┐                     │
          │         │ Plan entry and operating  │                    │
          │         │         strategy          │                    │
          │         └─────────────┬──────────────┘                   │
          │                       ▼                                  │
          │         ┌──────────────────────────┐  No go              │
          │         │          Review           │────────────────────┤
          │         └─────────────┬──────────────┘                   │
          │                       ▼                                  │
          │         ┌──────────────────────────┐                     │
          │         │ Market entry and operation│                    │
          │         └─────────────┬──────────────┘                   │
          │                       ▼                                  │
  ┌───────────────┐   ┌──────────────────────┐    ┌──────────────────┐
  │   Consider    │◀──│  Review and control  │───▶│  Withdraw from   │
  │   additional  │   │                      │    │  foreign markets │
  │foreign markets│   └──────────┬───────────┘    └──────────────────┘
  └───────────────┘              ▼
                     ┌──────────────────────┐
                     │Continue or expand     │
                     │     operations        │
                     └──────────────────────┘
```

The Dryden Press

TM 18-1 Total Amount Needed to Buy a Business

TOTAL AMOUNT NEEDED TO BUY A BUSINESS

Family Living Expenses	From last paycheck to takeover day	$ _____
	Moving expense	_____
	For three months after takeover day	_____
Purchase Price	Total amount (or down payment plus three monthly installments)	_____
Sales Tax	On purchased furniture and equipment	_____
Professional Services	Escrow, accounting, legal	_____
Deposits, Prepayments, Licenses	Last month's rent (first month's rent in Operating Expense below)	_____
	Utility deposits	_____
	Sales tax deposit	_____
	Business licenses	_____
	Insurance premiums	_____
Takeover Announcements	Newspaper advertising	_____
	Mail announcements	_____
	Exterior sign changes	_____
	New stationery and forms	_____
New Inventory		_____
New Fixtures and Equipment		_____
Remodeling and Redecorating		_____
Three Months' Operating Expense	Including loan repayments	_____
Reserve to Carry Customer Accounts		_____
Cash	Petty cash, change, etc.	_____
	Total	$ _____

Note: Money for living and business expenses for at least three months should be set aside in a bank savings account and not used for any other purpose. This is a cus help get through the start-up period with a minimum of worry. If expense money for a longer period can be provided, it will add to peace of mind and help the concentrate on building the business.

SOURCE: Reprinted with permission from Bank of America NT&SA, "How to Buy and Sell a Business or Franchise," *Small Business Reporter*, copyright © 1987, 9.

The Dryden Press

TM 19-1 Barriers to Succession Planning in Family Firms

BARRIERS TO SUCCESSION PLANNING IN FAMILY FIRMS

Founder/Owner	Family
Death anxiety	Death as taboo
Company as symbol	• Discussion is a hostile act
• Loss of identity	• Fear of loss/abandonment
• Concern about legacy	Fear of sibling rivalry
Dilemma of choice	Change of spouse's position
• Fiction of equality	
Generational envy	
• Loss of power	

SOURCE: Manfred F. R. Kets de Vries, "The Dynamics of Family-Controlled Firms: The Good News and the Bad News," *Organizational Dynamics* (winter 1993): 68.

The Dryden Press

TM 19-2 Pressures and Interests in a Family Business

	Inside the Family	Outside the Family
Inside the Business	**The Family Managers** Hanging onto or Getting Hold of Company Control Selection of Family Members as Managers Continuity of Family Investment and Involvement Building a Dynasty Rivalry	**The Employees** Rewards for Loyalty Sharing of Equity, Growth, and Success Professionalism Bridging Family Transitions Stake in the Company
Outside the Business	**The Relatives** Income and Inheritance Family Conflicts and Alliances Degree of Involvement in the Business	**The Outsiders** Competition Market, Product, Supply, and Technology Influence Tax Laws Regulatory Agencies

The Dryden Press

TM 19-3 A Checklist for Succession: Some Important Steps

A CHECKLIST FOR SUCCESSION: SOME IMPORTANT STEPS

For the Owners of Family-Run Firms

_____ Learn to delegate authority and decentralize operations.

_____ Develop an organizational chart.

_____ Plan for more than one successor—increase the possibilities.

_____ Establish a personnel development program.

_____ Encourage the potential successor to gain experience outside of the business.

_____ Do not neglect daughters.

_____ Keep plans updated—continually review the progress of the business and possible successors.

_____ Strategically plan for the future—do not always focus on putting out daily fires.

_____ Establish family business meetings to air issues.

For the Children of Family-Run Firms

_____ Announce your interest in taking over the family firm.

_____ Take responsibility for your personal development.

_____ Get a mentor (someone "outside" that you respect).

_____ Gain experience outside the family business.

_____ Get some accountability training—hold positions that teach responsibility and offer opportunities for decision making.

_____ Learn to blend family traditions with future business goals.

_____ Avoid family feuds—work with the family, not against it.

_____ Eliminate "Dad's (or Mom's) ghost"—prepare a clear takeover plan that eventually phases out older family leaders and allows changes.

The Dryden Press

TM 20-1 A Cause-and-Effect Diagram for Dealing with Unproductive Meetings

ENVIRONMENT
- Noisy
- Too Hot, Cold
- Poor Seating Arrangement
- No Coffee, Water
- Phone In Room
- Distractions in Window

TIME
- People Arrive Late
- Run Overtime
- Start Late
- People Leave Early
- Early/Late in the Day
- Postponed

RESOURCES/PEOPLE
- Decision Maker Not Present
- Poor Problem Solving Skills
- People Not Prepared
- Uninvited Guests
- Poor Visuals

COMMUNICATION
- Discussion Wanders
- Blocking Issues
- Boss Prevents Discussion
- Side Conversations
- Hidden Agendas
- Intimidation by Leader
- Hash Over Same Problem
- Long-Winded People
- Arguments
- Turf Protection

PROCEDURE
- Incomplete Agenda
- No Agenda
- Didn't Stick to Schedule
- No Organization
- No Introduction
- Don't Know Purpose
- No Follow-Up Action

→ Unproductive Meetings

The Dryden Press

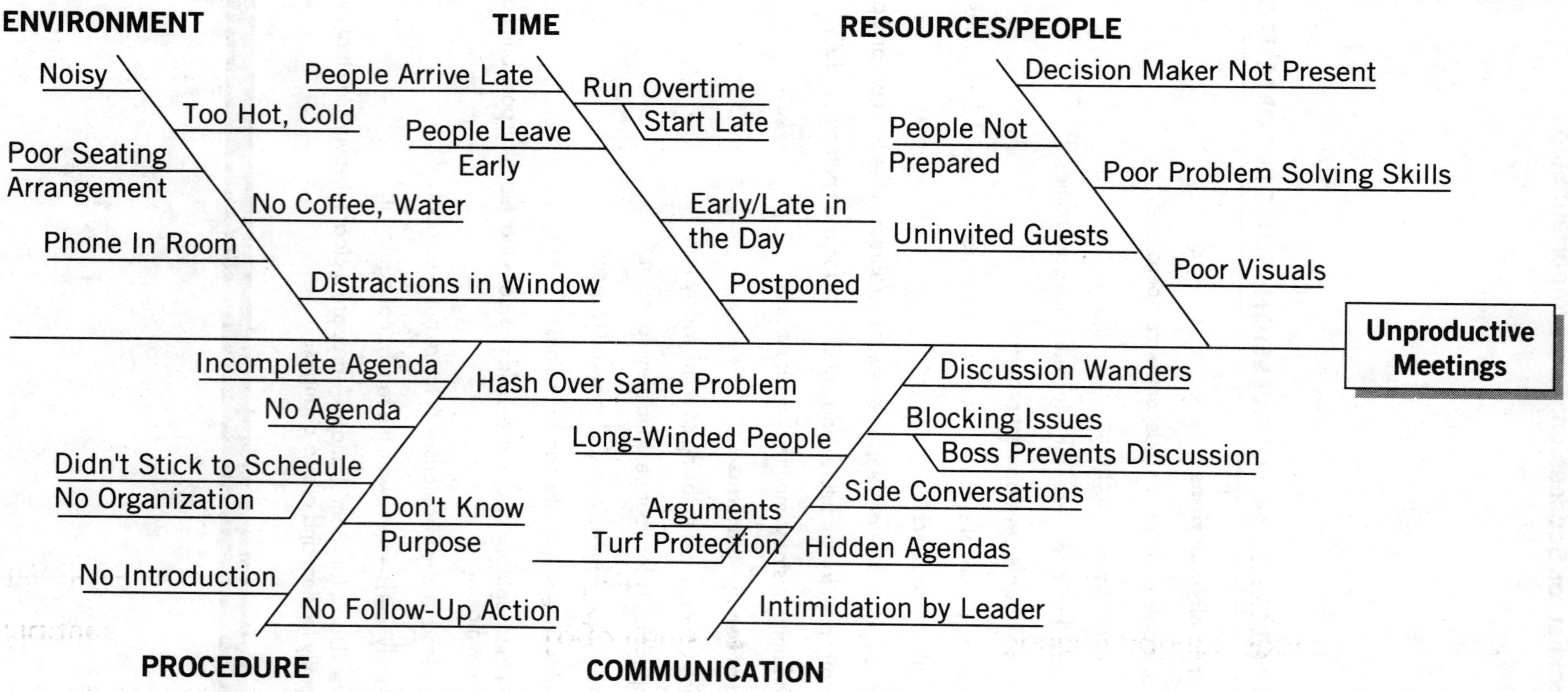

TM 20-2 Typical Rewards Total Quality Management Companies Use

TYPICAL REWARDS TOTAL QUALITY MANAGEMENT COMPANIES USE

Plaques	Logo items	Special parking space
Trophies	• hats	Special luncheon
Certificates	• shirts	Dinner with spouse or friend
Letter from CEO	• pens	Trip (local or distant)
Honor roll	• mugs	Seminar attendance
Letter to personnel file	• coasters	Pick-your-own-gift certificate
Picture in company paper	• shorts	Day off
Use of limousine	• decals	Cash
Savings bond	• paper weights	Tickets to special events
Banner for office	• desk sets	

The Dryden Press

TM 20-3   A Comparison of Constant Improvement and Innovation

A COMPARISON OF CONSTANT IMPROVEMENT AND INNOVATION

	Constant Improvement	**Innovation**
Effect	Long term and long lasting but not dramatic	Short term and dramatic
Pace	Small steps	Large steps
Time frame	Continuous and incremental	Intermittent and nonincremental
Change	Gradual and constant	Abrupt and volatile
Involvement	Everyone in the firm	A select few "champions"
Approach	Group efforts	Rugged individuals
Mode	Maintain and improve	Scrap and rebuild
Spark	Conventional know-how	Technological state-of-the-art breakthroughs, new inventions, new theories
Practical requirements	Little investigation, great effort to maintain improvement	Large investigation, little effort to maintain improvement
Effort orientation	People	Technology
Evaluation criteria	Process and efforts for better results	Results for profit
Advantage	Works well in slow-growth economy	Works well in fast-growth economy